Critical Perspectives on Food Sovereignty

This volume is a pioneering contribution to the study of food politics and critical agrarian studies, where food sovereignty has emerged as a pivotal concept over the past few decades, with a wide variety of social movements, on-the-ground experiments, and policy innovations flying under its broad banner. Despite its large and growing popularity, the history, theoretical foundations, and political program of food sovereignty have only occasionally received in-depth analysis and critical scrutiny. This collection brings together both long-standing scholars in critical agrarian studies, such as Philip McMichael, Bina Agarwal, Henry Bernstein, Jan Douwe van der Ploeg, and Marc Edelman, as well as a dynamic roster of early- and mid-career researchers. The ultimate aim is to advance this important frontier of research and organizing, and put food sovereignty on a stronger footing as a mobilizing frame, a policy objective, and a plan of action for the human future.

This volume was published as part two of the special double issue celebrating the 40th anniversary of *The Journal of Peasant Studies*.

Marc Edelman, James C. Scott, Amita Baviskar, Saturnino M. Borras Jr., Deniz Kandiyoti, Eric Holt-Giménez, Tony Weis, Wendy Wolford

Critical Agrarian Studies
Series Editor: Saturnino M. Borras Jr.

Critical Agrarian Studies is the new accompanying book series to the *Journal of Peasant Studies*. It publishes selected special issues of the journal and, occasionally, books that offer major contributions in the field of critical agrarian studies. The book series builds on the long and rich history of the journal and its former accompanying book series, the Library of Peasant Studies (1973–2008) which had published several important monographs and special-issues-as-books.

Critical Perspectives in Rural Development Studies
Edited by Saturnino M. Borras Jr.

The Politics of Biofuels, Land and Agrarian Change
Edited by Saturnino M. Borras Jr., Philip McMichael and Ian Scoones

New Frontiers of Land Control
Edited by Nancy Lee Peluso and Christian Lund

Outcomes of Post-2000 Fast Track Land Reform in Zimbabwe
Edited by Lionel Cliffe, Jocelyn Alexander, Ben Cousins and Rudo Gaidzanwa

Green Grabbing: A New Appropriation of Nature
Edited by James Fairhead, Melissa Leach and Ian Scoones

The New Enclosures: Critical Perspectives on Corporate Land Deals
Edited by Ben White, Saturnino M. Borras Jnr., Ruth Hall, Ian Scoones and Wendy Wolford

Rural Politics in Contemporary China
Edited by Emily T. Yeh, Kevin O'Brien and Jingzhong Ye

New Directions in Agrarian Political Economy: Global Agrarian Transformations, Vol. I
Edited by Madeleine Fairbairn, Jonathan Fox, S. Ryan Isakson, Michael Levien, Nancy Lee Peluso, Shahra Razavi, Ian Scoones, Kalyanakrishnan "Shivi" Sivaramakrishnan

Critical Perspectives on Food Sovereignty: Global Agrarian Transformations, Vol 2
Edited by Marc Edelman, James C. Scott, Amita Baviskar, Saturnino M. Borras Jr., Deniz Kandiyoti, Eric Holt-Giménez, Tony Weis, Wendy Wolford

Critical Perspectives on Food Sovereignty

Global agrarian transformations, volume 2

Edited by
**Marc Edelman, James C. Scott,
Amita Baviskar, Saturnino M. Borras Jr.,
Deniz Kandiyoti, Eric Holt-Giménez,
Tony Weis, Wendy Wolford**

Routledge
Taylor & Francis Group

LONDON AND NEW YORK

First published 2016
by Routledge
2 Park Square, Milton Park, Abingdon, Oxon, OX14 4RN, UK

and by Routledge
605 Third Avenue, New York, NY 10017, USA

First issued in paperback 2021

Routledge is an imprint of the Taylor & Francis Group, an informa business

British Library Cataloguing in Publication Data
A catalogue record for this book is available from the British Library

Typeset in Times New Roman
by RefineCatch Limited, Bungay, Suffolk

Publisher's Note
The publisher has gone to great lengths to ensure the quality of this reprint
but points out that some imperfections in the original copies may be apparent.

Disclaimer
Every effort has been made to contact copyright holders for their permission to
reprint material in this book. The publishers would be grateful to hear from any
copyright holder who is not here acknowledged and will undertake to rectify
any errors or omissions in future editions of this book.

ISBN 13: 978-1-138-12276-5 (pbk)
ISBN 13: 978-1-138-91650-0 (hbk)

Contents

CONTENTS

Citation Information

The chapters in this book were originally published in *The Journal of Peasant Studies,* volume 41, issue 6 (November 2014). When citing this material, please use the original page numbering for each article, as follows:

Chapter 1
Introduction: critical perspectives on food sovereignty
Marc Edelman, Tony Weis, Amita Baviskar, Saturnino M. Borras Jr, Eric Holt-Giménez, Deniz Kandiyoti and Wendy Wolford
Journal of Peasant Studies, volume 41, issue 6 (November 2014) pp. 911–931

Chapter 2
Historicizing food sovereignty
Philip McMichael
Journal of Peasant Studies, volume 41, issue 6 (November 2014) pp. 933–957

Chapter 3
Food sovereignty: forgotten genealogies and future regulatory challenges
Marc Edelman
Journal of Peasant Studies, volume 41, issue 6 (November 2014) pp. 959–978

Chapter 4
Diálogo de saberes *in La Vía Campesina: food sovereignty and agroecology*
María Elena Martínez-Torres and Peter M. Rosset
Journal of Peasant Studies, volume 41, issue 6 (November 2014) pp. 979–997

Chapter 5
Peasant-driven agricultural growth and food sovereignty
Jan Douwe van der Ploeg
Journal of Peasant Studies, volume 41, issue 6 (November 2014) pp. 999–1030

Chapter 6
Food sovereignty via the 'peasant way': a sceptical view
Henry Bernstein
Journal of Peasant Studies, volume 41, issue 6 (November 2014) pp. 1031–1063

Chapter 7
What place for international trade in food sovereignty?
Kim Burnett and Sophia Murphy
Journal of Peasant Studies, volume 41, issue 6 (November 2014) pp. 1065–1084

Chapter 8

Farmers' rights and food sovereignty: critical insights from India
Karine Peschard
Journal of Peasant Studies, volume 41, issue 6 (November 2014) pp. 1085–1108

Chapter 9

Life in a shrimp zone: aqua- and other cultures of Bangladesh's coastal landscape
Kasia Paprocki and Jason Cons
Journal of Peasant Studies, volume 41, issue 6 (November 2014) pp. 1109–1130

Chapter 10

Toward a political geography of food sovereignty: transforming territory, exchange and power in the liberal sovereign state
Amy Trauger
Journal of Peasant Studies, volume 41, issue 6 (November 2014) pp. 1131–1152

Chapter 11

Farmers, foodies and First Nations: getting to food sovereignty in Canada
Annette Aurélie Desmarais and Hannah Wittman
Journal of Peasant Studies, volume 41, issue 6 (November 2014) pp. 1153–1173

Chapter 12

The 'state' of food sovereignty in Latin America: political projects and alternative pathways in Venezuela, Ecuador and Bolivia
Ben McKay, Ryan Nehring and Marygold Walsh-Dilley
Journal of Peasant Studies, volume 41, issue 6 (November 2014) pp. 1175–1200

Chapter 13

Food sovereignty in Ecuador: peasant struggles and the challenge of institutionalization
Isabella Giunta
Journal of Peasant Studies, volume 41, issue 6 (November 2014) pp. 1201–1224

Chapter 14

Re-purposing the master's tools: the open source seed initiative and the struggle for seed sovereignty
Jack Kloppenburg
Journal of Peasant Studies, volume 41, issue 6 (November 2014) pp. 1225–1246

Chapter 15

Food sovereignty, food security and democratic choice: critical contradictions, difficult conciliations
Bina Agarwal
Journal of Peasant Studies, volume 41, issue 6 (November 2014) pp. 1247–1268

Please direct any queries you may have about the citations to
clsuk.permissions@cengage.com

Notes on Editors

Marc Edelman, Professor of Anthropology, Hunter College and the Graduate Center, City University of New York (CUNY).

James C. Scott, Sterling Professor of Political Science, Yale University, New Haven (USA).

Amita Baviskar, Associate Professor, Sociology Unit, Institute for Economic Growth, New Delhi (India).

Saturnino M. Borras Jr., Professor of Agrarian Studies, International Institute of Social Studies (ISS), The Hague (Netherlands).

Deniz Kandiyoti, Emeritus Professor in Development Studies, The School of Oriental and African Studies (SOAS), London (UK).

Eric Holt-Giménez, Executive Director, Food First, Oakland (USA).

Tony Weis, Associate Professor of Geography, The University of Western Ontario (Canada).

Wendy Wolford, Polson Professor of Development Sociology, Cornell University (USA).

Preface

A fundamentally contested concept, food sovereignty has – as a political project and campaign, an alternative, and a social movement – barged into global agrarian discourse over the last two decades.[1] Since then, it has inspired and mobilized diverse publics: workers, scholars, and public intellectuals, farmers and peasant movements, NGOs, and human rights activists in the North and global South. The term has become a challenging subject for social science research, and has been interpreted and reinterpreted in a variety of ways by various groups and individuals. Indeed, it is a concept that is broadly defined as the right of peoples to democratically control or determine the shape of their food system, and to produce sufficient and healthy food in culturally appropriate and ecologically sustainable ways in and near their territory. As such it spans issues such as food politics, agroecology, land reform, biofuels, genetically modified organisms (GMOs), urban gardening, the patenting of life forms, labor migration, the feeding of volatile cities, ecological sustainability, and subsistence rights.

The idea and practice of food sovereignty have generated vibrant discussions and debates within and between various circles among social movement activists and academics. For this reason, several academic institutions decided to forge an alliance with key activist think tanks and NGOs to organize a critical dialogue around this topic. The Yale Agrarian Studies Program and the International Institute of Social Studies (ISS) in The Hague took the lead among the academic institutions, while the Transnational Institute (TNI), Institute for Food and Development Policy or Food First, and the Dutch development agency Interchurch Organization for Development Cooperation (ICCO) took the lead among non-academic research and advocacy organizations. Other collaborators played a critical role in constructing the space for dialogue: Yale Sustainable Food Project, Yale South Asian Studies Council, Initiatives in Critical Agrarian Studies (ICAS), Misereor, Kempf Fund, and *The Journal of Peasant Studies*.

Two successful events were held. The September 2013 Yale University event brought together close to 300 leading scholars and political activists who are advocates of and sympathetic to the idea of food sovereignty, as well as those who are skeptical about the concept of food sovereignty, to foster a critical and productive dialogue on the issue. The keynote addresses were given by Paul Nicholson (La Vía Campesina), Teodor Shanin (The Moscow School of Social and Economic Sciences), Bina Agarwal (Manchester University), and Olivier de Schutter (then the UN Special Rapporteur on the Right to Food). The January 2014 ISS event in The Hague brought together more than 300 scholars

---

[1]Part of the text of this Preface draws from the conference blurbs used at the "Food Sovereignty: a critical dialogue" colloquiums held in September 2013 at Yale University and in January 2014 at the International Institute of Social Studies (ISS) in The Hague, the Netherlands.

and social movement activists mostly from across Europe – key speakers included Tania Li and Bridget O'Laughlin. The two events were accompanied by close to a hundred conference papers. The conference organizers also produced high quality video clips of the plenary speakers' speeches. These video clips are available at the organizers' websites.

The exchanges and debates at the two conferences were collegial and comradely, tackling serious issues that unite and divide conference participants. Most of the conference papers have been transformed into journal articles. There were at least four journal special issues that came out from this critical dialogue: *The Journal of Peasant Studies* (*JPS*) vol. 41, no. 5, edited by Madeleine Fairbairn, Jonathan Fox, S. Ryan Isakson, Michael Levien, Nancy Peluso, Shahra Razavi, Ian Scoones, and Kalyanakrishnan ("Shivi") Sivaramakrishnan, explored new directions in agrarian political economy. This volume established the context for the other *JPS* special issue, vol. 41, no. 6 in 2014, which focused on food sovereignty and was edited by Marc Edelman, James C. Scott, Amita Baviskar, Saturnino M. Borras Jr., Deniz Kandiyoti, Eric Holt-Giménez, Tony Weis, and Wendy Wolford. A special issue of *Globalizations* in 2015 was guest edited by Annie Shattuck, Christina Schiavoni, and Zoe VanGelder. Finally, a special issue of *Third World Quarterly* in 2015 was guest edited by Eric Holt-Giménez, Alberto Alonso-Fradejas, Todd Holmes, and Martha Robbins.

Routledge decided to publish, together with the Transnational Institute (TNI), the book editions of the special issues by *JPS* edited by Fairbairn, *et. al.* and Edelman, *et. al.* These are the present collections being introduced through this Preface. By explaining the origin of these collections, we hope that the readers will be able to follow the spirit of critical dialogue that produced these volumes, and contribute to the continuing dialogue. Finally, we hope that readers of these volumes will also view the accompanying video clips and read the other two related journal special issues.

Saturnino ("Jun") M. Borras Jr.
2 March 2015, The Hague

Introduction: critical perspectives on food sovereignty

Marc Edelman, Tony Weis, Amita Baviskar, Saturnino M. Borras Jr, Eric Holt-Giménez, Deniz Kandiyoti and Wendy Wolford

Visions of food sovereignty have been extremely important in helping to galvanize broad-based and diverse movements around the need for radical changes in agro-food systems. Yet while food sovereignty has thrived as a 'dynamic process', until recently there has been insufficient attention to many thorny questions, such as its origins, its connection to other food justice movements, its relation to rights discourses, the roles of markets and states and the challenges of implementation. This essay contributes to food sovereignty praxis by pushing the process of critical self-reflection forward and considering its relation to critical agrarian studies – and vice versa.

Over the course of more than two decades, visions of 'food sovereignty' have inspired (and been inspired by) a wellspring of social movements, on-the-ground experiments, policy innovations and – increasingly – heated debates. Even though proponents insist that food sovereignty is a 'dynamic process' rather than a set of fixed principles, until recently there had been little sustained interest in grappling with thorny questions of its origins, what its practical and conceptual limitations might be and what it would take to implement it now and in the future in economically, politically and ecologically diverse contexts. That reticence was perhaps rooted in the adoption of food sovereignty by transnational agrarian movements, such as *La Vía Campesina* (LVC), and the foot-dragging of sympathetic activists and researchers who were disinclined to challenge organizations representing peasants and leading figures within them.

Two conferences – at Yale University in New Haven in September 2013 and at the International Institute of Social Studies (ISS) in The Hague in January 2014 – widened and deepened growing debates.[1] Questions that scholar-activists had raised in off-the-record interviews with food sovereignty advocates and peasant leaders, or in hushed conversations in university corridors, exploded in fiery polemics – and received

---

[1]We gratefully acknowledge the vital contribution of James C. Scott, Co-Director of the Yale Agrarian Studies Program, who presided over key conference sessions and made frequent interventions in plenaries and informal discussions, always with his inimitable wit, good humour and profound insight.

in-depth analytical attention in some 90 papers, 15 of which are represented in this collection.[2] The active participation of numerous food sovereignty and peasant activists at these events and in authoring many of the papers made these much more than typical, run-of-the-mill academic conferences. What began as a dialogue in which academics asked 'Does food sovereignty have a future in critical agrarian studies?' was playfully flipped the other way by practitioners to ask 'Do critical agrarian studies have a future in food sovereignty?' Indeed, though diverse ideological standpoints led to some intense debates, a striking feature of these 'critical dialogues' was the enthusiasm that participants of every provenance and professional position displayed for engaging with each other's ideas in an atmosphere of mutual respect and appreciation. Readers of this collection will find that food sovereignty is a dynamic process after all, and one that increasingly intensifies its praxis and includes a much more profound process of self-reflection and a broad interrogation of key premises and heretofore unexamined assumptions.

Much of the early literature on food sovereignty involved a considerable dose of idealistic righteousness – and rightfully so, since the concept had contributed beyond anybody's initial expectations to galvanizing a broad-based and diverse movement around the need for radical changes in agro-food systems. Self-congratulatory celebrations of food sovereignty, however, too often went hand-in-hand with a certain inattention to underlying premises, policy implications and even the history of the idea itself. The critical dialogue in the pages below cranks up the intensity of the debates, leaving behind this oddly complacent past practice and raising difficult questions – including some for which there may be no immediate answers. While unable to capture the full breadth of the growing debate on the significance of food sovereignty as a mobilizing frame, policy objective and plan of action, this collection seeks to put academics, activists and of course activist-academics on a more solid footing as they engage and work with both agrarian studies and social movements struggling towards food sovereignty.

Challenging questions

To frame this introduction, we consider some of the most challenging questions:

(1) What are the origins of the concept of 'food sovereignty'? How does it relate to more conventional notions of 'food security'? What characterized the context in which food sovereignty emerged as a demand of social movements?

(2) How does long-distance or foreign trade fit into the food sovereignty paradigm, if at all? Is it possible to incorporate the millions of small farmers that produce commodities for export into a food sovereignty model and, if so, under what terms?

---

[2]In addition, two other journal special issues forthcoming in 2015 are based on the Yale and ISS colloquia: (a) *Globalizations* journal, guest edited by Annie Shattuck, Christina Schiavoni and Zoe Van-Gelder, and (b) *Third World Quarterly*, guest edited by Eric Holt-Giménez, Alberto Alonso-Fradejas, Todd Holmes and Martha Robbins. High-quality video recordings of all plenary talks at the Yale conference are available on the websites of the colloquium co-organizers and on YouTube. For the original conference papers, see: Yale University (2013), International Institute of Social Studies (2014) and Food First (2014).

(3) What role as a mobilizing concept can food sovereignty play in helping food-deficit nations move towards greater food self-sufficiency? And is this always possible or desirable?

(4) The Food and Agriculture Organization of the United Nations (FAO) estimates that urban agriculture helps to feed up to 800 million city dwellers – mostly in the poorest quintile (FAO 2002; Zezza and Tasciotti 2010). From 30 to 70 percent of urban families in poor countries engage in urban agriculture, so there is no question that it makes a significant contribution to the aggregate food supply (FAO 2010). What do the growing material and strategic importance of urban agriculture mean for the construction of food sovereignty? How can food sovereignty help bridge the land, resource, market and policy struggles of rural and urban producers?

(5) What will be required to administer food sovereignty and who will do it? Who is the sovereign in food sovereignty? What kinds of limitations or regulations on particular kinds of production or trade, if any, does food sovereignty imply?

(6) How much pluralism is acceptable in a food-sovereign society with respect to models of agricultural production, commerce and consumption? What are the obstacles to scaling up agroecology as a strategy of resistance to industrial agriculture and to centring agroecology as a normative farming style in the future? While individual farmers adopt complex farming *styles* that include industrial and agroecological practices, the political food sovereignty movement (e.g. La Vía Campesina and transnational, national and regional food sovereignty alliances) has largely adopted agroecology as a normative *form* of production. How will the centring/decentring of agroecology/industrial practices affect farming styles? What *mode* of production is under construction with agroecology and food sovereignty?

(7) What kinds of (land) property relations might characterize a food-sovereign society? What combinations of cooperative or collective practices and individual ones are likely to be most effective?

(8) How does food sovereignty address the complex agrarian transitions to modern food systems? How might it serve to stabilize livelihoods and labour flow to build in greater social resilience? What are the roles and realities of food workers, consumers and people in general in the construction of food sovereignty? Will food sovereignty be able to address situations where agriculturalists manifest a desire to enter, remain in or leave agriculture or where young rural people prefer not to become farmers?

(9) If food sovereignty is founded on 'rights', how does it relate to the many other rights-oriented food movements that do not necessarily embrace the food sovereignty framework?

(10) What difference does food sovereignty make within broader political-economic transformations? What impacts and implications does food sovereignty hold for transitions to a post-petroleum, post-growth and/or post-capitalist society?

1. Origins of 'food sovereignty'

The roots of 'food sovereignty' are much debated and shrouded in myth, as Edelman points out in this collection, while tracing the concept's origins to a Mexican government program in the early 1980s. In contrast, several of the other contributions echo versions of the established account that LVC 'first articulated' (Desmarais and Wittman) or 'mooted' (Agarwal) food sovereignty in 1996 at the Rome World Food Summit. Still others take a sociology-of-knowledge approach to the origins question, linking the beginnings of food sovereignty to the globalization of the 1970s (Bernstein), the Uruguay Round of the General Agreement on Tariffs and Trade (1986–1994), the predecessor of the World Trade Organization (WTO) (Burnett and Murphy) or the rapid concentration of giant seed corporations (Kloppenberg). What is clear amidst this cacophony of views is that visions of food sovereignty have evolved and that no consensus exists, a reality which many activists and scholars see as a virtue, a strength and a reflection and acknowledgment of on-the-ground diversity (as in, for example, Martínez-Torres and Rosset's celebration of the *'diálogo de saberes'* within LVC, van der Ploeg's analysis of the sources of peasant resilience or Desmarais and Wittman's invocation of the tremendous variety of national, regional and cultural identities that exist in a large country such as Canada). By critically scrutinizing varied interpretations of food sovereignty, as well as efforts to implement it, and by posing challenging and sometimes delicate questions, the contributions in this collection will no doubt contribute to the concept's further specification and evolution.

One area of intense political contention and scholarly debate concerns the distinction between 'food sovereignty' and 'food security'. The latter concept generally connotes simply adequacy of supplies and nutritional content, with the food itself produced and delivered under any conditions, including far-off, chemical-intensive industrial agriculture. This technocratic understanding of 'food security', typical of many intergovernmental organizations, has made it a target for food sovereignty activists and sympathetic academics. Indeed, some scholars go so far as to suggest that the food security versus food sovereignty opposition constitutes 'a global conflict' (Schanbacher 2010). This view is reflected in several contributions in this collection, including those by Martínez-Torres and Rosset, and McMichael. Bernstein accepts the food security versus food sovereignty dyad but sees it as one element of a broader set of problematical binaries central to agrarian populist discourse (e.g. industrial agriculture versus 'virtuous peasants'). The contributions by Edelman and Trauger each take a different tack, arguing that many of the numerous definitions of food security overlap significantly with conceptions of food sovereignty (e.g. in emphasizing 'culturally appropriate' food) and that in the early actions around food sovereignty activists either used both terms almost interchangeably or asserted that food sovereignty was a prerequisite for attaining genuine food security.

The peasant movements that adopted 'food sovereignty' as a rallying cry and political program in the early 1990s faced several common threats. These included: sudden market openings coupled with the evisceration or complete elimination of public-sector support for smallholding agriculturalists (e.g. commodities boards, state development banks and subsidized credit, extension and agronomic research programs); the consolidation of giant seed companies and increasing state efforts to tighten and enforce seed certification and intellectual property laws regarding crop genetic material; the criminalization of protest and of trafficking in prohibited goods (e.g. raw milk in the United States, farmer-grown seeds in Europe); and what Martínez-Torres and Rosset describe as 'territorial disputes with Capital and agribusiness' (Martínez-Torres and Rosset 2014, 980).

Several opportunities also characterized the context in which food sovereignty emerged as a demand of social movements. The most notable, analysed explicitly or assumed implicitly throughout this collection, is the rise of transnational agrarian movements (TAMs) and the coalitions that these formed with advocacy and donor non-governmental organizations (NGOs) in Europe and elsewhere. The presence of LVC and other TAMs at the 1996 Rome Food Summit and the creation of the International Planning Committee on Food Sovereignty, for example, were made possible by these alliances and were first steps in opening up spaces where peasants' voices could be heard in global governance institutions. Debates continue to roil the food sovereignty community about the ultimate usefulness of this engagement, but the food sovereignty idea would doubtless have had less traction without it.

2.   Does long-distance trade fit in the food sovereignty paradigm?

There are many good reasons why food sovereignty advocacy has tended to view long-distance or foreign trade of agricultural products in a negative light. The reconfiguration of land and social relations to produce commodities for export obviously has old roots in European colonialism, and in many places agro-export production continues to be predicated on and/or generative of severe land and social inequalities. Dependence on long-distance trading systems frequently amounts to a double-edged sword for smallholders and farm workers, with especially damaging impacts in many of the world's poorest countries. On one side is the extreme volatility of tropical agricultural commodities, long subject to frequent boom-bust swings. As Martin Khor (2000, 11) puts it: 'many developing countries still dependent on commodity exports have been trapped in a bad corner of the world trading system'. On the other side, rising imports of cheap (and frequently subsidized) surpluses from industrialized countries have glutted local markets and reshaped the nature of food provisioning, a dynamic that will inevitably be threatened by limits to fossil energy supplies at some point in the future (and in the meantime will be tied to ever-more-destructive forms of fossil energy extraction).

The increasing distance and durability of food is also deeply entwined with the mounting concentration of corporate power over global agro-food systems, and contains under-accounted atmospheric costs that must be understood in light of the urgency of reducing greenhouse gas (GHG) emissions and mitigating climate change. Industrialized agriculture is a major source of GHG emissions (e.g. from large machinery, fertilizers, pesticides, deforestation and intensive livestock operations) and the extreme specialization of landscapes means that both agro-inputs and outputs frequently travel over long distances. While the distance that food moves from farm to mouth is part of its climate impact, it is important to recognize that the nature of production typically has a much greater impact on emissions; or, to put it another way, 'food miles' are just one part of the much bigger environmental case against industrial agriculture (Weber and Matthews 2008). In contrast, labour-intensive and biodiverse small farms tend to reduce GHG emissions in production, enhance the capacity for carbon sequestration within landscapes and reduce the distance that food is transported. In short, there is much to be said for LVC's (Vía Campesina 2009) claim that small-scale farming 'cools the earth'.

Yet while the general motivation for 're-localizing' food systems as far as possible is clear enough, there is still a lot of imprecision about what 'as far as possible' ultimately means. Until recently, activists and scholars have been reluctant to consider this ambiguity. Burnett and Murphy's contribution provides probably the most explicit and detailed effort so far to bring the topics of long-distance and international trade into the food sovereignty conversation. One basic question here is what do we make of the millions of smallholders who produce agricultural commodities (and not only food) for export, particularly when they do so on the basis of relatively equitable land and social relations and sustainable multi-cropped or agro-forestry systems? Burnett and Murphy further point out that the centrality of food to the discussion may lead advocates of food sovereignty to neglect how smallholders cultivating export crops might face plummeting incomes if they were required to switch to growing staple foods for local markets (though we must also keep in mind how the explicit and implicit subsidization of cheap industrial foods grossly distorts relative prices, and how this distortion is not inevitable).

Another sticky issue for food sovereignty in relation to trade and distance, which Edelman points to, is the extent to which non-local dietary preferences can or should be challenged. While food cultures have historically been relatively place-based and tied to agricultural capabilities in a given region[3] – a connection that constitutes a central pillar of food sovereignty – calls for food sovereignty should not obscure the fact that some distance is inescapable, and that it is difficult to draw fixed lines to separate what is 'culturally appropriate' and might be permissible within a food sovereignty paradigm and what is not. The difference between fair trade coffee and Coca-Cola might seem plain enough to most, but translating this to policy and practice is far from straightforward, to say nothing of the even greyer area that lies between these two examples. The extent to which trade and distance (and the fossil energy consumption they entail) can be justified is complicated further by the matter of necessity or nutritional value versus luxury (and pure palate pleasure), in which case coffee, even if 'fairly traded', might not fare so well.

So far, most of the attention to multilateral governance in food sovereignty activism and scholarship has focused on attacking the institutionalization of corporate power, most centrally through the WTO. While this criticism is surely warranted, the failure to think with more specificity about the place of trade and distance in food sovereignty means that there has not been enough attention to the sorts of institutions that are needed to help small farmers secure more equitable, stable and democratic positions within trading networks. For Burnett and Murphy, this attention should include the WTO, and they challenge food sovereignty advocates to rethink the conventional stance ('WTO out of agriculture') and instead strategize how 'changes in the existing rules' might 'contribute to a broader food-sovereignty-based trade campaign'. They make the argument – highly controversial in the food sovereignty community – that 'it is possible to imagine the WTO as a place that counterbalances the power of those countries (and companies) that have set the rules to their benefit and to the detriment of small-scale producers and farm workers' (Burnett and Murphy 2014, 1080).

Outside of confronting the WTO, some of the hope for improving the equity and transparency of relations between small farmers and distant consumers has come to be vested in the expansion of fair trade networks. Food sovereignty advocacy has had a somewhat ambivalent relationship to fair trade networks and certification schemes, with attitudes located on a wide spectrum ranging from explicit support (as though they are a primary mechanism for managing trade in benign ways) to an unhelpful distraction (from the more important, structural work of contesting Free Trade Agreements and the WTO), to little more than 'greenwashing' (e.g. in the case of 'sustainable' palm oil) or 'poorwashing'. The latter view is buttressed by growing evidence that fair trade and other certification schemes frequently do little to improve small farmers' position in commodity chains, as well as often giving rise to troubling new forms of subordination and clientelism (Campbell and LeHeron 2007; Fisher 2007; Sylla 2014). A deeper concern is that fair trade networks and commodity certification schemes are, in their basic conception, pale shadows of earlier and much more ambitious, state-centred attempts to obtain fairer prices and more

---

[3]This was altered over long periods of time, of course, by dispersions of plants and animals that were accelerated dramatically by the European conquest of the Americas and the ensuing Columbian Exchange.

consistent, predictable market conditions through South-South supply management regimes, North-South development partnerships (e.g. the Lomé Agreement), and through the United Nations (UN) Conference on Trade and Development (Fridell 2013).

3. How will food-deficit regions move towards greater self-sufficiency?

Where agro-export-oriented large holdings continue to command significant portions of the best arable land, redistributive land reform remains the fundamental priority for any efforts to overcome food deficits and move towards greater self-sufficiency, together with increased public-sector investments in all of the smallholder-oriented supports needed to make agrarian reform successful (Borras 2008). But we must not assume that eschewing export production in the interests of strengthening local food production will tend towards progressive or redistributive outcomes. On the contrary, as the contribution by Paprocki and Cons indicates, this transformation can exacerbate other sorts of problems. Based on a carefully controlled study of two polders in Bangladesh – one subsistence-oriented and the other entirely given over to shrimp aquaculture – they argue that food sovereignty permits 'a full spectrum of agrarian classes to continue to be peasants, though it does not necessarily yield greater equality in agrarian class relations' (Paprocki and Cons 2014, 1111). In particular, despite some food sovereignty advocates' claims to the contrary, they suggest that the implementation of food sovereignty *per se* does little to address problems of landlessness.

Beyond the complex and contextually varied struggles for agrarian reform lies an array of other barriers to greater food self-sufficiency. Dependence on industrial food surpluses has dampened smallholder earnings in local markets, and over the longer term this has served to undermine the viability of small-scale farming – one of multiple reasons why many young people view the prospect of agrarian livelihoods in a negative light (White 2011). Food import dependence has also simplified diets in unhealthy ways, as a few varieties of wheat, maize and rice, along with a range of highly processed foods, have increasingly displaced more genetically diverse (and nutritionally rich) varieties of the 'big three' grains, 'minor' grains such as millets and quinoa, and whole foods in general. Such dietary changes are often assumed to be primarily a function of cheapness, with the expectation that food sovereignty advocacy will tend to be braced by strong preferences for 'local' and 'culturally appropriate' foods. Yet while cost has no doubt been pivotal, we must be careful not to underplay the extent to which dietary aspirations have been affected by long-term trade patterns and corporate branding, and the extent to which consumer preferences now lean towards processed products – from white bread and baked goods to fried chicken, packaged noodles and high-fructose corn syrup drinks – not only in urban areas but among smallholders and other rural people.

This implies that food sovereignty might not only be about defending food cultures but also about reinvigorating or even rebuilding them, and consciously working to enhance 'food literacy' and modify consumer tastes. Progressive food movements in the United States and Canada (including what Desmarais and Wittman call the new 'foodies') stress things like the need to eat seasonally within 'foodsheds' and to challenge the pervasive expectation that fresh produce will be available all year round. But it is possible that in food-deficit regions with large agrarian populations, food cultures are a bigger barrier to food sovereignty advocacy than is often appreciated.

Another underdeveloped dilemma in food sovereignty activism and scholarship is that some food-deficit regions and nations simply cannot produce enough food for current populations and have no choice but to engage in long-distance trade, with all of the vulnerability to food price volatility that this implies. This quandary is deepening with climate change (even before future emission and sequestration scenarios are considered), which now bears heavily on efforts to enhance food self-sufficiency – and in some cases is beginning to completely overshadow them. Many of the Low-Income Food-Deficit Countries identified by the FAO are the ones that are expected to be most adversely impacted by changes such as increasing average temperatures and aridity, greater weather extremes and rising sea levels. This is an exceedingly iniquitous dynamic: low-income countries are especially threatened by conditions they have done little to cause and could become still more dependent upon the food imports from the industrialized world that are part of its extremely disproportionate contribution to climate change (Weis 2010).

As suggested earlier, it is generally clear that efforts to move towards greater localization are consonant with the need to mitigate climate change. The relationship of food sovereignty to climate change – both in the urgency of the mitigation imperative and in the prospect that impacts might devastate the productive capacity of large areas of land – is in some ways a contemporary permutation of the old question of autarchy versus global transformation that animated debates among revolutionaries a century ago.

4.   Possibilities and limits of urban food production

One of the most compelling attractions of food sovereignty is the idea of fortifying (or rebuilding) direct, solidarity-based relationships between producers and consumers. In this, it seeks to address the environmental impacts of 'distancing' (in particular, from fossil energy consumption and GHG emissions noted earlier), while assuming that more intimate, even face-to-face, interactions could guarantee decent remuneration for food producers and also ensure affordable food prices for consumers. This prospect in turn assumes the co-existence of a 'floor price' and 'ceiling price', which are broadly and flexibly framed in moral economy terms. Such 'price bands' were long used by developing country governments of diverse orientations as a defence against unfair foreign competition (see, for example, Ffrench-Davis 2003, 218), though they have fallen out of favour in recent decades. While this is an admirable aspiration, it also presents perhaps one of the biggest challenges to food sovereignty as a political project because producer-consumer relationships are not only marked by the potential for solidarity, symbiosis and synergy, but can contain deep tensions and contradictions, as Bernstein, Agarwal and a number of other contributions in this collection point out. This solidarity/tension dilemma has multiple axes. A central axis is characterized by *rural-urban* divisions, which are growing beyond historic dimensions with so many people now living far from traditional food granaries. A second major axis, less recognized in the literature on food sovereignty, is marked *rural-rural* divisions, which reflects the need to account for the fact that most rural residents are now net food buyers, whether they are farmers or not. It is clear that prospects for producer-consumer solidarity must develop mechanisms for reconciling the desire for better remuneration from producers with the desire for affordable prices from consumers – which would mean resolving the age-old 'scissors' dynamic of rising costs and declining returns in agriculture.

Perhaps the most obvious way to reconcile these tensions is to bypass the various layers of brokers in the food system, such as food processors, traders, transport owners, financiers and petty merchants. But to go beyond scattered and mostly localized market arrangements between producers and consumers (internationalized mainly through fair trade), and work towards large-scale food system-wide reform, public policy carried out by the central state is essential. This leads us back to the contentious issue of the role of the state in food sovereignty (as discussed elsewhere in this introductory essay and in a number of contributions to this collection – e.g. contributions by McKay *et al.*, Giunta, and Bernstein), which includes questions about 'multiple sovereignties' (Edelman, this collection; Patel 2009) and 'competing sovereignties' (Schiavoni forthcoming).

This context partly explains how 'localization' has become a central imperative in food sovereignty, both to reduce the 'distancing' in the food system, as Clapp (2014) stresses, and to minimize the gap between production cost/mark-up and retail price. As has been stressed, the magnitude of urbanization is a central reason why geographical distance is such a challenge. However, as Robbins (forthcoming) argues, the matter of *spatial* distance is further complicated by the matter of *institutional* distance. This essentially implies that some social groups may live in close spatial proximity to sites of food production but face structural and institutional barriers that render food from these sites largely or wholly inaccessible for them. So while localization will undoubtedly remain an important aspect of food sovereignty, it should be understood not just as physical proximity, but also in relation to social, economic, political and cultural proximity.

Another aspect of localization that needs to be taken seriously stems from the fact that urban and peri-urban spaces are not only sites of consumption but are also increasingly key sites of food production (FAO 2002; McGregor, Simon, and Thompson 2005; Premat 2012). While 'urban agriculture' contributes only a small part of total food supply, it is estimated that it helps to feed up to 800 million people globally. More importantly, it is practiced by 30–70 percent of poor, urban populations in the world's poor countries, and is positively correlated with improved food security (FAO 2010; Zezza and Tasciotti 2010). Given the ongoing migrations of the rural poor to slums, the importance of urban agriculture will only increase. Especially in the fast-growing cities of the Global South, urban food production is difficult to quantify, since it stems mainly from independent livelihood initiatives by individuals or groups who squat on vacant lots to produce food for consumption and for the market.

However, the full value of urban and peri-urban food production goes beyond quantifying food output and also includes the potential to amplify solidarity with farmers. This potential is reflected in the fact that the urban and peri-urban-based food initiatives are important sources of political momentum in food sovereignty advocacy, given that such advocacy is motivated not only by an idea of solidarity with farmers in the distant countryside but also by immediate concerns around public health, access to healthy and affordable foods, dismantling racialized food systems, and the culture and lifestyle of food producers, food sellers, restaurant owners and consumers. Here, it must be acknowledged that the groups spearheading urban food initiatives are politically varied, and those conscious of food sovereignty are far from the majority, as is certainly the case in both Europe and North America (Holt-Giménez and Shattuck 2001; Román-Alcalá 2013),[4] though at the same time it is important to note that there are budding alliances between more radical urban-based 'food justice' movements and food sovereignty advocacy. A good example of this is the food justice movement in the United States, led by people from underserved communities of colour, which has a strong, historical affinity with food sovereignty (Holt-Giménez and Wang 2012).

In sum, there are many reasons that urban-based food initiatives should not be dismissed out of hand, and are fertile ground for enhancing alliances in the future.

---

[4]One strategic advantage that stems from this diversity is that some urban food initiatives involve social groups much closer to the dominant media, who possess considerable influence in shaping opinions about the dominant agro-food system.

5. Who will administer food sovereignty?

A central contribution of this collection is to tackle head-on questions that food sovereignty activists and scholars had often heretofore ignored or been reluctant to examine, with some notable exceptions including Beuchelt and Virchow (2012), Buisson (2013) and Hospes (2014). What, for example, will be required to administer food sovereignty and who or what will do it? Who is the sovereign in food sovereignty? And what kinds of limitations on particular kinds of production or trade does food sovereignty imply?

Trauger provides the widest ranging discussion of theories of sovereignty (as opposed to simply *food* sovereignty) in this collection. Her analysis highlights two dimensions that are central to the ongoing debates: the role in food sovereignty of states (or other governance mechanisms) and the role of markets (or other forms of allocating production factors and distributing outputs). Indeed, it is possible to locate most of the authors represented here in relation to their viewpoints on these two questions. Trauger argues that 'food sovereignty may implement its radical vision within the existing structures of the modern liberal nation state by working with, against and in between its juridical structures by reworking the central notions of sovereignty: territory, economy and power' (Trauger 2014, 1145). She further suggests that food sovereignty practices constitute 'a kind of civil disobedience' that can, at least temporarily, re-territorialize space, and cites as an example the 'overlapping sovereignties' that affect the traditional gathering and propagating of wild rice by the Anishinabe indigenous people in northern Minnesota.

Bernstein declares that the state 'is really "the elephant in the room" of … food sovereignty'. Desmarais and Wittman note how the question of the state's role has divided farm organizations in Québec, with some arguing that food sovereignty is synonymous with producers' control over the production process and others advocating versions of state-led food sovereignty. Advocates of the latter approach in Québec hope to counter federal government attempts to threaten provincial-level supply management mechanisms. Kloppenburg's innovative and controversial call for defending 'seed sovereignty' through a kind of open-source licensing similar to that used in the world of computer software depends entirely on contract law, which is, of course, a potentially powerful form of state authority. Trauger calls for enacting food sovereignty 'at multiple territorial scales' and asserts that its 'activities are always vulnerable to state power unless food sovereignty's economic and territorial alternatives are also written into the national state constitution' (Trauger 2014, 1148). Yet as Giunta shows in the case of Ecuador, the first in a small but growing list of countries which have incorporated food sovereignty principles into their national charters, the elevation of food sovereignty to the level of a constitutional norm has done relatively little to blunt the country's powerful agro-industrial interests (see also the contribution by McKay *et al.*).

Edelman's contribution raises several questions about the administration of food sovereignty that he claims require greater specification if implementation is to be effective. These include the limits on farm size, firm size and long-distance trade that are implied (but rarely specified) in most programmatic statements about food sovereignty, as well as the delicate politics of modifying consumer tastes for exotic products as economic localization progresses. Along with the contributions by Agarwal and by Burnett and Murphy, Edelman asks about the limits on producers' choices – to expand a successful small farm, for example, or to employ noxious chemicals – and who would enforce these limits.

Peschard raises another intriguing possibility in relation to states and supra-state levels of governance. Ambiguities in key international agreements, she asserts, particularly Trade-Related Aspects of Intellectual Property (TRIPS, part of WTO), may provide more room for manoeuvre and more development space than is usually appreciated, particularly when 'cunning states' (Randeria 2007), such as India, engage in foot-dragging or fail to implement the more draconian provisions of treaties they have ratified. Peschard, along with several others in this collection, points to the importance of unpacking the category 'state', with its diverse bureaucratic elements, its contradictory political and economic interests, its efficacy or inertia, its distinct levels of governance and its – at times – limited or overlapping sovereignty over key on-the-ground processes.

The state versus market dichotomy – central to the pioneering work of Polanyi (2001), among others – recurs throughout the debates in the pages that follow. Van der Ploeg, for example, sees food sovereignty as an alternative to the market economy. Peasants, he maintains, 'need the means and space' to fuel agricultural growth, improve livelihoods and increase food provision. Autonomy from input and credit markets 'allows peasant farms to produce for the markets, without being completely dependent on them'. He suggests that innovations that cannot be 'taken over' are central to food sovereignty, such as the system of rice intensification (SRI), a set of low-cost agroecological practices that has resulted in spectacular yield increases on small farms in several Asian countries and elsewhere. This vision of food sovereignty as an *alternative* to the market is not, however, shared by all contributors to this collection. Some, like Edelman, point to the Left's failure to analytically 'own' the often dismal experience of anti-market command economies under what used to be called 'actually existing socialism', while several others point to the necessity of markets that permit small producers to realize income and consumers to obtain a varied supply of foodstuffs (e.g. Burnett and Murphy, Giunta). These contributions, while approaching the market issue from widely divergent angles, share an appreciation for what Giunta, paraphrasing the Ecuadorian constitution, terms 'a dynamic and balanced relationship between society, state and market, in harmony with Nature' (Giunta 2014, 1214).

6.   The challenges of pluralism in a food sovereign society

Food sovereignty tends to hinge on a broad – but not always ideologically coherent – belief in democratic land control (for the emergence and promotion of smallholder farming) coupled with advocacy for farming systems that are both food securing and ecologically sustainable. This combination is often promoted together, though not always, and an agroecology-centric position is but one of various possible interpretations of food sovereignty. Other competing interpretations pivot on organic farming and/or fair trade-oriented agriculture, and some include views of more industrial but localized farming systems.

In recent years, agroecology has become much more systematically integrated into the food sovereignty discourse and practice, especially among social movement groups associated with LVC, which now explicitly advocates 'agroecology-based food sovereignty' and has developed an extensive agroecology training program. This echoes Altieri and Toledo's argument that the core principles of agroecology must provide the basis of any food sovereignty strategy, including

> recycling nutrients and energy on the farm, rather than introducing external inputs; enhancing soil organic matter and soil biological activity; diversifying plant species and genetic resources in agroecosystems over time and space; integrating crops and livestock and optimizing interactions and productivity of the total farming system, rather than the yields of individual species. (2011, 588)

This focus on agroecology as the productive basis for food sovereignty stands in fundamental tension with other alternative farming systems, such as more limited versions of organic farming and fair trade-oriented exporting which are popular among some food sovereignty advocates. For Altieri and Toledo (2011, 588), such alternatives are far too narrow, as 'organic farming systems … do not challenge the monoculture nature of plantations and rely on external inputs as well as on foreign and expensive certification seals', while 'fair trade systems destined only for agro-export, offer little to small farmers who in turn become dependent on external inputs and foreign and volatile markets'. Agroecology has come a long way since its original farming systems approach, both geographically (to include whole watersheds) and systemically (to encompass the whole food system). Its 'mission' has also expanded socially and politically, in part because it has come under ideological and economic attack, and it has become aligned towards food sovereignty at the same time that food sovereignty began to embrace agroecology (Holt-Giménez and Altieri 2013).

While agroecology prioritizes democratic land control along with food securing and ecologically sustainable farming practices, there are cases where these three objectives are assumed, though not in the context of an agroecology framework. Borras and Franco (2012a) sketch a possible set of dilemmas that may arise from the intersection of these three core elements of food sovereignty. In situations where the combination is indeed grounded in agroecology-based production, the task of food sovereignty movements is to consolidate and expand such ideal conditions. But these situations are rare. Much more common are situations where various combinations of these three elements are present. For instance, small farms with democratic land control by peasants may exist, and they may be producing maximum possible output from a given land area without using agroecological practices, employing instead inputs such as chemical fertilizers, pesticides, and genetically modified (GM) seeds. In other cases, peasants following agroecological practices might not have enough land to produce sufficient food (or other farm outputs to enable them to buy enough food) or might be making inadequate use of the land and other resources they control. The existence of such varied and less-than-ideal agro-food systems contributes to highly differentiated food sovereignty movements (Holt-Giménez and Shattuck 2011).

The degree of tolerance for pluralism is one of the biggest and most challenging questions confronting food sovereignty practitioners and researchers. If boundaries are set on farmer choice, what happens to farms that continue with some or many industrial inputs or practices? If agroecology is the aspiration, how can food sovereignty movements contribute to transitional efforts for less-than-ideal farms and farming landscapes? Will the idea of a '*diálogo de saberes*', as analysed by Martínez-Torres and Rosset in this collection, or the concept of 'unity in diversity' (Desmarais 2007) allow for a constructive interchange between the various social groups differentiated by their actually existing practices of food sovereignty? The answers to these questions are not obvious and will require careful empirical research and conceptual soul-searching.

7. Property and food sovereignty: from titles to the social relations of production

At the core of the food sovereignty vision is access to land. Redistributive land reform and what Borras and Franco (2012b) call 'land sovereignty' are generally considered a necessary foundation for creating a just food system in much of the world. In addition to land, others have added seed sovereignty (Bezner-Kerr 2010; Kloppenburg, this collection) as a way of recognizing both the importance of plant germplasm and challenging the increasing dominance of what Kloppenburg calls the 'Gene Giants' in controlling property rights over this basic resource.

Recently, this concern for access of various kinds has led to renewed efforts to provide secure tenure or title to land and seeds (Li 2012; Peters 2013). For a surprisingly diverse set of actors – from the Millennium Challenge Corporation of the US government to the FAO and Oxfam International to an array of social movements under the food sovereignty banner – titling has emerged as a key mechanism to address community and individual vulnerabilities. In the face of concerns over large-scale land deals, secure title seems necessary to ensure everything from progressive distribution (distribution from large to small landholdings, or from rich to poor) and access to resources to fair, prior and informed consent (FPIC), wherein companies are expected or obligated to consult with communities about their intentions to extract, produce or develop (FAO 2014; Franco 2014). This focus on secure property rights is often motivated by a desire to protect the most vulnerable community members, such as women and indigenous peoples, from dispossession. As Agarwal suggests in this collection, women face a variety of threats to their access to land, though they are still as likely to be dispossessed by male relatives (or relatives of an ex- or dead husband) as by a state or corporation. The struggle to include women on land titles has been relatively effective in Latin America (Deere and León 2001) though less so in Africa and Asia (but see Peters 2013 for an example of matrilineal societies where she argues that women would be prejudiced by the distribution of equal titles to male and female household heads).

In the discussion of (and practice around) property and secure access to land, there is of course the danger of assuming that (1) titles are the best means of securing access and (2) such access will necessarily provide the stability that will generate entrepreneurial or productive behaviour on the land in ways that align with the goals of either neoliberal rationality or food sovereignty. In the end, the property form may matter less than the struggle to have new forms documented and distributed – the key is the documentation (visibility and voice) and distribution (the move towards equality). Access, as Ribot and Peluso (2003) have argued, is a complicated and often contradictory and overlapping bundle of relations that is ultimately rooted in various forms of authority and power (see also Fairbairn 2013). Those who have the authority or power to dictate the conditions of access are able to circumvent or construct legal frameworks if they choose; indeed, titles may provide a legal means of foreclosure, alienation and expropriation (Mitchell 2009). Similarly, claims of having observed FPIC may allow external actors to operate in areas where otherwise they would have been viewed with suspicion or barred (Franco 2014). These troubling realities are among the main reasons why the landless movement in Brazil (the Landless Rural Workers Movement, or MST) officially rejects the government's attempt to provide new land reform beneficiaries with title to their land. In addition, the movement fears that in the context of Brazilian agriculture, with its focus on large-scale production, those receiving titles would become ineligible for state support, including credit and political representation provided to land reform beneficiaries but not to small holders.

Kloppenburg's analysis in this collection of the Open Source Seed Initiative (OSSI) provides an excellent example of the potential for open-access property regimes to allow wide distribution of seed technologies, even as the OSSI runs the danger of being drawn into the exclusionary world of contract law. Open-source seeds would unquestionably be a significant blow to corporate plant breeding in the early twenty-first century. As Kloppenburg notes, 'Negotiating the dense accumulation of intellectual property rights that potentially surrounds the material and methods of their work in order to assess and to obtain "freedom to operate" is now a substantial transaction cost for breeders' (Kloppenburg 2014, 1230). The dangers of open access are even more apparent in relation to land where the concept has been commonly understood as *res nullius* or land belonging to nobody, the thesis that underwrote the conquest of the Americas and which is currently being repurposed in the form of the 'yield gap', whereby land is considered to not be fully owned if its use does not lead to what is considered the highest possible yield when compared to global productivity standards. Assertions about yield gaps are a crucially important means of claiming that land in use is open-access land, available for those who promise to increase production levels.

Ultimately, there can be no single vision of the most appropriate form of property ownership for food sovereignty. Open access, public property, individual, communal, cooperative and collective ownership all have different merits in different contexts, and the best solution may be to recognize the merits of different property forms and allow for flexibility. Agarwal's piece in this collection cites LVC leader Paul Nicholson's preference for collective rights over individual land ownership (cited in Wittman 2009, 679), but this may be a difficult rule to force on farmers who have historically resisted large-scale, top-down collectivization efforts. Instead, attempts to integrate individual land ownership with various forms of collective organization and institutionalization, such as credit and machinery cooperatives, have the potential to build solidarity and benefit from economies of scale while allowing traditional or culturally appropriate ownership forms and norms to survive and multiply.

8. Food sovereignty, a multidimensional concept

Food sovereignty is inherently a multidimensional concept. The only way to be food sovereign is to develop networks of aggregation, processing, commercialization and distribution that are themselves linked to other sectors of the economy. Food sovereignty discourses have often focused narrowly on food and on farmers (and on idealized examples of these, as Bernstein notes in this collection), but if food producers and consumers are to be truly sovereign, then both will have to be supported by and incorporated into a variety of social, economic and political fora that go well beyond food itself. In other words, food sovereignty requires a healthy, sustainable and diverse rural economy that goes well beyond food production. Most if not all children of farmers want to be educated and to have the option of exploring non-farm occupations (White 2011) – to have the opportunity to become doctors and poets and mechanics as their interests and talents would allow. Food sovereignty will not offer a sustainable vision for the future if these activities and options are not part of the larger picture.

Contemporary life on the land in much of the world suffers from the historical legacies of urban bias and industrial development. Influential theorists and policy-makers have contended that agriculture generates only limited backward and forward linkages and that development, therefore, necessarily meant the rapid transition from rural economies to urban ones. Particular industries and urban areas were targeted for development while the rural poor (smallholders and the landless) were seen as sources of cheap labour and the wealthy landed classes were seen as producers of raw materials and cheap food. Food sovereignty advocates, as Agarwal indicates in this collection, argue that migration out of rural areas into urban ones has less to do with a rejection of farming *per se* than with a rejection of farming under the negative, insecure conditions fostered by urban bias. Visions of food sovereignty are a way of correcting this historical prejudice and revalorizing life on the land, but the attempt to revalorize small farms should not entail new anti-off-farm prejudices. If food sovereignty is to be more than simply a populist claim for a return to traditional life on the land, then the vision will need to accommodate flourishing rural economies that include industry, services and entertainment, a point on which Bernstein and McMichael agree.

If food sovereignty is to be the banner for a broader struggle, then the campaign for the sovereignty of food producers will need to be embedded in struggles for:

- the social function of property, which is about the collective obligation to organize the means of production, including land, seeds and capital, in ways that benefit society and nature as a whole;
- the social function of food and livelihood – or the 'right to be free of want', which is how, in a landmark legal case, the judicial system in the Brazilian state of Rio Grande do Sul interpreted the right of landless squatters to remain on their land (Houtzager 2005);
- the struggle to increase value and distribute according to need, which is embodied in the vision of food sovereignty to build agroindustry in rural communities to increase economies of scale, create forward and backward linkages and generate added value, all under the control of those who labour;
- the social function of political representation, which requires democratizing access to representation through building ties to sympathetic political forces.

Ultimately, these social functions can only be realized if they can be internalized and socialized, and so movements for food sovereignty will need to build educational programs and work to develop a collective will (Meek 2011; Tarlau 2013). It is also important to recognize that all of these struggles are contained within the struggle for access to land, but they are not necessarily visible if land is seen as a narrow 'thing', rather than as a set or web of articulated relationships situated in particular places and times. Rethinking food production might help to build a better and more just food system, but sustaining that and including people and sectors not directly (or willingly) linked to the land requires a much broader, multidimensional struggle for land, seeds, rural economies, education, representation, embedded markets and global, regional and local connections.

9. Food sovereignty and 'rights'

The food sovereignty movement focuses on the rights of farmers and consumers, usually seen as occupying the two ends of the food chain. This conception does not adequately recognize that the positions may often coincide, and that farmers in many countries are simultaneously food producers and buyers, peasants and proletarians. Increasing off-farm employment in rural areas and seasonal or long-term migration into urban settings means that, even in countries with large populations involved in agriculture, more and more farm households depend on purchased food, a dynamic that Agarwal analyses in this collection. Their stake in policies that make food affordable is a political hot-button issue; public discontent expressed through food riots – 51 instances in 37 countries over the last eight years – threatens political stability (World Bank 2014, 6). Social movements such as the Right to Food Campaign in India are based precisely on this notion of citizens' entitlement to food: that the state is the primary institution to which claims must be directed (Drèze 2004, 1726; Mander 2012). By asserting the right to food along with the rights to work, education and health, the campaign attempts to realize a democratic welfare state that is responsive and accountable to its poorest citizens. Its success is predicated upon a political calculus where the state is expected to privilege proletarian identities over peasant ones, a contradictory dynamic in which people may lose as farmers but gain as citizens. While the food sovereignty movement argues that a right to food that relies on industrial agriculture is unsustainable and plays into the hands of global agribusiness (see Trauger), many right-to-food activists remain sceptical about the food sovereignty movement's ability to address the issue of chronic hunger and malnutrition in an increasingly non-agrarian world. This challenge is easy to dismiss when it is posed by agribusiness, but harder to set aside when asked by rights activists. Food sovereignty activists, on the other hand (such as Desmarais and Wittman or Martínez-Torres and Rosset in this collection), argue that it is a broader concept than the right to food since it raises the issues of what food is produced, where, how and by whom.

The right to food, however, is an accepted principle in international law, legally binding for the 162 states that have ratified the 1966 International Covenant on Economic, Social and Cultural Rights, and the subject of various more recent specifications of states' obligations (although obviously not 'a guarantee', as Trauger observes). Several governments have incorporated it into law as well, some at the level of national constitutions (Golay 2011; Ziegler et al. 2011). While food sovereignty has also become a constitutional norm in various countries, as several contributions in this collection discuss (e.g. Giunta, McKay *et al.*), the concept is far from enjoying the legitimacy among international and national policy-makers that is the case with the right to food. Moreover, even when food sovereignty has achieved constitutional or other legal recognition, it has often been *in combination with* the right to food. Advocates of the latter approach have generally neglected to consider access to productive resources – and distributional questions more broadly – as part of the right to food. Food sovereignty supporters, in contrast, have given these elements a central place in their analyses. Nonetheless, the vastly greater international legitimacy of the right to food, as opposed to food sovereignty, suggests that it may be a more effective advocacy tool for building consensus and for beginning to resolve urgent crises related to food and agriculture – at least until food sovereignty makes further gains (see, for example, the analysis of the engagement of the former United Nations Special Rapporteur on the Right to Food, Olivier de Schutter, in Burnett and Murphy's discussion). As McMichael indicates, in his contribution to this collection, even the FAO's Committee on World Food Security, which opened to significant civil society participation in 2009 as a result of pressure from the International Planning Committee for Food Sovereignty, lacks explicit references to food sovereignty in its program and mandate. This observation echoes Beuchelt and Virchow (2012, 262–3), who point out that

> The International Labour Organization (ILO), the United Nations Environmental Programme (UNEP) and the World Bank have not worked further with the concept of food sovereignty. The United Nations Conference on Trade and Development (UNCTAD) also has no official definition, but the concept of food sovereignty is at least mentioned in some documents. The Food and Agriculture Organization (FAO) appears to deal more frequently with the concept of food sovereignty but no official FAO document contains the concept either … . The United Nations Human Rights Council (UNHRC) seems the only UN body which intensively discussed within its documents and meetings the concept of food sovereignty.

Supporters of food sovereignty tend to view it as a precondition for achieving the right to adequate food, but few have given in-depth attention to the questions that sympathetic critics, such as Beuchelt and Virchow, raise about the term's relative lack of acceptance among policy makers.

10.   Food sovereignty's agrarian question: what difference does food sovereignty make?

Food sovereignty has been at the centre of global resistance to capitalism since the 'Battle of Seattle' in 1999, in which a broad-based coalition of farmer, worker and environmentalist organizations brought the neoliberal project to establish the WTO to worldwide attention (Edelman 2009). The dramatic and tragic events of the 2003 protests against the WTO in Cancún, Mexico – in which South Korean farm leader Kun Hai Lee stabbed himself to death, claiming 'WTO kills farmers' – reflect the desperate human struggles that have given rise to the food sovereignty movement.

Over the last two decades, food sovereignty has captured the imagination of farmers, workers, consumers and citizens, staking out ideological territory of resistance and hope in the face of neoliberal projects for the unrelenting privatization, deregulation, corporatization and financialization of the world's economies. Much is expected of food sovereignty. Despite its broad political currency (or perhaps because of it), food sovereignty is often taken up as a set of demands, principles, policies, reforms and rights that together will somehow transform the neoliberal food regime, without identifying the profound structural changes needed in the capitalist economy and the liberal state for food sovereignty to feasibly exist. This oversight plagues many of the demands that adhere to food sovereignty (such as 'food democracy', 'food justice' and the 'right to food') with intractable political contradictions. While it is unreasonable for food sovereignty practitioners and scholars to assume the task of charting a global course through late capitalism, none of us can escape the need for political reflection on the particular role of food sovereignty in pushing this transition in a *post-capitalist* direction.

Trauger (this volume) tentatively open this door with a reflection on territory and strategies

> that work within, against and in between the powers of the sovereign liberal state. These include reframing property rights as use rights, engaging in non-commodified food exchanges and practicing civil disobedience to usher in reforms without compromising on essential elements of the food sovereignty agenda. (Trauger 2014, 1131)

Conclusions

The big questions are now on the table. Food sovereignty is entering its 'second generation', as Olivier De Schutter remarked at the Yale conference. This new stage will be marked by greater specificity and a refusal to seek refuge in vague and comforting platitudes. It will likely be characterized by an intensified and better-informed dialogue, increasingly complex alliances between producers and consumers, and greater integration with agroecology and with new paradigms of social and cultural change such as the Andean concept of *buen vivir* (Fatheuer 2011). The challenges remain daunting: corporate influence in politics at all levels and control of global food chains (and those for non-food agricultural products), as well as markets for inputs, especially seeds; the industrial 'cheap food' model on which too many consumers still rely out of necessity, preference or habit; the tenacious defence of globalized agricultural trade by influential states and powerful multilateral agencies, with their robust judicial apparatuses and dispute resolution and enforcement mechanisms; and the fact that biophysical threats to production from climate change are intensifying and beginning to wreak havoc on production in many of the world's poorest regions. Perhaps the largest overarching question is whether food sovereignty can generate transformational reforms – or the sort of 'nonreformist reforms' Jack Kloppenburg invokes (following Erik Olin Wright), implying 'social changes that are feasible in the world as it is … but which prefigure in important ways more emancipatory possibilities'.

References

Agarwal, B. 2014. Food sovereignty, food security and democratic choice: Critical contradictions, difficult conciliations. *Journal of Peasant Studies* 41, no. 6: 1247–68.

Altieri, M.A., and V.M. Toledo. 2011. The agroecological revolution in Latin America: Rescuing nature, ensuring food sovereignty and empowering peasants. *Journal of Peasant Studies* 38, no. 3: 587–612.

Bernstein, H. 2014. Food sovereignty via the 'peasant way': A skeptical view. *Journal of Peasant Studies* 41, no. 6: 1031–63.

Beuchelt, T.D., and D. Virchow. 2012. Food sovereignty or the human right to adequate food: Which concept serves better as international development policy for global hunger and poverty reduction?. *Agriculture and Human Values* 29, no. 2: 259–73.

Bezner-Kerr, R. 2010. Seed sovereignty: Unearthing the cultural and material struggles over seed in Malawi. In *Food sovereignty: Reconnecting food, nature & community*, eds. H. Wittman, A.A. Desmarais, and N. Wiebe, 134–51. Halifax, N.S.: Fernwood Publishing.

Borras, S. 2008. *Competing views and strategies on agrarian reform. Volume 1: International perspective*. Quezon City: Ateneo de Manila University Press.

Borras, S.M., and J.C. Franco. 2012a. Global land grabbing and trajectories of agrarian change: A preliminary analysis. *Journal of Agrarian Change* 12, no. 1: 34–59.

Borras, S., and J.C. Franco. 2012b. A 'land sovereignty' alternative? Toward a peoples' counter-enclosure. TNI Discussion Paper, July 2012.

Buisson, M. 2013. *Conquérir la souveraineté alimentaire*. Paris: l'Harmattan.

Burnett, K., and S. Murphy. 2014. What place for international trade in food sovereignty? *Journal of Peasant Studies* 41, no. 6: 1065–84.

Campbell, H., and R. LeHeron. 2007. Supermarkets, producers and audit technologies: The constitutive micro-politics of food, legitimacy and governance. In *Supermarkets and agri-food supply chains: Transformations in the production and consumption of foods*, eds. D. Burch and G. Lawrence, 131–53. Cheltenham: Edward Elgar.

Clapp, J. 2014. Financialization, distance and global food politics. *Journal of Peasant Studies* 41, no. 5. DOI:10.1080/03066150.2013.875536

Deere, C.D., and M. Leon. 2001. *Empowering women land and property rights in Latin America*. Pittsburgh, Pa: University of Pittsburgh Press.

Desmarais, A.A. 2007. *La Vía Campesina: Globalization and the power of peasants*. Halifax: Fernwood.

Drèze, J. 2004. Democracy and the right to food. *Economic and Political Weekly* 39, no. 17: 1723–31.

Edelman, M. 2009. Peasant-farmer movements, third world peoples, and the Seattle protests against the World Trade Organization, 1999. *Dialectical Anthropology* 33, no. 2: 109–28.

Edelman, M. 2014. Food sovereignty: Forgotten genealogies and future regulatory challenges. *Journal of Peasant Studies* 41, no. 6: 959–78.

Fairbairn, M. 2013. Indirect dispossession: Domestic power imbalances and foreign access to land in Mozambique. *Development and Change* 44: 335–56.

FAO. 2002. Feeding an increasingly urban world. *World Food Summit Five Years Later*. http://www.fao.org/worldfoodsummit/english/newsroom/focus/focus2.htm

FAO. 2010. Fighting poverty and hunger: What role for urban agriculture? http://www.fao.org/docrep/012/al377e/al377e00.pdf

FAO. 2014. Respecting Free, Prior and Informed Consent, Governance of Tenure Technical Guide 3.

Fatheuer, T. 2011. *Buen vivir: A brief introduction to Latin America's new concepts for the good life and the rights of nature*. Berlin: Heinrich Böll Foundation, Publication Series on Ecology No. 17.

Ffrench-Davis, R. 2003. *Entre el neoliberalismo y el crecimiento con equidad: tres décadas de política económica en Chile*. Santiago: J.C. Sáez.

Fisher, C. 2007. Selling coffee, or selling out? Evaluating different ways to analyze the fair-trade system. *Culture & Agriculture* 29, no. 2: 78–88.

Food First. 2014. *Food Sovereignty: A Critical Dialogue*. Video Gallery. http://foodfirst.org/publication/food-sovereignty-a-critical-dialogue/

Franco, J. 2014. *Reclaiming Free Prior and Informed Consent (FPIC) in the context of global land grabs*. Amsterdam: Transnational Institute.

Fridell, G. 2013. *Alternative trade: Legacies and the future*. Halifax: Fernwood.

Giunta, I. 2014. Food sovereignty in Ecuador: Peasant struggles and the challenge of institutionalization. *Journal of Peasant Studies* 41, no. 6: 1201–24.

Golay, C. 2011. *Droit à l'alimentation et accès à la justice*. Bruxelles: Bruylant.

Holt-Giménez, E., and M. Altieri. 2013. Agroecology, food sovereignty, and the new green revolution. *Agroecology and Sustainable Food Systems* 37, no. 1: 90–102.

Holt Giménez, E., and A. Shattuck. 2011. Food crises, food regimes and food movements: Rumblings of reform or tides of transformation? *Journal of Peasant Studies* 38, no. 1: 109–44.

Holt-Giménez, E., and Y. Wang. 2012. Reform or transformation? The pivotal role of food justice in the U.S. food movement. *Race/Ethnicity: Multidisciplinary Global Contexts* 5, no. 1: 83–102.

Hospes, O. 2014. Food sovereignty: The debate, the deadlock, and a suggested detour. *Agriculture and Human Values* 31, no. 1: 119–30.

Houtzager, P.P. 2005. The Movement of the Landless (MST) and the juridical field in Brazil, IDS Working Paper 248, Institute for Development Studies, University of Sussex.

International Institute of Social Studies. 2014. *Food Sovereignty: A Critical Dialogue*. Food sovereignty 2013/2014 conference paper series. http://www.iss.nl/research/research_programmes/ political_economy_of_resources_environment_and_population_per/networks/critical_agrarian_ studies_icas/food_sovereignty_a_critical_dialogue/

Khor, M. 2000. Globalization and the South: Some critical issues. Geneva: United Nations Conference on Trade and Development, Discussion Paper No. 147, April.

Kloppenburg, J. 2014. Re-purposing the master's tools: the open source seed initiative and the struggle for seed sovereignty. *Journal of Peasant Studies* 41, no. 6: 1225–46.

Li, T. 2012. What is land: Anthropological perspectives on the global land rush, paper presented at the Second International Conference on global Land Grabbing, Cornell University, October 17–19.

Mander, H. 2012. *Ash in the belly: India's unfinished battled against hunger*. New Delhi: Penguin Books.

Martínez-Torres, M.E., and P.M. Rosset. 2014. *Diálogo de saberes* in La Vía Campesina: food sovereignty and agroecology. *Journal of Peasant Studies* 41, no. 6: 979–97.

McGregor, D., D. Simon, and D. Thompson, eds. 2005. *The peri-urban interface: Approaches to sustainable natural and human resource use*. London: Routledge.

McKay, B., R. Nehring, and M. Walsch-Dilley. 2014. The 'state' of food sovereignty in Latin America: Political projects and alternative pathways in Venezuela, Ecuador, and Bolivia. *Journal of Peasant Studies* 41, no. 6: 1175–200.

Meek, D. 2011. Propaganda, collective participation and the 'war of position' in the Brazilian Landless Workers' Movement. *Studies in the Education of Adults* 43, no. 2: 164–80.

Mitchell, T. 2009. How neoliberalism makes its world: The urban property rights project in Peru. In *The road from Mont Pèlerin: The making of the neoliberal thought collective*, eds. Philip Mirowski and Dieter Plehwe, 386–416. Cambridge: Harvard University Press.

Patel, R. 2009. Grassroots voices: Food sovereignty. *Journal of Peasant Studies* 36, no. 3: 663–706.

Paprocki, K., and J. Cons. 2014. Life in a shrimp zone: aqua- and other cultures of Bangladesh's coastal landscape. *Journal of Peasant Studies* 41, no. 6: 1109–30.

Peters, E. P. 2013. Land appropriation, surplus people and a battle over visions of agrarian futures in Africa. *The Journal of Peasant Studies* 40, no. 3: 537–62.

Polanyi, K. 2001[1944]. *The great transformation: The political and economic origins of our time*. 2nd ed. Boston: Beacon Press.

Premat, A. 2012. *Sowing change: The making of Havana's urban agriculture*. Nashville, TN: Vanderbilt University Press.

Randeria, S. 2007. The state of globalization: Legal plurality, overlapping sovereignties and ambiguous alliances between civil society and the cunning state in India. *Theory, Culture & Society* 24, no. 1: 1–33.

Ribot, J.C., and N.L. Peluso. 2003. A theory of access. *Rural Sociology* 68: 153–81.

Robbins, M.J. (forthcoming). Locating food sovereignty: Geographical and sectoral distance in the global food system. *Third World Quarterly*.

Román-Alcalá, A. 2013. Occupy the farm: a study of civil society tactics to cultivate commons and construct food sovereignty in the United States. Paper presented at the Food Sovereignty: A Critical Dialogue International Conference September 14–15, Yale Program in Agrarian Studies.

Schanbacher, W.D. 2010. *The politics of food: The global conflict between food security and food sovereignty*. Santa Barbara, CA: Praeger.

Schiavoni, C. (forthcoming). Competing sovereignties in the political construction of food sovereignty. *Globalizations*.

Sylla, N. 2014. *The fair trade scandal: Marketing poverty to benefit the rich*. London: Pluto.

Tarlau, R. 2013. The social(ist) pedagogies of the MST: Towards new relations of production in the Brazilian countryside. *The Socialist Education Policy Analysis Archives* 21, no. 41: 1–23. http://files.eric.ed.gov/fulltext/EJ1015367.pdf

Trauger, A. 2014. Toward a political geography of food sovereignty: transforming territory, exchange and power in the liberal sovereign state. *Journal of Peasant Studies* 41, no. 6: 1131–52.

Vía Campesina. 2009. *Small scale sustainable farmers are cooling down the Earth*. Jakarta: Vía Campesina. http://viacampesina.org/downloads/pdf/en/EN-paper5.pdf

Weber, C.L., and H.S. Matthews. 2008. Food-miles and the relative climate impacts of food choices in the US. *Environmental Science and Technology* 42, no. 10: 3508–13.

Weis, T. 2010. The accelerating biophysical contradictions of industrial capitalist agriculture. *Journal of Agrarian Change* 10, no. 3: 315–41.

White, B. 2011. Who will own the countryside? Dispossession, rural youth and the future of farming. The Hague: International Institute of Social Studies, Valedictory Lecture, October 13.

Wittman, H. 2009. Interview: Paul Nicholson, La Via Campesina. *The Journal of Peasant Studies* 36, no. 3: 676–82.

World Bank. 2014. *Food Price Watch*. 5 (17), May.

Yale University. 2013. Agrarian Studies Conference. Food Sovereignty: A Critical Dialog. Conference Papers. http://www.yale.edu/agrarianstudies/foodsovereignty/papers.html

Zezza, A., and L. Tasciotti. 2010. Urban agriculture, poverty, and food security: Empirical evidence from a sample of developing countries. *Food Policy* 35: 265–73.

Ziegler, J., C. Golay, C. Mahon, and S.-A. Way. 2011. *The fight for the right to food: Lessons learned*. New York: Palgrave Macmillan.

Historicizing food sovereignty

Philip McMichael

To historicize food sovereignty is not simply to recognize its multiple forms and circumstances across time and space, but also to recognize its relation to the politics of capital in a crisis conjuncture. This paper traces the evolution of the food sovereignty vision from the initial stages of the food sovereignty countermovement to the present, arguing that food sovereignty politics have not only traveled from countryside to city as consumers/citizens anticipate ecological constraints and compensate for unequal food distributions, but also they have been confronted with transitions in the food regime following the recent food crisis. New enclosures, in the forms of land grabs and value-chains, administered by public-private 'governance' partnerships, have contradictory effects: threatening the peasant base of the food sovereignty countermovement, but also threatening to exacerbate the food crisis, as evidenced in recent food riot politics animated by the food sovereignty vision. As the food regime restructures, it reconditions the possibilities of food sovereignty politics. Arguably, the ultimate historicization of food sovereignty possibility is immanent in cumulative energy and climate feedbacks.

Introduction

To historicize food sovereignty is not simply to recognize its multiple forms and circumstances across time and space, but also to recognize its relation to the politics of capital in a crisis conjuncture. That is, the food sovereignty vision and movement today are conditioned by the contours of the food regime – now in crisis as its ability to continue to feed the world the illusion of 'food security' via 'free trade' has lost legitimacy in the wake of the recent and continuing global food crisis (McMichael and Schneider 2011). The crisis, in turn, has generated a heightened struggle between projects of corporate agricultural intensification, and an emerging ontological alternative in 'food sovereignty.'[1] Politically, this struggle extends from contention over land grabs, evictions and genetically modified organism (GMO) monocultures on the ground (cf Borras and Franco 2013), to discursive and tactical initiatives in and between the G8, the World Bank and the Food and Agriculture Organization (FAO). Under these circumstances, to historicize food sovereignty is to understand the shifting political landscape within and against which it must operate.

The author is grateful for the constructive comments of two anonymous reviewers.
[1]In many diverse manifestations: from agrarian movements (Borras, Edelman and Kay 2008) through CSA's, Slow Food and grass-roots fair trade (Fonte 2008, Friedmann and McNair, 2008, Jaffee 2007) seed networks in Europe (Corrado 2010, Da Via 2012, Bocci and Colombo 2013) and *in situ* conservation of Mexican maize culture (Fitting 2011), to the phenomenon of 'repeasantization' (Ploeg 2009).

While the term 'food sovereignty' emerged in the 1980s (Edelman 2013), the food sovereignty project emerged in the 1990s in the crucible of an intensifying global agrarian crisis exacerbated by trade liberalization and structural adjustment policies withdrawing support for domestic agricultural sectors across the global South. In other words, food sovereignty emerged as the antithesis of the corporate food regime and its (unrealized) claims for 'food security' via the free trade rules of the World Trade Organization (WTO). Food sovereignty's vision and intervention were governed by its positioning as an alternative principle of food security anchored in a democratic rebuilding of domestic agricultures, where possible, to overcome processes of deepening food dependency and depeasantization inflicted by corporate marketing of cheapened 'food from nowhere' (Bové and Dufour 2001). As this essay contends, the subsequent restructuring of the food regime alters the conditions of possibility for the food sovereignty movement.

Historicizing food sovereignty means charting its political-economic coordinates, but its actual forms are quite diverse, and its meaning has evolved with an elasticity implicating groups and practices beyond its roots in the countryside. In this sense, then, instances of food sovereignty organizing in turn provide a lens on elements of the contemporary conjuncture, straddling both rural and urban arenas. Knezevic (2014), for example, argues that anti-smallholder European Enlargement policies in the Balkan states have galvanized civic resistance via informalization, including proliferating urban farmers' markets, as an incipient form of food sovereignty appropriate to this episode of shock therapy. As Bové and Dufour of *La Confédération* Paysanne Européenne (CPE) observed of the food sovereignty movement:

> The strength of this global movement is precisely that it differs from place to place ... The world is a complex place, and it would be a mistake to look for a single answer to complex and different phenomena. We have to provide answers at different levels – not just the international level, but local and national levels too. History shows that each phase of political development has a corresponding institutional form: France's response to the Industrial Revolution was the nation-state; the WTO is the expression of this phase of the liberalization of world trade. (2001, 168)

This claim invokes the question of sovereignty, arguably compromised by WTO trade rules privileging transnational agribusiness over the possibility of national food policy. Under these circumstances, food 'sovereignty' employs a form of 'strategic essentialism' (see below), foreshadowing the more complex notion of the 'territory of self-determination', by which societies can be self-governing via their rural producers, agricultural capacities and domestic food needs.[2] In this regard, Polanyi anticipated food sovereignty when, observing competitive pressure on European producers from cheap New World grains in the late-nineteenth-century food regime, he remarked: 'it had been forgotten by free traders that land formed part of the territory of the country, and that the territorial character of sovereignty was not merely a result of sentimental associations, but of massive facts, including economic ones' (1957, 183–4).

To raise the 'territorial' question is to underline the salience and immanence of the food sovereignty movement. As argued below, the salience refers to the growing incidence of

---

[2]Menser (2014) argues territorial self-determination also requires a re-territorialization of class war, given the violent histories of the state system vis-à-vis indigenous populations. The recent *Land sovereignty manifesto: towards a peoples' counter-enclosure* represents a practical grounding of the food sovereignty theme in territorial terms (Borras and Franco 2012).

urban political unrest under conditions of food price volatility (with the possibility of rural/urban alliances). And the immanence refers to an unfolding global ecological crisis compressing time by space, as the unsustainability of energy, water and industrial food flows deepens and climate emergency unfolds.[3] I argue here that it is these palpable (and related) trends that food sovereignty addresses, as both countermovement and alternative to a crisis-laden food regime.

The food sovereignty countermovement

The recent 'food crisis' is a culmination of a deeper agrarian crisis associated with the long-twentieth-century food regime,[4] and its reproduction of capital's labor force via cheap food provisioning. How such provisioning is accomplished, and under what geopolitical relations and institutional rules, registers the food regime's cumulative forms (Friedmann and McMichael 1989). But the constant is a deepening metabolic rift[5] as food supply chains have lengthened and insulated consumers from ecosystem plundering and the environmental hazards of 'biophysical override' (Weis 2007). The central, agro-exporting principle of the food regime has served to displace producers by land grabbing on the one hand[6] and market predation on the other.[7] While the former process characterizes the capitalist era at large, a cheap food regime (characterized by food 'dumping') has only been institutionalized, *globally*, during the neoliberal era (Rosset 2006). Here, agro-exporting via *both* southern debt management and northern subsidies has eroded smallholder economy – precipitating a peasant countermovement, organized around the principle of 'food sovereignty' (McMichael 2005). This principle ultimately concerns the question of appropriate ways of living on Earth at a time of rising urban redundancy and ecosystem crisis.

However, the countermovement is not simply a peasant movement – one might say it is a movement informed by a peasant perspective underlining the importance of revaluing farming for domestic food provisioning and for addressing social inequalities. Hence the growing currency of 'food sovereignty' across the rural-urban divide. While the origins of 'food sovereignty' certainly lie in a peasant response[8] to a sharpening agrarian crisis

---

[3]For instance, the severity of drought in the American Southwest now portends a new 'dust bowl' devastating the land, crops and farm communities, and an EU commission predicts biannual occurrence of severe heat waves like that in 2003 by 2040 (Abramsky 2013).

[4]As the 'political face of global value relations' (Araghi 2003) the 'food regime' is a historically specific form of geo/political and human-ecological ordering premised on cross-border flows of (artificially) cheap food and energy.

[5]Marx's 'metabolic rift' refers to the disruption of soil and water nutrient cycles associated with urbanization and the progressive industrialization of agriculture (Foster 1999), inherent in capitalism as an 'ecological regime' (Moore 2011).

[6]Colonial land grabbing included requisitioning of subjects' grain reserves (Davis 2001).

[7]Dumping of northern foodstuffs in southern markets characterized the 1980s–1990s, and this has extended in the twenty-first century to the experience of Eastern European countries joining the EU and being subject to German and French supermarket colonization (La Vía Campesina 2013).

[8]Food sovereignty progenitor La Vía Campesina emerged at a 1992 meeting of farmers' organizations from Latin America and Europe in Managua. As founding member Paul Nicholson of the International Coordinating Committee put it: 'At that time, we issued a "Managua declaration" where we denounced the "agrarian crisis" and "rural poverty and hunger" resulting from the neo-liberal policies' (Nicholson, 2008, 456). Four years later, in Tlaxcala, Mexico, a Vía Campesina working group decided the term 'food sovereignty' was to be 'adopted by the whole movement and then defended publicly for the first time at the FAO World Food Summit in Rome' later in 1996 (Idem).

under the neoliberal project, the movement's political calculus has been governed by the demands of the historical conjuncture rather than a conventional peasant demand for agrarian reform *per se*.[9] The operative perspective is:

> In the context of food sovereignty, agrarian reform benefits all of society, providing healthy, accessible and culturally appropriate food, and social justice. Agrarian reform can put an end to the massive and forced rural exodus from the countryside to the city, which has made cities grow at unsustainable rates and under inhuman conditions.[10]

One of many such proclamations, this statement links the land question to the broader policy issue of producer rights, poverty elimination and reversal of the perversity of urban bias. Contrary to the classical agrarian question problematic, the movement privileges peasant agency in a programmatic approach to restoring the viability of the countryside for farming and addressing domestic food security – as governed by national democratic principles (McMichael 2013c). This has been a first step, anticipating ecological farming initiatives (see e.g. Rosset and Martinez-Torres 2012, Massicotte 2014).

From this perspective, processes of differentiation and depeasantization are not simply a trajectory calling into question the existence of peasantries; rather, they are forces calling into existence a peasant countermovement dedicated to protecting conditions of existence on the land. Such conditions may be quite heterogeneous, including contradictory relations (e.g. class, patriarchal, ethnic, debt). They constitute the historicity of the countermovement as it embodies a diversity of local challenges (Desmarais 2007, Wolford 2010). Nevertheless, its formative unity is conditioned by the violence of market hegemony as instituted in a combination of structural adjustment policies, WTO trade rules and an overriding episteme applying an economic calculus to a more complex set of cultural and ecological peasant 'practices' (cf Ploeg 2009, 19).

An historicized understanding would view this protective reflex as analogous to the 'canary in the mine', where 'the condition of the world's peasantries today is an indicator of a toxic combination of ignorance of the ecological and social harm to the planet by industrial agriculture, and its enabling policies of neo-liberalism' (McMichael 2008, 504). Peasant mobilization may be seen as the (not too) early warning of a socio-ecological catastrophe in the making – with a unique ability to name the problem. The uniqueness is the ability to problematize the current food regime as privileging industrial models and urban 'civilization' at the expense of ecosystems and their (*extant* and potential) stewards. The 'peasant' perspective, then, is essentially political, insofar as the defence of farming the land (as opposed to mono-cropping with chemicals) is in the interests of society as a whole.

Phenomenally, La Vía Campesina (2000) problematizes the food regime's 'massive movement of food around the world forcing the increased movement of people' in terms of displacement of farmers by unequal trade rules. *Substantively* (and historically) such dispossession is not simply of land, but of landed knowledge and ways of life critical to planetary health. From this perspective, the countermovement expresses a positive antithesis to corporate industrial agriculture: re-envisioning the conditions necessary to develop resilient and democratic forms of social reproduction, anchored in sustainable management of food systems by land users. That is, the advocacy of farming rights is framed within a broader

---

[9]This is a key point made by Mann (2014).
[10](Nyeleni 2006) Monsalve Suárez (2013) underlines this point in distinguishing between land rights and human rights – the latter involving states directly in addressing the socio-ecological function of land, including rights for the landless.

vision of how to rethink the ecological conditions and scale at which human communities can live, and survive. Instead of a 'dying echo of populist thought' this movement represents 'an active anti-systemic struggle' (Ajl 2013, 9).

Thus, at the time of Rio +20, La Vía Campesina declared:

> 20 years after the Earth Summit, life on the planet has become dramatically difficult. Expulsion from our lands and territories is accelerating, no longer only due to conditions of disadvantage imposed upon us by trade agreements and the industrial sector, but by new forms of monopoly control over land and water, by the global imposition of intellectual property regimes that steal our seeds, by the invasion of transgenic seeds, and by the advance of monoculture plantations, mega-projects, and mines.
>
> We should exchange the industrial agroexport food system for a system based on food sovereignty, that returns the land to its social function as the producer of food and sustainer of life, that puts local production of food at the center, as well as the local markets and local processing ... (2012a)

In other words, the current food regime stands in the way of human food security, democracy, ecosystem restoration, and livable scales where urban forms might be calibrated with rural proximity to repair and reduce the metabolic rift (Lappé 1971, Duncan 1996, Friedmann 2000, Schneider and McMichael 2010).

Accordingly, rather than center its politics in peasant claims alone, the movement chose a political target with a broader, conjunctural theme: the 'food security' claims of a privatizing trade regime. 'Food sovereignty' politicized this naturalized claim for market rationality in global food provisioning by invoking the 'collective rights already recognized by the UN [United Nations], such as the right to self-determination, the right to development and the right to permanent sovereignty over natural resources' (Claeys 2013) – in effect reasserting state sovereignty versus market rule as institutionalized in the WTO's Agreement on Agriculture (McMichael 2003). Use of the term 'sovereignty' was arguably a form of 'strategic essentialism', given the override of national sovereignty via WTO trade rules. It was a first step toward a subsequent, substantive claim for self-organizing food-secure systems as a collective right of citizens.

Three issues stem from this strategic intervention. First, food sovereignty centered on the collective 'right to produce food', meaning protection of farm sectors from trade 'dumping', and land sovereignty for land users and the landless (Borras and Franco 2012, Claeys 2013). Second, food sovereignty drew attention to the deceit of feeding the world with the claim of providing 'food security' through a marketplace in which a minority of the world's population participates.[11] And, third, food sovereignty's politicization of agri-food policy includes demands for a democratic resolution to the question of food security, anticipating a broader political alliance focusing on ecological and public health with respect to food systems (cf Lang and Heasman 2004, Wittman 2009, Claeys 2013, Andrée et al. 2014). The 'food sovereignty' initiative thus outlines a critique of the institutional structuring of the current, corporate food regime at the same time as it reformulates conditions necessary to a human rights-based form of food security. It reformulates a social

---

[11]This deceit was evident in the process of dispossession and displacement of millions of food producers during the 1990s in consequence of NAFTA (North American Free Trade Agreement) and WTO trade rules, an outcome informing the Millennium Development Goals (United Nations, 2000), and then again evident in the 'food crisis' of the late 2000s, in which world hunger figures almost reached the one billion mark (McMichael 2009b, McMichael and Schneider 2011).

contract appropriate to an era of ecological crisis: a sensibility captured in part by Wittman's term 'agrarian citizenship' (2009) – problematizing modernity's urban bias.[12]

While championing an International Convention on the Rights of Peasants, who include farmers, landless and indigenous people who work the land themselves, Paul Nicholson suggests, aptly, that the name La Vía Campesina refers to 'a process of peasant culture, a peasant "way"'. He continues, capturing the societal dimension of a peasant-inspired politics:

> The debate isn't in the word 'farmer' or 'peasant'. The debate is much more about the process of cohesion.... It is a process of accumulation of forces and realities coming together from the citizens of the entire planet. Food sovereignty is not just resistances, as there are thousands of resistances, but also proposals that come from social movements, and not just peasant movements. From environmental movements, among others, come many initiatives that develop proposals of recuperation, of rights, of policies. This is also an autonomous and independent process. There is no central committee, and food sovereignty is not the patrimony of any particular organisation. It's not La Vía Campesina's project, or even just a peasants' project. (Nicholson, 2009, 678–80)

It is in this sense that Edelman suggests 'peasantness' is a political rather than an analytical category (Edelman, 2009). That is, rather than a populist atavism, food sovereignty is a historical wedge in a crisis conjuncture to recognize and promote alternative socio-ecological relations to feed citizens rather than long-distance consumers.[13] In short, food sovereignty is a civilizational movement, combining a conjunctural critique of neoliberal 'food security' (equating agro-exporting with 'feeding the world') with long-held principles of self-determination reframed as democratic rights for and of citizens and humans (cf Claeys 2013). The central ethic – food as a human right, not a commodity – expresses the movement's potent politicization of neoliberal 'food security'.

The claim for a civilizational movement suggests that the long-term vision of food sovereignty elevates human security over the increasingly anachronistic principle of national security. This is where 'sovereignty' has multi-dimensional meaning. Initially a form of strategic essentialism for the food sovereignty movement, using the sovereignty idiom to reclaim lost juridical ground (including land) in the short term (the corporate food regime), it reformulates the meaning of 'sovereignty' in the long run. Reclaiming the right of national autonomy over food policy in effect problematizes the complicity of states in agro-export political economy. And this opens up the possibility of a longer-term issue of food security *territorialism* embedded in bioregional stewardship in the interests of human ecology – invoking a philosophy of 'agrarian citizenship' (cf Wittman 2009).[14] Thus the *Movimento dos Trabalhadores Sem Terra* (MST) works to link 'the struggle for the land with the struggle on the land' (Flávio de Almeida and Sánchez 2000), developing co-operative forms of rural labor, producing staple foods for the

---

[12]Which, interestingly, Davis (2010) reproduces in the notion of the Ark-like responsibility of the metropolis in combating climate change (but see Ajl 2013).
[13]Recent evidence establishes the relative/superior productivity of non-industrial, organic agriculture (e.g. Pretty *et al.* 2006, Badgley *et al.* 2007, IAASTD (International Assessment of Agricultural Science and Technology for Development) 2008).
[14]In 2000, the MST renamed its Sector of Production the Sector of Production, Cooperation and Environment, and published its *Commitment to land and life*, setting out its philosophical relationship with nature. This identity affirmed the rights claims of the 1988 Brazilian constitution, by which citizens' right to land carried a responsibility to fulfill a socially productive function including one of environmental sustainability (Wittman 2010, 286).

working poor and building alliances with, and offering livelihood security to, the urban unemployed (Wright and Wolford 2003).

While the food sovereignty drive for domestic food security may appear to promote a reactionary nationalism, its vision actually involves three historic steps: (1) revaluing humanty's agrarian foundations via a 're-territorialization' of (ecologically responsible) food production – substituting for food dependency on 'world granaries' organized by the food regime; (2) challenging the violence of the 'comparative advantage' principle in the state system, which enables agribusiness to construct (and reconstruct) world producing regions, promoting agro-exporting at the expense of the land and its inhabitants every-where, and (3) democratizating food systems with the potential to recalibrate urban and manufacturing forms as partners rather than predators of the countryside, and to eliminate the redundancy and disorder of inter-state competition in food provisioning.

Food regime crisis

The spike in world hunger in the late 2000s underscored the food insecure consequences of the food regime. The food crisis has strengthened initiatives within the United Nations to recalibrate the trade regime to legitimize domestic food security measures. In this post-global food crisis context, UN Right to Food *Rapporteur* De Schutter carried this initiative over to a recommendation to the WTO:

> WTO members should redefine how food security is treated in multilateral trade agreements so that policies to achieve food security and the realization of the human right to adequate food are no longer treated as deviations from but as recognized principal objectives of agricultural trade policy ... A more appropriate reframing of agricultural trade rules would explicitly recognize than market-determined outcomes do not necessarily improve food security .... (De Schutter, 2011b, 16, emphasis added)[15]

De Schutter followed up this Briefing Note with a report (De Schutter, 2009) regarding *Minimum principles* and measures to address the human rights challenge of what the World Bank termed 'large-scale land acquisitions', directed to states and investors involved in land grabbing and emphasizing investments that respect the environment, increase local food security and create employment via labor-intensive models (Claeys and Vanloqueren 2013, 195).

With respect to the food regime, Friedmann argues it embodies naturalized assumptions as 'implicit rules guiding relationships, practices and outcomes' (Friedmann, 2005, 234). One such assumption is that the market is the most efficient provider of food security in an uneven world. Here, moving food across borders is ideally a market operation, and adherence to the principle of comparative advantage guides WTO trade protocols (debili-tating smallholder agriculture). Friedmann's point is that when these assumptions are brea-ched, what was implicit or normalized may become explicit, problematic and contentious. Arguably, 'comparative advantage' as the rationale of market-driven 'food security' has become problematic and contentious as export bans and commandeering offshore land

---

[15]The recently concluded WTO Ministerial in Bali, December 2013, focused on the question of public procurement for domestic food security programs in the global South (largely at India's instigation), allowing a 'peace clause' limited to protecting extant (rather than future) reserves of 'traditional staple food crops' – arguably this does not alter the WTO trade regime, since the limited peace clause applies essentially to low-income (rather than global) consumers residing in the relevant countries.

for food supplies call the trade regime into question, triggering a process of restructuring (McMichael 2012, 2013a).

The food regime crisis embodies the entwined energy, climate and financial crises, crystallizing in a recent land grab for food and agrofuels (Houtart 2010), carbon sinks (Fairhead *et al.* 2012), water (Mehta *et al.* 2012) and as a new financial asset (Fairbairn 2013, Russi 2013). Capitalizing a new land frontier for agro-industrialization deepens capitalism's second contradiction (O'Connor 1998),[16] at the same time as it threatens the rights and habitats of people of the land.[17] Capitalizing grassland and forestland with agro-inputs degrades the natural foundations of production. Global fertilizer use is now intensified by agrofuels and the removal of cellulose fiber from fields (ETC 2009).[18] When displacement of food crops by agrofuels is paired with financial speculation on food futures and rising fertilizer costs,[19] the ability of the land-grab frontier to provide cheap energy and food supplies to reduce capital's costs of production and reproduction is likely to be short-lived.

The land grab signals the restructuring of the food/fuel regime, via transformation of its geography and governance, and a renewed challenge to the world's small producers. It contributes to a general process of relocation of food production to the global South, combining cost saving and state-sponsored 'agro-security mercantilism' (McMichael 2013a). The consequence is to reverse patterns of food circulation associated with the previous food regimes – originating in grain exports from the settler regions and then the global North in general (USA/Europe), with rising Southern agro-exporting creating a multi-centric geography of food and agrofuel circulation enabled by a complex of (hitherto soft law) rules and codes of conduct, beyond the jurisdiction of the WTO (McMichael 2012). Such land acquisition protocols (such as the Bank's Principles of Responsible Agricultural Investment) foreshadow global enclosure in the name of market rule. This process promises to reconstitute circulation patterns of commodities increasingly fungible as food, feed, fuel and plant matter.[20] Such a 'flex crop' syndrome is unlikely to tame an inflationary pressure on food prices, the consequences of which are discussed below.

The food crisis marks a key transitional moment with consequences for the political strategy of the food sovereignty movement. The World Food Summit in Rome, in June 2008, responding to a reversal of declining hunger rates attributed to the 2000 Millennium Development Goals, advocated the intensification of corporate agriculture (McMichael and

---

[16]Marsden points out that the assumption that 'sustainable intensification' resolves a 'yield gap' misleads insofar as the bioeconomic paradigm reproduces generic and aggregated solutions that override specific ecosystems and their sustainability (2012, 263).

[17]In this regard, Narula comments on the World Bank's approach to land acquisition: 'In many respects, the use of satellite imagery to identify investment-worthy sites stands as a metaphor for the Bank's current approach. Technocrats, physically and professionally removed from the land in question, use tools that are even further removed in time and space in order to assess land's current and potential value. This approach assumes that land and resources can be quantified by objective, distant images, and that the myriad uses, customs, and benefits informing the interests of land users can be captured, guaranteed, and marketized through written, formally-demarcated rights. These assumptions belie the complexity of land's real value to those who depend on it as a source of spiritual, social, and economic sustenance as well as a guarantor of rights' (Nanula, 2013, 169–70).

[18]FAOSTAT (Food and Agricultural Organization Statistics) reports from 1990–2002 China increased fertilizer usage 44 percent, India 33 percent, Pakistan 61 percent and Brazil 137 percent (Cribb 2010, 122).

[19]In addition to oil price inflation, peak phosphate (no substitutes) occurred in 1989 (Cribb 2010, 76).

[20]Borras *et al.* (2012) describe the materiality of these crops as 'flex crops'.

Schneider 2011). Parallel to the Summit, the International CSO (Civil Society Organizations) Planning Committee for Food Sovereignty drafted the *Terra Preta* Declaration,[21] stating:

> The serious and urgent food and climate crises are being used by political and economic elites as opportunities to entrench corporate control of world agriculture and the ecological commons. At a time when chronic hunger, dispossession of food providers and workers, commodity and land speculation, and global warming are on the rise, governments, multilateral agencies and financial institutions are offering proposals that will only deepen these crisis through more dangerous versions of policies that originally triggered the current situation .... Small-scale food producers are feeding the planet, and we demand respect and support to continue. Only food sovereignty can offer long-term, sustainable, equitable and just solutions to the urgent food and climate crises. (IPC, 2008)

The food crisis was indeed a turning point – precipitating a political mobilization of the opposing sides to the debate about the content and appropriate mechanisms of 'food security'. While WTO principles of free trade still held (but under critical scrutiny from key members (India, Brazil, China) of the recently formed Group of 20), the Rome Summit facilitated a shift toward overt public intervention in the name of 'feeding the world' projected to reach nine billion by 2050.

The World Bank's *2008 World development report* (2007) served as a template in identifying the African smallholder as the new object of 'agriculture for development',[22] setting the stage for a series of value chain initiatives, largely focused on Africa, from the Alliance for a Green Revolution in Africa (AGRA) to the African Agricultural Growth Corridors initiative associated with The New Alliance for Food Security and Nutrition (NAFSN) (Paul and Steinbrecher 2013, see also Patel 2013).

The challenge to small farmers is intensified here, as not only is some of their land subject to, or under consideration for, appropriation – for productive, speculative or even political motives (cf Kerssen 2012), but a more subtle 'grab' (control) is foreshadowed in the (primarily African) 'value-chain project'. The value-chain is a conduit of global value relations, drawing producers into competitive markets over which they have little or no control, in return for contracting for agri-food inputs (seed, fertilizer, chemicals) that extract new value from producers via their products and centralize agricultural knowledge as 'intellectual property', with increased exposure to debt and dispossession for producers, and reduction of local food security (McMichael 2013b). The value-chain project is likely to convert otherwise local farming into commodity-producing labor for a deepening global market in food and fuel. While the infrastructure and mode of circulation is still forming, it may well produce a similar outcome to the green revolution, where a sub-set of consumers and farmers prosper (for a time) without altering the incidence and/or geography of hunger (Patel 2013).[23]

---

[21]This author contributed to this draft.

[22]See special collection sections of *The Journal of Peasant Studies* 36, 3 (2009), and the *Journal of Agrarian Change* 9, 2 (2009) for critical reviews of the Bank's *2008 World development report*.

[23]Thus, Baltzer and Hansen found that the recent flurry of agricultural input subsidy programs directed at African smallholders mostly benefit 'less-poor and politically well-connected households as well as large input suppliers', 'mainly attack the symptoms of low input use and poor agricultural productivity rather than the underlying "disease" of high input procurement costs and market failures', and local elites 'may use subsidies as a tool to reach political objectives, input suppliers enjoy a stable demand and possibly greater market power', with the consequence that such input subsidy programs may become 'more entrenched in the political system and more subject to political manipulation and rent seeking' (2011, 31).

Food sovereignty politics

The emergence of a food/fuel regime, combined with 'agro-security mercantilism' as states override the WTO's 'free market' via direct investment offshore to secure non-trade based food supplies, has transformed the content and coordinates of the food regime. For the food sovereignty movement, at large, it is no longer simply the massive movement of food around the world but the massive movement of money for a global enclosure that now commands attention – from protecting rights to lands and common property resources to contesting governing principles characterized as a 'checklist of how to destroy global peasantry responsibly' (de Schutter 2011a). And, to the extent that food production is increasingly incorporated into (market or non-market) flows across borders to provision global consumers with purchasing power, 'food dependency' increases, rendering low-income urban and rural populations increasingly vulnerable to price hikes. These are the principal material conditions confronting the twenty-first-century food sovereignty movement.

The peasant countermovement already anticipated the recent food crisis, given its experience of the agrarian crisis stemming from structural adjustment policies fashioned in the 1980s against farm sectors in the global South. However, the mechanisms of depeasantization and deprivation have changed – with new enclosures for food, feed, fuel and offsets and financialized (speculative) prices substituting for the WTO-centered 'cheap' food market regime.

In these senses, the food crisis is not simply about hunger and food availability, but it is also an expression (and driver) of food regime restructuring, deepening its arsenal of weapons of dispossession. Such weapons may not be as subtle as the market mechanism is purported to be. But they continue to draw legitimacy from a capitalist narrative portraying the peasantry as an historical relic unfit for a productive modern world. And yet it is precisely the peasant experience and presence that is able to articulate not only the problem, but a solution to food regime contradictions that threaten ecosystem health and the fertility of the soil with industrial monocropping, and also the survival of humanity and other species. The unthinkable produces the thinkable. Who else could give voice to such calamity but the 'canary in the mine'? Thus, a founding member of La Vía Campesina, Nettie Wiebe, claimed:

> It's a movement of people of the land who share a progressive agenda. Which means we share the view that people – small farmers, peasants, people of the land – have a right to be there … . That it's our job to look after the earth and our people. We must defend it and we have to defend it in the global context..(quoted in Desmarais 2002, 98)

The crisis conjuncture refocused attention on the FAO's Committee on World Food Security (CFS) as the multilateral organization most appropriate to addressing the conditions of possibility of the food and hunger question. In this moment the IPC (International Planning Committee) for Food Sovereignty, with strong support from the Latin American region, negotiated a reform of the CFS whereby civil society would have an institutionalized voice through the newly formed Civil Society Mechanism (CSM), alongside member state delegations and a newly formed Private Sector Mechanism (PSM) (McKeon 2009). Despite its shortcomings (e.g. corporate membership, language of consensus, absence of explicit food sovereignty reference), the reformed CFS acknowledges the right to food, includes ongoing civil society input and recognizes the subsidiarity principle – all essential elements of food sovereignty. The key is that the CFS is a new space for debate at the global level informed by social movement and civil society representations of food security initiatives beyond the corporate (and often central government and international financial institution) vision. As La Vía Campesina claims:

> social movements now have a new international tool they can use when the time comes to demand from their governments local or national measures to stop land grabbing. An important methodological step has also been taken as the [voluntary] guidelines illustrate that direct participation in the drawing up of policies by the people most concerned by the topic is both possible and fruitful .... To have managed to withdraw from the hands of the World Bank the monopoly on the definition of policies in the area of land access and agrarian reform is a significant achievement. (2012b, 11)

However, it also acknowledges:

> For social movements participation in a body such as the CFS is a huge challenge for which they are not necessarily prepared, due in particular to their lack of familiarity with the culture of negotiation and tiny steps forward that lies at the heart of negotiations in a multilateral system. On some topics such as the FAO Voluntary Guidelines ... representatives of movements such as La Vía Campesina can rely on like-minded organizations. These collaborations are efficient as they respect the character and skills of the different parties. But on other subjects it may be impossible to monitor everything. An active participation in the Civil Society Mechanism may demand huge resources in time and people from social movements .... Representatives are also faced with the problem of the working language .... The other main difficulty is the discrepancy between what social movements experience on the ground and the documents discussed by the CFS. (8)

Nonetheless, on balance the reformed CFS has positive potential, providing opportunity for a food sovereignty presence via the Civil Society Mechanism, and particularly a forum for articulating the importance of domestic food security initiatives and smallholder support within a framework of human rights (see McKeon 2011). The CFS, in countering the World Bank's support for the rights of capital, has introduced debate on the rights of inhabitants on lands targeted for agricultural investment, underscoring the disproportionate role, and significance, of smallholder investment in farming systems. Key to this initiative are two alternative policy frameworks: the (Voluntary) Tenure Guidelines (designed to strengthen recognition of customary property tenure and address gender inequity), and the Minimum Human Rights Principle proposed by the UN Special Rapporteur for the Right to Food.

As above, the food regime crisis has refocused attention on the mechanisms of food security, as rising hunger and state-driven land grabs have together delegitimized 'free trade', deepening the crisis of the free trade architecture.[24] Space is opened for reformulations of food security that ultimately connect to support of small farmers via the principle of the right to food (as opposed to an investor-driven 'right to food' via land grabbing).

---

[24]The crisis has triggered two significant deregulatory initiatives. The Transatlantic Trade and Investment Partnership (TTIP) seeks (confidentially) to relax the EU's Precautionary Principle regarding food-associated chemicals (pesticides, packaging and additives), nano-technologies and GMOs, and to regulate procurement at the possible expense of local participatory food democracy initiatives defined as 'localization barriers to trade' (Hansen-Kuhn and Suppan 2013). The Trans-Pacific Partnership (TPP), which represents a regional 'free trade' agreement aimed at China's growing world influence, would intensify agricultural liberalization rules (in the wake of WTO paralysis), with a further end-run around domestic food security initiatives. Led by the US, the TPP is a confidential, corporate-focused initiative aimed at dismantling remaining market protections and it 'would expand protections for investors over consumers and farmers, and severely restrict governments' ability to use public policy to reshape food systems' (Karen Hansen-Kuhn, quoted in Muller et al. 2012, 3).

Arguably, this is the pivotal issue at stake at local as well as 'high-level' scales. With respect to the food insecurity fallout from the food crisis, de Schutter observed that adopting 'a human rights framework … may guide the redefinition of the policy priorities triggered by the current crisis. The question "for whose benefit?" is at least as important as the question "how to produce more?"' (2008).

In this reformulation context, however, the World Economic Forum and the G8 have countered with the NAFSN – composed of the African Union (AU), its planning body The New Partnership for Africa's Development (NEPAD), several African governments and over 100 companies. This initiative not only re-appropriates 'food security' in quantitative terms, but also regroups to reformulate governing mechanisms to commandeer African land, water and labor, and to monopolize seeds and markets, in effect threatening to undermine the CFS. As British Prime Minister David Cameron put it so bluntly, this initiative will 'unleash the power of the private sector', with a pledge of aid to the tune of US$22 billion, stipulating that recipient governments 'refine policies in order to improve investment opportunities' (quoted in Paul and Steinbrecher 2013). If the trade regime is vulnerable to price shocks and export bans, then *public-private partnerships*[25] based on direct, subsidized investment by agribusiness become *the new institutional mechanisms of the food regime.*

GRAIN's account of rice markets in Côte d'Ivoire is telling in terms of the current food regime trajectory: formerly self-sufficient in rice, the national rice company was privatized along with elimination of public support for agriculture via structural adjustment. By the 1990s, two-thirds of rice consumed was imported from Asia, but, with rice price inflation in 2008, local rice 'costs 15 percent less than imports...demand is growing … [and] women rice traders have recently formed several cooperatives and have even created brands for local rice' (2013, 1). To northern governments, donors and corporations, the re-establishment of control via *non-trade* solutions is irresistible. Thus:

> Under its Cooperation Framework, Côte d'Ivoire promises to reform its land laws and make other policy changes to facilitate private investment in agriculture. In exchange, it gets hundreds of millions of dollars in donor assistance and promises from eight foreign companies and their local partners to invest nearly US$800 million in the development of massive rice farms. (GRAIN 2013, 1)

Governance mechanisms for the NASFN include policy commitments by African states to facilitate access to key agricultural lands, using databases, resettlement policies and measures authorizing communities 'to engage in partnerships through leases or subleases' (5). *In other words, elites from the national down to the local level are being mobilized to participate in a process that La Vía Campesina might well rephrase as: 'the massive movement of money around the world is forcing the increased movement of people'.* Governance includes New Alliance partners confirming their 'intentions' to 'take account' of the CFS's responsible agricultural investment principles (RAIs) in formation, and the Tenure Guidelines (6). This follows a pattern of non-consultation with producer and civil society organizations and confidential Letters of Intent signed between companies and governments (Oxfam 2013, 6).

---

[25]To date, the G8 has signed Cooperation Framework Agreements (CFAs) since the New Alliance formed in May 2012 with Benin, Burkina Faso, Côte d'Ivoire, Ethiopia, Ghana, Malawi, Mozambique, Nigeria and Tanzania (Oxfam 2013, 3).

At the same time, the G8 threatens to override the CFS Tenure Guidelines (TGs) by launching a new transparency in land transactions initiative. While the Tenure Guidelines (which insist on Free, Prior and Informed Consent procedures to honor the rights of landed peoples), embody the legitimate requirements of the CFS, and to which states (including the G8) have committed, the G8's new initiative 'is attempting, yet again,[26] to enforce the principle that money and markets decide what is best for the world' (FIAN 2013). In short, political and corporate elites are maneuvering to compromise or even undermine the newly established authority of the CFS as the appropriate forum for global initiatives on land, food and nutrition. A corporate countermovement is in full swing, with the new grab for land accompanied by schemes for governing principles favoring an economic calculus over territorial rights of land users.

Not only has the crisis called the food/trade regime into question, but also its encouragement of land grabbing highlights the subordination of agricultural land to financial markets. The fetishization of agriculture via speculation in land as a financial asset, and episodes of land grabbing, is clearly on display. There is a direct, and an indirect, consequence for the countermovement. In the direct sense, the peasant movement (and allies) are confronted with ongoing construction of appropriation protocols, direct expropriation and expulsion from lands acquired by national or foreign interests. In this context, agrarian movements are substituting a human rights framework to defend territory and land access for the landless as an effective legal method of avoiding entrapment in a discourse of market-based rights – insisting that 'rights are social conquests' (Saragih, quoted in Monsalve-Suárez 2013, 277), and that 'the home states of these companies regulate the behavior of their companies abroad' (243). Reference to international human rights law brings into play international advocacy networks and international forums such as the CFS. This struggle has the potential to build on 'broader alliances among different actors, for instance, peasants, consumers, law professionals, policy makers and scientists, and on the capacity to simultaneously operate at different levels and arenas of action' (Ibid, 248). Land grabbing's open season is already focusing public attention on its violations of rights and sovereignty, irresponsibly threatening the world's peasantry and world food ecosystems resilience (see e. g. Pearce 2012, Kugelman and Levenstein 2013, Liberti 2013).

Indirectly, there are the more seductive methods of tenuous chaining of smallholders to new value circuits controlled by agribusiness and subsidized with public monies (McMichael 2013b). Alongside AGRA, for example, is the African Agricultural Growth Corridors initiative, associated with NAFSN. Many of the NAFSN-affiliated companies[27] represent 'the whole supply chain, from seeds, chemical inputs, production, processing, transport and trade to supermarkets' (Paul and Steinbrecher 2013, 2). The NAFSN goals are

> to identify suitable land for investors; to help the private sector to control and increase the use of agricultural inputs (fertilizers) and 'improved' (hybrid or GM [genetically modified]) seeds and halt the distribution of free and 'unimproved' seeds (farmer varieties, often well adapted to local conditions and needs); and to mobilize public largesse to assist investors'. (4)

Part of the latter includes northern pension funds, regarded as 'patient capital' for infrastructural and climate proofing investment and as a public complement to private investment by agribusiness. While such initiatives promise development opportunities for smallholders, it

---

[26]Following CFS rejection of the Bank's RAI principles, and substitution of the TGs and an RAI process.
[27]For example, Monsanto, Cargill, Dupont, Syngenta, Nestlé, Unilever, Itochu, Yara International, etc.

is argued they are more likely 'to put Africa's land, water and seeds [and labor] under the control of international traders and investors' (13).[28]

Impending challenges

Land grabbing via such direct or indirect methods is a recipe for intensifying the over-consumption/under-consumption relationship organizing the food regime (Patel 2007) by expelling more farmers into urban slums, and deepening food dependency as more land is commandeered for 'flex crops' for export. As such it will likely renew food rioting across the global South, contributing to the 'urbanization' of food sovereignty sensibilities (implicit in urban farming systems: endemic in the South and mushrooming now in the global North). Predictions of rising food prices associated with energy, soil and climate crises, financialization and land grabbing have the potential to not only politicize urban populations, but also to direct such politicization towards recognition of the importance of domestic agricultural sectors. As Araghi (2000) reminds us, the agrarian question reaches beyond the countryside to urban destinations of the dispossessed, and this connection operates in reverse as the strategic importance of agriculture to cities becomes clear.[29]

Arguably, the twenty-first-century agrarian question inverts the classical agrarian question's theoretical focus on proletarian political opportunity, converting the question of capital's reproduction to a question of the reproduction of the food producer (McMichael 2013c). In this context, we might consider how Karl Kautsky's formulation has turned. As he remarked at the turn of the twentieth century:

> What decides whether a farmer is ready to join the ranks of the proletariat in struggle is not whether he is starving or indebted, but whether he comes to market as a seller of labour-power or as a seller of food. Hunger and indebtedness by themselves do not create a community of interests with the proletariat as a whole; in fact they can sharpen the contradiction between peasant and proletarian once this hunger has been stilled and debts repaid, should food prices rise and make it impossible for workers to enjoy cheap food. (1988, 317)

The contemporary 'hunger regime' (Araghi 2003, 2009) is not only shared across the rural/urban divide, but food price inflation does not trigger disaffection between the urban proletariat and the peasantry; rather, it refocuses attention on the structuring of food systems and the politics of inequality. Thus:

---

[28]Mozambique, for example, is required to write legislation promoting 'partnerships' and to eliminate distribution of free and unimproved seeds, while 'any constraints on the behaviour of corporate investors in Africa (such as the CFS guidelines on land tenure) remain voluntary, while the constraints on host nations become compulsory' (Monbiot 2013). Oxfam reports a consistent pattern of land and water acquisition putting farmers at risk (and discounting CFS Tenure Guidelines), as well as promoting seed and input policies privileging the private sector and its intellectual property rights (2013, 7).

[29]Related to this, Cohen and Garrett note: 'in most countries, in cities other than the very largest "primary" ones, agriculture is even more fundamental. Merchants and mechanics provide agricultural inputs and tools. Traders dynamically connect city and countryside. In some cities, a notable proportion of urban residents farm for a living (most likely on land outside the city). In Egypt and Malawi, 10 per cent of urban dwellers outside major metropolitan areas claimed agriculture production as their main occupation .... As much as 40 per cent of the population of some African cities and up to 50 per cent in some Latin American cities engage in urban or peri-urban agriculture' (2009, 6, 8). See also Vanhaute (2011, 57–9).

In many different parts of the world – Egypt, Mexico, Mauritania and Bangladesh – rioter protest went beyond calls to reduce the price of food. The largely urban-based protests also critiqued the impact of existing globalization, international food regimes that transformed local systems of production and distribution, and political elites (authoritarian regimes) that benefited from the status quo … . And it was mostly among the urban poor that violent protest erupted with hundreds of deaths worldwide … . (Bush 2010, 121)

In Haiti, for example, where President Préval was ousted following an impassive response to rice price doubling in a single week, income inequality is second only to that of Namibia in global terms, and the cost of living was the key cross-class complaint. Formerly a rice exporter, Haiti imports about 82 percent of total consumption, and it is widely acknowledged (notably by Presidents Préval and Clinton, the latter bearing substantial responsibility) that Haiti lost its food security and food sovereignty following externally imposed neoliberal measures (Schuller 2008). Interestingly, Schuller equates Haiti to 'the canary in the mine', claiming:

Haiti needs to be seen as an early warning. Haiti's geopolitical position – especially its proximity to the US and its level of dependence on foreign aid – highlights the contradictions and flaws in the system of international aid and growing global food crisis. (2008)

Related to this condition of food dependency, *The New York Times* recently reported:

Across the Caribbean, food imports have become a budget-busting problem, prompting one of the world's most fertile regions to reclaim its agricultural past. But instead of turning to big agribusinesses, officials are recruiting everyone they can to combat the cost of imports, which have roughly doubled in price over the past decade. In Jamaica, Haiti, the Bahamas and elsewhere, local farm-to-table production is not a restaurant sales pitch: it is a government motto. (Cave 2013, 6)

This may not be about restoring or constructing a Caribbean peasantry, but food sovereignty is not simply about peasants – its salience is universal, but with distinctive local meaning. Food provisioning is the Achilles heel of government: 'failure to provide (food) security undermines the very reason for existence of the political system' (Lagi *et al.* 2011, 2). Under these conditions, the 'food sovereignty' slogan is no empty vision, its power stemming from the increasingly obvious shortcomings of a competitive state system embedded in a regime deepening the commodification of food. President Clinton understood this when he waxed Polanyian in his *mea culpa* of 2008: 'food is not a commodity like others … it is crazy of us to think we can develop a lot of these countries [by] treating food like it was a colour television set' (quoted in Patel 2010).

This sentiment gets to the point, namely that the food riot 'concerns the political economy of food provisioning. From a world-historical perspective, the food riot has always been about more than food – its appearance has usually signaled significant transitions in political-economic arrangements' (Patel and McMichael 2009, 11) – arguably, the world is at a crisis threshold as the political-economic arrangements and dependencies of the food regime are laid bare. The clustering of food riots, depicted in Figure 1, is indicative of a 'rebellion against the political economy of neoliberalism, as expressed in local and national settings' (11).

The Tunisian uprising of January 2011, which sparked the Arab Spring, called for bread and water without dictatorship'.[30] Gana's study of the Tunisian food riots, and the domestic

---

[30]Gulf states are particularly vulnerable, with food imports providing 60 percent of total demand (Cotula *et al.* 2011, S101). See also Loening and Ianchovichina (2011) on food dependency in the MENA (Middle East and North Africa) states.

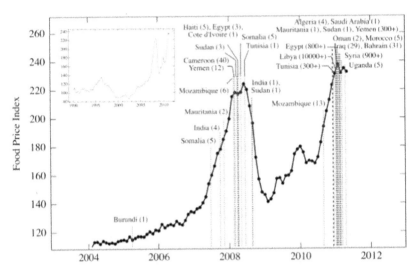

Figure 1. Food price inflation and protest.
The Food Price Index from January 2004 to May 2011, superimposed over a timeline of global mass unrest. The overall death toll associated with each event is reported in parentheses (Myerson 2012).

spatial inequalities linked to liberalization policies discriminating against the rural sector, concludes: 'the politicization of the protest movement indicates that people were making a direct link between political choices and development orientations and the deterioration of their living conditions' (2012, 207). Arguably, under these circumstances, there is an immanent politics of food sovereignty – given capital's need to reproduce its exploitative relations by colonizing land with energy-intensive agriculture, evicting peasantries and manipulating flex crops for profit. As Diamantino Nhampossa, coordinator of the National Peasants Union of Mozambique, remarked: 'These protests are going to end. But they will always come back. This is the gift that the development model we are following has to offer' (quoted in Patel 2010).[31]

How food politics unfold depends not only on the struggles between the corporate and agrarian movements over land and food rights, but also on the potential alliances between town and country prefigured in recent food riot patterning. Bush claims the Middle East offers several cases where 'urban and rural poor as well as the middle class demonstrated against spiraling food prices and persistent local corruption, repressive government and poverty', noting:

> Rioters knew too why governments had to be forced to mitigate the social costs of food inflation, why and how authoritarian regimes appeased transnational food companies, and how national food strategies impoverished food producers: low farm-gate prices were well-tested mechanisms to extract surplus for largely urban-based development. (Bush, 2010, 121, 123)

---

[31]A recent IFPRI (International Food Policy Research Institute) report regarding African vulnerability notes: 'Food security presents a serious challenge for the region because of high dependency on food imports, diminished capacity for generating foreign exchange to finance food imports, rising food demand driven by continued high population growth, and limited potential for agricultural growth because of severe water constraints and water resource management issues' (Breisinger et al. 2012, 2).

As political-economic elites continue to implement market solutions to food deficits, such political unrest will continue, providing growing credence to a politics of food sovereignty that connects food dependency to trade overriding stable domestic farm sectors.

Food rioting is just one indicator of crisis, but it draws attention to the perversity of 'emptying the countryside'[32] at a time of (market-based) food deficits, and the possibility of restoring the countryside with low-input agro-ecological farming to also address the interwoven energy and climate crises facing the world. Industrial agriculture's declining biophysical productivity (depletion of soil and nitrogen use efficiency) requires increased synthetic (fossil-fuel based) fertilizer applications when fertilizer costs have practically doubled since 1960 and energy prices are rising (Weis 2007, Cribb 2010, 76, Ploeg 2010). Figure 2 depicts the now close integration of food and energy prices.

Beyond rising energy prices inflating food prices, agro-industrialization's rising material costs (energy, ecosystem depletion) underscore the IAASTD's suggestion that agribusiness 'as usual is no longer an option', and its recognition of the salience of the food sovereignty countermovement's emphasis on multifunctional farming practices. La Vía Campesina now champions agro-ecology in anticipation of a deepening crisis of industrial agriculture, claiming 'To feed future populations, we must nurture the land' (2010, 6). Central to this project are knowledge-intensive practices that reduce chemical and other commercial inputs to farming, and restore local ecological knowledges as essential to both democratic and sustainable food systems (Rosset and Martinez-Torres 2012, Massicotte 2014).[33] This kind of intervention underscores the epistemic implications of the food sovereignty movement, in viewing the right to farm as both a democratic claim ('agrarian citizenship') as well as an assertion of the intricate relations between food, environment and social justice. Whereas capitalist modernity promotes 'agriculture without farmers' – extensive monocultures highly dependent on energy, mechanical and chemical inputs – the food sovereignty movement views the multi-functionality of farming as a cultural and ecological practice premised on skilled labor and the solidary economy of seed sharing. In this vision, restoring and sustaining soil and biodiversity are foundational to modern civilization, particularly in the Anthropocene Age.

> Thus La Vía Campesina claims integrated agroecological farming systems are widely recognized to be more adaptive and resilient to climate change, including droughts, hurricanes, temperature changes, and shifting planting dates. The higher level of on-farm diversity under agroecology means that if one crop is negatively affected, another one is likely to compensate for it. Mulch and green manures that cover soils protect them from erosion, high temperatures and conserve moisture. A diversity of varieties, as well as greater within variety genetic diversity, make peasant farms more able to adapt to changing conditions than homogeneous commercial agriculture. (2010, 11)

---

[32]If not always emptying the countryside, certainly discriminating against small farmers with rising input prices (linked to energy prices) and weak price and credit support compromises their ability to increase production when commodity prices rise (Patnaik 2008, El-Dukheri et al. 2011).
[33]Thus, La Vía Campesina notes its own research shows: 'agroecological farms are substantially more productive ... [and] a more integrated farm is one that combines crops and livestock, intercrops and rotates crops, employs agroforestry, and generally exhibits a higher level of functional biodiversity. Such systems are not only more productive but have far lower costs, especially in terms of expensive farm chemicals and machinery' (2010, 10).

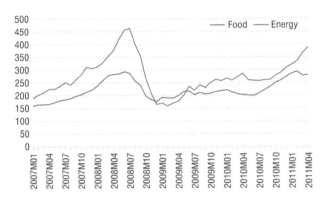

Figure 2.   International Food and Energy Prices (Index, current, US$2000–100).
Source: World Bank, DEC (Development Economics Vice-Presidency) prospects group (Loening and Ianchovichina 2011, 17).

Accordingly, the food sovereignty countermovement is developing agroecological schools and networks to assist farmers in conversion to or consolidation of ecological farming, and advocating publicly for reorientation of research and extension systems to support agroecological innovation and scaling up via farmer organizations (Ibid, 13). At the same time, peasant practices include constant innovation for survival on the land under conditions of climatic change. For example, ActionAid's report, *We know what we need: South Asian women speak out on climate change adaptation*, documents how farmers in the Ganges basin bordering Nepal, India and Bangladesh manage livelihoods under conditions of erratic monsoon patterns, evidencing 'that women in poor areas have started to adapt to a changing climate and can clearly articulate what they need to secure and sustain their livelihoods more effectively' (2007, 4). Pionetti has documented women's management of a 'seeds common' in the Deccan Plateau of South India, noting that:

> the continuous exchange of seeds for local crop varieties circulates genetic resources from one field to another within a village territory and beyond. The dynamic management of genetic resources enhances the stability of traditional agrosystems, increases the adaptation potential of local crops to evolving environmental conditions and limits the risk of genetic erosion. (2005, 154)

Meanwhile, conventional responses to climate change emissions, organized via carbon markets to promote the new 'green economy' trajectory, threaten to convert farmland into carbon sinks, intensifying the pressure on the food sovereignty movement to protect farmers and their land not only from cheap food and land grabbing, but now 'green grabbing' (Fairhead *et al.* 2012). Green grabbing deploys carbon trading as a method of environmental repair or caretaker services to resolve systemic problems: 'Thus tree farms are to replace peasants' fields and fallows, in order to absorb carbon dioxide emitted by the industrial system; tropical forests and the knowledge of their inhabitants are to provide services to Northern industry, researchers and tourists' (Lohmann 1993, 158). At the recent UN Climate Change conference in Warsaw, where the conversion of farmland to carbon sinks was on the agenda, La Vía Campesina stated its position:

> Rights over our farms, lands, seeds and natural resources need to remain in our hands so we can produce food and care for our mother earth as peasant farmers have done for centuries. We will not allow carbon markets to turn our hard work into carbon sinks that allow polluters to continue their business as usual. (2013)

Such climate-proofing threats to small farming and forest-dwellers will only intensify,[34] providing a new front in the struggle to build food sovereignty and value the natural world as a source of life rather than a carbon sink.

Conclusion

Returning to the food regime/food sovereignty dialectic, the overall point is that while the twentieth-century agrarian crisis has been expressed in various forms of peasant resistance (Wolf 1969, Rosset *et al.* 2006, Borras *et al.* 2008) and movements for reform of the agri-food system (Friedmann 2005, Patel 2007, Holt-Giménez and Patel 2009), it is only now, as a final enclosure ensues in the shadow of 'the nemesis effect', [35] rising energy and food prices and destabilization of human populations, that an ontological alternative is universally meaningful and necessary. The canary imagery suggests that at a historical moment like this, with its destructive neo-liberal market path-dependency, a seemingly unthinkable vision can emerge with such power as to remind us of our agrarian foundations. The reminder is driven by direct experience of dispossession, and the obvious deceit of feeding the world with assurances of market efficiency. The absent subjects in the original agrarian question have spoken through the food sovereignty intervention, shifting the focus from capital's expanded reproduction to the question of stewardship of the land as an act of social provision-ing and human survival.

As the corporate food regime has evolved – from dumping cheap (subsidized) food on increasingly unprotected farmers and appropriating land for agro-exports to a displacement of WTO trade rules by (governed) enclosure – the initial food sovereignty intervention has matured in vision and circumstance. Crisis lends credibility. But it also empowers new capital initiatives to roll back the claims and gains of the movement – a process enabled by the complicity of neo-liberalized states. This syndrome explains in part why food sover-eignty resonates in local communities experiencing austerity and/or food shortages, even while the civil society movement at the global level continues the fight for recognition and redistribution of both largesse and perspective. But states/governments will face the music as conditions deteriorate and new food price spikes spark cross-class/sector alliances.

While these alliances are momentary and/or incipient, it is likely they will consolidate under pressure of crisis, as the food question is understood for what it is: an enduring pol-itical relationship that cannot be reduced/fetishized to a question of 'how much'; rather, it is a political-ecological relationship. The fact that over half of the world's food is produced by small farmers, with some estimates up to 70 percent (ETC 2009), is a substantial rationale for advocating support for this producer class (e.g. reversing energy, agribusiness and export subsidies), including the urban 'peasantry'. Thus:

> By one estimate, some 200 million city dwellers produce food for the urban market, accounting for 15–20 per cent of total global food production... In West Africa, around 20 million house-holds (20 per cent of the urban population) are engaged in urban agriculture. They supply 60–100 per cent of the fresh vegetable market in those cities. (Cohen and Garrett 2009, 9)

This is a foundation for domesticating food security, and offers a palpable rejoinder to those who fetishize agro-exporting as the solution to global hunger. It should be a key part

---

[34]Cf McMichael (2009a).

[35]'Burdened by a growing number of overlapping stresses, the world's ecosystems may grow increas-ingly susceptible to rapid, unexpected decline' (Bright 1999, 12).

of a counter-narrative – one that also underscores the importance of regenerative local farming practices as solutions to the combined crises facing the planet. Not an easy task, but easier as conditions deteriorate?

Despite the temptation to (crudely) correlate ecological decline and heightened socio-ecological rationality, this paper is simply arguing that the inherent wisdom of food sovereignty, as a real utopia, inspires adjustments. It already has. And it is implicit and/or explicit in the association consumers, smallholders and urban classes make between the food regime and food insecurity. Communities are developing adaptive strategies that intersect with food sovereignty visioning, whether they call it food sovereignty or not. Often under the radar, nevertheless many of these initiatives reach toward resilient practices – not without contradiction, especially when neglecting social justice concerns. But these are the seeds of survival as the shit hits the fan. From transition town origins in Kinsale, Ireland, through the Detroit Black Community Food Security Network and D-town Farm, to a decentralized 'social movement rooted in communities across Mexico but linked to global food sovereignty efforts,' (Baker 2013, 3–4), political communities are forming in anticipation – building on knowledge networks such as *Moviemento Campesino a Campesino* (MCAC) and seed exchanges (Holt-Giménez 2006, Da Via 2012). In Canada, food sovereignty involves an increasing role of non-governmental organizations (NGOs) providing food access services – in new governance sites abandoned by the state (Martin and Andree 2014), giving rise to community food governance schemes (cf Friedmann 2011).

Such 'urbanization' of food sovereignty underscores the potential for linkages between rural and urban movements that implicitly understand the vulnerabilities of an ecologically compromised world and the socially bankrupt neoliberal vision of market solutions to the food question. The myopia of the current TTIP critique of local procurement as a 'trade barrier' is not only telling, but it also suggests a new stage of corporate market colonization: whereas the WTO prised open farm sectors in the global South for cheap imported food from the North at the expense of domestic producers, the emerging trade agreements target localized food systems in the name of 'free trade'.

Food sovereignty is, therefore, continually in dialectical tension with the food regime, and while the terms of the power struggle unfold across time and space, as argued above, it is ultimately about an ontological contest between distinct visions regarding agriculture: as an economic sector with producing units employing a short-term market calculus, or a landscape inhabited by farmers/pastoralists/fisherfolk geared to sustainable ecological relations. That is, while the struggle reflects a historic power inequality, it will be increasingly governed by a different order of historicization – the imminence of energy and climate feedbacks fundamentally altering the conditions of possibility of human survival.

References

Abramsky, S. 2013. Dust Bowl Blues. *The Nation,* 5/12 August, 14–19.
ActionAid. 2007. *We know what we need: South Asian women speak out on climate change adaptation.* Brighton, UK: Institute of Development Studies, Sussex University.
Ajl, M. 2013. The hypertrophic city versus the planet of fields. In: Neil Brenner, ed. *Implosions/ Explosions: towards a study of planetary urbanization.* Berlin: Jovis Verlag, pp. 2–19.
Andrée, P., J. Ayres, M. Bosia and M-J. Massicotte, eds. 2014. *Globalization and food sovereignty: global and local change in the new politics of food.* Toronto: University of Toronto Press.
Araghi, F. 2000. The great global enclosure of our times: peasants and the agrarian question at the end of the twentieth century. In: F. Magdoff, J.B. Foster and F.H. Buttel, eds. *Hungry for profit.* New York: Monthly Review Press, pp. 145–60.

Araghi, F. 2003. Food regimes and the production of value: some methodological issues. *The Journal of Peasant Studies*, 30(2), 337–68.

Araghi, F. 2009. Accumulation by displacement: global enclosures, the food crisis, and the ecological contradictions of capitalism. *Review*, XXXII(1), 113–46.

Badgley, C., Moghtader, J., Quintero, E., Zakem, E., Chappell, M.J., Aviles-Vazquez, K., Samulon, A. and Perfecto, I. 2007. Organic agriculture and the global food supply. *Renewable Agriculture and Food Systems*, 22(2), 86–108.

Baker, L. 2013. *Corn meets maize: food movements and markets in Mexico*. Boulder, CO: Rowman and Littlefield.

Baltzer, K. and H. Hansen. 2011. *Agricultural input subsidies in Sub-Saharan Africa: an evaluation*. Danida. international development cooperation. Denmark: Ministry of Foreign Affairs.

Bocco, R. and L. Colombo. 2013. Peasants' struggles for seeds in Italy and Europe. *The Journal of Peasant Studies*, 40(1–2), 270–76.

Borras, S., M. Edelman and C. Kay. 2008. *Transnational agrarian movements: confronting globalization*. Oxford: Wiley-Blackwell.

Borras, S. and J.C. Franco. 2012. A 'Land Sovereignty' Alternative? Towards a People's Counter-Enclosure. TNI Agrarian Justice Programme Discussion Paper, July.

Borras, S. and J.C. Franco. 2013. Global land grabbing and political reactions 'from below'. *Third World Quarterly*, 34(9), 1723–47.

Borras, S., J. Franco, S. Gómez, C. Kay and M. Spoor. 2012. Land grabbing in Latin America and the Caribbean. *The Journal of Peasant Studies*, 39(3–4), 845–72.

Bové, J. and F. Dufour. 2001. *The world is not for sale*. London: Verso.

Breisinger, C., O. Ecker, P. Al-Riffai and B. Yu. 2012. *Beyond the arab awakening. Policies and investments for poverty reduction and food security*. Washington, DC: IFPRI.

Bright, C. 1999. The nemesis effect. *WorldWatch*, May/June, 12–23.

Bush, R. 2010. Food riots: poverty, power and protest. *Journal of Agrarian Change*, 10(1), 119–29.

Cave, D. 2013. As cost of importing food soars, Jamaica turns to the Earth. *The New York Times*, August 4, 6.

Claeys, P. 2013. From food sovereignty to peasants' rights: An overview of Via Campesina's struggle for new human rights. *La Via Campesina's Open Book:* Celebrating 20 Years of Struggle and Hope. Available at: http://viacampesina.org/downloads/pdf/openbooks/EN-02.pdf

Claeys, P. and G. Vanloqueren. 2013. The minimum human rights principles applicable to large-scale land acquisitions or leases. *Globalizations*, 10(1), 193–8.

Cohen, M.J. and J.L. Garrett. 2009. The food price crisis and urban food (in)security. Human Settlements Working Paper Series. London and New York: iied/UNFPA. Available at: http://www.iied.org/pubs/display.php?o=10574IIED

Corrado, A. 2010. New peasantries and alternative agro-food networks: the case of Réseau Semence Paysannes. In: A. Bonanno, H. Bakker, R. Jussaume, Y. Kawamura and M. Shucksmith, eds. *From community to consumption: new and classical themes in rural sociological research research in rural sociology and development*, Volume 16. Emerald Publishing Group, pp. 17–30.

Cotula, L., S. Vermeulen, P. Mathieu and C. Toulmin. 2011. Agricultural investment and international land deals: evidence from a multi-country study. *Food Security*, 3(1), S99–S113.

Cribb, J. 2010. *The coming famine. The global food crisis and what we can do about it*. Berkeley: University of California Press.

Da Vía, E. 2012. Seed diversity, farmers' rights, and the politics of repeasantization. *International Journal of Sociology of Agriculture and Food*, 19(2), 229–42.

Davis, M. 2001. *Late Victorian holocausts. El Niño famines and the making of the Third World*. London: Verso.

Davis, M. 2010. Who will build the ark? *New Left Review*, 61, 10–25.

De Schutter, O. 2008. Building resilience: a human rights framework for food and nutritional security. 8 September, A/HRC/9/23. New York: United Nations.

De Schutter, O. 2009. Large Scale Land Acquisitions Leases: A Set of Minimum *Principles and Measures to Address the Human Rights Challenge. Addendum to the Report of the Special Rapporteur on the Right to Food to the Human Rights Council*. A/HRC/13/33/Add.2. Geneva: Human Rights Council.

De Schutter, O. 2011a. How not to think about land grabbing. *UN Special* Rapporteur on the Right to Food, Press Release. Brussels. Available at: http://www.srfood.org/en/how-not-to-think-about-land-grabbing

De Schutter, O. 2011b. The World Trade Organization and the post-global food crisis agenda. *Briefing Note 04*, November. Rome: FAO/United Nations.

Desmarais, A.A. 2002. The Vía Campesina: consolidating an international peasant and farmer movement. *The Journal of Peasant Studies*, 29(2), 91–124.

Desmarais, A.A. 2007. *La Vía Campesina. Globalization and the Power of Peasants*. Halifax: Fernwood Press.

Duncan, C. 1996. *The centrality of agriculture: between humankind and the rest of nature*. Montreal: McGill-Queen's University Press.

Edelman, M. 2009. Synergies and tensions between rural social movements and professional researchers. *The Journal of Peasant Studies*, 36(1), 245–65.

Edelman, M. 2013. Food sovereignty: Forgotten genealogies and future regulatory challenges. *Food Sovereignty: A Critical Dialogue*, International Conference, Yale University, September 14-15. Available at: http://www.yale.edu/agrarianstudies/foodsovereignty/papers.html

El-Dukheri, I., N. Elamin and M. Kherallah. 2011. Farmers' response to soaring food prices in the Arab region. *Food Security*, 3(1), S149–62.

ETC. 2009. Who Will Feed Us? *ETC Group Communiqué*, 102 (November). Available at: www.etcgroup.org.

Fairbairn, M. 2013. 'Like gold with yield': Evolving intersections between farmland and finance. *Food Sovereignty: a Critical Dialogue*, International Conference, Yale University, September 14-15. Available at: http://www.yale.edu/agrarianstudies/foodsovereignty/papers.html

Fairhead, J., M. Leach and I. Scoones. 2012. Green grabbing: a new appropriation of nature? *The Journal of Peasant Studies*, 39(2), 237–62.

FIAN. 2013. G8 should implement the CFS Tenure Guidelines rather than launch a new initiative aimed at increased transparency in land transactions.

Fitting, E. 2011. *The struggle for maize: campesinos, workers, and transgenic corn in the Mexican countryside*. Durham, NC: Duke University Press.

Flávio de Almeida, L. and F.R. Sánchez. 2000. The landless workers' movement and social struggles against neoliberalism. *Latin American Perspectives*, 27(5), 11–32.

Fonte, M. 2008. Knowledge, food and place. A way of producing, a way of knowing. *Sociologia Ruralis*, 48(3), 201–22.

Foster, J.B. 1999. Marx's theory of the metabolic rift: classical foundations for environmental sociology. *American Journal of Sociology*, 105(2), 366–405.

Friedmann, H. 2000. What on earth is the modern world-system? Foodgetting and territory in the modern era and beyond. *Journal of World-Systems Research*, 1(2), 480–515.

Friedmann, H. 2005. From colonialism to green capitalism: social movements and the emergence of food regimes. In: F.H. Buttel and P. McMichael, eds. *New directions in the sociology of global development* 11. Oxford: Elsevier, pp. 229–67.

Friedmann, H. 2011. Food sovereignty in the golden horseshoe region of Ontario. In: H. Wittman, A. A. Desmarais and N. Wiebe, eds. *Food sovereignty in Canada: creating just and sustainable food systems*. Halifax: Fernwood Press, pp. 169–89.

Friedmann, H. and P. McMichael. 1989. Agriculture and the state system: the rise and fall of national agricultures, 1870 to the present. *Sociologia Ruralis*, 29(2), 93–117.

Friedmann, H. and A. McNair. 2008. Whose rules rule? Contested projects to certify 'local production for distant consumers'. *Journal of Agrarian Change*, 8(2–3), 408–34.

Gana, A. 2012. The rural and agricultural roots of the Tunisian revolution: when food security matters. *International Journal of Sociology of Agriculture and Food*, 19(2), 201–13.

GRAIN. 2013. The G8 and land grabs in Africa. *Against the Grain*, March. Available at: www.grain.org

Hansen-Kuhn, K. and S. Suppan. 2013. *Promises and perils of the TTIP. Negotiating a transatlantic agricultural market*. Minneapolis: Institute for Agriculture and Trade Policy and Berlin: Heinrich Böll Foundation.

Holt-Giménez, E. 2006. *Campesino-a-Campesino: voices from Latin America's farmer to farmer movement for sustainable agriculture*. Oakland: Food First Books.

Holt-Giménez, E. and R. Patel, with A. Shattuck. 2009. *Food rebellions! Crisis and the hunger for justice*. Oakland: FoodFirst Books.

Houtart, F. 2010. *Agrofuels: big profits, ruined lives and ecological destruction*. London and New York: Pluto Press.

International Assessment of Agricultural Knowledge, Science and Technology for Development (IAASTD). 2008. *Executive summary of the synthesis report*. Available at: www.agassessment. org/docs/SR_Exec_Sum_280508_English.pdf.

International Planning Committee for Food Sovereignty. 2008. Civil society declaration of Terra Preta forum. 6 June. Available at http://viacampesina.org.en/index.php/main-issues-mainmenu-27/food-sovereignty-and-trade-mainmenu-38/534-civil-society-declaration-of-the-terra-preta-forum

Jaffee, D. 2007. *Brewing justice: fair trade coffee, sustainability and survival*. Berkeley, CA: University of California Press.

Kautsky, K. 1988 [1899]. *The agrarian question*, Vol. 2. London: Zwan Publications.

Kerssen, T. 2012. *Grabbing power: The new struggles for land, food and democracy in Northern Honduras*. Oakland: Food First Books.

Knezevic, I. 2014. Free markets for all: transition economies and the European Union's Common Agricultural Policy. In: P. Andreé, J. Ayres, M. Bosia and M-J. Massicotte, eds. *Globalization and food sovereignty*. Toronto: University of Toronto Press, pp. 228–52.

Kugelman, M. and S.L. Levenstein. 2013. *The global farms race: land grabs, agricultural investment, and the scramble for food security*. Washington, DC: Island Press.

Lagi, M., Bertrand, K.Z. and Yaneer, B.Y. 2011. *The food crises and political instability in North Africa and the middle east*. Cambridge, MA: New England Complex Systems Institute.

Lang, T. and M. Heasman. 2004. *Food wars: the global battle for mouths, minds, and markets*. London: Earthscan.

Lappé, F.M. 1971. *Diet for a small planet*. New York: Ballantine Books.

Liberti, S. 2013. *Land grabbing. Journeys in the new colonialism*. London and New York: Verso.

Loening, J.L., and E. Ianchovichina. 2011. *Middle East and North African countries' vulnerability to commodity price increases*. Washington, DC: World Bank.

Lohmann, L. 1993. Resisting green globalism. In: W. Sachs, ed. *Global ecology*. London and New Jersey: Zed Books, pp. 157–68.

Mann, A. 2014. *Power shift. Global activism in food politics*. Houndmills: Palgrave Macmillan.

Marsden, T. 2012. Third Natures? Reconstituting space through place-making strategies for sustainability. *International Journal of Sociology of Agriculture and Food*, 19(2), 257–74.

Martin, S. and P. Andree. 2014. A seat at the neoliberal table: from food security to food sovereignty in Canada. In: P. Andreé, J. Ayres, M. Bosia and M-J. Massicotte, eds. *Globalization and food sovereignty*. Toronto: University of Toronto Press, pp. 173–98.

Massicotte, M-J. 2014. Beyond political economy: Political ecology and La Vía Campesina's struggle for food sovereignty through the experience of the Escola Latinoamericana de Agroecologia (elaa), Brazil. In: P. Andreé, J. Ayres, M. Bosia and M-J. Massicotte, eds. *Globalization and food sovereignty*. Toronto: University of Toronto Press, pp. 255–87.

McKeon, N. 2009. *The United Nations and civil society. Legitimating global governance: whose voice?* London: Zed Books.

McKeon, N. 2011. Now's the time to make it happen: the U.N.'s committee on food security. In: E. Holt-Giménez, ed. *Food movements unite!*. Oakland: Food First Books, pp. 257–74.

McMichael, P. 2003. Food security and social reproduction: issues and contradictions. In: I. Bakker and S. Gill, eds. *Power, production and social reproduction*. New York: Palgrave Macmillan, pp. 169–89.

McMichael, P. 2005. Global development and the corporate food regime. In: F.H. Buttel and P. McMichael, eds. *New directions in the sociology of global development* 11. Oxford: Elsevier, pp. 229–67.

McMichael, P. 2008. The peasant as 'canary'? Not too early warnings of global catastrophe. *Development*, 51(4), 504–11. Special issue: Future of Agriculture.

McMichael, P. 2009a. Contradictions in the global development project: geo-politics, global ecology and the 'development climate'. *Third World Quarterly*, 30(1), 247–62.

McMichael, P. 2000b. A food regime analysis of the 'world food crisis'. *Agriculture and Human Values*, 26, 281–95.

McMichael, P. 2012. The 'land grab' and corporate food regime restructuring. *The Journal of Peasant Studies*, 39(3/4), 681–701.

McMichael, P. 2013a. Land grabbing as security mercantilism in international relations. *Globalizations*, 10(1), 47–64.

McMichael, P. 2013b. Value-chain agriculture and debt relations: contradictory outcomes. *Third World Quarterly*, 34(4), 671–90.

McMichael, P. 2013c. *Food regimes and agrarian questions*. Halifax: Fernwood Press.

McMichael, P. and M. Schneider. 2011. Food security politics and the Millennium development goals. *Third World Quarterly*, 32(1), 119–39.

Mehta, L., G.J. Veldwisch and J. Franco. 2012. Introduction to the special issue; water grabbing? Focus on the (re)appropriation of finite water resources. *Water Alternatives*, 5(2), 193–207.

Menser, M. 2014. The territory of self-determination, agroecological production, and the role of the state. In: P. Andreé, J. Ayres, M. Bosia and M-J. Massicotte, eds. *Globalization and food sovereignty*. Toronto: University of Toronto Press, pp. 53–83.

Monbiot, G. 2013. Africa, let us help – just like in 1884. *The Guardian*, 10 June.

Monsalve Suárez, S. 2013. The human rights framework in contemporary agrarian Struggles. *The Journal of Peasant Studies*, 40(1), 239–53.

Moore, J. 2011. Transcending the metabolic rift: a theory of crisis in the capitalist world ecology. *The Journal of Peasant Studies*, 38(1), 1–46.

Muller, A.R., A. Kinezuka and T. Kerssen. 2013. The trans-pacific partnership: a threat to democracy and food sovereignty. *Food First Backgrounder*, 19(2), 1–4.

Myerson, J.A. 2012. The real reason the Middle East is rioting. *Pacific Standard*, September 13. Available at: http://www.psmag.com/politics/why-the-middle-east-is-rioting-46792/

Narula, S. 2013. The global land rush: markets, rights and the politics of food. *Stanford Journal of International Law*, 49(1), 103–75.

Nyeleni. 2006. First Manifesto/Call of Social Movements and Civil Society toward the 'Land, Territory and Dignity' Forum, Porto Alegre, 6–9 March.

Nicholson, P. 2008. Vía Campesina: Responding to global systemic crisis. *Development*, 51(4), 456–59.

Nicholson, P. 2009. Interview with Hannah Wittman. *The Journal of Peasant Studies*, 36(3), 676–82.

O'Connor, J. 1998. *Natural causes*. New York: Guilford Press.

Oxfam. 2013. The new alliance: a new direction needed. *Oxfam Briefing Note*, September.

Patel, R. 2007. *Stuffed and starved: markets, power and the hidden battle over the world's food system*. London: Portobello Books.

Patel, R. 2010. Mozambique's food riots – the true face of global warming. *The Guardian*, 4 September.

Patel, R. 2013. The long green revolution. *The Journal of Peasant Studies*, 40(1), 1–63.

Patel, R. and P. McMichael. 2009. A political economy of the food riot. *REVIEW*, XXXII(1), 9–36.

Patnaik, P. 2008. The accumulation process in the period of globalization. *Economic and Political Weekly*, 28, 108–13.

Paul, H. and R. Steinbrecher. 2013. African Agricultural Growth Corridors and the New Alliance for Food Security and Nutrition. Who benefits, who loses? *EcoNexus* report, June. Available at: http://www.econexus.info/sites/econexus/files/African_Agricultural_Growth_Corridors_ &_New_Alliance_-_EcoNexus_June_2013.pdf

Pearce, F. 2012. *The land grabbers. The new fight over who owns the Earth*. Boston: Beacon Press.

Pionetti, C. 2005. *Sowing autonomy: gender and seed politics in Semi-Arid India*. London: iied.

Ploeg, J.D. 2009. *The new peasantries: struggles for autonomy and sustainability in an Era of Empire and globalization*. London: Earthscan.

Ploeg, J.D. 2010. The food crisis, industrialized farming and the imperial regime. *Journal of Agrarian Change*, 10(1), 98–106.

Polanyi, K. 1957. *The great transformation: the political and economic origins of our time*. Boston: Beacon Press.

Pretty, J., A.D. Noble, D. Bossio, J. Dixon, R.E. Hine, F.W.T. Penning de Vries and J.I.L. Morison. 2006. Resource conserving agriculture increases yields in developing countries. *Environmental Science and Technology*, 40(4), 1114–119.

Rosset, P. 2006. *Food is different: why we must get the WTO out of agriculture*. Halifax: Fernwood.

Rosset, P. and M-E. Martinez-Torres. 2012. Rural social movements and agroecology: context, theory and process. *Ecology and Society*, 17(3), 17. Available at: www.ecologyandsociety.org/vol17/iss3/

Rosset, P., R. Patel and M. Courville, eds. 2006. *Promised land. Competing visions of agrarian reform*. Oakland: FoodFirst Books.

Russi, L. 2013. *Hungry capital: the financialization of food*. Winchester, UK: Zero Books.

Schneider, M. and P. McMichael. 2010. Deepening, and repairing, the metabolic rift. *The Journal of Peasant Studies*, 37(3), 461–84.

Schuller, Mark. 2008. Haiti's food riots. *International Socialist Review* 59.

United Nations Development Programme. 2000. *Millennium Development Goals*. New York: United Nations.

Vanhaute, E. 2011. From famine to food crisis: what history can teach us about local and global subsistence crises. *The Journal of Peasant Studies*, 38(1), 47–66.

Vía Campesina. 2000. Bangalore Declaration of the Via Campesina, 6 October. Available at: http://viacampesina.org/main_en/index.php?option1=com_content&task=view&id1/453&Itemid1/428

Vía Campesina. 2010. Peasant and Family-Farm-based Sustainable Agriculture Can Feed the World. *Vía Campesina Views*, Jakarta, September.

Vía Campesina. 2012a. The people of the world confront the advance of capitalism: Rio +20 and beyond. Available at: http://viacampesina.org/en/index.php/actions-and-events-mainmenu-26/-climate-change-and-agrofuels-mainmenu-75/1248-the-people-of-the-world-confront-the-advance-of-capitalism-rio-20-and-beyond

Vía Campesina. 2012b. The Committee on World Food Security (CFS): A new space for the food policies of the world, Opportunities and Limitations. *LVC Notebook #4*.

Vía Campesina. 2013. Specific rights for peasants are also important for European farmers. Available at: http://viacampesina.org/en/index.php/main-issues-mainmenu-27/human-rights-mainmenu-40/1464-specific-rights-for-peasants-are-also-important-for-european-farmers.

Weis, T. 2007. *The global food economy. The battle for the future of farming*. London: Zed Books.

Wittman, H. 2009. Reworking the metabolic rift: La Vía Campesina, agrarian citizenship and food sovereignty. *The Journal of Peasant Studies*, 36(4), 805–26.

Wittman, H. 2010. Agrarian reform and the environment: fostering ecological citizenship in Mato Grosso, Brazil. *Canadian Journal of Development Studies*, 29(3–4), 281–298.

Wolf, E. 1969. *Peasant wars of the twentieth century*. New York: Praeger.

Wolford, W. 2010. *This land is ours now. Social mobilization and the meanings of land in Brazil*. Durham, NC: Duke University Press.

Wright, A. and W. Wolford. 2003. *To inherit the earth: the landless movement and the struggle for a new Brazil*. Oakland: FoodFirst Books.

Philip McMichael is a Professor and Chair of Development Sociology, Cornell University, and is a member of the Civil Society Mechanism in the Committee on World Food Security (CFS) of the Food and Agricultural Organization (FAO). Current research is on agrarian movements, land questions and food regimes. He is the author of *Settlers and the agrarian question* (1984), *Development and social change: a global perspective* (2012), and *Food regimes and agrarian questions* (2013), and editor of *Contesting development: critical struggles for social change* (2010).

Food sovereignty: forgotten genealogies and future regulatory challenges

Marc Edelman

'Food sovereignty' has become a mobilizing frame for social movements, a set of legal norms and practices aimed at transforming food and agriculture systems, and a free-floating signifier filled with varying kinds of content. Canonical accounts credit the Vía Campesina transnational agrarian movement with coining and elaborating the term, but its proximate origins are actually in an early 1980s Mexican government program. Central American activists nonetheless appropriated and redefined it in the late 1980s. Advocates typically suggest that 'food sovereignty' is diametrically opposed to 'food security', but historically there actually has been considerable slippage and overlap between these concepts. Food sovereignty theory has usually failed to indicate whether the 'sovereign' is the nation, region or locality, or 'the people'. This lack of specificity about the sovereign feeds a reluctance to think concretely about the regulatory mechanisms necessary to consolidate and enforce food sovereignty, particularly limitations on long-distance and international trade and on firm and farm size. Several regulatory possibilities are mentioned and found wanting. Finally, entrenched consumer needs and desires related to internationally-traded products – from coffee to pineapples – imply additional obstacles to the localisation of production, distribution and consumption that many food sovereignty proponents support.

> As is well known, criticizing one's friends is more demanding and therefore more interesting than to expose once again the boring errors of one's adversaries.
>
> –Albert O. Hirschman, *A Propensity to Self-Subversion* (1995, 58)

Introduction and disclaimers

Since the mid-1990s, 'food sovereignty' has emerged as a powerful mobilizing frame for social movements, a set of legal and quasi-legal norms and practices aimed at transforming food and agriculture systems, and a free-floating signifier filled with varying kinds of

---

I presented an earlier version of this paper at the International Conference on Food Sovereignty: A Critical Dialogue, Yale University, 14–15 September 2013, and at the Anthropology Colloquium, CUNY Graduate Center, 1 November 2013. I greatly appreciate the constructive comments I received from participants in both fora and from an anonymous JPS reviewer. The paper draws on research that over the years received support (for which I am most grateful) from the Wenner-Gren Foundation for Anthropological Research (Grants 5180 and 5627), the US National Science Foundation (Grants 9319905 and 0107491), and the PSC-CUNY Awards Program (Grants 668480 and 635290032).

content. It is at once a slogan, a paradigm, a mix of practical policies, a movement and a utopian aspiration. As a banner or frame it contributed to the formation of broad-based transnational coalitions, such as the People's Coalition on Food Sovereignty, based mainly in Asia (PCFS 2007), the International Planning Committee for Food Sovereignty, involved in pressuring the Food and Agriculture Organization (FAO) since 2002, and the Nyéléni Forum, which includes Vía Campesina and various other coalitions of peasants, pastoralists and fisherfolk. It has been the subject of regional presidential summit meetings, as in Managua in 2008 (Cumbre Presidencial 2008). As a set of policy prescriptions, measures intended to enhance 'food sovereignty' run the gamut from relatively convention-al types of protectionism to innovative forms of linking small-scale producers and consu-mers. 'Food sovereignty' has been incorporated in legal norms, sometimes at the level of national constitutions, in a growing number of nation-states, including Venezuela, Senegal, Mali, Nicaragua, Ecuador, Nepal and Bolivia (Beauregard 2009, Gascón 2010, 238–42, Muñoz 2010, Beuchelt and Virchow 2012) and localities (Sustainable Cities Col-lective 2011, Field and Bell 2013, 44). Some civil society organisations have sought to institutionalise food sovereignty at the international level through an international conven-tion that would supersede and obviate multilateral free trade agreements (PCFS and PAN AP 2004, Bové 2005, PCFS 2005, Windfuhr and Jonsén 2005, Claeys 2013, 4), though this initiative has languished in recent years.[1]

This paper acknowledges right up front that the idea of 'food sovereignty' has gained extraordinary traction and that it has contributed in numerous ways and in many parts of the world to the realization of a progressive agenda on food and agriculture issues. At the same time, the concept and the way it is typically understood have several evident limitations.[2] The paper cannot and does not pretend to cover the burgeoning literature on 'food sover-eignty'. Its objective instead is merely to broaden the discussion by briefly analysing several dimensions of 'food sovereignty' that thus far have received insufficient attention and that are arguably important in understanding the history of 'food sovereignty' and in advancing 'food sovereignty' policies. At the outset it is important to emphasise that the sceptical observations that follow are offered in a spirit of deep sympathy and solidarity with the food sovereignty project, which can only advance further if its proponents sharpen their critical focus and acknowledge how daunting the challenges are.

The origin story

All social groups have origin stories and myths. These serve to reaffirm shared identities and values, to mobilize and bind collectivities, to define adversaries and to connect the present to the past. Like other invented traditions, they are not necessarily about accurate historical reconstruction, but instead often serve to legitimise contemporary practices and doctrines (Hobsbawm 1983). Intellectual and social movements – and not just tribes or

---

[1]In contrast, an Intergovernmental Working Group of the United Nations (UN) Human Rights Council, mandated with drafting a Declaration on the Rights of Peasants and Other People Working in Rural Areas, held its first meeting in July 2013. The first draft under discussion contained several provisions related to food sovereignty (see Edelman and James 2011, Golay and Biglino 2013). A Convention on Food Sovereignty was one demand of the NGO Forum and allied social movements at the 2001 Rome +5 World Food Conference (Shaw 2007, 359).
[2]As Clapp warns, 'a broad conceptualization may work well in the early stages of a movement, but it is likely that the concept will need to be more precisely articulated, which may in turn cause it to lose some of its supporters' (2012, 176).

other imagined or epistemic communities – also typically have origin myths (McLaughlin 1999). Some of them are almost as fanciful as the tale about how the goddess Minerva was born fully-grown from the head of Jupiter, wearing her armour and accompanied by her wise owl.

In the case of 'food sovereignty', the canonical account is repeated more or less the same way in almost every analysis, whether by pro-food sovereignty scholar-activists (Windfuhr and Jonsén 2005, Martínez-Torres and Rosset 2010, 45–52, Wittman *et al.* 2010, Focus on the Global South 2013) or by sceptics (Beuchelt and Virchow 2012, 260, Hospes 2013). The following elements recur in most of the now very substantial food sovereignty literature:

(1) 'Food sovereignty' was first discussed by Vía Campesina at its Second International Conference at Tlaxcala, Mexico, in 1996.[3]
(2) Vía Campesina and its allies 'launched' or went public with a call for food sovereignty at the FAO-sponsored World Food Conference in Rome in 1996.
(3) They juxtaposed 'food sovereignty' to 'food security', which was seen as a contrary, deficient and 'mediocre' (Rosset and Martínez-Torres 2013, 6) concept, for reasons that will be elaborated below.
(4) The idea and practice of food sovereignty were refined at various international conclaves of peasant and farmer movements and other civil society organisations, including those in Havana (Foro Mundial 2001), Rome (NGO/CSO Forum 2002), Sélingué, Mali (Nyéléni Forum 2007), and Mexico City (Vía Campesina 2012).[4]

A few accounts of the history of food sovereignty provide greater specificity, though not much. Chaia Heller, for example, remarks that 'the precise origin of the term is unclear'. She notes, however, that 'On December 4, 1993, [the French] union paysans joined eight thousand other smallholders from across Europe to travel to Geneva, carrying a banner that for the first time read *Souveraineté alimentaire* (Food sovereignty)' (Heller 2013, 97).

There's an additional wrinkle to the food sovereignty origin story, which concerns academics who have written on the concept and its regional origins. In October 2012, Olivier De Schutter, the UN Special Rapporteur on the Right to Food, delivered a keynote address at the event where an annual Food Sovereignty Prize was awarded by the New York-based non-governmental organization (NGO) Why Hunger to several social movement groups. De Schutter began his speech to the audience of New Yorkers by remarking that 'the first researcher who actually used the concept of food sovereignty is somebody from New York. He is Marc Edelman in a book called *Peasants against globalization* in

---

[3]The proceedings volume from this meeting states, 'Food sovereignty, simply defined, is ensuring that land, water, seeds and natural resources are controlled by small and medium-sized producers. It is directly linked to democracy and justice' (Vía Campesina 1996, 21).
[4]A more complete listing of relevant meetings and framing documents is in Windfuhr and Jonsén (2005, 47–52). This process of refinement produced increasingly precise definitions, but also 'increasing levels of inconsistency' (Patel 2009, 666). Key ideas include protection for food producers, especially small-scale ones; regulation of agricultural production and trade; an end to dumping of developed-country surpluses in developing countries; sustainable, agro-ecological production practices; democratic control, by 'the people', 'local producers' or by those who 'produce, distribute and consume food'; management of resources, seeds and territories by small-scale food producers, and gender and other kinds of social equality. Occasionally, food sovereignty enthusiasts (Patel 2009, 666–7) acknowledge that such capacious framings contain internal or even 'fatal' contradictions, elisions and substantial doses of wishful thinking.

1999' (De Schutter 2012, Edelman 1999, 102–3).[5] Not long after, Priscilla Claeys, a member of the Special Rapporteur's research team and one of his PhD students, echoed this claim, albeit in less categorical terms, in an article in the journal *Sociology* (Claeys 2012, 849) and, more definitively, in a personal communication with the author (1 February 2013).[6]

Edelman had been unable to attend Why Hunger's Food Sovereignty Award event. Alerted by a colleague who was present, he viewed the video of De Schutter's keynote, feeling flattered of course but also experiencing a certain disbelief, since he didn't recall having 'used' 'food sovereignty' in *Peasants against globalization* (though he did remember that by the late 1980s peasant activists in Costa Rica occasionally employed the term).[7] He first went back to the index of the book and then to field notes and transcriptions of recorded interviews from the late 1980s and 1990s, where he found scattered references to '*soberanía alimentaria*', usually in relation to the dumping of US surplus maize, which undermined domestic producers.

In Central America, and especially in Costa Rica, these scattered mentions of 'food sovereignty' occurred (and gradually became more frequent) in a flow of much more commonly-used, related terms that peasant movements employed during their apogee in the late 1980s. At least as early as 1988, for example, the term 'food autonomy' ('*autonomía alimentaria*') was utilised by more radical Costa Rican peasant groups, such as the Atlantic Region Small Agriculturalists Union (Unión de Pequeños Agricultores de la Región Atlántica, UPAGRA), which was made up mainly of maize producers (La República 1988, 3). UPAGRA was the dominant force in a coalition of peasant movements called the Justice and Development Council (Consejo Justicia y Desarrollo), several leaders of which played key roles in founding Vía Campesina.

The politically centrist National Union of Small and Medium Agricultural Producers (Unión Nacional de Pequeños y Medianos Productores Agropecuarios, UPANACIONAL), similarly demanded,

> Food self-sufficiency [*autosuficiencia alimentaria*] and rejection of the importation of agricultural products at 'dumping' prices … [and the] promotion and the establishment of sovereignty in exports, so that these do not concentrate in the hands of transnational companies. (UPANACIONAL 1989, 2)

At least one UPANACIONAL leader attended some early Vía Campesina events, although his organisation later withdrew from most international work (Desmarais 2007, 182).

The documentary record of a roundtable held in early 1991 again indicates that Costa Rican rural activists employed the term 'food sovereignty' in relation to dumping and also to argue for 'sovereignty in exports' ('*soberanía en las exportaciones*') (Alforja 1991, 1, 7). They understood this as meaning that foreign firms ought not to control Costa Rica's agricultural export trade. Notably, at least two of the activists at the roundtable, including the

---

[5]The relevant section in the book was based on an article Edelman published in 1991 in the now-defunct journal *Peasant Studies* (not to be confused with the *Journal of Peasant Studies*). See Edelman (1991, 229). Edelman also mentioned 'food sovereignty' in another article (1998, 59) published one year before the book De Schutter mentioned.

[6]In another work, Claeys locates the origins of 'food sovereignty' in Central America in the mid-1980s (2013, 3).

[7]A few years later this was true in Honduras (and perhaps elsewhere in the region) as well. See Amador (1994).

one who spoke of 'soberanía alimentaria', were involved two years later in some of the earliest meetings of Vía Campesina. In April 1991, a letter that three other peasant leaders sent to the president of the republic similarly specified 'soberanía alimentaria' as an objective 'so that [the country] would not have to depend on surpluses from other countries that could vanish and the prices of which are subject to the international market' (Campos *et al.* 1991).[8]

Importantly, Central American governments of varying orientations occasionally used similar kinds of language at least as early as the 1960s (Boyer 2010, 322) and very explicitly in the 1980s. In Nicaragua, in 1983, for example, the Sandinista government's Ministry of Agricultural Development and Agrarian Reform (Ministerio de Desarrollo Agropecuario y Reforma Agraria, MIDINRA) produced a major 'Strategic Framework' that viewed 'food security' as (1) access to an adequate quantity and quality of food by the entire population and (2) national self-sufficiency (*autosuficiencia*) in the supply of food (Biondi-Morra 1990, 64).[9] In 1989, in Costa Rica, the then-Minister of Agriculture, an individual generally hostile to the peasant organizations, claimed 'to back the policy of self-sufficiency [*autoabastecimiento*] in [rice] and other basic grains' (La República 1989, 10A).

Another important source of 'food sovereignty' talk was the Food Security Training Program (Programa de Formación en Seguridad Alimentaria, PFSA), funded by the European Community, which held seminars in Panama for peasant activists from throughout Central America in late 1990 and 1991 (Edelman 1998, 57–62). This followed a related Food Security Program that focused on empirical research in the different countries of the region. While the abundant documentary materials these programs produced contain few, if any, mentions of 'soberanía alimentaria', the peasants who returned from the seminars sometimes began to use the term, although often almost interchangeably with 'seguridad alimentaria'.[10]

An important new tool for lexicographical research sheds additional light on the origins of 'food sovereignty' and also refutes once and for all De Schutter's notion that Marc Edelman was 'the first researcher who actually used the concept'. Google – ever respectful of norms governing intellectual property – usually won't let researchers view all of the pages it has scanned for its Google Books database, but it does provide a search tool called the Ngram Viewer that permits them to search for the relative frequency with which particular words or phrases appear in the texts.[11] It is possible, as well, to explore specific sources that employ the search term within delimited periods. Figures 1 and 2 provide a graphical representation of Ngram data for 'food sovereignty' and 'soberanía alimentaria' respectively. Both graphs show a steep increase in mentions of the search terms at the end of the 1990s, a reflection of the growing traction at that time of the food sovereignty concept as employed by Vía Campesina and its allies. Both graphs, however, also show a significant, though smaller, upturn in the early to mid-1980s. Scrutiny of this data complicates the origin story of food sovereignty still further.

---

[8]These leaders were from leftist and centrist organisations; none of them became involved in Vía Campesina.
[9]According to Spalding, 'In the absence of any competing, long-term national development plan, this MIDINRA document served as the main expression of the regime's economic vision' (1994, 73).
[10]As late as 2008, the declaration of the Latin American Presidential Summit on Food Sovereignty and Security also used the terms largely interchangeably (Cumbre Presidencial 2008).
[11]On the Ngram, see Egnal (2013) and Rosenberg (2013).

Figure 1. Relative frequency of 'food sovereignty' in Google Books English database, 1960–2009. Source: Google Ngram, 11 December 2013.

In 1983, the government of Mexico announced a new National Food Program (Programa Nacional de Alimentación, PRONAL) (Comisión Nacional de Alimentación 1984).[12] The first objective of PRONAL was 'to achieve food sovereignty', a concept that was understood as

> more than self-sufficiency in food; it implies national control over diverse aspects of the food chain, thus reducing dependency on foreign capital and imports of basic foods, inputs and technology. The key factor of this strategy is the adoption of a holistic focus on policies related to the phases of production, transformation, commercialisation, and consumption. (Heath 1985, 115)

While it is beyond the scope of this essay to discuss PRONAL in any depth, it is clear that the upward blips in the graphs in the mid-1980s are directly related to this Mexican government program and its rhetoric about 'soberanía alimentaria'.[13] Many researchers writing in English and Spanish – including Esteva (Esteva 1984, Austin and Esteva 1987), Heath (1985) and Sanderson (1986) – used the term in this context. The genealogical complication that this represents for the Vía Campesina food sovereignty origin story (and its near-universal acceptance by scholars) is obvious.[14] What is less clear (and probably unknowable) is whether Mexico exported the language of 'food sovereignty' to Central America, via mass media or actual contact between peasant movements or other civil society groups,

---

[12]Two years earlier, the phrase 'food sovereignty' appeared in discussions of Canada's food aid program, with one speaker asserting that 'the first test of any emerging nation's real sovereignty is food sovereignty' (Canadian Institute of International Affairs 1981, 107). The term, however, failed to gain traction at the time.

[13]Journalist Alan Riding charged accurately that PRONAL 'emerged as a SAM without money' (Riding 1986, 286). SAM – the Sistema Alimentario Mexicano – was the previous government's food program (dismantled in 1983), which tried simultaneously to provide support prices to farmers and subsidies to consumers, thus worsening an already critical fiscal deficit.

[14]Martínez-Torres and Rosset are right that '[f]ood sovereignty is a concept coined by actively appropriating and inventing language' (2010, 161). What they and other Vía Campesina activists fail to realise, however, is that the language appears to have been appropriated – even if indirectly – from PRONAL and Mexican President Miguel de la Madrid – surely not the most inspiring political-intellectual ancestor for these Mexico-based scholar-activists.

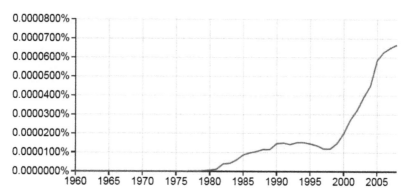

Figure 2.   Relative frequency of 'soberanía alimentaria' in Google Books Spanish database, 1960–2009.
Source: Google Ngram, 11 December 2013.

or whether the emergence of the term in Central America is a case of simultaneity of invention.[15]

How different is food security?

In 1996, Vía Campesina advanced 'food sovereignty' as an alternative to the FAO's concept of 'food security'.[16] Some analyses describe 'food sovereignty' versus 'food security' as a 'global conflict', characterised by 'fundamental antagonisms' (Schanbacher 2010, ix), others as a 'counterframe' (Fairbairn 2010, 26–7) or as part of a 'conflict between models' (Martínez-Torres and Rosset 2010, 169–70). Raj Patel points out that 'food sovereignty' was 'very specifically intended as a foil to the prevailing notions of "food security"' (2009, 665).[17]

But were these or are these diametrically opposed ideas? Even in the mid-1990s there were about 200 definitions of 'food security' in published writings (Clay 2003). One FAO

---

[15]On contacts in this period between Mexican and Central American peasant activists, see Boyer (2010) and Holt-Giménez (2006). It may be significant that the 1996 Vía Campesina conference that adopted a food sovereignty program was held in Mexico, where local movements would have been aware – at very least – of the De La Madrid government's rhetoric about 'food sovereignty'.

[16]The conventional view is typified by an editorial in the *Nyéléni Newsletter*:

food sovereignty is different from food security in both approach and politics. Food security does not distinguish where food comes from, or the conditions under which it is produced and distributed. National food security targets are often met by sourcing food produced under environmentally destructive and exploitative conditions, and supported by subsidies and policies that destroy local food producers but benefit agribusiness corporations. Food sovereignty emphasizes ecologically appropriate production, distribution and consumption, social-economic justice and local food systems as ways to tackle hunger and poverty and guarantee sustainable food security for all peoples. It advocates trade and investment that serve the collective aspirations of society. It promotes community control of productive resources, agrarian reform and tenure security for small-scale producers, agro-ecology, biodiversity, local knowledge, the rights of peasants, women, indigenous peoples and workers, social protection and climate justice (Focus on the Global South 2013).

[17]Fairbairn rightly suggests that 'food sovereignty is both a reaction to and an intellectual offspring of the earlier concepts of the "right to food" and "food security"' (2010, 15).

study sensibly advises that '[w]henever the concept is introduced in the title of a study or its objectives, it is necessary to look closely to establish the explicit or implied definition' (Clay 2003, 25). A number of those 200 or so definitions overlapped substantially with the emerging idea of 'food sovereignty'. And – as Patel acknowledges – 'food sovereignty is ... over-defined. There are so many versions of the concept, it is hard to know exactly what it means' (2009, 663).

'The concept of "food security"', according to Flavio Valente,

> was first utilised in Europe after World War I. In its origin it was profoundly linked to the concept of national security and to the capacity of each country to produce its own food so that it would not be vulnerable to possible politically- or militarily-related sieges [cercos], embargos or boycotts. (2002)[18]

'Food security' was considered part of the human rights agenda as early as the 1943 Hot Springs, Virginia, conference of allied governments, which gave rise to the FAO (Valente 2002, Shaw 2007, 8–10). Three decades later, the 1974 World Food Summit, held in the context of worsening scarcities, narrowed the definition of 'food security' to the 'availability at all times of adequate world food supplies of basic foodstuffs to sustain a steady expansion of food consumption and to offset fluctuations in production and prices' (quoted in Clay 2003, 27). Notably, this definition focuses on countries and on overall consumption rather than on the household or individual level. During this period, 'food security' became increasingly delinked from human rights concerns and centred instead on production and supply in relation to criteria of physical and nutritional necessity (Valente 2002, Shaw 2007). Over the next two decades, the FAO added additional elements to its definitions, including 'access' for all people, food safety and nutritional balance, and cultural preferences (Clay 2003). This new emphasis on consumption and on access by all people, including vulnerable populations, reflected the influential work on 'entitlements' of Amartya Sen (1981). Omawale, among others, has argued that Sen's concept of 'entitlement' constituted a 'bridge between the structural and human rights approach[es] to food in development' (Omawale 1984; see also Schanbacher 2010, 110–1). But entitlement theory also contributed to a shift in food security thinking away from the nation and toward the household or individual as the relevant secure or insecure unit (Fairbairn 2010, 24).

Some of the most frequently cited definitions of 'food security' developed in the 1980s and early 1990s contain elements that figure later in the idea of 'food sovereignty'. Take, for example, Solon Barraclough's definition, developed as part of a study sponsored by the United Nations Research Institute on Social Development:

> Food security can be defined as sustained and assured access by all social groups and individuals to food adequate in quantity and quality to meet nutritional needs. A food system offering food security should have the following characteristics: (a) capacity to produce, store, and import sufficient food to meet basic food needs for all groups; (b) maximum autonomy and self-determination (without implying autarky), reducing vulnerability to international market fluctuations and political pressures; (c) reliability, such that seasonal, cyclical and other variations in access to food are minimal; (d) sustainability such that the ecological system is protected and improved over time; and (e) equity, meaning, as a minimum, dependable access to adequate food for all social groups. (Barraclough 1991, 1)

---

[18]Fairbairn's idea that 'food security' is a relatively new concept, dating to the 1970s, clearly requires rethinking (2010, 22–3, 2012, 221).

Note the concern with 'autonomy and self-determination', 'sustainability' and protection of 'the ecological system', and 'equity'. Now compare Vía Campesina's 'original' – i.e., 1996 – statement at the Rome World Food Summit:

> Food security cannot be achieved without taking full account of those who produce food. Any discussion that ignores our contribution will fail to eradicate poverty and hunger. Food is a basic human right. This right can only be realized in a system where food sovereignty is guaranteed. Food sovereignty is the right of each nation to maintain and develop its own capacity to produce its basic foods respecting cultural and productive diversity. We have the right to produce our own food in our own territory. Food sovereignty is a pre-condition to genuine food security. (quoted in NGLS Roundup 1997)

Like the FAO definitions of 'food security', the relevant unit of sovereignty is the nation, and respect for cultural diversity is a paramount concern. The 'right to produce food' is indeed a novel addition, as is the mention of 'territory', a term that has historically figured in the demands of indigenous peoples but that here appears to refer to nation-states.

Perhaps more indicative of the slippage between 'food security' and 'food sovereignty' in 1996 is the NGO Forum Statement to the World Food Summit, titled 'Profit for few or food for all' and subtitled '*Food sovereignty and security* to eliminate the globalisation of hunger' (italics added). This extensive declaration highlighted six key elements, which are summarised in highly synthetic fashion here: (1) strengthening family farmers, along with local and regional food systems; (2) reversing the concentration of wealth and power through agrarian reform and establishing farmers' rights to genetic resources; (3) reorienting agricultural research, education and extension toward an agroecological paradigm; (4) strengthening states' capacity for ensuring food security through a suspension of structural adjustment programs, guarantees of economic and political rights, and policies to 'improve the access of poor and vulnerable people to food products and to resources for agriculture'; (5) deepening the 'participation of peoples' organizations and NGOs at all levels', and (6) assuring that international law guarantees the right to food and that food sovereignty takes precedence over macroeconomic policies and trade liberalization (NGO Forum 1996, see also Shaw 2007, 355–6).

By 2002, with the Rome +5 Summit and the formation of the International Planning Committee (IPC) for Food Sovereignty (a massive coalition of civil society organisations, including Vía Campesina), an important shift occurred in the prevailing 'food sovereignty' discourse. In particular, the IPC replaced 'nation' with 'peoples, communities, and countries' in its definition. As Otto Hospes (2013) points out, this 'suggests a pluralistic approach to the question of who is the sovereign'.

By 2007, the Declaration of the Nyéléni Forum for Food Sovereignty reduced the scope of sovereignty simply to 'peoples': 'Food sovereignty is the right of peoples to healthy and culturally appropriate food produced through ecologically sound and sustainable methods, and their right to define their own food and agriculture systems' (Nyéléni Forum 2007, 9). 'Healthy and culturally appropriate food', of course, was already part of earlier FAO definitions of 'food security'. As this and many other examples cited above suggest, in its origins and its contemporary expressions, 'food sovereignty' intersects considerably and sometimes even converges with 'food security'. Both have been protean concepts, frequently imprecise, always contested and in ongoing processes of semantic and political evolution.

The question of who is the sovereign in 'food sovereignty' is of crucial importance, since it is inevitably tied to the administration of food sovereignty. Is it the nation-state, a region, a locality or 'the people'? Is the meaning of 'food sovereignty' the same in a giant country (e.g., Canada) or a tiny one?[19] If the sovereign unit is a region defined as 'a local food ecosystem that bases its boundaries on ecological parameters like water flow, rather than on arbitrary state lines' (Field and Bell 2013, 59), then how will the relevant constituency be demarcated? What political institutions will administer 'food sovereignty'? How will these differ from existing state institutions? What processes will establish their democratic legitimacy?

Another rarely examined question is the meaning of 'sovereignty' itself and its relevance (or the lack of it) in an increasingly globalised world. Food sovereignty advocates face a paradox inasmuch as efforts to strengthen food sovereignty at the national level inevitably strengthen the states with which they are frequently in an otherwise adversarial relationship. Moreover, recent efforts to theorise sovereignty – even by critical scholars (e.g., Agamben 1998) who see institutionalised illegality, violence and 'biopolitical' domination of the citizenry as central to how states work – commonly hark back to conservative, pro-Nazi philosopher Carl Schmitt's hackneyed claim that the 'sovereign is he who decides on the state of exception' (2005 [1922], 1, 5). This deeply authoritarian premise would seem to have little to offer democratically-minded proponents of food sovereignty. It does, however, point squarely at an issue about which most food sovereignty advocates have been evasive at best, even those who conceive of the present moment as characterised by a 'conflict between models' (Martínez-Torres and Rosset 2010, 169–70). This is the question of the scope of the food sovereign's power and how it will be consolidated, maintained and enforced.

Long-distance trade and firm size

The ambiguous nature of the sovereign that characterises most discussions of 'food sovereignty' is suggestive of another set of problems that require specification if 'food sovereignty' is to make the leap from appealing slogan to on-the-ground policy.[20] The idea of 'food sovereignty' draws on a rich set of ideas and practices related to local 'food sheds', alternative food networks and the localisation of economies as a defence against globalisation. These include reducing 'food miles'; promoting direct marketing and geographical origin indications; local sourcing for restaurants and institutions such as schools, universities, hospitals, nursing homes and prisons, and maintaining greenbelts around urban areas. Food sovereignty advocates differ as to the role of market forces, though most insist that food is not simply a commodity. They also differ as to the role of long-distance and, especially, international trade in a food sovereign society, and have generally been silent on the question of small producers who depend on export production (of coffee, cacao, etc.) for their livelihoods (Burnett and Murphy 2013, 5–6). Some food sovereignty proponents explicitly call for tariff protections and 'an end to international trade agreements and financial

---

[19]Writing on Canada, Desmarais and Wittman stress 'unity in diversity' as a key principle of food sovereignty. They also point to the Canadian Wheat Board (CWB), which among other things was the country's major exporter, as an institution of 'food sovereignty' (2013). But they also acknowledge that importing countries would be unlikely to view the CWB that way. Indeed, part of the CWB's early success was that its single-desk buyer system eliminated competition among farmers, 'allowing them to achieve greater economic clout in the global grain trade' (Magnan 2011, 116).
[20]Of course some food activists, as Fairbairn (2012) indicates, view food sovereignty as largely a question of consumer choices and express little interest in its policy implications.

institutions that interfere with the sovereignty and sustainability of food systems' (Field and Bell 2013, 8–9).[21]

Imagine for a moment a flourishing small farm in a food sovereign society (Figure 3). It produces a wide variety of high-quality foods for nearby markets using sustainable agro-ecological practices. It does as much of the post-harvest processing, packaging, storage and transport as possible in order to capture value-added that would otherwise accrue to intermediaries, agroindustries and retailers. It pays a living wage and benefits to its hired hands and has excellent occupational safety and health standards. Perhaps it has direct links with urban or other consumers through weekly farmers' markets, farm stands or community supported agriculture (CSA) groups. It generates significant returns because of its varied production (which minimizes environmental and economic risks and generates year-round sales), its low-input (and thus low-cost) technological mix, its highly productive workforce (which appreciates the decent treatment), its financial backing from CSA sub-scriptions rather than commercial lenders (which lowers costs and protects against risks of price fluctuations, foreclosure, bad weather, pests and pathogens) and its savvy market-ing strategies (which also create a risk cushion and fuel further demand). It can, of course, reinvest those profits in the existing farm and in its amortisation fund and take some as income or worker bonuses. It may also decide that it wants to expand the scale of its oper-ations, purchasing or renting additional land and hiring more workers (or, if a cooperative,

Figure 3.   'Imagine a small farm … ' (Noyack, New York, USA, 2009).

---

[21]In 1996, Vía Campesina simply demanded the *renegotiation* of 'international trade agreements like GATT/WTO (General Agreement on Tariffs and Trade/World Trade Organisation), Maastricht, [and] NAFTA (North American Free Trade Agreement)' (Vía Campesina 1996, 23). Later, of course, it called for getting the 'WTO out of agriculture' (Rosset 2006). Food sovereignty advocates' views are evolving. Some 'see a gradual acceptance of trade under certain circumstances … , with the shift away from focusing primarily on local markets to integrating consideration for fairer trade' (Burnett and Murphy 2013, 4).

enlisting more associates). It might even decide that it wants to sell some of its products in markets on the other side of the country or abroad. How does a 'food sovereign' society, where 'the people define their own food and agriculture system', handle this type of dizzying success and these kinds of aspirations?

Like proponents of the many efforts to 'localise' economies in the face of globalisation (Hines 2000, Halweil 2002, Nonini 2013), 'food sovereignty' advocates rarely consider what sort of regulatory apparatus would be needed to manage questions of firm and farm size, product and technology mixes, and long-distance and international trade.[22] 'Food sovereignty' implies limits on all of these. Who would enforce those limits? One of the ironies of posing the question in these terms is that many food sovereignty enthusiasts favour abolishing or diminishing regulation of local trade and of preferred products (e.g., raw milk and raw milk cheeses). In this respect, their vision sometimes converges with that of the detested neoliberals, who tend to view all regulation as onerous for business, large and small. 'They [Maine farmers] don't need inspectors to make sure they are following good practices', Tony Field and Beverly Bell declare. '[K]eeping their neighbors, families, and long-time customers in good health is an even better incentive' (2013, 43).

Both post-Washington Consensus neoliberalism and food sovereignty movements manifest interest in decentralisation and local empowerment, albeit with very different rationales. The neoliberal vision backs decentralisation as a top-down method of institutional reform that increases 'efficiency' and (allegedly) empowers communities vis-à-vis higher orders of governance. Food sovereignty movements, on the other hand, favour decentralisation because it might create space for an alternative version of development based on small-scale farming and agroecology. The neoliberal approach assumes a congruence of interests between distinct classes of 'stakeholders', with the market resolving questions of trade and firm size. The food sovereignty approach is premised on an ongoing tension between market and society, but it prefers to assume – on the basis of what evidence is unclear – that the market can be kept at bay through direct democracy and 'the people' exercising control over 'their' food system. Again, the question of what that 'control' might look like is rarely specified in sufficient detail for it to become workable policy.

My concern here is with two specific imperatives – limiting firm and farm size and long-distance trade – both of which probably imply relatively draconian state control, though of what kind remains little discussed and unclear. It is worth examining briefly, however, the broader gamut of regulatory possibilities that might arguably be implemented in a food sovereign society. What kinds of control have been tried and what might be learned from these experiences? State-level anti-corporate farming laws in the United States have not been notably successful in stalling the advance of giant agribusinesses (CELDF n.d.). The commodities boards that existed in so many countries before the advent of neoliberalism (and that still survive in some places in hollowed-out form) were designed to provide price supports and to regulate foreign trade in a few, internationally traded products. Sometimes they were also in charge of supply management and reserves. Even if resources and political will could be mustered to resurrect and revitalise them, they would not likely be capable of administering the complex product mix of highly diversified food sovereign farms, or controlling the successful ones that might want to engage in long-distance trade or even move into potentially profitable monocultures. Ceilings on

---

[22]Ishii-Eitman (2009) and Burnett and Murphy (2013) are among the very few exceptions to this generalization. Mohan and Stokke (2000), Hinrichs (2003) and Robotham (2005) provide unusually thoughtful and grounded discussions of the complexities of constructing 'the local'.

farm size, which have been a feature of many agrarian reform programs, might begin to check the consolidation of large properties. But such measures have proven notoriously easy to circumvent through titling by different family members or separate corporate enti-ties.[23] Environmental protection and food safety agencies (and nongovernmental certifying organizations) could conceivably exercise some control over technology and the use of banned substances or practices, but these would require vastly greater resources in order to be effective and to overcome possible perverse incentives, such as 'cheating' with agro-chemicals or suborning inspectors. There is no indication that the 'local food policy coun-cils' hailed in some enthusiasts' analyses would be up to any of these daunting enforcement tasks (Halweil 2002, 8, Hassanein 2003, 79–80, Holt-Giménez et al. 2009, 170–1, Field and Bell 2013, 70). Some 'food sovereignty' advocates call for 'confederalism':

> Nurturing and strengthening citizen-centered food systems and autonomy calls for forms of political and social organisation that can institutionalise interdependence without resorting to the market or the central state. Confederalism involves a network of citizen groups or councils with members or delegates elected from popular face-to-face democratic assemblies, in vil-lages, tribes, towns and even neighborhoods of large cities. (Pimbert 2006, xii)

In this view, 'confederalism' would, if all goes well, be followed by a linking of federations and confederations that would produce 'a significant counter-power to the state and trans-national corporations' and result in a stage of 'dual power' (Pimbert 2006, xii, 26). This phrase is, of course, redolent of earlier historical experiences that ultimately did not go so well for small farmers.[24]

In an insightful 2008 essay, Boaventura de Sousa Santos pointed to a reciprocal myopia that afflicts both the heterogeneous progressive forces that come together in the World Social Forums (WSF) and traditional Marxists. On the one hand, 'the conventional left parties and the intellectuals at their service have stubbornly not paid any attention to the WSF or have minimized its significance'. On the other, 'the great majority of the activists of the WSF' – and by extension, one might add, 'food sovereignty' advocates – have shown 'contempt … for the rich left theoretical tradition, and … militant disregard for its renewal' (Santos 2008, 256–7). In thinking about the limitations of 'food sovereignty' as policy, it is necessary to go beyond Santos' affirmations and recognise that apart from their respective refusals to acknowledge the other, neither group has really grappled with the economic lessons that might be learned from what used to be called 'actually existing socialism'. This failure results in a notable short-sightedness when it comes to thinking through the implementation of 'food sovereignty' and particularly the need for strong regulatory over-sight of firm size and long-distance trade raised above.

The centrally planned economies were – and to the extent that they still exist, are – notoriously unsuccessful in providing their citizens with basic consumer goods and, in par-ticular, with sufficient fresh and varied foodstuffs. The stress and wasted time that people endured in a system that used queuing up, rather than purchasing power, as the rationing principle for basic goods were arguably an important aspect of the erosion of legitimacy that eventually contributed to those societies' demise (Shanin 1990, 71, Verdery 1996,

---

[23]In peri-urban areas in the United States, conservation and similar easements intended to preserve greenbelts and farmland have sometimes had the effect of creating ownership ceilings, even though this isn't their intention.
[24]See Lenin (1964 [1917]) and Stalin's unsurprisingly meretricious essay 'Dizzy with success' (Stalin 1955 [1930]).

26–9).[25] The Achilles' heel of the command economies was the 'plan indicator', a production goal that could be expressed in tonnes, metres, pairs (e.g., of shoes) or some other measure or combination of measures. In effect, 'the centre' set targets for enterprises and then negotiated its provision of inputs and the managers' delivery obligations. Frequently this led to hoarding of materials and labour, considerable waste and absurd outcomes, such as extra-heavy sheet metal and pipes (indicator in tonnes), oversupply of small shoe sizes and undersupply of large sizes (indicator in pairs), or overly bright light bulbs (indicator in watts) (Nove 1991, Verdery 1996). These results reflected two fundamental, unresolvable problems: first, the aggregation – for management and planning purposes – of impossibly large numbers of discrete products (e.g., types of light bulbs, sizes and styles of footwear) and second, the failure of the microeconomic signals from end users to be heard or to correspond to the specific products needed or desired.

The conclusion, which some 'food sovereignty' advocates may find lamentable, is (1) that market mechanisms, even if they frequently generate injustice and inequality, can be especially efficient at delivering a wide product mix to consumers, and (2) that micromanaging the consumer goods sector – and particularly the agriculture and food sector – has almost always proven counterproductive. This is not to say that supply management and commodities boards and so on are doomed – indeed, these or similar mechanisms will be essential for any meaningful version of food sovereignty – but rather to point very specifically to the strong regulatory control that will also be required to localise and domesticate trade and to maintain farm and firm sizes within tolerable bounds. But the onus is on food sovereignty enthusiasts to grapple with the history of the command economies and to come up with creative mechanisms that encourage diversity, that balance and meet the needs of producers and consumers, and that achieve the basic contours of a truly democratic 'food sovereign' production and distribution system. The issues of regulating trade and firm size that are implicit in so much of the food sovereignty literature are rarely acknowledged and have sadly received little or no serious attention.

Consumer taste in a food sovereign society

Kim Burnett and Sophia Murphy (2013) rightly draw attention to the food sovereignty movement's silence on the question of small producers who depend on export crops for their livelihoods and food security. They argue that having such producers shift from (sometimes) lucrative export crops to low-cost staples for domestic consumption risks exacerbating inequalities by reducing producers' incomes. Gerardo Otero et al. (2013, 265) point out that while many developing countries have become dependent on imports of industrially produced cereals and oils, the 'dependency' of developed countries is mainly in the sector of high-value 'luxury' foods that make only a small contribution to total nutritional intake. A related question concerns consumer tastes and needs (even if the latter are not strictly physiological, but socially constructed).

Sidney Mintz famously analysed the role of sugar imported from the Caribbean in fuelling the workforce that initiated the industrial revolution in England (1986). Together with

---

[25]Of course many, if not most, people didn't just line up, but also worked their connections and resorted to the illegal market economy to obtain otherwise scarce necessities. Cubans sardonically refer to this as 'sociolismo', a play on 'socialismo' and 'socio', which means 'partner' but which they commonly employ to mean 'buddy' or 'friend'.

stimulants – first tea and, somewhat later, coffee – caffeine and sugar became basic necessities in numerous countries where they were not produced. They powered workers (Jiménez 1995), actual and would-be elites (Roseberry 1996), and military machines (Haft and Suarez 2013). They kept innumerable sleep-deprived academics, policymakers and activists alert during interminable meetings. A food sovereign society could completely eschew these products, but in the event that prohibition of coffee and tea is not politically popular, long-distance international trade is essential for providing them (unless, of course, we contemplate anti-economic greenhouse production of these crops in cold climates).

If coffee, tea and cane sugar have been constructed as necessities, there is also the question of consumer predilections and whims – the construction of tastes for non-necessities – in a food sovereign society. In Costa Rica in the early 1980s, in the midst of the country's worst economic crisis since the 1930s depression, kiwis from Hawaii suddenly started to appear in supermarkets in upscale neighbourhoods, and frequent radio spots extolled the 'exoticness' and 'deliciousness' of this novel fruit. The seductive voice in the radio ads became the butt of comedians' jokes and impressions. The Archbishop denounced the squandering of scarce foreign exchange on kiwis and plaintively asked if there was a more delicious fruit in the world than Costa Rican pineapple, which, he reminded people, was cheap, abundant and locally produced.[26] This implicit plea for a kind of food sovereignty identified one problem, but masked another.

Food is not just a source of physiologically necessary nutrients but a major source of pleasure and sociality. Some food sovereignty proponents, such as Slow Food, make this a central part of their political (and culinary) practice, but most others – and especially those most concerned with policy – have given this dimension little systematic attention. Consumers in cold, Northern countries have come to enjoy not only pineapples and kiwis but an extraordinary cornucopia of perishable tropical fruits (and other products, e.g., chocolate, macadamia nuts, etc.). They have come to expect these delicacies all year round. Once they've tasted pineapple (or mangos or açaí or bananas), they are unlikely to take kindly to food sovereignty scolds who insist on their consuming only local products during those long northern winters.[27] The problem is not just how to reverse tastes constructed over long historical time, something that is probably close to impossible, but also how to build political support for 'the people' democratically exercising control over 'their' food system – that is, for food sovereignty. Limiting access to delectable exotic foods is almost certainly a poor road to consensus. An additional, related paradox is that food sovereignty as a set of diverse practices has advanced by incremental steps, while its advocates typically insist that nothing short of a complete overhaul of food and farming – along with associated changes in values – will be sufficient to reverse the juggernaut of corporate agriculture (Hassanein 2003).

Conclusion

Food sovereignty activists and scholars, almost without exception, attribute the invention of food sovereignty to Vía Campesina and accept the claim that 'food sovereignty' and 'food

---

[26] He was apparently unconcerned that pineapple was produced in pesticide-intensive monocultures.
[27] The ubiquitous plastic bags of mushy, tasteless Macintosh and 'Delicious' apples that were the main source of vitamin C during my childhood in 1950s and 1960s New York are but one dismal example of the alternative to long-distance trade. At least there were sometimes oranges from far-off Florida and California. The glories of summer included abundant local peaches, plums and berries.

security' are diametrically opposed concepts. This paper has shown instead that the prox-imate origins of the phrase are in a Mexican government program in the early 1980s and that its adoption by Central American peasant movements occurred in a context where for some time 'food security', 'food sovereignty' and several similar terms overlapped, blended into one another and were used largely interchangeably. Recent suggestions that the author of this paper was the first researcher to mention 'food sovereignty' are misplaced, since numerous Mexican and foreign scholars earlier analysed the Mexican government program mentioned above. Several, though not all, of the Central American activists who began to speak of 'food sovereignty' in the 1980s eventually went on to participate in the founding of Vía Campesina.

Food sovereignty proponents have been remarkably vague about who or what is 'the sovereign' in 'food sovereignty', with different organisations and theorists either disagree-ing, ignoring the issue entirely or shifting over time between pointing to the nation-state, a region, a locality or 'the people'. This question matters because it speaks to the crucial point of how a food sovereign society will be administered. Will a food sovereign society permit a successful small farm to expand its operations or to enter international markets? If so, up to what point? Who will draw the line and enforce it? There is an urgent need for devoting more attention to the political institutions needed for food sovereignty, as well as to the issues of how these will intersect with or differ from existing state institutions and how they will establish and maintain democratic legitimacy.

The nature of 'sovereignty' itself, similarly, is rarely scrutinised in the food sovereignty literature or by food sovereignty movements, most of which find themselves in adversarial relationships with the states in which they operate. The policies that would strengthen food sovereignty at the national level inevitably imply strengthening the states with which the movements are typically in conflict. The experience of the centrally-planned economies suggests that the strong state actions required to impose limits on farm and firm size and on long-distance and international trade could easily give rise to unintended consequences that would negatively affect both small agricultural producers and the consumers who sym-pathise with and depend on them.

The localisation of production and consumption that is central to most conceptions of food sovereignty raises a host of further problems that again have received far too little con-sideration. How much extra-local trade would be tolerated or encouraged? What will become of the millions of smallholders who depend for their livelihoods on export production and whose incomes would plummet if they were required to switch, say, from cacao or African palm production to cassava and maize? Localisation also raises fundamental pro-blems for consumers dependent on or even addicted to necessities, such as coffee, which are produced in far-off places. Both needs of this sort and predilections for other exotic pro-ducts are indicative of the extent to which food has deep cultural roots and meanings, formed over long historical time, that go beyond those typically adduced in the food sovereignty lit-erature. Attempts to reverse these tastes and needs would be extremely difficult and would doubtless raise widespread opposition to any food sovereignty program that sought to do so.

Food sovereignty advocates thus find themselves in an interesting and fertile moment. A proliferation of concepts, experiments and experiences provides abundant material for reflection and for practical efforts to solidify the paradigm on the ground and, hopefully, to scale it up. At the same time, the almost wilful neglect of some key theoretical and policy issues impedes further progress. If we are to imagine not only a successful small farm in a food sovereign society, but a successful food sovereign society built on a dynamic small farm sector, we need to devote considerably more attention to some of the challenges and paradoxes outlined above.

References

Agamben, G. 1998. *Homo sacer: sovereign power and bare life*. Stanford, CA: Stanford University Press.

Alforja, ed. 1991. *El campesino ve el ajuste estructural así. Reflexiones de Jorge Hernández (UPANACIONAL), Carlos Hernández (Consejo Justicia y Desarrollo), y Oscar Monge (UNAC)*. San José: Centro de Estudios y Publicaciones Alforja.

Amador, J. 1994. Author's interview with Jorge Amador, CNTC and COCOCH. Tegucigalpa: Honduras. July 29.

Austin, J.E. and G. Esteva. 1987. Final reflections. *In*: J.E. Austin and G. Esteva, eds. *Food policy in Mexico: The search for self-sufficiency*. Ithaca, N.Y.: Cornell University Press, pp. 353–373.

Barraclough, S.L. 1991. *An end to hunger? The social origins of food strategies*. London and Geneva: Zed Books, UNRISD, South Centre.

Beauregard, S. 2009. Food policy for people: incorporating food sovereignty principles into state governance. Case studies of Venezuela, Mali, Ecuador, and Bolivia [online]. Urban and Environmental Policy Department, Occidental College. Available from: http://www.oxy.edu/sites/default/files/assets/UEP/Comps/2009/Beauregard%20Food%20Policy%20for%20People.pdf [Accessed 19 May 2013].

Beuchelt, T.D. and D. Virchow. 2012. Food sovereignty or the human right to adequate food: Which concept serves better as international development policy for global hunger and poverty reduction? *Agriculture and Human Values*, 29(2), 259–273.

Biondi-Morra, B.N. 1990. *Revolución y política alimentaria: un análisis crítico de Nicaragua*. México, D.F.: Siglo Veintiuno Editores.

Bové, J. 2005. La réalité locale dépend aussi du contexte global. *In*: J. Duchatel and F. Rochat, eds. *ONU: droits pour tous ou loi du plus fort? Regards militants sur les Nations Unies*. Geneva: CETIM, pp. 366–368.

Boyer, J. 2010. Food security, food sovereignty, and local challenges for transnational agrarian movements: The Honduras case. *Journal of Peasant Studies*, 37(2), 319–351.

Burnett, K. and S. Murphy. 2013. What place for international trade in food sovereignty? Presented at the Food Sovereignty: A Critical Dialogue International Conference. Yale University.

Campos, C., Fernández, L., and T. González. 1991. Carta al Presidente de la República Licenciado Rafael Angel Calderón Fournier, 22 de abril de 1991.

Canadian Institute of International Affairs. 1981. *International Canada*. Ottawa: Canadian Institute of International Affairs and Parliamentary Centre for Foreign Affairs and Foreign Trade.

CELDF. n.d. Anti-corporate farming laws in the heartland [online]. Community Environmental Legal Defense Fund. Available from: http://www.celdf.org/anti-corporate-farming-laws-in-the-heartland [Accessed 29 Jul 2013].

Claeys, P. 2012. The creation of new rights by the food sovereignty movement: The challenge of institutionalizing subversion. *Sociology*, 46(5), 844–860.

Claeys, P. 2013. From food sovereignty to peasants' rights: An overview of via Campesina's struggle for new human rights. *In*: *La via Campesina's open book: Celebrating 20 years of struggle and hope*. Jakarta: Via Campesina, pp. 1–10.

Clapp, J. 2012. *Food*. Cambridge, UK: Polity Press.

Clay, E. 2003. Food security: Concepts and measurement. *In*: FAO, ed. *Trade reforms and food security: conceptualizing the linkages*. Rome: FAO, pp. 25–34.

Comisión Nacional de Alimentación. 1984. *PRONAL – Programa Nacional de Alimentación*. México, D.F.: Comisión Nacional de Alimentación.

Cumbre Presidencial. 2008. Cumbre Presidencial, Soberanía y Seguridad Alimentaria: Alimentos para la Vida, Managua, Nicaragua, 7 de mayo de 2008 [online]. Available from: http://www.iadb.org/intal/intalcdi/PE/2008/01655.pdf [Accessed 5 Aug 2013].

De Schutter, O. 2012. Food sovereignty prize address [online]. Food sovereignty prize. Available from: https://www.youtube.com/watch?v=qeht1Q-TwsI [Accessed 24 Nov 2012].

Desmarais, A.A. 2007. *La vía campesina: Globalization and the power of peasants*. Halifax, N.S.: Fernwood Publishing.

Desmarais, A.A. and H. Wittman. 2013. Farmers, foodies & first nations: getting to food sovereignty in Canada. Presented at the Food Sovereignty: A Critical Dialogue International Conference. Yale University.

Edelman, M. 1991. Shifting legitimacies and economic change: The state and contemporary Costa Rican peasant movements. *Peasant Studies*, 18(4), 221–249.

Edelman, M. 1998. Transnational peasant politics in Central America. *Latin American Research Review*, 33(3), 49–86.

Edelman, M. 1999. *Peasants against globalization: Rural social movements in Costa Rica*. Stanford, CA: Stanford University Press.

Edelman, M. and C. James. 2011. Peasants' rights and the UN system: Quixotic struggle? Or emancipatory idea whose time has come? *Journal of Peasant Studies*, 38(1), 81–108.

Egnal, M. 2013. Evolution of the novel in the United States: The statistical evidence. *Social Science History*, 37(2), 231–254.

Esteva, G. 1984. *Por una nueva política alimentaria*. Mexico, D.F.: Sociedad Mexicana de Planificación.

Fairbairn, M. 2010. Framing resistance: International food regimes and the roots of food sovereignty. *In*: H. Wittman, A.A. Desmarais, and N. Wiebe, eds. *Food sovereignty: Reconnecting food, nature & community*. Halifax, N.S.: Fernwood Publishing, pp. 15–32.

Fairbairn, M. 2012. Framing transformation: The counter-hegemonic potential of food sovereignty in the US context. *Agriculture and Human Values*, 29(2), 217–230.

Field, T. and B. Bell. 2013. *Harvesting justice: Transforming food, land, and agricultural systems in the Americas*. New York: Other Worlds & U.S. Food Sovereignty Alliance.

Focus on the Global South. 2013. Editorial: food sovereignty now! *Nyéléni Newsletter*, Mar, p. 1.

Foro Mundial. 2001. El Foro Mundial sobre Soberanía Alimentaria propone alternativas a las políticas alimentarias que generan hambre y malnutrición [online]. Available from: http://www.vivalaciudadania.org/forosocial/htm/foro8.htm [Accessed 12 Jan 2003].

Gascón, J. 2010. ¿Del paradigma de la industrialización al de la soberanía alimentaria? Una comparación entre los gobiernos nacionalistas latinoamericanos del siglo XX y los pos-neoliberales a partir de sus políticas agrarias. *In*: J. Gascón and X. Montagut, eds. *Cambio de rumbo en las políticas agrarias latinoamericanas? Estado, movimientos sociales campesinos y soberanía alimentaria*. Barcelona: Icaria Editorial, pp. 215–259.

Golay, C. and I. Biglino. 2013. Human rights responses to land grabbing: A right to food perspective. *Third World Quarterly*, 34(9), 1630–1650.

Haft, M. and H. Suarez. 2013. The marine's secret weapon: coffee [online]. *New York Times*. Available from: http://atwar.blogs.nytimes.com/2013/08/16/the-marines-secret-weapon-coffee/?_r=0 [Accessed 17 Aug 2013].

Halweil, B. 2002. *Home grown: the case for local food in a global market*. Washington, DC: Worldwatch Institute.

Hassanein, N. 2003. Practicing food democracy: A pragmatic politics of transformation. *Journal of Rural Studies*, 19(1), 77–86.

Heath, J.R. 1985. El Programa Nacional de Alimentación y la crisis de alimentos. *Revista Mexicana de Sociología*, 47(3), 115–135.

Heller, C. 2013. *Food, farms & solidarity: French farmers challenge industrial agriculture and genetically modified crops*. Durham: Duke University Press.

Hines, C. 2000. *Localization: a global manifesto*. London: Earthscan.

Hinrichs, C.C. 2003. The practice and politics of food system localization. *Journal of Rural Studies*, 19(1), 33–45.

Hirschman, A.O. 1995. *A propensity to self-subversion*. Cambridge: Harvard University Press.

Hobsbawm, E.J. 1983. Introduction: Inventing traditions. *In*: E.J. Hobsbawm and T.O. Ranger, eds. *The invention of tradition*. Cambridge: Cambridge University Press, pp. 1–14.

Holt-Giménez, E. 2006. *Campesino a campesino: voices from Latin America's farmer to farmer movement for sustainable agriculture*. Oakland: Food First Books.

Holt-Giménez, E., R. Patel, and A. Shattuck. 2009. *Food rebellions! Crisis and the hunger for justice*. Oakland, CA: Food First Books.

Hospes, O. 2013. Food sovereignty: the debate, the deadlock, and a suggested detour [online]. *Agriculture and Human Values*. Available from: http://link.springer.com/10.1007/s10460-013-9449-3 [Accessed 24 Jul 2013].

Ishii-Eiteman, M. 2009. Food sovereignty and the International Assessment of Agricultural Knowledge, Science and Technology for Development. *Journal of Peasant Studies*, 36(3), 689–700.

Jiménez, M.J. 1995. 'From plantation to cup': Coffee and capitalism in the United States, 1830–1939. *In*: W. Roseberry, L. Gudmundson, and M. Samper Kutschbach, eds. *Coffee, society, and power in Latin America*. Baltimore: Johns Hopkins University Press, pp. 38–64.

La República. 1988. Las medidas de presión se mantienen en firme – Gobierno pide calma a los agricultores. *La República*, 28 Jul, p. 3.

La República. 1989. El país no debe importar ni exportar arroz, dice Figueres. *La República*, 24 May, p. 10A.

Lenin, V.I. 1964. The dual power. *In*: *Collected works*, vol. 24. Moscow: Progress Publishers, pp. 38–41.

Magnan, A. 2011. The limits of farmer-control: Food sovereignty and conflicts over the Canadian Wheat Board. *In*: H. Wittman, A.A. Desmarais, and N. Wiebe, eds. *Food sovereignty in Canada: Creating just and sustainable food systems*. Halifax, N.S.: Fernwood Publishing, pp. 114–133.

Martínez-Torres, M.E. and P.M. Rosset. 2010. La Vía Campesina: The birth and evolution of a transnational social movement. *Journal of Peasant Studies*, 37(1), 149–175.

McLaughlin, N. 1999. Origin myths in the social sciences: Fromm, the Frankfurt school and the emergence of critical theory. *Canadian Journal of Sociology/Cahiers Canadiens De Sociologie*, 24(1), 109–139.

Mintz, S.W. 1986. *Sweetness and power: the place of sugar in modern history*. New York: Penguin Books.

Mohan, G. and K. Stokke. 2000. Participatory development and empowerment: The dangers of localism. *Third World Quarterly*, 21(2), 247–268.

Muñoz, J.P. 2010. Constituyente, gobierno de transición y soberanía alimentaria en Ecuador. *In*: J. Gascón and X. Montagut, eds. *Cambio de rumbo en las políticas agrarias latinoamericanas? Estado, movimientos sociales campesinos y soberanía alimentaria*. Barcelona: Icaria Editorial, pp. 151–168.

NGLS Roundup. 1997. The World Food Summit [online]. United Nations Non-Governmental Liaison Service. Available from: http://www.un-ngls.org/orf/documents/text/roundup/11WFS.TXT [Accessed 22 Mar 1997].

NGO Forum. 1996. Profit for few or food for all: food sovereignty and security to eliminate the globalisation of hunger [online]. Available from: http://www.foodsovereignty.org/Portals/0/documenti%20sito/Resources/Archive/Forum/1996/wfs+5_NGO_FORUM96.pdf [Accessed 30 Jun 2013].

NGO/CSO Forum. 2002. Food sovereignty: a right for all. Political statement of the NGO/CSO Forum for Food Sovereignty [online]. Available from: http://www.foodsovereignty.org/Portals/0/documenti%20sito/Resources/Archive/Forum/2002/political%20statement-eng.pdf [Accessed 22 Jun 2006].

Nonini, D.M. 2013. The local-food movement and the anthropology of global systems. *American Ethnologist*, 40(2), 267–275.

Nove, A. 1991. *The economics of feasible socialism revisited*. 2nd ed. London: HarperCollins Academic.

Nyéléni Forum. 2007. Nyéléni 2007: Forum for Food Sovereignty.

Omawale. 1984. Note on the concept of entitlement: Bridge between the structural and human rights approach to food in development. *In*: A. Eide, W.B. Eide, S. Goonatilake, J. Gussow, and Omawale, eds. *Food as a human right*. Tokyo, Japan: United Nations University, pp. 260–264.

Otero, G., G. Pechlaner, and E.C. Gürcan. 2013. The political economy of 'food security' and trade: Uneven and combined dependency. *Rural Sociology*, 78(3), 263–289.

Patel, R. 2009. What does food sovereignty look like? *Journal of Peasant Studies*, 36(3), 663–673.

PCFS. 2005. Draft – The People's Convention on Food Sovereignty [online]. Available from: http://www.archive.foodsov.org/resources/conventiondhaka.doc [Accessed 1 Aug 2013].

PCFS. 2007. People's Coalition on Food Sovereignty (PCFS) [online]. People's Coalition on Food Sovereignty. Available from: http://www.archive.foodsov.org/html/aboutus.htm [Accessed 1 Mar 2011].

PCFS and PAN AP. 2004. People's convention on food sovereignty. *In*: *Primer on people's food sovereignty*. Penang, Malaysia: People's Coalition on Food Sovereignty and Pesticide Action Network Asia and Pacific, pp. 35–45.

Pimbert, M.P. 2006. *Transforming knowledge and ways of knowing for food sovereignty*. London: International Institute for Environment and Development.

Riding, A. 1986. *Distant neighbors: a portrait of the Mexicans*. New York: Vintage Books.

Robotham, D. 2005. *Culture, society, and economy: bringing production back in*. Thousand Oaks, CA: Sage Publications.

Roseberry, W. 1996. The rise of yuppie coffees and the reimagination of class in the United States. *American Anthropologist*, 98(4), 762–775.

Rosenberg, D. 2013. Data before the fact. *In*: L. Gitelman, ed. *'Raw data' is an oxymoron*. Cambridge, MA: MIT Press, pp. 15–40.

Rosset, P.M. 2006. *Food is different: Why we must get the WTO out of agriculture*. Halifax, N.S.: Fernwood Publishing.

Rosset, P.M. and M.E. Martínez-Torres. 2013. Rural social movements and diálogo de saberes: territories, food sovereignty and agroecology. Presented at the Food Sovereignty: A Critical Dialogue International Conference. Yale University.

Sanderson, S.E. 1986. *The transformation of Mexican agriculture: international structure and the politics of rural change*. Princeton, N.J.: Princeton University Press.

Santos, B. de S. 2008. The world social forum and the global left. *Politics & Society*, 36(2), 247–270.

Schanbacher, W.D. 2010. *The politics of food: the global conflict between food security and food sovereignty*. Santa Barbara, CA: Praeger.

Schmitt, C. 2005. *Political theology: four chapters on the concept of sovereignty*. Chicago: University of Chicago Press.

Sen, A. 1981. *Poverty and famines: an essay on entitlement and deprivation*. Oxford: Oxford University Press.

Shanin, T. 1990. The question of socialism: A development failure or an ethical defeat? *History Workshop*, 30, 68–74.

Shaw, D.J. 2007. *World food security: a history since 1945*. New York: Palgrave Macmillan.

Spalding, R.J. 1994. *Capitalists and revolution in Nicaragua: opposition and accommodation, 1979–1993*. Chapel Hill: University of North Carolina Press.

Stalin, J.V. 1955. Dizzy with success: Concerning questions of the collective-farm movement. *In*: *Works*, vol. 12. Moscow: Foreign Languages Publishing House, pp. 197–205.

Sustainable Cities Collective. 2011. Maine town becomes first in US to declare food sovereignty [online]. Available from: http://sustainablecitiescollective.com/node/22295 [Accessed 2 Aug 2012].

UPANACIONAL. 1989. Planteamientos de UPANACIONAL frente a la agricultura de cambio. *Panorama Campesino*, 3, 1–17.

Valente, F.L.S. 2002. Um breve histórico do conceito de segurança alimentar no âmbito internacional [online]. *Red Interamericana de Agriculturas y Democracia*. Available from: www.riad.org/articulo.php3?id1=3a27eaaf3d0bc&id2=3a27eb5 [Accessed 24 Oct 2002].

Verdery, K. 1996. *What was socialism, and what comes next?* Princeton, N.J.: Princeton University Press.

Vía Campesina. 1996. La Vía Campesina: Proceedings from the II International Conference of the Vía Campesina, Tlaxcala, Mexico, April 18–21, 1996. Brussels: NCOS Publications.

Vía Campesina. 2012. International internal seminar on public policy for food sovereignty (preliminary report).

Windfuhr, M. and J. Jonsén. 2005. *Food sovereignty: towards democracy in localized food systems*. Warwickshire, UK: ITDG Publishing & FIAN.

Wittman, H., A. Desmarais, and N. Wiebe. 2010. The origins and potential of food sovereignty. *In*: H. Wittman, A.A. Desmarais, and N. Wiebe, eds. *Food sovereignty: Reconnecting food, nature & community*. Halifax, N.S.: Fernwood Publishing, pp. 1–14.

Diálogo de saberes in La Vía Campesina: food sovereignty and agroecology

María Elena Martínez-Torres and Peter M. Rosset

The transnational rural social movement La Vía Campesina has been critically sustained and shaped by the encounter and *diálogo de saberes* (dialog among different knowledges and ways of knowing) between different rural cultures (East, West, North and South; peasant, indigenous, farmer, pastoralist and rural proletarian, etc.) that takes place within it, in the context of the increasingly politicized confrontation with neoliberal reality and agribusiness in the most recent phase of capital expansion. This dialog among the 'absences' left out by the dominant monoculture of ideas has produced important 'emergences' that range from mobilizing frames for collective action – like the *food sovereignty* framework – to social methodologies for the spread of *agroecology* among peasant families.

Introduction

In the last 20 years we have seen the coming together of rural social movements and rural organizations from all over the world to form La Vía Campesina (LVC). LVC is a transnational social movement composed of national, regional and continental movements and organizations of peasant and family farmers, indigenous people, landless peasants, farm workers, rural women and rural youth, representing some 200 million families worldwide (Desmarais 2007, Martínez-Torres and Rosset 2008, 2010). Each component movement (i.e. the Latin American Coordination of Rural Organizations [CLOC], or Vía Campesina Thailand) and individual member organization comes to this global constellation with its own history, its own culture, and its own constellation of relationships with organizations inside and outside of LVC at the local, provincial, national and international level. LVC is not a single movement or organization, but rather is a constellation composed of many rural movements and organizations.

In this sense, LVC is a global 'space of encounter' among different rural and peasant cultures, different epistemologies and hermeneutics, whether East and West, North and South, landed and landless, farmer, pastoralist and farm worker, indigenous and non-indigenous, women, men, elders and youth, and Hindu, Muslim, Buddhist, Animist, Mayan, Christian and Atheist (Martínez-Torres and Rosset 2010, Rosset 2013). Representatives of this immense diversity come together to exchange, dialog, discuss, debate, analyze, strategize, build consensus around collective readings of reality, and agree on collective actions and campaigns with national, regional, continental or global scope.

Within this diversity there are many differences to work out, but it is remarkable that LVC has lasted 20 years without succumbing to internal fragmentation, as have many previous transnational alliances and movements (Martínez-Torres and Rosset 2010). How has this been possible? We argue that the process called *diálogo de saberes* in Spanish (Leff 2004), which roughly translates to 'dialog among different knowledges and ways of knowing', is key to the durability of the LVC constellation. It is a process whereby different visions and cosmovisions are shared on a horizontal, equal-footing basis. Part of it can be thought of a peasant/indigenous way of solving or avoiding conflicts, because there isn't one knowledge to be imposed on others.

This process of dialog happens on multiple levels, for example inside each member organization, and with its own constellation of relationships from the local to the international level (inside and outside of LVC), and then also when they come together as LVC. While there are differences, debates and conflicts, the latter are typically tabled for later consideration when tensions have abated. Organizations take mutual inspiration from the experiences and visions of others. In particular, *diálogo de saberes* is how LVC grows and builds areas of internal consensus, which are often new, 'emergent' proposals and ideas. As a recent LVC declaration put it, 'We ... have grown in our struggle, thanks to the exchange among cultures, to our processes, our victories and our setbacks, and to the diversity of our peoples' (LVC 2012).

It is our contention that the process of *diálogo de saberes* (DS) has also accelerated the recent shift toward the promotion of *agroecology* as an alternative to the so-called Green Revolution in many contemporary rural social movements that once argued for increased industrial farming inputs and machinery for their members (Altieri and Toledo 2011, Rosset *et al.* 2011). In this essay we describe this phenomenon in the historically specific context of La Vía Campesina.

The history of this evolution passes through the construction and elaboration of the *food sovereignty* framework by LVC, and has been critically molded by the ongoing internal encounter of DS. This encounter and dialog has been shaped by the increasingly politicized confrontation with neoliberal reality and agribusiness in its most recent phase of capitalist expansion (Martínez-Torres and Rosset 2010, Rosset 2013). In this process, member organizations have been informed by their experiences with *movement forms* of agroecology (i.e. *campesino-a-campesino* or farmer-to-farmer processes) and with their growing number of agroecology and political leadership peasant training schools in the Americas, Africa and Asia.

In an earlier paper (Rosset and Martínez-Torres 2012), we situated the rise of agroecology in LVC in the context of territorial disputes with Capital and agribusiness (Fernandes 2008a, 2008b, 2009), addressing the roles played in the current global disputes over natural resources by both *agroecology-as-farming* and *agroecology-as-framing*, as elements in the (re)construction of peasant territories. We saw this as re-peasantization through agroecology (in the sense of van der Ploeg 2008, 2010). In this paper we draw on the work of Enrique Leff (2004, 2011), Boaventura de Sousa Santos (2009, 2010) and agroecology pedagogues from an LVC member movement, the Landless Workers Movement of Brazil (MST), to explain the roles of DS in collective construction of mobilizing frames for resistance (Benford and Snow 2000) and for promoting on-the-ground, agroecology-as-farming (Tardin 2006, Martínez-Torres and Rosset 2010, Rosset and Martínez-Torres 2012). It is perhaps ironic that post-modern analysis helps us understand mobilization for quintessentially modernist goals, like the physical occupation and transformation of material territory.

Diálogo de saberes *(DS)*

In today's world, formal, instrumental and economic rationality are used as tools for domination, control, 'efficiency' and economization, generating what Boaventura de Sousa

Santos has called 'monocultures of knowledge' (Santos 2009, 2010). In the same vein, Enrique Leff (2004, 15) argues that 'theories and scientific disciplines construct paradigms that create epistemological obstacles to the integration of knowledges outside their disciplines ... Since metaphysics, dominant thinking has reified the world, enclosing it with rigid concepts and categories.'[1] In contrast, *diálogo de saberes* (DS) begins with the recognition, recovery and valorization of autochthonous, local and/or traditional knowledges, all of which contribute their experiences (Leff 2011). These knowledges are called 'absences' by Santos (2009, 2010) – left out of the dominant monoculture, and from the dialogs among the absences come 'emergences'. According to Leff:

> *Diálogo de saberes* is an opening and a call to subaltern knowledges, especially to those that sustained traditional cultures and today resignify their identities and position themselves in a dialog of resistance to the dominant culture that imposes its supreme knowledge. DS is a dialog with interlocutors that have been stripped of their own words and memory, traditional knowledges that have been buried by the imposition of modernity, and the dialog becomes an investigation, an exegesis, an hermeneutics of erased texts; it is a therapeutic politics to return the words and the meaning of languages whose flow has been blocked (Leff 2004, 26).

Leff (2004, 24) concludes: '*meaning* in the world, is reactivated in a potent movement unleashed through the *diálogo de saberes*, which is the exact opposite of the desire to fix the [unchanging] meaning of concepts in dictionaries and glossaries ... In *diálogo de saberes*, beings and knowledges from outside the time and space of positivist knowledge relate with one another' (Emphasis added).

We believe that LVC is a space where an enormous DS takes place, which puts the (re) appropriation and sharing of knowledges (the *absences* of Santos) into play. This leads to emergent discourses (the *emergences* of Santos) that question the dominion of mercantile and objectivizing rationality, the commodification of nature and economization of the world. In contrast to a totalitarian and uniform dominant world view, in the dialog of the absences the movements and organizations are constantly creating new, emergent knowledges and collective readings of reality (Santos 2009, 2010, Calle Collado *et al.* 2011, Sevilla Guzmán 2013). These come from dialog among the veritable 'ecology of knowledges' that exist among excluded peoples, and that are closely linked to and identified with their specific territories (Santos 2009, 2010, Cárdenas Grajales 2010).

Rosset (2013, 724) describes the evolution of LVC's positioning on land and territory, in a an example of what we are here calling DS:

> The inherent differences across this diversity have over time led to confrontation and debate, usually resolved in expanded visions and evolving collective constructions. The encounter with other rural cultures and actors outside of LVC has also profoundly affected thinking and visions ... [I]n March of 2006 [for] the first time ... LVC really engaged with the nonpeasant peer actors who share the rural territories that are contested in struggles for agrarian reform and the defense of land and territory. Of particular note was the encounter of LVC with groups of nomadic pastoralists, fisher folk and indigenous peoples. The collective analysis that was produced included a call to re-envision agrarian reform from a territorial perspective, such that the distribution of land to peasants would no longer mean a truncation of the rights of pastoralists to seasonal grazing areas, fisher folk to fishing sites, and of forest dwellers to forests.

---

[1]This and similar quotations have been translated from Spanish by the authors.

In this sense, and for the purpose of our discussion, we will define *diálogo de saberes* (DS) as:

> A collective construction of emergent meaning based on dialog between people with different historically specific experiences, cosmovisions, and ways of knowing, particularly when faced with new collective challenges in a changing world. Such dialog is based on exchange among differences and on collective reflection, often leading to emergent re-contextualization and re-signification of knowledges and meanings related to histories, traditions, territorialities, experiences, processes and actions. The new collective understandings, meanings and knowledges may form the basis for collective actions of resistance and construction of new processes.[2]

Leff (2004) distinguishes DS from concertations or stakeholder mediations where the goal and the outcome reflect some kind of compromise(d) solution, whose 'mid-point position' reflects the geometry of power (Massey 1991). We described in Martínez-Torres and Rosset (2010) how LVC rejects this kind of process, where they would be forced to find a mid-point with completely unacceptable positions. Through DS, even when grassroots groups dialog with intellectuals or scientists, 'new theoretical and political discourses are invented that interweave, hybridize, mimic, and confront each other in a dialog between communities and academy, between theory and praxis, between indigenous and scientific knowledge' (Leff 2004, 16).

In LVC, DS is both what we argue is a basic though non-explicit underlying process, and, in the case of CLOC South America, an explicit methodology[3]. In what they call *diálogo de saberes en el encuentro de culturas* ('DS in the encounter between cultures'), the Brazilian and other South American organizations in LVC are using a somewhat formal methodology based on Freire's (1984) dialogic methods for recognizing the different cultures and cosmovisions present in a given territory, and facilitating a process by which they collectively construct their understanding and positions (Tardin 2006, Toná 2009, do Nascimento 2010, Guhur 2010). The method is 'capable of creating horizontal relationships between technicians and peasants, between peasants and peasants, and between them and the society as a whole, based on philosophies, politics, techniques and methodologies that go hand in hand with emancipation and liberation' (Tardin, 2006, 1–2). It is based on a horizontal dialog between peers who have different knowledges and cosmovisions. They share their life histories, and engage in collective exercises to characterize the surrounding environment and space, to collect information (data) about the reality in that space, to systematically analyze that information and, using Freirian generating questions (Freire 1984), to move toward collective intervention to transform the reality, followed by a new sequence of reflection.

It is not a mere average or mid-point position that typically emerges from this kind of DS, but rather 'notions of development, biodiversity, territory, and autonomy emerge to configure strategies that mobilize social actions that legitimize rights which reinvent identities associated with the social re-appropriation of nature' (Leff 2004, 26). These are the emergences of Santos (2009, 2010), and many times serve as internal mobilizing frames (Benford and Snow 2000).

---

[2]Elaborated by the authors.

[3]In fact one could argue that La Vía Campesina itself is an emergence from the dialog among the absences (peasant, popular and indigenous peoples' organizations) that took place around the 500 Years of Resistance Campaign in the early 1990s, and through meetings of organizations in Managua, Mons and Tlaxcala, as described by Desmarais (2007), Martínez-Torres and Rosset (2010) and Rosset (2013).

From the DS inside LVC, and between LVC and other rural peoples (Rosset 2013), as well as with intellectuals and scientists, have come a series of emergent and mobilizing new ideas and processes. These range from emergent ways to understand changes in historical contexts, new processes to collectively transform reality in material territories, and new shared interpretive frames for internal mobilization and for the battle of ideas in the larger public imagination. Sevilla Guzmán (2013) and Calle Collado *et al.* (2011) have placed food sovereignty and new visions of agroecology among these 'emergences' from contemporary social movement dialogs.

DS and food sovereignty

Long-term trends toward consolidation in the global food system have been accelerated by recent decades of neoliberal policies – characterized by deregulation, privatization, cutbacks of essential services, open markets and free trade – and have led to a centralized pattern based on corporate producers of inputs, processors and trading companies, with production that is de-contextualized and de-linked from the specificities of local ecosystems and social relations (van der Ploeg 2008).

In support of this system, agribusiness, the World Bank, governments, finance banks, think tanks and elite universities create and put forth a framing language of efficiency, productivity, economies of scale, trade liberalization, free markets and 'feeding the world', all of which are purported to build *food security* (Rosset 2003, Borlaug 2007). This helps to build the consensus needed in society to gain control over territories and (re)configure them for the needs of industrial agriculture and profit-taking (Nisbet and Huge 2007, Rosset and Martínez-Torres 2012). This kind of unifying, economistic and 'scientific' rational is divorced from a social commitment to solve real problems of real people and the real environment (Guiso 2000), and imposes a knowledge monoculture that annuls diverse local and traditional knowledges, transforming these into what Santos (2009) calls 'absences' (Sevilla Guzmán 2013).

The food security discourse was challenged in the 1990s because, while it speaks to everyone's right to food, it says nothing about who produces what, how it is produced or where it is produced (Rosset 2003, Martínez-Torres and Rosset 2010). Thus the US government and transnational corporations (TNCs) could argue that food for the poor and hungry in the South should be sourced from where it has the lowest price per unit (i.e. industrial agriculture in the North), via 'one size fits all free trade policies', even as dumping that same food in South markets would undercut peasant farmers and increase the ranks of the poor and hungry (Rosset 2003).

A grand process of DS inside of, and led by, LVC led to the emergence of *food sovereignty* as a common framework that would allow diversity and take the specificity of each different place into account (i.e. the right of all countries and peoples to define their own policies). When farmer and peasant leaders from the Americas, Asia and Europe[4] met each other at the beginning of the 1990s, they discovered both their true diversity and the fact that they had common problems and common enemies from beyond national borders, and that they needed to struggle together. They found that they all had severe doubts concerning the concept of food security (Rosset 2003), and through a process of dialog over several years developed food

---

[4]African organizations joined later.

sovereignty as a banner for joint struggle (Desmarais 2007, Martínez-Torres and Rosset 2010, Rosset 2011). The framework emerged from those ongoing internal dialogs in the early 1990s, and was further elaborated at the International Forum for Food Sovereignty hosted by LVC in Nyéléni, Mali,[5] in 2007, to which LVC invited sister international movements of indigenous people, fisher folk, women, environmentalists, scholars, consumers and trade unions for a giant DS. Food sovereignty was defined there as:

> The right of peoples to healthy and culturally appropriate food produced through ecologically sound and sustainable methods, and their right to define their own food and agriculture systems. It puts the aspirations and needs of those who produce, distribute and consume food at the heart of food systems and policies rather than the demands of markets and corporations. It defends the interests and inclusion of the next generation. It offers a strategy to resist and dismantle the current corporate trade and food regime, and directions for food, farming, pastoral and fisheries systems determined by local producers and users. Food sovereignty prioritizes local and national economies and markets and empowers peasant and family farmer-driven agriculture, artisanal-fishing, pastoralist-led grazing, and food production, distribution and consumption based on environmental, social and economic sustainability. Food sovereignty promotes transparent trade that guarantees just incomes to all peoples as well as the rights of consumers to control their food and nutrition. It ensures that the rights to use and manage lands, territories, waters, seeds, livestock and biodiversity are in the hands of those of us who produce food. Food sovereignty implies new social relations free of oppression and inequality between men and women, peoples, racial groups, social and economic classes and generations ... There [must be] genuine and integral agrarian reform that guarantees peasants full rights to land, defends and recovers the territories of indigenous peoples, ensures fishing communities' access and control over their fishing areas and eco-systems, honors access and control by pastoral communities over pastoral lands and migratory routes ... (Nyéléni Declaration 2007).

Among the clear outcomes of the grand DS that was Nyéléni were the broadening of the concept[6] to address the concerns not just of farmers but also of fisherfolk, pastoralists, consumers and others, and the addition of issues of inequality and oppression among people. Wittman *et al.* (2010, 7) affirm that it effectively moved food sovereignty beyond the perspective of producers and production. They also highlight that the forum was able to construct a vision of food sovereignty where food is integral to local cultures, closes the gap between production and consumption, is based on local knowledge, and seeks to democratize the food system. It also helped solidify national and international coalitions beyond LVC. They conclude that: 'after Nyéléni, there was no doubt that we were now talking about a global food sovereignty movement that clearly understood the challenges ahead' (ibid.). Key pillars in the construction of food sovereignty for LVC have been, as reaffirmed in Nyéléni, agrarian reform and the defense of land and territory (Rosset 2013), the defense of national and local markets (Martínez-Torres and Rosset 2010), and agroecology (LVC 2010).

---

[5]See http://www.nyeleni.org for information on this event

[6]It may not be strictly correct to call food sovereignty a 'concept' or a 'paradigm', because it is an evolving process, framework or 'joint banner of struggle' with definitions that change over time as alliances are expanded and new actors are brought into the giant DS inside the food sovereignty movement.

DS and agroecology

While other actors came to agroecology from other angles (i.e. environmentalism, pest resistance to pesticides, consumer health, etc.),[7] LVC came to agroecology through the food sovereignty DS and through its internal dialog on land and territory (i.e. the *agrarian question*). A recent special *Grassroots voices* section of this journal (Rosset 2013) reviews the evolution of thinking over the past 20 years in LVC concerning agrarian reform, land and territory. This is also a process of DS, as described by Indonesian peasant leader Indra Lubis (cited in Rosset 2013, 758):

> It's quite important to see the experiences of those in Latin America, in Asia, in Africa, to learn from each other and exchange our strong spirits. LVC has a very successful methodology of working among peasants, among the landless, among small farmers, using the exchange of experiences to build unity across the diversity of national peasant organizations.

The ongoing DS on land and territory is key to understanding the emergence of agroecology, as this seems to be the result of dialogs among accumulated experiences with both the food sovereignty framework, and with concrete struggles for land and territory:

> The growing concern for the Mother Earth inside LVC has in turn resonated with a questioning of why we want land and territory and how we use it; in other words, 'Land for what?', or 'Territory for what?' While many organizations in the early years of their struggles called for more credit, subsidized agrochemicals and machinery for peasants, that is becoming less true ... Typically, agrarian movements that gained land through occupations and/or land reform from the State obtained poor quality, degraded land; land in which soil compaction and degradation are such that chemical fertilizers have little impact on productivity. This is land that can only be restored by agroecological practices to recover soil organic matter, fertility and functional biodiversity. Furthermore, many in the agrarian movements inside LVC, like the MST (Landless Workers' Movement of Brazil), began to ask what it means to bring 'the model of agribusiness into our own house'. By that they refer to the natural tendency of landless peasants, who had previously been farm workers for agribusiness, to copy the dominant technological model of production once acquiring their own land. Yet ... reproducing the agribusiness model on one's own land – by using purchased chemicals, commercial seeds, heavy machinery, etc. – will also reproduce the forces of exclusion and the destruction of nature that define the larger conflict ... Thanks to the gradual working out of this logic, and to the hard experiences of trying to compete with agribusiness on their terrain – that of industrial agriculture where who wins the competition is who has access to more capital, which is demonstrably not peasants who have recently acquired land – we can say today that, based

---

[7]In many cases, nongovernmental organizations (NGOs) and academics came to 'formal' agroecology before the large peasant organizations that belong to LVC. Eric Holt-Giménez (2009) thus referred to a divide between practitioners of agroecology supported by NGOs and advocates for agroecology within social movements. Rosset et al. (2011, 121) affirmed that this is changing. In some cases because of a certain 'territoriality' expressed by agroecology NGOs toward social movements whom they perceived as 'latecomers', the LVC agroecology process began relatively, though not completely, autonomously of NGOs. However the DS that began inside LVC has recently been opening toward many other actors in the world of agroecology, such as the Latin American Scientific Society for Agroecology (SOCLA), and can be seen, for example, in the participation of LVC-Brazil in the National Agroecology Articulation (ANA). The Global Agroecology Encounter of LVC (2012 in Thailand) recommended that similar processes of articulation be developed in Africa, Asia and Europe (LVC 2013a, 77). This historical sequence of being closed at first, and then opening up to alliances, follows the general pattern of LVC relationships with NGOs that we described in Martínez-Torres and Rosset (2010).

on LVC's series of agroecology encounters over the past five years, almost all LVC organizations now promote some mixture of agroecology and traditional peasant agriculture rather than the Green Revolution (Rosset 2013, 727).

What these processes of DS did was to essentially provoke reflection about, and call into question, a latent tendency of peasants and family farmers to apply elements of the dominant model of industrial agriculture on their own farms. From the beginning of its approach to the subject, LVC has seen agroecology as a technicism of little transcendence if divorced from food sovereignty and territory, which are the larger frames that gives it meaning (LVC 2013a). In a book written by, and largely for, LVC, Machín Sosa *et al.* (2013, 30) note that: 'for the social movements that compose La Vía Campesina, the concept of agroecology goes beyond ecological and productive principles. Other social, cultural, and political goals are incorporated into the agroecological vision'. In the words of a South Korean delegate from LVC: 'Agroecology without food sovereignty is a mere technicism. And food sovereignty without agroecology is hollow discourse'.[8]

The last five years have been a period of rapid development of an agroecology process inside LVC, in part as a product of an intense DS inside LVC facilitated by its Sustainable Peasant Agriculture Commission (Rosset and Martínez-Torres 2012, LVC 2013a). Part of the process has consisted of holding regional and continental 'Encounters of Agroecology Trainers'. These have been held in the Americas (2009 in Barinas, Venezuela, and 2011 in Chimaltenango, Guatemala), Asia (2010 in Colombo, Sri Lanka), Southern, Central and Eastern Africa (2011 in Shashe, Masvingo, Zimbabwe), West Africa (2011 in Techiman, Ghana) and Europe (2012 in Durango, Basque Country), as well as the first Global Encounter of Peasant Seed Farmers (2011 in Bali, Indonesia), and the First Global Agroecology Encounter (2012 in Surin, Thailand), culminating with the launching of the 'agroecology village' at the VI International Conference of LVC (2013 in Jakarta, Indonesia). The declarations from some of these meetings illustrate the growing place of agroecology in LVC (see LVC 2011a, 2011b, 2011c, 2013a, 2013b for examples).

This process has served several important purposes so far. One has been to help LVC itself to collectively realize the sheer quantity of ongoing experiences with agroecology, sustainable peasant agriculture and peasant seeds systems that are currently underway inside member organizations at the national and regional levels. The vast majority of organizations either already have some sort of internal program to promote agroecology and peasant seeds, or they are currently discussing how to create one. Another purpose these encounters have served is to elaborate detailed work plans to support these ongoing experiences and to link them with one another in an horizontal exchange and learning process. It also has been the space to collectively construct a shared vision of what agroecology means to LVC; in other words, the philosophy, political content and rationale that links organizations in this work.

In 2009, LVC defined what it called 'sustainable peasant agriculture' as follows:

The defense of the peasant-based model of sustainable agriculture is a basic issue for us. Peasant based production is not the 'alternative'. It is the model of production through which the world has been fed for thousands of years, and it still is the dominant model of

---

[8]Comment made by a Via Campesina participant at the First Global Agroecology Encounter of LVC (November 6–12, 2012, Surin, Thailand 2012).

food production. More than half of the population of the world works in the peasant agriculture sector, and the vast majority of the world's population depends on peasant based food production. This model, the peasant way ('la Vía Campesina'), is the best way forward to feed the world in the future, to serve the needs of our people, to protect the environment and to maintain our natural assets or common goods. Peasant based sustainable production is not just about being 'organic'. Peasant based sustainable production is socially just, respects the identity and knowledge of communities, prioritizes local and domestic markets, and strengthens the autonomy of people and communities … It is diverse, based on family farming and peasant agriculture. Production is developed and renewed based on the cultural roots of peasants and family farmers, men and women … Agroecological production methods, based on the notion of obtaining good quality food products without negatively affecting the environment, and while enhancing the conservation of soil fertility on the basis of a correct use of natural resources, and the smallest possible quantity of industrial chemicals, are part of it. Agroecology requires technological development that is based on both traditional and indigenous knowledge (LVC 2013a, 9–12).

By 2012, a lot of political debate and DS between different (cosmo)visions led to a new statement, that read in part:

As women, men, elders and youth, peasants, indigenous people, landless laborers, pastoralists and other rural peoples, we are struggling to defend and to recover our land and territories to preserve our way of life, our communities, and our culture. We are also defending and recovering our territories because the agroecological peasant agriculture we will practice in them is a basic building block in the construction of food sovereignty and is the first line in our defense of the Mother Earth. We are committed to producing food for people; the people of our communities, peoples and nations, rather than biomass for cellulose or agrofuels or exports to other countries. The indigenous people among us, and all of our rural traditions and cultures, teach respect for the Mother Earth, and we commit to recovering our ancestral farming knowledge and appropriating elements of agroecology (which in fact is largely derived from our accumulated knowledge) so that we may produce in harmony with, and take good care of, our Mother Earth. Ours is the 'model of life', of farms with farmers, of rural communities with families, of countrysides with trees and forests, mountains, lakes, rivers and coasts, and it stands in stark opposition to the corporate 'model of death', of agriculture without farmers and families, of industrial monoculture, of rural areas without trees, of green deserts, and of wastelands poisoned with agrotoxics and transgenics. We are actively confronting capital and agribusiness, disputing land and territory with them. When we control territory, we seek to practice agroecological peasant agriculture based on peasant seed systems in it, which is demonstrably better for the Mother Earth in that it helps to Cool the Planet, and it has been shown to be more productive per unit area than industrial monoculture, offering the potential to feed the world with safe and healthy, locally produced food, while guaranteeing a life with dignity for ourselves and future generations of rural peoples. Food sovereignty based on agroecological peasant agriculture offers solutions to the food, climate, and other crises of capitalism that confront humanity… (LVC 2013a, 69–70).

The language is much more influenced by indigenous cosmovisions and by the intensifying territorial dispute and need to differentiate peasant territories from those of agribusiness and extractive industries (Fernandes 2008a, 2008b, 2009, Fernandes *et al.* 2010, Rosset and Martínez-Torres 2012). Once again, we can call this an 'emergence' from the dialog among the 'absences', to use the language of Santos (2009, 2010).

A key and very illustrative point during the ongoing DS over agroecology – which contributed mightily to the evolution of the concept – was the 1st Continental Encounter of Agroecology Trainers of LVC in the Americas, that was held in 2009 on the campus of the 'Paulo Freire' Agricultural University Institute (IALA 'Paulo Freire'), created jointly by LVC and the government of Venezuela in Barinas, to give agroecology and political training to the daughters and sons of peasants and indigenous people. There a debate took place, in which three emblematic rural visions that coexist in LVC in Latin America con-fronted each other in the attempt to advance in the collective construction of a peasant agroecology, a debate which became a DS, which eventually produced emergent positions.

DS between peasant, indigenous and rural proletarian visions of agroecology

The organizations that belong to LVC and CLOC in Latin America can be loosely grouped into three crude and highly stylized – for the sake of argument – categories based on the mobilizing identity frame that these use in their struggles. Their positions and identities are more tendencies along a continuum, but we simplify here for explana-tory clarity. The most common are those organizations that use a *peasant* identity, thus focusing organizing efforts on people grouped by a mode of production or way of making their living. Even if such a peasant organization has mostly indigenous peasants as its membership base, it still typically organizes around 'farmer' issues of access to land, crop and livestock prices, subsidies, credit, etc.[9] Organizations that use a more *indigenous* identity typically organize around the defense of territory, autonomy, culture, community, language, etc.[10] Organizations that use a rural proletarian identity typically organize the landless to occupy land and/or organize rural labors into trade union formations.[11] The latter two types tend to be more radically anti-systemic than the conventional peasant organizations, while the proletarians are the most overtly ideological.

During the encounter that took place in Venezuela, it became clear that each of these kinds of organizations perceived agroecology very differently. The indigenous organiz-ations saw it as a synonym for highly diversified traditional farming systems on small plots of land, with practices, like planting dates, informed by traditional calendars based on the cosmos, passed down from the ancestors over millennia. The peasant organizations emphasized the family as the basic unit of organization in rural areas, and gave many examples of the *campesino-a-campesino* (farmer-to-farmer) methodology for spreading agroecology. The indigenous organizations responded that in their world, the community is the basic unit, and that rather than farmer-to-farmer methods that abstract a single family from their community and encourage them to make individual decisions, agroecol-ogy needs to be discussed in the community assembly. For the proletarians, on the other hand, whose basic organizing unit is the collective (of workers, of families, of militants), agroecology should be informed by science and knowledge transmitted in classrooms, where young people are trained as technicians to help their collectives of families transition to ecological farming, which would be practiced on large areas, possibly by collectivized families and workers. In other words, each type of organization had a remarkably different utopian vision, basic unit of organization and method of transmitting knowledge, as we show schematically in Table 1.

---

[9]Examples of this type of organization would the National Union of Autonomous Regional Peasant Organizations (UNORCA) in Mexico and National Association of Small Farmers (ANAP) of Cuba.
[10]Examples of this type of organization would be the National Indigenous and Peasant Coordination (CONIC) of Guatemala and the Bartolina Sisa National Confederation of Peasant, Indigenous and Native Women of Bolivia (CNMCIOB-BS).
[11]Examples of these kinds of organizations would be the Landless Workers' Movement (MST) of Brazil and the Rural Workers' Association (ATC) of Nicaragua.

Table 1. Peasant, indigenous and proletarian organizations, and agroecology.

Identity frame	Unit of organization	Transmission of knowledge	Emblematic struggles	Sources of affinity with agroecology
Indigenous	Community	Coded in cultural traditions	Defense of territory and construction of autonomy	Indigenous cosmovision and care for the Mother Earth
Peasant	Family	Experiential, farmer-to-farmer	Access to land, prices, subsidies, credit	Lower production costs, self-provisioning combined with marketing
Proletarian	Collective	Classrooms and technical assistance	Land occupations, strikes, transformation of the economic model	Socialist ideology, dispute with Capital

Despite sometimes intense debate and even raised voices on a few occasions, the delegates to the encounter, and thus these knowledges, were able to dialog with each other, and also with 'scientific' and 'expert' opinion in the form of technical staff and academic allies who were invited, creating what Guiso (2000) calls a collective hermeneutics.

The meeting was able to come up with elements of a new vision of agroecology, including a broad range of positions to be defended by LVC within this evolving framework (i.e. 'respect for the Mother Earth and Nature'), and those elements of other more technocentric visions that were to be rejected (i.e. 'the separation of human beings from Nature').[12]

Two issues could not be resolved, that of 'agroecology as an instrument of struggle for socialism', and 'the concept of scale in agroecological production' (LVC 2013a, 20). The issue of scale refers to the small family plot versus large collective settlement as different utopian visions of the indigenous and proletarian organizations, respectively. The difficulty in achieving consensus around the idea of socialism arose because some indigenous delegates felt that 'already existing socialism' had in the past not necessarily been hospitable for indigenous people. In the words of an indigenous leader who participated in the encounter, responding to the words of a leader from a proletarian organization:

Your *cosmovision* of historical materialism is an interesting one, and we could learn a lot from it. But first you must accept that is in fact a cosmovision, one among many, and that you can also learn from our cosmovisions. If you accept that, we can have a horizontal dialog.[13]

He went on to say:

We might agree to the idea of socialism as a goal, but first we need a debate about what we mean by socialism. Do we mean something like the communal and cooperative traditions of indigenous peoples? In that case, we might agree. Or do we mean certain examples of socialism in the past, where it did not go so well for us?

---

[12]The full list of positions to be defended or rejection can be found in LVC (2013a, 19–24).
[13]Author's notes from the encounter.

He then invited all the delegates to table the question of socialism in the construction of a collective vision of agroecology until the 2nd Continental Encounter, to be held two years later in Guatemala. Everyone agreed, and the organizers of the 2nd Encounter were tasked to organize a series of roundtable discussions between Marxist and Mayan intellectuals on historical materialism, indigenous cosmovision and agroecology, which effectively took place in 2011. The following is an extract from the declaration of that second encounter:

> We believe in agroecology as a tool in the construction of another way to produce and reproduce life. It is part of a socialist project, a partnership between workers and grassroots organizations, both rural and urban. It should promote the emancipation of workers, peasants, indigenous peoples and afro-descendents. True agroecology, however, cannot coexist in the context of the capitalist system. We affirm that agroecology is based on ancestral knowledge and practices, building knowledge through dialog and respect for different knowledges [*diálogo de saberes*] and processes, as well as the exchange of experiences and use of appropriate technologies to produce healthy foods that meet the needs of humankind and preserves harmony with *Pachamama* (the Mother Earth). We as La Vía Campesina, a multicultural network of organizations and movements, will continue to recognize and strengthen the exchange of experiences and knowledge among peasants, family farmers, indigenous peoples and afro-descendents, spreading and multiplying our training and education programs 'from Farmer-to-Farmer' ('campesino a campesino'), through both open, formal and informal education spaces as well as in community-based and territorial processes. We recognize the fact that this meeting has been held on Mayan territory, where the *campesino*-to-*campesino* movement began, based on a process that builds unity, erases borders and creates horizontal and comprehensive exchanges of experiences and knowledge. We understand that there are no standardized methods or recipes in Agroecology, but rather principles that unite us, such as organization, training and mobilization. Our quest to understand our world in relation to time, to its creative energies and forces and to our historical memories (of agriculture and humanity) is complemented by a historical materialist and dialectical interpretation of reality. Together we seek to develop our political and ideological understanding through a dialog among our cosmovisions to achieve structural change in Society, thus liberating us and achieving *buen vivir* (the indigenous concept of 'living well' in harmony with the Mother Earth) for our peoples (LVC 2013a, 47–8).

In other words, after a process of DS that was spread over two years and two continental encounters, a consensus was reached inside CLOC/LVC *in Latin America* that indeed recognizes historical materialism and diverse indigenous and other cosmovisions as equals.[14] These are issues and differences that literally broke other movements and alliances in the past, yet the praxis of DS has allowed LVC to move forward and gradually extend the area of consensus. Here we should be clear that the area of consensus in this case, and in general from processes of DS, is consensus around emergences, and not merely a midpoint between binomials.

This highlights an aspect we consider to be a crucial contribution of DS to the ability of LVC to survive for so long without major splits. We might call it a peasant, indigenous or community way of resolving conflicts. Barkin *et al.* (2009, 40) defined it as a 'new communitarian rurality', because it also includes a renewed emphasis on cooperation and strengthening rural communities. Since the founding of LVC, each time we have observed

---

[14]This particular consensus so far only extends to the Americas; it is worth noting that the declaration and new position statement produced a year later at the global agroecology encounter in Thailand contain no reference to socialism or historical materialism, though both express anti-capitalism (LVC 2013a, 54–78).

potentially divisive disputes, they have been tabled for discussion at a later time. Sometimes they are tabled for years, while they gradually work themselves out in the background, or until emotions are calmed. When they are taken up again later, the impasse is typically resolved by the emergence of something new, which extends the core area of consensus a little bit farther. With so many issues to address, no single issue can be allowed to shatter the space of dialog. The internal culture is such that the members do not push any given contradiction to the point of rupture. The space of LVC, like all human spaces, has power rifts, but these are downplayed. Time passes, and then issues are retaken. While things are heated, no resolution is attempted. This has created a 'safe space' to the point that organizations that cannot be together in the same room inside their home country can actually participate in a civil DS beyond their national borders in LVC meetings.

Agroecology as farming in La Vía Campesina

As discussed above, one reason why the organizations, movements and families that make up LVC are taking agroecology more and more seriously is that when land is acquired through struggle (through, for example land occupations, or via policy victories in favor of land redistribution), it is often degraded land. And when producers have used industrial farming practices, they have themselves incurred significant degradation. Faced with this reality, they are finding ways to manage or recover soils and agroecosystems that have been severely degraded by chemicals, machines, excessive mechanization and the loss of functional biodiversity caused by the indiscriminate use of Green Revolution technologies. Severe degradation means that even the ability to mask underlying causes with ever higher doses of chemical fertilizers and pesticides is limited, and the cost of doing so is becoming prohibitive, as prices of petroleum-derived farm inputs have soared in recent years. This situation has paved the way to adopt agroecological principles and practices as alternatives for small farmers (LVC 2010, Rosset and Martínez-Torres 2012).

The route of transition towards agroecology as a form of agricultural production is a difficult one in multiple aspects. The loss of knowledge is one, the demobilizing nature of top-down extension is another, and the stacked deck in favor of the industrial agriculture model is another (Rosset *et al.* 2011). DS has been a way to break through those barriers.

The fact that agroecology is based on applying principles in ways that depend on local realities means that the local knowledge and ingenuity of farmers must necessarily take a front seat, as farmers cannot blindly follow pesticide and fertilizer recommendations prescribed on a recipe basis by extension agents or salesmen. DS is proving to be the way in which both the mobilizing frame is constructed and the transformation of farming practice is achieved. DS is important to the latter as peasants most overcome the 'de-skilling' that took place when the Green Revolution essentially replaced peasant knowledge with the 'mental monoculture' of step-by-step formulae and 'recipes' imposed by agricultural extension agencies and agrochemical company sales staff (Freire 1970, 1973, Rosset *et al.* 2011, Martínez-Torres 2012).

Emphasis on the struggle for autonomy is echoed time and again, as organizations and families stress the advantages offered by agroecology in terms of building relative autonomy from input and credit markets (by using on-farm resources rather than purchased inputs), from food markets (greater self-provisioning through mixing subsistence and market crops), and even by redirecting outputs toward local and ecological or organic markets where farmers have more influence and control (and thus greater autonomy from global markets). In other words, in LVC, agroecology is part of what van der Ploeg (2008, 2010) calls *re-peasantization* (Rosset and Martínez-Torres 2012).

A form of DS that has become a central methodology for promoting farmer innovation and horizontal sharing and learning is the *campesino-a-campesino* (farmer-to-farmer, or peasant-to-peasant) methodology (Holt-Giménez 2006, Rosset *et al.* 2011). While farmers innovating and sharing goes back to time immemorial, the contemporary and formalized version was developed locally in Guatemala and spread through Mesoamerica beginning in the 1970s. *Campesino a campesino* (CAC) is a social process methodology, that is based on farmer-promoters who have innovated new solutions to problems that are common among many farmers or have recovered/rediscovered older traditional solutions, and who use their own farms as their classrooms to share them with their peers. Dialog takes place when visiting the farm of a peer, seeing, touching, feeling, even tasting an alternative practice as it is actually functioning on that farm, allowing peasants to imagine and translate it into their own vision. Later, on their own farm, they may test it out and/or adapt it in their own way, with their own creativity, sometimes recreating the practice but sometimes coming up with completely new practices/solutions.

In Cuba, for example, this methodology has allowed an LVC member organization, the National Association of Small Farmers (ANAP), to build a movement that in a bit more than a decade has helped about one half of the nations' peasants to transition to ecological farming. LVC has prioritized the documentation and socialization of this experience (Rosset *et al.* 2011, Machín Sosa *et al.* 2013), and exchange visits by peasants from other countries and continents to learn firsthand from it (LVC 2013c). Thus, a farmer-to-farmer agroecology process has been transformed into a 'farmer organization-to-farmer organization' process. Of course, no other organization can or would blindly copy the Cuban example because the reality of each country is different, but rather it is taken as an important input or contribution to a larger process of DS. This farmer organization-to-farmer organization DS process, built on exchange visits and documentation and sharing of experiences, is how those organizations that are new to agroecology learn from those with more experience.

The DS on agroecology inside LVC has increasingly been organized on a systematic basis. The first step has been to use the agroecology encounters to collectively identify, and then launch processes to self-study, document, analyze and horizontally share, the lessons of the best cases of agroecology inside the movement. Products of these processes can include written studies and videos, and but also more targeted exchange visits. An example is the Zero Budget Natural Farming movement (ZBNF) in Southern India. At the First Continental Encounter of Agroecology Trainers in LVC in Asia, held in Sri Lanka in 2010, delegates from India made what seemed to be extravagant claims about this grassroots agroecological movement that had grown rapidly in the southern state of Karnataka (Babu 2008, Palekar n.d.). The ZBNF movement is partially a response to the acute indebtedness in which many India peasants find themselves.[15] The debt is due to the high production costs of conventional Green Revolution-style farming, as translated into budgets for bank credit, and is the underlying cause of the well-known epidemic of farmer suicides (Mohanty 2005).

---

[15]ZBNF is a movement that started independently from LVC. As it grew, however, it increasingly drew in large numbers of peasant families that belong to the Karnataka State Farmers' Association (KRRS), which is a member of LVC. KRRS soon began to champion ZBNF.

The idea of ZBNF is to use agroecological practices based totally on resources found on the farm, like mulching, organic amendments and diversification, to break the stranglehold of debt on farming households by purchasing zero off-farm inputs. According to LVC farmer leaders in South Asia, several hundred thousand peasant families had joined the movement, and were routinely harvesting more with much lower costs than when they had earlier used conventional farming practices. At the Encounter, delegates from East and Southeast Asia were openly skeptical of these claims, to which the Indian delegates responded by extending an invitation to all of the LVC organizations in Asia to send delegates on a farmer organization-to-farmer organization exchange visit to Karnataka. They also offered to head up a process by which an Indian and foreign LVC team would study and document the ZBNF movement. The exchange visit subsequently took place, and by 2013 at the Global Agroecology Encounter in Thailand, delegates from several other Asian countries reported on growing experiments with variants of ZBNF in their countries, as a result of the exchange and DS process. The South Asia region of LVC has now opened an international peasant agroecology training school based on ZBNF methods, with local ZBNF farmers as part of the teaching staff, using farmer-to-farmer methodology.

Zimbabwe is an emblematic case for LVC that brings together the resolution of a long-standing territorial dispute (between dispossessed black peasants and white colonist farmers) through land reform driven by land occupations, DS, agroecology and the construction of food sovereignty. The Zimbabwe Organic Smallholder Farmer's Forum (ZIMSOFF) is a recent member of LVC, yet they now host the International Operative Secretariat (IOS) that just moved there from Jakarta. Their president, Elizabeth Mpofu, who is an emerging global leader in LVC, is an agroecology promoter from Shashe in the Masvingo agrarian reform cluster. Before founding ZIMSOFF she was a leader in the Association of Zimbabwe Traditional Environmental Conservationists (AZTREC). AZTREC was (and is) a national alliance of demobilized liberation fighters ('war veterans') who were promised but never received land, traditional spiritual leaders and traditional indigenous authorities. All had struggled together in the war of liberation, but had been partially left out of the new Zimbabwe, due the failure to deliver on land reform, and by the imposition of modern state structures that left traditional authorities powerless and ignored indigenous culture. The very idea of AZTREC was to promote a DS between disposed peasants, traditional indigenous authorities and spirit healers, to recover traditional farming knowledge and use it as building block for 'endogenous development' to be constructed through the struggle to recover lost land and by practicing ecological farming (Rosset 2013). AZTREC was instrumental in planning the nationwide wave of land occupations that led to the government's often maligned but basically misunderstood and ultimately successful national land reform program (see Scoones *et al.* 2010, Cliffe *et al.* 2011, Moyo 2011).

The First Encounter of Agroecology Trainers in the Africa 1 Region of LVC[16] was held in Shashe in Masvingo province, Zimbabwe, in 2011. Shashe is an intentional community created by formerly landless peasants from AZTREC who engaged in a two-year land occupation before being awarded the land by the land reform. A cluster of families in the community are committed to practicing and promoting agroecological farming, and set up the Shashe Endogenous Development Training Centre. At this center they hosted the encounter of LVC organizations from Southern, Central and Eastern Africa in which all

---

[16]'Africa 1' denotes one of the nine regions in the geographical organization of LVC, and is composed of peasant organizations from Southern, Eastern and Central Africa.

participants were able 'to witness first hand the successful combination of agrarian reform with organic farming and agroecology carried out by local small-holder farming families' (LVC 2011a).

LVC has since decided to create four new international peasant agroecology training schools in Africa. One will be at the Shashe center, and the other schools will be in Mali, Niger and Mozambique. With these new schools, LVC will have more than 40 peasant agroecology and political training schools in the Americas, Africa, Asia and Europe (see Rosset and Martínez-Torres 2012 for further discussion). These schools are slated to play a key role over the coming time period in facilitating the DS-based agroecology process inside LVC in the various regions of the world (LVC 2013a, 76–8).

Conclusions

Diálogo de saberes in LVC has been a grand dialog of absences from the dominant monoculture of ideas. Through the process of DS, LVC has been able to avoid fragmentation and create emergent mobilizing frames like food sovereignty, construct its own evolving vision of agroecology, and generate territorial processes also based on DS to disseminate agroecological farming practices. To quote Enrique Leff (2004, 23):

> The true potential of DS is not in the generation of 'consensus' among perspectives that erases difference through 'rational' communication and negotiation among 'interests', but rather its capacity to produce dialectical synthesis. DS is real communication between beings constituted and differentiated by their knowledges ... a Pleiad of cultural beings constituted by their own identities, each with their 'denominations of origin', yet at the same time these are reinvented as they differentiate themselves (by resisting and desisting) from the unitary global thought and identity. This encounter between beings in the ideology of knowledges is the spark that ignites human creativity, where cultural diversity leads to discursive innovation and the hybridization of rationalities and meanings that produce branching processes that weave together diverse pathways of thought and [collective] action.

Above all, the shared vision that is emerging through ongoing DS is making agroecology into a socially activating tool for the transformation of rural realities through collective action, and is a key building block in the construction of food sovereignty. In the 'Jakarta Call' issued at the VI International Conference held in June of 2013, LVC called agroecology 'our option for today and for the future' (LVC 2013b). In the agroecology booklet prepared for the conference, the new challenges facing agroecology were summarized in a call for the movement to defend the vision built through DS:

> One of our tasks has been to come to a common understanding of what agroecology and agroecological peasant agriculture mean to us. This is particularly important now because agroecology itself is under dispute by corporations, governments and the World Bank, with the scientists and intellectuals who knowingly or unwittingly work for them. This neoliberal attempt to co-opt agroecology can be seen in government 'organic agriculture' programs that promote monoculture-based organic exports for niche markets, and subsidize companies to produce organic inputs that are even more expensive than the agrotoxics whose costs led to the debt-trap so many rural families find themselves in. It can also been seen in the so-called 'climate smart agriculture' of the World Bank that, similar to REDD (Reduction of Emissions from Deforestation and Forest Degradation) for forests, would allow TNCs to become the owners of the soil carbon in peasant fields, dictating the production practices to be permitted, all as a pretext to allow large corporate polluters to keep polluting and heating the planet. We believe that the origin of agroecology lies in the accumulated knowledge and wisdom of rural peoples, organized in a dialog among different kinds of knowledge ('*diálogo de saberes*') to produce the 'science', movement, and practice of agroecology. Like seeds,

then, agroecology is a heritage of rural peoples, and we place it at the service of humanity and Mother Earth, free of charge or patents. It is 'ours', and it is not for sale. And we intend to defend what we mean by agroecology, and by agroecological peasant agriculture, from all attempts at cooptation (LVC 2013, 70).

References

Altieri, M.A. and V.M. Toledo. 2011. The agroecological revolution in Latin America: rescuing nature, ensuring food sovereignty, and empowering peasants. *Journal of Peasant Studies*, 38 (3), 567–612.

Babu, R.Y. 2008. Action research report on subhash palekar zero budget natural farming [online]. Research Report, Administrative Training Institute, Mysore, India. Available from: http://www.atimysore.gov.in/PDF/action_research1.pdf [Accessed 30 August 2013].

Barkin, D., M.E. Fuente and M. Rosas. 2009. Tradición e innovación. Aportaciones campesinas a la orientación de la innovación tecnológica para forjar sustentabilidad. *Trayectorias*, 11(29), 39–54.

Benford, R.D. and D.A. Snow. 2000. Framing processes and social movements: an overview and assessment. *Annual Review of Sociology*, 26, 611–39.

Borlaug, N. 2007. Feeding a hungry world. *Science*, 318(5849), 359.

Calle Collado, A., M. Soler Montiel and M. Rivera Ferre. 2011. La democracia alimentaria: soberanía alimentaria y agroecología emergente. In: A. Calle Collado, ed. *Democracia radical: entre vínculos y utopías*. Barcelona: Icaria, pp. 213–38.

Cárdenas Grajales, G.I. 2010. El conocimiento tradicional y el concepto de territorio. *Revista NERA*, 2, 1–12.

Cliffe, L., *et al.* 2011. An overview of fast track land reform in Zimbabwe. *Journal of Peasant Studies*, 38(5), 907–38.

Desmarais, A.A. 2007. *LVC. Globalization and the power of peasants*. London, UK, Ann Arbor, MI, Halifax, NS: Fernwood Publishing and Pluto Press.

do Nascimento, L.B. 2010. Dialogo de saberes, tratando do agroecossistema junto a uma família no município de Iporá-go. Master's Thesis, Universidade Federal do Paraná, Brazil.

Fernandes, B.M. 2008a. Questão Agraria: conflictualidade e desenvolvimento territorial. *In:* A. M. Buainain, ed. *Luta pela terra, reforma agraria e gestão de conflitos no Brasil*. Campinas, Brazil: Editora Unicamp, pp. 173–224.

Fernandes, B.M. 2008b. Entrando nos territórios do território. *In:* E.T. Paulino and J.E. Fabrini, eds. *Campesinato e territórios em disputas*. Sao Paulo, Brazil: Expressão Popular, pp. 273–301.

Fernandes, B.M. 2009. Sobre a tipologia de territórios. *In:* M.A. Saquet and E.S. Sposito, eds. *Territórios e territorialidades: teoria, processos e conflitos*. Sao Paulo, Brazil: Expressão Popular, pp. 197–215.

Fernandes, B.M., C.A. Welch, C. A. and E.C. Gonçalves. 2010. Agrofuel policies in Brazil: paradigmatic and territorial disputes. *Journal of Peasant Studies*, 37(4), 793–819.

Freire, P. 1970. *Pedagogy of the oppressed*. New York: Seabury Press.

Freire, P. 1973. *Extension or communication?* New York: McGraw.

Freire, P. 1984. La educación como práctica de la libertad. Mexico: Siglo XXI.

Guhur, D.M.P. 2010. Contribuições do diálogo de saberes à educação profissional em agroecologia no MST: desafios da educação do campo na construção do Projeto Popular. Master's Thesis, Universidade Estadual de Maringá, Brazil.

Guiso, A. 2000. Potenciando la Diversidad. Diálogo de saberes, una práctica hermenéutica colectiva. *Revista Aportes*, 53, 57–70.

Holt-Giménez, E. 2006. *Campesino a campesino: voices from Latin America's farmer to farmer movement for sustainable agriculture*. Oakland, CA: Food First Books.

Holt-Giménez, E. 2009. From food crisis to food sovereignty: the challenge of social movements. *Monthly Review*, 61(3), 142–56.

Leff, Enrique. 2004. Racionalidad ambiental y diálogo de saberes. Significancia y sentido en la construcción de un futuro sustentable. *Polis. Revista Latinoamericana*, 7, 1–29.

Leff, Enrique. 2011. *Aventuras de la epistemología ambiental: de la articulación de ciencias al diálogo de saberes*. Mexico: Siglo XXI.

LVC (La Vía Campesina). 2010. Sustainable peasant and family farm agriculture can feed the world [online]. Vía Campesina Views No. 6. Available from: http://viacampesina.org/downloads/pdf/en/paper6-EN-FINAL.pdf [Accessed 12 August 2013].

LVC (La Vía Campesina). 2011a. 1st encounter of agroecology trainers in Africa Region 1 of LVC, 12–20 June 2011, Shashe Declaration [online]. Available from: http://viacampesina.org/en/index. php?option=com_content&view=article&id=1098:1st-encounter-of-agroecology-trainers-in-afri ca-region-1-of-la-via-campesina-&catid=23:agrarian-reform&Itemid=36 [Accessed 12 August 2013].

LVC (La Vía Campesina). 2011b. Peasant seeds: dignity, culture and life. Farmers in resistance to defend their right to peasant seeds [online]. LVC – Bali Seed Declaration. Available from: http://viacampesina.org/en/index.php?option=com_content&view=article&id=1057:peasant-see ds-dignity-culture-and-life-farmers-in-resistance-to-defend-their-right-to-peasant-seeds&catid= 22:biodiversity-and-genetic-resources&Itemid=37 [Accessed 12 August 2013].

LVC (La Vía Campesina). 2011c. 2nd Latin American encounter on agroecology. Final Declaration [online]. Available from: http://viacampesina.org/en/index.php?option=com_content&view= article&id=1105:2nd-latin-american-encounter-on-agroecology&catid=23:agrarian-reform&Ite mid=36 [Accessed 12 August 2013].

LVC (La Vía Campesina). 2012. Bukit Tinggi declaration on agrarian reform in the 21st century [online]. Available from: http://viacampesina.org/en/index.php/main-issues-mainmenu-27/ agrarian-reform-mainmenu-36/1281-bukit-tinggi-declaration-on-agrarian-reform-in-the-21st-cen tury [Accessed 12 August 2013].

LVC (La Vía Campesina). 2013a. From Maputo to Jakarta: 5 years of agroecology in La Vía Campesina [online]. Jakarta: La Vía Campesina. Available from: http://viacampesina.org/ downloads/pdf/en/De-Maputo-a-Yakarta-EN-web.pdf [Accessed 12 August 2013].

LVC (La Vía Campesina). 2013b. The Jakarta call [online]. Available from: http://viacampesina.org/en/ index.php/our-conferences-mainmenu-28/6-jakarta-2013/resolutions-and-declarations [Accessed 14 August 2013].

LVC (La Vía Campesina). 2013c. La Via Campesina Agroecology trainers in Cuba. Available from: http://viacampesina.org/en/index.php/main-issues-mainmenu-27/sustainable-peasants-agriculture- mainmenu-42/1541-cuba-la-via-campesina-agroecology-trainers [Accessed 23 December 2013].

Machín Sosa, B., et al. 2013. Agroecological revolution: the farmer-to-farmer movement of the ANAP in Cuba [online]. Havana and Jakarta: ANAP and La Vía Campesina. Available from: http://viacampesina.org/downloads/pdf/en/Agroecological-revolution-ENGLISH.pdf [Accessed 12 August 2013].

Martínez-Torres, M.E. 2012. Territorios disputados: tierra, agroecologia y recampesinización. Movimientos sociales rurales en Latinoamerica y agronegocio [online]. Paper presented at the 2012 Conference of the Latin American Studies Association, San Francisco, CA, 23–26 May 2012. Available from: http://lasa.international.pitt.edu/members/congress-papers/lasa2012/files/ 4305.pdf [Accessed 30 August 2013].

Martínez-Torres, M. E. and P.M. Rosset. 2008. La Vía Campesina: transnationalizing peasant struggle and hope. In: R. Stahler-Sholk, H.E. Vanden and G.D. Kuecker, eds. Latin American social move- ments in the twenty-first century: resistance, power, and democracy. Lanham, MD: Rowman & Littlefield, pp. 307–22.

Martínez-Torres, M.E. and P.M. Rosset. 2010. La Vía Campesina: the birth and evolution of a trans- national social movement. Journal of Peasant Studies, 37(1), 149–75.

Massey, D. 1991. A global sense of place. Marxism Today, 35(6), 24–9.

Mohanty, B.B. 2005. We are like the living dead: farmer suicide in Maharashtra, Western India. Journal of Peasant Studies, 32(2), 243–76.

Moyo, S. 2011. Three decades of agrarian reform in Zimbabwe. Journal of Peasant Studies, 38(3), 493–531.

Nisbet, M.C. and M. Huge. 2007. Where do science debates come from? Understanding attention cycles and framing. In: D. Brossard, J. Shanahan and T.C. Nesbitt, eds. the public, the media and agricultural biotechnology. Wallingford, UK: CABI International, pp. 193–230.

Nyéléni Declaration. 2007. Nyéléni Declaration [online]. Available from: http://www.nyeleni.org/ spip.php?article290 [Accessed 31 May 2013].

Palekar, S. n.d. The philosophy of spiritual farming: zero budget natural farming. Revised 4th ed. Amravati, Maharashtra, India: Zero Budget Natural Farming Research, Development & Extendion Movement.

Rosset, P.M. 2003. Food sovereignty: global rallying cry of farmer movements [online]. Institute for Food and Development Policy Food First Backgrounder 9(4), 1–4. Available from: http://www. foodfirst.org/node/47 [Accessed 31 May 2013].

Rosset, P.M. 2011. Food sovereignty and alternative paradigms to confront land grabbing and the food and climate crises. *Development*, 54(1), 21–30.

Rosset, P.M. 2013. Re-thinking agrarian reform, land and territory in La Vía Campesina. *Journal of Peasant Studies*, 40(4), 721–75.

Rosset, P.M., *et al.* 2011. The campesino-to-campesino agroecology movement of ANAP in Cuba: social process methodology in the construction of sustainable peasant agriculture and food sovereignty. *Journal of Peasant Studies*, 38(1), 161–91.

Rosset, P.M. and M.E. Martínez-Torres. 2012. Rural social movements and agroecology: context, theory, and process [online]. *Ecology and Society*, 17(3), 17. Available from: http://www.ecologyandsociety.org/vol17/iss3/art17/ [Accessed 30 Sept 2013].

Santos, B.S. 2009. *Una epistemología del sur*. Mexico: Siglo XXI.

Santos, B.S. 2010. *Descolonizar el saber, reinventar el poder*. Montevideo: Ediciones Trilce.

Scoones, I., *et al.* 2010. *Zimbabwe's land reform: myths and realities*. Suffolk, UK: Boydell & Brewer.

Sevilla Guzmán, E. 2013. El despliegue de la sociología agraria hacia la agroecología. *Cuaderno Interdisciplinar de Desarrollo Sostenible*, 10, 85–109.

Tardin, J.M. 2006. *Considerações sobre o Diálogo de Saberes* (mímeo). Sao Paulo: Escola Latino-Americana de Agroecologia.

Toná, N. 2009. O Diálogo de Saberes, na Promoção da Agroecologia na Base dos Movimentos Sociais Populares. *Revista Brasileira de Agroecolgoia*, 4(2), 3322–5.

van der Ploeg, J.D. 2008. *The new peasantries. Struggles for autonomy and sustainability in an era of empire and globalization*. London: Earthscan.

van der Ploeg, J.D. 2010. The peasantries of the twenty-first century: the commoditization debate revisted. *Journal of Peasant Studies*, 37(1), 1–30.

Wittman, H., A.A. Desmarais and N. Wiebe. 2010. The origins and potential of food sovereignty. In: H. Wittman, A.A. Desmarais and N. Wiebe, eds. *Food sovereignty: reconnecting food, nature and community*, Halifax, NS: Fernwood Publishing, pp. 1–14.

María Elena Martínez-Torres is researcher and professor in Society and Environment at the *Centro de Investigaciones y Estudios Superiores en Antropología Social – Unidad Sureste* (CIESAS-Sureste) and author of the book *Organic coffee: sustainable development by Mayan farmers* (Ohio University Press, 2006).

Peter M. Rosset is researcher and professor in Agriculture, Society and the Environment at *El Colegio de la Frontera Sur* (ECOSUR) in Mexico, and researcher at the *Centro de Estudios para el Cambio en el Campo Mexicano* (CECCAM). He is also co-coordinator of the Land Research Action Network (www.landaction.org).

Peasant-driven agricultural growth and food sovereignty

Jan Douwe van der Ploeg

Department of Rural Sociology, Wageningen University, Wageningen, the Netherlands

The concept of food sovereignty presents us with an important theoretical and practical challenge. The political economy of agriculture can only take up this gauntlet through improving its understanding of the processes of agricultural growth. It is very difficult to address the issue of food sovereignty without such an understanding. Developing such an understanding involves (re)combining the political economy of agriculture with the Chayanovian approach. This paper gives several explanations (all individually valid but stronger in combination) as to why peasant agriculture results in sturdy and sustainable growth and also identifies the factors that undermine this capacity. The paper also argues that peasant agriculture is far from being a remnant of the past. While different peasantries around the world are shaped and reproduced by today's capital (and more specifically by current food empires), they equally help to shape and contribute to the further unfolding of the forms of capital related to food and agriculture. It is important to understand this two-way interaction between capital and peasant agriculture as this helps to ground the concept of food sovereignty. The article argues that the capacity to produce enough food (at different levels, distinguishing different needs, and so on) needs to be an integral part of the food sovereignty discourse. It concludes by suggesting that peasant agriculture has the best potential for meeting food sovereignty largely because it has the capacity to produce (more than) sufficient good food for the growing world population and that it can do so in a way that is sustainable.

Introduction

Food matters. It rallies people and it often induces unexpected changes in society. Food is contested and can be the object of 'food wars' (Lang and Heasman 2004). Food shortages and food riots show that the *quantity* and *availability* of food do matter to people, just as food scandals and associated scares make clear that the *quality* of food also concerns people a lot. Abruptly imposed limitations on exports in some major food-exporting countries and scarcities (or at least the fear of them) have once again put the *origin* of food production on the agenda: where does our food come from and how secure is its supply? Of equal importance are questions of *whom* and *how*: what is the identity of the producers and what is their style of farming? These questions cover a wide range of

I am very grateful to the participants in the Yale Conference on Food Sovereignty (2013) who stimulated me, with their comments and questions, to further develop this paper. I am indebted to the anonymous reviewers who helped me very much in fine-tuning the different lines of argumentation. I thank Nick Parrott for his valuable help in upgrading the different versions of this text.

issues that include gender relations, food safety, animal welfare and the attractiveness and accessibility of the countryside.

While there are a number of urgent questions that concern consumers, the same is also true for the producers of food. These questions emerge from, and contribute to, diverging agricultural development trajectories. They include what is to be produced, by whom, for whom and where, how, under what conditions, who gets the benefits and what is done with these benefits? Some food producers are arriving at solutions that are quite at odds with the conventional wisdom and this is leading them to structure their farms differently. At the same time new coalitions with consumers are emerging (e.g. farmers producing for local peasant markets and consumers who prefer zero-miles food, and so on).

Questions about the direction, nature and impact of agricultural development are also disputed at national and international levels. The questions being asked include: how, and to what extent, can agriculture contribute to economic growth; how can it increase employment, contribute to the generation of income and, consequently, strengthen the domestic market; and how can it contribute to the preservation of landscapes, cultural heritage, the maintenance of biodiversity and counteract climate change? A short glimpse at the agenda of say the Committee of World Food Security (CFS) of the Food and Agricultural Organization (FAO) of the United Nations quickly shows how multidimensional the current food question is (see, for example, HLPE 2013).

All this clearly indicates that there are serious misgivings among producers, consumers, national and international communities, about the efficacy of 'the market' as a co-ordinating principle. There is widespread concern about the outcomes that result from the 'free' functioning of today's markets for agricultural and food products (Weis 2010).

In this context the notion of food sovereignty (FS) is emerging as a strategic counter-point.[1] Food sovereignty is coming to be seen as a far better guiding principle for the production, processing, distribution and consumption of food than the market. FS is, as yet, not completely crystallized. It is more of a concept 'under construction'. One of the most prominent features of this process of construction is the central involvement of grass root organizations (International Commission 2013). Despite its 'infancy', FS shows the potential for becoming an overarching concept that is capable of strongly mobilizing people around the world. This is largely because it shows the promise of integrating a wide range of issues, including the quality, quantity, availability and origin of food, the identity of the producers and the style of farming. Food sovereignty offers food producers the prospect of regaining their dignity and improving their livelihoods. Another strength of FS is that it promises to address, in a coherent way, different levels, including those of national and international communities. The concept might also contribute to a rethinking of agriculture's role in wider issues such as the nature and rhythm of economic growth, levels of employment, climate change, etc.

The concept of food sovereignty, as it has been developed so far, is also important in that it (1) helps to build bridges between urban consumers and farmers; (2) triggers active food democracy by inviting and stimulating local actors to co-design their food

---

[1]The notion of counterpoint has been developed by Wertheim (1974), who linked it to the genesis and growth of social movements. A counterpoint is a value, probably not yet very explicit, that contrasts with the dominant values and can become the starting point of a process of contestation. The term originally stems from music, where a counterpoint signals the beginning of a new rhythm or a new melody.

systems; (3) strengthens (as opposed to atomizing) social relations; (4) helps reduce the insecurity, instability, volatility and dependency created by global commodity markets; and (5) helps agricultural producers to pursue more agroecological production methods.[2]

This paper explores one of the many aspects of the notion of FS: the interrelation between agricultural development and FS. I specifically ask what type of agricultural growth best fits with FS? This question does not just concern the *quantities* of food produced – but also affects issues of food quality, democracy, sustainability and resilience.

The dominant discourse ('we need to double world food production') increasingly translates the need for agricultural growth into a programme centred on capital and technology. This can only lead to a further industrialization of agricultural production processes and also assumes a continuation of existing dietary patterns. These two phenomena are almost seamlessly interwoven with the current food regime. Yet it is obvious that such a programme is intrinsically unsustainable (Tittonell 2013). It will result in the opposite of what it claims or pretends it will achieve. However, in rejecting such a programme, we should not throw the baby out with the bathwater. The banner of agricultural growth (and associated themes such as rural poverty, food prices and food distribution) should not exclusively belong to the dominant discourse. Such questions are not a 'nettle that FS prefers to avoid' (Bernstein 2013, 25). When re-thought, re-modelled and re-dimensioned, such issues can play an integral and coherent part in the FS discourse. Attention to production and growth does not imply that issues such as redistribution, a reduction of losses, changes in dietary patterns and bio-energy are of secondary importance. A focus on the former will strengthen the latter. However, to adequately address food production and agricultural growth some obstacles need to be removed.

Some obstacles to understanding the concept of food sovereignty

The political economy of agriculture and food, as it stands today, critically lacks a set of concepts (a sub-theory) for studying, analysing and explaining processes of agricultural growth. In this respect there is an 'intellectual deficit' (Bernstein 2010, 300). I think this deficit resides in a series of conceptual handicaps that together have far-reaching consequences that cannot be remedied simply by resetting some of 'the limits of inherited conceptions' (Bernstein 2010, 300). I briefly discuss some of these handicaps below. These relate to the *type* and *origins* of agricultural growth, as well as the *level* on which it is realized.

First, we have to take into account that agriculture needs to be understood as co-production, i.e. the ongoing interaction, intertwinement and mutual transformation of *humanity* and *living nature*. Consequently, concepts such as growth, development, productivity and increases in productivity cannot be reduced, without a clear specification, to notions that reflect just one side of the complex mechanics of agriculture. For example, when talking about productivity it is crucial to specify whether one is referring to labour productivity, the productivity of land (or, more generally, the productivity of the natural resources implied in the agricultural process of production) or the productivity of *all* these resources taken together (i.e. total factor productivity). This is important, especially since these different types of productivity are not necessarily aligned with each other. Increases in one type

---

[2]I am strongly indebted to Olivier de Schutter, the UN Special Rapporteur on the right to food, who introduced these points in his opening address of the Yale Conference on Food Sovereignty, held on 14–15 September 2013 at Yale University.

might very well be detrimental for another.[3] The same applies to growth. Agricultural growth may result in an increase of the total amount of food and other agricultural products being produced (this notably occurs when the agricultural frontier moves forward and/or when physical yields are improved, i.e. when the productivity of land is increased).[4] But agricultural growth might equally occur alongside a stagnation or even a reduction of the total amount being produced (this is the case when growth mainly or solely materializes as increases in labour productivity and associated increases in profits). It goes without saying that the *trajectory* that agricultural growth (or the development of productive forces) takes is crucial for any debate about food sovereignty. This point highlights a major weakness of agrarian political economy. As pointed out by Bernstein (2010, 302), attention is generally strongly focused[5] on 'increases in the productivity of *labour*' (emphasis added) and 'economies of scale', and the latter are thought to be the only possible vehicle for attaining the former. Thus, when the debates on food sovereignty (and the need to greatly increase the total amount of food being produced on the global level)[6] raise the issue of the specific agricultural development trajectory (i.e. the form or type of agricultural growth), it is clear that the political economy of agriculture is particularly ill-equipped for addressing this new and major issue.

The concept of *land productivity* is complex and difficult to define and measure. The choice of one measure (say money) may favour the capitalist farm, while the use of another (say calories) may favour the peasant farm. In the most general sense, land productivity refers to the wealth produced per unit of land. This of course critically depends on the perception of social wealth. Does it just refer to the marketed production or does it include production that is re-used in the farm (or consumed by the farming family and/or shared with others who assisted in the harvest and/or left for those who come to reap remnants and leftovers)? Is it expressed in monetary terms or in terms of gross or net nutritional content produced per hectare? How to include the heat produced by cattle (in many parts of the world this is used for heating the peasant's house)? Often physical yields (e.g. production per hectare in kilogram) are used as a measure to assess the levels of, and differences in, land productivity. Under *ceteris paribus* conditions this might be adequate;[7] mostly, however, there are structural differences that make such straightforward comparisons misleading. In smallholdings, mixed cropping is the rule (the

---

[3]Increases in labour productivity may run counter to increases in land productivity (although this is not necessarily the case). Equally, increases in land productivity may translate into increased or decreased labour productivity. The specific combinations have varied historically and geographically (Hayami and Ruttan 1985) and their effects depend strongly on prevailing politico-economic conditions. Important examples are discussed in Geertz (1963).

[4]Although this is not necessarily the case. There may be negative feed-back effects, such as increased production in one place triggering marginalization somewhere else.

[5]Excluding some worthy recent contributions, especially from political ecology (e.g. Jansen, 1998; Feuer, 2012).

[6]This raises the question of what is to be done. Asking this question does not preclude us from asking equally important questions such as where, and how and by whom this is to be done. In reality the 'what' question presumes the other questions. One characteristic of the hegemonic discourse is that it does not pay much attention to the questions of how, where and by whom. The hegemonic discourse simply translates the need to increase food production into the need for more capital investment and more patentable scientific innovation.

[7]But even then the devil might be in the detail. When different varieties of the same crop are used, small but important differences might be overlooked, making the comparison unsatisfactory. Compared with peasant agriculture, large scale farms often use varieties that have a higher water content, which contributes to higher yields. A further difference might be that in peasant agriculture

Mexican *milpa* being exemplary for its biophysical and nutritional value), in large hold-ings monocultures dominate. For each single crop, then, the yield might be lower in the smallholder plot. However, when all crops are taken together and assessed in calories or in energy units then one hectare with mixed cropping might render far higher results than one hectare of specialized farming. This means that if a high-yield corn monocul-ture displaces a traditional milpa landscape, the yield goes up, but the productivity of the land goes down. The time dimension should also be taken into account. Over time the productivity of single monoculture crops may decline greatly (due to an exhaustion of natural resources). However, this effect might remain invisible when input use is con-tinuously increased or production is relocated to, as yet, unexhausted areas. It goes without saying that all these complexities can considerably complicate the debate on the 'inverse relationship' (which I will briefly address later in this text). In this paper I will use yields as the main, though not the only, yardstick, but I do so with all required precautions.

Secondly, political economy basically perceives agricultural growth (in whatever form) as being a *derivate* of processes of technological development that originate in science and which are transmitted towards the agricultural sector through extension and/or the activities of agro-industries. Thus, the origins of growth are considered to be exogenous to the agricultural sector: they reside elsewhere. By the same token, factors *internal* to the agricultural sector are seen as impeding growth, or even blocking it completely. Examples of such thinking include assumptions about the 'backwardness of peasants', the nature of intra-sectoral relations (e.g. the *latifundio-minifundio* complex), the relations between a large-scale agro-export sector and a subsistence sector that contributes to 'structural involution' (Geertz 1963), the urban bias that shapes agrarian policies (Lipton 1977) and the 'law of diminishing returns'. Such views reduce the perceived role of farmers to that of *adopting* technological progress developed elsewhere and embodied in specific commodities being supplied by upstream agro-industries and/or in new insights and ideas propagated by rural extensionists. Their only role in this *schema* is to slow down and minimize the potential for growth by being uncooperative in realizing the potentials entailed in the technologies that have been designed for them to adopt. Hence, just as we need to introduce the centrality of *land* productivity[8] into the current debate, we also have to introduce (and to theoretically sub-stantiate) the possibility that farmers *themselves* may very well develop the 'productive forces' – as they have done throughout the ages (Mazoyer and Roudart 2006).

A third handicap resides in the complex micro-macro relations that characterize the agricultural sector. Single units of production (located at the micro-level) might grow considerably, whilst the agricultural sector as a whole (the macro level) stagnates or even regresses. This might occur when, for example, the expansion (or growth) of these single units occurs through the take-over of other units that have higher levels of land productivity. This may appear to be, at first sight, an irrelevant technicality. However, it is at the core of the food sovereignty issue. It is also critically related to

---

stalks, leaves, and even the roots might be considered as the relevant part of total production, whilst in large scale farming only the kernels count.

[8]That is, increases in the productivity of natural resources which simultaneously translate into increases in labour productivity. Following Hayami and Ruttan (1985) this trajectory is often referred to as the 'Asian model' (as opposed to the 'American model'). The trajectory of agricultural develop-ment in China, over the last 40 years, highlights the potentials of this 'Asian model' – which is far from exhausted. Recent developments in China are discussed later in this paper.

the land grabbing issue. To clarify this point it is important to recognize that being embedded in (and subordinated to the overall logic of) capitalism does *not* imply that *all* agriculture is *capitalist* agriculture. In *capitalist agriculture* all the resources, including the labour force, are commodified: the heart of the process of production is based on capital-labour relations. Alongside this model there is *peasant agriculture* (producing commodities for the downstream markets, but grounded on low levels of commoditization of the main resources)[9] and *entrepreneurial agriculture* (grounded on a far-reaching commoditization of the main resources, but not of the labour force).[10] Generally, peasant farms have lower levels of *total* production (for the farm as a whole) than entrepreneurial and capitalist farms. This is largely due to them being of a far smaller scale, but is also related to differences in their internal logic. However, when looking at *land* productivity – the most important lens from the perspective of environmental sustainability – peasant farms generally achieve higher levels of production per unit of land than capitalist or entrepreneurial farms.[11] This translates into more wealth (more value added) being generated per labour object (per hectare, per animal, etc.) in peasant agriculture than in entrepreneurial or capitalist agriculture. This is also the case because the cost structures are different and the differences would be even more pronounced if the externalized costs of different farming systems were accounted for. If considerable portions of peasant agriculture are taken over by expanding entrepreneurial and/or capitalist units of production (or swallowed up by newly created units), then the expanding or newly created *units* may record a considerable growth in production, but the *agricultural sector as a whole* might experience a decline – because the high level of land productivity achieved by the peasant units has been replaced by the lower levels achieved by the entrepreneurial and capitalist farms. This is precisely what has occurred in Europe over recent decades, where the reallocation of milk quotas from small and low cost peasant units towards large, entrepreneurial farms led to the total income (realized with these quotas) declining by at least 21 percent (van der Ploeg 2003, 307, 2008, 123). Similar shifts from peasant to entrepreneurial agriculture are now being envisioned as the way forward for the Global South (as will be discussed later).

Historically, differences in land productivity have been central in the debate on what is known as the 'inverse relationship'. This debate focuses on two interrelated questions. First, is there an *empirical* relation that runs from highly intensive smallholder agriculture to extensive, large scale agriculture? Second, can such a difference, if it exists, be

---

[9]This point of view has been largely absent in Anglo Saxon peasant studies, but has had an influence on the political economy of agriculture and the views of the radical left elsewhere. In the Mediterranean area this point of view was widely accepted and developed as early as the 1930s and 1940s. Emilio Sereni, one of the organic intellectuals closely related to the Italian peasantry, noted in his thoughts developed in the years of armed resistance that 'for peasant producers [resources such as] manure are to be considered as a means of production, and not as capital' (Sereni 1956, 76). 'Manure is produced within the farm and it is normally re-used within the farm without circulating in the market – hence, it never assumes the form of a commodity' (Sereni 1956, 75). He also noted that: 'a further proliferation of the commodity nature of agriculture occurs through and implies a growing dependency on the market' (Sereni 1956, 77).

[10]I consider peasant agriculture to be an expression of Petty Commodity Production (PCP), and entrepreneurial agriculture as an expression of Simple Commodity Production (SCP).

[11]For a recent contribution see Larson et al. (2012). Whether or not peasant agriculture can unfold its productive potentials greatly depends, as I will argue in the following section, on politico-economic conditions and the nature of technologies. It is not an ontological issue: it is time, as I will argue later, to move the debate beyond the 'inverse relationship'.

translated into calls for egalitarian land reform that redistributes land from large holdings to landless people and smallholders? There have been some excellent contributions to both these questions. These range from the pioneering studies of the Comite Interamericano de Desarrollo Agricolo (highlighted in CIDA 1966 and 1973 and summarized in Feder 1973), via the meticulous synthesis of Berry and Cline (1979), to the recent work of Larson et al. (2012). By contrast Sender and Johnston (2004) and Woodhouse (2010) argue that much of the observed inverse relationship is the result of misinterpretation and that redistribution of the land to smallholders would have highly negative consequences.

The debate on the 'inverse relationship' clearly intersects with the current debates on food sovereignty and the possible contribution of peasant agriculture. The problem with the historical debate is that it has frequently evolved into polarized and fixed positions that imbue the different sides of the equation with ontological properties. One camp has attributed peasant agriculture with an intrinsic superiority. The opposite position views peasant farming as intrinsically backwards. The dialectical relation between reality and potentiality (between 'what-is' and 'what-can-be') has been neglected by both camps. Equally, the social relations of production have generally been ignored: relatively little attention has been paid to questions of what makes one form of farming more productive than others at some times (and less productive at other times)?

The current hegemonic discourse proposes the need for 'small' and 'large farms' (read peasant and corporate farms) to coexist alongside each other (e.g. IFAD 2010). The need to greatly increase total food production is used to argue that both 'small' and 'large' units need room to develop and to contribute, as much as possible, to 'feeding the world'. In reality, this proposed 'coexistence' legitimizes a situation in which entrepreneurial and capitalist farms are crowding peasant farms out of the market. As a consequence, the growth of total production (at the macro level) is *slowing down*. This runs diametrically counter to food sovereignty. Hence, a conceptual framework is needed to deal adequately with the complex relations between the micro and macro level and the associated aggregation problems.

These three handicaps jointly lead to one central conclusion: the political economy of agriculture fails to positively identify the factors located within the agricultural sector itself that induce, sustain and/or strengthen (and thus explain) the process of agricultural growth. Equally, it fails to provide the conceptual tools needed to distinguish and explain different levels of agricultural growth. This applies to both capitalist and peasant agriculture – the two realities on which the political economy of agriculture centres most of its attention. And it is particularly applicable when we take into account relations with nature and the possibility of drawing on agroecology. While the search for profits (increasing the return on investments) is central to capitalist agriculture, this does not result *per se* in steady and ongoing increases of total agricultural production, since this search may well involve a relentless exploitation of man and nature. It is neither clear (nor theoretically explained) why this search for profits sometimes goes in one direction (increasing yields, for instance), and at other times, in a different one (e.g. increases in scale). The same applies to peasant agriculture: there is no capacity to theoretically explain how, when, why, under what conditions and to what degree peasant agriculture can materially engage in enlarging the total amount of food (and other agricultural products) being produced. To date, the political economy of agriculture has failed to theoretically explain the (potential) sustainability of peasant farming compared with the often destructive mechanics of capitalist farming. Equally it has, as yet, not elaborated the conceptual instruments that can positively identify the factors that make peasant agriculture more capable of sustaining growth and thus contributing to the rising needs of a growing world population that is increasingly located in large metropolises.

Five reasons that explain the productive potential of peasant agriculture – and how its materialization is sometimes frustrated

Growth is intrinsic to peasant agriculture (but it can get blocked)

Peasant farms tend to continuously and persistently expand their production Creativity, long-term experimentations, aggregated knowledge and its exchange through extended networks[12] result in yield increases, more intensive cropping schemes, improved soil management, etc. The search for emancipation meant to improve their own livelihood and that of the next generation, translates into, and partly occurs through, continuous and persistent increases in total production. Peasant agriculture is not only a system for value creation it is also a system that tends to permanently enlarge the amount of created value.

Peasant farms develop their production because this is the way in which they can fulfil their emancipatory aspirations.[13] The mechanisms on which peasant-driven agricultural growth is grounded basically come down to a continual upgrading of the natural and social resources used for agricultural production and a constant improvement in the 'technical efficiency' of the process of production. The latter means that the ratio between resources used and production realized increases: i.e. the input-output ratio is improved.[14] Craftsmanship, peasant knowledge and the quality of the resources are the decisive factors here.

Although, under specific conditions, peasants may acquire the property of some of their neighbours, systematic take-overs of the land and other resources are not part of peasant communities and they do not generally figure in processes of peasant-driven agricultural growth. Thus, growth at the level of the single peasant farms translates positively into agricultural growth at the macro level, i.e. into an increased supply of food (and other agricultural products). This represents a strategic difference with entrepreneurial agriculture, where growth occurs as much through take-overs as through technological progress. This means that the individual agricultural enterprise may expand considerably, but that in the sector as a whole growth can be zero (or even negative). The same also applies to capitalist farming: the aim of which is to achieve increases in the rate of return, which could even translate into extensification.[15]

In order to be able to develop production at the farm level peasant families need the means and the 'space' (Halamska 2004) to do so. Space refers to the politico-economic room needed to successfully develop production and translate the results back into an effective improvement of one's own livelihood. More specifically, we can conceptualize this space as being

---

[12]Later in this text I characterize such elements as being part of the constructive capacity of the peasantry.

[13]Improved livelihoods, improved prospects to face difficult circumstances whenever these emerge, more opportunities for the children, more cattle and especially 'beautifully bred' animals that will enlarge the status of their owner, abundant amounts of high quality seed to exchange with others, etc.

[14]'Technical efficiency' (see Yotopoulos 1974 for an extended discussion), is a widely used concept in agrarian sciences. However, it critically overlooks the dimension of time. It would be better, therefore, to use a notion as 'ecological efficiency' that includes the sustainability of resource-use.

[15]Evidently, the possibilities for take-overs depend very much on the economic and institutional environment in which farms are located. The same applies for profit-maximization and the way it relates to total output at farm level.

composed of the reigning social relations of (and in) production.[16] If the means and space are available an ongoing (if not persistent) agricultural growth will be the outcome. However, peasant-driven agricultural growth might also slow down, get blocked or even be reversed. This will usually be due to external reasons which, on the whole, have been very well documented and analysed in agrarian political economy. But regression might be also be triggered by internal reasons, i.e. highly authoritarian relations between fathers and sons (as beautifully exemplified in the novel of Giovanni Ledda about *Padre Padrone* (1975)) which may provoke the desertion of young men. Oppressive gender relations (often coupled with religious fundamentalism) may have similar effects: they cause mothers to advise their daughters 'to marry anyone other than a peasant'. In many rural parts of the Mediterranean area this has led to considerable social desertification. Exploitative gender relations can also lead to very negative connotations about farming among women, as in many African examples of women doing the farm labour and men controlling the farm income (de Schutter 2013).

Thus far I have identified sets of elements that respectively regard: the *translation* of emancipatory aspirations into increased levels of production; the *mechanisms* that materially allow for and sustain such increases and the required *space* (and means, etc.) to effectively do so. I will now briefly illustrate each of these sets. By developing them further I think that they can constitute the basis of the much needed theory to explain agricultural growth (especially the peasant driven type). Such a theory would also contribute to further strengthening the food sovereignty discourse.

The best possible way to theorize the translation of emancipatory aspirations into increases in production (i.e. to understand resistance and cultural repertoire as drivers of agricultural production) is to seriously re-examine the work that A.V. Chayanov did in the early twentieth Century (Chayanov 1966). The nucleus of this work is illustrated in Figure 1. The uninterrupted lines represent 'utility', i.e. the possibility to satisfy needs and aspirations (this utility diminishes per unit of product as the total level of production grows) and 'drudgery', i.e. the energy and hardship needed to realize a particular level of production (this drudgery increases with the further growth of total production). At point E1 the two lines are in equilibrium. This point determines the level of production P1. Now, if utility is enlarged beyond the immediate consumption needs of the family (for example to include the creation of a more productive farm that is more able to meet the needs of the farming family), a new utility curve is defined (the dotted line), leading to the establishment of a new equilibrium (E2) and, consequently, a new level of production (P2). This allows the family farm to move beyond satisfying its members' immediate consumption needs, and to engage, for instance, in capital formation (i.e. creating the ingredients of the more productive farm). Thus, the aspiration for emancipation translates into, and occurs through, enlarged production and material improvements to the resource base. This might also result from a redefinition of drudgery. A farmer knowing that his or her current production might open up the possibility, in the near future, of working according to an improved balance, will probably find the drudgery as less burdening and troublesome. Thus, a new 'drudgery line' emerges that defines a new equilibrium and corresponding level of production. It is also possible that utility and drudgery might both be perceived differently, creating the possibility of E3 and P3.[17]

---

[16]Here there is an interesting link with the earlier work of Chayanov. The development of productive forces, including substantial yield increases, often will require new, additional space. In this respect Chayanov (1988, 142) argued that increases in yields de facto require 'new relations of production'.
[17]This is just one balance taken out of a far wider series of balances (both internal and external to the peasant farm) that are discussed in van der Ploeg (2013).

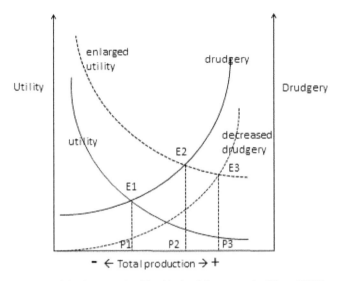

Figure 1. The balance of drudgery and utility (derived from van der Ploeg 2013).

In everyday life, complexities such as the ones shown in Figure 1 are governed through cultural repertoires (consisting of values, norms, shared beliefs and experiences, collective memory, rules of thumb, etc.) that specify recommended responses to different situations. Put differently: the active assessment and re-assessments of 'Chayanovian' balances involve judgements based in the *moral economy* (Scott 1976). These are decisive. The moral economy is not external to the 'economic machine': it is essential to the 'machine's' performance.

From an analytical point of view, the mechanisms used to enlarge production at the farm level, and which contribute to increase net productivity per unit of land[18] come down to the following:

- The application of more working hours, more inputs and improved tools[19] per object of labour (i.e. per unit of land, per animal, per fruit tree, etc.).
- The fine-tuning of the agricultural process of production (i.e. bringing different growth factors in line). This involves experience, constant observation and interpretation, local knowledge, etc.
- The systematic improvement of resources (especially the objects of labour): augmenting soil fertility, building irrigation and drainage systems, breeding better cows, selecting plants to obtain higher yielding varieties, strengthening the complementarity between species, making better manure, building new and better buildings, obtaining more knowledge, joining existing or creating new networks, etc.
- Innovativeness, i.e. the searching for and development of new insights, new practices, new seeds, new machinery, etc. Here, goal-oriented experimentation, an

---

[18]For Chayanov (1988, 144) the increase of yields was part of the 'development of productive forces'; he perceived yield increases as 'a progressive phenomenon'.
[19]The latter two, inputs and tools, are often summarized and presented as (part of) 'capital'. This is acceptable as long as one recognizes that we are not talking here about capital in the Marxist sense.

open eye for deviations and an overall ordering of the farm as a 'patchwork', allowing for unexpected interactions and surprises, are important prerequisites.
- A specific calculus that moves peasant agriculture to yield levels that are higher than the ones that result from, and are compatible with, the search for the highest rate of return that characterizes entrepreneurial and, especially, capitalist agriculture.

Together these mechanisms result in and sustain continual increases in land productivity (and as an effect of this, labour productivity may rise as well). These mechanisms are central (although not exclusive) to peasant-driven agricultural growth. In other trajectories (e.g. entrepreneurial agriculture), other mechanisms (such as the integral application of exogenous technological models – exemplified by the Green Revolution package – and the take-over of neighbouring farms) are central, whilst the working time per object of labour is typically reduced and the 'chaos' needed for novelty production is avoided. Technologies that strongly increase labour productivity and which standardize as much as possible the labour process are at the heart of the dynamics of capitalist agriculture (Weis 2007). Thus, different technologies are developed and used (as convincingly discussed by Bray 1986) and the productive forces (land, labour, knowledge, animals, machineries) implied in each constellation are moulded in concrete phenomena that are distinctively different (van der Ploeg 2008).

In order to translate the longing for an improved livelihood through the indicated mechanisms into increased production (that renders more value added, which will help to satisfy a greater range of needs), peasants need the means and space to do so. It is here that the political economy of agriculture, as it stands today, is important. To put it bluntly, if nearly all the extra value that results from yield increases is taxed or appropriated by others, there is little sense in strongly developing production (to engage in, for example, the drudgery of improving soil fertility). If the flow of water is diverted by landlords or neighbouring corporate farms, the search for improved plant varieties becomes pointless. The same applies to the means. If farm gate prices are so low that no savings can be generated (and banks are unwilling to provide credit on acceptable terms) then the means to acquire diesel, or a tractor, or to have the old tractor repaired, are lacking. A lack of space and scarcity of means often go together: an increased volatility in markets (and insecurity about demand) is likely to translate into negative prospects that do not justify the peasant investing in the farm.

Taking these different arguments and considerations together we can conclude that peasant agriculture contributes more (just as it potentially can contribute far more in the decades to come) to total agricultural growth and, consequently, to the provision of food, than other mode of agricultural production. However, this only applies if, and when, sufficient space and means are available. If the required space and means are lacking, this potential for growth and increased supplies of food becomes blocked.[20]

China is an intriguing, albeit contradictory, example of peasant-driven agricultural growth. Here the peasantry has been re-establishing itself since the beginning of the 1980s and has achieved impressive agricultural development (Gulati and Fan 2007).

---

[20]Collectivization is one of the most drastic mechanisms for reducing, if not completely eliminating, such space. The prominent communist peasant leader and intellectual Emilio Sereni wondered 'whether the productive structures of soviet agriculture, just as the ones of other socialist countries, always and everywhere contribute to the dynamic requirements of the productive forces in agriculture' (Sereni 1967).

During this period China has witnessed an impressive reduction of poverty, and agricultural production has continuously grown. This is in stark contrast to sub-Sahara Africa, which has seen a stagnation of agricultural production and an absolute increase of people living on or below the 1 dollar a day poverty level (see Li Xiaojun et al. 2012). Although some aspects of China's agricultural growth are highly problematic (e.g. the elevated use of chemical fertilizers, the rise of 'pig factories' and the soaring importation of soy beans as discussed in Schneider 2011 and Weis 2013), peasant driven growth is the main driver of rural development in China (Ye et al. 2010). The centrality of peasant agriculture also defies the models used in the West (be it the neo-classical or the ones of the radical left) to explain the presumed backwardness of peasant agriculture. Previously, the question of 'Who will feed China' (Brown 1995) was widely discussed in the West. The answer is now abundantly clear. So far it has been the *nong min*, the peasants from China and they are doing a remarkably good job of it (van der Ploeg et al. submitted). To understand and explain this impressive result, we have to build a better understanding of peasant-driven agriculture into our theories.[21]

Peasant agriculture embodies resilience (although in the end it may be broken)

Peasant farms are often located in remote, inhospitable or marginal areas that are completely unattractive to entrepreneurial and capitalist farms.[22] They also often face difficulties and adverse conditions and are able to continue to produce when the others have long before capitulated.[23] In short: peasant farms are far more resilient and more shockproof than capitalist and/or entrepreneurial farms. This makes them a far better vehicle for guaranteeing food sovereignty than other modes of agricultural production.

The resilience of peasant farming is due to the way it is structurally rooted in wider society. Peasant farms are essentially grounded on natural and social resources that are controlled by the peasant unit itself. They are relatively autonomous from the main upstream markets (van der Ploeg 2010) – a feature that is currently being strongly promoted by agroecological and peasant movements. This structural feature allows peasant farms to produce for the markets, without being completely dependent on them. In terms of food sovereignty this is a strategic feature. By contrast, entrepreneurial and capitalist farms are to a large extent, or even completely, grounded on commodities. Consequently, they are run as a financial operation. They are basically about getting money in order to acquire the needed resources, which are transformed into products to be sold. Entrepreneurial and capitalist farming are essentially about converting money into more money and often degrade the foundations of production in the process. This is in sharp contrast to peasant farms that use the available, self-owned and controlled, natural and social resources for production and

---

[21]The argument that peasant agriculture has considerable developmental potential is also supported by the Brazilian and India experiences (Schneider and Niederle 2010, Cunningham 2009). Other important cases are cotton in West Africa (Tschirley et al. 2010), rice in Vietnam (Jaffee et al. 2012) and specific groups of Africa's rural poor (Hazell 2004, Fraser 2009)

[22]As for example in the inhospitable baldios in the North of Portugal, the tropical rice polders in Western Africa (locally called bolanhas) or, more generally, the hilly and mountainous pasture lands in considerable parts of the world. Not only is it too costly (too labour intensive) for capitalist and entrepreneurial farms to operate here, they also cannot exert sufficient control (let alone control-at-a-distance). 'The art of not being governed' (Scott 2009) perfectly describes this incompatibility of control and peasant farming in complex and difficult eco-systems.

[23]Europe witnessed this during the agricultural crises of the 1880s and the 1930s (Bieleman 2010).

then sell the marketable surplus to obtain money. If the benefits of operating an entrepreneurial or capitalist farm turn out to be lower than the costs, the farm enterprise will be deactivated – if possible.[24] By contrast in such a situation the peasant farm will resolutely continue.

Volatility is inherent in the world market for food and agricultural products, the more so as this market comes to be increasingly controlled by food empires. This volatility is generating a new set of unexpected effects.

Recently Oostindie et al. (2013) analysed the 2007–2010 period for a constant sample of 1000 dairy farms taken from a data set of all dairy farms maintained by Alfa, one of the agencies responsible for elaborating farm accountancy records. The data describe the farms, their economic structure and performance over time. In the second half of 2008 and in the first half of 2009 all these farms faced a dramatic decrease of the prices paid for the milk, from an average level of some 35 to less than 25 €/100 kg of milk. However, the impacts of this sudden shock were highly differentiated. Some farms could absorb this shock relatively easy. In 2009, 25 percent of the farms showed an average margin between benefits and costs of +14.55 €/100 kg of milk: others faced a negative cash flow, with 25 percent having an average margin of −9.70 €/100 kg of milk.

The authors identified the group that was able to fare reasonably well through the period of low milk prices as peasant-like farms, whilst the group that experienced negative cash flows showed the features of entrepreneurial agriculture. The first group was far more multifunctional than the second: their farms did not depend on one single market but had diversified. Equally, the peasant farms were, on average, smaller than the entrepreneurial ones; they used less external inputs and invested less in new technologies: their level of depreciation was 5.61 €/100 kg of milk as opposed to 14.25 for the entrepreneurial farms. Finally, the peasant farms were far less indebted: they paid 2.19 €/100 kg milk as interest on loans versus €7.15 for the entrepreneurial farms.[25] In normal years (with good milk prices) the peasant farms realized family incomes more or less equal to those of the (larger) entrepreneurial farms. In bad years (2008 and 2009) however, they were the only ones with a positive income while the entrepreneurial farms were confronted with a negative income. The latter were unable to meet their obligations to the banks and other providers, the more so since they hardly had any reserves.

This huge problem was resolved by the banks who decided to refinance the debts and to provide additional credit to resolve the most immediate concerns. However, in 2012, volatility hit again. This time this was not due to a decrease in milk prices but a consequence of sharp and substantial increases in the prices for feed, fodder, energy and fertilizers. In the meantime banks faced the need to recapitalize themselves as formalized in the Basel III agreements. Consequently, it was no longer possible for them to refinance debts in 2012 and many large dairy farms had to be de-activated. They are currently for sale.

The study by Oostindie et al. (2013) highlights an important reversal and shows a range of unexpected effects that might occur on a wider scale in the future, which could have serious consequences for food sovereignty. For a long time it has been thought that

---

[24]It might be possible that delivery contracts or obligations towards the banks coerce the farm to continue anyway.
[25]'The highest liabilities-to-assets ratio was found in farms in Denmark and the Netherlands, with 56% and 36% respectively' (European Commission 2010, 4). The total debts of Dutch farmers amount to some €38 billion. This is roughly 19 times as high as the sector's total yearly income. Debts are distributed in a highly unequal way – the highest levels (both absolutely and relatively) are found in the entrepreneurial pole of Dutch agriculture.

large, entrepreneurial farms were more able than smaller peasant units to compete on world markets. This was indeed the case so long as the regulatory schemes entailed in agrarian policies gave strong support to this segment – through, for example, price support and protection – whilst environmental costs could be externalized. However, in deregulated markets that are controlled by food empires and show high levels of volatility, this is no longer the case. Ironically, it is the peasant farms that are more able to face, and respond, to high levels of volatility and the associated insecurities and risks.

This discussion has three main implications for food sovereignty. First, the possibility of the sudden elimination of parts of the productive capacity is an immediate and considerable threat for FS, although in the longer term it might turn out to be an opening for FS. Secondly, peasant agriculture is better placed to face up to and deal with high levels of price volatility. Thirdly, the proposal to extend entrepreneurial farming across large zones of the Global South (as articulated by food empires and multilateral organizations) is ludicrous. It poses a very real threat to food sovereignty.

Does resilience come with a price? According to some observers the price to be paid for this resilience based on distantiation is high: 'It seems hard [….] to avoid the conclusion that new peasants' "autonomy" from markets […] is to be achieved by relative poverty of income' (Woodhouse 2010, 418). This 'unavoidable' conclusion rests on the misinterpretation of two facts that I discussed several years ago in *The new peasantries* (2008). First: 'if all resources used on the farm had to function as capital (i.e. generate at least the average level of profitability) and all labour was to be remunerated as wage labour, then nearly all Dutch farms […] would go broke'. Second: '40 percent of Dutch farming families derive less than the minimum income from farming' (van der Ploeg 2008, 448).

Woodhouse's reasoning is based on a strange reversal. Since peasant farms in the Netherlands are indeed *distantiated* from the main upstream markets (meaning that buildings, animals, machines, etc., do not have to function as capital, labour is not remunerated as wage labour and no rent or lease is paid on the land) – they do not go broke. They function very well, provide an income that is often acceptable and they are better equipped (as discussed above) to face adverse circumstances. But they would go broke if they had to pay for all the factors of production and non-factor-inputs – as does a capitalist farm. In short: distantiation from the upstream markets does not come with a price. It does not lower the farm income. Rather, it helps to increase and to sustain the farm income. Then the second observation: it is true that 40 percent of Dutch farmers derive less than the legal minimum wage from farming. Is this intrinsic to peasant farming? Is it the price to be paid for autonomy? Among this 40 percent there is a considerable sub-group that actively opts to have a small farm and to combine this with another job. Then there are entrepreneurial farmers who face very high financial burdens that almost completely 'consume' the available income. And finally there are many peasants who do have incomes that are too low. The point though is that without distantiation their income would be even lower than it actually is. Said differently: without distantiation it would not be just 40 percent, but say 80 percent, of Dutch farmers whose income would be below the legal minimum wage. As said before, agrarian political economy is not always helpful for understanding peasant realities. Peasants do not 'pay' for autonomy (and the resilience it brings), they benefit from it.

This issue is both theoretically pertinent and of huge political importance. Institutions such as the World Bank, development NGOs, universities and the main food empires are currently developing and disseminating classification schemes that have, regardless of the many minor differences, one central point in common. They view agricultural development as a unilinear and selective process – as a ladder to modernity (see Figure 2, developed by the Syngenta group, which reduces development to 'incremental stages of agricultural

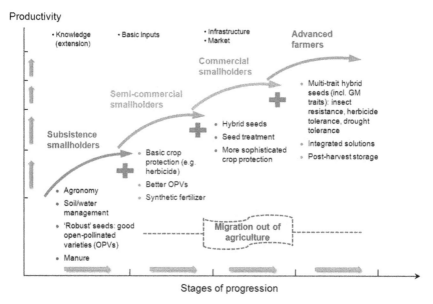

Figure 2.   The imperial view of agricultural development.
Source: Zhou (2010, 4).

intensification'). This selective process favours a minority of farmers who have access to more resources than others and excludes the majority of smallholders (see, for example, Zhou 2010, Berdegue and Fuentealba 2011). This latter group is assumed to move (or to be moved) to the cities whilst their resources are used to strengthen the smaller group. The process is also selective in the sense that development for the minority group that stays on the land, consists of taking over the package sold to them by the different food empires. This makes them into 'advanced farmers'.

The problem with classification schemes like these is that they do not necessarily have to be 'true' in order to be applied and implemented. Such models currently structure the agrarian policies of nation states, the credit policies of banks, the pricing policies of agro-industries and the mechanics of bargaining by farmers' unions. When systematically applied (and/or imposed) they can do considerable damage (van der Ploeg 2003).

Peasant farming continuously reinvents itself, especially in periods of crisis (but it might prove too burdensome to rebuild it)

Apart from resisting difficult periods, peasant farmers also have the capacity to reinvent and materially rebuild farming in a way that helps to immunize themselves against the circumstances and relations induced during and by a crisis. Peasants can carve, together with others, pathways that help them to survive and go beyond a crisis that otherwise would destroy the agricultural sector. They do so by materially rebuilding the practice of farming and by changing the patterns in which this practice is embedded.

A well-known example of this phenomenon is the deep European agricultural crisis of the 1880s that was provoked by massive imports from cheap grain from Canada and, especially, the USA. This crisis was met, notably in the north-west of Europe by a large-scale switch from growing grains towards new forms of cattle, pig and chicken raising

Figure 3.   Specialized farms producing for global markets.

that were based on the cheap imports (Bieleman 2010). Thus, an initial threat, cheap imports, was reversed into a benefit although the tying of livestock feeding to transatlantic shipments of industrial grains did sow the seeds of a future crisis. Another important response was the development of farmers' cooperatives. These could, of course, not change the markets, but they definitely changed the relations between farming and the markets.[26] The agricultural crisis of the 1930s eventually resulted in another re-patterning of the set of relations in which farming was embedded. The first forms of national agricultural policies were agreed upon and progressively implemented. These were the forerunners of what would become the European Union's Common Agricultural Policy (CAP), although the process of getting there was far from uninterrupted.

As a consequence of the current agricultural crisis (that has been partly induced by the general economic and financial crisis and partly caused by internal mechanisms) farms can no longer reproduce themselves solely through the markets. This is especially the case for large, specialized farms producing for the main commodity markets (see Figure 3). They produce *for* the market but reproduction *through* the market is becoming increasingly difficult, if not impossible, for them. Prices are, on the whole, too low, whilst their costs are too high. Their main outlets (both internal and export markets) have suffered considerable contractions; volatility means that prospects are insecure and investments are increasingly risky and often not possible, especially, since banks have reduced the amount of capital they are prepared to invest in agriculture.

At the same time, we are witnessing the emergence of a new constellation that consists of redesigned and materially rebuilt farms that are able to escape from the crisis and are laying the foundations for a new, post-crisis agriculture (see Figure 4). These are multifunctional farms, which mainly base themselves on the use of their own resources (new forms of cost reduction play an important role here). They are creating new services and new products which are increasingly sold through new, nested markets – often actively and jointly constructed by farmers and consumers (van der Ploeg et al. 2012). Pluriactivity (also known as multiple job holding) is another common feature, chosen not only for economic necessity but also because it brings social benefits.

In analytical terms this implies a major change: instead of being built on just one circuit for reproduction (a main commodity market), farming is now increasingly grounded on several circuits for reproduction. These additional circuits not only reduce reliance on global markets, which offer less attractive prospects than before, they also sustain new ways of farming that include biophysical and socio-economic realities that differ greatly from those of specialized farming, which is solely tuned to the world market. In the

---

[26]It is telling that in the Mediterranean parts of Europe (where the peasantry was marginal and latifundia types of agriculture dominated the scene) another response emerged: a massive outmigration.

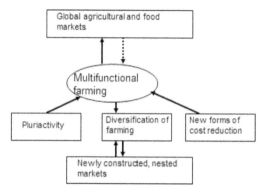

Figure 4.   Multifunctional farming grounded on a wider set of circuits for reproduction.

context of FS it is interesting that the newly created markets are mostly (but not exclusively) domestic ones. This helps to shift agriculture away from the stifling export-orientation encouraged by neo-liberal policies. The domestic market has increasingly become an important arena for generating growth in the 'smallholder' sectors of agriculture (HLPE 2013).

A theoretically important aspect of this is that the turn towards multi-functionality (and the associated emergence of new products, new services and new markets) is being driven by the constructive and creative capacity of the peasantry. Peasant agriculture is not just about producing products, nor does it just involve the endless repetition of routines that result in such products. Peasant agriculture entails a constructive capacity: it includes mechanisms that are used to make agriculture grow, face adverse conditions, and regenerate and even enhance the biophysical basis of production. And when the 'normal' level of resilience does not suffice, this constructive capacity is employed to re-design and materially rebuild agriculture through the development of new products, services and markets.[27]

The creation of new processes of production within and by peasant agriculture is a slow but constant process – but this accelerates in periods of crisis. At such times there is a more urgent need to jump over the crisis-induced limitations by designing and building new pro-cesses of production that are superior (more productive, generating more value added, allowing for more control by the direct producers, more flexible, etc.) to the existing ones. Theoretically, the creation and further unfolding of such new, superior, processes of production equates to the development of productive forces. For the peasants involved in this process this evidently implies a considerable burden. Thus, we encounter another Chayanovian balance at the level of peasant agriculture as a whole: a balance between burden and benefits. The burden is felt now, whilst the benefits are still to come (i.e. they are anticipated benefits). Thus, the balance spans a period of time. If the time span becomes too long, the burden may start to become too stressful. And if benefits are too low for the burden involved, it could also go terribly wrong. However, despite these poten-tial traps it is peasants who develop the productive forces, doing so according to Chayano-vian balances that link them, and others, to the politico-economic and ecological conditions under which they operate.

---

[27]In terms of STS (Science and Technology in Society) we are talking here about 'architectural inno-vations' that reconfigure an existing system (see, for example, Henderson and Clark 1990).

Peasant agriculture builds on, and enriches nature (but sometimes there is no space to do so)

Peasant agriculture can deal with, and builds upon, biodiversity. By doing so it manages and further enriches agro-biodiversity. This has been abundantly and convincingly documented in the rapidly expanding literature on agroecology (for recent examples see Altieri et al. 2011, Altieri and Toledo 2011). It is important to note that the surge in agroecological practices is not limited to the Global South – it is equally widespread in the Global North (although often known under other names such as farming economically, low external input agriculture, natural cycle farming, permaculture, regenerative agriculture, and so on). The shift towards agroecological practices is not a one-off step, but an ongoing process that proceeds progressively. Agroecological farming is neither static, nor does it (necessarily) show lower yields than conventional farming. It is also not necessarily subject to diminishing returns.[28]

The re-grounding of farming on resources located in local ecosystems and controlled by peasant producers themselves (or by communities of peasant producers) entails a re-introduction of nature into the agricultural production process. Agriculture is, literally, being re-grounded on ecological capital (Guzman Casado et al. 2000). This re-grounding implies many different steps and possibilities. These include the development of ecological structures at micro and meso levels (i.e. within the farm and at local/regional level; Visser 2000). Such an ecological structure might be an existing (and probably extended) pattern of hedgerows, ponds, small pieces of fallow land between meadows, all of which contain specific natural values. But it might also be created anew, in a goal-oriented way (Primdahl 1999). Another aspect is the revitalisation of food webs, that is the intricate 'web' of micro-organisms, worms, herbivores, parasitoids, insects, moles and birds – that provide 'a network of consumer-resource interactions among a group of organisms, populations or aggregate trophic units' (Smeding 2001, 84). Such food webs improve and sustain productive capacity by, for example, enhancing the nitrogen delivery capacity of the subsoil, suppressing pests and increasing resilience against diseases. But they may also sustain a range of 'higher order natural values', such as birds of prey. In his discussion on food webs Smeding argues that

> one important solution [...] for agriculture in the industrialised countries could be the development of farming systems that are economically based on [the] utilisation of biodiversity and that also harbour conservation worthy species. (Smeding 2001, 131, see also Altieri 1999, Almekinders et al. 1995)

Healthy and well-developed food-webs, embedded in robust ecological structures can also considerably strengthen the resilience of plant-animal production systems, and reduce the levels of stress, which pose a major problem in today's agricultural production systems. In synthesis, through extended re-grounding, agricultural production is (once again) based on the local ecology. Re-basing agriculture on ecological capital restores the relation with nature, rebuilds agricultural cycles that enlarge sustainability, and (re-)produces a wider array of specific natural values. The production of 'green services' (landscape, natural values, a healthy environment, clean water, mitigation of global warming,

---

[28]In a later section of this paper I touch on the question of whether agroecological practices are 'class neutral' or not (re. Bernstein 2013), i.e. whether they are especially, or only appropriate, for peasant agriculture or whether they might be also incorporated in entrepreneurial and capitalist farming.

etc.) and the production of agricultural commodities are no longer separated (or at best 'positioned alongside each other'), but become mutually reinforcing, with one being a condition for the other and vice versa (Gerritsen 2002).

This process of re-grounding can be understood as a further extension of the defence mechanisms discussed above. But whilst pluriactivity and farming economically are basically an endeavour to disconnect agricultural production from financial capital and the circuits controlled by it, extended re-grounding takes this process further by firmly re-establishing ecological capital as the bedrock for agricultural production.

Extended re-grounding can result in a range of mutually re-enforcing economic benefits. The more that agriculture is grounded on food webs, the more variable costs (especially those related to fertilization and crop protection) can be reduced. This allows a further unfolding of the style of farming economically, whilst maintaining levels of pro-ductivity (for an exemplary case see Brussaard et al. 2003). Increased resilience and reduced stress in the plant and animal systems generally translate into fewer harvest losses, diseases and pests and a reduction in expenditure on herbicides, pesticides, veterinary services and medicines. Equally, there is generally a positive effect on the longevity of livestock, which is in considerable contrast with the accelerated 'turn-over time' of animals in entrepreneurial and capitalist farming. An extended longevity also contributes to increased benefits and reduced costs, together with a significant improvement in food quality. Thus, through making a turn towards agroecology, peasant agriculture is consistently increasing the contribution it makes to food sovereignty.

A theoretically important point here is that living nature, as shaped and re-shaped within and through the process of co-production, comes to the fore as a major productive force. It is a productive force that can be moulded in different (and partly contrasting) ways and directions (Visser 2010).

In many instances, however, the rebuilding of peasant agriculture on nature is blocked by the many regulatory schemes that are tuned to industrial types of farming and at odds with the dynamics of peasant agriculture (Marsden 2003).

Peasant agriculture can contribute to society at large (but its capacity to do so might be weakened)

Although any estimation is seriously hindered by conceptual problems and by inadequate databases, it is not too bold to claim that there are, on a world-scale, some 0.6 billion peasant units of production.[29] In OECD countries their number is declining (although large interregional disparities might be noted); in developing countries the absolute numbers are increasing and many people depend partly or even completely on peasant agriculture.

China alone has at least 200 million smallholder units (Dan 2006, FAO 2010, 2012), a small part of which is currently engaged in up-scaling towards larger, often co-operative, enterprises. Although these Chinese peasant farmers only utilize 10 percent of the total amount of the world's agricultural land, they produce 20 percent of all food in the world. This is an important indication of the productivity that can be realized through small-holder agriculture.

---

[29]IFAD (2010) indicates that, worldwide, some 450 million small-scale farmers provide a livelihood to around two billion people. However, it can be argued that IFAD's definition of a smallholder is too limited as it only includes units of production of two hectares or less.

Brazil, another major agricultural powerhouse, has a dual agricultural structure. Along-side large holdings (capitalist and entrepreneurial units) there is an extensive smallholder sector consisting of nearly 4.4 million peasant units (some 85 percent of the total farm units). Brazilian agricultural census data shows that, between 1996 and 2006, the number of smallholdings increased by some 400,000 units (MDA 2009). These newly-created peasant farms cover a total area of 32 million hectares, 'which equals the total agricultural area of Switzerland, Portugal, Belgium, Denmark and the Netherlands taken together' (Cassel 2007, 4). In Brazil, peasant units cover 24.3 percent of the total agricultural area, while the large corporations control 75.7 percent. Despite this, the smallholders produce 38 percent of the total value of production. Expressed in absolute terms corporate agriculture produces an average of 358 Reais per hectare per year and smallholder agriculture 677 Reais/ha/year. Moreover, such smallholder agriculture makes a strategic contribution to food security, producing 58 percent of all milk, 50 percent of all chicken and 59 percent of pork. They also grow 38 percent of the country's coffee, 46 percent of its maize, 70 percent of the beans (an important popular dish) and 87 percent of the cassava (MDA 2009).

Evidently, the data from China and Brazil cannot be generalized to other countries. In other countries and regions quite contrasting constellations might exist. When it comes to agriculture and food production, *heterogeneity* is, both between, and within, countries, overwhelming. Nonetheless, when it comes to numbers, productivity and contribution to food sovereignty smallholder agriculture repeatedly emerges as a significant reality that should not be ignored.

Peasant agriculture can also contribute considerably to overall economic growth; directly through increases in production and productivity and, indirectly, by forming a large (part of the) internal market, especially in developing countries (Delgado 1997, Mazoyer and Roudart 2006). When producing sufficiently and achieving higher incomes peasant farmers will considerably spur the sale of the 'wage goods' produced by urban industries. In periods of economic crisis this is a strategic feature. If, alongside the need to increase total agricultural production, there is also a considerable need to enlarge rural employment and/or to raise rural incomes then peasant agriculture definitely has more potential than entrepreneurial and capitalist forms of agriculture. For Brazil, for example, the peasant sector (which only uses 24 percent of the available land) generates 74 percent of all agricultural employment.

Peasant-driven agricultural growth can also be 'the engine of rural non-farm growth' (Haggblade et al. 2007). The Chinese experience is a case in point (Zhang et al. 2006, Mohapatra et al. 2007). The different growth linkages (the mechanisms that link agricultural growth and overall development) are strong in countries where peasant agriculture dominates. It has been shown that 'estate-led agricultural growth' generates the weakest 'consumption linkages' (Haggblade and Hazell 1989, Janvry and Sadoulet 1993), but that these linkages are strong in peasant agriculture.

The role of peasant-driven agricultural growth in poverty alleviation has already been mentioned (in the comparison of China and Africa). Worldwide there are 1.4 billion poor people (living on less than US$1.25 a day). Seventy percent of them are located in the countryside and are dependent, in one way or another, on farming (IFAD 2010). The amelioration of their situation represents a moral duty in itself. Beyond this, substantial improvements in these rural people's purchasing power can significantly act as the engine of growth for the internal market and thus help to alleviate the effects of the current economic crisis. The performance of China is again a case in point.

When smallholder agriculture plays a central role in contributing to the required increases in overall production, it simultaneously makes an important contribution to poverty alleviation and the consolidation and strengthening of internal markets.

Smallholder agriculture is, on the whole, more energy-efficient than other forms of agricultural production (Netting 1993, Pimentel 2009a, 2009b). The following figures, which translate the consumption of carbon energy into calories, illustrate this point. 'Peasant type' smallholder agriculture generates 4–10 calories of food for each calorie of energy consumed. In 'Green Revolution type' smallholder agriculture the figure is 2–5 calories of food per calorie of energy consumed. By contrast, large-scale corporate agriculture of the 'hi-tech type' only produces 1/10th to 1/20th calorie per calorie consumed (Rajesware S. Raina 2011, Table 1). These figures are supported by earlier studies that compared energy-use efficiency in meat production in Italy (Ventura 1995) and water-use efficiency in the north of Portugal (van den Dries 2002).

Peasant agriculture is, in many places, essential for natural resource management and, in other places, it makes a significant contribution to the maintenance of natural resources (soil productivity, landscapes, water, biodiversity, carbon-capture, and so on). Under the right conditions it does so in highly efficient ways. These characteristics can contribute to avoiding major geo-hydrological problems (land or mudslides), can help to mitigate climate change and preserve sweet water reserves.

One of the major ecological distortions linked to the current organization of agricultural production at the global scale is the abandonment of meadows and pasturelands for extensive grazing in hills and mountains, coupled with the use of fertile arable land to produce grains for fattening cattle, concentrated in large feed-lots and for feeding chickens and pigs in factory farms (Weis 2013). The concentration of cattle in these feedlots (and the use of cheap grains) exerts competitive pressure on smallholder herdsmen, provoking the abandonment of meadows and pastures. Supporting these peasants would help remove such a distorted structure.

Alongside the (classical) points discussed so far, there is a new generation of benefits created by today's peasantries. These cannot easily be grasped in economic terms – they mostly relate to the way society is patterned and they afford the promise of attractive and resilient alternatives to the regulatory systems imposed by state apparatuses, supranational bodies and large corporations. Take today's markets. These are extended and rigid systems for making commodities flow in specific ways. The major features of these market systems include articulated centre/periphery relations, command centres that exert control-at-a-distance over extended spaces and large areas of social life, multiple sets of dependency relations, and a centralized appropriation of the generated value added.[30] In contrast to these features, the nested markets that are emerging in many places represent an emerging alternative that goes far beyond their current mechanics and impact. Nested food systems are the equivalent of smart grid systems, which offer a promise for de-centralized and democratically governed energy production and consumption. Nested food systems are locally centred but can be mutually connected whenever the need to do so arises. They are also flexible, have low losses and high efficiency levels. Above all they offer the promise of including and benefiting more than just small minorities of producers and consumers (as is currently the case). They have the potential to include all producers and all consumers.

---

[30]I have illustrated some of these features in my analysis of the Parmalat empire (now part of the French Lactalis group) (van der Ploeg 2008, chapter 4). See also Russi (2013) and Clapp (2012).

Secondly, it is also important to note that new forms of peasant agriculture and the newly emerging nested markets are, to a degree, 'self-governing spaces' that are able to distantiate themselves (at least partly) from the impact of stifling regulatory schemes. They allow the actors involved far more space to realize their aspirations in a more fully fledged way. With a further unfolding of peasant agriculture the possibilities for self-government might be rolled out over far larger areas of social life (just as, in the past, the networking capacities of Italian *mezzadri* 'travelled' to other sectors of the economy).

Capital and labour, food empires and peasantries

Capital and labour are mutually entwined with each other. There is not just a one-sided set of relations between capital and labour (independent/dependent, exploiting/exploited, powerful/powerless, leading/following, dominant/subordinate). Labour shapes and impacts upon capital as much as capital shapes and impacts upon labour. And what applies to capital and labour generally, applies to food empires and peasantries specifically. Food empires and today's peasantries are mutually entwined with each other through the many interactions in which they both engage: sometimes these are cooperative, at other times they involve conflict. Capital does not necessarily have a privileged role in these encounters, nor are the peasantries merely dependent or always the losers within the equation. Instead, sometimes specific peasantries take the lead and capital has to react and try to reconquer lost terrain. Peasantries and food empires are the two opposing poles in a relationship characterized by many-sided struggles (Cleaver 2000).[31]

Generally speaking, food empires create and reproduce peasantries: without a relatively autonomous resource base and without work being structured as a self-valorizing activity, it is impossible to produce and to keep producing under the conditions currently imposed by capital (the squeeze on agriculture, volatility, etc.). But as much as capital creates today's peasantries, it also simultaneously tends to destroy them. More specifically, food empires currently relate to the peasantries through:

(1) *The systematic disassembling of the resource base on which peasant farming is grounded*. This process has been unfolding for a long time and through different mechanisms. Seeds are currently one of the most contested foci of the disintegration of previously 'organic' constellations as their production and distribution is externalized from farming and new forms of control are established (Kloppenburg 2010).

(2) *The intensification of extraction processes*. This indicates how the social wealth produced in the primary sector is increasingly appropriated by, and centralized in, food empires. Food processing is one of the most profitable industrial sectors, which explains why large chemical groups, such as DSM, have moved into food processing.

(3) *The takeover of strategic resources, such as land, water, genetic materials, market outlets, etc*. Food empires control and condition entire markets, partly because they own the infrastructure of these markets. The points of entry, exit and of conversion

---

[31]The operaismo tradition goes a step further by claiming that labour classes (including the peasantries) are the dynamic motor of capital; capital is just a 'function' of labour (Tronti 1979, Moulier 1989, Hardt and Negri 2000). My own position is that, according to historical circumstances, it is sometimes labour and sometimes capital that takes the lead.

are all controlled by food empires. Consequently, they can, through a temporary or permanent closure of one particular entry point, cut large groups of producers out of the market. The fear of this happening can be a powerful weapon influencing the relations between food empires and peasantries.

Together these relations place a constant pressure on income levels and an ongoing threat to the continuity of the farm (as discussed above, farms can no longer be reproduced solely through the markets), an elimination of the possibility to run the farm independently and a denial of the dignity of those working on the farm. Food empires induce redundancy within agriculture. Food products become anonymous, processes of agricultural production and food processing become footloose, and areas of production become interchangeable, whilst the peasantries working in them might suddenly find that they are superfluous. Instead of being proud and independent producers with an autonomous resource base, there is the real possibility of farming being reduced to a simple conversion (governed by an alien script) of purchased commodities (inputs) into commodities to be sold (produce) or even becoming completely redundant.[32]

Thus, food empires induce the aspirations for emancipation discussed in the previous section, which, in turn, translate into the search to (1) augment production, (2) increase resilience, (3) re-invent farming in order to face up to the crisis, (4) build upon nature, and (5) positively contribute to society at large. The aspiration for emancipation is not a 'divine' trait, it is not solely a subjective notion – it is an effect induced among the peasantries by capital and its influence. Ironically, this effect helps the peasantry to develop strategies to effectively counter capital.[33] The redundancy, poverty and insecurity induced by capital, are denied and subsequently translated into responses. This is what John Holloway (2010, 18) refers to as 'negation-and-creation', which involves 'moving against-and-beyond' (Holloway 2010, 19). It is here that the constructive capacity of the peasantry (which I referred to in the previous section) comes to the fore and which clearly entails 'the counterposing of a distinctly different logic here and now to the logic of capitalism' (Holloway 2010, 26). Food empires disrupt the continuity of peasant production (through extraction, grabbing, etc.); this is countered by the peasantries, through productive increases that follow a different logic (not aiming at maximizing rates of return but more on securing their own subsistence), just as the disassembling of the resource base is countered by rebuilding farming on nature, and so on. In the words of Cleaver: 'Many peasant struggles quite self-consciously set out to elaborate new ways of being, new relationships among people and between humans and nature' (Cleaver 2000, 17).[34]

The impact of peasant struggles can be far-reaching. In Italy, for instance, in 1930 capitalist farmers (who only constituted 2.8 percent of the population actively engaged in farming at the time) controlled 53.8 percent of all land and, very significantly at the

---

[32]This is exactly what the scheme of classification (in Figure 2) both illustrates and hides. The fear of being dismissed from farming figures here as 'migration out of agriculture', whilst the other fear (of losing the autonomous resource base and being reduced to just an 'entrepreneur') is entailed in the move from 'semi-commercial smallholder' to 'advanced farmer'. The loss of the autonomous resource base figures here as the change from 'robust seeds' to 'multi-trait hybrid seeds (including GMOs)'.

[33]This is notably the case when it comes, for example, to creating new products, services and new, nested, markets for selling them.

[34]'Positive forms of struggle [...] not just resist capital but [...] create alternatives to it' (Cleaver 2000, 18).

time, 61.4 percent of all cows (which then played a central role in providing traction power). Eighty years later (in 2010), 4.1 percent of all farms were partly run using wage labourers – but now these farms only control 9.0 percent of all the land. This remarkable change, that especially occurred in the years immediately after the second World War and continued during the decades that followed, resulted from social struggles that combined the emancipatory relations of the rural population into 'a material force able to impact considerably on the structure of our society' (Sereni 1956, 63).[35]

Bernardi recalls the nature of this struggle: 'in an economic context characterized by frequent battles between the government and the peasant movement […] the laws of agrarian reform […] provoked, between 1950 and the midst of the 1970s, an expansion of peasant properties of 3,000,000 hectares' (Bernardi 2007, 272). At the same time 'the yields of the different cultures registered average increases of 30 percent' (Bernardi 2007, 272). Sereni added: 'although we cannot neglect the relative limits imposed by the framework and laws of capitalist society [….], it is undeniable that the actions of the masses succeeded in imposing a land reform upon the ruling classes' (Sereni 1955, 1).

Peasant struggles can also proceed in a 'silent' (or 'stealthy') way. In this vein (Mamonova et al. forthcoming, 4) describe how the share of peasant production in total agricultural production has risen in Russia, over recent decades, from 26.3 to 45.0 percent.

Just as capital impacts upon the peasantries, the peasantries impact upon capital. According to Cleaver, 'studies on peasants in Mexico, Nigeria and elsewhere[36] [have] demonstrated how their unwaged work contributed to the expanded reproduction and how their struggles, often autonomous of those of waged workers, had the power to rupture such accumulation' (Cleaver 2000, 17).[37] This point has also been made by Friedmann who noted that social movements act as 'engines of regime crisis and formation' (Friedmann 2005, 229), while in the same vein McMichael refers to 'the key role of workers and farmers in shaping […] food regimes' (McMichael 2013, 13).

Shaping capital, or more specifically, shaping food empires occurs at many different levels and through a range of mechanisms.[38] I shall briefly refer to some of them here. A first, widely known mechanism centres on the takeover (and appropriation) of symbols and practices developed in peasant struggles. The early development of organic farming was, in many countries, driven by sturdy endeavours from peasants who believed it was the only way forward (Hollander 2012). They effectively developed what capital and imperial science declared to be impossible and irrelevant: farming without resort to chemical

---

[35]The Communist Party and the mezzadri linked to it played a central role in these struggles. Antonio Gramsci suggested as early as 1924, to found an 'association for the defence of peasants'. Emilio Sereni prepared the foundation of this 'alliance' (of peasants, rural workers, shareholders, etc.) during the years of resistance, but it was only in 1955 that the radical 'Alleanza Nazionale dei Contadini' (closely related to the Partito Comunista Italiano (PCI)) was actually established. Later on, Emilio Sereni (a member of the central committee of the PCI and a minister in the immediate post war years) became its Secretary General.

[36]Cleaver refers here to de Rouffignac (1985) and Agbon (1985).

[37]Together with other 'autonomist' Marxists, Cleaver proposes a broadened notion of the 'working class' that includes the peasantries.

[38]There is a wide array of mechanisms that can be used to 'disrupt' food empires. These range from (1) national and international campaigns that react to contaminated or otherwise dangerous food products (as in the 'Nestlé baby killer campaign'), via (2) demonstrations in front of factories and supermarkets and (3) building alternatives (as in on-farm processing and direct selling through farmers' markets), to (4) the active reduction of dependency (as occurs through the agro-ecological movement).

inputs. Nonetheless, they succeeded – only to see their emblems[39] increasingly taken over by large entrepreneurial farms, food processing industries and large retail organizations. Now we have 'green' supermarkets, and food industries process a wide range of organic products. However, without the increasingly successful sub-sector of organic peasants such phenomena would not have become a reality.[40] In more general terms: the development of multifunctional farming and the associated construction of new, nested markets, constrain food empires from engaging in venomous campaigns against the emerging alternatives and the promises they entail, and copying some of its symbols and methods. This demonstrates that (1) peasant movements often have the lead and capital is obliged to follow and (2) that peasant based movements really do have the ability to pattern different socio-material realities.

A second mechanism (now becoming increasingly more important) is the design and development of novelties that cannot be taken over. A case in point is the System of Rice Intensification (SRI), 'a set of practices and principles (originally developed in Madagascar) in response to diverse agroecological and socio-economic conditions faced by farmers' (Stoop 2011, 445; see also ILEIA 2013). 'SRI emerged in relative isolation from the international mainstream of rice agronomy' (Maat and Glover 2012, 132). Each single practice intuitively seems to be counter-productive – SRI involves planting very young seedlings, widely spacing individual tillers, alternating between wet and dry soil moisture regimes (instead of permanent flooding), the use of organic rather than mineral fertilizers and frequent weeding. However, together these changes have produced spectacular jumps in yields that are accompanied by considerable cost decreases (together these factors explain the wide dissemination of SRI, which is now practised in many countries). SRI is a disembodied technological change. It does not involve inputs that can be sold. Neither is it a script that can be standardized. Instead it requires to be intelligently adapted to local ecological circumstances. SRI differs, as do all other agroecological practices, fundamentally from Green Revolution technologies. Like agroecology, it is a definite move away from the model that views more plants per hectare and more fertilizer as the ways to achieve higher grain yields. In contrast to the varieties promoted by the Green Revolution, the cultivars used in SRI are selected according to their tillering features, with the emphasis on their ability to develop an abundant root system.[41] These larger and more active root systems increase drought tolerance, as well as efficiency in nutrient uptake – and thereby reduce fertilizer use (Stoop 2011, 448). At the same time, building a healthy supply of soil organic matter strengthens the beneficial associations between the roots and soil biota. By building on nature in this way (see also the previous section) peasants have a definite effect on major food empires who face actual and potential decreases in the sale of 'miracle seeds', fertilizers, pesticides, etc. Peasants 'advance' in

---

[39]Other emblems that have been systematically taken over are those that refer to artisanality, genuineness, animal welfare, etc. These are features that food empires cannot materially produce, but which they need to maintain their relations with consumers. As such they take these over (or 'rob' them, as some say).

[40]I leave aside the question whether or not peasant struggles to develop organic farming have been in vain. I only note that many of the original organic peasant producers have re-invented their farms and networks (whilst continuing to produce in an organic way) and thus continued their search for emancipation.

[41]This is an important contrast with the photo-insensitive short-straw cultivars that were at the heart of the Green Revolution. 'Modern' rice cultivation, as defined in and by the Green Revolution, involved a shift away from solar energy and human labour towards a greatly increased use of fossil energy in the form of chemical fertilizers. SRI builds again on soil biology, solar energy and local knowledge.

a way that definitively differs from the trajectory outlined in Figure 2 and by doing so they slow down accumulation by agro-industries.

A third mechanism through which the peasantry affect and partly re-shape capital might be found in the phenomenon of 'milk-strikes'. This type of peasant struggle (not only restricted to milk but also including other food products) has been used to put pressure on the food industry to which the product was delivered and to (re-)negotiate the farm-gate price and other conditions. This type of struggle started in the late 1960s in France[42] and swept across all of Europe in the following decades. It was one of several factors that triggered the search for interchangeable food production areas. In this respect, peasant struggles unwittingly contributed to the very creation of food empires. Peasant struggles, aiming to obtain better terms of exchange, can trigger new modes of accumulation that offer worsened terms, thereby triggering new struggles. Evidently, this cannot be repeated endlessly. At a certain moment the last resort will be reached.

Fourthly, new accumulation modalities might also occur through operations at the level of the (supra-national) state. The explicit objective of the Mansholt Plan (which aimed at the large-scale modernization of European agriculture) was to replace peasant farms by newly created, large-scale entrepreneurial farms. One of the underlying, but hidden, motivations was that peasant farms were considered to be far too intensive and should be replaced with large entrepreneurial farms that produced more extensively, thereby slowing down the overall growth of production and consequently reducing the financial support provided by the European Community. Thus, the high intensity of peasant agriculture triggered a policy that aimed to eliminate (or at least greatly reduce) this sector.[43] Ironically, this policy failed in two respects – at least at the level of the EU as a whole. From the 1970s onwards new technologies appeared on the market that simultaneously augmented intensity levels and labour productivity. These technologies fitted very well into the newly emerging entrepreneurial farms and thus contributed to enormous overproduction. In addition, the peasantry was far too resilient to disappear. The latter feature continues to exert a major imprint on the Common Agricultural Policy.

A few conclusions

Empirically, peasant agriculture plays a major role in the national economy of many countries, particularly (but not only) in less developed countries. Delgado (1997, 145) notes that

smallholding farming in sub-Saharan Africa is thought at present to account for 70% of total employment, 40% of total merchandise exports, and 33% of GDP on average, although the shares are much higher in many countries of the region. One-third to two-thirds of value

---

[42]Earlier expressions of the phenomenon emerged in the Second World War when milk strikes were used, in for example Friesland in the Netherlands, to resist German razzias against Jewish people.
[43]This same mechanism can be found in areas were the peasantry was able to gain and to combine both economic and political strength (as in Catacaos in Peru in the 1970s and 1980s and the Algarve in Portugal in the second half of the 1970s). Although impressive growth was realized in these areas (in employment, incomes, investments, production, and so on) this newly created strength was broken and the newly developed productive structures dismantled. Since then, regression and underdevelopment have been the rule – which is highly detrimental for the process of capital accumulation. The historical parallel is clear. In 1917 Chayanov wrote that 'the peasant farm is to be the basis for the construction of a new agriculture in Russia' (Chayanov 1988, 137). However, the Russian peasantry was nearly eradicated and Russia paid a very high price for this – until today.

added in manufacturing depends on the supply of agricultural raw material, mostly from small-holders. Furthermore, primary agricultural commodities account for large shares of total merchandise exports in the region, again mostly from smallholders [....]. Despite these achievements, economic conditions for smallholders in sub-Saharan Africa have been especially tough.

If we turn our attention from sub-Saharan Africa to (say) Europe, we also encounter situations in which peasant agriculture is important – for a variety of reasons, most of which are different from those that exist in Africa. The same holds true in Asia, Latin America and, for that matter, in America, where there are nearly 2 million smallholdings[44] alongside fewer than 300,000 large-scale farms. In many places, the balance between small and large holdings continues to be precarious.

If the analysis contained in the previous sections is correct then it is true that the different peasantries of this world are politically far stronger than is normally suggested and/or believed to be the case. They control, *trotzdem Alles*,[45] significant parts of agricultural production and the food supply. This is potential power. In addition, they are, as we have seen, engaged in a struggle to enlarge their autonomy. In this respect, Cleaver refers to the 'hitherto neglected autonomous activity of workers and peasants' (Cleaver 2000, 15), in which 'self-valorization' occurs and 'newness and otherness' are being created (Cleaver 2000, 18).

The importance and potential strength of the peasantries of the world increasingly reside in their capacity to establish and secure food sovereignty. The stronger they become (i.e. the more they actively engage in different social struggles), the more they will be able to ensure food sovereignty. And in so doing they will transform agriculture and have a positive effect on considerable parts of society at large.

The struggle for food sovereignty is not just starting now. It has historical roots that run deep. In the years preceding the Russian Revolution, Chayanov developed, together with radical political movements such as the *narodniki,* a transitional project for Russian agriculture that had three clear objectives:[46] (1) increase agricultural production as much as possible, thus contributing to the overall growth of the national economy;[47] (2) strive to maximize the productivity of agricultural labour; and (3) distribute national income more equitably. In Chayanov's view this transition critically needed to be driven forward by the peasantry itself.[48] Nowadays this appears to be merely of historical interest.

---

[44]According to the definitions used by the USDA there are 1,995,000 small farms in the USA. This corresponds to 91% of all American farms. Their number is increasing (by 118,000 between 2002 and 2007). The USDA's Commission on Small Farms stated; 'we are convinced of the necessity to recognize the small farm as the cornerstone of our agricultural and rural economy' (quoted in HLPE 2013, 28).

[45]This expression was used by Rosa Luxemburg and Clara Zetkin to characterise class struggle, and more specifically, the relation between personal dedication and class struggle. A close literal translation is 'in spite of everything'.

[46]In the Anglo-Saxon world the work of Chayanov is known mostly through the 1966 Thorner edition. German translations of his work (from 1923 and 1924) and the highly valuable Italian edition (1988) of his work on the 'Economy of labour' (from 1917) have rarely been used (see van der Ploeg 2013). Here I use his work from 1917.

[47]'The entire future of our country [....] depends on the rapid and energetic progress of our agriculture and especially whether or not it is able 'to cultivate two spikes of grain wherever just one spike is growing now' (Chayanov 1988, 154).

[48]'Before us there are millions of peasants, with their own habits, their own ideas about farming. These are men that nobody can command. They do whatever they do according to their own willingness and according to their own concepts' (Chayanov 1988, 155).

However, some 90 years later China defined almost exactly the same principles in its *San Nong* policy (the 'three rural principles' that guide agricultural policy). The first principle is *Nong Ye* which means to produce as much as possible in order to satisfy the national needs for food. It is identical, although the wording is somewhat different, to the first objective of Chayanov's transitional project. Improvement of land productivity is central here. *Nong Ming*, the second principle, refers to peasants and their incomes – incomes that are to be increased through improvements in labour productivity (i.e. objective 2 of Chayanov). *Nong Cun*, finally, refers to the liveability of rural villages, to the quality of rural life and it is an evident echo of objective 3: the equitable distribution of national income.

Chayanov's transitional project is thus not only of historical interest. It is alive and kicking today in the Chinese *San Nong* policy (and the many shortcomings, contradictions and conflicts that accompany it). It is also present in many other initiatives located elsewhere. The struggle for food sovereignty has been a long one and it will certainly be with us for many decades to come. There will be many changes – just as in the past. But one thing will remain constant: that is, the strategic centrality of the peasantries of this world. Without them there will be no food sovereignty.

References

Agbon, E. 1985. Class and economic development in Nigeria 1900-1980. Dissertation (PhD). University of Texas, Austin.

Almekinders, C.J.M., Fresco, L.O., Struik, P.C. 1995. The need to study and manage variation in agro-ecosystems. *Netherlands Journal of Agricultural Science*, 43, 127–142.

Altieri, M.A. 1999. The ecological role of biodiversity in agroecosystems. *Agriculture, Ecosystems and Environment*, 74, 19–32.

Altieri, M.A., F.R. Funes-Monzote, and P. Petersen. 2011. Agroecologically efficient agricultural systems for smallholder farmers: contributions to food sovereignty. *Agron. Sustain. Dev.*, 1–13. doi:10.1007/s13593-011-0065-6.

Altieri, M.A. and V.M. Toledo. 2011. The agroecological revolution in Latin America: Rescuing nature, ensuring food sovereignty and empowering peasants. *The Journal of Peasant Studies*, 38(3), 587–612.

Berdegue, J. and R. Fuentealba. 2011. *Latin America: the state of smallholders in agriculture*, Paper presented at the IFAD Conference on New Directions for Smallholder Agriculture 24-25 January, 2011.

Bernardi, Emanuele. 2007. Dall'Alleanza Contadini alla CIA, Confederazione Italiana Agricoltori, un'esperienza nella rappresentanza agricola in Italia. *In: Istituto Alcide Cervi, Annali, 29/2007*, pp. 271–280.

Bernstein, H. 2010. Introduction: some questions concerning the productive forces. *Journal of Agrarian Change*, 10(3), 300–314.

Bernstein, H. 2013. Food sovereignty: a sceptical view, Conference paper #1, International Conference 'Food Sovereignty: A Critical Dialogue', Yale University, September 14-15, 2013.

Berry, R.A. and W.R. Cline. 1979. Agrarian Structure and Productivity in Developing Countries. A study prepared for the International Labour Office within the Framework of the World Employment Programme, The John Hopkins University Press, Baltimore and London.

Bieleman, J. 2010. *Five Centuries of Farming: A short history of Dutch agriculture*. Wageningen, Netherlands: Wageningen Academic Publishers, 1500–2000.

Bray, F. 1986. *The rice economies: Technology and development in Asian societies*. Oxford: Blackwell.

Brown, L.R. 1995. Who Will Feed China? Wake-Up Call for a Small Planet (Worldwatch Environmental Alert Series), World Watch Institute, Washington.

Brussaard, L., W. Rossingh, and H. Wiskerke. 2003. Special Issue of *NJAS. Wageningen Journal of Life Sciences*, 51, 3–7.

Cassel, G. 2007. A atualidade da Reforma Agraria. *Jornal Folha de Sao Paulo* (04-03-2007) p. 4.

Chayanov, A.V. 1966. *The Theory of Peasant Economy* (D. Thorner et al., editors, Manchester University Press, Manchester.

Chayanov, A.V. 1988. *L'economia di lavoro, scritti scelti*, a cura di Fiorenzo Speroto, Franco Angeli/ INSOR, Milan.

CIDA (Comite Interamericano de Desarrollo Rural). 1966. *Tenencia de la tierra y desarollo socio-economico del sector agricola: Peru*. Washington, DC.

CIDA. 1973. Bodennutzung und Betriebsfuhrung in einer Latifundio–landwirtschaft. In: E. Feder (ed.) *Gewalt und ausbeutung, lateinamerikas landwirtschaft*. Hamburg, Germany: Hofmann und Campe Verlag, pp. 162–218.

Clapp, J. 2012. *Food*, Cambridge, UK/Malden, MA, USA: Polity.

Cleaver, H. 2000. *Reading capital politically*. Cardigan Centre, Leeds: Anti/Theses.

Cunningham, K. 2009. Connecting the milk grid: smallholder dairy in India, ch. 17. In: D.J. Spielman and R. Pandya-Lorch, eds. *Millions fed: Proven successes in agricultural development*. Washington: IFPRI, pp. 1–42.

Dan, G. 2006. Agriculture, rural areas and farmers in Beijing. Beijing: Vhina Intercontinental Press.

Delgado, C. 1997. The role of smallholder income generation from agriculture in sub-Saharan Africa. In: L. Haddad, ed. *Achieving food security in Southern Africa: New challenges, new opportunities*. Washington, DC: IFPRI, pp. 145–173.

van den Dries, A. 2002. *The art of irrigation; the development, stagnation and re-design of farmer managed irrigation systems in Northern Portugal*. Wageningen: Wageningen University.

European Commission. 2010. *EU Farm economics overview*. Brussels: FADN.

FAO. 2010. 2000 World census of agriculture. Main results and metadata by country (1996-2005), Rome.

FAO. 2012. Trends and impacts of foreign investment in developing country agriculture, Rome.

Feder, E. 1973. *Gewalt und Ausbeutung, lateinamerikas landwirtschaft*. Hamburg, Germany: Hoffmann und Campe Verlag.

Feuer, H. 2012. Pre-Industrial Ecological Modernization in Agro-Food and Medicine: Directing the Commodification of Heritage Culture in Cambodia, *PhD thesis*, Rheinischen Friedrich-Wilhelms-Universität zu Bonn.

Fraser, A. 2009. *Harnessing Agriculture for Development*. London, Oxfam International. 75 p. Available from: http://www.oxfam.org/en/policy/harnessing-agriculture-development.

Friedman, H. 2005. From colonialism to green capitalism: social movements and the emergence of food regimes. In: F.H. Butel and P. McMichael, eds. *New directions in the sociology of global development* 11:229-67, Oxford: Elsevier.

Geertz, C. 1963. *Agricultural involution*. Berkeley, CA: University of California Press.

Gerritsen, P.R.W. 2002. *Diversity at Stake: A farmers' perspective on biodiversity and conservation in western Mexico*. Wageningen: Circle for Rural European Studies, Wageningen University.

Gulati, A. and S. Fan. 2007. *The Dragon and the Elephant: Agricultural and rural reforms in China and India*. Baltimore: John Hopkins University Press.

Guzman Casado, G.I. et al. 2000. *Introduccion a la agroecologia como desarrollo rural sostenible*. Madrid: Barcelona; Mexico: Ediciones Mundi-Prensa.

Haggblade, S. and P. Hazell. 1989. Agricultural technology and farm-nonfarm growth linkages. *Agricultural Economics*, 3(4), 345–364.

Haggblade, S., P. Hazell, and P. Dorosh. 2007. Sectoral growth linkages between Agriculture and the rural non-farm economy. In: S. Haggblade, P. Hazell and T. Reardon, eds. *Transforming the rural non-farm economy*. Baltimore: Johns Hopkins University Press, pp. 141–182.

Halamska, M. 2004. A different end of the peasants. *Polish Sociological Review*, 3(147), 205–268.

Hardt, M. and A. Negri. 2000. *Empire*. Cambridge, Mass: Harvard University Press.

Hayami, Y. and V. Ruttan. 1985. *Agricultural Development: An international perspective*. Baltimore: John Hopkins.

Hazell, P. 2004. *Smallholders and pro-poor agricultural growth*. Paris: OECD.

Henderson, R.M. and K.B. Clark. 1990. Architectural innovation: the reconfiguration of existing product technologies and the failure of the established firms. *Administrative Science Quarterly*, 35(1), Special Issue: Technology, Organizations, and Innovation, 9–30.

HLPE (High Level Panel of Experts). 2013. *Investing in Smallholder Agriculture for Food Security*, HLPE Report 6, June 2013, CFS Committee on World Food Security, Rome: FAO.

Hollander, D. 2012. *Tegen beter weten in. De geschiedenis van de biologische landbouw en voeding in Nederland (1880-2001)*. Utrecht: Universiteit van Utrecht.

Holloway, J. 2010. *Crack capitalism*. London/New York: Pluto Press.

IFAD (International Fund for Agricultural Development). 2010. Rural Poverty Report 2011, New realities, new challenges, new opportunities for tomorrow's generation, Rome: IFAD.

ILEIA. 2013. *'SRI, much more than more rice'*, Special Issue of Farming Matters, March 2013.

International Commission on Sustainable Peasant Agriculture of la Via Campesina. 2013. *From Maputo to Jakarta : 5 Years of Agroecology in La Vía Campesina*, La Via Campesina, n.p.

Jaffee, S., Nguyen, V.S., Dao; The Anh and Nguyen Do A. T. et al. 2012. *Vietnam Rice, Farmer and Rural Development: From successful growth to prosperity*. Washington, DC: World Bank. 160 p.

Jansen, J. 1998. *Political ecology, mountain agriculture and knowledge in honduras*. Amsterdam: Thela.

de Janvry, A. and E. Sadoulet. 1993. Market, state, and civil organizations in Latin America beyond the debt crisis: The context for rural development. *World Development*, 21(4), 659–674.

Kloppenburg, J. 2010. Impeding dispossesion, enabling repossession: biological open source and the recovery of seed sovereignty. *Journal of Agrarian Change*, 10(3), 367–388.

Lang, T. and M. Heasman. 2004. *Food wars: The global battle for mouths, minds and markets*. London: Earthscan.

Larson, D.F., K. Otsuka, T. Matsumoto and T. Kilic. 2012. Should African rural development strategies depend on smallholder farms? An exploration of the inverse productivity hypothesis, *Policy Research Working Paper 6190*, Agricultural and Rural Development Team, Development Research Group, World Bank, Washington.

Ledda, G. 1975. *Padre padrone, l'educazione di un pastore*. Rome: Feltrinelli.

Lipton, M. 1977. *Why Poor People Stay Poor: urban bias in world development*. London: Temple Smith.

Li Xiaoyun, Qi Gubo, Tang Lixia, Zhao Lixia, Jin Leshan, Guo Zhanfeng, and Wu Jin. 2012. *Agricultural development in China and Africa, A comparative analysis*. Oxon/New York: Earthscan/Routledge.

Maat, H. and D. Glover. 2012. Alternative Configurations of Agronomin Experimentation. *In:* J. Sumberg and J. Thompson (eds), *Contested Agronomy*. London: Routledge.

Mamonova, N., O. Visser, and M. Spoor. Forthcoming. The Re-emerging Peasantry in Russia: 'peasants-against-their-own-will', 'summertime peasants' and 'peasant-farmers'. The Hague: ISS.

Marsden, T. 2003. *The condition of rural sustainability*. Assen: Royal Van Gorcum.

Mazoyer, M. and L. Roudart. 2006. *A history of world agriculture*. London: Earthscan.

McMichael, P. 2013. Food Regimes and Agrarian Questions, Agrarian Change and Peasant Studies Series, 3, Halifax and Winnipeg: Fernwood Publishing.

MDA (Ministério do Desenvolvimento Agrário). 2009. *Agricultura Familiar no Brasil e O Censo Agropecuário 2006*. Brasília: MDA.

Mohapatra, S., S. Rozelle, and R. Goodhue. 2007. The rise of self-employment in rural China: Development or distress? *World Development*, 35(1), 163–181. doi:10.1016/j.worlddev.2006.09.007.

Moulier, Y. 1989. Introduction. In: A. Negri, ed. *The politics of subversion*. Cambridge: Polity.

Netting, R. 1993. *Smallholders, householders: farming families and the ecology of intensive, sustainable agriculture*. Palo Alto, USA: Stanford University Press.

Oostindie, H., J.D. van der Ploeg, and R. van Broekhuizen. 2013. *Buffercapaciteit: Bedrijfsstijlen in de melkveehouderij, volatiele markten en kengetallen*. Wageningen: WUR/ALFA.

Pimentel, D. 2009a. Energy inputs in food crops production in developing and developed nations. *Energy*, 2, 1–24. doi:10.3390/en20100001.

Pimentel, D. 2009b. Reducing energy inputs in the agricultural production system. *Monthly Review*, 61(03), 1–11.

Primdahl, J. 1999. 'Agricultural landscapes as production and living places: On the owner's versus producer's decision making and some implications for planning'. *Landscape and Urban Planning*, 46(1–3), 143–150.

Rajesware, S. Raina. 2011. *Agriculture and trade after the peak oil*. New Delhi and Heinrich Böll Stiftung, Berlin: Centre for Policy Research.

de Rouffignac, A.L. 1985. *The contemporary peasantry in Mexico: A class analysis*. New York: Praeger.

Russi, L. 2013. *Hungry Capital, The financialization of food*. Winchester/Washington: Zero Books.

Schneider, M. 2011. Feeding China's Pigs, Implications for the Environment, China's Smallholder Farmers and Food Security, Insititute for Agriculture and Trade Policy (IATP) Minneapolis.

de Schutter, O. 2013. The agrarian transition and the 'feminization' of agriculture, paper presented to the Food Sovereignty Conference, Yale University, September 14-15, 2013, Conference Paper # 37.

Schneider, S. and P. Niederle. 2010. Resistance strategies and diversification of rural livelihoods: the construction of autonomy among Brazilian family farmers. *The Journal of Peasant Studies*, 37(2), 379–405.

Scott, J.C. 1976. *The moral economy of the peasant*. New haven, NJ: Yale University Press.

Scott, J.C. 2009. *The art of not being governed: An anarchist history of upland southeast Asia*. New Haven: Yale University Press.

Sender, J. and D. Johnston. 2004. Searching for a weapon of mass production in Rural Africa: Unconvincing arguments for land reform. Journal of Agrarian Change, 4(1–2), 142–164.

Sereni, E. 1955. Una nuova fase nella lotta per la terra, in: Riforma Agraria, Rivista di economia e politica agraria, anno III, numero 11-12, nov. dic. 1955, pp 1-10.

Sereni, E. 1956. *Vecchio e Nuovo nelle Campagne Italiane*. Roma: Editore Riuniti.

Sereni, E. 1967. Impresa coltivatrice e problemi agrari del socialismo. Critica marxista, 5(1), 78–105.

Smeding, F.W. 2001. *Steps Towards Food Web Management on Farms*. Wageningen: Wageningen University.

Stoop, W. 2011. The scientific case for system of rice intensification and its relevance for sustainable crop intensification. *International Journal of Agricultural Sustainability*, 9(3), 443–455.

Tittonell, P.A. 2013. *Farming systems ecology: Towards ecological intensification of world agriculture*. Wageningen: Wageningen University.

Tronti, M. 1979. Lenin in England. *Red Notes*, 1979, 1–6.

Tschirley, D.L., C. Poulton, N. Gergely, P. Labaste, J. Baffes, D. Boughton, and G. Estur. 2010. Institutional diversity and performance in African cotton sectors. *Development Policy Review*, 28(3), 295–323.

van der Ploeg, J.D. 2003. *The virtual farmer, past, present and future of the Dutch Peasantry*. Assen: Royal Van Gorcum.

van der Ploeg, J.D. 2008. *The New Peasantries: Struggles for autonomy and sustainability in an era of empire and globalization*. London: Earthscan.

van der Ploeg, J.D. 2010. The peasantries of the twenty-first century: the commoditisation Debate revisited. *The Journal of Peasant Studies*, 37(1), 1–30.

van der Ploeg, J.D. 2013. *Peasants and the Art of Farming, a Chayanovian Manifesto*, Agrarian Change and Peasant Studies Series 2, Halifax and Winnipeg: Fernwood Publishing.

van der Ploeg, J.D., S. Schneider, and Y. Jingzhong. 2012. Rural development through the construction of new, nested markets: comparative perspectives from China, Brazil and the European Union. *Journal of Peasant Studies*, 39(1), 133–173.

van der Ploeg, J.D., Y. Jingzhong, W. Huifang, and W. Chunyu. submitted. *Peasant managed agricultural growth in China: mechanisms of labour-driven intensification*.

Ventura, F. 1995. Styles of beef cattle breeding and resource use efficiency in Umbria. In: J.D. van der Ploeg and G. van Dijk, Eds. *Beyond modernization: The impact of endogenous rural development*. Assen, The Netherlands: Royal Van Gorcum.

Visser, A.J. 2000. Prototyping on farm nature management, a synthesis of landscape ecology, development policies and farm specific possibilities. *Aspects of Applied Biology*, 58, 299–304.

Visser, J. 2010. *Down to earth, a historical-sociological analysis of the rise and fall of 'industrial' agriculture and of the prospects for the re-rooting of agriculture from the factory to the local farmer and ecology*. Wageningen: Wageningen University.

Weis, T. 2007. *The global food economy: The battle for the future of farming*. London: Zed Books.

Weis, T. 2010. The accelerating biophysical contradictions of industrial capitalist agriculture. *Journal of Agrarian Change*, 10(3), 315–341.

Weis, T. 2013. The meat of the global crisis. *Journal of Peasant Studies*, 40(1–2), 65–86.

Wertheim, W.F. 1974. *Evolution or revolution: The rising waves of human emancipation*. London: Penguin Books.

Woodhouse, P. 2010. Beyond industrial agriculture? Some questions about farm size, productivity and sustainability. *Journal of Agrarian Change*, 10(3), 437–453.

Ye, J., J. Rao, and H. Wu. 2010. Crossing the river by feeling the stones: rural development in China. *Rivista di economia agraria*, LXV(2), 261–294.

Yotopoulos, P.A. 1974. Rationality, efficiency and organizational behaviour through the production function: Darkly. *Food Research Institute Studies*, XIII(3), 263–273.

Zhang, J., L., Zhang, S., Rozelle, and S. Boucher. 2006. Self-employment with Chinese characteristics: the forgotten engine of rural China's growth. *Contemporary Economic Policy*, 24(3),
446–458.

Zhou, Y. 2010. *Smallholder agriculture, sustainability and the Syngenta foundation*. Syngenta
Foundation for Sustainable Development, n.p.

Jan Douwe van der Ploeg is currently professor of Transition Studies at Wageningen University in
the Netherlands and adjunct professor of Rural Sociology at the China Agricultural University in
Beijing. Among his recent publications are *The New Peasantries* (Earthscan, 2008) and *Peasants
and the Art of Farming: a Chayanovian Manifesto* (Ferrnwood Publishing, 2013). He combines
research in European agriculture with research of agricultural systems in the Global South.

Food sovereignty via the 'peasant way': a sceptical view

Henry Bernstein

This paper attempts to identify and assess some of the key elements that 'frame' food sovereignty (FS): (1) a comprehensive attack on corporate industrialised agriculture, and its ecological consequences, in the current moment of globalisation, (2) advocacy of a (the) 'peasant way' as the basis of a sustainable and socially just food system, and (3) a programme to realise that world-historical goal. While sharing some of the concerns of (1), I am sceptical about (2) because of how FS conceives 'peasants', and the claim of some of its leading advocates that small producers who practice agroecological farming – understood as low (external)-input and labour-intensive – can feed the world. This connects with an argument that FS is incapable of constructing a feasible programme (3) to connect the activities of small farmers with the food needs of non-farmers, whose numbers are growing both absolutely and as a proportion of the world's population.

Introduction

'Food sovereignty' (hereafter FS) is conceived as 'the right of nations and peoples to control their own food systems, including their own markets, production modes, food cultures and environments...as a critical alternative to the dominant neoliberal model for agriculture and trade' (Wittman *et al.* 2010, 2). This conception is closely associated with *La Vía Campesina* and those who support it, and it serves simultaneously as a slogan, a manifesto and a political project, and aspires to a programme of world-historical ambition. This paper attempts to identify and assess some of the key elements that 'frame' FS:

A first version of this paper was written for the international conference on 'Food Sovereignty: A Critical Dialogue' held at Yale University, 14–15 September 2013. I am grateful to Jens Lerche and Edouard Morena for recent stimulating conversations on this and associated themes, and to two anonymous reviewers of the first draft. The version published here had to be submitted in advance of the conference, and would have been further revised in the light of its stimulating exchanges. I am also fortunate to have received comments on the original draft (both before and after it was revised) from Jairus Banaji, Jun Borras, Andries Du Toit, Deborah Johnston, Deborah Levenson Estrada, Peter Mollinga, Bridget O'Laughlin, Carlos Oya, Pauline Peters and Phil Woodhouse. Taken together they offered many valuable suggestions and asked pointed questions, which (always the way?) pulled in different directions. Several of those named asked (in the words of one of them): 'now that we are convinced that these FS theorists are wrong, now what?'. Indeed, and the work of analysis, understanding and 'critical dialogue' continues. Of course, I remain solely responsible for shortcomings of exposition and argument.

(1) as a comprehensive attack on corporate industrialised agriculture for its devastations, both environmental and social;

(2) as the restatement and extension, in conditions of contemporary globalisation, of that foundational trope of agrarian populism: the social and moral superiority of 'peasant' (or 'small-scale') farming, and now centre-stage its ecological superiority too;

(3) as a programme for the constitution of a new, sustainable and socially just world food order, 'reconnecting food, nature and community' (Wittman *et al.* 2010).

In effect, these elements constitute a kind of thesis and antithesis, although whether they satisfy the conditions of a transformational synthesis is another matter, considered below. They register the impact in recent decades of political ecology on political economy, while the classic questions of (activist) political sociology – what is to be done, by whom and how? – add to the mix of issues in advancing any programme of FS.

Trying to assess the claims of FS, both analytical and evidential, in the span of a single article presents certain difficulties. First is the sheer quantum of the literature generated by FS, magnified by the internet sites of the many organizations committed to it. Here the collection of popular essays edited by Hannah Wittman, Annette Aurélie Desmarais and Nettie Wiebe (2010b) in which the principal North American, or North American-based, champions of FS are well represented, provides many of my examples of FS argument and prescription.[1]

Second, the FS literature encompasses versions of virtually all processes and patterns of agrarian change in the world today, sweeping up many diverse dynamics and struggles into its overarching framework of the vicious and the virtuous. As a result, the exposition in this article connects, or collides, with a series of major issues, debates and relevant literatures – for example, concerning primitive accumulation, the theoretical bases of histories of capitalism, political ecology, 'peasants' and 'rural community' – that I can mostly only reference rather than deal with fully.[2]

Third, FS advocacy is typically constructed from statements about the global, on one hand, and, on the other hand, what I call 'emblematic instances' of the virtues of 'peasant'/small-scale/'family' farming as capital's other. The two are often connected, so that the individual 'peasant' farm (and 'community') exemplifies the way forward to save the planet, to feed its population in socially more equitable and ecologically more sustainable ways. Each of such 'emblematic instances' deserves further scrutiny and assessment, which cannot be undertaken here, although ways of doing this are illustrated. Interrogating the construction of capital's other – in general and in particular – is the principal emphasis of the paper, at the cost of disregarding other aspects like those that seek to incorporate large(r) farmers and small-scale urban food cultivation ('gardening') into FS.

---

[1] FS is experiencing its own 'literature rush', in the term applied by Oya (2013b) to the associated topic of 'global land grabbing' (see also note 5 below).

[2] Carlos Oya has pointed out to me that arguments and evidence from political economy may be less familiar to some readers than the stirring discourse and simplifications of much of the FS literature. I take his point and can only suggest that there are accessible introductions to some of the key ideas of both materialist and Chayanovian agrarian political economy in the first two titles of the series of 'little books on big ideas' about *Agrarian change and peasant studies*, namely Bernstein (2010a) and Ploeg (2013), respectively.

Food sovereignty: when and why?

The key historical focus of FS analysis and prescription is the conjuncture of 'globalisa-tion' since the 1970s. There is a strong case that a new phase of global capitalism with new modalities of accumulation started to emerge from that time which, among other things, (belatedly) changed inherited conceptions of the agrarian question centred on 'national' paths of the development of capitalism in the countryside and its contributions to industrialisation (Bernstein 1996/7).[3] A list of some of the key themes in the discussion of globalisation and its impact on agriculture comprises (drawing on Bernstein 2010a, 82–4):

(1) trade liberalisation, shifts in the global trade patterns of agricultural commodities, and associated battles within and around the World Trade Organization (WTO);

(2) the effects on world market prices of futures trading in agricultural commodities, that is, speculation spurred by 'financialisation';

(3) the removal of subsidies and other forms of support to small farmers in the South as 'austerity' measures required by neoliberalism, thus reduction of government and aid budgets for (most) farming together with promotion of 'export platforms', especially of animal feeds and high-value commodities (horticultural and aquatic);

(4) the increasing concentration of global corporations in both agri-input and agro-food industries (in the terms of Weis 2007), marked by mergers and acquisitions, and the econ-omic power of fewer corporations commanding larger market shares;

(5) new organisational technologies deployed by these corporations along commodity chains from farming through processing and manufacturing to retail distribution, e.g., the 'supermarket revolution' in the global sourcing of food and market shares of food sales, and the recent entry of major supermarket chains into China, India and other parts of the South;

(6) how these technologies combine with corporate economic power to shape and constrain the practices (and 'choices') of farmers and consumers;

(7) the push by corporations to patent intellectual property rights in genetic material, under the provisions of the WTO on Trade-Related Aspects of Intellectual Property Rights (TRIPS), and the issue of corporate 'biopiracy';

(8) the new technical frontier of engineering plant and animal genetic material (genetically modified organisms or GMOs) that, together with specialised monoculture, contributes to the loss of biodiversity;

---

[3] 'Belatedly' needs qualification in that Marxist (and marxisant) debate of the agrarian origins and development of capitalism has centred for some time on two contending models of (1) 'national' paths of transition and (2) the formation of a world market/world economy as intrinsic to transitions to capitalism (see Bernstein 2013a, a review essay of Banaji 2010). In the current context of globa-lisation, FS represents a re-turn to the national (and nationalist?).

(9) the new profit frontier of agrofuel production, dominated by agribusiness corporations supported by public subsidies in the USA and Europe, and its effects for world grain supplies available for human consumption;

(10) health consequences, including the rising levels of toxic chemicals in 'industrially' grown and processed foods, and the nutritional deficiencies of diets composed of 'junk foods', fast foods and processed foods; the growth of obesity and obesity-related illness, together with continuing, possibly growing, hunger and malnutrition;

(11) the environmental costs of all of the above, including levels of fossil-fuel use, and their carbon emissions, in the ongoing 'industrialisation' of food farming, processing and sales, for example, the distances over which food is trucked and shipped from producer to consumer, and for many high-value horticultural commodities air-freighted;

(12) hence issues of the 'sustainability' or otherwise of the current global food system in the face of its 'accelerating biophysical contradictions' (Weis 2010): its continued growth or expanded reproduction along the trajectories noted.

Each of these vast themes is well rehearsed today and constitutes an arena in which different perspectives clash and the assessment of relevant evidence is a demanding task, as ever. That challenge cannot be undertaken here, due to limits of space (and the author's competence). Anticipating some of what follows, I note one instance in relation to arguments about continuing, possibly growing, hunger and malnutrition. This is often, and rightly, attributed to dynamics of inequality and poverty: who goes hungry and why is a matter of crises of reproduction within what I call 'classes of labour' (below), the millions who 'cannot *buy* or produce enough food' (Oxfam 2010, 2, emphasis added), of whom the former include many of the rural as well as urban poor. Further, in terms of the (in)capacity to buy food (enough food, good enough food), this is also often, and rightly, claimed as the result of relations of *distribution* (who gets what) across contemporary capitalism, *not* the result of any shortfall in aggregate world food production (e.g., Altieri and Rosset 1999). The difference between *buying* food and *producing* it for self-consumption is often elided, however (with a strong preference of FS for the latter). We can also note that the consumption of fast foods has particular class dimensions that vary across regions, and can ask, for example, whether the availability of a much wider range of foods, including those available year-round thanks to international trade, is intrinsically a bad thing.

In sum, the topics listed are central to the comprehensive opposition of FS to a 'corporate industrialised agriculture' that is increasingly global in its drivers, modalities and effects, that registers a 'changing relationship to food imposed by the industrialization of (agricultural) production and the globalization of agricultural trade' (Wittman *et al.* 2010a, 5), and results in 'food insecurity, fossil-fuel dependence and global warming' (McMichael 2010, 172).

On one hand, this encompassing criticism points to an intensification of some long-evident tendencies of capitalist agriculture, including the pace of technical change in farming (especially 'chemicalisation') and in its upstream and downstream industries driven by the accumulation strategies of agri-input and agro-food corporations (and their powerful lobbies in the formation of public policy); and the differential effects for farming and food consumption in North and South, and how they are shaped by international divisions of labour and trade in agricultural commodities.

On the other hand, recent FS (and other 'green'-inspired) analysis has highlighted novel features of the current order of globalisation, in which perhaps quantitative now transforms into qualitative change, especially concerning key aspects of technology, for example, the growing privatisation and corporate control of seeds[4] together with their genetic engineering and associated consequences (spanning 4–8 in the list above), generating the concept of 'seed sovereignty' as a component of FS (notably Kloppenburg 2010a, 2010b); and the 'agrofuels boom' (9 in the list above) which Holt-Giménez and Shattuck (2010, 80, 86 and *passim*) characterise as a distinct and profound new 'agrarian transition', driven by 'classic capitalist overproduction' and a falling rate of profit in agribusiness, and collapsing the (previous) 'industrial link between food and fuel' (see also McMichael and Scoones 2010, Weis 2010).

In combination with this thrust of argument from political ecology, FS similarly emphasises the social effects of 'neoliberal globalisation', for example, the dietary and health consequences of industrialised food (10 in the list above; and see Lang and Heasman 2004); a rising incidence of hunger and malnutrition, whether aggregate world food availability is adequate (as suggested above) or declining due to the diversion of grain to animal feeds and agrofuels (again 9 and 10 above; see Bello and Baviera 2010); and the ongoing or intensified dispossession of the world's peasants or small farmers: 'the literal displacement of millions of families from the land and their rural communities' (Wittman *et al.* 2010a, 9), 'the present massive assault on the remaining peasant formations of the world' (Friedmann 2006, 462), the 'corporate food regime' that 'dispossess[es] farmers as a condition for the consolidation of corporate agriculture' (McMichael 2006, 476), and 'absolute depeasantisation and displacement' through a wave of 'global enclosures' that marks the current moment (Araghi 2009, 133–134).

The last is the most central theme of that major (principal?) strand of FS literature that appeals to peasant farming as the alternative to (increasingly) corporate, industrial and global capitalist agriculture. Displacement of peasant farmers today is presented as a consequence of pressures on their social reproduction from the withdrawal of public support (3 above; Desmarais 2007, Bello and Baviera 2010) and from trade liberalisation (1 above; and see Bello 2009) – both standard components of neoliberal policy agendas, albeit 'dumping' of subsidised food exports from the North has a longer history. Further, dispossession is also a direct consequence of 'land grabbing': a new wave of 'global enclosures' [in Araghi's (2009) term] by transnational agribusiness, sovereign wealth funds and private financial entities, in collusion with governments in (and beyond) the South to establish large-scale enterprises dedicated to export production of food staples and agrofuels (Borras *et al.* 2011).[5]

In short, considering world agriculture today entails a far larger cast of agents/'actors' than those who feature in debates of the origins and early development of capitalist farming as processes 'internal' to the countryside and centred on classes of landed property, labour (both peasant and wage labour) and emergent agrarian capital. They now incorporate, on one hand, an enormously wide range of types of farming by social class relations (capitalists, petty commodity producers, 'subsistence' or 'survivalist' farming, each with their own specificities and diversity), and diverse (rural) classes of labour including 'subsistence' or 'survivalist' farmers. On the other hand, they also incorporate, as indicated, different types

---

[4]Which started from the 1930s in the USA with the development of hybrid maize seed, hence anticipating the subsequent Green Revolution, as detailed in the outstanding study by Kloppenburg (2004).
[5]Edelman (2013) and Oya (2013b) provide necessary and valuable correctives to typically exaggerated claims about 'global land grabbing', including important issues in producing and using evidence.

(and scales) of capital in the various moments of the overall circuits of capital and its expanded reproduction – financial, productive, commercial – as well as states and supra-state bodies (the WTO, the World Bank).

The highly topical (and contested) contemporary themes outlined connect, of course, with longer histories of capitalism and agriculture, aspects of which I sketch next.

Capitalism versus the peasant

The genesis of 'capitalism versus the peasant' (Bello and Baviera 2010, 69) is Marx's famous sketch of 'so-called primitive accumulation' as ' ... nothing else than the process which divorces the producer from the ownership of the conditions of his own labour' (Marx 1976, 874 and Ch. 27 *passim*).[6] Bello and Baviera (2010, 73) refer to a 'centuries-long process of displacement of peasant agriculture by capitalist agriculture', and Handy and Fehr (In Wittman *et al.* 2010) sketch English enclosures from the sixteenth century (before Britain's 'first industrial revolution') and especially between the mid-eighteenth and mid-nineteenth centuries, when (capitalist) 'high agriculture' emerged (in tandem with industrialisation). They also contest views that capitalist farming achieved any advances in yields over contemporary small-scale farming in the period(s) in question.

Beyond continuing debate of the origins of capitalist farming, stimulated especially by the work of Robert Brenner (1976, Ashton and Philpin 1985), some variant or other of primitive accumulation is widely applied in analyses of the restructuring of social relations of land and labour, its drivers, modalities and effects (intended and unintended), in the vast and diverse colonial zones of the 'three continents' (Latin America, Asia and Africa) at different historical moments of the formation of a capitalist world economy.[7]

Industrialisation of the food system

Wittman *et al.* (2010a, 5) suggest 'two hundred years of industrialization of the food system', that is, several centuries after the original emergence of agrarian capitalism and

---

[6]Marx regarded dispossession of the peasantry as a necessary but not sufficient condition of the development of capitalist farming: 'the only class created directly by the expropriation of the agricultural population is that of the great landed proprietors' (Marx 1976, 905), hence something further is required for a transition to capitalism. For some scholars (e.g., Byres 2006, Heller 2011), this came about, in effect, through 'primitive accumulation from below'. The concept of 'primitive accumulation', not least as necessary to capitalism throughout its history, has made a major comeback, stimulated by David Harvey's notion of 'accumulation by dispossession' in a crisis of over-accumulation in global capitalism since the 1970s (Harvey 2003). 'Is there any busier notion at the moment than that of primitive accumulation (and its analogues and extensions)? That is, busy in the elasticity of its definitions, its expanding range of applications and the claims made for it. To make sense of the proliferating claims for, and debates about, primitive accumulation, it helps to distinguish different ways in which the concept is put to work: a combination of the substance given to the concept, how it is deployed, and the evidence used to illustrate or support its different uses' (Bernstein 2013c, a preliminary survey that I hope to develop). The most lucid guide to, and assessment of, this current busyness that I have read is by Derek Hall (2012).

[7]See Bernstein 2010a (Ch. 3), and references therein. In a passing acknowledgement of longer histories of class-based agrarian civilisations, Raj Patel (2010, 191) suggests that 'the political situation has *never* been favourable to those who produce food; its new global context merely compounds a millenia-old disenfranchisement', although the meanings of 'disenfranchisement' and spaces for enfranchisement today are very different from, say, medieval India or Europe or Egypt in late antiquity (Banaji 2001).

about a half-century or so before the periodisation suggested below.[8] Holt-Giménez and Shattuck (2010, 85–6) propose that current neoliberal globalisation, specifically the 'agrofuels boom', 'closes a historical chapter in the relation between agriculture and industry that dates back to the Industrial Revolution' – a chapter with two parts. Initially 'peasant agriculture effectively subsidized industry with cheap food and cheap labour', while 'Later on, cheap oil and petroleum-based fertilizers opened up agriculture to industrial capital. Mechanization intensified production, keeping food prices low and industry booming. Half of the world's population was pushed out of the countryside and into the cities'. The motif of 'cheap food' signalled by Holt-Giménez and Shattuck is a central thread running through the political economy of capitalism and agriculture with implications for FS, as we shall see.

International food regimes (IFRs)

The FS framework is typically informed by notions of capitalism as 'world system' that occupy a spectrum from agit-prop invocations to the more analytical. 'Capitalism' – or its current phase of globalisation – is named as the source of corporate industrialised agriculture, with different emphases on various aspects or moments of the histories of capitalism, as just illustrated. Sometimes 'capitalism' becomes simply a synonym for industrialised agriculture, or is interchangeable with ideologies of 'modernity' (and modernising projects) – based in certain conceptions of rationality, efficiency and the conquest of nature – held to constitute (and explain?) the global food order (thesis) that FS defines itself against (antithesis).[9]

The most potent analytical framework available to FS is that of the political economy of international food regimes (IFRs) from the 1870s, developed by Harriet Friedmann and Philip McMichael (and deployed by Weis 2007 and Fairbairn 2010, among others). McMichael has recently provided a 'genealogy' of the concept, in which he considers its origins and its subsequent developments and extensions to include 'social movement, eco-logical and nutritional science relationships' (2009, 140). The IFR approach offers 'a unique comparative-historical lens on the political and ecological relations of modern capit-alism writ large' (McMichael 2009, 142).

Here there is space only for some brief observations. First, it is interesting that Fried-mann's and McMichael's original work was historical research on agriculture in two sites of the first 'settler-colonial' IFR from the 1870s to 1914, namely the USA (Friedmann 1978a, 1978b) and Australia (McMichael 1984), as distinct from the great agrarian zones of the 'three continents' where the 'peasant question' was manifested most sharply in colonial conditions and thereafter. In effect, peasantries are largely missing from the first century of Friedmann and McMichael's accounts of IFRs, other than as affected by the patterns of trade they established.[10] McMichael observes that 'the twentieth-century ideal typical model' of 'national agro-industrialisation' (2009, 145, 141) was prefigured by 'settler

---

[8]Wittman (2010, 92) also suggests the 'turn of the twentieth century' as a key moment marked by 'the invention of the internal combustion engine and innovation in affordable gas-powered farm implements...', while Ploeg (2013) dates the promotion/generalisation of 'modernisation' of farming from around the mid-twentieth century.

[9]The implicit reduction of capitalism to particular conceptions of modernity is a common Foucauldian syndrome, in which forms of 'governmentality' generated by different historical experiences of capit-alism are treated as detached from it, as are the beliefs and practices of bureaucrats and planners who exercise 'the rule of experts' (Mitchell 2002).

[10]Not least 'cheap' wheat exports in the second IFR (to which they were central) and thereafter, as noted above.

states'. This is all the more poignant as in effect those states lacked peasantries, hence a need for 'peasant elimination', as Kitching put it (2001, 148 and Chapter 10 *passim*).[11]

Second, the first IFR coincided with (1) the transition from the first to second industrial revolution, that is, from an economy based in iron, coal and steam power to one increasingly based in steel, chemicals, electricity and petroleum, which vastly accelerated the development of the productive forces in farming,[12] as well as in food processing, storage and transport: conditions of the first IFR, (2) a shift in the locus of the development of modern capitalist agriculture or 'agribusiness' (as distinct from farming, see further below) from the western European sites of early agrarian transitions to the USA (on which see Cronon 1991, Post 1995), and (3) a new tripartite international division of labour in agricultural production and trade, centred on the USA and other settler-colonial countries (Canada, Argentina, Australia), Europe, and the (mostly) colonial tropics (Friedmann and McMichael 1989).[13]

Third, there are differences between Friedmann and McMichael concerning what has replaced the second IFR, the 'mercantile-industrial food regime' (in Friedmann's term) under US hegemony from the 1940s to early 1970s. These differences are discussed by McMichael (2009, 151–4), in which he argues that a third 'corporate' IFR has consolidated, while Friedmann proposes an emergent 'corporate-environmental' food regime:

> Led by food retailers, agrofood corporations are selectively appropriating demands of environmental, food safety, animal welfare, fair trade, and other social movements that arose in the interstices of the second food regime. *If it consolidates*, the new food regime promises to shift the historical balance between public and private regulation, and to widen the gap between privileged and poor consumers as it deepens commodification and marginalizes existing peasants.' (Friedmann 2005, 227–8, emphasis added)

Two points to conclude here. One is that the collapse of the second IFR in the early 1970s (Friedmann 1993) coincided exactly with the moment of the emergence of 'neoliberal globalisation' (above). The other is that McMichael now ties his analysis of food regimes, and especially the current corporate regime, to strong advocacy of FS, which connects with celebrations of 'resistance'.[14]

---

[11]None of this means that such settler states did not engage in the violent dispossession of indigenous peoples; on the USA see Byres (1996, Ch. 5), and on slavery, while 'non-capitalist' in his view, as nonetheless central to the development of American capitalism, see Post (2003, 2011). Rosa Luxemburg's view of primitive accumulation in North America and South Africa as 'the struggle against peasant economy' signified the destruction of largely subsistence-oriented *settler* farming (1951, Ch. 29).

[12]The invention of chemical fertilisers, and other agricultural chemicals, and their impact on the productivity of land (yields); the development of scientific plant and animal breeding (facilitated by new knowledge of genetics and its applications), similarly impacting on yields; the invention of the internal combustion engine and its use in tractors and other farm machines, transforming the productivity of labour.

[13]This also corresponds, of course, to the periodisation of Lenin's *Imperialism* (1964). Coming from a different direction, Jairus Banaji (2010, 333) designates the late nineteenth century as 'the watershed of agrarian capitalism' marked by the 'rapid evolution' of the 'discernibly modern' capitalist agricultural enterprise and its labour regimes; the 'gravitational pull of European and American industry wrought changes in the distant countrysides they drew on through local trajectories of accumulation and dispossession' (Banaji 2010, 360).

[14]In effect, a 'greening' of food regime analysis through the 'discovery' of peasant virtue, especially as articulated by *La Vía Campensina*.

'Resistance'

There are many and complex debates concerning the 'persistence of the peasantry' in the epoch of capital, including its current phase of globalisation, in which peasant 'resistance' features in different registers and on different scales:

> manifested in struggles over land, rent, taxes, debt, forced cultivation, labour conscription, and the various forms of control that colonial and independent states sought to impose on small farmers in the name of progress – whether the mission of colonialism to 'civilize' peoples of colour, or 'modernizing' agriculture as an element of strategies for economic development. (Bernstein 2010a, 96, and 95–7 passim)

The larger and heroic scale of resistance is exemplified in Eric Wolf's *Peasant wars of the twentieth century* (1969) with its case studies of Mexico, Russia, China, Vietnam, Algeria and Cuba from the 1900s to the 1960s. The smaller, mundane, scale is exemplified by James C. Scott's *Weapons of the weak* (1985), a study of a village in Malaysia in the late 1970s. Scott argued, with intentional provocation, that the continuous and cumulative effects of 'everyday forms of peasant resistance' within socially differentiated rural localities do more to improve the conditions of peasant farmers than occasional, more widely recognized, episodes of overt conflict and rebellion.

'Resistance' invoked in FS discourse resonates both these scales; on the smaller scale the commitment of peasants to continue farming in certain ways, informed by agroecological wisdom and values of autonomy, community and social justice, in the face of the corrosive effects of capital and 'modernising' states. As, it is claimed, corrosion becomes onslaught in the current neoliberal moment of intensified global enclosure/dispossession (above), then peasant resistance – to cheap food imports, land-grabbing, tendencies to market monopoly and other impositions of agribusiness on ways of farming – has become more widespread, connected and organised, leading to the heroic scale of a 'global agrarian resistance' (McMichael 2006) in which *La Vía Campesina*, in the vanguard of 'transnational agrarian movements' (Borras *et al.* 2008a), is usually credited with coining the slogan of FS.

One should also note here the more recent coinage of 'resistance of the third kind', which refers primarily to how (small) farmers exploit any 'room for manoeuvre' (or 'adaptive' rather than 'reactive' change and innovation) in the commodity markets they inhabit (Schneider and Niederle 2010). Somewhat confusingly, this is framed by Ploeg *et al.* (2012, 153–7) with reference to 'everyday forms of resistance', as restated by Kerkvliet (2009) – that is, Scott-type 'resistance' of the mundane kind – and to the Chinese notion of 'rightful resistance' (O'Brien and Li 2006).[15] I return to 'resistance of the third kind' below.

And (any) 'achievements' of capitalist agriculture?

In 1750 (roughly the onset of the first industrial revolution) world population was some 750 million people (approximately half of whom were Chinese). In 1950, world population was 2.5 billion. It grew to 6 billion in the next 50 years, and is projected to rise to some 9 billion

---

[15]The most common causes of protest in rural China that O'Brien and Li (2006) consider are illegitimate types and levels of taxation demanded by various tiers and agencies of the local state, other depredations by party and state cadres, and corrupt practices in village elections. Two of their key concerns are the analysis of opportunities for such rightful resistance and perceptions of its promises and dangers.

by the middle of this century. Such expansion was not possible without the extraordinary development of productivity in capitalist farming. As Robert Brenner (2001, 171–2) put it, only capitalism was able to generate 'a process of self-sustaining economic development characterized by rising labour productivity in agriculture' that overcame the two great prior obstacles in world history: the long-term tendency of population to outrun food supply and the inability of urban population, and non-agricultural labour, to grow beyond a highly limited proportion of total population, in effect phases A and B of the Malthusian cycle.[16] This does not mean that the development of capitalist agriculture provides the sole explanation for the growth of world population any more than other important elements of this 'big picture', namely greatly improved levels of nutrition for many, if not all, and the contributions of forms of medicine generated by capitalist 'modernity'. Nevertheless, both point towards the remarkable development of scientific knowledge and its applications in the era of capital, and the multiple and interrelated social innovations that made possible the expansion of the scale of human existence and, I would argue, its richness.

Of course, none of this is the consequence of any intent on the part of capital to improve the human condition. Its driving force, from its emergence to today, is profit, or in Marx's terms, the necessary and ever-growing expansion of value. This works through contradictions intrinsic to, and connecting, the constitutive dynamics of capital (competition between capitals, tendencies to crisis), between capital and those it exploits (class conflict) and oppresses (democratic struggles), and between capitalism and nature (O'Connor 1998, Foster 2000, J.W. Moore 2010, 2011). Any dialectical view of the historical career of capital as both destruction and creation (Berman 1983) provides a different perspective to those binaries that view capitalism *only* as destructive.

And destructive of what? To put the question differently, and more specifically: when did the rot of capitalist agriculture set in? (1) Is it inscribed in (all) experiences of capitalist agriculture from its very beginning?[17] (2) Is it inscribed in capitalism more generally? (3) Does it 'only' become an issue with the industrialisation of farming and/or its corporatisation and/or its globalisation (depending on how these three dimensions of contemporary capitalist agriculture are periodised, individually or jointly)? The arguments for FS, as noted, typically focus most strongly on the current period, while its most comprehensive elaborations – declaring an alternative episteme and rationality in the relations (or mutual constitution) of society and nature – point towards an affirmative answer to the first two versions of the question, hence lead to another: what was it that 'the rot' of capitalist agriculture set into, that is, what forms of precapitalist society?[18] Were the latter always and necessarily 'superior' to capitalism, on social, moral and/or ecological

---

[16]Wittman (2010, 92) recognises that with the industrialisation of farming, at least from the early twentieth century (see note 8 above) 'the ability to produce more food, faster and with less labour, became a reality'. Her timing falls exactly within the period of the first IFR, spearheaded by a 'historically unprecedented class' of commercial *family* farmers in the settler colonial countries ('diasporas') of the Americas and elsewhere (Friedmann 2005, 295–6).

[17]From which Duncan's idiosyncratic and original argument dissents (Duncan 1996).

[18]In a sense this is to 'scale up' Oya's point (2013b) that so many claims about 'global land grabbing' proceed without any adequate 'baseline' evidence of what is deemed to change (for the worse) as a result of 'land grabs' that actually happen. The logical implication of some 'green' analysis, whether explicit or implicit, is to turn the clock back on industrialisation itself (and to return to pre-industrial levels of population?).

grounds? In turn this leads to a further question, and the most central: who or what is capital's other in the current stage of world history?

Capital's other

In the discourse of FS, capital's other is personified by 'peasants', 'poor' peasants, small farmers, sometimes small- and medium-scale farmers, 'peasants, farmers, farm workers and indigenous communities' (McMichael 2010, 168), and (most generically?) 'people of the land' (Desmarais 2002). They qualify as capital's other by virtue of an ensemble of qualities attributed to them, which include their sustainable farming principles and practices, their capacity for collective stewardship of the environments they inhabit (Wittman 2010, 94), their 'peasant frugality' (McMichael 2010, 176) and 'their vision of autonomy, diversity and cooperation' versus the dependence, standardisation and competition imposed on farming by 'the forces of capital and the market' (Bello and Bavieri, in Wittman *et al.* 2010, 74). They are the bearers of 'indigenous technologies' that 'often reflect a worldview and an understanding of our relationship to the natural world that is more realistic and sustainable than those of western European heritage' (Altieri 2010, 125), and provide the basis for 'revalorizing rural cultural-ecology as a global good' (McMichael 2006, 472). All these and other such qualities combine to represent, or express, a radically different episteme to that centred in market relations and dynamics, an 'alternative modernity' to that of capitalist agriculture based in an ecologically wise and socially just rationality (McMichael 2009).

These representations, of course, are located in older, and much contested, notions of 'peasants' and a (or the) 'peasant way', proclaimed by agrarian populism, namely

> the defence of the small 'family' farmer (or 'peasant') against the pressures exerted by the class agents of... capitalism – merchants, banks, larger-scale capitalist landed property and agrarian capital – and indeed, by projects of state-led 'national development' in all their capitalist, nationalist and socialist variants, of which the Soviet collectivisation of agriculture was the most potent landmark. (Bernstein 2009, 68)

Much FS advocacy amounts to a topical restatement of 'taking the part of peasants' (Williams 1976), now informed by political ecology, in a new period of globalising capitalist agriculture. As is common with (binary) conceptions of such an entity and its 'other', it is not always clear which comes first; there is always the intriguing question of the materials from which, and method by which, the other is constructed.[19] In this case, I suggest, the wholly positive construction of the other incorporates an abstraction of 'peasant economy' (or 'peasant mode of production') combined with what one may term 'emblematic instances' of the practices of the peasant 'rank and file' (McMichael 2010, 168), whether within or without the FS 'movement'.[20] Here I confine myself to several kinds of issues concerning who the 'peasants'/small farmers/people of the land are,

---

[19]Another intriguing question, also beyond the scope of this paper, is the formation of discourse (ideology) through the mutual interactions of farmers' organisations and sympathetic intellectuals. The latter typically claim only to articulate in more scientific language what farmers already think, do, feel and say, which farmers' organisations then adopt and recycle to show that intellectuals ('experts') support their views and demands. Morena (2011) is an illuminating exploration of this dynamic in the French *Confédération Paysanne*.
[20]The most significant theorisation of 'peasant economy' remains that of A.V. Chayanov (1966), first published in 1924–5. Chayanov was committed to the development of peasant farming through new ('modern') technologies and forms of social organisation.

before moving on to consider the kinds of measures envisaged to turn FS into a viable movement of transformation of the 'world food system'.

Who are the 'peasants'?

The first issue is (1) whether peasants', 'poor' peasants/small farmers, sometimes small farmers or small- and medium-scale farmers or all (?) farmers, farm workers, indigenous communities, 'people of the land', are synonyms;[21] (2) if so, whether they are adequate synonyms for *social* categories that we can recognise and use to think with, and (3) whether the social categories indicated, or implied, by these labels are internally coherent and useful.[22] For example, are there differences between 'peasants' and 'small farmers'?[23] Who are 'poor peasants', and does the signifier 'poor' distinguish those so described from others who are not 'poor'? If so, what is the substance of that distinction?[24] On the other side of this 'stretching' of categories, are there social differences between small and medium farmers? Or does their lumping together simply serve to construct a common 'other' to large-scale farming?[25] And what of farm workers? Borras and Franco (2010, 116) note 'the distinct class interests of the rural labourers', and Patel (2010, 190) signals the centrality to agrarian capitalism of the relation between 'farm owner and farm worker' who have different interests ('farm owner' here presumably encompassing small and medium farmers).

---

[21]Jack Kloppenburg (2010a, 370) is unusual in confronting, and trying to deal with, this issue (as others): 'Whatever their differences, all producers of horticultural and agronomic crops put seeds in the ground. A Nicaraguan *campesino* might plant soybeans by hand on half a hectare, while an Iowa farmer could be using John Deere's DB60 planter to simultaneously sow 36 rows of soybeans on 2500 acres. But both producers could well be planting seed purchased from Monsanto – or saved from a previous harvest. They find themselves in similar structural positions in relation to Monsanto and Syngenta and DuPont...'. This statement thus encompasses *all* farmers from very small to very large, illustrated by a commodity that itself may be part of the problem for many FS advocates, and certainly when it is monocropped on 2500 acres.

[22]Patel (2010, 186) notes 'tensions between different geographies of citizenship...not only between producers and consumers but within the bloc of "small farmers" itself, along axes of power that range from patriarchy to feudalism', although he does not pursue this further nor consider dynamics of commodification and their effects, notably differentiation (on which see below).

[23]'What constitutes a 'small farmer' is properly a *social*, hence relational, issue. To simply use *size* measures of farm – say, 2 ha (Altieri 2008, also cited by McMichael 2010) – across the vast range of ecological and social conditions of farming is not helpful. The 'smallest of the small' by average farm size is no doubt in China where 50 percent of farmers cultivate only from 0.03–0.11 ha of arable land, and less than 3 percent cultivate more than 0.67 ha, according to Li (2012, 15; see also Li *et al.* 2012). Whether such small (tiny)-scale farming offers support for the 'peasant way' is another matter. The extremely high yields of such small farms in China are based in irrigation, widespread use of hybrid seeds [and, increasingly, genetically modified (GM) seeds?], massive (excessive?) applications of chemical fertilisers, and extremely intensive labour. This means that gaps between yields in China and sub-Saharan Africa, say, are much greater than gaps in labour productivity (Bernstein 2012c, and calculations from Li 2012). A revised version of Bernstein (2012c) will appear in a volume edited by Lawyer Kafureka and Giuliano Martiniello, to be published by the Makerere Institute of Social Research, Kampala.

[24]According to the claims of the 'peasant way', those small farmers who are willing and able to practise agroecological farming will be less poor than those who are not (see further below). One wonders if the persistence and centrality of evocations of (unspecified) 'poor' farmers resonate another central motif, that of their 'exploitation'/oppression by corporate agribusiness capital.

[25]In the interests of coalition building? And especially in farming zones in the North where *La Vía Campesina* is present or wants to be?

Are all peasants the same (doing things the same way)? #1

Do all peasants/small farmers exemplify the qualities of the 'other' listed above? If not, then those who do might be regarded as a kind of vanguard of the 'peasant way'. There are occasional glimpses of this issue. For example, Miguel Altieiri, a leading exponent of agroecology within FS, recognises that 'a proportion of medium- and small-scale farmers are conventional' (2010, 122).[26] He then gives the ('emblematic') instance of farmers using polycultures on Central America hillsides, and in the face of adverse climatic conditions thereby incurring 'lower economic losses than *neighbours* using monocultures' (Altieri 2010, 124–5, emphasis added).[27] One would like to know more about those who practise diversified farming and those (including their neighbours) who practice 'conventional farming': whether they differ in any significant socioeconomic terms. If not, then presumably they do what they do as a result of *choice* – 'good' choice and 'bad' choice respectively.[28]

Further, one should ask whether the fact that some ('vanguard') peasants/small farmers exemplify the virtues of 'autonomy, diversity and cooperation' (separately or jointly) in their farming, while others do not, is a result of 'choice' or *lack of choice*. Certainly both are possible, but to understand when, where and why they occur (and may change), requires close investigation of the conditions of constraint and opportunity that different categories of small farmers confront. In turn this entails consideration of ecological and market conditions, and of the class differentiation of small (and medium) farmers.

---

[26]And a major proportion? Elsewhere (Bernstein 2010a, 97), I noted that some 'peasants' in colonial Africa 'themselves initiated new paths of specialized commodity production. Polly Hill's study (1963) ... provides a well-known example of the self-transformation of "subsistence" farmers into commodity producers. Moreover, Hill was clear that over time the more successful [cocoa growers]...became capitalist farmers. More generally, rather than simply being either passive victims or active opponents of colonial imposition, many peasants tried to *negotiate* the shift towards commodity production (commodification of subsistence) they confronted, in more or less favourable circumstances, mobilizing larger or smaller resources of land and labour, with greater or lesser success. The same applies to responses to the impositions of "national development" following independence from colonial rule.' A key suggestion in this passage can be extended, namely that not all small farmers are either *passive victims* or *active opponents* of neoliberal globalisation (or different phases of capitalism that preceded it). This binary of victim/resistance hero further breaks down when, as so often, the leaders of specific moments and movements of 'resistance' come from the ranks of the rich and middle peasantry or more successful commodity producers, for example, the central role of 'middle peasants' in Wolf's political sociology of 'peasant wars of the twentieth century' (1969), and for a more recent example, the case of 'New Farmers' Movements' in India in the 1980s (Brass 1994), led by rich peasants/capitalist farmers, which campaigned for better producer prices and larger input and other subsidies, much like farm lobbies in the North.

[27]Altieri draws on a survey of hillside farmers after Hurricane Mitch in Central America, reported in Holt-Giménez (2006, 67–76); see also the latter's careful Appendix B (Holt-Giménez 2006, 89–97), which includes some indications of reasons given for adoption and non-adoption of agroecological practices – among the latter is shortage of household labour time.

[28]This also seems to be the thrust of Jan Douwe van der Ploeg's proposal of 'new peasantries' in both South and North (2008, see especially Ch. 2 and 10), and his contrast between 'the peasant principle', aiming for at least 'relative' autonomy from markets, and 'the entrepreneurial mode' of farming which embraces commodity production. Both apparently are a matter of 'choice' (values, etc.) – again 'good' and 'bad' respectively – with his most interesting discussions centred on the conditions and effects of such choice in very different types of farming. The value of his work over a long period is that it combines knowledge of farming practices – what farmers do – in different parts of the world, often from first-hand research, and taking seriously (diverse) patterns of commodification.

Are all peasants the same (doing things the same way)? #2

My basic position in this last regard is that there are no 'peasants' in the world of contemporary capitalist globalisation. The reasoning of this position has been argued extensively elsewhere (in most accessible fashion in Bernstein 2010a), and would be tedious to repeat here. Its principal points include processes of the 'commodification of subsistence' in capitalism, the transformation of peasants into petty commodity producers, the consequent internalisation of commodity relations in the reproduction of farming households, and inherent tendencies to class differentiation of petty commodity production, whether farming is practised as the sole or principal basis of household reproduction or combined with other activities – in other branches of petty commodity production (including crafts and services) and/or, most importantly, the sale of labour power. Other closely related dynamics are the (near) ubiquity of 'off farm' income for all classes of farmers (albeit typically from different sources, and for different purposes, according to class) – so-called 'pluriactivity' (below) – and of rural labour markets on which much 'peasant' farming depends, including in sub-Saharan Africa where it has been largely ignored in both research and policy (Oya 2013a).

All these processes generate a 'relentless micro-capitalism' of petty commodity production in the countryside (in the term applied by Mike Davis 2006, 181, to the urban 'informal economy'), that long preceded the 'macro-capitalism' of corporate agriculture/agribusiness, if now increasingly connected with it. Of course, such processes, so schematically outlined, work in extremely diverse ways between and within different farming groups and areas and over time. Their concrete investigation, I suggest, provides an essential component of understanding who farms, in what conditions, and in what ways – issues signalled above – and how that affects how much they produce for their own consumption and for commodity exchange, hence available to non-farmers, on which more below.

One important conclusion of applying this perspective from political economy is that there are far fewer petty commodity producers able to reproduce themselves primarily, let alone exclusively, from their own farming in the world today than the numbers of 'peasants' claimed by FS advocates. Those numbers typically include all those who engage in some farming, however marginal, as an element in their reproduction (estimated at over 60 percent of 'farmers' in India, for example), and who do not contribute to the net marketed surplus of food. Sometimes such numbers also count all enumerated as 'rural' in censuses and surveys including those without access to land, those not engaged in ('own account') farming, and those who otherwise rely on 'footloose labour' for their reproduction (Breman 1996). This also means that large sections of rural people in today's South, perhaps the majority in most places, are better understood as a particular component of 'classes of labour' rather than 'farmers' in any determinate and useful sense.[29]

---

[29]Classes of labour comprise 'the growing numbers ... who now depend – directly *and indirectly* – on the sale of their labour power for their own daily reproduction' (Panitch and Leys 2001, ix, my emphasis). There are no reliable estimates of the numbers of rural labour migrants in the two countries with the largest 'peasant' populations in the world, China and India. In China official statistics count as farmers 'those formally registered by the government as rural residents', including some '150 million people registered as peasants who work away from home in industry and services ... and another 150 million who work off-farm near home' (Huang *et al.* 2012, 142). In this extreme case, 'rural labour beyond the farm', as I term it, comprises perhaps some 300 million workers officially designated as 'peasants'! On rurally-based classes of labour in India, see Lerche (2010, 2013); also Harriss-White (2012) who 'takes the part of the petty commodity producer', both rural and urban, while arguing that the peasantry in India has disappeared even though class differentiation in the countryside measured by agrarian accumulation is more or less frozen, in her view.

For this reason I am also sceptical about many guesstimates of the number and pro-portions of populations (especially non-farmers) supplied with food staples from small-scale farming, together with associated claims that because there are so many peasants/small farmers even modest increases in their output would add substantially to aggregate food supply (e.g., Altieri 2008, 2010). Is there any systematic evidence for either of these crucial positions? In posing this question I should make it clear that my scepticism does not extend to those I would classify as dynamic petty (and not so petty) commodity producers. As an agricultural economist wrote about sub-Saharan Africa:

> if access to markets [as promoted by neoliberal 'reform' but long preceding it] were much or all of the story, then all farmers in any given locality should be able to benefit. But do they? Social differentiation among the peasantry is no longer a fashionable area of inquiry, so case studies published during the last decade tend to be weak on such differences. What is reported, though, confirms our worst fears: differences are substantial. When and where farm economies blossom, it seems that *the great bulk of the marketed surplus comes from a small fraction of the farmers* ... (Wiggins 2000, 638, emphasis added)

And peasant 'community'?

Peasant 'community' is another central and potent trope in (some) discourses of agrarian populism that is carried into FS. The principles attributed to it include cooperation (as above), reciprocity, egalitarianism and the values of (highly) localised identity.[30] Its emble-matic instances frequently centre on food, for example in the sharing and exchange of seeds (Isakson 2009, Altieri 2010, Bezner Kerr 2010), pooling of labour in cultivation,[31] and redistribution of food from households with a surplus, when this occurs, to those with a deficit, as well as instances of (political) solidarity. At the same time, 'community'

---

[30]Among the many discursive functions of notions of 'community' is that of an original state of grace, whose integrity can only be violated by 'external' malevolence. This was a common trope in 'doc-trines of development' (Cowen and Shenton 1996) applied in colonial Africa to try to limit class for-mation and manage social order, based in ostensibly indigenous authority ('indirect rule'; see also Cowen and Shenton 1991, and note 33 below). There is more than an echo of this in some populist views of the subversion of peasant community by the 'external' forces of market and state. More gen-erally, invocations of 'community' (and the local) often seem to resemble the young Marx's view of religion as 'the heart of a heartless world, and the soul of soulless conditions' (Marx 1843/2009) – and the opium of some intellectuals? There is a broader theoretical issue here which can only be signalled rather than discussed further, stemming from the Chayanovian construction of 'peasant economy' from a model of the *individual* household. This generates two problems. One is the analysis of the 'inside' of the household: its mode of economic calculation or its 'logic', 'rules' and the 'balances' it strives for, in the terms of Ploeg's restatement of a Chayanovian perspective (Ploeg 2013), but *not its social relations*, most evidently those of gender which Ploeg largely omits. The other is the problem of formulating on this basis any adequate collective notion of 'peasants' beyond an aggregate of individual households. Is it significant that the collective term 'peasantry' is relatively little used these days (an exception being the title of Ploeg 2008)? 'Peasantry', in fact, tends to be applied much more, and more accurately, to those historic cases in which peasants *can* be defined as a *class* (of labour) in relation to classes and institutions of surplus-appropriating (precapitalist) landed property (feudalism, and the like). In short, there is a strategic analytical vacuum here which generalised and ideologically appealing, if little specified, notions of 'community' serve to fill (or conceal).

[31]Although pooling of labour, once a reciprocal customary practice, can become a means of 'dis-guised' exploitation between households differentiated as a result of commodification, as Mamdani (1987) pointed out and illustrated.

usually exemplifies a 'strategic essentialism' (Mollinga 2010) in FS discourse, as in popu-list discourse more widely, which obscures consideration of contradictions within 'communities'.

In short, it remains (like so much else) under-theorised; whether class differentiation is strongly marked or not, 'community' and its reproduction is always likely to involve ten-sions of gender and intergenerational relations. The former are widely recognised, the latter less so.[32] In their brilliant comparative essay on 'intergenerational tensions resulting from two differently configured crises of social reproduction' in Côte d'Ivoire and Sierra Leone, Chauveau and Richards (2008, 546, emphasis added) conclude that

> In the one case (class-stratified agrarian communities on the western flank of the Upper Guinea Forest), failure fully to incorporate a social underclass has resulted in iconoclastic violence tar-geting customary rural institutions.... In the other case – the egalitarian communities at the core of the UGF – room for expansion on an extensive forest frontier gave lineage heads scope to adapt custom to their financial requirements for reproducing a younger generation. Urban econ-omic failure then forced this younger generation back home, and a crisis of reincorporation resulted.... A fundamental contrast between the ethnic violence associated with the war in Côte d'Ivoire and the class-based violence targeted against chiefly families in Sierra Leone, perpetrated by *two groups of young men otherwise similar in their poverty and hyper-mobility*, thus comes into focus.

The point, of course, is not that this applies in the same ways and in equal measure to all rural communities, rather that Chauveau and Richards theorise and distinguish, in consider-able depth, two particular instances of the contradictions of rural community that may be 'extreme' but are not necessarily 'exceptional', to deploy the formulation of Mahmood Mamdani (1987). A similar point seems to be implied by Saturnino Borras and Jennifer Franco (2010, 115, emphasis added) when they note that in many places the 'rural poor do not have access to and/or control over land resources, which are usually under the control of landed classes, the state *or the community*', the last presumably referring to those 'local elites' constituted within, or through, the social inequalities of 'community'.[33]

Capital's (agroecologial) other and its 'emblematic instances'

There have been important developments in agroecology in recent decades that subvert inherited equilibrium concepts of environmental processes, not least in the semi-arid

---

[32]In FS literature, see, for example, Bezner Kerr (2010) and the Movimento dos Trabalhadores Sem terra (Landless Workers Movement - MST) activist Itelvina Masioli, who emphasises 'all the patriar-chal values that are so strong in our rural societies' (Masioli and Nicholson 2010, 41). Theorising gender relations involves more than acknowledging their centrality, of course; for a fine example of confronting the intricate ways in which gender and class dynamics intersect in a particular social context, see O'Laughlin (2009).

[33]This is a hot topic in South Africa and elsewhere in sub-Saharan Africa, because of the (growing?) claims on 'community' land and other resources made by chiefs – on South Africa, see Claassens (2013), and, on Ghana, Grischow (2008), who shows the alarming replay of ideologies of colonial indirect rule in the 1920s and 1930s in today's development discourses of 'community' and its 'social capital'. In her essay on Malawi, Rachel Bezner Kerr (2010, 134, 147) suggests that 'the social dynamics surrounding seeds are an important element in struggles for food sovereignty between men and women, different generations, [and] communities' as well as 'the state, scientists and private corporations', and that while 'Community and kin networks remain a viable and important source of seed for many smallholder farmers... these networks are fraught with contestations that leave landless peasants, young women and AIDS-affected families with less access and control over seed'.

tropics, and contribute to a better understanding of the farming practices of those who inhabit them. For sub-Saharan Africa, a key work in this respect was the long-term historical study by Fairhead and Leach (1996) of the 'forest-savanna mosaic', albeit a study limited by its neglect of political economy as was much of a collection they inspired to challenge 'received wisdom on the African environment' (Leach and Mearns 1996, and see Bernstein and Woodhouse 2001). Interestingly, some key 'emblematic instances' of the virtues of small-scale farming centre on areas of high population densities, for example 'along the Sahara's edge, in Nigeria, Niger, Senegal, Burkina Faso and Kenya' (Lim 2008), and in the Central Plateau of Burkina Faso and southern Niger (Reij 2006; both authors cited by McMichael 2010).

All this research contributes to longstanding debate between views of Africa as both 'over-populated' and 'under-populated'. The former is associated with Malthusian 'crisis narratives' of environmental degradation ('over-grazing' and 'desertification', 'deforestation' in the expansion of cultivation frontiers). The latter is associated with various counter-Malthusian currents. For example, Boserup (1965) famously associated African female-centred farming systems with low population densities, hence the lack of demographic pressure on land-intensive types of technical innovation, while the study of Machakos District in Kenya by Tiffen et al. (1994) reported a six-fold growth of population over six decades with increases in the productivity of land as well as growth of incomes, signalled in the title of their book as *More people, less erosion*.[34]

This study serves as an emblematic instance for Lim (2008), although he does not cite it (and strangely includes Machakos on the edge of the Sahara). How convincingly Tiffen et al. (1994) provide an example of capital's other is another matter. First, their thesis is that this happy outcome – 'Malthus controverted' (Tiffen and Mortimore 1994) – is driven by neither agroecological nor 'community' values but is the result of farmers seizing *market* opportunities and investing in conservation to enhance land-intensive productivity and the profit it yields, helped by provision of such public goods as education which do not 'distort' market signals. In short, they did not see farmers in Machakos as capital's other but rather as exemplars of *Homo economicus*. Second, and putting aside this interpretation, a subsequent study by Andrew Murton (1999) presented three strategic qualifications to the *evidence* for the Tiffen thesis. First, he investigated the distribution of non-farm income, of investment in conservation and farm productivity, and of land, in Machakos, which revealed aspects of social differentiation missed (or ignored) by Tiffen and her co-workers.[35] Second, funds from urban employment provided the strategic source of farm and conservation investment. Third, this has an important historical/generational aspect (easily and often overlooked), namely that the pioneers of such investment were in a far stronger position to reproduce and expand their farming enterprises than poorer contemporaries and subsequent generations. Murton presents a picture of Machakos comprising both Boserup-type innovation under demographic pressure and productivity growth by wealthier farmers (the success story highlighted by Tiffen) and a reproduction

---

[34]Note also Clark and Haswell (1964), one of a number of counter-Malthusian, and indeed natalist, texts by the Roman Catholic Clark, a pioneering economic statistician and development economist, in this case co-authored with an agricultural economist of West Africa. The 'under-population' position has been overtaken by current rates of demographic growth in sub-Saharan Africa, the highest of any major region, as are its rates of urbanisation (Severino and Ray 2011). Pauline Peters (2004) provides a valuable survey and analysis of class and other social dynamics driving increasing conflict over land in sub-Saharan Africa.

[35]See also the critical comments by Dianne Rocheleau (1995).

squeeze on the poor who experience 'a detrimental and involutionary cycle of declining yields, declining soil fertility and diminishing returns to labour, as first phase conservation and productivity gains are overtaken by population growth' (Murton 1999, 34). This example illustrates issues of political economy that need to be investigated for (other) 'emblematic instances' of the rationality ('good practice') of (undifferentiated) 'peasants'/small farmers claimed by FS advocates.[36]

This applies to another pertinent African example, concerning land rehabilitation and water conservation in the Sahel following the droughts of the 1970s, presented as an emblematic instance of peasant 'adaptation' to adverse ecological conditions by McMichael, above, citing a two-page presentation by Reij (2006). In a fuller study, published by International Food Policy Research Institute (IFPRI) (a CGIAR (Consultative Group on International Agricultural Research) institution), Reij *et al.* (2009, 1) analyse 'two agroenvironmental success stories in the West African Sahel': 'the relatively well-documented story of farmer-managed soil and water conservation...in the densely populated Central Plateau of Burkina Faso', and 'the still incompletely documented story of farmer-managed restoration of agroforestry parklands in heavily populated parts of Niger' since the mid-1980s. They attribute success to a 'win-win' coalition of 'charismatic leaders, both farmers and development agents' who 'played key roles in diffusing the innovations', Reij *et al.* (2009, 9) supportive government policy and public investment, the role of NGOs, and Dutch, German, IFAD and World Bank project funding; in short, a rather broader coalition of actors than the peasants exclusively highlighted by McMichael (2010, 175–6) – and a coalition that transgresses the boundaries of the FS binary?

Whatever the achievements of land rehabilitation in the Sahel, they are highly labour-intensive and the aggregate yield gains reported by Reij *et al.* (2009) in a region of growing population, and population density, do not suggest a sizeable surplus available to feed non-farmers.[37] The last also applies to a different kind of emblematic instance, in a very different context, provided by Ryan Isakson's account (2009) of *milpa* – maize, legumes, squash and herb polyculture – in the highlands of Guatemala. He argues that *milpa* cultivation contributes to (global) 'food sovereignty' through the 'conservation of agrodiversity'. At the same time, he shows that it is 'subsistence-oriented' and 'self-sufficient', *and* combined by those who practise it with the sale of labour power, increasingly through long-distance labour migration, and petty commodity production in farming and crafts (as well as active involvement in land markets, both locally and further afield in Guatemala). In effect, the reproduction of *milpa* cultivation is possible only through (necessary) engagement in commodity relations. How, and how much, its practitioners are able to negotiate such engagement may leave them some space for 'choice', including their rejection of 'the complete commodification of food' and the uncertainties of dependence on markets for obtaining food (Isakson 2009, 755). However, and the other side of this same coin, *milpa* cultivation does *not*

---

[36]In this respect, contrast, for example, the study by Fairhead and Leach (1996), cited earlier, with that of H.L. Moore and Vaughan (1994). The issues advised here are exemplified in a new generation of theoretically informed and empirically grounded agrarian political economy, for example, the important series of articles on Senegal by Carlos Oya (2001, 2004, 2007); see also Mueller (2011), Oya's more general surveys of agriculture in sub-Saharan Africa (2010, 2012), and the excellent survey of Southeast Asia by Hall *et al.* (2011).

[37]Also, the 'relatively high labour demand of "improved indigenous" methods used in the Sahel to bring "degraded" soils back into cultivation – between 40 and 80 work-days per hectare treated with *tassa* or *zwai* pits – will evidently strongly favour those capable of hiring labour' (Woodhouse 2012, 109).

contribute to FS in the sense of producing food surplus to the needs of those who pursue 'self-provisioning'.

In short, what I termed above an abstract and unitary conception of 'peasants' is actualised in FS discourse through farming practices that exemplify their virtues as capital's other: the 'emblematic instance' of acroecological principles at work. Many (most?) of these instances or illustrations concern what Robert Chambers (1983) called 'resource poor farmers' who, in his conception, typically inhabit difficult (and remote) rural environments, thereby leaving out those who are 'resource poor' because of processes of differentiation.[38] These emblematic instances deployed by FS are usually short on socioeconomic detail (Isakson being an exception), but they suggest that (1) virtuous farming is practised mainly by the poorest farmers who confront major ecological and social constraints rather than 'choosing' to farm how they do and 'choosing' to remain poor, pace the virtues of 'frugality';[39] (2) what they do is mostly low-(external) input and highly labour-intensive 'subsistence' farming – precisely the virtues acclaimed by FS, and undoubtedly requiring great knowledge, ingenuity and skill,[40] and/or (3) a key condition of possibility of these ways of farming is activity in, and income from, other types of integration in commodity relations, and especially labour migration (often not reported or considered).

For FS, those viewed as the rearguard of farmers, the standard of 'backwardness', in conventional narratives of modernity, become the vanguard; in Robert Chambers' biblical invocation, 'putting the last first' (1983). When capital's (agroecological) other is exemplified by practices of 'subsistence', 'self-sufficiency' and 'self-provisioning' versus surplus production, this suggests a fundamental problem for FS.

A different kind of emblematic instance is provided by a sub-category of farmers different from the great majority in arid West Africa and Central American uplands. They are no doubt mostly 'dynamic petty (and not so petty) commodity producers' (above), held to exemplify Ploeg's 'peasant principle', that is, they aim to (1) minimise external inputs, hence the degree of their integration in upstream markets (domination by upstream capitals), (2) find ways of selling their commodities other than in markets dominated by food 'Empire' capitals, and (3) create new (commodity) products and services, both food and non-food (e.g., agro-tourism). This is the space of 'resistance of the third kind', manifested in 'adaptive' change and innovation as noted earlier, on which I can only comment briefly here.

First, one must note that some of these emblematic instances centre on highly specialised commodity production, like the Parmesan cheese and *Chianina* beef producers of Italy (Ploeg *et al.* 2012). Second, some rely on state support of various kinds, and indeed small- (and medium-) farmer-friendly policies and funding are a central plank of (new) 'Rural Development' (Ploeg *et al.* 2012). Third, spaces of 'room for manoeuvre' in markets are

---

[38]Indeed the (second) 'emblematic instance' of land reclamation in the Sahel (above) fits very well with concerns and programmes within 'mainstream' development to reach and support 'resource poor farmers', and to ameliorate/end rural poverty, especially when this proceeds through 'participatory' methods of research, innovation and community mobilisation, of which Chambers (1983, Chambers *et al.* 1989) has long been a leading advocate.

[39]And, of course, 'choosing' to leave the countryside and/or to leave farming, not the same thing as Murphy's ethnography of Wanzai County, Jiangxi Province, China, shows so well (Murphy 2002). For different views of rural out-migration as an issue in the generational reproduction of farming by two scholars of Southeast Asia, see Rigg (2006) and White (2011).

[40]As well as 'drudgery', in Chayanov's term. Kitching (2001, 147) suggests that peasants are 'the historically classical and demographically dominant example of people who are poor *because* they work so hard'.

a concern for capitals of all scales – large, medium and small. Some large-scale farmers, depending on circumstances, have shifted to low- and no-tillage cultivation when subject to cost-price inflation of machinery and fuel. Fourth, the pragmatic edge of 'resistance of the third kind'/'rightful resistance' is subsumed, together with many types of economic calculation and practice, under the encompassing belief that what unites all farmers, at least potentially, is the pursuit of more or less significant 'autonomy' from markets, their 'dull compulsions' (in Marx's term) and disciplines. This claim from first principles that what farmers do (throughout modern history? history *tout court?*) is driven by the desire for autonomy is a matter of faith, in which there are believers and non-believers. Fifth is the vexed question of so-called 'pluriactivity' (a term of bureaucratic resonance and maybe provenance too?), and the highly contentious assumption that periodic or regular waged and salaried work is a(nother) kind of *choice* that rural families make in order to continue to produce, and to live, as more or less autonomous/independent farmers.[41] This leads Ploeg and Ye (2010) to a strikingly benign interpretation of rural labour migration and its driving forces in China since the 1980s.[42]

Finally, the principal thrust here is again to champion the success of yield-enhancing types of farming, largely ignoring issues of labour productivity which, nonetheless, is likely to be substantially higher in emblematic instances of the second kind than of the first.[43]

Transforming the world food system?

FS aims for an 'ecological basis of citizenship', an 'agrarian citizenship' that responds to 'specialization with diversification, to efficiency with sufficiency and to commoditization with sovereignty' (Wittman 2010, 91, 95) and calls for a radical 'democratization of the food system in favour of the poor and underserved' (Holt-Giménez and Shattuck 2010, 76, also McMichael 2010, 174), that includes relocalising markets and governance (Fairbairn 2010, 27). How this might be achieved includes the challenges of regulating transnational agribusiness and international trade in order to 'protect' 'domestic food production' and small farmers as 'guardians of the commons' (McMichael 2010, 170–2), and the challenges for 'agrarian citizens' to enact 'horizontal relationships within and between communities (social capital) and local ecologies (ecological capital) as well as connecting vertically with broader communities encompassing "humanity" and the "environment"' (Wittman 2010, 103).[44] A common term for realising the ambitions of the passage from local to national and global is 'scaling up'.

---

[41] A step forward, in my view, would simply be to replace 'pluriactivity' with the descriptive term 'part-time farmers'. The latter, of course, would contain a very wide range of types in class and other social terms from, say, urban professionals who do 'weekend farming' to the marginal farmers/'footloose labour' of the countrysides of the South. They could then be identified, distinguished, researched and explained more adequately, rather than subsumed as so many instances of 'pluriactivity'.

[42] Interpretations of change in contemporary rural China as part of a process of primitive accumulation, variously conceived but centred on industrial and urban development, are provided by Harvey 2003, Walker and Buck 2007, Pun Ngai and Lu Huilin 2010, and Webber 2012; see also Rachel Murphy's ethnography of *How migrant labour is changing rural China* (2002; cited in note 39 above) and note 29 above.

[43] Schneider and Niederle (2010, 390, note 11) point out that one 'Rural Development' initiative, Brazil's 'More Food Programme – linked to the second kind of emblematic instance – 'financed the purchase of almost 13,000 tractors for family farmers across the country' in the space of nine months.

[44] To characterise local farming systems in terms of 'social *capital*' and 'ecological *capital*' is a discursive own goal – seeing like capital? (McMichael 2009, 162).

Farming and agriculture

It is useful to start here with a distinction between 'farming' and 'agriculture', alluded to earlier but not yet explained. While farming is what farmers do and have always done – with all the historical diversity of forms of farm production, their social and ecological conditions and practices, labour processes, and so on – agriculture or the 'agricultural sector' emerged in the period of industrial capitalism from the 1870s sketched above, and was manifested in the first IFR. By 'agriculture' I mean

> farming *together with* all those economic interests, and their specialized institutions and activities, 'upstream' and 'downstream' of farming that affect the activities and reproduction of farmers. 'Upstream' refers to how the conditions of production are secured before farming itself can begin. This includes the supply of instruments of labour or 'inputs' (tools, fertilizers, seeds) as well as markets for land, labour, and credit – and crucially, of course, the mobilization of labour. 'Downstream' refers to what happens to crops and animals when they leave the farm – their marketing, processing and distribution and how those activities affect farmers' incomes, necessary to reproduce themselves. Powerful agents upstream and downstream of farming in capitalist agriculture today are exemplified by agri-input capital and agro-food capital respectively. (Bernstein 2010a, 65 and Ch. 4 *passim*)

This gives an analytical purpose to the distinction, which I have followed consistently in the text of this paper, rather than the common practice of using 'farming' and 'agriculture' as synonyms.

The distinction is highly relevant to any FS programme, and also points towards another fundamental problem signalled earlier. First, capital's other in FS discourse centres above all (and sometimes, it seems, exclusively) on (re-)affirming particular types of *farming* against *agriculture* in the forms of its most recent development: corporate, industrial and global. What then are its programmatic proposals?

'Scaling up' #1

The answer appears more straightforward, 'upstream' when the model of virtue is farming that is intensive in terms of (indigenous) knowledge *and* labour, and using 'organic and local resources' hence independent of 'external inputs', especially agro-chemicals (Altieri 2010, 120). In effect, little is required upstream than cannot be sourced locally, and enhanced via the 'scaling up' of 'farmer-to-farmer' networks to share and disseminate knowledge of agroecological good practices, including sharing seeds.[45] At the same time, it is often explicit that the goal of this type of farming is indeed self-provisioning of households and local communities, for which food sovereignty guarantees their food security (and social reproduction).

'Scaling up' #2

There remain two further critical questions, therefore. The first, already touched on, is whether a surplus to their own food needs, and how much of a surplus, low (external)-

---

[45]'Family' labour supply as an 'upstream' constraint is often overlooked, though see notes 27, 31 and 37 above; also, for example, in Brazil 'When the [MST] communities...do achieve access to land, the huge majority hardly have enough labour power' (Masioli and Nicholson 2010, 36). A major issue lurking here, hinted at earlier and that remains unavoidable, and perhaps irresolvable, for a general (Chayanovian-type) model, is the supply and uses of labour, and returns to labour, within the individual 'family' labour farm.

input, labour-intensive producers, geared to 'self-provisioning' (and autonomy), can provide to those who are not food growers, the majority of the world's population today, to satisfy their food security. Even supposing that an adequate surplus was possible, the second question that follows is the downstream one: how will that surplus reach non-farmers and on what terms? In effect, the rather large jump in 'scaling up' from individual and local small farm production to feeding 'broader communities' like 'humanity' (*sic*, Wittman, 2010) points to 'the market question' in which capitalism registers an unprecedented achievement in human history, resolving Phase B of the Malthusian cycle (above) if, as always, in profoundly contradictory and unequal ways. This also points to relations between the (non-identical) pairings/oppositions of rural and urban, and agricultural and industrial, on which FS has little to say to date, other than to remark on the predatory nature of the urban on the rural, and to hope that 'protecting' more labour-intensive (and presumably more remunerative) small-scale farming would help stem migration from the countryside (and encourage 're-peasantisation'). Some FS advocates recognise the urgency of the downstream, for example, 'Food sovereignty was not designed as a concept only for farmers, but for people...[there is a] need to strengthen the urban-rural dialogue' (Wittman *et al.* 2010, 7, quoting *La Vía Campesina*), and FS advocates 'technical and material alternatives that suit the needs of small-scale producers and low-income consumers' Altieri (2010, 129).

However, does FS have any answer to the downstream question, other than formulations of more 'equitable' (socially or nationally 'owned'?) markets: 'the right of nations and peoples to control...their own own markets' (Wittman *et al.* 2010, p. 2), 'marketing and processing activities' that operate through 'equitable market opportunities': 'fair trade, local commercialization and distribution schemes, fair prices and other mechanisms that link farmers and consumers and consumers more directly and in solidarity' (Altieri 2010, 130), and so on? This is a wish list that slides past, rather than confronts, the contradictions intrinsic to all commodity relations and markets, and expresses the larger problem of FS before the central issue, explained so clearly by Woodhouse (2010). That concerns the relationships between (1) the productivity of labour in farming, (2) farm incomes, and (3) food prices for those who have to buy their food (including many rural people) – what can (approximately) be termed the questions of production, rural poverty and food distribution.

The first, productivity of labour, is key because it focuses attention on how many people each person farming (or farming household, community, etc.) can feed beyond satisfying her/their own food security.[46] This does not require embracing any 'hyper-productivity' of labour in industrial agriculture (Weis 2010), but it does require avoiding the fetish of the inverse relationship of farm size and yield (commended by Altieri 2010, 122; see Woodhouse 2010 and references therein). The second element – farm incomes – is, or should be, central to the FS programme [as it is to Ploeg's (2013) 'Chayanovian manifesto'; Altieri (2010), 126, 130, on the 'very poor', also emphasising rural employment creation], however tempered by favoured 'values' of frugality and sufficiency; indeed, as noted earlier, it resonates a longstanding concern within 'standard' development

---

[46]Acknowledged implicitly by Altieri (2010, 126–8) who contrasts the case (limiting case, in my view) of (now rare) *chinampa* wetland cultivation of maize in Mexico from which 'each farmer can support twelve to fifteen people', with terrace cultivation in highland southern Peru 'requiring about 350–500 worker days per hectare in a given year'. Most cultivation by poor farmers in the South, like the large numbers in the arid and semi-arid tropics, comes much closer to Altieri's second example of labour intensity (and productivity) than his first example.

discourse to ameliorate/end rural poverty (famously, Lipton 1977 and the debate on 'urban bias' it provoked; see more recently IFAD 2011). The third element centres on how markets would work, and what kinds of market reforms could plausibly meet the needs of *both* small farmers and food consumers, especially low-income consumers (Altieri 2010). If capital has a long history of sacrificing ecology in order to make food 'cheap' (to reduce the reproduction costs of labour, hence wages), the vast numbers of poor (net) food consumers today, urban and rural, need affordable as well as adequate supplies of (healthy) food. The most obvious way to try to end the poverty of small farmers is to *subsidise* their production; there are various historical examples of this, and it is recommended once more in contemporary conditions by Julio Boltvinik (2012).[47] Other things being equal, however, this would raise the price of food (as Boltvinik recognises), hence a need too to *subsidise* the food requirements of the vast numbers of poor consumers (of which there are also some experiences). This seems to be a nettle that FS prefers to avoid grasping. It certainly implies a central role for governments that I come back to shortly.

Traditional and modern technologies

Altieri (2010) uses the term 'traditional' comprehensively to characterise and commend the virtues of 'peasant'/small-scale farming, and the agroecological wisdom accumulated in its knowledges and practices. Its productivity 'may be low, but the cause appears to be social, not technical' (Altieri 2010, 126), although what this means is not clear. Beyond enhancing the capacities of small farmers based in 'tradition' through farmer-to-farmer 'scaling up', he also refers to 'the millions of poor farmers yet untouched by modern agricultural technology' (Altieri 2010, 131), although it is not clear here whether he considers this a good thing or a bad thing. If the latter, then what 'modern agricultural technology' might poor farmers benefit from, and how will it reach them?

Probably the single most potent focus of current dispute concerning the virtues and vices of 'traditional' and 'modern' technologies is GM seed. GMOs are almost universally condemned by FS, but a more nuanced view is found in the innovative and careful work of Jack Kloppenburg. In exploring the concept of 'seed sovereignty' as a programmatic possibility in the form of a 'protected' versus 'open access' commons, he points to a wider potential constituency than farmers, especially progressive plant scientists (one of the inspirations of ideas about 'open source' seed innovation, exchange and multiplication). He also advises rethinking 'rejectionist positions towards the techniques and products of biotechnology... A failure to distinguish between biotechnology and *corporate* biotechnology has too often led to impoverishment of debate' along the fault lines of binary utopias and dystopias (Kloppenburg 2010a, 381). Kloppenburg's approach suggests a perspective on farming

---

[47]Boltvinik's paper will be published in a forthcoming collection from Zed Books, edited by him, Farshad Araghi and Susan Archer Mann, which also contains a revised version of Bernstein (2012b) that engages with Boltvinik's argument concerning 'peasant persistence and poverty'. More generally, the exposure of farmers to the vagaries of both subsidy regimes and price fluctuations seems to have been considered more concretely for market dynamics in the North, for example, by Nicholson (Masioli and Nicholson 2009, 40) on milk production in the Basque country where 'the bad news is that we are losing a lot of farmers today. And not only small family farmers, but big farmers also cannot compete'. He also points to the problem of European countries like Austria and France that have (some) policies apparently conducive to sustainability and others that encourage agro-industry and competitive export agriculture.

technologies that transcends the binary of 'traditional' and 'modern', itself inherited from much criticised paradigms of 'modernisation'.[48]

And the state...

This is really 'the elephant in the room' of the programmatic aspirations of FS, and one little problematised or explored beyond appeals to states to intervene to support small farmers, and more broadly to resolve the 'tensions between socially equitable development and eco-logically sound conservation' (Altieri 2010, 131). This would encompass a range of effec-tive policies and practices, from regulating international (and domestic) trade in food commodities, to protecting and promoting small-scale farming, to 'scaling up' from the local to the national – *and* to subsidise both (small) farm incomes and consumer prices for food sourced from small farmers (above)? – in short, a list of demands that no modern state has satisfied.

This appeal to such comprehensive and progressive state action is launched in a histori-cal context in which most states most of the time are deeply implicated in the ongoing march of capitalism (and once state socialism) 'against the peasant', as some FS analyses emphasise. Indeed, as indicated earlier, the immediate target of much agrarian populism historically – as movements as well as ideology – was not capitalism but rather the state. Perhaps this is why McMichael (2010, 171, emphasis added) describes 'agrarian citizen-ship' as a *'tactic* appealing to the authority of the state to protect farmers', albeit a 'tactic' that has to confront a fundamental *strategic* lacuna in any plausible political programme.[49]

There are few examples to date of governments claiming to adopt FS. Wittman *et al.* (2010a, 9) provide a summary of Ecuador where the 'Organic Law on the Food Sovereignty Regime' in 2009 was partly vetoed by the country's president 'citing concerns about the ban on GMOs, consequences of changes in land ownership structures and issues related to the production of agrofuels'. Moreover, the month before the law on FS, the National Assembly passed a new Mining Law 'to spur extraction in new areas by national and inter-national companies'. Probably Venezuela is a more appropriate test case, with very differ-ent assessments of its experience in pursuit of (national) FS since the late 1990s by Schiavoni and Camacaro (2009) and Kappeler (2013).[50]

---

[48]If now stood on its head: from modern 'good'/traditional 'bad' to traditional 'good'/'modern 'bad'. This is a common effect of how such binaries work in the construction of ideology; see also Oya (2013b, 514–5).

[49]He continues that agrarian citizenship is 'a strategic intervention in the politics of development insofar as it advocates for peasant-farmer rights to *initiate* social reproduction of the economic and ecological foundations of society' – an eloquent formulation that makes no advance concerning the modalities of achieving the (programmatic) aim it articulates.

[50]Analysing the effects of government policies always presents demands of methods and evidence. A topical instance relevant here is the critical assessment of the FAO's latest *State of Food Insecurity* (2012) by a collective organised by Small Planet (2013). The latter suggests seven countries as examples of reducing hunger significantly, a somewhat unlikely group comprising Ghana, Thailand, Vietnam, Indonesia, Brazil, China and Bangladesh (and from which Venezuela is absent). Their success is attributed to progressive policies concerning farming and/or social protection, and the report cites Oxfam (2010) as one of its sources. Here is part of what Oxfam (2010, 25–6, emphases added) said about Vietnam: 'The take-off started with agricultural land reform, followed by labour-intensive manufacturing development and, more recently, promotion of electronics and high-tech sectors in *the hope of becoming an industrialized country* by 2020. *Integration into the global market* facilitated the increases in exports and foreign investment. Once a rice importer, Viet Nam

And some boundary issues

FS distances itself from other perspectives on farming, agriculture and food, to reinforce its distinctiveness and its radicalism – to guard its 'boundaries', so to speak. Thus its central binary: agroecological 'peasant' farming versus corporate industrial agriculture, the (rural) local versus the global of capital, sustainability versus unsustainability, and so on. One important instance of this is the opposition to 'food security' as articulated by 'mainstream' international organisations (e.g., Fairbairn 2010, McMichael 2010). Another is the dangers of the 'greening' of agribusiness and parts of its food system to defuse the demands of environmental movements and to maintain/expand market shares and profits (Fairbairn 2010, 18, citing Friedmann 2005). More specific examples include warnings against the seductions of promoting niche production in the South for the higher end of Northern consumer markets (Altieri 2010, 130–1), 'green' land-grabbing that displaces farmers (and pastoralists), turning them into 'conservation refugees' (Wittman 2010, 102, see also Brockington 2009, and the contributions to the themed issue of the *Journal of Peasant Studies* 39(2), Fairhead *et al.* 2012); the methods of 'climate proofing' advocated by 'the development industry...as a new profit frontier' (McMichael 2010, 174), and the problems of ostensibly more inclusive (private) property rights in biological materials (Kloppenburg 2010b).

However, the radical project of FS cannot be adequately imagined, let alone feasibly pursued, while ignoring or bypassing so much of the agrarian history of the modern world, other than to frame it through selective aspects of agriculture in contemporary neo-liberal globalisation, and sometimes in the longer histories of 'capitalism against the peasant'. Several relevant examples noted in passing include the apparently dismissive stance of FS advocates towards the wide range of perspectives and policies concerning farming and agriculture in modern history, and the rich and complex *experiences* of their operation, for example, in support of the interests of (small) farmers/petty commodity producers and/or food consumers, or against them, or – as is so common, or ubiquitous – contradictory in their conceptions, modalities, and effects.

As a political project, FS both promotes emblematic instances of (organised) political 'resistance' (among others, Desmarais 2002, McMichael 2006, Wittman 2010 on campaigns against 'green deserts') and confronts a classic issue of radical politics: how the FS movement positions itself in relation to the established powers of states and international bodies (the UN, the FAO, IFAD, the CGIAR, the World Bank) in order to try to push them in the direction it desires, with all the dangers of co-option and compromise, of the blurring of boundaries, that might entail.[51]

From project to programme?

The 'downstream' problem is well stated by Altieri (2010, 128–9, emphases added):

---

is now the *second biggest exporter* in the world. How has this been achieved? Public support to smallholder agriculture was an important factor. The de-collectivization of property and the *opening up to fertilizer imports (use of which tripled due to lower prices)* allowed food production to increase exponentially.'

[51]In the specific case of the struggle against agrofuels, Holt-Giménez and Shattuck (2010, 87) attempt to grasp this nettle with their (unlikely) suggestion that there are 'potential allies from those sectors in the food and energy industries (e.g., some petroleum companies, the meat industry and supermarket chains) that oppose agrofuels' albeit that they also 'seek to concentrate their own power over food systems'.

The development of sustainable agriculture requires significant structural changes *in addition to* technological innovation and farmer-to-farmer solidarity. This is impossible without *social movements* that create the *political* will among decision-makers to dismantle and transform the institutions and regulations that presently hold back sustainable agricultural development...ecological change in agriculture cannot be promoted without comparable *changes in the social, political, cultural and economic* arenas that conform [sic] and determine agriculture.[52]

Here I can only note the complexities inherent in the sociology of such movements, and that bear on the politics of forging and pursuing a viable programme. Some of that analytical agenda has been well defined by some FS advocates, or at least sympathisers, concerning movements at local and national levels (e.g., Edelman 2002, Conclusion) and transnationally (e.g., Borras *et al.* 2008b). One aspect of complexity is the intricate class contours of 'peasant' countrysides, how they intersect with inequalities of gender, generation and ethnicity (for example, *indigènes* and 'strangers' in so many rural locales in sub-Saharan Africa), and the effects for multi-class social movements. Another aspect of complexity is the diverse range of issues and sometimes conflicting goals – more and less specific, larger and smaller, bearing on different social interests – that are bracketed together as expressions of a unitary 'peasant way'.

A different issue in the construction of a (global) social movement focussed on a common programme is that of international leadership, organisation and direction, especially in the face of the massively concentrated powers invested or complicit in the global food system, and the global effects of its 'accelerating biophysical contradictions'. Here it is striking that one of *La Vía Campesina*'s 'central characteristics is the in-principle absence of a policy-making secretariat...of a sovereign authority dictating what any member organization can do' (Patel 2010, 193). There may be very sound grounds for this, philosophically and practically, but it also has consequences, as indicated by Joan Martinez-Alier. A central foundation of his construction of Ecological Economics is the incommensurability of values, hence opposition to the market-based 'pricing' (or shadow pricing) of environmental 'goods' and effects central to conventional Environmental Economics. Nonetheless, he concludes *The environmentalism of the poor* (Martinez-Alier 2002, 271, emphasis added) with a notion of 'procedural power which, in the face of complexity is able nevertheless to *impose* a language of valuation determining which is the bottom-line in an ecological distribution conflict', and then asks 'Who then has the power to decide the procedure ... ? Who has the power to simplify complexity, ruling some languages of valuation out of order?'. Could it be that a new FS 'International in the making' or 'global agrarian resistance' needs a politbureau after all?

Conclusion

This paper concludes, for better or worse, with a stronger scepticism about aspects of FS than I had when I started writing it, albeit with considerably more interest in, and sympathy for, its agroecologists, their empirical knowledge of what farmers do and their activities as practitioners, than for its aspirations to 'grand theory' and its feel-goodism, sacrificing pessimism of the intellect to optimism of the will.[53] The grounds for that scepticism, I trust, are clear. They include a critique of any 'peasant way', of beliefs that 'peasants'

---

[52]And Patel (2010, 194): 'the prerequisites [for FS]...are a society in which the equality-distorting effects [sic] of sexism, patriarchy, racism and class power have been eradicated'.
[53]On which see, in a different context, some sharp reflections by Michael Burawoy (2010, 2011), on which I draw in Bernstein (2013b).

practising low (external)-input and labour-intensive farming, can feed current and projected world population, and of a failure of FS on the 'downstream' side necessary to move it forward from its constitutive binary, thesis and antithesis, towards a synthesis that yields a programme of 'transformation'. Moreover, I have argued that this failure is *intrinsic* given that FS discards crucial elements of agrarian political economy, of the political economy of capitalism more broadly, and of modern history, in order to establish its thesis and especially its antithesis: capital's other. And I have found the failure particularly surprising, and alarming, in relation to both the theorisation and historical investigation of the conditions of reproduction of peasantries (small farmers/petty commodity producers), including the lack of socioeconomic analysis of those acclaimed for their agroecological virtue. This might, in part, be an effect of the role in providing a key analytical 'frame' for FS of food regime analysis, given that its origins are located above all in the shaping of world food markets by the development of export agriculture in 'settler colonies' that lacked peasantries (as noted earlier).[54]

However, this scepticism is *not* a rejection of all that FS advocacy points to and bundles together. First, FS is only one instance, albeit a potent one, in challenging materialist (agrarian) political economy to take environmental change seriously, and in doing so to abandon mechanistic conceptions of farming in its own heritage (see Bernstein 2010b). Second, as noted, FS sweeps up so many topical issues and instances of struggle on which one can take a differentiated, and sympathetic, stance without accepting the overarching ('totalising'?) ambition of FS to transform the world food system via capital's other. Examples range from opposition to the inequalities of international trade in food and other agricultural commodities (and its highly selective 'liberalisation') and to aspects of international agribusiness, to support for resistance to 'land grabbing' for food farming, agrofuels, and mining. Such resistance is typically socially heterogeneous, involving multi-class movements, whose assessment always requires a 'concrete analysis of a concrete situation' rather than the ('verificationist') accumulation and celebration of the 'emblematic instance'. What counts here, as always, is trying to grasp the social dynamics and contradictions that generate such movements and that pervade them. Third, scepticism about FS does not preclude support for some instances of redistributive land reform, nor for those among (rurally-based) classes of labour whose farming, however marginal, is often crucial to their reproduction.[55] The point is that sympathy and solidarity in all such instances does not have to be predicated on, nor lead to, any belief in humanity's salvation through small-scale farming, and indeed is obscured by it.

References

Altieri, M.A. 2008. Small farms as a planetary ecological asset: five key reasons why we should support the revitalization of small farms in the Global South [online]. Available from: http://www.foodfirst.org/en/node/2115 [Accessed 2 April 2013].

---

[54]It might also be seen as 'ethnocentric' in this respect, as Peter Mollinga suggested to me (personal communication). The colonies in question were those of European settlement, and farming in Asia and Africa is largely ignored (more so perhaps than Latin America given its proximity to the North American epicentre of the first two IFRs).

[55]As should be clear from my review (Bernstein 2012a) of Scoones *et al.* (2010) on Zimbabwe, the world's most comprehensive redistributive land reform for a long time, creating spaces for the revival and expansion of dynamic petty commodity production and 'accumulation from below' (see also Scoones *et al.* 2012, and Hanlon *et al.* 2013) and for 'survivalist' farming that contributes to the reproduction of (rural) 'classes of labour'.

Altieri, M.A. 2010. Scaling up agroecological approaches to food sovereignty in Latin America. *In*: Wittman, Desmarais and Wiebe, eds. pp.120–33.

Altieri, M.A. and P. Rosset. 1999. Ten reasons why biotechnology will not ensure food security, protect the environment and reduce poverty in the developing world. *AgBioForum*, 2(3/4), 155–62.

Araghi, F. 2009. The invisible hand and the visible foot: peasants, dispossession and globalization. *In*: Akram-Lodhi and Kay, (eds) *Peasants and globalization. Political economy, rural transformation and the agrarian question*. London: Routledge, pp. 111–147.

Aston, T.H. and C.H.E. Philpin, eds. 1985. *The Brenner debate. Agrarian class structure and economic development in pre-industrial Europe*. Cambridge: Cambridge University Press.

Banaji, J. 2001. *Agrarian change in late antiquity: gold, labour and aristocratic dominance*. Oxford: Oxford University Press.

Banaji, J. 2010. *Theory as history. Essays on modes of production and exploitation*. Leiden: Brill.

Bello, W. 2009. *The food wars*. London: Verso.

Bello, W. and M. Baviera. 2010. Capitalist agriculture, the food price crisis & peasant resistance. *In*: Wittman, Desmarais and Wiebe, eds. pp. 62–75.

Berman, M. 1983. *All that is solid melts into air. The experience of modernity*. London: Verso.

Bernstein, H. 1996/7. Agrarian questions then and now. *Journal of Peasant Studies*, 24(1/2), 22–59.

Bernstein, H. 2009. V.I. Lenin and A.V. Chayanov: looking back, looking forward. *Journal of Peasant Studies* 36(1), 55–81.

Bernstein, H. 2010a. *Class dynamics of agrarian change*. Halifax, NS: Fernwood.

Bernstein, H. 2010b. Introduction: some questions concerning the productive forces. *In*: H. Bernstein and P. Woodhouse, eds. Special issue on Productive forces in capitalist agriculture: political economy and political ecology. *Journal of Agrarian Change*, 10(1), 300–14.

Bernstein, H. 2012a. Review of Scoones et al., 2010. *Journal of Agrarian Change*, 12(1), 170–3.

Bernstein, H. 2012b. Agriculture/industry, rural/urban, peasants/workers: some reflections on poverty, persistence and change. Paper Presented at the International Workshop on Poverty and Persistence of the Peasantry, El Colegio de México, 13–15 March.

Bernstein, H. 2012c. Sub-Saharan Africa and China: preliminary notes for comparison and contrast. Paper Presented at the workshop on The Land Question: Capitalism, Socialism and the Market, Makerere Institute for Social Research, Kampala, 9–10 August.

Bernstein, H. 2013a. Historical materialism and agrarian history. *Journal of Agrarian Change*, 13(2), 310–29.

Bernstein, H. 2013b. Doing committed social research: what are the dangers? *China Journal of Social Work*, 6(1), 69–81.

Bernstein, H. 2013c. Primitive accumulation: what's in a term? Presentation at the Workers and Punks University May Day School, Ljubljana, 26 April–1 May.

Bernstein, H. and P. Woodhouse. 2001. Telling environmental change like it is? Reflections on a study in sub-Saharan Africa. *Journal of Agrarian Change*, 1(2), 283–324.

Bezner Kerr, R. 2010. Unearthing the cultural and material struggles over seed in Malawi. *In*: Wittman, Desmarais and Wiebe, eds. pp.134–51.

Boltvinik, J. 2012. Poverty and persistence of the peasantry. Background paper for International Workshop on Poverty and Persistence of the Peasantry, El Colegio de México, 13–15 March.

Borras, S.M., Jr., M. Edelman and C. Kay, eds. 2008a. *Transnational agrarian movements confronting globalization*. Special issue of *Journal of Agrarian Change*, 8(1–2).

Borras, S.M., Jr., M. Edelman, and C. Kay. 2008b. Transnational agrarian movements: origins and politics, campaigns and impact. *Journal of Agrarian Change* 8(2–3), 169–204.

Borras, S.M.Jr. and J.C. Franco. 2010. Food sovereignty & redistributive land policies: exploring linkages, identifying challenges. *In*: Wittman, Desmarais and Wiebe, eds. pp. 106–19.

Borras, S.M., Jr., R. Hall, B. White and W. Wolford, eds. 2011. *Forum on global land grabbing*. Special issue of *Journal of Peasant Studies*, 38(2).

Boserup, E. 1965. *The conditions of agricultural growth: the economics of agrarian change under population pressure*. London: Allen & Unwin.

Brass, T., ed. 1994. *New farmers' movements in India*. Special issue of *Journal of Peasant Studies*, 21(3/4).

Breman, J. 1996. *Footloose labour. Working in India's informal economy*. Cambridge: Cambridge University Press.

Brenner, R. 1976. Agrarian class structure and economic development in pre-industrial Europe. *Past and Present*, 70, 30–74.

Brenner, R. 2001. The Low Countries in the transition to capitalism. *Journal of Agrarian Change*, 1 (2), 169–241.

Brockington, D. 2009. *Celebrity and the environment: fame, wealth and power in conservation*. London: Zed Books.

Burawoy, M. 2010. From Polanyi to Pollyanna: the false optimism of global labor studies [online]. *Global Labour Journal*, 1(2), 301–13. Available from: http://digitalcommons.mcmaster.ca/globallabour/vol1/iss2/7 [Accessed 2 September 2012].

Burawoy, M. 2011. On uncompromising pessimism: response to my critics [online]. *Global Labour Journal*, 2(1), 73–77. Available from: http://digitalcommons.mcmaster.ca/globallabour/vol2/iss1/8 [Accessed 2 September 2012].

Byres, T.J. 1996. *Capitalism from above and capitalism from below. An essay in comparative political economy*. London: Macmillan.

Byres, T.J. 2006. Differentiation of the peasantry under feudalism and the transition to capitalism: in defence of Rodney Hilton. *Journal of Agrarian Change*, 6(1), 17–68.

Chambers, R. 1983. *Rural development. Putting the last first*. London: Longman.

Chambers, R., A. Pacey and L.A. Thrupp, eds. 1989. *Farmer first: farmer innovation and agricultural research*. London: Intermediate Technology Publications.

Chauveau, J.-P. and P. Richards. 2008. West African insurgencies in agrarian perspective: Côte d'Ivoire and Sierra Leone compared. *Journal of Agrarian Change*, 8(4), 515–52.

Chayanov, A.V. 1966. *The theory of peasant economy*. D. Thorner, B. Kerblay and R.E.F. Smith, eds. Homewood, IL: Richard Irwin for the American Economic Association.

Claassens, A. 2013. Recent changes in women's land rights and contested customary law in South Africa. *In*: B. Cousins, H. Bernstein, B. O'Laughlin and P. Peters, eds. Special issue on *Agrarian change, rural poverty and land reform in South Africa since 1994, Journal of Agrarian Change*, 13(1), 71–92.

Clark, C. and M. Haswell. 1964. *The economics of subsistence agriculture*. London: Macmillan.

Cowen, M.P. and R.W. Shenton. 1991. The origin and course of Fabian colonialism in Africa. *Journal of Historical Sociology*, 4(2), 143–74.

Cowen, M.P. and R.W. Shenton. 1996. *Doctrines of development*. London: Routledge.

Cronon, W. 1991. *Nature's metropolis. Chicago and the Great West*. New York: W.W. Norton.

Davis, M. 2006. *Planet of slums*. London: Verso.

Desmarais, A.-A. 2002. The *Vía Campesina*: consolidating an international peasant and farm movement. *Journal of Peasant Studies*, 29(2), 91–124.

Desmarais, A.-A. 2007. *La Vía Campesina. Globalization and the power of peasants*. Halifax, NS: Fernwood Publishing.

Duncan, C.A.M. 1996. *The centrality of agriculture. Between humanity and the rest of nature*. Montreal, QC: McGill-Queen's University Press.

Edelman, M. 2002. *Peasants against globalization. Rural social movements in Costa Rica*. Stanford, CA: Stanford University Press.

Edelman, M. 2013. 'Messy hectares': questions about the epistemology of land grabbing data. *Journal of Peasant Studies*, 40(3), 485–501.

Fairbairn, M. 2010. Framing resistance: international food regimes & the roots of food sovereignty. *In*: Wittman, Desmarais and Wiebe, eds. pp. 15–32.

Fairhead, J. and M. Leach. 2006. *Misreading the African landscape. Society and ecology in a forest-savanna mosaic*. Cambridge: Cambridge University Press.

Fairhead, J., M. Leach and I. Scoones, (Guest Editors). 2012. 'Green Grabbing': a new appropriation of nature? *Journal of Peasant Studies* 39(2).

FAO. 2012. *The state of food insecurity in the world 2012*. Rome: FAO.

Foster, J.B. 2000. *Marx's ecology. Materialism and nature*. New York: Monthly Review Press.

Friedmann, H. 1978a. Simple commodity production and wage labour on the American plains. *Journal of Peasant Studies*, 6(1), 71–100.

Friedmann, H. 1978b. World market, state and family farm: social bases of household production in the era of wage labour, *Comparative Studies in Society and History*, 20(4), 545–86.

Friedmann, H. 1993. The political economy of food: a global crisis. *New Left Review* 197, 29–57.

Friedmann, H. 2005. From colonialism to green capitalism: social movements and emergence of food regimeso. *In*: F.H. Buttel and P. McMichael, eds. *New directions in the sociology of global development*. Amsterdam: Elsevier, pp. 227–64.

Friedmann, H. 2006. Focusing on agriculture: a comment on Henry Bernstein's 'Is there an agrarian question in the 21st century?' *Canadian Journal of Development Studies*, 27(4), 461–5.

Friedmann, H. and P McMichael. 1989. Agriculture and the state system: the rise and decline of national agricultures, 1870 to the present. *Sociologica Ruralis*, 29(2), 93–117.

Grischow, J.D. 2008. Rural 'community', chiefs and social capital: the case of Southern Ghana. *Journal of Agrarian Change*, 8(1), 64–93.

Hall, D. 2012. Rethinking primitive accumulation: theoretical tensions and rural Southeast Asian complexities. *Antipode*, 44(4), 1188–208.

Hall, D., P. Hirsch and T. Li. 2011. *Powers of exclusion. Land dilemmas in Southeast Asia*. Singapore: National University of Singapore Press.

Handy, J. and C. Fehr. 2010. Drawing forth the force that slumbered in peasants' arms. *In*: Wittman, Desmarias and Weibe, (Eds). *The Economist, high agriculture and selling capitalism*.

Hanlon, J., J. Manjengwa and T. Smart. 2013. *Zimbabwe takes back its land*. Sterling, VA: Kumarian Press.

Harriss-White, B. 2012. Capitalism and the common man: peasants and petty production in Africa and South Asia. *Agrarian South: Journal of Political Economy*, 1(2), 109–60.

Harvey, D. 2003. *The new imperialism*. Oxford: Oxford University Press.

Heller, H. 2011. *The birth of capitalism. A twenty-first century perspective*. London: Pluto.

Hill, P. 1963. *The migrant cocoa farmers of southern Ghana*. Cambridge: Cambridge University Press.

Holt-Giménez, E. 2006. *Campesino a campesino. Voices from Latin America's farmer to farmer movement for sustainable agriculture*. San Francisco: Food First Books.

Holt-Giménez, E. and A. Shattuck. 2010. Agrofuels and food sovereignty: another agrarian transition. *In*: Wittman, Desmarais and Wiebe, eds. pp. 76–90.

Huang, P.C.C., G. Yuan and Y. Peng. 2012. Capitalization without proletarianization in China's agricultural development. *Modern China*, 38(2), 139–73.

IFAD (International Fund for Agricultural Development). 2011. *Rural poverty report 2011. New realities, new challenges: new opportunities for tomorrow's generation*. Rome: IFAD.

Isakson, R. 2009. *No hay ganancia en la milpa*: the agrarian question, food sovereignty, and the on-farm conservation of agrobiodiversity in the Guatemalan highlands. *Journal of Peasant Studies*, 36(4), 725–59.

Kapeler, A. 2013. Perils of peasant populism: why redistributive land reform and "food sovereignty" can't feed Venezuela. Paper presented to the international conference on 'Food Sovereignty: A Critical Dialogue', September 14–15, Yale University, Connecticut, USA.

Kerkvliet, B.J.T., 2009. Everyday politics in peasant societies (and ours). *Journal of Peasant Studies*, 36(1), 227–45.

Kitching, G. 2001. *Seeking social justice through globalization. Escaping a nationalist perspective*. University Park, PA: Pennsylvania State University Press.

Kloppenburg, J.R., Jr. 2004. *First the seed. The political economy of plant biotechnology*, 2nd edition. Madison, WI: University of Wisconsin Press.

Kloppenburg, J.R., Jr. 2010a. Impeding dispossession, enabling repossession: biological open source and the recovery of seed sovereignty. *Journal of Agrarian Change*, 10(3), 367–88.

Kloppenberg, J.R., Jr. 2010b. Seed sovereignty: the promise of open source biology. *In*: Wittman, Desmarais and Wiebe, eds. pp. 152–67.

Lang, T. and M. Heasman. 2004. *Food wars. The global battle for mouths, minds and markets*. London: Earthscan.

Leach, M. and R. Mearns, eds. 1996. *The lie of the land. Challenging received wisdom on the African environment*. Oxford: James Currey.

Lenin, V.I. 1964 [1916]. *Imperialism, the highest stage of capitalism. Collected Works. Volume 22*. Moscow: Progress Publishers.

Lerche, J. 2010. From 'rural labour' to 'classes of labour': class fragmentation, caste and class struggle at the bottom of the Indian labour hierarchy. *In*: B. Harriss-White and J. Heyer, eds. *The comparative political economy of development: Africa and South Asia compared*. London: Routledge, pp. 64–85.

Lerche, J. 2013. The agrarian question in neoliberal India: agrarian transition bypassed? *In*: A. Shah, J. Lerche and B. Harriss-White, eds. Special issue on *Agrarian transition and Left politics in India, Journal of Agrarian Change*, 13(3), 382–404.

Li Xiaoyun, 2012. What can Africa learn from China's experience in agricultural development? Unpublished paper, Beijing.

Li Xiaoyun, et al. 2012. *Agricultural development in China and Africa. A comparative analysis.* London: Routledge.

Lim, Li Ching. 2008. Sustainable agriculture pushing back the desert [online]. Available from: http://www.i-sis.org.uk/desertification.php. [Accessed 2 November 2011].

Lipton, M. 1977. *Why poor people stay poor.* London: Maurice Temple Smith.

Luxemburg, R. 1951 [1913]. *The accumulation of capital.* London: Routledge and Kegan Paul.

Mamdani, M. 1987. Extreme but not exceptional: towards an analysis of the agrarian question in Uganda. *Journal of Peasant Studies,* 14(2), 191–225.

Martinez-Alier, J. 2002. *The environmentalism of the poor.* Cheltenham: Edward Elgar.

Marx, K. 1843/2009. *Introduction to A contribution to the critique of Hegel's philosophy of right* [online]. Available from: http://www.marxists.org/archive/marx/works/1843/critique-hpr/intro.htm [Accessed 2 February 2010].

Marx, K. 1976. *Capital,* Volume 1. Harmondsworth: Penguin Books.

Masioloi, I. and P. Nicholson. 2010. Seeing like a peasant. Voices from *La Vía Campesina. In:* Wittman, Desmarais and Wiebe, eds. pp. 33–44.

McMichael, P. 1984. *Settlers and the agrarian question. Foundations of capitalism in colonial Australia.* Cambridge: Cambridge University Press.

McMichael, P. 2006. Reframing development: global peasant movements and the new agrarian question. *Canadian Journal of Development Studies,* 27(4), 471–83.

McMichael, P. 2009. A food regime genealogy. *Journal of Peasant Studies,* 36(1), 139–70.

McMichael, P. 2010. Food sovereignty in movement: addressing the triple crisis. *In:* Wittman, Desmarais and Wiebe, eds. pp.168–85.

McMichael, P. and I. Scoones, eds. 2010. *Biofuels, land and agrarian change,* Special issue of *Journal of Peasant Studies,* 37(4).

Mitchell, T. 2002. *Rule of experts. Egypt, techno-politics, modernity.* Berkeley: University of California Press.

Mollinga, P. 2010. The material conditions of a polarized discourse: clamours and silences in critical analysis of agricultural water use in India. *Journal of Agrarian Change,* 10(3), 414–36.

Moore, H.L. and M. Vaughan. 1994. *Cutting down trees. Gender, nutrition and agricultural change in the Northern Province of Zambia, 1890–1990.* London: James Currey.

Moore, J.W. 2010. The end of the road? Agricultural revolutions in the capitalist world-ecology, 1450–2010. *Journal of Agrarian Change,* 10(3), 389–413.

Moore, J.W. 2011. Transcending the metabolic rift: a theory of crises in the capitalist world-ecology. *Journal of Peasant Studies* 38(1), 1–46.

Morena, E. 2011. The Confédération Paysanne as 'peasant' movement: re-appropriating 'peasantness' for the advancement of organisational interests. PhD Dissertation, King's College, University of London.

Mueller, B.E.T. 2011. The agrarian question in Tanzania: using new evidence to reconcile an old debate. *Review of African Political Economy,* 38(127), 23–42.

Murphy, R. 2002. *How migrant labour is changing rural China.* Cambridge: Cambridge University Press.

Murton, A. 1999. Population growth and poverty in Machakos District, Kenya. *Geographical Journal,* 165(1), 37–46.

O'Brien, K. and L. Li. 2006. *Rightful resistance in rural China.* Cambridge: Cambridge University Press.

O'Connor, J. 1998. *Natural causes. Essays in ecological Marxism.* New York: Guilford Press.

O'Laughlin, B. 2009. Gender justice, land and the agrarian question in Southern Africa. *In:* Akram-Lodhi and Kay (eds.). *Peasants and globalization. Political economy, rural transformation and the agrarian question.* London: Routledge, pp. 190–213.

Oxfam. 2010. *Halving hunger still possible?* Briefing Paper 139. Oxford: Oxfam.

Oya, C. 2001. Large- and middle-scale farmers in the groundnut sector in Senegal in the context of liberalization and structural adjustment. *Journal of Agrarian Change,* 1(4), 124–63.

Oya, C. 2004. The empirical investigation of rural class formation: methodological issues in a study of large- and mid-scale farmers in Senegal. *Historical Materialism,* 12, 289–326.

Oya, C. 2007. Stories of rural accumulation in Africa. Trajectories and transitions among rural capitalists in Senegal. *Journal of Agrarian Change,* 7(4), 453–93.

Oya, C. 2010. Agro-pessimism, capitalism and agrarian change: trajectories and contradictions in sub-Saharan Africa. *In*: V. Padayachee, ed. *The political economy of Africa*. London: Routledge, pp. 85–109.

Oya, C. 2012. Contract farming in sub-Saharan Africa: a survey of approaches, issues and debates. *Journal of Agrarian Change*, 12(1), 1–33.

Oya, C. 2013a. Rural wage employment in Africa: methodological issues and emerging evidence. *Review of African Political Economy*, 40(136), 251–73.

Oya, C. 2013b. Methodological reflections on 'land grab' databases and the 'land grab' literature 'rush'. *Journal of Peasant Studies*, 40(3), 503–20.

Panitch, L. and C. Leys. 2000. Preface. *In*: L. Panitch and C. Leys, eds. *The socialist register 2001*. London: Merlin Press.

Patel, R. 2010. What does food sovereignty look like? *In*: Wittman, Desmarais and Wiebe, eds. pp. 186–96.

Peters, P.E. 2004. Inequality and social conflict over land in Africa. *Journal of Agrarian Change*, 4 (3), 269–314.

Ploeg, J.D. van der. 2008. *The new peasantries. Struggles for autonomy and sustainability in an era of empire and globalization*. London: Earthscan.

Ploeg, J.D. van der. 2013. *Peasants and the art of farming. A Chayanovian manifesto*. Halifax, NS: Fernwood.

Ploeg, J.D. van der. and J.Z. Ye. 2010. Multiple job holding in rural villages and the Chinese road to development. *Journal of Peasant Studies*, 37(3), 513–30.

Ploeg, J.D. van der, J.Z. Ye and S. Schneider. 2012. Rural development through the construction of new, nested, markets: comparative perspectives from China, Brazil and the European Union. *Journal of Peasant Studies*, 39(1), 133–73.

Post, C. 1995. The agrarian origins of US capitalism: the transformation of the northern countryside before the Civil War. *Journal of Peasant Studies*, 22(3), 380–445.

Post, C. 2003. Plantation slavery and economic development in the antebellum southern United States. *Journal of Agrarian Change*, 3(3), 289–332.

Post, C. 2011. *The American road to capitalism: studies in class structure, economic development and political conflict, 1620–1877*. Leiden: Brill.

Pun Ngai and Lu Huilin. 2010. Unfinished proletarianization: self, anger, and class action among the second generation of peasant-workers in present-day China. *Modern China* 36(5), 493–519.

Reij, C. 2006. More success stories in Africa's drylands than often assumed [online]. Paper presented at the Forum sur la Souveraineté Alimentaire, Niamey, 7–10 November. Available from: http://www.roppa.info/IMG/pdf/More_success_stories_in_Africa_Reij_Chris.pdf [Accessed 9 November 2012].

Reij, C., G. Tappan and M. Smale. 2009. *Agroenvironmental transformation in the Sahel. Another kind of 'Green Revolution'*. Discussion Paper 00914. Washington: IFPRI.

Rigg, J. 2006. Land, farming, livelihoods, and poverty: rethinking the links in the rural South. *World Development*, 34(1), 180–202.

Rocheleau, D. 1995. More on Machakos. *Environment*, 37(7), 3–5.

Schiavoni, C. and W. Camacaro. 2009. The Venezuelan effort to build a new food and agriculture system [online]. *Monthly Review* 61(3). Available from: http://monthlyreview.org/2009/07/01/the-venezuelan-effort-to-build-a-new-food-and-agriculture-system [Accessed 5 February 2013].

Schneider, S. and P.A. Niederle. 2010. Resistance strategies and diversification of rural livelihoods: the construction of autonomy among Brazilian family farmers. *Journal of Peasant Studies*, 37(2), 379–405.

Scoones, I., *et al.* 2010. *Zimbabwe's land reform. Myths and realities*. Harare: Weaver Press.

Scoones, I., *et al.* 2012. Livelihoods after land reform in Zimbabwe: understanding processes of rural differentiation. *Journal of Agrarian Change*, 12(4), 503–27.

Scott, J.C. 1985. *Weapons of the weak. Everyday forms of peasant resistance*. New Haven, CT: Yale University Press.

Severino, J.-M. and O. Ray. 2011. *Africa's moment*. Cambridge: Polity Press.

Small Planet. 2013. *Framing hunger. A response to* The State of Food Insecurity in the world 2012.

Tiffen, M. and M. Mortimore. 1994. Malthus controverted: the role of capital and technology in growth and environmental recovery in Kenya. *World Development*, 22(7), 997–1010.

Tiffen, M., M. Mortimore and F. Gichuki. 1994. *More people, less erosion. Environmental recovery in Kenya*. Chichester: John Wiley.

Walker, R. and D. Buck. 2007. The Chinese road. Cities in the transition to capitalism. *New Left Review II*, 46, 39–66.

Webber, M. 2012. *Making capitalism in rural China*. Cheltenham: Edward Elgar.

Weis, T. 2007. *The global food economy. The battle for the future of farming*. London: Zed Books.

Weis, T. 2010. The accelerating biophysical contradictions of industrial capitalist agriculture. *Journal of Agrarian Change*, 10(3), 315–41.

White, B. 2011. Who will own the countryside? Dispossession, rural youth and the future of farming [online]. Valedictory Lecture, ISS, The Hague, 13 October. Available from: http://www.iss.nl/fileadmin/ASSETS/iss/Documents/Speeches_Lectures/Ben_White_valedictory_web.pdf [Accessed 7 January 2012].

Wiggins, S. 2000. Interpreting changes from the 1970s to the 1990s in African agriculture through village studies. *World Development*, 28(4), 631–62.

Williams, G. 1976. Taking the part of peasants. *In*: P. Gutkind and I. Wallerstein, eds. *The political economy of contemporary Africa*. Beverly Hills, CA: Sage, pp. 131–54.

Wittman, H., A.A. Desmarais and N. Wiebe, eds. 2010. *Food sovereignty. Reconnecting food, nature and community*. Oakland, CA: Food First.

Wittman, H. 2010. Reconnecting agriculture & the environment: food sovereignty & the agrarian basis of ecological citizenship. *In*: Wittman, Desmarais and Wiebe, eds. pp. 91–105.

Wittman, H., A.A. Desmarais and N. Wiebe. 2010. The origins and potential of food sovereignty. *In*: Wittman, Desmarais and Wiebe, eds. pp. 1–14.

Wolf, E. 1969. *Peasants wars of the twentieth century*. New York: Harper and Row.

Woodhouse, P. 2010. Beyond industrial agriculture? Some questions about farm size, productivity and sustainability. *Journal of Agrarian Change*, 10(3), 437–53.

Woodhouse, P. 2012. Water in African agronomy. *In*: J. Sumberg and J. Thompson, eds. *Contested agronomy: agricultural research in a changing world*. London: Routledge, pp. 102–15.

Henry Bernstein is Emeritus Professor of Development Studies at the School of Oriental and African Studies, University of London, and Adjunct Professor at the College of Humanities and Development, China Agricultural University, Beijing. He was Editor, with Terence J. Byres, of the *Journal of Peasant Studies* from 1985–2000, and Founding Editor, again with Terence J. Byres, of the *Journal of Agrarian Change* in 2001, of which he became Emeritus Editor in 2008. His 'little book on a big idea', *Class dynamics of agrarian change* (2010), has been published in Chinese, Japanese, Portuguese, Spanish and Turkish editions with translatio0 ns in Bahasa and French forthcoming.

What place for international trade in food sovereignty?

Kim Burnett and Sophia Murphy

International agricultural commodity trade is central to the livelihoods of millions of farmers across the globe, and to most countries' food security strategies. Yet global trade policies are contributing to food insecurity and are undermining livelihoods. Food Sovereignty emerged in part as the articulation of resistance to the World Trade Organization's Agreement on Agriculture (AoA) and the imposition of multilateral trade disciplines on domestic agriculture policy. While not explicitly rejecting trade, the food sovereignty movement is identified with a strong preference for local markets. It challenges existing international trade structures, and on the whole its official position on trade remains ambiguous. We argue that trade remains important to the realization of the livelihoods of small-scale producers, including peasants active in the Food Sovereignty movement. It also matters for food security. That it remains underexplored by the movement risks marginalizing millions of smallholder producers, and risks overlooking opportunities to shape trade rules along more food sovereign lines. The authors suggest further development of the movement's position on trade is strategically important.

Introduction

The Food Sovereignty Movement (FSM) emerged in part in resistance to the model of globalization that was institutionalized in the Uruguay Round of trade agreements (URA) and the establishment of the World Trade Organization (WTO) in 1995. Since its inception, the FSM has contested the WTO's legitimacy as an institution for the governance of food and agriculture. The connection between the FSM's origins and its rejection of the WTO has created the impression that the movement is opposed to international trade. This is inaccurate; the movement has objected to the privileged place given to trade in food and agriculture policy and law, and has objected to the multilateral rules that govern trade, but the FSM is not opposed to trade *per se*. Nonetheless, it is our view that there is confusion about what

Sophia Murphy is the grateful recipient of a Vanier Canada Graduate Scholarship and a scholarship from the Trudeau Foundation. She thanks both for their support. Kim Burnett expresses gratitude to the Canadian Social Sciences and Humanities Council for a Joseph-Armand Bombardier CGS Doctoral Scholarship, #767-2008-1014 and to the Centre for International Governance Innovation in Waterloo, Ontario for funding through Balsillie Fellowships. The authors also thank Stuart Clark for his comments on the paper and Hannah Wittman for helping put the paper on track early on in the process. The article is in large part the result of many years of conversation, debate and heated argument with many, many people in many parts of the world. The authors are indebted to all who took the time to engage. Thank you.

kind of trade would be 'all right' in a food sovereignty model and an insufficient consideration on the part of the FSM of what lies beneath the label 'international trade' in particular (namely, numerous and varied markets operating in complex interrelationships) as well as insufficient consideration of how best to regulate those markets.

We argue that the FSM should strive for a clearer and more considered stance on international trade. That stance should take account of the diverse needs and interests of hundreds of millions of smallholder farmers and farm workers around the world. These livelihoods are dependent on export markets and despite many inherent challenges, those involved do not necessarily want to exit international markets. We see three changes to the context of agricultural trade that support a re-examination of the costs and opportunities of engaging in advocacy on multilateral trade. First, who trades which commodities with whom and how, has changed markedly in the past 15 years. Second, the WTO appears to be adapting to some extent to this new context, which also includes changes in the balance of global geo-political power and changes in how the institution relates to civil society. Third, the FSM itself has begun to say more about trade and the conditions under which it should take place. The moment seems propitious for a fresh look at the FSM's strategy on trade.

The FSM has argued international trade should be regulated at the UN, not the WTO. The authors agree the WTO has many limitations in its structure, founding principles and in its negotiating culture. Nonetheless, we see opportunities at the WTO to contribute to a broader food-sovereignty-based trade campaign. We suggest the FSM consider the potential for changes in the existing rules and the difference such changes could make to the lives of smallholders, farm workers and their communities.

Our intention is to raise questions that are important to the FSM but not yet sufficiently discussed by the movement. To that end, the paper begins with an examination of the FSM and its history with regard to trade. We then consider some ways in which the movement's ambiguous position on trade excludes the needs and interests of smallholder farmers and farm workers whose livelihoods depend on trade. We look at changes in trade and at the WTO and assess the movement's stated preference for the UN to house trade negotiations and agreements. Finally, we explore the possibilities for a more engaged FSM strategy on trade.

Food sovereignty: a movement and a concept

Food sovereignty as a movement is a relatively new transnational social movement and advocacy network of peasants, farmers, fisher folk, and other peoples dependent on agricultural production for their livelihoods. The movement originated in the Americas and Europe and expanded quickly to Asia, and later to Africa and other parts of the world (Holt-Gimenez 2010, 204). FSM emerged as a political movement when La Via Campesina (LVC) used the term to assert itself as an international voice for peasant organizations at the World Food Summit in Rome in 1996. In just 15 years, the movement has become a leading transnational agrarian movement of peasant[1] organizations, lead in large part by LVC. As of 2010, the FSM represented primarily marginalized rural people from over 150 social movements and 79 countries, including 12 African countries and several

---

[1]La Via Campesina in fact defines themselves as an international movement of 'peasants, small- and medium-sized producers, landless, rural women, indigenous people, rural youth and agricultural workers' (Via Campesina 2007). For simplicity, the term 'peasants' is used in this paper to include all of these groups.

countries in South and East Asia (Holt-Gimenez 2010). The movement has become a pivotal force in working to safeguard the rights, dignity and livelihoods of millions of the most vulnerable persons and communities across the world.

LVC introduced the concept of food sovereignty as an alternative to the expansion of capitalist agricultural production and neoliberal globalization of agricultural markets. The emergence of LVC coincided with the birth of the WTO and the coming into force of the URA Agreement on Agriculture (AoA). Under the banner of food sovereignty, LVC members articulated their rejection of the WTO and all it stood for with the slogan: 'WTO out of agriculture.' They were not just rejecting the AoA, but all the agreements that affected agriculture, understanding that just taking agriculture out of the WTO (i.e. removing the AoA) would not keep agriculture free from WTO rules.[2] The slogan was an assertion that agriculture was their space, as producers, and they should have a voice in how the space should be managed. LVC was not just articulating a critique of the AoA's rules and asserting that globalization should not dictate domestic agricultural policies. The organization's wider point was to assert the primacy of agriculture, to allow governments space to support agricultural sectors rather than liberalize them, to insist on the importance of including producers' voices in governance mechanisms and to reject the corporate control of commodity markets. From early on, LVC refused to acknowledge the legitimacy of the WTO. The organization chose instead to devote what scarce resources it had for multilateral advocacy to the UN system.[3]

LVC defined food sovereignty at its inception as, 'the right of each nation to maintain and develop its own capacity to produce its basic foods, respecting cultural and productive diversity' and, 'the right to produce our own food in our own territory' (in Desmarais 2007, 34). The organization later added, 'the right of people to define their agricultural and food policy' to the definition (in Desmarais 2007, 34). The movement and the concept became more formalized at the 2007 Forum for Food Sovereignty (Nyéléni) in Mali. The Nyéléni Declaration contains the most commonly recognized definition of food sovereignty today:

> Food sovereignty is the right of peoples to healthy and culturally appropriate food produced through ecologically sound and sustainable methods, and their right to define their own food and agriculture systems. (Nyéléni 2007)

The forum also established the movement's central focal areas, including land and agrarian reform, market protections for peasants, sustainable and agro-ecological agricultural production, greater control for peasants over seeds and resources, and women's rights (Nyéléni 2007, Holt-Gimenez and Shattuck 2011).

Trade and food sovereignty

From the inception of the FSM through Nyéléni to today, international trade has been a central focus of the movement's political work, which is critical of the structures of trade, and of the rules institutionalized in international trade agreements. The movement

---

[2]Interview by Kim Burnett with Nettie Wiebe, International Coordinating Committee member of the North American/Mexican region in LVC from 1996–2001.

[3]This is based on first-hand observation of LVC statements made in trade and agriculture strategy meetings among civil society organizations, including the series of meetings co-hosted by CSOs at the World Council of Churches in Geneva over a number of years starting in 1998, in which Sophia Murphy was an organizer, facilitator and participant as an advisor on trade and agriculture for the Institute for Agriculture and Trade Policy, an NGO based in Minneapolis, USA.

is not, however, hostile to trade. Indeed, a number of the farmers' organizations associated with the FSM have members whose crops are sold in international markets – ROPPA in West Africa, for example, and the National Family Farm Coalition in the United States. As the FSM has evolved, it has taken a clearer position that it accepts trade under certain circumstances.

Trade under certain circumstances

Broadly, the FSM allows for trade where domestic production cannot meet needs, and where agriculture gives priority to providing food for domestic populations with the surplus available for export (Via Campesina 2010). Windfuhr and Jonsén (2005, 32) observe,

> [the] food sovereignty framework is a counter proposal to the neo-liberal macroeconomic policy framework. It is not directed against trade *per se*, but is based on the reality that current international trade practices and trade rules are not working in favour of smallholder farmers...

Similarly, the third pillar in the Declaration of Nyéléni rejects trade and its institutions when qualified as harmful: 'governance structures, agreements and practices that depend on and promote unsustainable and inequitable international trade and give power to remote and unaccountable corporations' (IPC 2009). The movement calls for trade rules that permit the protection and support of small-scale producers, as well as mechanisms such as supply management, commodity agreements, quotas, etc. in support of food security and sustainable livelihoods (Pimbert 2009). These requests in fact mirror many agricultural policies adopted historically by most of what are today industrialized countries (see Chang 2003, Stiglitz 2007, Rodrik 2007).

Some in the FSM also promote 'fairer trade'. At the Nyéléni forum, the declaration states: 'Fair trade initiatives and other arrangements should be supported' (Nyéléni 2007). At the same conference, transparent trade was promoted, where trade, 'guarantees just incomes to all peoples as well as the rights of consumers to control their food and nutrition'. More recently, the Nyéléni newsletter included a promotion of socially just trade:

> Food sovereignty emphasizes ecologically appropriate production, distribution and consumption, social-economic justice and local food systems as ways to tackle hunger and poverty and guarantee sustainable food security for all peoples. It advocates trade and investment that serve the collective aspirations of society. (Nyéléni 2013)

Notably, LVC, in its 2013 Jakarta Call, cites 'fair trade between countries' as one of the principles of food sovereignty moving forward (Via Campesina 2013b). Yet these are all passing references. The FSM remains vague on what 'fairer' trade should look like.

A report affiliated with the *Réseau des organisations paysannes et de producteurs de l'Afrique de l'Ouest* (ROPPA, which in English translates as the Network of Farmers' and Agricultural Producers' Organisations of West Africa) gives a more comprehensive position on trade in traditional commodities and food sovereignty (Koning and Jongeneel 2006).[4] ROPPA is an association of West African peasant associations, a member of LVC,

---

[4]It's not clear how the report is connected to ROPPA, and how connected it is to the Food Sovereignty movement. However the report does bear the ROPPA logo and ROPPA is a prominent member of the movement.

and active in the FSM. The report considers how cotton and cocoa production can be integrated into food sovereignty principles through the Economic Community of West African States (ECOWAS), in particular to increase farm-gate prices of these commodities. The authors propose three foundational pillars for autonomy and empowerment in export markets: (a) end dependence on importing markets; (b) involve farmer organizations; and (c) include production controls. Because the United States dominates a large share of the cotton market (roughly 20 percent), international supply management is considered impossible to coordinate, and a shift to processing and selling cotton for the ECOWAS market is deemed necessary (Koning and Jongeneel 2006). The authors do not demonstrate that the domestic demand necessary for this approach to be feasible exists.

For cocoa, the report recommends an international supply control arrangement, which the authors argue is possible because developed countries do not produce cocoa, and there are no close substitutes, giving producers more market power. Recognizing challenges (for example, free riders), the authors argue these can be overcome with the right incentives (Koning and Jongeneel 2006). While the report does not demonstrate a commitment across countries, and is largely conceptual, it does think through how export commodity production can be compatible with the principles of food sovereignty.

Overall, there is little evidence that the FSM works with small-scale farmers whose production is exported and no clear agenda is presented for them. This leaves the conditions where trade is integral to food security unaccounted for. It also leaves ambiguous the precise circumstances in which trade is acceptable to the movement, and makes it possible to identify contradictions in what is said under a food sovereignty banner. This in turn leaves uncertain what place there is within food sovereignty as a concept and as a movement for small-scale producers whose production is exported. It is probably fair to say that the movement does not yet have a position on international trade itself, but that it has taken a position against certain norms and practices around trade.

Local markets first

The FSM clearly prioritizes local market exchange over global trade, in part as a direct response to neoliberal globalization and the tenets of agricultural liberalization that have accompanied it (Rosset 2006, Nyéléni 2007, Wittman et al. 2010). The original definition of food sovereignty put out by Via Campesina in 1996 focused on the rights of nations to develop their capacities to produce their own food. Assertion of this right has been consistent through to Nyéléni, where the forum called for 'localizes food systems' as the third of six pillars of food sovereignty. The pillar promotes a bridging of the distance between producers and consumers and a re-localization of decision-making (IPC 2009). Elsewhere at Nyéléni, it was established that policies should prioritize production for local consumption, and imports should not displace this (Nyéléni 2007).

The movement's prioritization of local markets, promotion of greater self-sufficiency and condemnation of the WTO could lead to the perception that the movement is against trade *per se*. In fact, it would be more accurate to say that the movement's concern is with structures of agricultural production and trade; that is, structures governed by policies promoting liberalization and privatization and entrenching transnational corporate power, which the FSM, with reason, sees as harmful to hundreds of millions of small-scale producers. This analysis motivates the FSM's demand that governments have greater autonomy in their domestic policy-making.

The perception of the movement as against international trade is exacerbated by strongly critical views of trade expressed by proponents of food sovereignty. The

Oakland Institute's materials about food sovereignty link production of coffee, cocoa, and other 'colonial legacy' products to hunger and poverty (Oakland Institute, ND). Peter Rosset documents how export-oriented trade supports the interests of large, wealthy and expanding farms at the expense of small-scale farmers and peasants, who are displaced by the expansion of export trade onto marginal lands with poor soil quality and difficult growing conditions (Rosset 2006, 5). Holt-Gimenez and Shattuck (2011) criticize what they label 'mainstream' fair trade[5] and classify it as part of the corporate food regime. The authors acknowledge that some within an 'Alternative Fair Trade' movement take 'progressive and often radical positions on the issues of food and justice', but the distinction only seems to further underline that most of the fair trade movement fails to take a progressive stance.

Views such as these contribute to the impression – a vague but definite sense – that the FSM rejects trade, and risks oversimplifying the motives and interests of small-scale farmers producing for export markets (which we elaborate on below). In our view, the FSM would benefit from more debate and some clarification on how the movement views trade, the needs and political objectives of small-scale producers engaged in export, and the place of these producers under food sovereignty.

Opposition to the WTO

If the FSM has been ambivalent about trade, its rejection of the WTO as a legitimate institution for governing agricultural trade is crystal clear (Rosset 2006, Holt-Gimenez 2010, Wittman et al. 2010, Via Campesina 2013a, 2013b). Forged in part in reaction to the WTO and the Uruguay Round Agreements (URA), FSM sees the WTO as an illegitimate, undemocratic institution embedding the neoliberal governance of agricultural production and trade, at the expense of peasant and small-scale producers. This deep resistance to the WTO is evident in analyses such as this from Peter Rosset:

> The WTO and other trade liberalization agreements are by nature designed from the ground up to favor the removal of barriers to trade, rather than its regulation in the public interest, and the non-transparent, anti-democratic, superpower-dominated mechanisms they use are unlikely to make anything else possible (Rosset 2006, 77).

Peter Rosset and Maria Elena Martinez invoke 'collective defiance' as a characterization of social movements, citing LVC's defiant attitude to the WTO and World Bank (Rosset and Martinez 2005, 5). In the preparations for the WTO's Ministerial Conference in Bali in December 2013, LVC members are still clearly articulating their strong rejection of the WTO and the underlying interests it is seen to represent (Via Campesina 2013a, 2013b). LVC emerged with a strong critique that the GATT Uruguay Round negotiations[6] were deeply undemocratic and marginalized developing countries and, within countries, the voices of social movements, especially farmers and peasants. LVC's critique targeted the WTO agreements almost immediately, and also the structural adjustment policies of the World Bank and the IMF, which they saw as emerging from the same economic logic.

---

[5]Which they qualify as 'corporate expansion and individual "consumption-as-politics", divorced from political organizing' (Holt Gimenez and Shattuck 2010, 115).
[6]GATT (or the General Agreement on Tariffs and Trade) was the forum in which multilateral trade negotiations took place until the WTO was established in 1995, at which time the GATT became one of the agreements administered by the WTO.

Overall, the existing and expanding structures of global agricultural production and trade were decried as economically, culturally, socially and politically harmful to peasants, small-scale farmers, indigenous peoples and other food producers and to be root causes of poverty, hunger and landlessness around the world (Desmarais 2007, Rosset 2009, Wittman et al. 2010). In this analysis, international trade is an instrument of oppression, part of a larger economic structure that disadvantages the South against the North, the peasant against the transnational grain trader, and local cultural preferences against global consumer culture, embodied by McDonald's, Walmart and Carrefour.

Yet trade matters

Tens of millions of small-scale producers and farm workers earn their living from crops raised for export, and from a food sovereignty perspective, this makes trade important. The FSM has not explained how such producers might make the transition to a new livelihood, nor whether it is a transition that the producers involved actually want to make. The food sovereignty principle that agriculture is for feeding local communities before trade raises questions about where export commodities fit, particularly commodities that are not staple foods, such as cocoa and coffee. Five million small-scale farmers grow almost 90 percent of the world's cocoa while 25 million people produce 80 percent of the world's coffee (Fairtrade Foundation 2013). While primarily grown on plantations using labourers, commodities such as tea, sugar and bananas are also grown by millions of small-scale farmers (Fairtrade Foundation 2013). These livelihoods leave much to be desired, but are too important to people's survival to dismiss or ignore.

Meanwhile, evidence shows that many producers selling in export markets express interest in improving conditions, and especially their economic bargaining power, in the markets they already know (Murphy 2010, Wolford 2010, Vorley et al. 2012). A recent IIED/Hivos study of smallholder agency in globalized markets makes the point that both farmers' organizations and, especially, NGOs, sometimes pursue an ideological agenda that neglects the stated economic preferences of the smallholders concerned (Vorley et al. 2012).

Indeed, many studies, rooted in critical analysis, demonstrate that the interests of small-scale farmers vary (Borras 2008, Murphy 2010, Wolford 2010, Hivos/IIED final 2012). Many small-scale farmers may prefer producing within the existing global structures, even seeing production for exports as prestigious (Singh 2002). Concern for the nature of markets today does not necessarily translate into a desire to confront the global system, but instead leads to demands for space to equitably integrate into the global system:

> Many small-scale farmers themselves are less preoccupied with critiques of global power and more interested in their rights as economic actors. That is, they want to improve their bargaining position in the markets they buy from and sell to, they want laws that accommodate their needs … they want programmes and support structures to help them better meet the demands of the most promising markets … They also want some protection from loan sharks, from unscrupulous middlemen, from dumped agricultural imports, and from landowners who flout the law, or bend it to suit their interests. (Murphy 2010, 27)

Wolford's (2010) examination of Brazil's Landless Workers Movement (MST in Portuguese, and a member of the FSM) and the differences among members in the north and south of the country found that sugarcane producers in the north, who joined the movement in the late 1990s, preferred to return to sugarcane production over switching to agricultural self-sufficiency. This was in contrast to the small-scale producers from the south, who had joined MST earlier in the movement's history. Ultimately, Wolford concludes that while the MST wanted to move farmers out of sugarcane production on the grounds it is an 'exploitative crop', settlers in the North knew the crop, how to grow it, and how to access its markets. Wolford ascribes this commitment to sugarcane production to "common sense"; that is, decisions motivated more by unconscious and taken-for-granted intuitions emergent from traditions, socialization and institutional influences than by deliberation and reflection. (Wolford 2010, 22–23). They were more comfortable with the risks in the sugarcane sector than with those of home gardens. Knowing the associated risks and power relations in sugarcane, when prices were right, growing sugarcane and acquiring reliable wages was their preference, over domestic production oriented towards greater self-sufficiency (Wolford 2010).

Another example can be found in West Africa, where Kuapa Kokoo, a Ghanaian cocoa cooperative, represents over 40,000 farmers across 1300 Ghanaian villages (Kuapa Kokoo N.D.) and produces 10 percent of Ghana's cocoa supply. It is the country's only cooperative licensed to export cocoa. The cooperative became Fairtrade[7] certified through Fairtrade International (FLO) two years after its creation. Shortly after, it became a majority share-holder of what is today Divine Chocolate, an independent 100 percent certified Fairtrade chocolate company. The chocolate is produced in Germany, operations are based in London, but the profits return to the cooperative in Ghana. In many ways, Divine embodies the sort of fair trade promoted by the FSM.

But Divine Chocolate goes further: the cooperative has publically celebrated the Fair-trade certification of major transnational companies including Nestlé and Cadbury (Divine Chocolate 2011), despite these companies' limited commitment to fair trade and the fact that they are competitors in the same market. But 98 percent of Kuapa Kokoo's production is for conventional markets, and their support for the mainstream adoption of fair trade language appears to demonstrate a broader objective to also improve the market conditions under which it operates. Producers in developing countries demonstrate a range of motivations for producing for fair trade markets, some social and community driven, but they are motivated by other factors as well, including acquiring higher prices, greater financial access, and a more reliable market (Reynolds et al. 2007).

True certified fair trade products represent a niche market and their potential to be scaled-up and replicated is limited by structural constraints. But fair trade products and the efforts of the market can be considered an important part of the process of change, even part of a broader fair trade movement (Reynolds et al. 2007). In many ways the market mechanism creates new normative and discursive framings that challenge claims of the benefits of free trade and current commodity chain relations. As Bacon points out, while imperfect, fair trade does embody elements of a Polanyian Double Movement, that is, a social movement that emerges in confrontation of existing economic structures that embed society in markets, engendering harmful socioeconomic impacts, with an effort to re-embed markets in society (Bacon 2010). Fair trade markets also provide important opportunities for farmers, most of whom have too few market alternatives, and are evidence that not all small-scale producers are pursuing the same model of governance. These examples demonstrate smallholder farmers resisting radical and ideological change and instead looking for practical opportunities. This raises questions about representation in

---

[7]Fairtrade (one word) is used to denote the FLO certification program. Fair trade two words is used for the concept of fair trade and the broader movement.

the FSM, and how the many production practices that the movement promotes can all find their place.

Representation and smallholder exporters[8]

Food sovereignty holds that people should define their policies in a democratic system, the specifics of which should be determined by context. Diverse outcomes are expected and welcomed (Patel 2009, 663, Nyéléni 2013). The model clearly includes space to produce for export markets. But at the same time, food sovereignty is committed to a number of core tenets, which include prioritization of production for domestic food consumption and a strict resistance to transnational corporations. The requirement to respect these principles presumably constrains the choices people have in shaping their food production and consumption choices. In other words, there are uncertainties around the boundaries food sovereignty sets on 'allowed' choices. The boundaries are not firm on many issues, but on trade there are some clear parameters, linked, as we saw above, to the unambiguous rejection of the WTO, and the critiques of mainstream fair trade markets but without a clear idea of what exactly 'true' fair trade would look like.

Principles of representation are complex. LVC emerged as an alternative peasant voice, challenging those who claimed at the time to represent the voices of peasants: IFAP (the International Federation of Agricultural Producers) and certain NGOs, who often spoke in the name of the smallholder producers they worked with in the global South.[9] The FSM saw IFAP as representing the often large-scale farmers who benefited from the neoliberal, capitalist structures of agricultural production and trade (Desmarais 2007, Borras 2008, 2010, Holt-Gimenez 2010). Meanwhile, although NGOs are recognized to have been useful when peasant organizations were unable to participate in governance forums, there were tensions around what role NGOs should play as peasant voices came forward to speak for themselves (Desmarais 2007, 23). Today, the FSM works selectively and on carefully defined terms with a small number of NGOs, such as the Foodfirst Information and Action Network (FIAN), the Land Research Action Network (LRAN), and the Inter-Church Organisation for Development Cooperation (ICCO) and (until recently), Oxfam-Novib (Borras et al. 2008).

To claim representation, however, by the account of many, including supporters, is to engage in the exclusionary (Borras 2008, Boyer 2010, Wolford 2010). Borras (2008, 268) makes the critique that the movement is relatively absent in national and local settings, and that, despite its intentions to the contrary, it fails to represent peasants across class, political and ideological divides, as well as in many geographical areas. Others have found the movement's efforts at the international level were not aligned with the understandings of peasants at the ground level (Windfurh and Jonsén 2005, Boyer 2010). Boyer's study in Honduras specifically argues that members at the local level felt that the movement's objectives in international spaces did not reflect their understandings and needs, causing tensions (Boyer 2010). In her case study on the MST in Brazil, Wolford's (2010) main finding is that the appearance of representation necessitates contradictions and exclusion of interests within a movement. She does not see this as necessarily problematic; but more a natural

---

[8]Representation is a big issue. Here we only discuss smallholders, but issues related to consumers would also be an important element as well, one affected by trade. It is simply beyond the scope of this contribution to include this here.

[9]IFAP has since been dissolved. A new organization with a broadly similar constituency has emerged in its place: the World Farmers Organization.

tendency for tension, and a disjuncture between a public façade and actual engagement, which for Wolford is a normal part of activism. She also recognizes, however, that an over-simplified ideal of representation is not without consequence. In the case of the Brazilian MST trying to integrate sugar cane producers in the north, the challenge proved to be the assumption on the part of organizers that once joining the MST, sugarcane growers would come to share the movement's ideals. This proved not to be the case and sugarcane farmers eventually withdrew from the movement.

Given the limits of representation, although recognizing its importance for political movements, the question arises of how to regulate an international trade system that serves the broader interests of smallholders, within and outside of the FSM. The movement advocates the establishment of an equitable system that empowers smallholders as economic actors in markets, while allowing for diverse ways of engaging in agricultural production. The question is not just one of how to construct a system of trade that is true to FSM's vision, but also how such a trade system might emerge from current structures of international trade. The governance of international trade has undergone significant change since LVC emerged. Resilient food systems – and their producers and consumers – need many markets; the global trade rules dictate a single market. Can this change?

Agricultural trade in international markets

Free trade theory argues that a division of labour and specialization will encourage systems of production and exchange based on comparative advantage, maximizing efficiency and reducing costs. The claim of free trade is that the removal of government interventions such as tariffs, subsidies and market protections will allow consumers and producers to follow their economically rational self-interest, which in turn will create a 'first best' single market in which welfare is maximized. While obviously important, this theory of trade is ultimately unpersuasive on a number of counts, from the empirically measurable irrationality of many market actors when assessed against economists' expectations (Thaler and Sunstein 2009) to the challenges of unequal distribution that mar so many supposedly 'free' markets (Stiglitz 2007). Agricultural trade is in fact characterized by large political and economic power asymmetries (Clapp, 2009, Koning and Pinstrup-Andersen 2007, Morrison and Sarris 2007) and is dominated by modes of production that pose huge ecological challenges (see UNCSD 2011, UNCTAD 2013).

Despite these limitations in theory and practice, international trade remains important in agriculture; indeed, it has been vital to communities, countries and empires for thousands of years in many parts of the world. Trade can form part of an important safety net, guarding against local crop failures. If one region does not get the harvest it needs, then another can provide some of its surplus. Trade can also make it possible for human settlements to exist in places where the food available locally would not be sufficient for a large population. Trade has allowed people to enjoy different foods and different tastes, enriching diets. People trade food for other goods, too, thereby diversifying their economies. Trade can create ecological efficiencies, allowing a more intelligent distribution of stresses on natural resources such as land and water than do the political boundaries of nation states (see for example the discussion of Caroline Saunders and others of the energy use and emissions of New Zealand's agriculture – Saunders et al. 2006). Trade in some form is a given – the challenge lies in how to align trade rules with food sovereignty's broad principles.

The rules that govern international trade were first negotiated at the end of the Second World War, and were signed in 1947 as the General Agreement on Tariffs and Trade (GATT). GATT did not exclude agriculture but first the United States and then the

European Community successfully secured an exemption from GATT rules for their agriculture sectors (Wilkinson 2006). This exemption lasted until the URA, which concluded in 1994 with a revised version of GATT and a standalone Agreement on Agriculture (AoA) as well as a number of other agreements that have determined the evolution of agricultural trade and investment over the past 13 years, including Trade-Related Intellectual Property Rights (TRIPs), Trade-Related Investment Measures (TRIMs), and the General Agreement on Trade and Services (GATS). Before the URA, international agricultural markets were largely dominated by governments and state-trading boards, although a handful of private grain traders were also present and important (Morgan 1979). Much of the trade in international markets was residual. This meant agricultural commodity markets were relatively thin (supplies were limited) but the major exporters held large stocks, which stabilized international prices (Galtier 2013).

The changing face of international trade

International trade has evolved significantly since 1994. It is less about an exchange of goods between two firms from clearly identified countries and increasingly about what are called global value chains (GVC),[10] in which one or more firms organize the production of a good – say green beans – by engaging directly with producers (or their cooperatives of local buyers) and overseeing all stages of processing through to the point of final sale (usually a supermarket shelf). John Humphrey and his colleagues were among the first to describe this phenomenon in the post-URA world, looking at the role of supermarkets in shaping production and demand (Dolan and Humphrey 2000, Humphrey and Schmitz 2001).

The emergence of vertically integrated GVCs in international trade, including agricultural commodity trade, has a complex history, linked to innovations in communication, storage and transportation as well as policy changes within countries and at the multilateral level. The AoA was a catalyst for these changes, as were GATS, TRIMs and TRIPs, and the Agreement on Sanitary and Phytosanitary Standards (SPS). Change came from outside the WTO trade agreements, too, from bilateral and regional trade agreements and national policies to shift power from the state to the private sector.

As these changes have taken effect, the US and EU no longer dominate as exporters and importers in international agricultural commodity markets (Bureau and Jean 2013). Brazil, Argentina, Thailand, India, the Ukraine, Russia and China are among the countries that have emerged as big producers, buyers and sellers of agricultural commodities (Daviron and Douillet forthcoming). An estimated 69 percent of LDC food imports in 2006–2007 came from other developing countries (cited in Mold and Prizzon 2011).

While the source of food exports has shifted, private traders have consolidated their power. Four companies control an estimated 75–90 percent of all cereal trade in international markets (Murphy et al. 2012).[11] The privatization of the Canadian and Australian wheat boards,[12] an outcome aggressively sought by the private grain firms through domestic and multilateral lobbying efforts, has led to takeovers by the already dominant commodity traders, further reducing competition for farmers and consumers alike. New companies are emerging, as Hopewell (2013) discusses in relation to Brazil and as Schneider (2011) and Peine (2013) describe in China. These firms will no doubt change

---

[10]The term value chain was first coined by Porter (1985).
[11]These are Archer Daniel Midland, Bungee, Cargill and Louis Dreyfuss.
[12]The Canadian Wheat Board has lost its monopoly but will remain a voluntary public firm until 2016.

the landscape over time, but for now they appear to be copying the global model set by existing agribusiness.

Demand for food continues to grow, reflecting dietary shifts in middle-income countries as they increase both meat consumption (creating demand for feed), and the consolidation of biofuels markets, powered by mandates and subsidies in the US and EU. This demand is shaping what is grown, what is traded, who to and at what price. Meanwhile, as demand grows, so does waste. In one widely cited report, as much as half of all food produced is estimated to be thrown away – nearly two billion tonnes per year globally (IME 2013). According to a recent UNEP report, 'If current population and consumption trends continue, humanity will need the equivalent of two Earths to support it by 2030.' (Moomaw et al. 2012). This demand (and much of the waste) comes from relatively affluent consumers who are less sensitive to price increases. As the global food price crisis (discussed below) illustrated, it is the poor who have absorbed price shocks and uncertain demand (Dawe and Timmer 2012, McCreary 2012). All of this fuels unstable politics and mounting pressure for change, as evident in local fights over resources, food riots, and the dramatic spike in foreign investment in land, too often accurately characterized as land grabs.

The food price crisis

In 2007–2008, food commodity prices doubled, hitting their highest levels in 30 years or more (Wise and Murphy 2012). Governments began to question the idea that international markets were a sound basis for food security. Their doubts were fuelled by a stream of analysis on the failings of international commodity markets, including a report prepared by eight inter-governmental agencies for the Group of 20 richest economies on price volatility (IAWG 2011); the CFS High Level Panel of Experts report on the same topic (HLPE 2011); and public statements such as the 2009 G20 L'Alquila Declaration, which many more governments and agencies than the G20 membership also signed (Wise and Murphy 2012). National policies started to change: food importers such as Saudi Arabia significantly increased their food reserves, while other countries, such as Uganda and Senegal, invested in stockholding infrastructure to support improved marketing and distribution of domestic production (ActionAid 2012).

Changes at the WTO

Meanwhile, the WTO itself has undergone some changes. Although the epitome of globalization in some circles, the WTO has proved in some ways a surprisingly flexible institution. Today, the dominant economic powers at the WTO are the United States, the European Union, Brazil, India, and China. The so-called Quad of negotiators that dominated talks in the 1980s and 1990s (the United States, Europe, Canada and Japan) is no longer relevant (Hopewell 2013). Economically less powerful states have begun to cooperate and to challenge the more powerful. For example, the Group of 33 (G33) countries, a group of developing countries, large and small, led informally by the Philippines, Indonesia and to some extent India, has emerged as a decisive voice on agriculture. Some of the G33's demands, articulated around the objective of protecting national food security and providing support to 'resource-poor, low-income farmers', are aligned with the principles of food sovereignty. The G33 fought for the right to raise tariffs, at least temporarily, and to protect certain agricultural commodities from import liberalization (Khor 2008b). These positions were one of the reasons the WTO negotiations broke down in

July 2008. Contestation of US cotton subsidies, led by Brazil but involving African cotton producers, also contributed to the negotiation stalemate (Khor 2008a, 2008b).

There is also a G20 in the context of the agriculture negotiations, separate and not entirely aligned with the G33, which is led by agricultural exporters such as Brazil and Argentina. G20 proposals target industrialized countries for further tariff concessions while also remaining committed to opening markets in the South for their exports. Among this group, Brazil in particular has emerged as a trading powerhouse with a strong presence in the WTO negotiations. Brazil has led two successful challenges, one against the United States (on cotton) and the other against the European Union (on export subsidies for the sugar industry) using the WTO's Dispute Settlement Mechanism. Brazil is not a typical developing country in the context of agriculture, yet the fact that a developing country could force a trading powerhouse to change its laws (or, as the US chose to do, pay a fine) is an indication that the institution does not only represent the interests of industrialized countries' agri-businesses.

In addition to changes in the political balance of power within the WTO, there have been changes in relation to civil society engagement. In 1998, Scholte et al. argued CSOs could carve out a stronger democratic space if they focused on sustained and substantial advocacy with the organization (Scholte et al 1998). In the decade after the WTO was founded, procedural changes supported this view. The WTO General Council agreed to dramatically improve public access to documents and to create some space for civil society, including accreditation procedures to give CSOs more consistent access to the organization. It seems reasonable to suppose that this change was in part the result of the pressure created by NGOs, who would post negotiating texts and other documents on their websites, sometimes even giving governments access to the texts before the WTO secretariat could do so.[13] These changes were in some ways small, and many of them were informal. They were made possible by the relationships some NGOs developed with government delegates and with the WTO secretariat staff.[14] They did not change the fundamental disagreements on what trade policies would be best but they made it possible to have an open debate on some issues.

The work of the Special Rapporteur (SR) on the Right to Food, Olivier de Schutter, illustrates the possibilities for engagement. In 2011, the SR engaged directly and publicly with the WTO, setting out some challenges to the trade rules from a right-to-food perspective and making proposals on where the rules should be reformed to better support national food security strategies (de Schutter 2011). Among the SR's recommendations was a call for the rules to allow the establishment of public food reserves – a call that was then reflected in the G33 proposal on public food stocks in 2012. This is not in itself evidence of a direct causal relationship, but given the SR's close engagement with the FSM, it is interesting both that he chose to engage in an uncompromised but constructive way with the WTO, and that at least some number of governments heard what he had to say.

Before the food crisis broke, many countries were already unhappy with the Doha proposals for agriculture, as evidenced in the G33 and G20 proposals. The crisis then showed the vulnerability of poor countries that depended on international markets for food security.

---

[13]Evaluations of the Institute for Agriculture and Trade Policy's (IATP's) trade work include quotations from government negotiators acknowledging their gratitude for the documents and analysis of what they might imply.

[14]This observation is based on Sophia Murphy's first-hand involvement in WTO negotiations as a senior policy advisor with IATP, between 1997 and 2008, as well as on her consulting work with civil society organizations, government and the UN.

It also shone a light on the one-sidedness of rules that gave exporters significant policy space and importers so much less (Sharma 2011). The differences among negotiators grew irreconcilable in the wake of the crisis and agriculture was central to the collapse of the Doha negotiations in 2008.

It is still an open question whether the Doha negotiations will ever be completed. Whether or not they are completed, the shifts in political focus and balance of power observed in the last five or so years suggest the WTO offers room for manoeuvre that the FSM might want to consider. There are some specific advantages to the multilateral trade system, as well as costs to ignoring the system, despite its significant challenges.

For the FSM, what role for the WTO?

Food sovereignty, too, has evolved and taken root in the last 15 years. A number of governments have integrated food sovereignty into their constitutions or laws, including Ecuador, Venezuela, Mali, Bolivia, Nepal and Senegal (Wittman et al. 2010, 8). A growing number of constituencies are choosing food sovereignty as a way to express their dissatisfaction with the food systems with which they must interact. National and sub-national food sovereignty movements have emerged, adding depth and complexity to a project that began as an international exchange among peasant organizations. Can this evolving and changing FSM see opportunity in international trade regulation to advance its agenda?

While rejecting the WTO as a forum, the FSM accepts the need for multilateral discussion of trade and proposes the UN, especially the Food and Agriculture Organization (FAO), to be the appropriate forum in which governments should determine the rules by which to govern global food and agriculture. The FSM judges the UN to be more democratic than the WTO, more accessible to civil society and thus more likely to represent the interests of diverse stakeholders. LVC in particular has invested significant time and political energy in a successful bid to create a voice for small-scale producers at both FAO and the International Fund for Agricultural Development (IFAD), two of the three Rome-based food agencies.[15] This work has been led by the International Planning Committee for Food Sovereignty (IPC) and most recently culminated with an important role for civil society, and within that for producers, as part of the renewal of the UN Committee on World Food Security (CFS) in 2009 (Brem-Wilson 2010).

The appeal of the FSM emphasis on the UN as the forum that should govern all aspects of agriculture, including trade, has appeal. The UN has a better basis from which to integrate trade into a broader vision of agriculture and food as having political and cultural, as well as material, importance.

The FAO has changed in the years since LVC started building their multilateral presence, responding to heavy criticism by reforming and amending its work to renew its place as an important institution for the governance of food and agriculture. Food security has moved to the top of the global policy agenda, and definitions of food security have also evolved importantly in the years since the 1996 World Food Summit. Not least, the right to food has now a prominent place in the international debate, as evidenced by the range and depth of the issue-based reports coming from the office of Olivier de Schutter, the UN Special Rapporteur on the Right to Food. The reformed Committee on World Food Security

---

[15]The third is the World Food Programme.

(CFS) is tackling some of the biggest challenges to global food security at its annual meetings, with governments, civil society, and the private sector all at the negotiating table.

Nonetheless, the proposal that the FAO becomes the forum for international trade negotiations is not persuasive. The FAO has no mandate to govern agricultural trade. And while isolating agricultural trade policy from broader agricultural policy is highly problematic, so, too, is the proposal that agricultural trade rules can somehow be isolated from other trade discussions. This is especially so now that trade encompasses so many aspects of the economy, from the rules that govern the movement of labour, to intellectual property rights, to investment. Somehow the trade rules for agriculture, while having to respect agriculture and its specificities, are going to have to come to terms with other sectors and economic priorities as well. Agriculture's future is intimately bound to the future of other sectors of the economy. FAO is simply not equipped to allow an integrated discussion of this kind.

The WTO does have a mandate to govern trade, and not just in the eyes of the dominant economic powers. Other countries seek to participate actively at the WTO, whether as part of formal groups such as the Least Developed Countries or the African Union, or in more fluid groups built around negotiating positions, such as the G20 and G33.

While the struggle to renew and re-empower the UN remains of obvious importance to the FSM objectives, a shorter-term objective could also be to support those countries that want to change the WTO from within. The risk of not engaging is to lose an opportunity to strengthen small-scale producer voices in negotiations that shape the rules determining producers' livelihoods. Many of those small-scale producers live in some of the now more dominant countries: Brazil, India and China especially. While China presents enormous challenges for organizing civil society, both India and Brazil have well-developed and articulate civil society organizations that are active in influencing national policy, including trade policy. If the FSM ignores this avenue, it both loses an opportunity and allows others, especially agri-business, to dominate that chance to influence policy.

This position has echoes of the debate between 'insider' and 'outsider' strategies that were prominent around the time of the Seattle Ministerial in 1999. Our view echoes those of Green (2012) and others who argue that an engagement within policy spaces and a confrontation from outside of them are necessary. The significant changes in the balance of power within the WTO over the last decade suggest the costs and opportunities of engagement by NGOs as 'insiders' need to be revisited. As a consensus-based organization, moving slowly closer to universal membership (although not yet there), the WTO's authority is not trivial. The organization is led less by the secretariat than most UN agencies and is in that sense more accountable to the members, who are ultimately the spokespeople of (mostly) elected governments. While continuing to advocate for changes at the UN that would curb and direct trade policy (especially through the CFS), why not simultaneously push for a change that could lead to new multilateral trade rules at the WTO?

The dissolution of the WTO meanwhile could create a void in international trade governance that would risk strengthening plurilateral agreements among the richest economies. The trend towards more fragmentation in international systems is highly detrimental to the realization of food security. In such contexts, weaker states lack the space in which to cooperate and build alliances with one another, leaving them more vulnerable to the whims of the more powerful countries. The outcomes of too many bilateral and regional free trade agreements attest to this (for example, the Central America Free Trade Agreement.).

Many will question the extent to which the WTO can be made more democratic. Changes in accreditation, access to negotiating documents and meeting summaries, and the creation of a public forum for open debate give some ground for hope. In addition to the evolving and improved channels for civil society engagement, developing countries have emerged as stronger and more able negotiators. Meanwhile the political context has changed markedly to a more critical examination of modern globalized agricultural systems. The situation is far from perfect but so are the alternatives.

One question is the extent to which the WTO as an institution for the negotiation of trade agreements can be separated from the pursuit of a specific agenda, often called 'corporate globalization' (Hopewell 2013). It is possible to imagine multilateral trade rules that encourage and support a plurality of markets and that empower governments to negotiate policy spaces for these markets in the interests of their citizens, in the interests of food security and sustainable poverty reduction. In some small way, the space the G33 has sought to carve out with its proposal to exempt expenditures on public grain reserves from limits under WTO spending controls is a step in this direction. We think it is possible to imagine the WTO as a place that counterbalances the power of those countries (and companies) that have set the rules to their benefit and to the detriment of small-scale producers and farm workers. Such a WTO would move away from a mandate of increased liberalization to increased consideration of the needs of specific markets and supporting special and differential treatment, special products, commodity agreements, and other measures as seems useful to protect the public interest, broadly speaking, and the rights and interests of producers and farm workers more specifically.

Conclusion

This paper begins a process of considering why trade should be integrated into a vision for food sovereignty. The FSM's ambiguous, unclear and sometimes contradictory position on trade lends to misunderstandings about the movement's vision for trade and how it might be realized, which in turn may close political doors and result in fractures within the movement. As the movement evolves and takes on an increasingly important (and more broadly based) political role, rethinking where, with whom, and with which institutions to engage also takes on some urgency. Engagement with trade offers not only new ways to realize food sovereignty, as it has been defined, but also ways to round out and further develop the concept of food sovereignty itself. Dialogue with small-scale export producers will be an important part of this, to understand their interests and their motivations, and to use this understanding to broaden the scope of food sovereignty. Whether producing for fair trade markets, or traditional or non-traditional agricultural commodity chains, some fieldwork evidence suggests that these producers are motivated to continue their engagement in export markets. Millions of farmworkers, too, are working to improve their working conditions, but are also protective of their jobs. They perceive international trade to be important for their livelihoods.

We suggest the movement reconsider its dismissal of the WTO. The literature on social movements and political change argues that contentious issues require contentious politics, which are essential for opening doors where opportunities for engagement are absent. Yet the literature simultaneously argues that movements should be open to opportunities for structural changes when such opportunities arise (Gaventa and McGee 2010, Tarrow, 2011). There appear to be cracks in the edifice of the WTO today: opportunities that were not evident 20 years ago. These could present important opportunities to transform not only the rules of trade but the way in which those rules are determined, with some potential for the principles of food sovereignty to be integrated.

We remain cautious in making these arguments. Our hope is to contribute some perspective, grounded in theory and analysis, that may be of use to the FSM as it continues to act against the dominant structures of agricultural production and trade that have been harmful to small-scale producers and farm workers everywhere. We hope work will continue on forging a stronger strategy, one that includes a place for trade.

References

ActionAid. 2012. Cobwebbed: international food price crisis and national food prices. Some experiences from India,' ActionAid International and the International Food Security Network.

Bacon, C.M. 2010. Who decides what is fair in fair trade? The agri-environmental governance of standards, access, and price. *Journal of Peasant Studies*, 37(1), 111–147.

Borras, S.M., Jr. 2008. La Via Campesina and its global campaign for agrarian reform. *Journal of Agrarian Change*, 8(2–3), 258–289.

Borras S.M., Jr., M. Edelman, and C. Kay. 2008. Transnational agrarian movements: origins and politics, campaigns and impacts. *Journal of Agrarian Change*, 8(2–3), 169–204.

Borras, S.M., Jr. 2010. The politics of transnational agrarian movements. *Development and Change*, 41.5, 771–803.

Boyer, J. 2010. Food security, food sovereignty, and local challenges for transnational agrarian movements: the Honduras case. *Journal of Peasant Studies*, 37(2), 319–351.

Brem-Wilson, J. 2010. The reformed Committee on World Food Security. A briefing paper for civil society. Facilitated by the International Planning Committee for Food Sovereignty, with the support of the Center Internazionale Crocevia, and Mundubat.

Bureau, J.C. and C. Jean. 2013. Do yesterday's disciplines fit today's farm trade? Challenges and policy options for the Bali ministerial conference. ICTSD issue paper. Geneva.

Chang, H.J. 2003. *Kicking away the ladder: development strategy in historical perspective*. London, UK: Anthem Press.

Clapp, J. 2012. *Food*. Cambridge, UK: Polity Press.

Daviron, B. and M. Douillet. Forthcoming. Major players in international food trade and world food security. Research and Information System for Developing Countries (RIS), Delhi and the Global Development and Environment Institute, Tufts University, Boston.

Dawe, D. and C.P. Timmer. 2012. Why stable food prices are a good thing: lessons from stabilizing rice prices in Asia. *Global Food Security*, 1(2), 127–133.

De Schutter, O. 2011. The World Trade Organization and the post-global food crisis age. Activity Report. Office of the UN Special Rapporteur on the Right to Food. November.

Desmarais, A.A. 2007. *La Via Campesina: globalization and the power of peasants*. Canada. Black Point: Fernwood.

Divine Chocolate. 2011. Divine Chocolate Welcomes Latest Major Chocolate Brand to Fairtrade Certification. *Divine News*. 5 October. Available from: http://www.divinechocolate.com/us/newsid/160/divine-chocolate-welcomes-latest-major-chocol.aspx [Accessed April 2012].

Dolan, C. and J. Humphrey. 2000. Governance and trade in fresh vegetables: the impact of UK supermarkets on the African horticulture industry. *Journal of Development Studies*, 37(2), 147–76.

Fairtrade Foundation. 2013. Powering UP smallholder farmers to make food fair. Available from: http://www.fairtrade.org.uk/includes/documents/cm_docs/2013/F/FT_smallholderpercent20report_2013_lo-res.pdf [Accessed May 2013].

Galtier, F. 2013. Gérer l'instabilité des prix alimentaires dans les pays en développement. *A Savoir* No. 17. Agence Française de Développement. France.

Gaventa, J. and R. McGee. 2010. *Citizen action and national policy reform: making change happen*. London: Zed Books.

Green, D. 2012. *From poverty to power - how active citizens and effective states can change the world*. 2nd Edition. Oxford, UK: Practical Action Publishing and Oxfam; Kindle Edition.

HLPE. 2011. *Price volatility and food security*. A report by the high level panel of experts on food security and nutrition for the committee on world food security. Rome: FAO.

Holt-Gimenez, E. 2010. Grassroots voices: linking farmers' movements for advocacy and practice. *Journal of Peasant Studies*, 37(1), 203–236.

Holt-Gimenez, E. and A. Shattuck. 2011. Food crisis, food regimes, and food movements: rumblings of reform or tides of transformation. *The Journal of Peasant Studies*, 38(1), 109–144.

Hopewell, K. 2013. New protagonists in global economic governance: Brazilian agribusiness at the WTO. *New Political Economy*, 18(4), 603–623.

Humphrey, John and Hubert Schmitz. 2001. Governance in Global Value Chains. IDS Bulletin 32(3). Institute for Development Studies. Sussex University. UK.

IAWG: Interagency Working Group. 2011. Options for promoting responsible investment in agriculture, Interagency Working Group on the Food Security Pillar of the G-20 Multi-year Action Plan on Development.

Institution of Mechanical Engineers (IME). 2013. *Global food. Waste not, want not*. London: IME.

International Planning Committee for Food Sovereignty (IPC). 2009. What is the IPC. Available from: http://www.foodsoveoreignty.org/Aboutus/WhatisIPC.aspx [Accessed May 2013].

Khor, M. 2008a. Trade: Africans played pivotal role at turning point of WTO negotiations. *North South Development Monitor* (SUNS), No. 6531, August 5.

Khor, M. 2008b. 'Agriculture: Falconer report says WTO talks failed on political factor'. TWN Info Service on WTO and Trade Issues *North South Development Monitor* SUNS No. 6537, August 18.

Koning, N. and R. Jongeneel. 2006. Food sovereignty and export crops: Could ECOWAS create an OPEC for sustainable cocoa? *Forum on Food Sovereignty*. ROPPA. West Africa.

Koning, N. and P. Pinstrup-Andersen (eds). 2007. *Agricultural trade liberalization and the least developed countries*. Dordrecht, The Netherlands: Springer.

Kuapa Kokoo. N.D. Available from: http://www.kuapakokoo.com/index.php?option=com_content&view=article&id=48&Itemid=56 [Accessed April 2012].

McCreary, I. 2012. Food Reserves in India. Report for the Canadian Foodgrains Bank. Winnipeg, Canada.

Mold, A. and Prizzon, A. 'Two steps forward, one step back: LDCs and the challenges of South-South trade in times of 'Shifting Wealth'' *Trade Negotiations Insights*. Volume 10. No. 8. November 2011. International Centre for Trade and Sustainable Development. Geneva.

Moomaw, W., T. Griffin, K. Kurczak and J. Lomax. 2012. The critical role of global food consumption patterns in achieving sustainable food systems and food for all, *UNEP Discussion Paper*, United Nations Environment Programme, Division of Technology, Industry and Economics, France. Available from: http://www.humanmedia.org/dcc/pdf/unep_food_report_2012.pdf

Morgan, D. 1979. *Merchants of grain: the power and profits of the five giant companies at the center of the world's food supply*. New York: Viking.

Morrison, J. and Sarris, A. (eds) 2007. *WTO rules for agriculture compatible with development*. Rome: FAO.

Murphy, S. 2010. Changing perspectives: small-scale farmers, markets and globalization. IIED/HIVOS Working Paper. UK and the Netherlands. Available from: http://www.hivos.net/content/download/37718/244245/file/Sophia_Murphy-Web.pdf

Murphy, S., Burch, D. and Clapp, J. 2012. Overview and Part 1: The ABCD commodity traders, pp. 5–21 in Cereal secrets: The world's largest grain traders and global agriculture. UK: Oxfam Research Report. Available from: http://www.oxfam.org/sites/www.oxfam.org/files/rr-cereal-secrets-grain-traders-agriculture-30082012-en.pdf

Nyéléni. 2007. Declaration of Nyéléni. Available from: http://www.nyeleni.org/spip.php?article290 [Accessed March 2011].

Nyéléni. 2013. Editorial: food sovereignty now! *Nyéléni Newsletter* Number 13, March. Available from: http://www.nyeleni.org/DOWNLOADS/newsletters/Nyeleni_Newsletter_Num_13_EN.pdf [Accessed May 2013].

Oakland Institute. N.D. Food Price Crisis: A Wake Up Call for Food Sovereignty. *Policy Brief*. Available from: http://www.oaklandinstitute.org/content/food-price-crisis-wake-call-food-sovereignty [Accessed May 2013].

Patel, R. 2009. What does food sovereignty look like? *The Journal of Peasant Studies*, 36(3), 663–673.

Peine, E.K. 2013. Trading on pork and beans: Agribusiness and the construction of the Brazil-China-soy-pork commodity complex. *In*: H.S. James Jr, ed. *The ethics and economics of agrifood competition*. Dordrecht: Springer Science + Business Media, pp. 193–210.

Pimbert, M. 2009. *Towards food sovereignty*. London: IIED. Available from: http://dlc.dlib.indiana.edu/dlc/bitstream/handle/10535/5851/14.855IIED.pdf

Porter, M. 1985. *Competitive advantage: creating and sustaining superior performance*. New York: The Free Press (Simon and Schuster).

Raynolds, L., Murray, D.L. and Wilkinson, J. 2007. *Fair trade: the challenges of transforming globalization*. London: Routledge.

Rodrik, D. 2007. *One economics, many recipes*. Princeton: Princeton University Press.

Rosset, P. 2006. *Food is different*. Nova Scotia: Fernwood.

Rosset, P. 2009. Fixing our global food system: food sovereignty and redistributive land reform. *Monthly Review* 61(3), 114–128.

Rosset, P. and Martinez, ME. 2005. Participatory evaluation of La Via Campesina, for the Norwegian Development Fund and La Via Campesina. Norwegian Development Fund, Oslo. Available from: http://www.norad.no/en/tools-and-publications/publications/publication?key=117349 [Accessed May 2013].

Saunders, C., Barber, A. and Taylor, G. 2006. Food Miles – Comparative Energy/Emissions Performance of New Zealand's Agriculture Industry. Agribusiness and Economics Research Unit: Research Report 285. Lincoln University. New Zealand.

Schneider, M. 2011. *Feeding China's pigs: implications for the environment, China's smallholder farmers and food security*. Minneapolis: Institute for Agriculture and Trade Policy.

Scholte, J.A., R. O'Brien and M. Williams. 1998. The WTO and Civil Society. CSGR Working Paper No. 14/98. Centre for the Study of Globalisation and Regionalisation, University of Warwick, Coventry.

Sharma, R. 2011. Food export restrictions: Review of the 2007-2010 experience and considerations for disciplining restrictive measures. *FAO Commodity And Trade Policy Research Working Paper* No. 32. May. Rome: FAO.

Singh, S. 2002. Contracting out solutions: political economy of contract farming in the Punjab. *World Development*, 30(9), 1621–1638.

Stiglitz, J. 2007. *Making globalization work*. New York: W.W. Norton and Co.

Tarrow, S.G. 2011. *Power in movement: social movement sin contentious politics*. 3rd Edition. New York, NY: Cambridge University Press.

Thaler, R.H. and C.R. Sunstein. 2009. *Nudge*. New York: Penguin.

UNCSD. 2011. Food security and sustainable agriculture. *Rio 2012 Issues Briefs* No. 9. New York: UN Commission on Sustainable Development Secretariat. December.

UNCTAD. 2013. *Trade and environment review 2013*. Geneva: UNCTAD.

Via Campesina. 2007. "The International Peasant's Voice". Wednesday, July 11th, online at http://www.viacampesina.org/main_en [Accessed 30 March, 2008]

Via Campesina. 2010. Towards a common agriculture and food policy 2013 within a food sovereignty framework. Available from: http://www.eurovia.org/spip.php?article274&lang=fr [Accessed May 2013].

Via Campesina. 2013a. End the WTO and the (sic) STOP the new wave of Free Trade Agreements. Available from: http://viacampesina.org/en/index.php/actions-and-events-mainmenu-26/10-years-of-wto-is-enough-mainmenu-35/1389-end-the-wto-and-the-stop-the-new-wave-of-free-trade-agreements [Accessed May 2013].

Via Campesina. 2013b. The Jakarta Call. Available from: http://viacampesina.org/en/index.php/our-conferences-mainmenu-28/6-jakarta-2013/resolutions-and-declarations/1428-the-jakarta-call. [Accessed August 2013].

Vorley, B., Del Pozo-Vergnes, E. and Barnett, A. 2012. *Small Producer Agency in the Globalised Market: Making Choices in a Changing World*. UK and the Netherlands: IIED/HIVOS. Available from: http://pubs.iied.org/16521IIED.html

Wilkinson, R. 2006. *The WTO: crisis and governance of global trade*. London: Routledge.

Windfuhr, M. and J. Jonsén. 2005. *Food sovereignty: towards democracy in localized food systems*. Warwickshire: FIAN International/ITDG Publishing.

Wise, T. and S. Murphy. 2012. Resolving the food crisis: Assessing global policy reforms since 2007. Boston: GDAE and Minneapolis: Institute for Agriculture and Trade Policy. Available from: http://iatp.org/files/2012_01_17_ResolvingFoodCrisis_SM_TW.pdf

Wittman, H., Desmarais, A.A. and Wiebe, N. 2010. *Food sovereignty: reconnecting food, nature and community*. Nova Scotia: Fernwood.

Wolford, W. 2010. *This land is ours now: social mobilization and the meanings of land in Brazil*. North Carolina: Duke University Press.

Kim Burnett is a SSHRC-funded doctoral student with the University of Waterloo's Global Governance program. Her research focuses on governance of agricultural production and trade, examining how Fair Trade and Food Sovereignty challenge neoliberal structures of agricultural production and trade, and with what efficacy. Kim worked in the private, public and non-profit sectors before her studies, was a research fellow with Oxfam America in 2009, and has held research contracts with Oxfam America and World Vision. Kim authored a recently published article in *Geopolitics* on Fair Trade and Food Sovereignty responses to governance opportunities after the global food crisis.

Sophia Murphy has 20 years' experience in public policy analysis. She is a writer, researcher and occasional teacher whose work is focused on agriculture, market power and food systems. She is a PhD student at the Institute for Resources, Environment and Sustainability at the University of British Columbia, working on trade and food security. She has a Trudeau Foundation scholarship and a Vanier scholarship from the Canadian Government. Sophia is a member of the High Level Panel of Experts to the UN Committee on World Food Security. She is also a member of the ActionAid USA board.

Farmers' rights and food sovereignty: critical insights from India

Karine Peschard

Farmers' access to and rights over seeds are the very pillars of agriculture, and thus represent an essential component of food sovereignty. Three decades after the term *farmers' rights* was first coined, there now exists a broad consensus that this new category of rights is historically grounded and imperative in the current context of the expansion of intellectual property rights (IPRs) over plant varieties. However, the issue of their realization has proven so thorny that even researchers and activists who are sympathetic to farmers' rights now express growing skepticism regarding their usefulness. In this article, I explore this debate through a case study of India's unique Protection of Plant Varieties and Farmers' Rights (PPV&FR) Act. Based on an analysis of advances and setbacks in implementing the PPV&FR Act and a discussion of other relevant pieces of legislation, I argue that the politics of biodiversity and IPRs in India in recent years has been characteristic of the cunning state, and that this has seriously compromised the meaningful implementation of farmers' rights.

Introduction

Farmers' rights – understood as farmers' right to freely access, use, exchange and sell crop genetic resources – are a key dimension of food sovereignty.[1] They are also the object of an important debate among scholars and activists.[2] It is widely acknowledged that the concept is ambiguous and its implementation fraught with difficulties. As a result of the slow progress made in realizing farmers' rights in the last 25 years, a number of researchers, while agreeing with farmers' rights in principle, have grown increasingly critical of their usefulness in practice (Borowiak 2004; Kloppenburg 2004; Bertacchini 2008).

This research was supported by a postdoctoral fellowship of the Social Sciences and Humanities Research Council of Canada. I wish to thank Shalini Randeria, Marc Edelman, Anitha Ramanna, Priscilla Claeys and two anonymous reviewers for their comments on an earlier draft of this article, as well as the organizers and participants in the conference *Food sovereignty: a critical dialogue*, held at Yale on 14–15 September 2013, for stimulating discussions. The usual disclaimer applies.
[1]In a recent press release, La Via Campesina states that 'with or without the [International Treaty on Plant Genetic Resources for Food and Agriculture, ITPGRFA] Treaty, in line with or against national laws, La Via Campesina will continue to exercise, in a very concrete way, Farmers' Rights over their seeds, because it is the very first step for food sovereignty' (Via Campesina 2013).
[2]See, for example, Montecinos (1996), Bennett (2002), Borowiak (2004), Kloppenburg (2004) and Kneen (2009, 66–75). For a review of the literature up to 2005, see Andersen (2005).

It is important to distinguish farmers' rights from the emerging category of peasants' rights. The expression *farmers' rights* was coined in the 1980s in the context of the emerging debate over the contribution of farmers to the maintenance of plant genetic resources for agriculture, and was subsequently developed within the ambit of the Food and Agriculture Organization (FAO).[3] It refers to farmers' rights over crop genetic resources and associated knowledge. The more recent expression *peasants' rights* is closely associated with La Via Campesina's Declaration of Rights of Peasants – Women and Men (2009) currently under discussion at the United Nations (UN) Human Rights Council (UNHRC 2012).[4] The concept of peasants' rights includes, but is not limited to, farmers' rights over crop genetic resources; it encompasses a much broader range of rights, such as the right to life and an adequate standard of living, land, freedom of association and access to justice.[5] Another key difference between the two concepts is that while farmers' rights are framed as intellectual property rights, peasants' rights are framed as human rights. The present article discusses efforts to implement farmers' rights in India. Peasants' rights, which are still at the stage of discussion at the UN, have not yet entered the public debate in India.

India is a key case study to explore the global politics of farmers' rights. Most countries in the Global South adopted plant variety legislation modelled on the International Union for the Protection of New Varieties of Plants (UPOV)[6] following the coming into force of the World Trade Organization Agreement on Trade-Related Aspects of Intellectual Property Rights (WTO/TRIPS). In contrast, India developed its own *sui generis* legislation – the Protection of Plant Varieties and Farmers' Rights (PPV&FR) Act, 2001. The inclusion of farmers' rights in the new legislation was a direct result of civil society mobilization and lobbying.[7] It is broadly regarded as one of the most progressive farmers' rights legislation worldwide.

---

[3]For a detailed history of the concept of farmers' rights, see Andersen (2005).

[4]In February 2012, the UN Advisory Committee to the Human Rights Council adopted a draft Declaration on the rights of peasants and other people working in rural areas, largely based on La Via Campesina's Declaration of Rights of Peasants – Women and Men (see Via Campesina 2009; UNHRC 2012). On the ongoing negotiation of an international Declaration (and, eventually, Convention) on the rights of peasants at the UN, see Edelman and James (2011), Claeys (2012), Golay (2013) and Edelman (2014).

[5]Several articles of La Via Campesina's Declaration of the Rights of Peasants touch, directly or indirectly, upon farmers' rights over seeds, notably Article 5 ('Right to seeds and traditional agricultural knowledge and practice'); Article 9 ('Right to the protection of agricultural values') and Article 10 ('Right to biological diversity'). For a comprehensive list of peasants' rights, see UNHRC (2012).

[6]Created in 1961 and revised in 1972, 1978 and 1991, the International Union for the Protection of New Varieties of Plants (UPOV) is an inter-governmental organization that enforces intellectual property rights on plant varieties, known as plant breeders' rights.

[7]In the context of this article, I use 'civil society' to refer to those individuals and organizations that have been actively involved in the public debate over farmers' rights in India. Some of these organizations were founded as early as the late 1970s, others in the late 1990s. They describe themselves as 'non-profit organizations working on environmental and social issues', 'grassroots organizations' or 'research and advocacy organizations'. While they are not farmers' organizations, they work closely with farmers' communities toward food security, sustainable agricultural practices and the preservation of agricultural biodiversity. With the exception of large rallies of 18,000 to 200,000 farmers organized in Delhi in 1993 against the General Agreement on Tariffs and Trade (GATT) negotiations and Dunkel Draft (Gupta 1998, 291), farmers' organizations are conspicuous by their absence in the farmers' rights debate. The reasons behind this are beyond the scope of this essay, but would warrant further research.

With its unique farmers' rights legislation and *sui generis* system, India has been the object of considerable interest among scholars and policymakers. (Cullet and Kolluru 2003; Ramanna 2006; Santilli 2009, 350–6) For the most part, the literature discusses the legislation from a formal point of view.[8] Given pervasive discrepancies between the law and its implementation, any meaningful discussion of farmers' rights must imperatively tackle what is actually happening on the ground. Moreover, discussions of the implementation of the PPV&FR Act are scant and limited in scope: they focus on what has been achieved so far (Gautam *et al.* 2012), on the intricacies of implementation (Ramanna and Smale 2004; Kochhar 2010; Kumar *et al.* 2011), on trends in applications filed for plant variety protection (Kochupillai 2011; Lushington 2012) and on whether the Act is likely to attract private investment in plant breeding (Ravi 2004). While these analyses are important, a thorough assessment of farmers' rights requires broadening the analysis beyond the technicalities of implementation to include the broader policies and politics of farmers' rights to genetic resources in India, and this is what this article attempts to do.

Twelve years into the implementation of the PPV&FR Act, this paper takes stock of the progress made in realizing farmers' rights in India and attempts to explain how the high levels of mobilization that surrounded the drafting of the legislation gave way to disillusionment and skepticism. As Kochhar (2010, 281) observes,

> an insignificant number of applications filed for the registration and protection of prevailing farmers' varieties for further commercial use is surprising, particularly when huge public opinion was built up before the enactment of PPV&FR Act to provide for extensive farmers' rights under the new *sui generis* PVP [plant variety protection] law.

Based on interviews with key participants in the debate – researchers, nongovernmental organizations (NGOs) and officers of public agencies responsible for implementing the Act – I argue that this is in large part due to the ambiguous role played by the Indian state, whose stance and action on the issue of farmers' rights have been characteristic of the cunning state.[9] The concept of the cunning state was proposed by Randeria (2003a, 2003b, 2003c, 2007; Randeria and Grunder 2010) to suggest that we should approach the role of some states in the new architecture of global governance as neither weak nor strong, but able to 'capitalize on their perceived weakness in order to render themselves unaccountable both to their citizens and to international institutions' (Randeria 2003a, 3). The ambivalent politics of cunning states is evidenced in the case of farmers' rights in India by the government's controversial decision to join UPOV shortly after the PPV&FR Act was passed, the fact that several pieces of legislation introduced since 2001 seem to undo the farmers' rights provisions of the PPV&FR Act and, more recently, the government's stance in the first national case of biopiracy involving the use of local varieties of eggplants in the development of Bt brinjal. The lack of a clear political will on the part of the Indian state to effectively enforce the legislation and protect farmers' rights has

---

[8] A notable exception is Ramanna (2006), a detailed case study based on interviews with the different actors in the farmers' rights debate in India. However, it was published in the early stages of the Act, and thus does not address the issue of its implementation.

[9] This article is based on research conducted between 28 January and 8 March 2013 in New Delhi, Chandigarh (Union Territories), Hyderabad and Medak district (Andhra Pradesh) and Pune (Maharashtra). In total, I conducted 18 interviews with NGOs (seven), researchers (five), government officials (three), farmers (two) and a representative of industry. I also participated in related events, such as a biodiversity festival and a farmers' assembly, and visited village seed banks.

led to a break of trust between the state on one hand, and farmers and civil society on the other.

In the first part of the article, I set the stage for the discussion to follow by tracing the broad lines of the global debate over farmers' rights and giving an overview of the Indian farmers' rights legislation and what is unique about it. In the second, more substantive, part of the article, I discuss advances and setbacks in implementing farmers' rights in India since the passing of the PPV&FR Act in 2001. Broadening the analysis to other important policies and pieces of legislation passed during the same period, I then develop the argument that the politics of farmers' rights in India have been characteristic of the cunning state and that this has compromised their meaningful implementation. In the conclusion, I sum up advances and impasses in the implementation of the PPV&FR Act, and suggest how emerging alternatives, such as Open Source seed systems and the proposed UN Declaration on the Rights of Peasants, could open up new avenues for the realization of farmers' rights in India.

The vexed issue of farmers' rights

It is widely acknowledged that the concept of farmers' rights is ambiguous and its implementation fraught with difficulties. One problematic dimension is the lack of an accepted definition. Most official documents pertaining to farmers' rights do not actually define the term (FAO 1989, 2001). They establish that these rights arise from farmers' historical and contemporary contribution to plant breeding. They do not, however, specify who the rights holders are (apart from the fact that they are not individuals but communities), or what they are entitled to.

This vagueness has given rise to diverging interpretations. Some narrowly equate farmers' rights with 'plant back rights', the right to save seeds from a harvest to sow the next crop. The International Treaty on Plant Genetic Resources for Food and Agriculture (ITPGRFA), also known as the Seed Treaty, establishes the right to the protection of traditional knowledge, the right to equitable benefit sharing and the right to participate in decision making (Art. 9.1). It adds that 'Nothing in this Article shall be interpreted to limit any rights that farmers have to save, use, exchange and sell farm-saved seed/propagating material, subject to national law and as appropriate' (FAO 2001, Art. 9.2). Peasant movements, for their part, have a more encompassing understanding of the term. In the Declaration on the Rights of Peasants, rights over crop genetic resources include, for example, the 'right to determine the varieties of the seeds they want to plant' (Art. 5.1), the right to reject varieties of plants which they consider to be dangerous economically, ecologically and culturally (Art. 5.2), and the right to grow and develop their own varieties and to exchange, give or sell their seeds (Art. 5.8) (Via Campesina 2009). In an attempt to seek a compromise between these different conceptions, Andersen (2006, 5) suggests the following working definition:

> Farmers' Rights consist of the customary rights that farmers have had as stewards of agro-biodiversity since the dawn of agriculture to save, grow, share, develop and maintain plant varieties, of their legitimate right to be rewarded and supported for their contribution to the global pool of genetic resources as well as to the development of commercial varieties of plants, and to participate in decision-making on issues that may affect these rights.

This definition avoids the controversial issue of farmers' right not only to save and exchange, but also to *sell* seeds. It also recognizes farmers primarily as stewards, or conservers, of plant genetic resources, rather than as breeders.

The key fault line in the debate concerns the vexed relationship between farmers' rights and intellectual property rights (IPRs). Some observers believe that farmers' rights and IPRs can be reconciled. Those who defend this view tend to conceive of farmers' rights within the conventional property rights framework. According to Cullet and Kolluru (2003, 12–3), for example, 'farmers' rights are based on the recognition that all economic actors should have commercial rights over their knowledge, and not only one specific category of inventors'. Farmers' rights should thus grant farmers full property rights over their knowledge, including the right to commercialize it.[10] In contrast, in an official position statement, La Via Campesina states that farmers' rights 'are eminently collective; they should therefore be considered as a different legal framework from those of private property and intellectual property' (Via Campesina 2001). In the Declaration of Rights of Peasants, it asserts the right to reject intellectual property of crop genetic material. Article 10.4 ('Rights to biological diversity') reads:

> Peasants (women and men) have the right to reject intellectual property rights of goods, services, resources and knowledge that are owned, maintained, discovered, developed or produced by the local community. They cannot be forced to implement those intellectual property rights. (Via Campesina 2009)

There is also significant disagreement as to the potential for realizing farmers' rights. Borowiak (2004), for example, argues that, contrary to breeders' rights, farmers' rights prove difficult to enact because they involve collective rather than individual knowledge, historical as well as current contributions, and traditional knowledge rather than new knowledge. 'Because farmers' rights do not actually contest breeders' rights per se, proponents tend to implicitly concede the legitimacy of the IPRs regime' (Borowiak 2004, 532). This is the conclusion reached by Santilli (2009, 351–2, my translation) in the Indian case: 'the recognition of intellectual property rights on farmers' varieties, even through a *sui generis* system, ended up legitimizing the position in favour of such rights (on commercial varieties) held by the private commercial seed sector representatives'. The danger, concludes Borowiak (2004, 511), is to legitimize the inequities it claims to address. To paraphrase Escobar (1994, 220), farmers are acknowledged as having rights on seeds only to the extent that they agree to treat seeds as capital. Despite FAO's insistence that breeders' rights and farmers' rights are 'parallel and complementary rather than opposed' (FAO 1987, 2–3), this is far from obvious. As Borowiak (2004, 534) shrewdly concludes, 'the reality is that TRIPS and breeders' rights have the force of capital behind them whereas the FAO and farmers' rights do not'.[11] Interestingly enough, a government official at the Indian Council for Agricultural Research made a similar comment.[12]

The evolution of Kloppenburg's thought on farmers' rights is interesting. In the revised 2004 edition of *First the seed*, he devotes a whole new chapter to plant biotechnology in the twenty-first century, in which he recognizes being overly optimistic with regards to the Seed Treaty 16 years earlier. The ITPGRFA was signed in 2001 and came into force in 2004. Its objectives are similar to those of the Convention on Biological Diversity (CBD) –

---

[10]On reconciling farmers' rights and breeders' rights, see also Alker and Heidhues (2002), Verkey (2007) and Winter (2010).

[11]On the role of multinational corporations in drafting the TRIPS Agreement, see Sell (1999) and Matthews (2002).

[12]Indian Council for Agricultural Research (ICAR), interview with the author, New Delhi, 26 February 2013.

conservation, sustainable use and benefit sharing – but, as its name indicates, it is specifi-cally concerned with genetic resources for food and agriculture. Both the CBD and the Seed Treaty are based on the premise that countries have sovereign rights over their genetic resources, as opposed to the former principle of genetic resources as the common heritage of humanity. At that time, and for reasons of realpolitik, Kloppenburg supported the shift toward national sovereignty over genetic resources. As he concludes, however, 'although so-called Farmers' Rights were recognized, they remain rhetorical constructs, and peasant farmers and indigenous peoples have been subjected to a new round of appro-priationist initiatives' (Kloppenburg 2004, 336). In a recent article, he offers a sharp critique:

> However appealing in conception, farmers' rights as they have actually been implemented in international fora have been little more than a rhetorical sleight of hand, a means of diverting activist energies into prolonged negotiations with corporate lobbyists and state bureaucrats. The final result of 12 years of talks was, in 2001, approval of an International Treaty on Plant Genetic Resources for Food and Agriculture (ITPGRFA) that neither effectively impedes genetic dispossession nor provides any material recompense for what is being taken. (Kloppenburg 2010, 373)

The growing skepticism surrounding the farmers' rights approach makes all the more important and timely a critical assessment of what national farmers' rights legislations have achieved so far. In the next section, I present an overview of the Indian Protection of Plant Varieties and Farmers' Rights Act, 2001, widely regarded as the most far-reaching farmers' rights legislation worldwide (Andersen and Winge 2008, 5).

India's farmers' rights legislation

Like the majority of countries in the Global South, India did not offer intellectual property in plant varieties prior to joining the WTO. The 1970 Indian Patent Act explicitly excluded agriculture and horticultural methods of production from patentability (GOI 1970). Conse-quently, India had to substantially revise its legislation in order to fulfil its new obligations under the TRIPS Agreement.[13]

The first draft of the plant variety protection bill, introduced in 1993, made no mention of farmers' rights. This draft met with considerable opposition and prompted mass demon-strations (termed *beej satyagraha* or seed protest) by farmers (Seshia 2002, 2745). Revised drafts were introduced in 1997, 1999 and 2000. From January to August 2000, a Joint Parlia-mentary Committee held public consultations throughout India. After a seven-year struggle and five drafts, the PPV&FR Act was finally passed in 2001 (Sahai n.d.[2]; Rangnekar 1998). The PPV&FR Act differs in substantial ways from the initial drafts. Civil society suc-ceeded in having several of its demands incorporated into the legislation, notably the *sui generis* system and the chapter on farmers' rights. It also succeeded in including farmers' right to sell seeds of protected varieties, the most fiercely resisted demand (Sahai 2001).

India's legislation is unique worldwide for it combines plant breeders' rights with elements of the CBD and Seed Treaty. In other words, India developed a truly *sui generis* (literally 'of its own kind') legislation. Significantly, farmers' rights are acknowl-edged in the very title of India's new law: the Protection of Plant Varieties and Farmers'

---

[13]As Seshia (2002, 2745) points out, Indian industry associations were calling for plant variety pro-tection prior to the WTO, and the Indian legislation should therefore not be seen strictly as the outcome of the TRIPS Agreement.

Rights (PPV&FR) Act, 2001. Chapter VI of the Act is devoted to farmers' rights. A farmer has the right to save, use, sow, resow, exchange, share or *sell* seeds, *including from protected varieties*, as well as harvested materials, 'in the same manner as he was entitled before the coming into force of this Act' (Art. 39.1).[14] The only restriction is that a farmer cannot sell branded seeds of a protected variety if they are labelled as such. This provision is usually understood as meaning that farmers can sell seeds in a generic form without a label but cannot compete with breeders and seed companies by selling under a brand name (Cohen and Ramanna 2007).

Farmers are recognized as breeders alongside public and private breeders, and are entitled to IPR protection of their varieties. Farmers' varieties are defined as those that have been traditionally cultivated and evolved by farmers in their fields, or those that are wild relatives, or land races of a variety about which farmers possess common knowledge (Art. 2 l). Farmers can register their varieties and are exempt from paying fees. The criteria for registration are the same as for public and private breeders – distinct, uniform and stable – except for the novelty criterion, which does not apply to farmers' varieties.

One salient feature of the Act is the recognition of extant (or existing) varieties as eligible for protection alongside new ones. Extant varieties include those notified under the Seeds Act, farmers' varieties, varieties in the public domain and varieties about which there is common knowledge (Art. 2j). This is a significant departure from UPOV and conventional IPR law, whose rhetoric is precisely to reward innovation and investment. According to Seshia (2002, 2745), extant varieties are mostly those in the public domain, and the rationale behind their inclusion was to strengthen the position of the public sector in establishing plant breeders' rights (PBR) over its varieties.

Besides new, farmers' and extant varieties, the Act provides for a fourth category – essentially derived varieties (EDV).[15] As its name indicates, EDV are essentially identical to the parent variety except for certain specific traits. EDV was added as an afterthought, and it remains a vague category whose definition is open to interpretation. According to some observers, the rationale was that it could provide some protection to publicly bred varieties that had been only slightly modified (S. Seshia 2001, cited in Cohen and Ramanna 2007). According to others, it was introduced under industry pressure and could be used to restrict farmers' rights. For example, a company could prevent farmers from developing a new variety using a protected variety by arguing that the new variety is in fact an EDV.[16]

The Act includes a number of innovative provisions pertaining to farmers' rights. For example, farmers cannot be held responsible for infringing breeders' rights if they can demonstrate that they did so unknowingly, a provision meant to protect farmers who are not yet aware of the new breeders' rights legislation. Moreover, seed companies are obligated to inform farmers of the expected yield of their varieties, and farmers are entitled to compensations if the seeds do not perform as advertised.[17]

---

[14]A farmer is defined in the PPV&FR Act as any person who cultivates crops himself or herself or through direct supervision, or who conserves and adds value to wild species or traditional varieties through selection and identification of their useful properties (Art. 2 k).

[15]Interestingly, EDV is a concept taken from UPOV 1991, of which India is not a member.

[16]Biswajit Dhar, Director, Research and Information Systems for Developing Countries, interview with the author, New Delhi, 5 March 2013.

[17]This provision takes on a special dimension in the context of the wave of farmers' suicides that has plagued the Indian countryside in recent years. While the causes defy simplistic explanations, spurious seeds and crop failure in a context of economic precariousness are important dimensions of the problem (Stone 2002).

The Act also includes provisions for benefit sharing. Farmers who are engaged in the conservation of genetic resources and their improvement through selection are entitled to receive benefits through the National Gene Fund. Upon registering varieties, private and public breeders are obligated to declare if they have used genetic resources maintained by indigenous or farmers' communities in the process, and the latter are entitled to receive benefits. Indigenous and farmers' communities can also make claims to the National Gene Fund when they believe that this has been the case. Any person, governmental or non-governmental agency can make a claim on behalf of a community. These provisions are innovative and represent one of the first attempts to incorporate the CBD's access and benefit-sharing provisions into a national legislation.

India also revised its legislation on industrial property to comply with the WTO TRIPS Agreement by introducing successive amendments to the Indian Patent Act in 1999, 2002 and 2005. The Patent Act (1970) allowed patents on processes but not on products, and excluded plants and agricultural methods.[18] With the 2002 amendment, products can now be patented. Moreover, a method or process for modifying a plant can now be counted as an invention and therefore patented. Patents are allowed on microorganisms, as well as on microbiological, biochemical and biotechnological processes, which means that methods of genetic engineering and genetically engineered organisms can be patented. It excludes from patentability plants and animals, in whole or in part, other than microorganisms, but including seeds, varieties, species and essentially biological processes for production or propagation of plants and animals (GOI 2002b). However, case law in other countries shows that even if patents are not allowed on higher life forms like plants, companies have successfully claimed *de facto* rights over the plants that incorporate a patented gene.[19] The Act also excludes discoveries and any invention derived from traditional knowledge. Patents have direct implications for farmers' rights since they are exclusive rights that prevent farmers from saving and exchanging seeds.

More than seven years elapsed between the introduction of the first draft, in 1993, and the passing of the PPV&FR Act, in 2001. Farmers' rights were only included in the PPV&FR Act after strong civil society pressure and lobbying, and their implementation raised a new set of challenges.

Twelve years on: advances and setbacks in implementing farmers' rights in India

The PPV&FR Act was passed by Parliament in 2001 and received presidential assent the same year, but the government delayed the Act's regulations until December 2006, effectively preventing its implementation. According to Ghose (2004), the main reason for delaying its implementation was the government's controversial decision to join UPOV and the ensuing Public Interest Litigation (this is discussed in more detail below). In any case, the PPV&FR Authority became functional with the Gazette notification and the appointment of the Chairperson of the Authority in November 2005. The registration

---

[18]The Patent Act (1970) excluded from patentability 'any process for the (…) treatment of animals or plants to render them free of disease or to increase their economic value or that of their products' (Art. 3).
[19]In the Monsanto vs. Schmeiser case, for example, the Canadian Supreme Court ruled that the issue of how Roundup Ready canola had landed on Schmeiser's property – whether through genetic contamination or otherwise – was ultimately irrelevant. Monsanto's patent on a gene extended to the plant of which it is a part, thus blurring the distinction between patents on trangenic cells or genes, and patents on plants (Cullet 2005, 105).

process for plant varieties came into effect in May 2007. The same year, the National Gene Fund was constituted. Finally, in February 2009, the PPV&FR Authority issued the first registration certificate.[20]

According to the latest statistics (February 2013), the PPV&FR Authority has received a total of 4284 applications for the registration of different categories of varieties (extant, new, farmers and EDV). Most applications come from the private sector (1799), followed by farmers (1387) and the public sector (1098). For the period 2007–2011, applications for the registration of farmers' varieties only accounted for 0.09 percent of the total number of applications. The lower pace of filing for farmers' varieties is generally accounted for by a lack of awareness of the new legislation among farmers, and the difficulty for them to deal with complex registration procedures (Lushington 2012, 126–7). Starting in 2012, there was a marked increase in the number of applications for farmers' varieties (32 percent of all applications, up from 0.09 percent).[21] However, applications were overwhelmingly for rice – 1404 out of 1460 (PPV&FR Authority 2013c) – and the increase reflects the intensified efforts of a small number of organizations more than the broadening of the process across India.

Out of these applications, 459 certificates have been issued for public varieties, 101 for private varieties and only six for farmers' varieties (PPV&FR Authority 2013a). Another eight farmers' varieties are awaiting registration at the time of writing.[22] The six varieties that have been granted registration under the Act are four varieties of rice and two of bread wheat (PPV&FR Authority 2013b).[23] Even though there is no data or even estimates of the number of farmers' varieties in existence in India, this is a dismayingly low number. Moreover, it is unlikely to change now that the grace period for the registration of extant varieties – five years from the date of notification of the crop species – is coming to an end. After the grace period, only new farmers' varieties will be eligible for plant variety protection.

As for the other farmers' rights provisions of the Act, results are also mixed. As we have seen, civil society formally has a say in the implementation of the PPV&FR legislation. The PPV&FR Authority includes representatives from the government, an agricultural university, the seed industry, a farmers' organization, a women farmers' organization and an indigenous organization. However, these provisions have not so far translated into meaningful participation.[24] As for the National Gene Fund, its impact has been limited. Benefit-sharing mechanisms have not been acted upon as yet, and proceeds are being redistributed in the form of an award to a small number of farmers and farmers' communities (five per year)

---

[20]Introducing plant variety protection is not a simple task. It requires setting up a complex infrastructure for processing applications, including guidelines for each crop species and for the different categories of applications, as well as for conducting distinctiveness, uniformity, stability (DUS) testing and in field grow-out tests, national and field gene banks, an appellate tribunal for resolving disputes surrounding plant variety registration, benefit sharing, compulsory licensing and the payment of compensation (Gautam *et al.* 2012, 20).

[21]Compiled from data in Lushington (2012) and PPV&FR Authority (2013a).

[22]Registrar General, PPV&FR Authority, interview with the author, New Delhi, 4 March 2013.

[23]The four varieties of rice are Tilak Chandan, Hansraj, Indrasan and Dadaji HMT; the two varieties of bread wheat are KUDRAT 9 and Wheat Ravi No. 1.

[24]Among the NGO representatives interviewed, no one knew who the farmers' and women farmers' representatives to the PPV&FR Authority were or even that there was one. When I asked officials at the PPV&FR Authority, I was told that the position for farmers' representative was currently vacant but that someone would be nominated shortly (Registrar General, PPV&FR Authority, interview with the author, New Delhi, 4 March 2013).

in recognition for their contribution to the preservation of agricultural biodiversity (PPV&FR Authority 2012).

In view of the low numbers of farmers' varieties registered, efforts have been made in recent years to increase the number of applications under this category. The PPV&FR Authority implemented a number of initiatives to reach out to farmers and increase awareness of the Act, such as conducting regional workshops and opening regional offices.[25] The PPV&FR Authority has also simplified the registration process. Farmers are exempted from paying fees for the registration of farmers' varieties and they are required to submit only half the quantity of seed material specified for a new variety. Regarding distinctiveness, uniformity, stability (DUS) criteria, the uniformity level for farmers' varieties cannot exceed double the number of off-types (any seed or plant that deviates in one or more characteristics from the variety as described) specified for new varieties, and the variety is deemed to meet the stability criteria if it meets the uniformity criteria (GOI 2009).

It is difficult to calculate the ratio of applications to registration because a variety can be found at any of the different stages of the registration process, a long process that takes between eight and 20 months. Nonetheless, farmers' varieties clearly have a lower ratio of registration to applications than public or private varieties. Although criteria have been relaxed for farmers' varieties, the fact remains that the DUS criteria used to assess commercial varieties are not suited to farmers' varieties. Commercial cultivars presuppose a high level of genetic uniformity and stability not found – nor considered desirable – in farmers' varieties bred for diversity and resilience (Navdanya 2013). This reflects the fact that commercial and farmers' varieties are inscribed in different paradigms (intensive vs. low-input farming) and obey distinct needs and logics.

The fact that the number of farmers' varieties registered remains low in spite of these efforts points to a broader problem. Indeed, a thorough understanding of the farmers' rights issue requires more than a formal analysis of the number of applications and the practical impediments to the registration of farmers' varieties; it requires an examination of the broader policies and politics of farmers' rights. As I explore below, an important part of the explanation for the low number of applications for farmers' varieties is a certain ambivalence toward the Act on the part of farmers and NGOs, possibly as a result of a series of contradictory governmental decisions and policies since the passing of the PPV&FR Act.

Farmers' rights beyond the PPV&FR Act

The first hint that the government was not unequivocally intent on implementing the new legislation came less than a year after the passing of the Act. In May 2002, the Indian cabinet expressed interest in joining the International Union for the Protection of New Varieties of Plants (UPOV). This decision came as a shock to those who had campaigned for a *sui generis* legislation.[26] Indeed, in order for India to join UPOV, it would have to amend its plant variety protection legislation to conform to the UPOV 1978 Convention. This would have negated all that had been achieved with the PPV&FR Act, since UPOV has no concept of farmers' rights. This decision on the part of the Indian cabinet is hard to explain, but it is clear that it was under strong external pressure. In the wake of the passing of the PPV&FR Act, UPOV was keen to get such an important country as India on board and prevent the

---

[25]See the PPV&FR Authority Annual Reports for a summary on these initiatives. (PPV&FR Authority n.d.).
[26]Suman Sahai, Director, Gene Campaign, interview with the author, New Delhi, 24 February 2013.

Indian model from becoming an alternative for other countries in the Global South. The UPOV Secretariat at the time made an offer to open an exception and allow India to join UPOV 1978. Indeed, since April 1999, countries had to join the latest, and more restrictive, 1991 Convention. The 1991 UPOV Convention extends protection from 15 to 20 years, does not include a breeders' exemption – the right to use a protected variety to develop a new variety – and extends protection to 'all plant varieties and products including those that are derived' (Art. 1). This means that protection is extended to harvested materials; farmers are no longer allowed to exchange or sell such material, and can only save seeds if national governments, with the consent of the breeder, allow limited exceptions. UPOV 1991 also allows 'dual protection', meaning that a product can be covered simultaneously by a patent and plant breeders' rights.[27]

However, the offer to join UPOV 1978 was not made in writing. According to a seasoned observer, UPOV is a member-driven organization and it is questionable whether the Secretariat offer would have been tenable.[28] In any case, Gene Campaign, an Indian NGO that has played a key role in the farmers' rights debate in India, filed a Public Interest Litigation (PIL) challenging the government decision on the grounds that India was under no obligation to join UPOV, and that doing so would constitute a violation of its own legislation (the PPV&FR Act and the Constitution) as well as of the CBD and Seed Treaty, of which India is a signatory (Gene Campaign 2003; Sahai n.d.[1]). In response to the PIL, the government backtracked and denied its intention to join UPOV, which put a temporary end to the PIL. The matter of India joining UPOV has since become dead letter, and India continues to hold observer status.[29]

As this example illustrates, we must look beyond the PPV&FR legislation in order to fully understand the challenges of implementing farmers' rights in India. Indeed, a number of bills and amendments passed since 2001 have direct implications for farmers' rights, notably the Biological Diversity Act, the Seeds Bill, the Biotechnology Regulatory Authority of India Bill and the National Food Security Act.[30]

A year after the passing of the PPV&FR Act, India enacted the Biological Diversity Act to fulfil its commitments as a party to the CBD (GOI 2002a). The Biological Diversity Act, 2002, creates a National Biodiversity Authority (NBA) to oversee the implementation of the Act and to advise the government on matters related to biological diversity. The NBA is responsible for regulating access to and use of genetic resources in India. In line with the CBD, the Act asserts national sovereignty over natural resources by imposing strict

---

[27]Few countries, such as the United States, allow the protection of plant varieties under patent law. However, as evidenced by the evolution of UPOV conventions, the tendency, over time, has been to expand the scope of plant breeders' rights to make them more akin to utility patents.

[28]Biswajit Dhar, Director, Research and Information Systems for Developing Countries, interview with the author, New Delhi, 5 March 2013.

[29]Contrary to Santilli's (2009, 350, my translation) suggestion that the fact that UPOV has not responded to India's interest in joining 'reveals that UPOV will probably not accept a *sui generis* system for the protection of plant varieties, distinct from its own', the immediate reason for India not joining UPOV is the filing of a Public Interest Litigation. This is not to say that UPOV would accept a *sui generis* system; in fact, it almost certainly would not, since it goes against the trend towards stronger plant breeders' rights evident in the latest UPOV Convention (1991).

[30]To add to the complexity, different ministries, each with its own goals and institutional culture, are responsible for implementing these laws. For example, the seeds policy comes under the authority of the Ministry of Agriculture, the Ministry of Environment and Forest is responsible for implementing the Biological Diversity Act and the Ministry of Science and Technology is in charge of the regulation of agricultural biotechnology.

conditions on foreigners' access to biological resources and related knowledge. However, it has also been criticized as alienating indigenous farmers from their resources by centralizing control and creating a burdensome bureaucracy (Cullet and Kolluru 2003). The PPV&FR Act and the Biological Diversity Act have distinct objectives. The PPV&FR Act aims 'to provide for the establishment of an effective system for the protection of plant varieties, the rights of farmers and plant breeders, and to encourage the development of new varieties of plants', whereas the Biological Diversity Act aims to regulate access to biological resources and associated knowledge, and ensure equitable sharing of the benefits arising from their use. However, there is some overlap between the two pieces of legislation, as both are designed to protect biological wealth and to regulate the IPRs involved. Both, for example, have provisions related to benefit sharing and the disclosure of the origin of biological materials.

A draft Seeds Bill was also introduced in 2004 to replace the Seeds Act, 1966 (GOI 2004). The stated goal of the bill is to create a regulatory environment conducive to the growth of the seed industry, and it is in many ways at odds with the PPV&FR Act. The proposed Seeds Bill made the registration of varieties mandatory. It stated that 'no seed of any kind or variety shall (...) be sold unless it is registered' (Art. 13.1) and that 'no producer shall grow or organize the production of seed unless he is registered as such by the State government' (Art. 21.1). Registration, however, is a long and costly process for farmers. In any case, farmers' varieties would likely not meet registration standards because they respond to a logic different from that of commercial varieties. The bill did not distinguish between a seed company and a farmer who barters seeds with his neighbour, and required that both be registered:

> Every person who desires to carry on the business of selling, keeping for sale, offering to sell, *bartering*, import or export or otherwise supply any seed (...) shall obtain a registration certificate as a dealer in seeds from the State Government. (Art. 22.1, emphasis added)

The bill also gave seed inspectors extensive search powers and stipulated fines for the exchange and barter of unregistered seeds.

Critics of the draft Seeds Bill, 2004, argued that it undermined most of the pro-farmer provisions of the PPV&FR Act, and that it would benefit multinational and large Indian seed companies (through sales of exported seeds) but would be detrimental to farmers (Zaidi 2005). They pointed out that some of its provisions were an assault on the informal seed market and were in direct contradiction to the PPV&FR Act. Indeed, Article 43.1 stated that

> nothing in this Act shall restrict the right of the farmer to save, use, exchange, trade or sell his farm seeds and planting material, except that he shall not sell such seed or planting material under a brand name or which does not conform to the minimum limit of germination, physical purity, genetic purity (...).

While the first part of the Article complied with the PPV&FR Act, the second part about meeting registration standards did not. Most farmer-selected varieties do not meet criteria for physical and genetic purity; they tend to be genetically unstable, which is precisely what makes them highly adapted to specific soils and cultivation systems. Moreover, many safeguards for farmers' rights present in the PPV&FR Act were not included in the Seeds Bill, 2004, which did not provide for innocent infringement, for benefit-sharing in cases where farmers' varieties were being used in the development of commercial cultivars, or for redress in case of spurious seeds (GRAIN with Sharma 2005; Zaidi 2005).[31]

The bill met with an outcry and a list of amendments was introduced in 2010 following the recommendations of a Standing Committee on Agriculture (PRS 2010). The amendments corrected the most glaring inconsistencies with the PPV&FR Act, by (1) deleting the requirement for farmers to conform to the prescribed minimum limits of germination, physical purity and genetic purity, (2) expanding the definition of a farmer (who is exempted from compulsory registration of seeds) to include any person who conserves or adds value to traditional varieties and (3) setting up a Compensation Committee where farmers can claim compensation if seeds fail to perform to expected standards. As of October 2013, it had not yet been passed.[32]

Another bill that is relevant to farmers' rights is the Biotechnology Regulation Act of India (BRAI) Bill (GOI 2013a). The BRAI Bill was introduced in Parliament despite strong opposition on 22 April 2013. It regulates the research, manufacture, importation and use of products of modern biotechnology. The bill has been denounced as favoring the interests of the biotechnology industry at the expense of biosafety. It creates a single-window clearing house for genetically modified (GM) crops in the form of a three-member committee under the authority of the Ministry of Science and Technology. Critics point out that this puts the Ministry of Science and Technology in a position of conflict of interest, since it becomes both a promoter and regulator of GM crops. Critics also argue that the Bill takes away power from state governments (under the Constitution of India, agriculture is a state subject). The bill is also criticized for bypassing the Right to Information Act (RTI), 2005, since some information related to GM crops would be considered 'confidential commercial information'. Finally, the bill does not include any provision for long-term independent impact assessment or need assessment (Coalition for a GM-Free India 2013). This pro-industry bill sends another strong signal that the government is favoring the interests of the commercial seed industry.

Finally, the National Food Security Bill has been the object of considerable debate since its inception in December 2011. Setting aside all opposition, the Indian cabinet promulgated an ordinance on 3 July 2013 and the bill was passed on 12 September 2013 as the National Food Security Act (NFSA) (GOI 2013b). The NFSA set up an ambitious program aimed at providing subsidized grains to two-thirds of India's 1.2-billion population who are food insecure. Laudable though the aim might be, the bill has been severely criticized as a missed opportunity for food security and farmers, and as expanding people's dependence on government welfare rather than tackling the structural roots of malnutrition and hunger (Kothari 2012). For example, it makes no provision for the production of food or the support of small and marginal farmers through the local procurement of 'coarse grains'.[33] 'Coarse grains' refers to cereal grains other than wheat and rice – such as millets, barley and sorghum – that are highly nutritious and better adapted to marginal environments but have been traditionally neglected by public policies bent on high-yielding

---

[31]The only mechanism for redress is to turn to a local consumer court, an option already available under the 1986 Consumer Protection Act.

[32]Another relevant act is the Geographical Indications Act, 1999, which came into force in 2003. According to Ramanna (2006, viii), depending on the way it is implemented, it could be either beneficial to farmers, if it enables them to claim rights for agricultural goods originating in a specific region, or it could be detrimental if it restricts farmers' access to the protected goods.

[33]Food activists advocate substituting the negatively connoted 'coarse grains' by 'nutritious grains' but the latter has not yet made its way into common parlance.

varieties.[34] NGOs such as the Deccan Development Society and the Millet Network of India have long advocated the cultivation of traditional varieties of millets and their inclusion in the Public Distribution System, but their demands have not made their way into the NFSA.[35] The NFSA also raises concern that increased demand and higher government payments for staples like wheat and rice may lead to a decrease in agricultural diversification.[36]

In sum, after the passing of the PPV&FR Act, 2001, a series of controversial government decisions and pieces of legislation sent contradictory signals regarding the government's will to implement farmers' rights. The first such signal was the cabinet's unexpected decision to join UPOV, in 2002, in direct contradiction to efforts to devise a *sui generis* legislation. Both the amended Seeds Bill, 2004, and the Biotechnology Regulatory Authority of India (BRAI) Act, 2013, are widely perceived as promoting the interests of the commercial seed industry over those of farmers. The Seeds Bill, 2004, in particular, included provisions that undermined the rights conferred to farmers under the PPV&FR Act. Finally, the National Food Security Act, 2013, has been interpreted as a missed opportunity to promote farmers' rights by linking, for example, this ambitious scheme to local food production.

Farmers' rights and the cunning state

India's decision to join UPOV in the wake of the PPV&FR Act can be interpreted as a desire to please and appease civil society at home by passing a strong farmers' rights legislation, all the while ceding to international pressure to join UPOV and appease another constituency – the national seed industry. However, as we have seen, this decision was not only totally contradictory but ultimately impracticable.

Randeria's analysis of the cunning state offers interesting insights into the role of countries such as India in the global politics of intellectual property rights over genetic resources. As she suggests, 'cunning states (…) lack neither [bargaining power nor technical expertise] but prefer to make sub-optimal use of the limited space currently available for autonomous policy formulation and implementation within the WTO framework' (Randeria 2007, 7). As she is careful to specify,

> this is not to suggest that their sovereignty is not being externally constrained and internally contested. It is my argument that, within these limits, there is considerably more space for setting national agendas than is conceded by cunning states, which lack the political will, rather than the space, for autonomous policy-making. (Randeria 2007, 6)

This argument is borne out by the fact that India was initially intent on introducing a legislation based on UPOV 1978. It is important to stress that both options – UPOV 1978 and a *sui generis* legislation – were consistent with its obligations under the TRIPS Agreement.

---

[34]Coarse grains have recently attracted the interest of private corporations. For example, the Syngenta Foundation, in partnership with Bioversity and the Consultative Group on International Agricultural Research (CGIAR), has a Payments for Agrobiodiversity Conservations Services (PACS) program targeting Indian varieties of millets (Syngenta n.d.).
[35]The Deccan Development Society (DDS n.d.) has been a pioneer in the revalorization of millet-based farming and food systems in India. See also the website of the Millet Network of India (MINI n.d.)
[36]For a critique of the National Food Security Act, see the Right to Food Campaign (n.d.)

Most government officials are well aware that the ambiguity surrounding certain provisions of the TRIPS Agreement allows for a multitude of possibilities. As the Indian Minister for Commerce and Industry put it eloquently at the time:

> we are all aware that the text of the TRIPS is a masterpiece of ambiguity, couched in the language of diplomatic compromise, resulting in a verbal tight-rope walk, with a prose remarkably elastic and capable of being stretched all the way to Geneva. (Ministry of Commerce and Industry 2002, 2)

One prime example is the fact that the meaning of 'an effective *sui generis* system for plant varieties' in Article 27(3)b of the TRIPS Agreement was entirely open to interpretation. In fact, there is no agreed upon understanding of that phrase to this day.[37] This ambiguity gave countries considerable flexibility to develop a system truly 'of its own kind' (especially for countries which, like India, are not members of UPOV), but few countries took advantage of it. India is among the few countries[38] that exploited the flexibility allowed by the TRIPS Agreement to introduce a protection of plant varieties legislation better adapted to its reality, but it only did so under pressure from civil society.

The importance of political will (and the lack of it) is evidenced when one contrasts the Indian government's stance on the issue of farmers' rights with its stance on the issue of generic drugs. In April 2013, in a much-awaited decision, the Supreme Court of India ruled that, under India's anti-evergreening provisions, the patent sought by Novartis for a new version of its cancer drug Glivec did not represent a true innovation. Evergreening refers to the myriad ways in which pharmaceutical companies use the law and related regulatory processes to extend their patents, particularly on blockbuster drugs, beyond the period of time that would normally be permissible under the law. In practice, the Supreme Court decision means that generic drug manufacturers can continue producing generic versions of the drug (Harris and Thomas 2013). Food is as critical as health, and the Indian state could similarly argue that seeds are a matter of public interest and intervene to regulate royalties and seed pricing.[39] However, it has chosen not to do so. A number of factors explain why the Indian state is more inclined to defend access to generic drugs than access to seeds. For one thing, wealthy urban patients represent a more influential constituency than poor rural farmers.[40] More importantly perhaps, the interests of its thriving Indian generic drug industry are at stake.

India's stance on biopiracy nationally and internationally also illustrates cunning states' ambivalent role. India has consistently taken a strong stance against biopiracy in international negotiations at the WTO, World Intellectual Property Rights Organization (WIPO) and on the Nagoya Protocol on Access and Benefit-Sharing. It has championed the most stringent option of 'disclosure as a TRIPS obligation' and supported efforts at

---

[37] According to Article 27(3)b, 'However, Members shall provide for the protection of plant varieties either by patents or by an effective *sui generis* system or by any combination thereof' (WTO 1994). On the lack of an agreed upon interpretation of the meaning of 'an effective *sui generis* system for new plant varieties', see World Trade Organization (2008).
[38] With the exception of Costa Rica and Ethiopia in their national legislation, and the African Union as a whole, the countries that recognize farmers' rights are mostly located in Asia (Bangladesh, Malaysia, Nepal, Pakistan, the Philippines and Thailand). See the Farmers' Rights Project (n.d.)
[39] In India, the State government of Andhra Pradesh has recently introduced a bill asserting its right to monitor the pricing of seeds and royalties (Kurmanath 2013).
[40] While the issue of access to seeds affects all farmers, it is a more pressing concern for small farmers who rely on farm-saved seeds.

developing an international legal instrument for the disclosure of the origin of biological materials and associated traditional knowledge when they are the objects of intellectual property claims. This has pitted India against the European Union, which agrees with the disclosure requirement in principle, but wants any legal consequences to fall outside the purview of patent law, and against the United States, which argues that this should be addressed under national, not supranational, legislation (TWN 2013).

In contrast to its proactive stance in international negotiations on traditional knowledge and biological material, India has a mixed record on the protection of farmers' rights and its resources against biopiracy. The first case of biopiracy involving India's natural resources to draw public attention after the coming into force of the WTO involved turmeric. In this case, the publicly funded Indian Council for Scientific and Industrial Research (CSIR) successfully challenged, in 1997, the patent granted by the US Patent and Trademark Office (USPTO) on the grounds that it did not meet the criterion of novelty (turmeric has been used in India for thousands of years for healing wounds and rashes) (Shiva 1997). However, the Indian state failed to challenge the patent granted to a US transnational corporation by the European Patent Office on the Neem tree, an evergreen found all over India, whose seeds have pesticidal properties. Instead, the legal challenge was taken up by a civil society coalition that challenged the patent on the grounds that the seeds of the Neem tree were traditionally used as a bio-pesticide. The European Patent Office struck down the patent after a five-year long legal battle on the grounds that it lacked novelty, since a similar process already existed in India. Ironically, as Randeria (2007, 8–10) points out, although the coalition's objective – the revocation of the patent – was met, the decision dismissed the argument regarding traditional knowledge and the rights of agricultural communities, and reduced the case to a dispute between Indian and American industrialists. In the case of Basmati rice, the Indian government only challenged the US corporation RiceTec patent when forced to do so by the Indian Supreme Court following a Public Interest Litigation. Moreover, when it did, it only protected the interests of Indian Basmati rice exporters and not those of its farmers and breeders. When RiceTec withdrew the claims relevant to Indian rice exporters, the Indian government simply dropped the case. However, following a transnational civil society campaign, the USPTO struck down 15 of the 20 patent claims (Caduff and Randeria 2010, 295). The most recent case involves a patent obtained by Monsanto in Europe on Indian melons with a natural resistance to the Cucurbit yellow stunting disorder virus. The Indian government did not take legal action and a coalition led by the Indian NGO Navdanya and the European NGO No Patents on Seeds challenged the patent on the grounds that Monsanto had not applied for authorization to access germplasm as required under the Biodiversity Act, that it represented an abuse of patent law since European patent law does not allow patents on conventional breeding and, finally, that the patents would severely restrict farmers and plant breeders (No Patents on Seeds 2011). While it did not challenge the European patent, the National Biodiversity Authority announced in June 2013 its intention to oppose Monsanto's application for the same patent before the US Patent Office on the grounds that it involves the misappropriation of Indian melon germplasm (Sood 2013b). Taken together, these cases reveal the inconsistent role of the Indian government in challenging foreign patents on Indian bio-resources.

Another characteristic of cunning states is the discrepancy that exists between national and international discourse, official positions and actions, and the law and its enforcement. In consonance with its position on the disclosure of the source of origin of biological materials, India is one of a handful of countries that have enacted domestic disclosure rules (along with Brazil, China and Peru).[41] However, it has not shown the same readiness to enforce these rules. The first national case of biopiracy involves the use of local varieties of brinjal (the Indian term for eggplant) in the development of Bt brinjal (Laursen 2012). Bt brinjal was developed by a public agricultural university (the University of Agricultural Science in Dharwad, Karnataka State), Mahyco-Monsanto Biotech (MMB)[42] and a private consulting firm (Sathguru Management Consultants Private Limited). As in the case of Basmati rice and Neem tree, it is civil society that first raised the issue, alerted authorities and pressured the government into action. In 2010, the Indian NGO Environment Support Group filed a complaint with the Karnataka Biodiversity Board (KBB), alleging that the developers of Bt Brinjal had not applied to the National Biodiversity Authority (NBA) for the authorization to use local varieties of eggplants, in violation of India's National Biodiversity Act.[43] The KBB initially supported the complaint, but later washed its hands of the matter, referring it to the NBA (Sood 2012).

Foot-dragging on the part of the NBA prompted the Environment Support Group to file a Public Interest Litigation against the Ministry of Environment and Forest, the NBA and the KBB demanding that they 'perform their statutory duties under the Biological Diversity Act, 2002 with regard to existing cases of biopiracy' (High Court of Karnataka 2012). The NBA and KBB finally filed a criminal complaint in November 2012 after the High Court issued notice to them. However, the same month, in a controversial move, the Karnataka government announced the transfer of the two officers who were empowered by the KBB to file a criminal complaint in the case, a decision that suggests that there is no will to pursue the case on the part of public authorities (ESG 2013; Sood 2013a). The case is currently on hold: on 3 January 2013, four of the accused obtained a six-month stay of criminal proceedings. Curiously enough, one of the accused in the Bt Brinjal case was appointed in May 2013 as the new chairperson of the PPV&FR Authority – a clear indication of where the central government stands on the case.

If cunning states' strategies may help them navigate the intricacies of global politics and international environment and trade negotiations, they are not without consequences at home, where they risk alienating civil society. The ambiguous politics of the Indian state regarding IPRs and biodiversity have led to disillusionment and skepticism, even among some activists who previously supported the PPV&FR Act. Indeed, given the government's mixed record on farmers' rights and biopiracy, many activists express disenchantment with the role of the government and public sector. As one long-time environmental activist and researcher put it: 'we disagree with Green Revolution policies, but at least at that time the government was to some extent working for the public good; nowadays, it works for private interests'.[44]

---

[41]According to section 25(1) of the Patents Amendment Act, 2005: 'Where an application for a patent has been published but a patent has not been granted, any person may, in writing, represent by way of opposition to the Controller against the grant of patent on the ground – ... (j) that the complete specification does not disclose or wrongly mentions the source or geographical origin of biological material used for the invention'.

[42]Mahyco-Monsanto Biotech (MMB) is a 50:50 joint venture between Mahyco (the Maharashtra Hybrid Seed Corporation) and the US company Monsanto.

[43]According to the Biological Diversity Act, 2002, 'No person shall apply for any intellectual property right by whatever name called in or outside India for any invention based on any research or information on a biological resource obtained from India without obtaining the previous approval of the National Biodiversity Authority before making such application' (Art. 6.1).

[44]Grassroots organizer, Environmental NGO, interview with the author, Pune, Maharashtra, 23 February 2013. On the changing role of the Indian state since 1991, see Gupta and Sivaramakrishnan (2010).

Adding to the unease is the uncertainty surrounding the legal status of genetic resources held by the National Bureau of Plant Genetic Resources (NBPGR). Part of the Indian Council of Agricultural Research (ICAR), NBPGR is responsible for the exchange, quarantine, collection, conservation, evaluation and systematic documentation of plant genetic resources. Most of these resources have been collected from farmers over the years and are held in trust by the NBPGR. In October 2012, the Indian Council of Agricultural Research (ICAR) moved a controversial proposal to make this material available to private seed companies (it is currently available only to research institutes) but was forced to backtrack following the public outcry (Sharma 2012). In this broader policy context, some farmers and NGOs are wary of registering their varieties with the PPV&FR Authority, especially since this involves giving a sample of the variety for the purpose of characterization[45] and storage in a national gene bank. In the absence of a clear will on the part of the government to keep genetic resources in the public sector, farmers fear that their varieties may end up in the hands of the private sector. There exists a precedent: in late 2002, Syngenta, the Switzerland-based multinational corporation, entered into an agreement with a state agricultural university (*Indira Gandhi Krishi Vishwavidyalaya*, IGKV) in the Indian State of Chhattisgarh to gain access to 20,000 paddy varieties in the custody of the university. A coalition of grassroots organizations launched a campaign that led to the demise of the agreement (Lutringer 2009). A certain wariness toward the post-liberalization state is evident in NGO workers' insistence that the state is not the owner of plant genetic resources but their caretaker. It is also evident in their emphasis on the role of communities in the management of plant genetic resources. As one grassroots activist and researcher puts it, 'if you can't rely on the government or on the private sector, that only leaves communities'.[46]

Disillusionment with the public sector translates into mixed feelings about the Indian legislation and a broader critique of the farmers' rights discourse. Some activists argue that farmers' rights should be understood in much broader terms, and not as 'vestigial rights'.[47] The Indian farmers' rights legislation 'might be more progressive than what is found elsewhere but the principle – exclusive rights – is actually wrong'.[48] The need 'to move beyond farmers' rights' is another recurring theme: 'the whole rights framework[49] is very restrictive [for farmers], we should talk about autonomy and sovereignty, not rights'.[50]

These quotes by Indian activists echo the current debate on the pertinence of the rights-based approach.[51] One of its most prominent critics is Brewster Kneen (see also GRAIN

---

[45]Morpho-agronomic characterization consists in the analysis of germplasm, using descriptors developed by organizations such as the FAO International Plant Genetic Resources Institute (IPGRI) and UPOV. This data is then used to elaborate the 'passport' of a specific variety.

[46]Grassroots organizer and researcher, Environmental NGO, interview with the author, Pune, Maharashtra, 23 February 2013.

[47]Executive Director, Sustainable Agriculture NGO, interview with the author, Hyderabad, 14 February 2013.

[48]Director, Rural Grassroots Organization, interview with the author, Medak district, Andhra Pradesh, 10 February 2013.

[49]It must be noted that these comments are made with reference to India's PPV&FR Act, in which farmers' rights are conceived as IPRs, and not to current efforts to frame peasants' rights as human rights.

[50]Director, Rural Grassroots Organization, interview with the author, Medak district, Andhra Pradesh, 10 February 2013.

[51]For a concise overview of the different positions in the debate, see Edelman (2014, 13–5).

2007). In The Tyranny of Rights, Kneen (2009, 66) describes the term farmers' rights as 'certainly one of the most pernicious constructs of the rights language':

> The assertion of Farmers' Rights is intended to create the legal space for farmers to maintain these traditional practices in the face of efforts, by both states and corporations, to enclose this space and occupy it with hybrids, patented varieties and corporate agents while outlawing the traditional practices. Thus Farmers' Rights are functionally a reactive claim for an exception to the capitalist laws of private property. (Kneen 2009, 69)

This analysis is shared by many Indian activists, who recognize the limits of what can be achieved even with outstanding legislation. In this context, the emerging discussion around food sovereignty is perceived as a possible way out of the impasse. As one long time farmers' rights activist puts it, 'if a community is food sovereign and seed sovereign, farmers' rights are not very important'.[52] Navdanya (2013, 35) defines seed sovereignty as self-governance by farming communities in the sphere of informal exchange and, in the market sphere, as the recognition in law of the sovereign rights of farmers. While food security is widely discussed (as witnessed by the debate around the food security bill), discussion on the issue of food sovereignty is embryonic in India: it is limited for the time being to a small circle of farmers' organizations and grassroots NGOs that have close links to La Via Campesina and the global food sovereignty movement. According to one grassroots activist, food sovereignty, which implies community control over resources, does not go down well in India where 'the State is sovereign, not its people'.[53]

Within these circles, there is an emerging discussion of Open Source Seeds, conceived as an alternative to farmers' rights as formulated in the PPV&FR Act.[54] Open Source Seeds are still at the stage of conceptual discussions in India, but a small network of activists and researchers has launched a number of initiatives. The Centre for Sustainable Agriculture (CSA), based in Hyderabad, and the Alliance for Sustainable and Holistic Agriculture, a network of organizations across the country, launched an Open Source Campaign and produced a working document. (CSA n.d.) The guiding principle is that rights should not be exclusive and should not prevent further innovation. As is the case with open source software, material transfer agreements should specify that any variety derived from such material is also open source (the so-called viral effect). CSA is working with farmer-breeders and lawyers to establish an open source legal system, while at the same time dialoguing with the government (in particular, the NBPGR) to have public resources, including all the existing germplasm held by public agricultural universities, declared as open source. While individual scientists within the public breeding system may be open to discussing open source, institutions are wary of doing so.[55] In the prevailing climate of liberalization and strengthening of IPRs, these initiatives clearly go against the general trend and promise to be an uphill battle.

---

[52]Director, Rural Grassroots Organization, interview with the author, Medak district, Andhra Pradesh, 10 February 2013.
[53]Grassroots organizer, interview with the author, Medak district, Andhra Pradesh, 12 February 2013.
[54]For an overview of Biological Open Source and seeds, see Kloppenburg (2010).
[55]Executive Director, Sustainable Agriculture NGO, interview with the author, Hyderabad, 14 February 2013.

Conclusion

Farmers' rights and food sovereignty: lessons from India

The lengthy and heated debate over the formulation of India's PPV&FR Act has raised a number of important issues, such as how to recognize and reward farmers' innovations and how to define farmers' rights in legal terms.[56] The very notion of farmers as 'rights-holders' is an outcome of this process. And while many grassroots initiatives by Indian NGOs aimed at documenting and supporting farmers' breeding and conservation practices predate the debate over farmers' rights, the latter gave them new momentum.

There is no question that farmers enjoy significant rights under India's Protection of Plant Varieties and Farmers' Rights Act (2001) – at least on paper. However, important questions remain as to its implementation. Beyond technical or practical limitations such as the lack of awareness and resources, there exists a deeper barrier to the realization of farmers' rights in India. Indeed, meaningful implementation of these rights is dependent on a close working relationship between the public authorities in charge for implementing the legislation on one hand, and farmers and their representatives on the other. However, in the current policy context in which the general thrust is toward the liberalization of Indian agriculture, the kind of trust required for such a relationship is lacking. Stated differently, the very political and economic climate that led to the introduction of plant variety protection – and thus created the need for farmers' rights in the first place – is not conducive to their meaningful implementation.

Farmers' rights activists in India have been largely successful in the fight over the plant variety protection legislation. However, for reasons discussed in this article, the initial optimism surrounding the adoption of the PPV&FR Act has given way in recent years to wariness and skepticism. In this context, farmers' rights activists are increasingly channelling their efforts into grassroots initiatives for the preservation of farmers' varieties, all the while searching for alternative avenues for the realization of farmers' rights. One of these avenues, which I have briefly discussed, is open source seed systems. Another avenue, which La Via Campesina and its allies are pursuing through the proposed UN Declaration on the Rights of Peasants, is to frame the right to seeds and genetic resources as a human right. This strategy presents its own challenges. According to Claeys (2012, 853),

> the legalization of social struggles carries a number of potentially negative impacts that the movement is well aware of: the transformation of the movement's struggle in technical debates to be solved in specialized arenas, the demobilization of movement activists, and the loss of autonomy.

However, it also opens up new possibilities for both definition and implementation. On a conceptual level, the negotiations on a Declaration on the Rights of Peasants could be seen as an opportunity to redefine farmers' rights over their seeds in a way that further challenges the limitations of conventional property rights. On a strategic level, it opens up the possibility for civil society to resort to the Supreme Court and international instruments to bring pressure to bear on the state for the realization of farmers' rights. In a country like India, where a progressive Supreme Court has been successful in holding the state accountable to its citizens,[57] this may represent a promising avenue.

---

[56]Thank you to Anitha Ramanna for drawing my attention to these positive impacts of the farmers' rights debate in India.
[57]For example, the Supreme Court has, in recent years, interpreted the right to food as part of the right to life, and directed the Central Government to design an employment guarantee scheme, upgrade education as a right and draw up a right to information act. See Chandhoke (2007, 45–6).

References

Alker, D., and F. Heidhues. 2002. Farmers' rights and intellectual property rights: reconciling conflicting concepts. In *Economic and social issues in agricultural biotechnology*, ed. R.E. Evenson, V. Santaniello, and D. Ziberman, 61–92. Wallingford: CABI.

Andersen, R. 2005. *The history of farmers' rights: a guide to central documents and literature.* Lysaker, Norway: The Fridtjof Nansen Institute.

Andersen, R. 2006. *Realizing farmers' rights under the international treaty on plant genetic resources for food and agriculture. Summary of findings from the farmers' rights project, Phase 1.* Lysaker, Norway: The Fridtjof Nansen Institute.

Andersen, R., and T. Winge. 2008. *Success stories from the realization of farmers' rights related to plant genetic resources for food and agriculture.* Lysaker, Norway: The Fridtjof Nansen Institute.

Bennett, E. 2002. The summit-to-summit merry-go-round. *Seedling* July: 3–10.

Bertacchini, E. E. 2008. Coase, Pigou and the potato: Whither farmers' rights?. *Ecological Economics* 68: 183–93.

Borowiak, C. 2004. Farmers' rights: intellectual property regimes and the struggle over seeds. *Politics & Society* 32, no. 4: 511–43.

Caduff, C., and S. Randeria. 2010. Reinventing the commons. In *Turn over. Cultural turns in der soziologie*, ed. S. Frank and J. Schwenk, 289–305. Frankfurt: Campus Verlag.

Centre for Sustainable Agriculture (CSA) n.d. *Open source seed systems.* http://agrariancrisis.in/wp-content/uploads/2012/08/Open-Source-Seed-Systems-1.01.pdf [accessed July 8, 2014].

Chandhoke, N. 2007. Engaging with civil society: The democratic perspective. NGPA Working Paper Series, London School of Economics.

Claeys, P. 2012. The creation of new rights by the food sovereignty movement: the challenge of institutionalizing subversion. *Sociology* 46, no. 5: 844–60.

Coalition for a GM-Free India. 2013. Critique of the biotechnology regulatory authority of India (BRAI) bill, 2013. New Delhi: Coalition for a GM-Free India. http://indiagminfo.org/wp-content/uploads/2011/09/brai-2013-coalition-critique.pdf [accessed October 8, 2013].

Cohen, M.J., and A. Ramanna. 2007. Public access to seeds and the human right to adequate food. In *Global obligations for the human right to food*, ed. G. Kent, 161–90. Maryland: Rowman and Littlefield.

Cullet, P. 2005. Monsanto v Schmeiser: a landmark decision concerning farmer liability and transgenic contamination. *Journal of Environmental Law* 17, no. 1: 83–108.

Cullet, P., and R. Kolluru. 2003. Plant variety protection and farmers' rights. Towards a broader understanding. *Delhi Law Review* 24: 41–59.

Deccan Development Society (DDS). n.d. http://www.ddsindia.com [accessed July 7, 2014].

Edelman, M. 2014. Linking the rights of peasants to the right to food in the United Nations. *Law, Culture and the Humanities* 10, no. 2: 196–211.

Edelman, M., and C. James. 2011. Peasants' rights and the UN system: Quixotic struggle? Or emancipatory idea whose time has come?. *Journal of Peasant Studies* 38, no. 1: 81–108.

Environment Support Group. 2013. Transferring prosecuting officers exposes Indian and Karnataka governments weak intent to tackle biopiracy by Mahyco/Monsanto and others. Press release, Bangalore, 9 March. http://www.esgindia.org/campaigns/press/transferring-prosecuting-officers-expose.html [accessed October 8, 2013].

Escobar, A. 1994. Welcome to cyberia: notes on the anthropology of cyberculture. *Current Anthropology* 35: 211–31.

Farmers' Rights Project. n.d. http://www.farmersrights.org [accessed July 8, 2014].

Food and Agriculture Organization. 1987. Report by the Chairman of the Working Group on its Second Meeting, Report of the Second Session of the Commission on Plant Genetic Resources, CL 91/14, Appendix F.

Food and Agriculture Organization. 1989. Resolution 5/89. Farmers' Rights. Report of the Conference of FAO. 25th Session. Rome, 29 November.

Food and Agriculture Organization. 2001. International Treaty on Plant Genetic Resources for Food and Agriculture. Rome, 3 November.

Gautam, P.L., A.K. Singh, M. Srivastava, and P.K. Singh. 2012. Protection of plant varieties and farmers' rights: a review. *Indian Journal of Plant Genetic Resources* 25, no. 1: 9–29.

Gene Campaign. 2003. *Oppose UPOV! save farmers! Gene campaign's legal action against Indian government.* New Delhi: Gene Campaign.

Ghose, J.R. 2004. Saving seeds or saving face? Seed acquisition mechanisms among farmers in Jharkhand, India and sui generis protection. http://ranaghose.com/research/sssf.pdf [accessed October 8, 2013].

GOI (Government of India). 1970. Patents Act, 1970. Act No. 39.

GOI (Government of India). 2001. Protection of Plant Varieties and Farmers' Rights Act, 2001. Act No. 53.

GOI (Government of India). 2002a. Biological Diversity Act, 2002. Act No. 18.

GOI (Government of India). 2002b. Patents Amendment Act, 2002. Act No. 38.

GOI (Government of India). 2004. Seeds Bill, 2004.

GOI (Government of India). 2009. The Gazette of India Extraordinary. Part II, Section 3, Sub-section (i). G.S.R. 452 (E). June 30.

GOI (Government of India). 2013a. Biotechnology Regulatory Authority of India (BRAI) Bill. Bill No. 57.

GOI (Government of India). 2013b. National Food Security Act, 2013. Act No. 20.

Golay, C. 2013. Legal reflections on the rights of peasants and other people working in rural areas. Background paper. Prepared for the first session of the working group on the rights of peasants and other people working in rural areas (15–19 July 2013). http://www.ohchr.org/Documents/HRBodies/HRCouncil/WGPleasants/Golay.pdf [accessed February 17, 2014].

GRAIN. 2007. What's wrong with rights?. *Seedlings* October: 2–23.

GRAIN, with D. Sharma. 2005. India's new seed bill. *Seedling* July: 22–7.

Gupta, A. 1998. *Postcolonial developments: agriculture in the making of modern India*. Durham, NC: Duke University Press.

Gupta, A., and K. Sivaramakrishnan. 2010. *The state of India after liberalization: interdisciplinary perspectives*. New York: Routledge.

Harris, G., and K. Thomas. 2013. Low-cost drugs in poor nations get a lift in Indian court. *The New York Times*, 1 April.

High Court of Karnataka. 2012. Public interest litigation, writ petition No. 41532/2012, High Court of Karnataka at Bangalore. http://www.esgindia.org/sites/default/files/campaigns/press/esg-pil-biopiracy-hc-kar-oct-2012-final-.pdf [accessed October 8, 2013].

Kloppenburg, J. 2004 [1988]. *First the seed: the political economy of plant biotechnology, 1492–2000*. Madison: The University of Wisconsin Press.

Kloppenburg, J. 2010. Impeding dispossession, enabling repossession: biological open source and the recovery of seed sovereignty. *Journal of Agrarian Change* 10, no. 3: 367–88.

Kneen, B. 2009. *The tyranny of rights*. Ottawa: Ram's Horn.

Kochhar, S. 2010. How effective is sui generis plant variety protection in India: some initial feedback. *Journal of Intellectual Property Rights* 15: 237–84.

Kochupillai, M. 2011. India's plant variety protection law: historical and implementation perspectives. *Journal of Intellectual Property Rights* 16, no. 2: 88–101.

Kothari, A. 2012. No food security without ecological and livelihood security. Infochange News and Features, May. http://www.infochangeindia.org/environment/politics-of-biodiversity/no-food-security-without-ecological-and-livelihood-security.html [Accessed 16 July 2013].

Kumar, P.S., S.M. Khan, M. Hora, and M.P. Rao. 2011. Implementation of Indian PPV&FR Act and Rules: inadequacies leading to avoidable litigation. *Journal of Intellectual Property Rights* 16: 102–6.

Kurmanath, K.V. 2013. AP asserts its right on seed price, royalty payouts. *The Hindu Business Line* 25 March.

Laursen, L. 2012. Monsanto to face biopiracy charges in India. *Nature Biotechnology* 30, no. 1: 11.

Lushington, K. 2012. The registration of plant varieties by farmers in India: a status report. *Review of Agrarian Studies* 2, no. 1: 112–28.

Lutringer, C. 2009. Acting on institutions to preserve agricultural biodiversity: the Syngenta controversy in Chhattisgarh. In *The changing identity of rural India: a socio-historic analysis*, ed. E. Basile and I. Mukhopadhyay, 259–86. London: Anthem Press.

Matthews, D. 2002. *Globalizing intellectual property rights: the TRIPS agreement*. London: Routledge.

Millet Network of India (MINI). n.d. http://www.milletindia.org [accessed July 7, 2014].

Ministry of Commerce and Industry. 2002. *India and the WTO. A monthly newsletter of the Ministry of Commerce and Industry (May)*. New Delhi: Government of India. http://commerce.nic.in/writereaddata/publications/wto_may2002.pdf [accessed October 11, 2013].

Montecinos, C. 1996. Sui generis: a dead end alley. *Seedling* 13, no. 4: 19–28.

Navdanya. 2013. The law of the seed. http://www.navdanya.org/attachments/Latest_Publications1. pdf [accessed October 9, 2013].

No Patents on Seeds. 2011. Opposition to Monsanto's patent on Indian melon. International coalition 'No patents on seeds' concerned about abuse of patent law. 3 February. http://www.no-patents-on-seeds.org/en/information/news/opposition-monsanto-s-patent-indian-melon [accessed July 31, 2013].

Protection of Plant Varieties & Farmers' Rights (PPV&FR) Authority. 2012. Annual report 2011–12. PPV&FR Authority, Department of Agriculture & Co-operation, Ministry of Agriculture, Government of India.

Protection of Plant Varieties & Farmers' Rights (PPV&FR) Authority. 2013a. Implementation of the protection of plant varieties and farmers' rights act, 2001. Updated Status – February, 6p.

Protection of Plant Varieties & Farmers' Rights (PPV&FR) Authority. 2013b. List of registered certificates issued, updated 31.05.2013. http://www.plantauthority.gov.in [accessed July 10, 2013].

Protection of Plant Varieties & Farmers' Rights (PPV&FR) Authority. 2013c. Status of crop wise applications, updated 14.06.2013. http://www.plantauthority.gov.in [accessed July 10, 2013].

Protection of Plant Varieties & Farmers' Rights (PPV&FR) Authority. n.d. Annual Reports 2008–2013. http://www.plantauthority.gov.in [accessed July 7, 2014].

PRS. 2010. Official amendments to the Seeds Bill, 2004. PRS Legislative Research. Centre for Policy Research. http://www.prsindia.org/uploads/media/Note%20on%20official%20Amendments% 20in%20Seeds%20Bill%202004.pdf [accessed October 9, 2013].

Ramanna, A. 2006. The farmers' rights project - background study 4. Farmers rights in India - A Case Study. FNI Report 6/2006. Lysaker, Norway: The Fridtjof Nansen Institute.

Ramanna, A., and M. Smale. 2004. Rights and access to plant genetic resources under India's new law. *Development Policy Review* 22, no. 4: 423–42.

Randeria, S. 2003a. Between cunning states and unaccountable international institutions: social movements and rights of local communities to common property resources. Social Science Research Center Berlin (WZB) Discussion Paper No. SP IV 2003–502.

Randeria, S. 2003b. Cunning states and unaccountable international institutions: legal plurality, social movements and rights of local communities to common property resources. *European Journal of Sociology* 44, no. 1: 27–60.

Randeria, S. 2003c. Glocalization of law: environmental justice, World Bank, NGOs and the cunning state in India. *Current Sociology* 51: 305–28.

Randeria, S. 2007. The state of globalization. Legal plurality, overlapping sovereignties and ambiguous alliances between civil society and the cunning state in India. *Theory, Culture & Society* 24: 1–33.

Randeria, S., and C. Grunder. 2010. The (un)making of policy in the shadow of the World Bank: infrastructure development, urban resettlement and the cunning state in India. In *Policy worlds*, ed. C. Shore, S. Wright, and D. Però, 187–204. London: Pluto Press.

Rangnekar, D. 1998. Tripping in front of UPOV: plant variety protection in India. *Social Action* 48, no. 4: 432–51.

Ravi, S.B. 2004. Effectiveness of Indian sui generis law on plant variety protection and its potential to attract investment in crop improvement. *Journal of Intellectual Property Rights* 9: 553–48.

Right to Food Campaign. n.d. http://www.righttofoodindia.org [accessed July 7, 2014].

Sahai, S. 2001. India: plant variety protection, farmers' rights bill adopted. http://www.twnside.org. sg/title/variety.htm [accessed October 11, 2013].

Sahai, S. n.d.[1]. Gene Campaign public interest litigation to protect farmers' rights. http://www. genecampaign.org/articles/gc_publicinterest_protectfarmer.pdf [accessed October 8, 2013].

Sahai, S. n.d.[2]. Why India should have sui generis IPR protection on plant varieties. http://www. genecampaign.org/articles/whyIndia_have_suigeneris_iprprotection.pdf [accessed July 19, 2013].

Santilli, J. 2009. *Agrobiodiversidade e direitos dos agricultores*. São Paulo: Peirópolis & Instituto Internacional de Educação do Brasil.

Sell, S.K. 1999. Multinational corporations as agents of change: the globalization of intellectual property rights. In *Private authority and international affairs*, ed. A.C. Cutler, V. Haufler and T. Porter, 169–97. New York: State University of New York.

Seshia, S. 2002. Plant variety protection and farmers' rights: law-making and cultivation of varietal control. *Economic and Political Weekly* 37: 2741–7.

Sharma, D.C. 2012. ICAR prepares to open India's plant gene bank to private companies. *Mail Online*, November 25. http://www.dailymail.co.uk/indiahome/indianews/article-2238319/ICAR-prepares-open-Indias-plant-gene-bank-private-companies.html [accessed October 11, 2013].

Shiva, V. 1997. The turmeric patent is just the first step in stopping biopiracy. *Third World Network* 86. http://www.twnside.org.sg/title/tur-cn.htm [accessed July 22, 2013].

Sood, J. 2012. Whose germplasm is it? *Down to Earth*, 15 October.

Sood, J. 2013a. Biopiracy case turns intense. *Down to Earth*, 28 February.

Sood, J. 2013b. India to confront Monsanto in US. *Down to Earth*, 15 June.

Stone, G.D. 2002. Biotechnology and suicide in India. *Anthropology News* 46, no. 5: 5.

Syngenta. n.d. PACS/biodiversity Overview. http://www.syngentafoundation.org/index.cfm?pageID=482 [accessed October 17, 2013].

Third World Network. 2013. TWN info service on intellectual property issues. February 26. http://twnside.org.sg/title2/intellectual_property/info.service/2013/ipr.info.130203.htm [accessed July 8, 2014].

UNHRC Advisory Committee. 2012. Final study of the Human Rights Council Advisory Committee on the advancement of the rights of peasants and other people working in rural areas, A/HRC/19/75. http://ap.ohchr.org/documents/dpage_e.aspx?si=A/HRC/19/75 [accessed February 21, 2014].

Verkey, E. 2007. Shielding farmers' rights. *Journal of Intellectual Property Law & Practice* 2, no. 12: 825–31.

Via Campesina. 2001. The position of Via Campesina on biodiversity, biosafety and genetic resources. *Development* 44, no. 4: 47–51.

Via Campesina. 2009. Declaration of rights of peasants – women and men, document adopted by the Via Campesina International Coordinating Committee in Seoul, March 2009. http://viacampesina.net/downloads/PDF/EN-3.pdf [accessed July 5, 2013].

Via Campesina. 2013. The International Seed Treaty: A resolution in support of Farmers' Rights. Press Release, 3 October. http://www.twnside.org.sg/title2/biotk/2014/btk140101.htm [accessed February 18, 2014].

Winter, L. 2010. Cultivating farmers' rights: reconciling food security, indigenous agriculture, and TRIPS. *Vanderbilt Journal of Transnational Law* 43, no. 1: 223–54.

World Trade Organization. 1994. Agreement on Trade Related Aspects of Intellectual Property Rights (TRIPs). 1994. *Marrakesh Agreement Establishing the World Trade Organization*, Annex 1C, Legal Instruments - Results of the Uruguay Round Vol. 31; 33 I.L.M. 1197, 1201, 15 April.

World Trade Organization. 2008. TRIPS: Reviews, Article 27.3(B) and Related Issues. Last updated: November 2008. http://www.wto.org/english/tratop_e/trips_e/art27_3b_background_e.htm [accessed July 19, 2013].

Zaidi, A. 2005. Seeds of despair. *Frontline* 22, no. 16.

Karine Peschard is a postdoctoral fellow at the Graduate Institute of International and Development Studies, in Geneva, where she conducts comparative research on farmers' rights in Brazil and India. Her research interests are centred on global capital, contemporary peasant movements, food sovereignty, agricultural biotechnology, intellectual property rights and biodiversity.

Life in a shrimp zone: aqua- and other cultures of Bangladesh's coastal landscape

Kasia Paprocki and Jason Cons

This essay questions the possibilities of food sovereignty for producing a radical egalitarian politics. Specifically, it explores the class-differentiated implications of food sovereignty in a zone of ecological crisis – Bangladesh's coastal Khulna district. Much land in this deltaic zone that had previously been employed for various forms of peasant production has been transformed by the introduction of brackish-water shrimp aquaculture. This has, in turn, caused massive depeasantization and ecological crisis throughout the region. Through an examination of two markedly different polders (embanked islands) – one which has been overrun by shrimp production and one that has resisted it – we ask how coastal communities and their members have variously negotiated their rapidly changing ecologies and food systems based on their relative class position and access to land. We highlight the multiple meanings that peasants from different classes ascribe not just to shrimp, but also to broader questions of adaptation, community and life in uncertain terrains. We show that while food sovereignty in non-shrimp areas has averted the depeasantization affecting shrimp areas, it has not necessarily led to greater equality in agrarian class relations. To achieve such ends, we suggest that a broader conception of agrarian sovereignty provides a critical and necessary corollary to self-determination in agricultural production.

Introduction

This essay questions the analytic and political project of 'food sovereignty' by looking at class-differentiated responses to ecological crisis in two markedly different polders (embanked islands) in Bangladesh's shrimp zone. Much of the literature on food sovereignty

Our deepest thanks to the community researchers in Khulna for their collegiality and enthusiasm in conducting this research. Special thanks also to David Bruer at Inter Pares and the Department of Foreign Affairs, Trade and Development Canada, as well as the Atkinson Center for a Sustainable Future-Oxfam Rural Resilience Project at Cornell, for making this project possible. Thanks also to Khushi Kabir for her vision in planning and making the project happen, and to the Nijera Kori staff for their partnership in executing the research. Thanks in particular to Rezanur 'Rose' Rahman, from whom we have learned a great deal, and whose passion for the movement is a constant inspiration. Earlier drafts of this essay were presented in Fall 2013 at the Yale Agrarian Studies conference on Food Sovereignty and at the workshop, 'Bangladesh: contested pasts, competing futures' at the University of Texas, Austin. We thank these audiences for their generous feedback and engagement. We thank Erin Lentz, Townsend Middleton and David Rojas for their helpful comments on earlier drafts.

makes a strong argument for self-determination in food production. The implication of this work is that when peasants have control over their production choices, they have more choice in general – to lead healthier lives, to make more independent economic choices, to be more strategic about balancing subsistence and market integration. Yet, if food sovereignty is a *political* project organized around resisting the neoliberal food regime, its use as an *analytic* to explore the practices of self-determination has been more limited. Indeed, explorations of food sovereignty have often been overdetermined by the broader political project – reducing the complexities and vagaries of peasant politics to opposition to neoliberalism. We join others in suggesting that such overdetermination tends to problematically flatten critical divisions amongst the peasantry (Akram-Lodhi 2007, 560).

In order to reinsert such differentiation back into the debate, and indeed to indicate why it is important, we here focus on the ways class radically reshapes relationships to food, to subsistence and to hopes for better futures within communities.[1] We do this by comparing one space which is ostensibly food sovereign – Polder 22, an island in Southern Bangladesh's Khulna district that has successfully resisted the incursion of shrimp aquaculture – with one that is markedly non-food sovereign – Polder 23, an island which been overrun with shrimp production. Within these communities, we pay particular attention to those individuals whose livelihoods are most precarious – 'the subalterns among subalterns' (Wolford 2010, 11). Specifically, we focus on the landless.

We explore the differentiated meanings of food sovereignty in a context where landlessness, as opposed to smallholder production, is a central animating political concern. This is true in Bangladesh broadly, where approximately 48 percent of the rural population is functionally landless (owning less than 0.05 acres of land) (The World Bank 2002). As we will show, these dynamics are particularly important in the context of shrimp. Indeed, the central difference between the two polders we compare here might be usefully described in terms of access to productive agricultural land. In Polder 23, effectively, residents cannot access land for uses other than shrimp production. Narratives of life within the polder highlight the social consequences of a lack of food sovereignty and a range of miseries linked to what Adnan has recently described as two-way or recursive primitive accumulation (Adnan 2013), whereby depeasantization is a *consequence* as well as a *precondition* of expanding capitalist production. In other words, an absence of food sovereignty in Polder 23 – linked to the historical emergence of shrimp aquaculture – has led to absolute depeasantization. By this, we mean that the majority of the middle- and low-income residents of the polder have been displaced to pursue industrial and other labor in urban areas; the rest have been transformed into low-wage workers in industrial aquaculture in the polder.

In contrast, in Polder 22, residents have actively prevented the transformation of their agricultural lands into shrimp fields. In so doing, they have produced a context of, arguably, food sovereignty within which communities are more central to making decisions about the shape of agricultural production and market integration. Yet, as the experience of landless peasants within the polder show, food sovereignty does not yield egalitarian social politics. We argue that such a politics would necessitate land policy reform more specifically focused on achieving what Borras and Franco have recently termed 'land sovereignty' (Borras and Franco 2012), a crucial dynamic in reframing a broader conception of agrarian sovereignty. Thus, contrary to analyses that see food sovereignty as a radically egalitarian

---

[1]Our claim, of course, is not that class is the only category of differentiation that matters amongst the peasantry. Rather, we argue that it is one critical dimension in understanding the vagaries and differential impacts of food sovereignty and its lack in rural communities in Bangladesh.

political platform (Patel 2006; Martínez-Torres and Rosset 2010), we argue that food sovereignty allows a full spectrum of agrarian classes to continue to be peasants, though it does not necessarily yield greater equality in agrarian class relations.

Equally important to our argument is the context of ecological, as well as capitalist, crisis. Khulna is a region in the throes of multiple overlapping ecological crises. On the one hand, climate change – both actual experienced forms of climate-related transformation such as increased vulnerability to tropical storms and cyclones, and discursive forms, such as the support of international non-governmental organizations (iNGOs) for increased shrimp production as a form of sustainable livelihood in the face of climate change (Food and Agriculture Organization 2010; The World Bank 2011) – has dramatically transformed both the physical and the risk landscape for smallholders, landless laborers and other peasants in the region (McMichael 2009a; Yu et al. 2010; Tanner and Allouche 2011; Watts 2011; Ahmed 2013; Shaw, Mallick, and Islam 2013). On the other, the transition to shrimp aquaculture in Khulna over the past 30 years has radically transformed access to land, quality of land and ability to remain on the land. These twin crises throw the class implications of food sovereignty into stark relief. In this context of ecological crisis, a lack of food sovereignty results in depeasantization for poorer agrarian classes (Araghi 2001, 2009).[2] The presence of food sovereignty, conversely, allows people to remain as peasants, though not necessarily to thrive or transcend inequitable class relations.

Our conceptualization of food sovereignty is grounded in James Scott's classic analysis of the 'subsistence ethic' in *The moral economy of the peasant*. Scott positions the subsistence ethic as the technical and social arrangements that mitigate risk to ensure the survival of a peasant family. The subsistence ethic positions exploitation, or understandings thereof, as the violation of these arrangements, resulting in a threat to household survival. The moral economy of the peasant is, as Scott argues, 'a phenomenological theory of exploitation' that revolves around minimum needs for subsistence security (1976, 161). For Scott, thus, the subsistence ethic marks a threshold of exploitation beyond which survival – or survival as peasant producers – is no longer possible. It is, thus, a framing of moral economy that focuses on the thin line between persistence and eradication.[3] Marc Edelman persuasively argues that Scott's argument shares key resonances with the food sovereignty debate. Indeed, he suggests that, in the context of transnational peasant movements, the moral economy of the peasant has been 'broadened to the "right to continue being agriculturalists"' (2005, 332).

Edelman's point resonates strongly in both Polder 22 and 23, where arguably peasant conceptualizations of food sovereignty generalize the subsistence ethic from the family to the community level.[4] Yet, as we suggest, the right to remain agriculturalists does not,

---

[2]On the implications of this argument to the broader debate over peasant differentiation and the agrarian question of the twenty-first century, we concur with McMichael that 'to represent the prospects of the peasantry solely through the lens of the capital relation is problematic because it reproduces a *telos* regarding the transience of peasantries, and tends to foreclose possibility of *campesino* resistances to capitalism' (2006, 412). We thus retain the distinction between absolute depeasantization (through which rural dwellers are forced to leave rural communities entirely), and transitions of production relations within rural communities, which may nevertheless be classified as 'proletarianization' (Harriss 1987; Bernstein 2004, 2006).

[3]Our argument here doesn't seek to endorse Scott's reading of moral economy over others, which are more focused on micropolitics and microdifferentiation within and across communities. Rather, we are interested in the subsistence ethic because it highlights the contrast between existence and non-existence of individuals, families and communities in peasant agriculture.

[4]Which is not to say that Scott's work is not attentive to community politics and relations vis-à-vis subsistence. Rather, we are suggesting that the notion of food sovereignty generalizes and reframes

necessarily, imply egalitarian rural politics. Rather, as our respondents repeatedly high-lighted, it suggests that the mitigation of risk through the provision of food within the community is preferable to the risks borne at both the family and community level by production that does not ensure the minimal subsistence consumption by the community. The moral economy of the peasant in the context of food sovereignty thus does not ensure a radical agrarian politics, or equitable distributions of land, food or other goods. It merely ensures subsistence and the maintenance of the community at large and the class politics within it. As scholars equally concerned with social justice *within* peasant communities as in relation to them, we suggest that this is not enough. As Borras argues, 'acknowledging such differ-ences [within communities], rather than ignoring or dismissing their significance, is an important step toward finding ways to ensure truly inclusive and effective representation in decision-making and demand-making' (Borras 2008, 276–7). As such, attending to the differential effects of food sovereignty allows us to explore the possibilities of a broader agrarian sovereignty – a possibility to which we return in our conclusion.

Methods

Research for this essay was carried out in summer of 2013 and draws on over 100 inter-views conducted in two villages in each polder. It is part of a larger project that traces the experience of displacement and shrimp-aquaculture in Khulna. This research was carried out in partnership with *Nijera Kori*, Bangladesh's largest landless movement. It is worth noting, particularly in light of our argument, that the reform prescriptions suggested by land sovereignty are firmly on the advocacy agenda of Nijera Kori and its broad network. Nijera Kori seeks distributive land reform through campaigns for the distri-bution of common (*khas*) lands among the landless – a mandate already established in Bangladesh's constitution, but which has largely remained dormant without broad-scale and persistent advocacy from community groups and individuals. Re-distributive land reform is sought by Nijera Kori through campaigns for better implementation of land ceiling laws and land use policies, along with policy advocacy for reform and implemen-tation of share tenancy and land tenure laws, indigenous land rights, and restitution of con-fiscated minority lands. We return to the question of Nijera Kori's strategies for securing land sovereignty in the conclusion of this paper.

The research was conducted using a participatory research approach we call commu-nity-based oral testimony.[5] In June of 2013, we met with groups of landless laborers from villages in each polder and worked collectively to establish a research agenda for examining agrarian change in Khulna and to train them in the use of basic unstructured interviewing techniques. For a two-week period following this training, these community researchers then interviewed their neighbors and other residents of their respective villages, digitally recording narratives, testimonies, and oral histories spanning the history and pre-history of shrimp in the region. While researchers, as members of Nijera Kori's local groups, were all landless, they conducted interviews that cut across class and landless/landed divides within the polders.

While all of the community researchers were members of Nijera Kori landless collec-tives in their villages, they conducted interviews with both fellow members (at various

---

the concept of a subsistence ethic at a community scale. As we show here, this is particularly marked and critical in the context of broad-based ecological crisis.
[5]For a more detailed discussion, see Cons and Paprocki (2010).

levels of involvement) as well as non-members, resulting in a diversity of testimonies among various classes, professions and political orientations. In coding and analyzing the accumulated data, we identify both cohesion and rupture in the narratives of the movement in this region. Moreover, we draw out memories and oral histories that both emphasize the different ways that pasts and presents are narrated across class boundaries and attend to the ways that the breakdown in community life and livelihoods are remembered similarly by both landed and landless community members. As Wolford writes, 'even subaltern narratives of dispossession and mobilization are complicated and themselves have to be read against the grain' (Wolford 2010, 27). Indeed, while our approach captures strikingly similar sets of narratives of loss in Polder 23, the picture in Polder 22 emerges as more complicated. Accounts offered by respondents with different access to land problematize reports of the overwhelming success of the anti-shrimp farming movement in Polder 22, suggesting that the movement still has much to accomplish before its benefits are shared equally by all residents.

In contrast to approaches to food sovereignty that take a broadly political economic view or constitute discussions of sovereignty at a national scale, this research firmly situates food sovereignty within specific communities navigating multiple crises. As Wolford argues, 'theoretically locating actors within spatial structures, and analyzing how the two are mutually constituted, is a useful way of incorporating actors and actions, as they are embedded in agency and structure, contingency and context, space and time' (Wolford 2003, 168). To this end, our approach at once foregrounds the experiences and analyses of individuals as key observers of catastrophic agrarian transformations and provides an intimate view of the ways that transformations in capitalist accumulation in coastal Bangladesh are constituted at both broad and local scales. In doing so, we further foreground a key critique of progressive political agendas such as food sovereignty that frame the agrarian question as a struggle for survival between peasants and capitalism – namely, that they risk being insufficiently attentive to the vagaries of intra-community inequalities and injustices.

Green pasts, blue presents

A brief historical framing is useful in understanding the contemporary state of shrimp production in Khulna. In his recent examination of shrimp and primitive accumulation in Noakhali District (to the east of Khulna), Adnan (2013) highlights the multiple and recursive historical processes that facilitated the rise of shrimp. As he writes,

> As compared to the pre-eminent role of deliberate dispossession in Marx's analysis of enclosure, the evidence on land grabs in Noakhali shows the operation of alternative forms of primitive accumulation, embodying different degrees of intentionality. On the one hand, there are clear instances of deliberate expropriation of poor peasant lands by private interest groups and agencies of the state. On the other, comparable outcomes have resulted indirectly from the working out of complex processes triggered by policy and development interventions that were primarily concerned with other objectives. (Adnan 2013, 122)

This reading of primitive accumulation is also apt for Khulna, though the processes whereby displacement and land-grabbing took place there were markedly distinct from those in Noakhali.

Beginning in the 1960s and lasting through the 1980s, the Coastal Embankment Project (CEP), carried out with funds from the World Bank and implemented largely by Dutch engineers, built mud embankments around numerous islands in Khulna's delta region

(Quassem and van Urk 2006).[6] The purpose of the embankments was to protect the interiors of these islands from semi-regular salt-water storm surges and to transform the region from a food-secure to a food-exporting region (Choudhury, Paul, and Paul 2004). The embankments facilitated wide-scale adoption of Green Revolution dwarf-varietal rice, which largely replaced indigenous varietals throughout the region.[7] From the 1980s, structural adjustment programs in Bangladesh imposed by the International Monetary Fund (IMF) and the World Bank encouraged the adoption of export-oriented agricultural policies in the country. As Adnan (2013, 105–16) traces, throughout the 1980s, major international banks and development agencies began to fund and promote commercial shrimp production in Bangladesh, addressing rising international demand by strengthening supply chains linking Bangladesh to markets throughout the world.

Government and international support for shrimp exports combined with pre-existing transformations in Khulna's coastal landscape to produce a markedly violent environment (Peluso and Watts 2001; Guhathakurta 2008). Indeed, following Stonich and Vandergeest, we argue that the 'characteristics of industrial shrimp farming create situations of enormous tension and opportunities for violence' (2001, 261). Beginning in the 1980s, cartels of businessmen and large landholders, primarily residing outside of the region, began to recognize the polders as ideal spaces for brackish-water shrimp production. In many polders, the transition from agriculture to aquaculture was facilitated by armed representatives of these groups taking over and controlling sluice gates designed to facilitate drainage in the polders and using them to flood the islands (a process also accomplished by drilling holes through the embankments to the salt water outside). Once a polder is flooded, the embankment ensures that the entire area remains waterlogged (unless local anti-shrimp community groups or village committees can regain control of the sluice gates to let the water out).

Thus, a project that had been conceived of as a high-modernist remaking of a landscape to facilitate agricultural productivity was transformed into a mechanism to facilitate new forms of capitalist accumulation at the expense of agriculture (Scott 1998). Over the ensuing 30-year period, brackish-water shrimp aquaculture has come to completely dominate land use within many polders in this region, motivated by the expansion of Bangladesh's frozen shrimp export industry, which tripled in size between 1988 and 2008 (Paul and Vogl 2011). The encroachment of salt water and pressure from powerful land owners, often supported by both hired goons and local politicians, have forced many landless groups off of the land and forced many smallholders to either sell or lease their land for shrimp production (while many report being rarely or never compensated for their land once it has been flooded and taken over by neighboring shrimp production). These transformations have heralded a range of structural shifts in social relations that have produced a range of confrontations and conflicts (see below and Guhathakurta 2008).

---

[6]The CEP formally ran from 1961 to 1979. However, it is important to note that this project represented neither the beginning nor the end of embanking projects in the region. Other projects involved in embankment construction in Khulna include the Delta Development Project, which operated in Khulna during the 1980s and, most recently, the ongoing Asian Development Bank-funded Coastal Rehabilitation Project. As Sur (2010) notes, the embankments in Polder 22 were constructed by the Bangladesh Water Development Board.

[7]This project was one in a long line of large-scale institutional projects designed to re-engineer the deltaic landscape that is now Bangladesh, shaped by various political agendas (Boyce 1990; Haque and Zaman 1993; Lewis 2010).

The environmental impacts of shrimp aquaculture, chief among which include aquifer and soil salination (Primavera 1997; Deb 1998; Paul and Vogl 2011), have further contributed to processes of depeasantization in the polders, making small-scale agriculture difficult to impossible in many of the most active shrimp zones (Guimaraes 1989). The social and ecological crisis heralded by shrimp has been further exacerbated by climate change in the area. Many of the embankments in the shrimp zone have been critically weakened by shrimp farmers drilling through the walls to bring in salt water (Brammer 1990). This puts polders with high levels of shrimp aquaculture at heightened risk from increasingly frequent cyclones in the region (Barraclough and Finger-Stitch 1996; Choudhury, Paul, and Paul 2004).

This is not to say that there has been no resistance to shrimp in the area. Indeed, several polders have taken active roles in reclaiming food and land sovereignty. Perhaps the most well-known example of this was the landless movement in Polder 22. In 1990, a local landless leader named Karunamoyee Sardar was shot and killed while leading a protest movement against Wajad Ali, a local shrimp boss who was attempting to open the polder to shrimp production (Sur 2010). Karunamoyee's death galvanized the landless movement in Polder 22 and there have been no further attempts to bring shrimp production inside the polder's embankments.

The absence of shrimp in Polder 22 has led to comparatively low levels of landlessness within the polder (30 percent, as opposed to 84 percent in Polder 23). Moreover, it has made Polder 22 a safer place to live in the context of climate change, as its embankments have not been compromised by shrimp aquaculture. Indeed, as residents report, people from surrounding regions often take shelter in the polder when the region is threatened by cyclones and other dramatic climatic events. Yet it has also placed other forms of pressure on residents. Many landless laborers displaced from neighboring polders have moved to Polder 22 in an attempt to reestablish agricultural livelihoods.[8] This has taxed land and water resources within the island. To explore the differential impacts between Polder 22 and other polders in Khulna's shrimp zone, we now turn to Polder 23, a space that has been completely overrun by brackish-water shrimp aquaculture.

Polder 23

Polder 23 is a seemingly paradigmatic case of what is at stake in discussions over food sovereignty. A space in which agriculture has been completely overwhelmed by aquaculture, the polder offers a vivid tale of shrimp and of ecological transformation – one that speaks of displacement, dispossession and insecurity. Falling in Khulna's Paikgacha Upazilla, the polder is approximately 5852 hectares in size with a population of approximately 22,000.[9] Eighty-four percent of residents in Polder 23 are landless as a result of the expansion of commercial shrimp cultivation. Indeed, the vast majority of the polder's arable land has been transformed into *gher* leases (shrimp farming plots). This transformation is apparent from even a cursory glance at the polder landscape. In contrast to the intensive use of land in much of rural Bangladesh, Polder 23 appears to be barren (see Figure 1). Brackish water stretches across the horizon, punctuated by short mud embankments demarcating *gher* plots and the stilted huts used by those who monitor the *ghers* to prevent shrimp

---

[8]A process that may contribute to the inegalitarian politics we explore below.
[9]More than 13,000 of whom live in Paikgacha town, a booming market town largely organized around shrimp exports.

Figure 1.   View from inside Polder 23.

theft. The remaining villages in Polder 23 are crowded onto thin spits of land hemmed in by brackish plots that often come within feet of houses and courtyards. Villages are in comparatively poor repair. While many *baris* (households) have tiny vegetable plots, residents report that little grows in them because of soil salination. Chickens run through the villages, but it is rare to see larger livestock.

   Arguably, Polder 23 represents a space of ecological crisis, bordering on ecological collapse. Residents of the two villages in which research for this paper was conducted report that there remains almost no agriculture outside of shrimp. Whereas before the advent of *bagda* (tiger prawn) production,[10] the polder grew numerous varietals of rice, both indigenous and hybrid, now little rice grows. Residents report that freshwater fish cultivation – a vital source of protein throughout Bangladesh – is impossible. There is little land available for livestock grazing. Fruit-producing trees no longer grow (see Figure 2). As one resident reported:

> [Shrimp production] started in 1983. Before leasing, people would grow rice. Many people built brick houses from the profit of selling rice. People used to have fish, cows, and they were very generous. When the rich people would catch fish, they would give the small fish to the poor people, but they do not do it anymore. Everyone is in crisis now. During 1985, 1986, and 1987, right after the lease had started, I have seen it with my own eyes that all the trees were becoming dry because of salt in the land. There was a storm on 23rd November 1988. After that storm [flood] all the fruit-trees have died, except for some date-trees. It is really

---

[10]Bagda is the primary form of shrimp production in Polder 23. Bagda are grown in brackish water.

Figure 2.   View from inside Polder 23.

hard for us to survive. If a woman wants to buy a sari, it costs her 250 to 300 taka [US$3.20–3.80]. It is not possible to buy a sari, when you need to spend money on food. People constantly make decisions between food and other necessities, and most of the time, the decision about food wins.

The collapse of livelihood options in Polder 23 for the majority of landless laborers has a range of cascading consequences. Prior to the incursion of shrimp into the polder, residents claim that it was possible even for sharecroppers and day laborers to achieve household self-sufficiency by combining wage labor with farming on the polder's *khas* (common) land. Now, the majority of land within the polder, including *khas* land, has been overrun with shrimp. As a result, residents report not just a decline in the availability of nutritious foods, but a shortage of labor opportunities, an inability to pay the fees necessary for sending children to school and a marked increase in indebtedness both to local moneylenders and to microcredit organizations.[11]

Shrimp aquaculture has displaced many from the polder. When asked about the residents of the polder who had been landless before the advent of shrimp, respondents used words such as *dhongsho, bilupto, shesh* (destroyed, extinct, finished). Remaining residents are primarily smallholders who have been transformed into wage laborers as their land has been degraded or they have been pressured to sell or lease out their land at miniscule prices to larger shrimp cultivators. Many who have left the polder have moved to *bastis* (slums) in

---

[11]For more on microcredit indebtedness in contemporary Bangladesh, see Cons and Paprocki (2010) and Karim (2011).

Khulna city seeking employment in the brick-making industry. Many others, as residents recounted, make seasonal trips to India to seek employment in construction. Those who remain eke out livings through low-paying day labor in the *ghers* where constant exposure to salt water and to the chemicals used in shrimp aquaculture yields a range of health problems from skin rashes to infections. Residents report that little *khas* (common) land remains in Polder 23, and that this land has been almost uniformly absorbed by larger land owners involved in shrimp. The lack of access to *khas* land means that residents of Polder 23 now must travel regularly to Paikgacha to purchase household necessities – food, fuel and water – once harvested within the polder. The advent of shrimp has, as such, heralded a new wave of primitive accumulation in Polder 23 – on the one hand, enclosing land for incorporation into new forms of capitalist production and, on the other, forcibly incorporating the displaced into a set of asymmetric market relations and transforming a set of public goods into commodities (Marx 1992; Adnan 2013).

If the lack of food sovereignty in Polder 23 has had grave consequences for landless laborers, it has also had significant impacts in the notion of community throughout the polder. While moderate landholders have, indeed, benefited from using their land for shrimp leases, most respondents agree that the influx of shrimp has eroded social cohesion and more community oriented ways of living.[12] As one respondent put it:

> Before people weren't always running to work in the shrimp farm, women were free in the afternoon and they would sit together in the fields and chat. During the month of Poush [December–January] you would look at the beautiful rice fields and chat with your friends. Now you don't have time as you are always running after money. Now you don't have the time to sit and listen to people. Before you had rice in your home, you had cows, you had fish in the pond. People were not as worried and were happier.

Residents of the polder repeatedly make similar arguments contrasting life before shrimp with life in its wake. Shrimp aquaculture in Polder 23 has been complicit not just in the transformation of livelihoods, but also in the transformation of communities. Indeed, the shift to shrimp in narratives of residents of Polder 23 is explicitly framed as simultaneously a personal/household and community level crisis. Notably, this nostalgia for life prior to the shrimp was shared across class boundaries in the polder. Residents repeatedly commented on the decline of community activities within the polder, from the disappearance of community plays (*jatra*), to the absence of sporting events such as horse racing, to a loss of the leisure to spend time with one's neighbor.

Such nostalgic reminiscences would be easy to dismiss as romanticization, particularly in light of experiences in Polder 22 (discussed below). However, landless residents of Polder 23 were acutely aware of, and vocal about, the differences between poverty in a context of food sovereignty versus its lack. As one put it:

> There is a significant difference between our current poverty and poverty in the past. In old days, we didn't have any scarcity of food. There were no leases in the *bil* [low lands], so were able to catch a lot of *mach* [fish] such as *shoil, gojal, koi, bain, puti* and *chingri* to feed our family … Since fish were available, the selling price of the caught fish would not be more than 2 to 3 taka if we decided to sell them in the market. But now these fishes are very rare and expensive. A lot of people that are ages of 25–30 have never seen some of the fish I talked about. One day my elder son asked me about *gojal mach* and *koi mach*, so

---

[12]On the transformation of social and ecological relations through the expansion of industrial agriculture, see Wittman (2009).

I showed him a tilapia fish and explained that *koi mach* is kind of like tilapia *mach*. One day, I got some *koi mach* for him from the Paikgacha Bazaar, which cost me 17 taka for 250 very tiny *koi mach*. I just wanted to show my son what *koi mach* look like. In the old days, we used to have cows, so we could drink milk. We were healthy and had energy then, but now we do not have that.

Such framings clearly articulate an erosion of not just community but of the quality and security of life in shrimp-producing zones. In this context, residents speak not just of salt water and sweet water (*labon* and *mishti pani*), but indeed of salt and sweet land and areas (*jommi* and *elaka*). They speak to the incursion of shrimp aquaculture as a process that produces both *ex situ* and *in situ* displacement, or, as Feldman and Geisler suggestively put it, 'diminishments in the capacity to socially reproduce lives and livelihoods' (Feldman and Geisler 2012, 974). On the one hand, the landscape has been depopulated, forcing former peasants to seek precarious employment in urban areas on a permanent or semi-permanent basis. On the other, aquaculture has radically transformed the landscape for residents who remain, undermining, eroding and compromising not just land, but a range of social and economic capacities linked to it.

Indeed, even those who were profiting from shrimp expressed a desire to recapture agrarian pasts. As one respondent who leased his land for shrimp explained when asked about the future of the area:

I do not know what to say. I hope that the next generations do not have to go through this kind of hardship that my generation or I went through. I want to see the fields full of rice, backyards full of vegetables and people without any hardship. Remember, I mentioned another village where they do not have the *gher* system. Every family from that village has fruit trees. When we went there they cooked vegetables from their own garden, brought us *bel* [fruit] and milk so that we could make *shorbot* [a dairy and fruit drink]. They are happy. They do not have any problems with food. They understand the repercussion of doing lease business. Leasing seems absurd to them. If they grow rice for one year, they can feed their family for two years. I went to a relative's house in Til Danga a few months ago. In Til Danga, poor people protested against leasing, but the people that have 10–15 *bighas* of land [3–5 acres] wanted to lease. But the rich people later realized that leasing is not good for them, as well, so they joined the poor people and started protesting against the *gher* system. There is no *gher* in that area now. I think it was a better decision for them. People can have cows, drink milk, and eat fruits.

The narratives of residents of Polder 23 thus capture a critique of the utter loss of food sovereignty. This loss indeed links to both nostalgia for and desire to return to forms of peasant agriculture. This narrative is regularly and directly framed as a desire for self-determination, an ability to make individual- and community-level decisions about agricultural production, as well as a bleak vision of a future without it. The loss of control over land and production has had devastating impacts throughout the polder, transforming the lives of both those who benefit from shrimp aquaculture as well as those who have been transformed into a proletarian workforce for maintaining it. Polder 23 offers an urgent portrait of the loss of agricultural self-determination. It is a space of acute subsistence crisis. The breakdown of Scott's subsistence ethic here, indeed, denotes the demise of peasant livelihoods in Polder 23.

Polder 22

In *The Moral economy of the peasant*, Scott discusses the 'safety-first rule' which is founded on the mitigation of risk to ensure subsistence, explaining that 'a critical assumption of the safety-first rule is that subsistence routines are producing satisfactory results. What if they are not? Here the rationale of safety-first breaks down' (Scott 1976, 26). This framing of subsistence as survival is also a critical assumption of the food sovereignty paradigm, which suggests that peasants are best equipped to mitigate risks and ensure subsistence through reliance on local food production, often through traditional production relations. As such, it is critical to examine the rationale and transformation of food sovereignty under conditions of crisis (ecological, as in Khulna, economic or otherwise). Under these conditions, is it appropriate to assume that food sovereignty and traditional production relations are sufficient to ensure the 'survival of the weakest' (Scott 1976, 43)? If they are not, what can be made of the food sovereignty paradigm in the context of crisis?

Polder 22 provides a compelling case through which to examine these questions. The polder is at the center of Bangladesh's shrimp aquaculture production region. As such, it is surrounded by other Polders whose embankments hold vast tracts of industrial shrimp farms. It is roughly 2812 hectares in size with a population of 10,700, 30 percent of which is landless. In contradistinction to the stark landscapes in shrimp-intensive polders, Polder 22 is an island of green (see Figure 3). Viewed from outside, one can see an embankment covered with grass, dense groves of mangrove trees and other florae, along with people working, children playing and numerous small homesteads within. In contrast to Polder 23 and other shrimp areas in the region, Polder 22 appears socially, economically and agronomically analogous to other villages in rural Bangladesh. Yet, in part because of its situation within Khulna's shrimp zone, the polder is also under various forms of pressure due to broader regional ecological shifts. The relative food sovereignty and non-salinated land within it have encouraged many people from surrounding polders

Figure 3.   Interior of Polder 22.

to migrate into it. This has placed pressure not just on land use within Polder 22, but also on access to resources such as fresh water which are no longer available in surrounding environs. Such shifts may, indeed, be inflecting the class politics within the polder that we discuss below.

Residents of Polder 22 as well as those who live outside are acutely aware of both the pleasant aesthetics of this landscape as well as the wide-ranging benefits it affords its residents. They are also acutely aware of the history of struggle that has preserved the polder as a shrimp-free zone. In Horinkala, one of the largest villages in the polder, is a shrine to Karunamoyee Sardar depicting her leading a march against the shrimp bosses. On the anniversary of her death at the hands of shrimp businessmen (7 November 1990), the polder and the shrine are sites of convergence for landless laborers in the region and, indeed, for anti-shrimp activists throughout Bangladesh and beyond.

Highest among the list of benefits offered by this fertile environment free of shrimp farms is the ability to produce and consume one's own food and other household requirements. This collective understanding of food sovereignty as an ideal is expressed by individuals in Polder 22 from across the class spectrum. To that end, residents of Polder 22 repeatedly articulate the importance of their capacity to produce and consume without participating in the market. One landless woman explained,

> even if I don't have money now to go to the market, I can make do. But if they [in the shrimp areas] don't have money in their hands, they have no way to survive. But we can get by for a week. So there is a huge difference between our area and theirs.

Another resident, a landless day laborer, echoes this value, explaining how this subsistence is made possible in practice:

> Just doing shrimp farming has caused so much harm to this country, for the people and for the trees … For us, we see that even if we don't go to the bazaar for a week, we can make do. We pick spinach, vegetables from the fields, catch fish from the ponds. But those who do shrimp farming, for them they don't have the option to grow their own food.

More generally, these statements also demonstrate the collective understanding that it is the ability of a community to produce its own food that ensures the (relative) subsistence security of its members. Importantly to the present argument, much of this collective understanding is based on the recognition that it is difficult (if not impossible) for marginal farmers in Khulna to *earn* enough money in their own communities through their own labor to feed a family. As such, the ability to produce the food and other necessities for a family's subsistence is what enables a smallholding family living at the margins to survive. One farmer, asked whether Bangladesh can achieve the goal of national 'food self-sufficiency' (*khaddo shongshompurno*) through the shrimp industry, explains:

> no, not at all, because for every taka I earn, I end up spending 500 taka … There is no security [with shrimp farming]. You can't grow trees, there won't be any rice; you can't raise cows or get firewood or grow vegetables, fruits, anything. It's harmful in every way, the only thing you gain is a little money.

These statements suggest that the values created by food sovereignty extend beyond simple market decisions and food production and encompass a broader understanding of life, community and survival. Food sovereignty results in a series of additional social and economic values which facilitate consumption and promote sustainable livelihoods.

The benefits of collective control over the ecological landscape, both tangible and intangible, figure highly among the advantages people describe of living in Polder 22. One farmer explained,

> The trees give us oxygen and also during the months of Choitro and Boishakh [March–May], when the sun and the heat on our heads is intense, after working we rest by sitting under the trees. So sitting under the trees we get oxygen and we are able to live because of this oxygen. Our bodies also feel comfort under the shade. But in the salt areas there are no trees, no vegetation. Where will they get their oxygen from? When we have a big storm, the trees protect our houses. If we didn't have trees, we would have been washed away from this land, there wouldn't be anyone left in Polder 22. Just because of the trees, the oxygen, because of being able to raise cows, goats, hens and ducks, we are surviving.

This farmer's testimony cogently articulates the inherent relationship between a vibrant landscape hospitable to trees and other vegetation and the social and economic life of its inhabitants. In this way, a political ecology of food sovereignty recognizes that the ability of a community to define its own agricultural systems is accompanied by benefits that may be illegible outside of farmer-based production systems (Boyce 1996; Altieri 1998; Escobar 1999; Isakson 2009). In this sense, 'survival' and resilience to ecological crises may take on different meanings relative to the epistemological position that circumscribes them.

Beyond these ecological benefits, chief among the values of food sovereignty articulated by residents of Polder 22 is the ability of smallholders to meet all of their families' subsistence needs by producing rice, vegetables and fruits on their own land. Testimonies from small and medium landholders in Polder 22 unambiguously demonstrate the value of food sovereignty for those with access to sufficient resources to take advantage of a locally self-reliant food system. However, while the benefits of food sovereignty to smallholding farmers are clear, how are these impacts differentiated across the agrarian landscape based on class and land tenure? *What does it mean to be land-poor in the context of food sovereignty?* In comparison to the landless poor in Polder 23 who struggle to persist in the face of adverse labor markets and rampant depeasantization, landless peasants in Polder 22 enthusiastically recognize their own advantages from their community's food sovereignty. One landless day laborer explained,

> If shrimp cultivation had continued in this polder, then we would have been destitute, unable to eat and left to die, because we would not have had any work. If I didn't have work, how would I have eaten? With the end of shrimp cultivation, we benefitted a lot, our village, my home. Now we have mango trees and berry trees growing within my homestead, and we can eat their fruits. Moreover, in terms of work, in the month of Poush (December/January), we can cut rice paddy, which we can survive on for up to 6 months. But if there was still shrimp cultivation, then we couldn't grow rice. So this has benefitted me. We are able to keep two goats and a cow. If shrimp cultivation was still continuing, I would not have had all this.

This farmers' testimony speaks to the many advantages of food sovereignty for day laborers in Polder 22 – specifically, the ecological possibility of growing fruit trees for subsistence production and the environment hospitable to grass for grazing livestock on open access state property.[13] Along with access to these resources, the availability of opportunities

---

[13]Common property regimes in Bangladesh, though theoretically regulated by the country's constitution, are governed in practice through local negotiation, patronage relations and the persistent agitation of those who, from radically different positions of power, seek to lay claims to resources. They are also, importantly, deeply circumscribed by the particular ecology of the region, characterized by

for day labor provides the above respondent's family with sufficient rice to survive through half the year. On this latter point, however, it becomes clear that even community 'food sovereignty' does not prevent the poorest from dependence on selling their labor to wealthier landed peasants for their families' survival.

Rather, landlessness is a central factor for determining the advantages an individual may derive from community food sovereignty, and is itself determinate of both the self-sufficiency of and capacity for a family's consumption. While some families considered 'landless' lack agricultural land, they may possess enough land within their homestead to produce fruits or other vegetables for managing their subsistence, such as the day laborer quoted above. However, others lacking even this homestead land face more tenuous existence. One woman who, along with her husband, depends on day labor to earn money to buy food and other household necessities, explains, 'when both of us work throughout the week then that is a good week. If we do not get enough work, we go hungry for 2 days, eat for 2 days'. Similarly, many day laborers in Polder 22 articulate their experience of food sovereignty as distinctly different from that of most smallholders, insofar as it is not defined by the security and self-sufficiency afforded by stable landholding. The result is often the inability to engage actively in the collective social and political life that shapes the sovereign food system on which the community is founded. One landless laborer, asked about the advantages of food sovereignty and lack of shrimp production in Polder 22, explained, 'I work constantly in other people's fields. I never get to hear much about that. I don't have the time or opportunity to listen to other people'. In contrast to smallholders who discuss the collective political empowerment that gives rise to and is facilitated by food sovereignty, the marginality experienced by this day laborer is evident.

In Polder 22, food sovereignty carries specific benefits for all members of the community – it allows for the survival of peasant production for most residents, particularly in contrast to the absolute depeasantization of Polder 23. However, and crucially, these benefits are acutely differentiated by class. The image of idyllic farm life proposed by the notion of food sovereignty of subsistence food production and production relations characterized by self-determination may hold some truth for some members of the community. But it is not shared across the agrarian landscape. For the landless and land-poor, the experience of food sovereignty is deeply circumscribed by inequitable sharecropping arrangements, patterns of circular migration and often-precarious livelihoods. Many landless workers cite the 'reverse *tebhaga*' system as indication of their relatively tenuous economic conditions. This refers to a sharecroppers' movement in Bengal in the 1940s known as the Tebhaga Movement, which sought the right of sharecroppers to retain two-thirds of their harvested crop, as opposed to the customary one-half (the rest of course going to the landlord) (Cooper 1988; Hashmi 1992; Sarkar 2010; Majumdar 2011). Under the reverse *tebhaga* system operating today in Polder 22 and surrounding areas, sharecroppers retain only one third of their

---

transient alluvial deposits (*chars*) which cause the constant formation and erosion of land, at once creating and curtailing opportunities for claims-making. Thus, the ability of landless people to gain access to *khas* lands is largely dependent on their ability to mobilize both individually and collectively. In Polder 22, landless collectives (including both members and non-members of Nijera Kori) have successfully secured access to multiple tracts of *khas* land which is collectively cultivated by a group of 26 members for a period of approximately 9 months of each year. In addition to this, landless collectives work voluntarily to build and maintain modest embankments that protect an additional ring of *khas* land around the polder. Seasonal cultivation and casual livestock grazing on this land provides a source of livelihood to many of the community's marginalized residents,

harvest, even as they are required to bear all the expenses of farming, buying seeds and other inputs, and all additional labor costs. As such, most landless people in Polder 22 report that they are unable to recover their costs from sharecropping, and find it preferable to work as day laborers on the land of others.

In addition to day labor in the village, the majority of those who don't have sufficient landholdings support their families throughout the year through circular labor migration. Some of them leave for extended periods to work in Kuwait and other Gulf states, though the majority migrate to other rural areas in Bangladesh for agricultural harvests, to urban areas to work as construction workers and rickshaw drivers or to peri-urban areas to work in brick fields. One day laborer describes the practice of circular agricultural migration:

> Some people work in the area, but some go outside, to work in the field, cutting rice, they go for a month or two, then they come home. That's how they support their family. They go to Gopal-ganj to cut rice. The *mohajon* [money-lender] comes to take them to work in different places, they go away for weeks, or months. If they come home every week, the travel gets too expens-ive, then they won't have any money left over. So say if 10 people go somewhere where they found work, they will send one of them to come back to the village with money for all the families. The next week someone else comes home, carrying money from everyone.

In addition to stories of agricultural labor such as this one, others describe urban labor, such as one laborer who says 'some people also go to Khulna city to Sattar's shipyard for ship breaking. Basically a lot of people go out for work. If there were more opportunities to earn in Polder 22, it would be more convenient for all of us'. What is conspicuous in this and other stories of labor migration from Polder 22 is that while landless men are continuously compelled to leave to earn money to support their families, their wives and children stay in the village, where social reproduction continues apace. These dynamics exhibit a move toward off-farm wage labor and proletarianization, yet not in the extreme forms of absolute depeasantization evident in Polder 23 (Harriss 1987). Thus, though the work of a migrant laborer from Polder 22 may often be identical to the work of a landless person who has been forced to leave Polder 23, the difference is significant: food sovereignty in Polder 22 serves to preserve the survival of the landless family within the agrarian landscape, while the lack of food sovereignty results in absolute depeasantization for the landless in Polder 23.

Towards an agrarian sovereignty

These two case studies shed light on both the conditions of peasants today in diverse rural political economies, as well as the results and implications of contemporary rural peasant movements. As Edelman describes in his discussion of twenty-first-century peasant move-ments, the political imperatives of peasant moral economies have expanded to include the right to persist as peasant agriculturalists (Edelman 2005, 332). For the landless people of Polder 22, food sovereignty has in many ways facilitated the fulfillment of this right, rela-tive to their counterparts in Polder 23 and other areas taken over by shrimp aquaculture and the most extreme processes of depeasantization. However, even as food sovereignty facili-tates the possibility for a full spectrum of agrarian classes to continue being agriculturalists, testimonies from Polder 22 indicate that this vision is insufficient to ensure the stability and security of their lives and livelihoods.

Insofar as food sovereignty in Polder 22 denotes relative autonomy from neoliberal agro-industrial food systems and capitalist export markets more generally, the community's residents are relatively shielded from the most precarious implications of transition to shrimp export production. As McMichael has written of the current industrial food regime, 'within the terms of the development narrative, rendered more virulent under neoliberalism, the elimination of peasant agriculture is understood to be inevitable' (McMichael 2009b, 284). Indeed, we can see in Polder 22 that relative independence from industrial agriculture has the remarkable benefit of facilitating the survival of peasant agriculture in that community, and that this survival is extraordinary in a region in which peasant agriculture has been all but eradicated. However, the class inequality which remains, and the continued instability of the livelihoods of the poorest, call into question the sufficiency of food sovereignty as a theorized causal process for preventing all forms of agrarian dispossession, of which neoliberal development is only one driver (Adnan 2013, 123). In other words, if the point is to strive for social justice for peasants and peasant communities, food sovereignty is necessary, but not sufficient.

But what might an alternative framing look like? What kind of peasant politics might yield a more equitable agrarian landscape? And is such a landscape possible against the backdrop of the suite of contemporary and historical processes of agrarian change accumulating in Bangladesh's coastal landscape? Here, we would like to raise the question of a broader mode of agrarian sovereignty recently posed by Akram-Lodhi (2013). Akram-Lodhi suggests that to transform the contemporary food regime, a more expansive ambit of concerns than those raised by food sovereignty alone will be necessary. Akram-Lodhi's framing argues for an agrarian sovereignty that links producers and consumers. Here, we develop a slightly different understanding. We ask whether mere survival is an adequate starting point for reimagining politics.[14] Reading food sovereignty through the lens of Scott's subsistence ethic, and against the narratives of residents of Polder 22 and 23, we argue that it is limited as a mechanism for reconstructing political community, particularly a community grounded in egalitarian social relations. An agrarian mode of bare life might be a starting point for political engagement, but it cannot be the endpoint. An alternative politics of agrarian sovereignty, in contrast, must be predicated on a series of open questions about possible agrarian presents and futures and what forms of self-determination must be engaged to bring them about.

While the testimonies from community members in Polders 22 and 23 attest to the importance of self-determination in food production for agrarian communities, at the same time they speak to the precarious livelihoods of the most marginal members of

---

[14]It is worth noting that there are remarkable similarities between food sovereignty – as described by Scott's subsistence ethic – and the debate over sovereignty opened by Agamben's *Homo sacer* (1998). Agamben's argument famously identifies those excluded by the 'sovereign exception' as being cast from *bios* – humanity defined as inclusion in political community – into *zoe* – humanity defined only as biology, or 'bare life'. This framework and the debate over sovereignty that it has engendered have been, by and large, overlooked in the literature on food sovereignty. A full examination of those linkages is beyond the scope of this paper. However, there are interesting resonances between food sovereignty and discussions of humanitarianism over the meaning of humanitarian sovereignty and the purpose of exercising that sovereign power. Authors such as Ticktin (2006) and Agier (2011) have critiqued the nature of humanitarian sovereignty as reducing the conception of humanitarian aid to one of bare life – mere survival. Others have reframed this critique, arguing that the purpose of humanitarian intervention is and should be defined by an imperative towards bare life: to keeping people alive and getting out of the way so that those affected by humanitarian catastrophe can author their own forms of community and politics (Weizman 2012). The question of whether bare life can serve as an effective platform for political intervention, advocacy or activism in the context of peasant politics is one that we would suggest is latent, yet crucial in the food sovereignty debate.

these communities, and their acute vulnerability to ecological crises. This latter concern in particular suggests that even as rural social movements (and the scholars, activists and policy makers that support them) advocate for food sovereignty in the face of a global industrial food regime, they must also be conscious of the insufficiency of such a framework to attend to the needs of *all* rural classes facing ecologies in crisis. This concern is increasingly important, as Edelman explains; for the peasantries of the twenty-first century, 'the subsistence crisis has become a permanent state' (Edelman 2005, 336).

The political implications of this analysis are that while attention to food systems and advocacy for food sovereignty are important and can have powerful impacts, these strategies fall short if they are insufficiently attentive to dynamics of land and class. As our case demonstrates, this essentialism does a disservice to rural social movements and the diverse actors of which they are composed. As Wolford has noted of analyses of such social movements, 'we tend to recognize the different initial subject positions of these mobilized actors but then romantically imagine that these differences fall away once a movement is formed' (Wolford 2010, 7). Our attentiveness to the diversity within rural communities in Khulna seeks to direct attention to the ways in which the global struggle for food sovereignty could better reflect their diverse needs and aspirations. For the landless community members in both Polder 22 and 23, their lack of land rights has resulted in dispossession and, for those in Polder 22, their ability to take advantage of rights to food sovereignty has been constrained in the absence of a more comprehensive set of agrarian rights.

This analysis leads us to support Borras and Franco's appeals to 'land sovereignty' as an important corollary to food sovereignty. As Borras and Franco explain,

> taking seriously the historic demands for land by the various strata of working peoples, what is needed is an alternative frame that better expresses a truly pro-working poor class bias in land issues – especially the core idea of the rural working classes being able to exercise full and effective control over the land where they live and work. (Borras and Franco 2012, 6)

The case of Polder 22 and 23 suggests that combining land sovereignty with food sovereignty may be precisely the alternative frame necessary to achieve sustainable and equitable agrarian reform in rural Bangladesh. If we are to embrace McMichael's argument that 'the transformation of rural subjectivity [through agrarian social movements] is not confined to defending property or territory, but includes re-envisioning the conditions necessary to develop sustainable and democratic forms of social reproduction' (McMichael 2009c, 308), then a more inclusive framing is clearly necessary.

This brings us back to the strategies and vision of Nijera Kori, Bangladesh's landless movement and our partners in this research. Nijera Kori and the landless collectives of which it is composed have actively led the process of reimagining alternative agrarian futures and sovereignties in Khulna and elsewhere in rural Bangladesh.[15] Along with a coalition of civil society organizations loosely organized as the Association for Land

---

[15]As documented by Adnan (2013) in Bangladesh's Noakhali district, Nijera Kori has mobilized on behalf of the rights of the landless to *khas* lands with varying degrees of success. In Noakhali, landless groups gained the rights to collectively cultivate *khas* lands through local campaigning and squatting on newly formed *char* lands, as well as the support of national-level advocacy groups. These campaigns were fraught with the obstacles of multiple and competing regimes of power, requiring complex and often competing strategies on the part of local stakeholders. Thus, in Khulna, as in Noakhali, the process of reimagining agrarian futures entails challenging both old and new power structures which threaten the ability of landless peoples to survive and thrive.

Reform and Development, Nijera Kori promotes a vision for agrarian reform in Bangladesh that is distinct from common developmentalist and neoliberal models of land reform, i.e. land reform which is managed by the state, or land reform managed through the market (Byres 2004; Borras 2006). Neither does it propose that egalitarian agrarian reform can be achieved through securing property rights (O'Laughlin 2009).

Many of the land reform platforms advocated by Nijera Kori involve what Borras and Franco call *social movement or community-led distributive and redistributive land reform*. This entails active campaigns initiated from within local communities by production cooperatives and village committees, with support from local landless collectives, advocating for reforms through both national campaigns and localized struggles. One example is through multi-scalar organizing around the national land use policy, which theoretically prohibits agricultural land from being converted to use for aquaculture. It is often only through collective organizing and direct agitation that the prevention of such conversion is made possible. *Khas* land distribution, which takes both distributive and re-distributive forms, similarly requires localized collective organizing and national advocacy directed at state policy reform. Even as land access itself remains critical for individuals engaged in agricultural production, truly equitable land sovereignty is impossible in the absence of the distribution of the benefits of such access across the spectrum of agrarian classes. Here, too, the possibilities for transforming production relations are grounded in local collective work. To that end, Nijera Kori groups are pursuing projects such as collective cultivation, cooperative economic ventures and the establishment of seed banks for safeguarding community capacity for autonomous cultivation.

The process of reimagining agrarian futures through agrarian sovereignty is an ongoing and unfinished struggle. However, in the face of the ecological crisis confronting Khulna and its inhabitants, it is precisely through the collective generation of strategies for pursuing change that communities might address inequitable power structures – globally, nationally and locally – and thus facilitate the possibility of equitable agrarian futures in the region. The implications of such work, particularly for life in Khulna's shrimp zone, are urgent. They represent a collective set of possibilities for peasant production in the deltaic region that encompass both survival and, perhaps, social justice.

References

Adnan, S. 2013. Land grabs and primitive accumulation in deltaic Bangladesh: Interactions between neoliberal globalization, state interventions, power relations and peasant resistance. *Journal of Peasant Studies* 40, no. 1: 87–128.

Agamben, G. 1998. *Homo sacer: Sovereign power and bare life*. Stanford: Stanford University Press.

Agier, M. 2011. *Managing the undesirables: Refugee camps and humanitarian government*. Oxford: Polity.

Ahmed, N. 2013. Linking prawn and shrimp farming towards a green economy in Bangladesh: Confronting climate change. *Ocean & Coastal Management* 75: 33–42.

Akram-Lodhi, A.H. 2007. Land reform, rural social relations and the peasantry. *Journal of Agrarian Change* 7, no. 4: 554–62.

Akram-Lodhi, A.H. 2013. How to build food sovereignty. *Food Sovereignty: A Critical Dialogue*, 14–15 September, Yale University, New Haven, CT.

Altieri, M.A. 1998. Ecological impacts of industrial agriculture and the possibilities for truly sustainable farming. *Monthly Review* 50, no. 3: 60–71.

Araghi, F. 2001. The great global enclosure of our times: Peasants and the agrarian question at the end of the twentieth century. In Hungry for profit: The agribusiness threat to farmers, food, and the environment, eds. F. Magdoff, J.B. Foster, and F.H. Buttel, 111–47. New York: Monthly Review Press.

Araghi, F. 2009. The invisible hand and the visible foot: Peasants, dispossession and globalization. In *Peasants and globalization: Political economy, rural transformation and the agrarian question*, eds. A.H. Akram-Lodhi and C. Kay, 111–147. London and New York: Routledge.

Barraclough, S., and A. Finger-Stich. 1996. *Some Ecological and Social Implications of Commercial Shrimp Farming in Asia*. UNRISD Discussion Paper 74. United Nations Research Institute for Social Development, Geneva, and World Wide Fund for Nature-International, Gland, Switzerland.

Bernstein, H. 2004. 'Changing before our very eyes': Agrarian questions and the politics of land in capitalism today. *Journal of Agrarian Change* 4, nos. 1–2: 190–225.

Bernstein, H. 2006. Is there an agrarian question in the 21st century? *Canadian Journal of Development Studies* 27, no. 4: 449–60.

Borras, S.M., Jr. 2006. The underlying assumptions, theory, and practice of neoliberal land policies. In Promised land: Competing visions of agrarian reform, eds. P. Rosset, R. Patel and M. Courville, 99–128. Oakland: Food First Books.

Borras, S.M., Jr. 2008. La Vía Campesina and its global campaign for agrarian reform. *Journal of Agrarian Change* 8, nos. 2–3: 258–89.

Borras, S.M., Jr. and J.C. Franco. 2012. *A 'Land Sovereignty' Alternative? Towards a People's Counter-Enclosure*. TNI Agrarian Justice Programme Discussion Paper, July. Amsterdam: Transnational Institute.

Boyce, J. 1996. Ecological distribution, agricultural trade liberalization, and *in situ* genetic diversity. *Journal of Income Distribution* 6, no. 2: 265–86.

Boyce, J.K. 1990. FORUM: Birth of a megaproject: Political economy of flood control in Bangladesh. *Environmental Management* 14, no. 4: 419–28.

Brammer, H. 1990. Floods in Bangladesh: Geographical background to the 1987 and 1988 floods. *The Geographical Journal* 156, no. 1: 12–22.

Byres, T.J. 2004. Neo-Classical Neo-Populism 25 Years On: Déjà Vu and Déjà Passé. Towards a Critique. *Journal of Agrarian Change* 4, nos. 1 and 2: 17–44.

Choudhury, N.Y., A. Paul, and B.K. Paul. 2004. Impact of coastal embankment on the flash flood in Bangladesh: A case study. *Applied Geography* 24, no. 3: 241–58.

Cons, J., and K. Paprocki. 2010. Contested credit landscapes: Microcredit, self-help and self-determination in rural Bangladesh. *Third World Quarterly* 31, no. 4: 637–54.

Cooper, A. 1988. *Sharecropping and sharecroppers' struggles in Bengal 1930-1950*. Calcutta: KP Bagchi & Company.

Deb, A.K. 1998. Fake blue revolution: Environmental and socio-economic impacts of shrimp culture in the coastal areas of Bangladesh. *Ocean & Coastal Management* 41: 63–88.

Edelman, M. 2005. Bringing the moral economy back in … to the study of 21st-century transnational peasant movements. *American Anthropologist* 107, no. 3: 331–45.

Escobar, A. 1999. Whose knowledge, whose nature? Biodiversity, conservation, and the political ecology of social movements. *Journal of Political Ecology* 5: 53–82.

Feldman, S., and C. Geisler. 2012. Land expropriation and displacement in Bangladesh. *Journal of Peasant Studies* 39, nos. 3 and 4: 971–993.

Food and Agriculture Organization. 2010. 'Climate-Smart' Agriculture: Policies, Practices and Financing for Food Security, Adaptation and Mitigation. *The Hague Conference on Agriculture, Food Security and Climate Change*, 31 October-5 November, The Hague.

Guhathakurta, M. 2008. Globalization, class and gender relations: The shrimp industry in southwestern Bangladesh. *Development* 51, no. 2: 212–19.

Guimaraes, J.P.d.C. 1989. Shrimp culture and market incorporation: A study of shrimp culture in paddy fields in Southwest Bangladesh. *Development and Change* 20: 653–82.

Haque, C.E., and M. Zaman. 1993. Human responses to riverine hazards in Bangladesh: A proposal for sustainable floodplain development. *World Development* 21, no. 1: 93–107.

Harriss, J. 1987. Capitalism and peasant production: The green revolution in India. In *Peasants & peasant societies*, ed. T. Shanin, 227–46. Oxford: Basil Blackwell.

Hashmi, T.u.-I. 1992. *Pakistan as a peasant Utopia: The communalization of class politics in East Bengal, 1920-47*. Boulder: Westview Press.

Isakson, S.R. 2009. No hay ganancia en la milpa: The agrarian question, food sovereignty, and the on-farm conservation of agrobiodiversity in the Guatemalan highlands. *Journal of Peasant Studies* 36, no. 4: 725–59.

Karim, L. 2011. *Microfinance and its discontents: Women in debt in Bangladesh.* Minneapolis: University of Minnesota Press.

Lewis, D. 2010. The strength of weak ideas? Human security, policy history, and climate change in Bangladesh. In *Security and development,* eds. J.-A. McNeish and J.H.S. Lie, 113–29. Oxford: Berghahn Books.

Majumdar, A. 2011. *The Tebhaga movement: Politics of peasant protest in Bengal 1946-1950.* Delhi: Aakar Books.

Martínez-Torres, M.E., and P.M. Rosset. 2010. La Vía Campesina: The birth and evolution of a transnational social movement. *Journal of Peasant Studies* 37, no. 1: 149–75.

Marx, K. 1992. *Capital: Volume 1: A Critique of Political Economy.* London: Penguin Books.

McMichael, P. 2006. Peasant prospects in the neoliberal age. *New Political Economy* 11, no. 3: 407–18.

McMichael, P. 2009a. Contemporary contradictions of the global development project: Geopolitics, global ecology and the 'development climate'. *Third World Quarterly* 30, no. 1: 247–62.

McMichael, P. 2009b. A food regime genealogy. *Journal of Peasant Studies* 36, no. 1: 139–69.

McMichael, P. 2009c. Food sovereignty, social reproduction and the agrarian question. In *Peasants and globalization: Political economy, rural transformation and the agrarian question,* eds. A.H. Akram-Lodhi and C. Kay, 288–312. London and New York: Routledge.

O'Laughlin, B. 2009. Gender justice, land and the agrarian question in Southern Africa. In *Peasants and globalization: Political economy, rural transformation and the agrarian question,* eds. A.H. Akram-Lodhi and C. Kay, 190–213. London and New York: Routledge.

Patel, R. 2006. International agrarian restructuring and the practical ethics of peasant movement solidarity. *Journal of Asian and African Studies* 41, nos. 1–2: 71–93.

Paul, B.G., and C.R. Vogl. 2011. Impacts of shrimp farming in Bangladesh: Challenges and alternatives. *Ocean & Coastal Management* 54: 201–11.

Peluso, N.L., and M. Watts, eds. 2001. Violent environments. Ithaca: Cornell University Press.

Primavera, J.H. 1997. Socio-economic impacts of shrimp culture. *Aquaculture Research* 28: 815–27.

Quassem, M., and A. van Urk. 2006. Participatory flood management: Comparative study of the dutch and Bangladesh experience. In *Floods, from defence to management,* eds. E. van Beek, M. Taal and J. van Alphen, 133–46. London: Taylor & Francis.

Sarkar, S.C. 2010. *The sundarbans: Folk deities, monsters and mortals.* New Delhi: Social Science Press.

Scott, J.C. 1976. *The moral economy of the peasant.* New Haven: Yale University Press.

Scott, J.C. 1998. *Seeing like a state: How certain schemes to improve the human condition have failed.* New Haven: Yale University Press.

Shaw, R., F. Mallick, and A. Islam, eds. 2013. *Climate change adaptation actions in Bangladesh.* Tokyo: Springer.

Stonich, S., and P. Vandergeest. 2001. Violence, environment, and industrial shrimp farming. In *Violent environments,* eds. N.L. Peluso and M. Watts, 261–86. Ithaca: Cornell University Press.

Sur, M. 2010. Chronicles of repression and resilience. In *Freedom from fear, freedom from want? Re-Thinking security in Bangladesh,* eds. H. Hossain, M. Guhathakurta and M. Sur, 47–61.

Tanner, T., and J. Allouche. 2011. Towards a new political economy of climate change and development. *IDS Bulletin* 42, no. 3: 1–14.

Ticktin, M. 2006. Where ethics and politics meet: The violence of humanitarianism in France. *American Ethnologist* 33, no. 1: 33–49.

Watts, M. 2011. Ecologies of rule: African environments and the climate of neoliberalism. In *The deepening crisis: Governance challenges after neoliberalism,* eds. C. Calhoun and G. Derluguian, 67–92. New York: New York University Press.

Weizman, E. 2012. *The Least of all possible evils: Humanitarian violence from Arendt to Gaza.* New York and London: Verso Books.

Wittman, H. 2009. Reworking the metabolic rift: La Vía Campesina, agrarian citizenship, and food sovereignty. *Journal of Peasant Studies* 36, no. 4: 805–26.

Wolford, W. 2003. Families, fields, and fighting for land: The spatial dynamics of contention in rural Brazil. *Mobilization* 8, no. 2: 157–72.

Wolford, W. 2010. *This land is ours now: Social mobilization and the meanings of land in Brazil.* Durham: Duke University Press.

World Bank. 2002. *Poverty in Bangladesh: Building on progress.* Washington, DC: World Bank and Asian Development Bank.

World Bank. 2011. *Climate-Smart agriculture: Increased productivity and food security, enhanced resilience and reduced carbon emissions for sustainable development*. Washington, DC: World Bank.

Yu, W., et al. 2010. *Climate change risks and food security in Bangladesh*. London: Earthscan.

Kasia Paprocki is a PhD candidate in Development Sociology at Cornell University. Her research focuses on development, agrarian dispossession and resistance in rural Bangladesh.

Jason Cons is a Research Assistant Professor in the Lyndon B. Johnson School of Public Affairs at the University of Texas, Austin. His research focuses on the India-Bangladesh border and on agrarian change in rural Bangladesh.

Toward a political geography of food sovereignty: transforming territory, exchange and power in the liberal sovereign state

Amy Trauger

The failures of food security and other policies to guarantee the right to food motivate the calls for the radical reforms to the food system called for by food sovereignty. Food sovereignty narratives identify neoliberal state policies and global capital as the source of the food insecurity, and seek new rights for producers and consumers. However, the nature of territorial state power and the juridical structures of the (neo)liberal state may mute the more radical aims of food sovereignty. An engagement with literature on liberal sovereignty illustrates the primacy of the neoliberal market to the exercise of liberal sovereignty by the modern nation-state. The rights of the state to govern trade, often in the interests of capital, and the rights of trade and commerce often trump the citizen's right to food. Reading political theory against the practice of food sovereignty offers insight into solutions for food sovereignty that work within, against and in between the powers of the sovereign liberal state. These include reframing property rights as use rights, engaging in non-commodified food exchanges and practicing civil disobedience to usher in reforms without compromising on essential elements of the food sovereignty agenda.

1.   Introduction

In March of 2011, the town of Sedgewick, Maine, passed a 'food sovereignty' ordinance granting residents the 'right to produce, process, sell, purchase, and consume local foods of their choosing' (Town of Sedgewick, Maine 2011). Provoked by the implementation of the US Food Safety and Modernization Act, which constrained production and distribution practices in Maine in new ways, and inspired by discourses of food sovereignty, the citizens of Sedgewick passed an ordinance that allowed them to establish autonomy over the exchange of food stuffs in their town, and not without consequence. Several farmers have recently been brought up on charges of selling raw milk without a license, and fines have been leveled against farmers, reframed as criminals (Bangor Daily News 2011). The food sovereignty ordinances enacted in Maine encountered limits to the rights of citizens to shape the rules governing food production. Their efforts to decentralize

The author would like to thank Amy Ross and the 2012 Graduate Seminar on Sovereignty in the Department of Geography at the University of Georgia for helping me think through the ideas in this paper. I would also like to thank three anonymous referees and Jun Borras for valuable comments on previous versions of this paper. The author would also like to thank the University of Georgia Research Foundation and the Department of Geography for its generous financial support of field research for this project in 2010 and 2013.

decision-making and prioritize the rights of small-scale farmers and consumers ultimately constituted a criminal de/re-territorializing of sovereign state space (Kurtz 2013). The failures of the food sovereignty ordinance in Maine to secure a space of autonomy for producers and consumers to exchange food outside of federal regulations beg questions about the nature of territorial power and the way appeals for rights in the juridical structures of the (neo)liberal state may not be productive for food sovereignty.

The efforts by the citizens of Sedgewick, Maine, are linked conceptually to peasant movements that operate under the banner of food sovereignty to end hunger and poverty. The primary effort of these movements is to establish authority for decision-making that would support viable agricultural livelihoods for millions of the world's peasants, and thus guaranteeing them a certain right to food. The United Nations Declaration on Human Rights, Article 25(1), asserts that 'everyone has the right to a standard of living adequate for the health and well-being of himself and of his family, including food, clothing, housing … ' (United Nations, 2014) Yet, in spite of state-based food security programs, an estimated 870 million people do not have enough food to meet their needs and suffer from chronic undernourishment (UNFAO 2013). The vast majority of people suffering from hunger and hunger related causes live in the least developed countries, and all people suffering from hunger in either the developed or developing world live in extreme poverty and may receive some form of food aid. Many of those in the developing world are landless former peasants or farmers struggling to live off the exports of commodities to the global North. Clearly, the right to food is not a guarantee, and it is available only to those who are willing and able to pay for, or otherwise receive, legally sanctioned food.

The failures of food security and other policies to guarantee the right to food are at the heart of the radical reforms called for by food sovereignty to end hunger and secure sustainable livelihoods for small-scale farmers. Food sovereignty narratives identify modern notions of property rights and global capitalist markets as the source of the problems in the food system and demand more rights for producers and consumers. These narratives are clear that reform in the food system requires rethinking the neoliberal market as a mechanism for state-based food security initiatives, and implicates the state for its policies that marginalize small producers in the interests of capital. The calls for radical solutions, however, do not adequately engage with the problems that the modern liberal state presents for food sovereignty. Working through these tensions requires an understanding of what is meant by liberal sovereignty and how it works in relationship to power, territory and the economy. In this paper, I position food sovereignty as a progressive rejection of modern liberal state sovereignty that draws on alternative notions of power, territory and economy to establish new modes of decision-making as well as generate new subjectivities.

2.   The political-economic context of food sovereignty's emergence

Many food sovereignty scholars identify the enclosure acts in Great Britain in the 1700s and 1800s that privatized common lands and forced thousands of peasants off the land and into factories as a pivotal moment in the modernization of agriculture (Dawson 2010). This spatial shift in land ownership facilitated and paralleled the transition from agrarian, feudal (or otherwise 'traditional') societies toward an urbanized, rationalized capitalist society structured politically through the nation-state and its biopolitical functions (Foucault 1978; Habermas 1987). According to Harvey (1990, 12) 'scientific domination of nature promised freedom from scarcity, want and the arbitrariness of natural calamity'. The modernist assumptions about the separation of nature and society also normalized new allegiances to the state and its guarantee of food security through innovations in agricultural science (Russell 1966).

Modernity is also characterized by the production of unequal social relations, in particular the production of racial categories through natural science (Gilroy 1993), as well as the gendered division of labor in the production of public and private space (Landes 1988). Modernity, with its emphasis on 'rational' urban dwelling and wage labor relations, also constructed the urban-rural divide that normalizes the countryside as the ideal site for the peasantry and food production (Murdoch and Pratt 1993). Perhaps more powerful than practice, the discursive power of modernity, or the creation of subjects who wish to become autonomous individuals free from the constraints of external authority, is perhaps modernity's greatest accomplishment (Habermas 1987; Appadurai 1996). Modernity is thus able to reproduce itself through the desires of those who desire to become and remain fixed in the dualities between nature and culture or urban and rural (to name a few) that characterize modern life (Latour 1993). The power of this narrative has transformed societies everywhere.

Since the end of World War II, agricultural production in nearly every part of the world has transitioned to some degree to a modernist agricultural system characterized by a vertically integrated market (versus subsistence) economy of food (Friedmann 1993). Decision-making power about some of the most fundamental aspects of life – land, seed and food supplies – is now concentrated in the hands of national states, supranational organizations and transnational corporations (Goodman and Watts 1997). The commodification of food, in the second food regime (Friedmann and McMichael 1989), has resulted in the vertical integration and the concentration of power in a few very large firms with national governments increasingly tailoring food regulation to the demands of agribusiness. Social movements, like food sovereignty, signal discontent with the policy status quo, and politically contest the governance of food and agricultural production (McMichael 2009).

Food sovereignty is often thought of as a response to 'crises' in the global economic system and the socio-ecological systems that support and sustain peasant agriculture (Rosset 2008). Food sovereignty discourse attends to the issues of power asymmetries in the food system that benefit global capital. National state governments and supranational organizations work together, largely through territorial-state policies, such as structural adjustment programs, to enroll small-scale producers in the global economy (Patel and McMichael 2009). These neo-colonial processes normalize modernist development paths to engage as many people as possible in urban/industrial sectors, accumulate through dispossession and facilitate the capitalist transformation of the countryside (Bello 2009; Pimbert 2009). This process has impoverished and made millions of people hungry through removing them from the land and moving them into wage-labor relations in the global economy.

State-run food security programs, premised on the notion that people should have access to safe, adequate and appropriate food, emerged with the development of the welfare state in the 1960s, primarily in more developed countries. In the US, food security policies emerged as a response to both the overproduction of commodities and widespread poverty during the Great Depression (Allen 1999). This model has since expanded to many more states, particularly during the Cold War era. Additionally, the technological changes brought to bear on agriculture via the Green Revolution in developing countries were an exercise in philanthrocapitalism justified by mitigating food insecurity (Morvaridi 2012). The development of policies that employ market mechanisms to distribute food to the poor are consistent with neoliberal notions of the subject which position the individual as responsible for nutritional intake via purchasing food or receiving it as food aid

(Barrett 2002). Subsidies for commodities produced in the developed world also produce surplus to be used as a tool of foreign policy and artificially suppress food prices to facilitate growth and profit in other economic sectors (Selowsky 1981).

Research has shown that in nearly every context, food aid alleviates the short-term need for food in an emergency, but initiates a long-term pattern of dependence (Levinsohn and McMillan 2007). The global circulation of commodities, such as rice or maize, reduces local prices, lowers farmers' incomes and ultimately undermines domestic production. Both the depression in income and the loss of domestic production set up conditions for dependency on the foreign source of food. Additionally, policies such as subsidies for production encourage over-supply in countries from which the aid comes, and thus creates a positive feedback loop resulting in the maintenance of a system that keeps the world's poorest people in poverty. Export models of agricultural development, such as the production of coffee, also produce situations of vulnerability in which farmers could potentially grow a commodity they can neither consume, nor sell if global prices decline below the costs of production. This means that both food aid (the production of consumers) and export orientation models of development (the production of commodities) are part of the 'spatial fix' – the transnational restructuring of space via capitalist transformation of the countryside (Harvey 2003).

Food safety legislation connects the capitalist transformation of the countryside to the state and its food security programs in tangible ways. Food safety standards are a key mechanism for governing global trade in commodities (Dunn 2003). Harmonization between countries is specifically designed to reduce barriers to trade and promote free trade. Standards, however, when based on the science of hygiene, often facilitate the production of food in ways that benefit multinational capital and marginalize small-scale producers (Kurtz, Trauger, and Passidomo 2013). Food safety legislation is an effective way for states to steer agricultural production toward large-scale production models, such as those privileged in the contentious Food Safety Modernization Act (FMSA) in the United States. The FSMA is designed to prevent food contamination, rather than react to its occurrence. This has meant the implementation of food safety practices that were never appropriate for small-scale production, and which have made it cost-prohibitive for most farmers, and sparked resistance, such as that in Sedgewick, Maine.

In short, food security, through its market mechanisms, the (over)production of global commodities and the territorial state-based policies that promote them, has contributed to dependency on the modernist industrial model of agriculture. These policies have undermined the livelihoods of small holders globally and generated new inequities and disconnections between producers and consumers. The state, through its policy mechanisms on food security or food safety, is a vehicle for promoting and continuing certain agricultural practices. These practices nearly always work to the benefit of the transnational corporations who have strategic advantages in commoditized, industrialized agriculture, and neoliberal policy supports them rather than producers or consumers. Corporate rights, the right of the liberal state to govern and the primacy of private property all support this regime of truth, rights and power in favor of capital. In what follows, I will also demonstrate how the state and the market have also worked to blunt the edge of social movements to change the neoliberal, modernist paradigm of the corporate food regime.

2.1. The alternativeness of the alternatives

Market relations are implicit in all the so-called sustainable alternatives that have emerged in the second half of the twentieth century (Buck, Getz, and Guthman 1997; Hinrichs 2000).

The emergence of organic agriculture in the 1980s and its widespread adoption as a federal program in the 2000s signaled a change on both the part of the producer and consumer to reject environmentally damaging practices, although sales of certified organic products remain small. The development of standards for fair trade similarly signaled a rejection, largely by consumers, of unfair labor practices and unfair prices for global commodities, such as coffee and bananas. Sales in Europe are higher than anywhere else, and command a larger and growing market share (Renard 2003). The globalization of organic production and the success of the fair trade model fit well within the neoliberalization of the global food economy. Consumers pay more for a product in the belief that they are doing good, but have little or no control over how benefits are distributed or accrued on the other end of the supply chain (Trauger and Murphy 2013; Trauger forthcoming). Far from addressing the failures of the market to ensure justice for consumers and producers, organic and fair trade have scaled up the governance of food from the state regulatory apparatus to supranational non-governmental organizations (NGOs) who govern within a voluntary auditing system. These consumer-driven and market-based initiatives, and their codification into labels and certifications, have only made organic and fair-trade agriculture 'safe for capitalism' (Guthman 1998, 150).

Other efforts to 'draw attention to the severe shortcomings of commodifying food' (McMichael 2009, 163) include civic agriculture and the (re)localization of food production and consumption. Conventional, industrial-scale agriculture produces cheap food and fungible commodities and keeps consumers separated socially and geographically from the places of food and commodity production, effectively making them ignorant of and disconnected from production practices. Civic agriculture, as an alternative form of entrepreneurship, emphasizes local food systems as a livelihood strategy for small-scale farmers in the global North. Examples include community gardens, farmer's markets, Community Supported Agriculture (CSA), box schemes, and pre-ordered and bulk meat purchases, among many other innovative production and distribution strategies (Lyson 2004) of the kind that the Maine food sovereignty ordinance was designed to protect. Civic agriculture is designed to promote community social and economic development in ways that commodity agriculture, which participates in global-scale markets, does not (Lyson and Guptill 2004). It accomplishes this through short supply chains premised on trust, transparency and reciprocity, also known as 'embeddedness' (Winter 2003).

Civic agriculture aims to promote its objectives by connecting producers and consumers through direct marketing or locality-based food processing and procurement. Locality-based food systems, however, have a tendency to produce a two-class food system in which those who produce the food cannot afford to purchase it. The marketness and instrumentalism of capitalism, however, continue to leave middle-class consumers with more power and privilege than farmers or lower-income consumers (Hinrichs 2000). Local food systems in the global North also trend toward a 'defensive' (Winter 2003) or 'unreflexive' (DuPuis and Goodman 2005) stance against global capitalism, without interrogating how marketness reproduces the inequality that embeddedness set out to disrupt. The emphasis on the transformative potential of individual purchasing decisions in a local market also is consistent with the neoliberal agenda of self-care and the modernist paradigm of individual autonomy and rationality (Guthman 2008a).

Social movements on behalf of the poor and hungry often tend to see capital behind the production of inequities in the food system, and tailor their responses accordingly (Hinrichs 2000; Levkoe 2006). Food justice or community food security activism seek to decommodify food, but these forms of activism often include charity as a problematically racist and elitist approach to food injustice (Anderson and Cook 1999; Guthman 2008b). Charity models are consistent with neoliberal food policies because the distributed food is often surplus commodities. Furthermore, the distribution of surplus food, particularly in the form of 'reclaimed foods', does not challenge the current economic structures of the food system that produced hunger and surplus in the first place (Poppendieck 1999). Similarly, food justice movements that focus on equity as a goal are unclear or agnostic about what action is to be taken to achieve that goal (Gottlieb and Joshi 2010). Other avenues toward dealing with food injustice and food system inequities that are clear about methods often involve disciplining racialized bodies to engage in food-related self-care as neoliberal subjects (Guthman 2008a; Slocum et al. 2011). Additionally, very few, if any, forms of food activism specifically target neoliberal policies, and thus fail to engage with the state-based policies that develop and promote markets (Alkon and Mares 2012).

Food sovereignty builds on the successes of the social movements that have come before it and seeks remedies for the failures of those movements to achieve food security for all. This is evidenced in food sovereignty's emphasis on organic methods, producer control over prices, the development of local markets and anti-hunger politics. It also identifies some of the key reasons for the failures of those movements to guarantee the right to food for all. It does this by specifically challenging the hegemony of market-based social relations and neoliberal policies in the food system (Alkon and Mares 2012). Food sovereignty narratives identify rights as central to power in the food system, including more decision-making rights for farmers, the rights to trade and the rights of women and minorities (Pimbert 2009; Fairbairn 2010). Food sovereignty aims to return control of productive resources to farmers, and the control of food distribution to communities (Holt-Gimenez and Peabody 2008; Patel 2009; Wittman, Desmarais, and Wiebe 2010). This is a different from past activism in a number of ways. Food sovereignty targets transnational capital directly and, by extension, the state-based policies that promote it. It acknowledges that food security on its own is a failure and that additional rights are required beyond the right to food. It makes connections between the rights and responsibilities of producers and consumers to determine the content and character of the food system.

2.2. Histories of food sovereignty

What we said in 1997 is not what we say it is now.

– Paul Nicholson, La Via Campesina, 2013

The concept of food sovereignty has gained considerable traction in a political struggle for progressive reform in the food system (Edelman 2014). It has been widely adopted in a variety of places and contexts, and while effective in mobilizing change, it is broad in its scope and ambition (Clapp 2012). Food sovereignty was developed conceptually in a Latin America context, and was publicly unveiled at the Rome World Food Conference in the NGO Response to the Rome Declaration on World Food Security. This NGO response articulated food sovereignty largely as the 'rights of nations' (Agarwal 2014) to determine their food systems and policies. It also included a six-point plan for ending hunger and articulated the conditions under which food security might be achievable by and for nations. This includes cultural projects such as strengthening family farms and NGO participation in policy, political agendas towards reducing the concentration of wealth and power and strengthening the capacities of nations to provide food security, ecological objectives of decreasing the environmental impacts of agriculture and economic projects geared toward decentralizing and democratizing trade.

Edelman (2014) and others (Patel 2009; Schanbacher 2010) assert that in this document and in general, food sovereignty is positioned against 'food security'. In the NGO statement, however, food sovereignty is positioned as a prerequisite to achieving food security. Article 6 states that 'International law must guarantee the right to food, ensuring that food sovereignty takes precedence over macro-economic policies and trade liberalization'. Point 6.1 declares that 'each nation must have the right to achieve the level of food sufficiency and nutritional quality it considers appropriate without suffering retaliation of any kind … ' Point 6.2 asserts that 'all countries and peoples have the right to develop their own agriculture. Agriculture fulfills multiple functions, all essential to achieving food security' (World Food Summit, 1996). Far from being the antithesis of food security, food sovereignty demands the political rights to govern agriculture and trade as a prerequisite for food security.

This first definition of food sovereignty was subsequently elaborated on in various meetings of NGOs and civil society organizations. These include the Foro Mundial in 2001, the meeting in Selengue, Mali, in 2007 and a meeting of La Via Campesina in 2012. The Nyéléni Declaration articulated the most frequently invoked definition of food sovereignty, which is:

> Food sovereignty is the *right of peoples* to healthy and culturally appropriate food produced through ecologically sound and sustainable methods, and their right to define their own food and agriculture systems. It puts the aspirations and needs of those who produce, distribute and consume food at the heart of food systems and policies rather than the demands of markets and corporations.
>
> (Nyéléni 2007:9 pp. 1-73, emphasis added).

Agarwal (2014) notes that this shift from 'nations' to 'peoples' is significant in that it positions food sovereignty as all-encompassing, embracing everyone in the food chain as a potentially powerful actor. This big-tent vision, however, contains some potentially damning contradictions. Patel (2009), Agarwal (2014) and others have elaborated on these at length, such as the tension between individual and collective rights and tensions between national and local food self-sufficiency. These tensions have yet to be resolved in any global-scale narrative or policy, and are often worked out on the ground in food sovereignty practice. The shift from 'nations' to 'peoples' is not just a semantic move to make food sovereignty more inclusive, however. It also signaled a shift from disentangling national-scale food policies from transnational capital (which took up three of the six points in the 1996 declaration) to an interest in local action to assert and maintain political autonomy at multiple scales.

The Nyéléni Declaration was a key moment in transnational organizing as it brought together a select group of 500 delegates from a variety of organizations in 80 different countries to specifically address how to craft an international agenda for resistance and to assert political autonomy at a local level. In the Nyéléni definition of food sovereignty, the interests and rights of producers, distributors and consumers are privileged, as is the ability of 'local communities' to determine their food systems to mitigate hunger in all its forms. It also includes a 'right to food security', the transformation of social relationships, particularly between genders and races, and the 'sharing of productive resources' free from threats of 'expulsion and privatization' (Nyéléni 2007, 13). This definition has a lot for scholars to wrestle with, but I interpret it as a questioning of the modernist project, or what the Nyéléni documents identify as the 'whole fabric of global economics and society' (17).

The Nyéléni definition demands the right to determine the nature of politics, economies and social relationships in any given community with the right to non-interference from other parties, including the state. This is, by any definition, political autonomy and a declaration of self-determination. An oft-quoted statement from one of the Nyéléni delegates underscores this interpretation well. The anonymous delegate is recorded in the documents as saying:

> All peoples that want to be free and independent must produce their own foods. Food sovereignty is more than just a right; in order to be able to apply policies that allow autonomy in food production, it is necessary to have political conditions that exercise autonomy in all territorial spaces: countries, regions, cities and rural communities. Food sovereignty is only possible if it takes places at the same time as *political sovereignty of peoples.*
>
> (Nyéléni 2007, 16, emphasis added)

It is probably fair to say that other, more violent measures to question modernity and to obtain political autonomy are emergent on a global stage, coincident with food sovereignty (Barber 1992). To understand the motivations and the forms of resistance to modern state and capital hegemony taken by food sovereignty requires a deeper reading of the documents emergent from transnational organizing around food sovereignty.

2.3. *The Nyéléni definitions*

Delegates to the Nyéléni forum in Mali identified seven general areas of modern agriculture that are constitutive of the problem of food insecurity, and how these areas might be changed to facilitate political autonomy in the name of food security.[1] Working groups convened to answer questions about what food sovereignty was 'fighting for', 'fighting against' and 'what we can do about it' (Nyéléni 2007, 25). For the purposes of this paper I focus on three themes that relate to the political economic alternatives that food sovereignty proposes: (1) local markets and international trade, (2) access to and control over natural resources and (3) sharing territories and land. These themes cover some of the basic areas of decision-making power over the food economy of a community, alternative modes of access to land and the production of social relationships premised on equality and fairness that I elaborate on in Section IV below.

Food sovereignty seeks to redefine relationships regarding markets, trade and the exchange of food (Nyéléni 2007, 25–27). The Nyéléni delegates identified that 'currently trade is based on an unsustainable production system and is controlled by TNCs' (25). The trade agreements that characterize the corporate food regime are premised on the philosophies of free trade, and in the delegates' view, this has destroyed livelihoods and local economics. These neoliberal policies, rather than guaranteeing the right to food, are in fact the source of food insecurity. The Nyéléni delegates recommend returning democratic control of food distribution to producers and consumers, and implementing 'autonomous control over local markets' (26). They identify local food production, food cooperatives, local processing and solidarity economies as key mechanisms toward this end. They also 'propose to governments, policies that protect local production and markets … eliminate corporate control and facilitate community control' (27). These policies, if implemented, would effectively subvert federal or national authority in favor of local control. In short, the delegates identified that rescaling, decentralizing and democratizing decision-making

---

[1]Nyéléni, 2007. The seven themes are: local markets and international trade policies, local knowledge and technology, access to and control over natural resources, sharing territories and land, conflicts and natural disasters, social conditions and forced migration and production models.

about markets are required for autonomy. Surplus is to be appropriated for the local community, as opposed to transnational capital, if it is appropriated at all.

Additionally, food sovereignty tackles the issue of land reform and the problem of privatization in radical ways (Nyéléni 2007, 33–25). The delegates identified access to land as a key right required for food sovereignty, as well as a resource that is unevenly distributed by discriminating against the poor, women and indigenous people. They write, 'A genuine agrarian reform is needed that allows us continued rights of access to and control over our territories' (33). The delegates argue for upholding 'the legal and customary rights of peoples and communities for access to local, communal resources' (34) and include 'access to and control over our seed varieties' (34) as a key element of autonomy. They also identify an 'alternative economic system among local producers' such as that identified above as key to keeping land under community control. They also seek to ensure women's access to land and work toward the recognition of indigenous peoples as key actors in deciding issues of access and control of all productive resources including water, land and seed. They conclude with a simple statement: 'We will fight privatization and patenting' (35). In summary, the equitable sharing of productive resources, through alternative frameworks of use and access and through decommodifying and de-privatizing property, form the basis for food sovereignty's solution to the problem of accessing land.

According to the Nyéléni delegates, privatization forms the basis of modernist notions of space in the nation-state and produces unequal social relations (Nyéléni 2007, 35–27, 56–60). The Nyéléni delegates are clear about the way their episteme of territory and power departs from the geographical imaginary of the nation-state. They write, 'we define territories beyond geopolitical boundaries' (35) and acknowledge traditional forms of knowledge, land use and land access rather than the rules of the nation-state. They stress 'sharing territory' over owning or privatizing territory. They resist 'all forms of expulsion' whether of indigenous people or migrants in another rejection of the prerogatives of the territorial nation-state. They instead will work to end discrimination, particularly against women, indigenous people, migrants and future generations from accessing land. The Nyéléni delegates also stress that traditional ecological knowledge, a strong civil society and alternative economic systems will be the basis for decision-making over resources and exchange. They argue that conflicts over territories are generated through privatization and the liberalization of land markets that leave some with much and many with too little. The key, they conclude, to making all of this possible is 'decision-making power at the local level' (60).

As compelling as these visions are, they do not adequately confront the political realities of liberal sovereignty, namely, the territorialization of space and national economies under the governance of the modern nation-state. Additionally, the privatization of property is enshrined as a central right in liberal democracies and facilitates the development of a capitalist economy (Smith 1863). The collective right to access, use or share land thus stands directly opposed to a political and economic system premised on the primacy of private property rights. Given that capitalism and liberal states have been mutually constituted in the project of modernity (Patel and McMichael 2009; Barkan 2013), any appeal to the state for rights to trump state/interstate laws in trade or to undermine private property are paradoxical. The appeal to rights from the state (and thus also to give the state rights to 'decide the exception' as discussed below) thus leaves food sovereignty vulnerable to failure of some essential elements of its vision. For example, if the redistribution of land is achieved without addressing the issue of privatization via the market-based nature of land sales to peasants, the conditions that generate inequality as identified by the Nyéléni delegates remain in place (O'Laughlin et al. 2013).

The appeal for expanded rights for farmers to access productive resources is clear, but very little is said about who or what that guarantor of use or access rights could be (Patel 2009; Schanbacher 2010), especially when those rights counter the rights of the state to uphold private property rights and the interests of capital to have them. Scholars agree that the radical demands of food sovereignty are disciplined and muted by liberal states (Patel 2009, 669), but there is a tendency in much of the food sovereignty narratives and literature to continue to see the state as the guarantor of rights. This seems to be a fundamentally backward-looking view toward the Cold War era of state-driven food security initiatives which have failed. These arguments for more regulation and state oversight essentially call for the displacement of the power of transnational capital with territorial state-based policies, without addressing that those policies can and may still drive and promote the circulation of transnational capital. Also, rights granted by the state give the state the power to determine when, if and how those rights will be granted (Agamben 2005).

A serious tension then lies between those who advocate that the state/capital is the problem and cannot be the solution, and those who argue that the state can be a source of solutions if only we do it differently. The Nyéléni documents appeal to states for changes to policies, and the implementation of new policies to protect the interests of small holders and communities, at the same time that they demand autonomy from state oversight. Because state overthrow is not a popular option, the answer to this tension, as proposed by many food sovereignty scholars, then, is to *do democracy better* by broadening or expanding rights to individuals. This solution does not question whether the way liberal democracy is currently practiced may actually be part of the problem, given the way that it concentrates power and rights in a sovereign state, and upholds the primacy of modernist notions of trade and private property. Doing democracy differently or better may not adequately address the problem of food insecurity, if the way that state power and capital work through the technology of sovereignty is not also addressed as well. That is to say, peasant rights to land or individual rights to food, no matter how broad, will always be trumped by the sovereign's right to govern, usually in the interests of capital. The right to food and the right to govern are thus at odds in a liberal state when the objective of food sovereignty is to decommodify food and decentralize authority over decision-making.

3. Theories of sovereignty

Another rarely examined question is the meaning of 'sovereignty' itself.

– Marc Edelman (2014, 12)

Sovereignty as a concept has long figured into geopolitical thought, particularly as it relates to the development of the modern nation-state after the Peace of Westphalia. Taylor (2000, 766) defines sovereignty 'as a condition of final and absolute authority in a political community'. Typically, this political community has been the 'nation', and sovereignty refers to the state's (sometimes democratic) control over a certain delimited territory. Historically, sovereignty territorialized the nation-state, in terms of controlling what lies within its boundaries in its internal spatiality, but also in its reciprocal relations with other nation-states who recognize it (and are recognized) as sovereign in external relations (Brenner 1999; Benhabib 2004; Agnew 2009). The powers that inhere to the sovereign state give it the right 'to kill or to allow to live' (Mbembe 2003, 11) that which it is able to 'capture' or appropriate (Delueze and Guattari 1987) with the right to non-interference in these decisions by external actors (Storey 2001). The sovereign right to kill cultivates a parallel function in the sovereign right to foster and manage life, or what Foucault (1978) refers to as biopower. The management of life as a power held by the state is predicated on the sovereign right to decide what constitutes life, which makes those it can 'capture' subject to the state valuations of life (Agamben 2005). In short, the sovereign is that which holds the power to value and foster life according to the political or economic usefulness of its life (or death) (Rose 2007).

The actual practice of sovereignty is far more contested than the discourses that surround it might suggest; sovereignty in action is rarely absolute (Agnew 2009; Elden 2010). While having real effects, sovereignty is a social construction that makes the territorial national state possible (Storey 2001; Nyers 2006; Agnew 2009). The degree to which territorial boundedness figures into the sovereign power of the state is a matter of much debate (Ong 2007; Agnew 2009). These debates reveal the way in which the myth of the territorial basis of the Westphalian state system is increasingly challenged, and is being replaced with a network ontology in which sovereignty is an emergent property of social relations. In this model, sovereignty emerges from neoliberal economic relationships between states, which extend the reach, or hegemony, of individual national states into the economic or political space of other territorial states in imperial ways (Hardt and Negri 2001; Agnew 2009). Some would say that the rise of supranational arrangements constructs new geographies of power that erode the power of the territorial sovereign state (Anderson 1996). Others, however, argue that the nation-state is often strengthened rather than weakened with the rise of globalization, and that global capital mobilizes certain powers of the nation-state to control resources, territory and people (Watts 2000; Agnew 2005; Ong 2007). Without doubt, however, the contemporary era presents challenges to existing ideas about the spaces and territories of the nation-state, particularly with regard to what constitutes authority and autonomy over space in transnational, if not post-national, political arrangements (Appadurai 2003; Benhabib 2004). What remains is a carefully maintained fiction about the territorial basis of the sovereign state.

Nyers (2006, xii) suggests that this fiction is a product of 'statism' as a social movement, 'so powerfully successful that the state has become normalized as the only authentic community that can serve as a site for political activity'. The state is created through the repeated performance of activities that produce its powers, such as those associated with citizenship, allegiance and belonging. Benhabib (2004) writes, 'Citizenship and practices of political membership are the rituals through which the nation is reproduced spatially … to ensure the purity of the nation in time through the policing of its contacts and interactions in space' (18). Through this normalization and naturalization of the state, alternative political practices, such as self-governance or popular self-rule, are rendered 'unacceptable or unthinkable' (Nyers 2006, xii). What constitutes the normative (the order of the state) necessarily produces the non-normative (the chaos outside the order of the state) which, according to Schmitt (1922), must be guarded against. The 'state of exception', or totalitarian rule, is thus invoked in emergency situations to prevent the collapse of the state into chaos (Schmitt 1922). Agamben (2005) extends the idea of the state of exception to suggest that it is no longer necessary to invoke exceptions in emergencies; the current state of political affairs is characterized by the suspension of civil liberties in order to sustain the sovereign power of the state.

The state of exception, according to Ong (2007), is selectively used to generate 'overlapping or variegated sovereignties' (19) in which there are exemptions to state sovereignty (for transnational corporations) to produce value for capital. Similarly, McCarthy and Prudham (2004) suggest that the meaning of neoliberalism emerges through its practice as a form of governance that facilitates the development of markets, rather than as a preexisting philosophy informing forms of governance that favor an absence of regulation.

Ong's framing of neoliberalism as a Schmittian state of exception allows for the creation of 'sites of transformation where market-driven calculations are being introduced in the management of populations and the administration of special spaces' for capital (2007, 4). While Ong (2007) makes visible the links between transnational capital and state powers of exception, Barkan (2013) argues that the state and the corporate body have never been separate. In fact, 'corporate capitalism emerges as a mode of liberal government' and this 'clarifies how reforms unwittingly reinvest the sovereign power they seek to subvert' (13). Together, Ong and Barkan advance an understanding of sovereignty that is bracketed from its basis as a singularity of power over territory, and also demonstrate how liberalism and transnational corporate capital are so deeply intertwined they cannot be approached as separate entities.

In the case of the United States, the constitution arose from a need for a centralized authority granting certain federal powers of supremacy over states. The Commerce Clause (US Constitution n.d. Article I, Section 8, Clause 3) describes one of the powers granted to Congress which is to 'regulate commerce with foreign Nations, and among the several States and with the Indian tribes' (sic). This clause effectively gives federal authority to govern all economic affairs within the United States as well as with other national-states. The degree to which the federal government is involved in economic matters between groups has varied over time according to the way the Supreme Court has interpreted these powers. According to the decisions made in the early twentieth century in response to challenges to the Commerce Clause, Congress was given the power to regulate interstate commerce and to 'protect and advance' the interstate commerce, in order to 'prevent interstate trade from being destroyed or impeded by the rivalries of local governments' (Shreveport Rate Cases 1914). When this is the law of the land, trade that is not sanctioned by the federal government is outlawed, regardless of the rights of individuals to the food of their choosing.

That the federal government would protect its right to regulate and ban interstate commerce over people's right to food was made clear in a recent case involving the transport of raw milk into Georgia from South Carolina. The case was brought by the Farm-to-Consumer Legal Defense Fund (FTCLDF) against the Food and Drug Administration (FDA) for its attempt to criminalize the sale of raw milk across state lines. Unpasteurized milk is legal to produce and sell to customers in South Carolina, but not to people who live in Georgia. Thus, consumers in Georgia sought to purchase it outside the state, which according to the FDA is in violation of the Interstate Commerce Clause. The case against the FDA was thrown out on technical grounds, but not before the lawyers for the FDA elaborated on the 'right to food' versus the right of the federal government to regulate commerce. They argued that

> substantive due process does not protect, or even recognize, rights to foods of one's choosing or rights to physical health, and that extending constitutional protection to such rights would place the matter outside the arena of public debate and legislative action.
>
> (Kurtz, Trauger, and Passidomo 2013, 142)

In short, the rights to food that the plaintiffs asserted as fundamental were considered secondary to the interests of government to regulate, promote and protect trade.

The framing of sovereignty as also produced through, and productive of, the actions and state protection of capital is instructive for understanding how the transnational food regime works. It also helps to understand why and how appeals to the liberal state for rights are not necessarily viable solutions to the food security crises identified by food sovereigntists.

Rights in a neo/liberal state are required to be translated back through a market-based economy so that they can continue to support the normal order of the state. In the raw milk case cited above, the rights of government *to govern* trumped the rights of individuals to food. That the decision to outlaw the trade in raw milk across state lines benefits the interests of capital (the pasteurizers who control the supply chain) and not the producers or the consumers is an overlooked side note in this case, but a significant one. Thus, any alternatives that are not easily controlled by the neoliberal order and the associated sovereign powers of exception granted by the state are simply rendered illicit and illegitimate, thus criminalizing and capturing those who produce and exchange food outside of the neoliberal order (van der Ploeg 2009, 266). How then to avoid capture?

Avoiding capture might draw on the ways in which territory is enrolled and acted upon in the liberal sovereign state. Elden (2010) describes territory as a technology of power in which space is produced by the state in order to measure and control the population and the resources (i.e. life) within its bounds. Territorial formations are thus geographical expressions of power upon which the state intends to make a permanent claim. Storey (2001), however, suggests that territory is always and already a temporary spatial strategy as competing interests may appropriate space over time. An example of territory temporarily mobilized to avoid capture by the biopolitical state is the temporary autonomous zone (TAZ) (Bishop and Williams 2012). Also known as 'freezones', TAZs offer a space of bounded autonomy for dissidents and free thinkers, and often operate at the political and economic margins of the state for the purposes of expanding the range of normative discourses (Bey 2003). These spaces are often strongly associated with anarchist politics, but are animated by discourses of action that move away from state overthrow and toward creating spaces of freedom, self-reliance and mutual aid (Bishop and Williams 2012).

Sovereignty is a specifically spatial and social strategy mobilized by the modern state to claim territory, in the attempt to subject life within the bounds of that territory (and in some cases, beyond) to the biopolitical power of the state. Sovereignty, while having real effects, especially over the rights to foster life, is a contested social construction which produces 'imaginaries' of subjection, boundedness and power. Citizens participate in the daily life of the state, and in so doing create and reify its structures (Holston 1998; see also Wittman 2010). Therefore the exercise of sovereignty by the state over citizens is hardly absolute, and this partiality opens up opportunities for organizations and individuals organizing under the banner of food sovereignty to (re)territorialize space in non-violent resistance. The notions of sovereignty from (geo)political theory can inspire action to shift the balance of power between producers/consumers over rights to decision-making powers about life and death. This struggle invokes specifically geographic technologies of power, such as territory and space, to produce new modes of belonging and allegiance. This is both a forward-looking and innovative episteme of power and territory that pays attention to a different form of democracy than that practiced by the liberal sovereign state.

4. Transforming/resisting liberal sovereignty

According to Benhabib (2004), allegiance, citizenship and sovereignty are co-produced through the repeated performances of individuals and communities across space and time. The performances also (re)produce territory and the economy for the sovereign state as well as (re)generate the structures/networks of power used by the state. Thus, food sovereigntists might contest state/capital sovereignty by refusing to perform the sovereignty of the liberal state, or performing what Nyers (2006) calls the 'unthinkable' by not commodifying food, or not adhering to laws regulating food production. Perhaps these collective anti-sovereign performances can be framed through Deleuzian *assemblages* of actions knit together through a kind of Nancian *being in common* or what Hardt and Negri (2004) more recently refer to as the *multitude*. By this I mean to say that rather than being subject as a citizen to territorial state rule dictating the collective behavior of producers and consumers, alternative notions of governance and the economy may bring people together (even across national boundaries) in novel ways. In this context, the forms of power that are available to activists are non-violent refusals to participate in what Nyers calls the 'social movement of statism' through civil disobedience.

In addition to the way food sovereignty challenges norms of exchange, land and decision-making practices, it also is a powerful narrative of alternative modernity (or anti-modernity) that questions modernist subjectivity as much as it challenges the practices of modernity that have failed to produce 'freedom from want' (Harvey 1990, 12). The discourse of food sovereignty also generates anti-modern subjects who work against the social movement of statism, and perform an alternative sovereignty against but, unfortunately, within the liberal state. In a positive light, food sovereignty might recapture meanings of sovereignty and citizenship that have less to do with transnational capital and its enabler, the territorial state, and more to do with 'popular self-rule' (Agnew 2009, 48). Seen more negatively, liberal sovereignty retains the power to make the exception, and invokes it, as Ong (2007) suggests, to produce variegated sovereignties. In what follows, I elaborate on some ways in which food sovereignty actions challenge liberal sovereignty, as well as how the (neo)liberal state is troubling to many of the objectives of food sovereignty.

4.1. *Territory, economy and power*

Food sovereignty resists the continued enclosure of land and other commons, such as seed, which its defenders argue perpetuates the centralization of power and control of agriculture by states and corporations. Property reform, then, is a central pillar of food sovereignty demands, but O'Laughlin et al. (2013) caution that land redistribution can, paradoxically, lead to the reconcentration of wealth in the hands of those who receive land via land reforms, and lead to other undesirable outcomes such as the loss of waged agricultural labor and the relegation of farmers to land unfit for farming. Traditional land reform tends to focus on renegotiating who owns discrete parcels of land, and is in contrast to many of the Nyéléni narratives which stress that 'access', 'sharing' and 'rights to use' are more central than owning or (re)distributing land. In addition, the episteme of ownership that land can be claimed, exchanged and transferred from one person to the next is antithetical the idea that land (or other kinds of capital) can be used without paying for it or without paying for the privilege of using it.

This is not to say that agrarian reform or land reform is not necessary, but rather the episteme of ownership needs to be rethought. Land reform that enrolls peasants in a market-based economy after the fact of land reform perpetuates the inequalities that already exist within the society that led to landlessness, poverty and hunger. This is well documented in a number of comprehensive studies of land reform, including Wolford's (2010a, 2010b) work on the Movimento dos Trabalhadores Sem Terra (MST) or the Landless Workers Movement in Brazil. According to Wolford (2010a), state involvement and (mis)management of land reform privileged the already powerful and led to the exacerbation of existing inequalities. The Brazilian state's interest in promoting agrarian reform was not out of goodwill toward peasants, but to enroll them in the market-based economy for sugar cane, as part of the market liberalization occurring at the time throughout Latin America (Kurtz 2004). The redistribution of land gave some farmers some access to some land, but their lack of interest, at least in the North, in cultivating sugar cane for the market led to their further marginalization in the economy (Wolford 2010b).

A conceptual shift away from commodification and privatization may require rethinking the relationship between capital and the benefits one receives from it. Owning or accessing land for members of the MST did not necessarily benefit them if they did not wish to work as sharecroppers in sugarcane. Wider freedoms must also be associated with access to capital, as elaborated by Borras and Franco (2012) on the rights that are prerequisite to land sovereignty. Rather than rejecting western property rights, they argue that land sovereignty allows for 'plural' rights, 'encompassing communal, community, state and/or private property rights' (7), which echoes Patel's (2009) 'overlapping geographies' or maybe, less positively, Ong's (2007) 'variegated sovereignties'. Ribot and Peluso (2003) identify a key distinction between access as 'the ability to derive benefits from things' and ownership as 'the right to benefit from things' that may also be instructive to food sovereignty.

Land reform occurs in a variety of forms with a variety of outcomes, but remaining true to the vision of autonomy from state and market imperatives as 'the right to *derive* benefits' from capital remains a key feature of food sovereignty. I would also add that the right to derive benefits must come with a guarantee that capital does not come with strings attached to the neoliberal market economy. Collective land rights or usufruct rights are antithetical to capitalism, which relies on privatization and an episteme of ownership of capital, and which generates inequality in a class-based system. Refusing to participate in privatization is part of what Nyers (2006) calls the 'unthinkable' for the state, the undermining of the central structures upon which it rests. But this is exactly what food sovereignty is asking us to think about. Food sovereignty can and does change the terrain for struggle over decision-making in the food system by (re)territorializing space to engage alternative notions of ownership and decision-making. All social struggles are spatial (Martin and Miller 2003) and changing the terrain, figuratively or literally, upon which a struggle is engaged may ultimately change the outcomes of the struggle as well.

Food sovereignty narratives call for 'alternative economic systems' and 'solidarity economies' as necessary for changing an asymmetrical trade scheme. Food sovereignty also resists the production of inequality that so many local and organic food systems continue to perpetuate. J.K. Gibson-Graham (2006) suggests practicing this through a *being in common* that is achieved through the interdependence of a variety of economic subjects and objects. This is accomplished via the conscious and deliberate re/negotiation of foundational economic ideas and practices, the development of new economic languages and the creation of new economic subjects, which food sovereignty accomplishes through its transnational organizing and localized markets. This strategy also suggests engaging with the principle of subsidiarity, which encourages decision-making at the lowest scale and between the fewest people possible, such as agreements between producers and consumers about what food is safe to consume (Feagan 2007). Persisting with such alternatives even when it is illegal, such as raw milk sales in Maine or Georgia, constitutes a kind of civil disobedience, used to leverage more autonomy or power from the liberal state. This strategy also exploits gaps in the power of the sovereign state, and reterritorializes space for food sovereignty, however temporarily.

In what follows, I offer a few examples of food sovereignty based on the practices surrounding wild rice by Anishinabe tribal members in northern Minnesota. These practices illustrate the way in which food sovereignty may implement its radical vision within the existing structures of the modern liberal nation state by working with, against and in between its juridical structures by reworking the central notions of sovereignty: territory, economy and power. Until the rights to govern are granted to people and communities, rights to food are taken, often illicitly, in order to provide food, protect natural capital and exercise collective decision-making against the interests of capital. These examples include ways to work against the primacy of private property rights through fighting for and acting on the right to access to territory, the (re)development of an anti/post-capitalist subjectivity with gift economies, and the use of civil disobedience to both obtain food and produce political subjects oriented toward shared power and community food security.

4.2. *White Earth Tribe of Anishinabe, Minnesota*

Food sovereignty's struggles over space fall under the political strategy that Patel (2009) refers to as the 'overlapping geographies' of cosmopolitan federalism, in which multiple authorities engage in the governance of space. Indigenous Treaty Rights in the US may be considered alternative norms of property and use of resources that can inform democratic decision-making about how to use land in similar ways. The Treaty Rights sometimes enjoyed by tribal members include the rights to hunt, fish and grow rice on land and water from which Native Americans were expelled in the nineteenth and twentieth centuries in Minnesota, and which they no longer own. In 1837, the Chippewa/Ojibwe tribes of the Upper Midwest (under duress) ceded 3 million acres of territory to the United States, while retaining hunting, fishing and ricing rights. Wild rice is a grain endemic to the lakes and ponds of the Upper Midwest, and has provided a staple food for the Ojibwe (of which the Anishinabe are a part) for centuries. While imperfect and a totally inadequate reparation for genocide, a mechanism does exist within the liberal state to grant overlapping sovereignties to those whom it recognizes as other sovereigns, with an associated package of rights for using resources on land they do not own.

Unfortunately, these rights are threatened by the actions of both federal and state governments, largely due to their interests in protecting the commercial ricing, sport fishing and hunting industry in Minnesota. According to primary sources in the White Earth Tribe, state Department of Natural Resources (DNR) officials harass native ricers and fishers when they assert their Treaty Rights off the reservation. The state conservation officials will issue citations, which are usually dismissed in state and district courts because access to and use of those lands is a federal-level dispute. The citations, however, are a strategy of harassment that poses intimidating barriers to native ricers and costs them money and time in unnecessary legal entanglements. One respondent says,

> I was stopped at a gas station by a DNR official and asked for ricing permits, simply on the basis of having a canoe and a push pole in the truck. When we refused to cooperate, the officer called for reinforcements, but finally just gave us a warning based on our canoe not having a state registration sticker. He had to find something.

In spite of harassment, tribal members continue to assert their rights off the reservation, as well as engaging in other acts of civil disobedience to govern their resources. According to other White Earth respondents, the number of lakes with rice in them off the reservations has declined since the state established authority over their management. On the reservation, the tribe manages the rice crop and encourages the seeding of lakes, which is the depositing of wild rice grains in the lake, and is widely practiced on the reservation. A respondent told me that they have always made sure that they left some rice 'for the lake' and often take varieties from one lake to another to encourage cross breeding. This action is deemed an illegal activity off the reservation by the state of Minnesota, and can only be practiced by state conservation officials. The criminalization of these acts is an assertion of the neoliberal hegemony of the sovereign state. Even if it grants tribal members some use rights, it does not grant governance rights, especially when this might interfere with capital accumulation from the commercial ricing and sport fishing industries. This is more akin to Ong's (2007) 'variegated sovereignty' than Patel's (2009) 'overlapping sovereignties' in that the state retains the right to invoke a state of exception, and does not grant any decision-making authority.

While the White Earth tribe is by no means food secure, food security in the view of many on the reservation does not arise from and is currently not possible through the state. Community-based decision-making around food security that is rooted in traditional knowledge and practices is demonstrated in the 'gift economy' of wild rice on the White Earth Indian Reservation. Up until the middle of the twentieth century, the communal and inter-tribal ricing season in the autumn would supply each family with enough rice to eat for one year and a small amount for trading. Anything left would be distributed among the families in the tribe, particularly to those without able-bodied adults and to the elderly. This practice, now dramatically changed, continues in the ritual gifting of rice in nearly every social interaction. For example, wild rice is given to the host, particularly elders, whenever a person is invited to a home. It is also evident in the ritualized exchanges of rice at tribal gatherings such as a drum ceremony, which was criminalized and forbidden until 1978. While this gift economy has been disrupted by the dramatic disruptions that colonialism, racism and genocide have brought the Anishinabe tribes, a subjectivity based on the non-monetary exchange and circulation of food in the interests of food security persists. These transactions also cannot be regulated or criminalized by the state because they are non-commodified exchanges.

In the absence of any state intervention of any kind, neoliberal or otherwise, community-based solutions are required, and the White Earth tribe has, through the reclaiming of old, previously outlawed, practices, invoked traditions of harvesting and sharing rice as a form of food security. The tribal governance of resources constitutes a kind of autonomous zone, through which tribal interests can (but do not always) trump the interests of capital. These autonomous zones extend off the reservation when tribal members act on the right to rice for subsistence means in spite of the resistance to this from the state. The sustainable use of the lakes for ricing requires collective decision-making within and across tribes about yields and management of rice production. The forms of power that are invoked against the illegal actions of the sovereign state (e.g. the illicit act of seeding lakes) can only be seen as civilly disobedient. These are instructive examples for thinking through how food sovereignty reconfigures notions of power (through disobedience), economy (through acting on rights to subsistence and non-commodified food exchanges) and shared access to property through overlapping zones of authority (tribal, state, federal) over territory. The ongoing interest in the state to support commercial fishing and ricing, against the needs and rights of tribal members for subsistence, suggests that there are very deep waters into which food sovereignty must step to assert its rights to food security.

5. Conclusions

Food sovereignty is a narrative about returning decision-making control to producers and consumers in the food system to mitigate the negative externalities of capital and state control of food, including hunger and food insecurity. The right to food is always already not met for the poor and landless in the world because the rights of capital, as they are encoded in the constitutions of liberal states, trump the rights of individuals and communities. Food sovereignty challenges modernist notions of power and autonomy that lead neoliberal subjects to believe that geopolitical power is fixed and total in its manifestations, and the opportunity for subverting the power of the state is possible only through the reform of liberal rights and policies. This myth persists even while food sovereignty asserts that there are possibilities and sites for transformation through alternative ways of thinking about the territories, economies and power that underpin the liberal state. This paper has attempted to make more explicit the connections between territory and power in the liberal state, and demonstrated how troubling privatization of capital is for food sovereignty, as well as how central it is for liberal sovereignty.

Food sovereignty action, often civilly disobedient, constitutes a re-territorialization of power that the state may or may not have the political will to resist. The partiality of sovereignty in the liberal state presents possibilities to subvert its power, and challenges the 'social movement of statism' that (re)creates its existence. While the state may look the other way at the re-territorializing of power for a time, the interventions of food sovereignty are almost always threatened and temporary. The sovereign state retains the power to determine the exception, and thus food sovereignty activities are always vulnerable to state power unless food sovereignty's economic and territorial alternatives are also written into the national state constitution. Thus, perhaps the most essential part of the process to shift the scale of decision-making away from the state and toward communities, tribes and cities is to generate visions of the state as mutable, flexible and open to the possibilities offered by food sovereignty. The narratives of food sovereignty require the creation of a different kind of sovereign state, one that attends to the needs of small-scale producers, the poor and nature, rather than capital. This may be possible if the rights of communities to govern are granted through the constitution, rather than a series of additional rights for individuals.

The engagement with literature on liberal sovereignty illustrates the primacy of the neoliberal market to the exercise of liberal sovereignty by the modern nation-state. The rights of the state to govern trade, often in the interests of capital, and the rights of trade and commerce often trump the citizen's right to food. The solution then cannot be to give people more or expanded rights when those rights are already not guaranteed, due to an oversized reliance on a neoliberal market to provide food to citizens. The rights of communities or other collectives to determine the nature of their food economy need to be made paramount to the rights of liberal states to govern trade and the rights of capital to appropriate surplus via the mechanisms that promote markets. It is arguable that a state that privileges the rights of communities or farmers is a different kind of state altogether, one that perhaps recognizes the power of people to govern, and one that recognizes that capital resources are troubling to equity when they are owned. That this is possible is revealed through the illicit behaviors of people organizing around food sovereignty, with illegal raw milk sales or illegal seeding of lakes. The sovereignty of the state is not the absolute that some versions of political theory suggest and that the state would like to perpetuate about itself. Acting on this reality opens up opportunities for disobedience as well as spaces for the creation of alternatives. The state is a living, mutable social construction, that with effort and creativity can be changed.

In 2008, Ecuador became the first country to codify food sovereignty in its constitution. The legislation includes bans on transgenic seeds and natural resource extraction in protected areas and a variety of disincentives to monoculture agriculture. It also establishes barriers to food imports, encourages organic production and reforestation initiatives. The law draws on legislation that recognizes the 'Rights of Nature', a new strategy being used to defend human and natural communities from environmental harm caused by the appropriation of resources in the interests of capital. Since 2008, Venezuela, Mali, Bolivia, Nepal and Senegal have integrated food sovereignty into their national constitutions or laws. What this means for the future of these states, who are legislating themselves out of an interconnected and interdependent global capitalist economy, and potentially undermining the structures supporting private capital in liberal sovereignty, remains to be seen. What is evident from reading political theory against the actions of food sovereignty in local places, however, is that the rights of community, such as those identified in the Maine food sovereignty ordinances, or collective land rights, cannot be defended adequately if a national-scale constitution moots those rights. Thus, food sovereignty law must also be enacted at multiple territorial scales if policy is to be effective, or it will remain an illicit, temporary and threatened, albeit powerful, form of civil disobedience.

Food sovereignty is clear about decommodifying food and transforming the political-economic foundations of the global food system/corporate food regime. Food sovereignty is also clear about the production of alternative subjectivities and the transformation of society. Food sovereignty is as much about changing systems of production as it is about something more fundamental and perhaps more ontologically threatening to capitalist modernity: the transformation of meaning, primarily around the meaning of capital, exchange and decision-making authority. All of these differences set food sovereignty outside the existing social movements for change in the food system, in terms of both what is resisted and how it is resisted. The narrative is less about how poor people have a right to food and more about how buying and selling land generates inequities that lead to poverty. It is about how people have rights to make decisions about production and consumption activities, and not just rights to food. It is also a narrative about how people have rights to a particular kind of life, and that corporations and transnational capital kill. It is a much more fundamental narrative, and it implicates both the state and capital for having complicity in bringing death and disease to the food system. It also looks elsewhere for solutions.

References

Agamben, G. 2005. *State of exception*. Chicago: University of Chicago Press.

Agarwal, B. 2014. Food sovereignty, food security and democratic choice: Critical contradictions, difficult conciliations. *The Journal of Peasant Studies*, doi: 10.1080/03066150.2013.876996.

Agnew, J. 2005. Sovereignty regimes: Territoriality and state authority in contemporary world politics. Annals of the Association of American Geographers 95, no. 2: 437–461.

Agnew, J. 2009. *Globalization and sovereignty*. Lanham, MD: Rowman & Littlefield Publishers, Inc.

Alkon, A. H. and T. M. Mares. 2012. "Food sovereignty in US food movements: Radical visions and neoliberal constraints. *Agriculture and Human Values* 29, no. 3: 347–359.

Allen, P. 1999. Reweaving the food security safety net: Mediating entitlement and entrepreneurship. *Agriculture and Human Values* 16, no. 2: 117–129.

Anderson, J. 1996. The shifting state of politics: New medieval and postmodern territorialities?. *Environment and Planning D: Society and Space* 14: 133–153.

Anderson, M. D., & J. T. Cook. 1999. Community food security: Practice in need of theory?. *Agriculture and Human Values* 16, no. 2: 141–150.

Appadurai, A. 1996. *Modernity al large: Cultural dimensions of globalization* (Vol. 1). Minneapolis: University of Minnesota Press.

Appadurai, A. 2003. Sovereignty without territoriality: Notes for a postnational geography. In *The Geography of Identity*, ed. by P. Yaeger, 40–58. Ann Arbor: University of Michigan.

Bangor Daily News. 2011. State sues Blue Hill farmer for selling unpasteurized milk at farmers' markets. http://bangordailynews.com/2011/11/16/news/hancock/blue-hill-farmer-cited-for-violating-state-law/ (accessed February 12, 2012).

Barber, B. 1992. Jihad vs. McWorld. *The Atlantic Monthly* 269, no. 3: 53–65.

Barkan, J. 2013. *Corporate sovereignty*. Minneapolis: University of Minnesota Press.

Barrett, C.B. 2002. Food security and food assistance programs. *Handbook of Agricultural Economics* 2: 2103–2190.

Bello, W. 2009. *The food wars*. London: Verso.

Benhabib, S. 2004. *The rights of others: Aliens, residents, and citizens*. Cambridge: Cambridge University Press.

Bey, H. 2003. *The temporary autonomous zone: Ontological anarchy, poetic terrorism*. 2nd Ed. New York: Autonomedia.

Bishop, P., and L. Williams. 2012. *The temporary city*. London: Routledge.

Borras, S. M., and J. C. Franco. 2012. A 'land sovereignty' alternative? Towards a peoples' counter-enclosure. *Transnational Institute*.

Brenner, N. 1999. Beyond state-centricism? space, territoriality, and geographical scale in globalization studies. *Theory and Society* 28: 39–78.

Buck, D., C. Getz, and J. Guthman. 1997. From farm to table: The organic vegetable commodity chain of Northern California. *Sociologia ruralis* 37, no. 1: 3–20.

Clapp, J. 2012. *Food*. Cambridge, UK: Polity Press.

Dawson, A. 2010. Introduction: New enclosures. *New Formations* 69, no. 1: 8–22.

Delueze, G., and F. Guattari. 1987. *A thousand plateaus*. B. Massumi, trans. Minneapolis: University of Minnesota Press.

Dunn, E.C. 2003. Trojan pig: Paradoxes of food safety regulation. *Environment and Planning A* 35, no. 8: 1493–1511.

DuPuis, E.M., and D. Goodman. 2005. Should we go 'home' to eat?: Toward a reflexive politics of localism. *Journal of Rural Studies* 21, no. 3: 359–371.

Edelman, M. 2014. Food sovereignty: Forgotten genealogies and future regulatory challenges. *Journal of Peasant Studies*. doi: 10.1080/03066150.2013.876998.

Elden, S. 2010. Land, terrain, territory. *Progress in Human Geography* 34, no. 6: 799–817.

Feagan, R. 2007. The place of food: Mapping out the 'local' in local food systems. *Progress in Human Geography* 31, no. 1: 23–42.

Fairbairn, M. 2010. Framing resistance: International food regimes and the roots of food sovereignty. In *Food Sovereignty: Reconnecting food, nature and community*, ed. by H. Wittman, A.A. Desmarais, and N. Wiebe, 15–32. Halifax: Fernwood Publishing.

Foucault, M. 1978. Part five: right of death and power over life. In *The History of Sexuality, Volume One*, 135–159. New York: Vintage Books.

Friedmann, H. 1993. The political economy of food: A global crisis. *New Left Review* 29–57.

Friedmann, H., and P. McMichael. 1989. Agriculture and the state system: The rise and decline of national agricultures, 1870 to the present. *Sociologia Ruralis* 29, no. 2: 93–117.

Gibson-Graham, J. K. 2006. *A postcapitalist politics*. Minneapolis: University of Minnesota Press.

Gilroy, P. 1993. *The black atlantic: Modernity and double consciousness*. Cambridge: Harvard University Press.

Goodman, D., and M. Watts, eds. 1997. *Globalising food: Agrarian questions and global restructuring*. London: Routledge.

Gottlieb, R., and A. Joshi. 2010. *Food justice*. Cambridge: MIT Press.

Guthman, J. 1998. Regulating meaning, appropriating nature: The codification of California organic agriculture. *Antipode* 30, no. 2: 135–154.

Guthman, J. 2008a. Neoliberalism and the making of food politics in California. *Geoforum* 39, no. 3: 1171–1183.

Guthman, J. 2008b. Bringing good food to others: Investigating the subjects of alternative food practice. *Cultural geographies* 15, no. 4: 431–447.

Habermas, J. 1987. *The philosophical discourse of modernity*. Cambridge: Polity Press.

Hardt, M., and A. Negri. 2001. *Empire*. Cambridge: Harvard University Press.

Hardt, M., and A. Negri. 2004. *Multitude: War and democracy in the age of empire*. New York: Penguin.

Harvey, D. 1990. *The condition of postmodernity: An enquiry into the conditions of cultural change*. Malden, MA: Blackwell.

Harvey, D. 2003. *The new imperialism*. Oxford: Oxford University Press.

Hinrichs, C.C. 2000. Embeddedness and local food systems: Notes on two types of direct agricultural market. *Journal of Rural Studies* 16, no. 3: 295–303.

Holston, J. 1998. Spaces of insurgent citizenship. In *Making the invisible visible: A multi-cultural planning history*, ed. by L. Sandercok, 37–56. Berkeley: University of California Press.

Holt-Gimenez, E. and L. Peabody. 2008. From food rebellions to food sovereignty: Urgent call to fix a broken food system. *Food First Backgrounder* 14, no. 1: 1–6.

Kurtz, M. J. 2004. *Free market democracy and the Chilean and Mexican countryside*. New York: Cambridge University Press.

Kurtz, H. 2013. Scaling biopolitics: enacting food sovereignty in Maine (USA). Yale Food Sovereignty: A Critical Dialogue." Conference Paper # 40. http://www.yale.edu/agrarianstudies/foodsovereignty/pprs/40_Kurtz_2013.pdf [Accessed November 18, 2013].

Kurtz, H., A. Trauger, and C. Passidomo. 2013. The contested terrain of biological citizenship in the seizure of Raw Milk in Athens, Georgia. *Geoforum* 48: 136–144.

Landes, J. B. 1988. *Women and the public sphere: In the age of the french revolution*. Ithaca: Cornell University Press.

Latour, B. 1993. *We have never been modern*. Cambridge: Harvard University Press.

Levinsohn, J., and M. McMillan. 2007. Does food aid harm the poor? Household evidence from Ethiopia. In *Globalization and poverty*, edited by A. Harrison, 561–598. Chicago: University of Chicago Press.

Levkoe, C. Z. 2006. Learning democracy through food justice movements. *Agriculture and Human Values* 23, no. 1: 89–98.

Lyson, T. A. 2004. *Civic agriculture: Reconnecting farm, food, and community*. Lebanon, NH: University Press of New England.

Lyson, T. A., and A. Guptill. 2004. Commodity agriculture, civic agriculture and the future of US farming. *Rural sociology* 69, no. 3: 370–385.

Martin, D. G., and B. Miller. 2003. Space and contentious politics. *Mobilization: An International Quarterly* 8, no. 2: 143–156.

McCarthy, J., and S. Prudham. 2004. Neoliberal nature and the nature of neoliberalism. *Geoforum* 35, no. 3: 275–283.

Mbembe, A. 2003. Necropolitics. *Public Culture* 15, no. 1: 11–40.

McMichael, P. 2009. A food regime genealogy. *The Journal of Peasant Studies* 36, no. 1: 139–169.

Morvaridi, B. 2012. Capitalist philanthropy and the new green revolution for food security. *Food Security* 19, no. 2: 243–256.

Murdoch, J., and A.C. Pratt. 1993. Rural studies: Modernism, postmodernism and the 'post-rural'. *Journal of Rural Studies* 9, no. 4: 411–427.

Nyéléni. 2007. Proceedings of the forum for food sovereignty held in selengue. Mali, February 23-27.

Nyers, P. 2006. *Rethinking refugees: Beyond states of emergency*. New York: Routledge.

O'Laughlin, B., H. Bernstein, B. Cousins, and P.E. Peters. 2013. Introduction: Agrarian change, rural poverty and land reform in South Africa since 1994. *Journal of Agrarian Change* 13, no. 1: 1–15.

Ong, A. 2007. *Neoliberalism as exception: Mutations in citizenship and sovereignty*. Chapel Hill: Duke University Press.

Patel, R. 2009. What does food sovereignty look like?. *Journal of Peasant Studies* 36, no. 3: 663–706.

Patel, R. and P. McMichael. 2009. A political economy of the food riot. *Review* XXXII, no. 1: 9–35.

Pimbert, M. 2009. Towards food sovereignty. Gatekeeper 141. London: International Institute for Environment and Development.

van der Ploeg, J. D. 2009. *The new peasantries: Struggles for autonomy and sustainability in an Era of empire and globalization*. London: Routledge/Earthscan.

Poppendieck, J. 1999. *Sweet charity?*. New York: Penguin.

Renard, M. C. 2003. Fair trade: Quality, market and conventions. *Journal of Rural Studies* 19, no. 1: 87–96.

Ribot, J.C., and N.L. Peluso. 2003. A theory of access. *Rural Sociology* 68, no. 2: 153–181.

Rose, N. 2007. *The politics of life itself*. Princeton: Princeton University Press.

Rosset, P. 2008. Food sovereignty and the contemporary food crisis. *Development* 51, no. 4: 460–463.

Russell, E.J. 1966. *A history of agricultural science in Great Britain, 1620-1954*. New York: George Allen and Unwin Ltd.

Schanbacher, W.D. 2010. *The politics of food: The global conflict between food security and food sovereignty*. Santa Barbara: Praeger International.

Schmitt, C. 1922. *Political theology, four chapters on the concept of sovereignty*. George Schwab (trans.), Chicago: University of Chicago Press.

Selowsky, M. 1981. Income distribution, basic needs and trade-offs with growth: The case of semi-industrialized Latin American countries. *World Development* 9, no. 1: 73–92.

Shreveport Rate Cases. 1914. 234 U.S. 342. https://supreme.justia.com/cases/federal/us/234/342/case.html [Accessed January 15 2014].

Slocum, R., J. Shannon, K. V. Cadieux, and M. Beckman. 2011. 'Properly, with love, from scratch' Jamie Oliver's food revolution. *Radical History Review* 110: 178–191.

Smith, A. 1863. *An inquiry into the nature and causes of the wealth of nations*. London: A. and C. Black.

Storey, D. 2001. *Territory: The claiming of space*. Harlow: Prentice Hall.

Taylor, P. 2000. Sovereignty. In *The dictionary of human geography*, ed. by R. Johnston, D. Gregory, G. Pratt, and M. Watts, 766–767. Malden, MA: Blackwell.

Town of Sedgewick, Maine. 2011. Local Food Ordinance. www.sedgwickmaine.org/images/stories/local-food-ordinance.pdf [Accessed February 12, 2012].

Trauger, A. Forthcoming. Is bigger better? Organic and fair trade banana production in the dominican republic. *Annals of the Association of American Geographers*.

Trauger, A., and A. Murphy. 2013. On the moral equivalence of global commodities: placing the production and consumption of organic bananas. *International Journal of Sociology of Agriculture and Food* 20, no. 2: 197–217.

UNFAO. 2013. http://www.worldhunger.org/articles/Learn/world%20hunger%20facts%202002.htm [Accessed October 10 2013].

United Nations. 2014. *United Nations Declaration on Human Rights, Article 25 (1)* available at: http://www.un.org/en/documents/udhr/ [Accessed October 22, 2013].

US Constitution. n.d. Const. art. I, § 8.

Watts, M. 2000. *Struggles over geography: Violence, freedom and development at the millennium*. Hettner-Lectures, 3. Heidelberg, Germany: Department of Geography, University of Heidelberg.

Winter, M. 2003. Embeddedness, the new food economy and defensive localism. *Journal of Rural Studies* 19, no. 1: 23–32.

Wittman, H., A. A. Desmarais, and N. Wiebe, eds. 2010. *Food sovereignty: Reconnecting food, nature and community*. Halifax: Fernwood Publishing.

Wolford, W. 2010a. Participatory democracy by default: land reform, social movements and the state in Brazil. *The Journal of Peasant Studies* 37, no. 1: 91–109.

Wolford, W. 2010b. *This land is ours now: Social mobilization and the meanings of land in Brazil*. Chapel Hill: Duke University Press.

World Food Summit, 1996. *Rome Declaration on Food Security*. http://www.converge.org.nz/pirm/food-sum.htm. [Accessed July 4, 2014].

Amy Trauger is an Associate Professor of Geography at the University of Georgia in Athens. Her work has focused on women farmers, sustainable agriculture and the alternativeness of alternative agriculture. She is pursuing a research trajectory in food sovereignty and is currently working on the book *'We want land to live': space, territory and the politics of food sovereignty* to be published by UGA Press in the Geographies of Justice and Social Transformation Series.

Farmers, foodies and First Nations: getting to food sovereignty in Canada

Annette Aurélie Desmarais and Hannah Wittman

This paper examines how the concept and framework of food sovereignty has been incorporated in food policy agendas across diverse sectors of Canadian society, particularly in the work and discourse of the National Farmers Union, Québec's Union Paysanne, Food Secure Canada and movements for Indigenous food sovereignty. This analysis highlights both the challenges to conceptualizing food sovereignty and the tensions in defining inclusive policies that engage with food sovereignty at distinct, and often overlapping, scales. We critically assess how the 'unity in diversity' principle of food sovereignty functions in the Canadian context, paying particular attention to the policy implications of debates about the meaning of food sovereignty. What is most evident in examining the demands of a wide range of actors using food sovereignty language in Canada is a shared aim to reclaim a public voice in shaping the food system and a growing convergence around ideals of social justice, environmental sustainability and diversity. But, if food sovereignty is about fundamental transformation of the food system, it is yet in initial stages in this country.

Introduction

While there is a growing body of literature on food sovereignty at a global level, much less is known about what food sovereignty movements look like in specific places and how their expression is largely shaped by local dynamics. This contribution provides a critical analysis of how a diverse range of intentions, strategies, tactics and discourses collide under the 'big tent' of food sovereignty in Canada. We look at how the concept and framework of food sovereignty has been incorporated in food policy agendas across diverse sectors of Canadian society. This analysis highlights both the challenges to conceptualizing food sovereignty and the tensions in defining inclusive policies that engage with food sovereignty at distinct, and often overlapping, scales. The ways different actors engage with food sovereignty in Canada requires re-thinking traditional and legal conceptions of sovereignty as more than the ability of a territorially bounded entity to exercise power through domination, a view that perhaps might be more theoretically relevant in national policies

The authors are grateful to Dawn Morrison and other members of the BC Working Group on Indigenous Food Sovereignty for ongoing conversations on the intersection between agrarian and indigenous visions of food sovereignty. We also thank Anelyse Weiler for research assistance and the two external reviewers for helpful suggestions to improve the paper.

for food security. Instead, engaging with the concept of food sovereignty as it has evolved among grassroots actors requires a critical engagement with a new politics of possibility. This involves reconsidering and reframing concepts of collective political will, appropriate authority, governance, self-determination, solidarity, and individual and collective rights (Alfred 1999, Shaw 2008).

Food sovereignty was initially introduced in Canada through the work of the National Farmers Union (NFU) and the Union Paysanne, the two Canadian members of La Vía Campesina. The NFU is unique among Canadian farm organizations: it is the only national, direct-membership, voluntary farm organization in Canada to have been created by an act of Parliament. The NFU describes itself as 'working for people's interests against the corporate control of the food system' (NFU, n.d). Unlike other Canadian commodity farm organizations, it represents farmers producing all kinds of foodstuffs in all regions of the country, except for Quebec.[1] The NFU, as a founding member of La Vía Campesina, actively participated in the key Vía Campesina debates in the early 1990s about the emergent concept of 'food sovereignty'. However, it took years before the NFU began using food sovereignty in its domestic work within Canada. Meanwhile, the concept of food sovereignty was central to Québec's Union Paysanne when that organization was formed in 2001. The Union Paysanne includes farmers, researchers, students, consumer groups and eco-tourism businesses that joined together to build alternatives to '*malbouffe*' and industrial agriculture.[2] The Union Paysanne emphasizes a peasant agriculture that involves 'a human-scale agriculture and vibrant rural communities' (Union Paysanne n.d.) and engages in concerted efforts to link producers and consumers.[3] Initially, discussions of food sovereignty in Canada remained focused primarily on agricultural production and agricultural trade policy issues.

This changed after the Nyéléni International Forum for Food Sovereignty held in 2007 in Sélingué, Mali. In addition to representatives of the NFU and the Union Paysanne, a range of other Canadian organizations that were members of Food Secure Canada – a national civil society alliance involved in work on food security and sustainable food systems – attended the event. This diverse range of actors returned home committed to working together to consolidate a national food sovereignty movement. This commitment led to the pan-Canadian People's Food Policy Project (PFPP), launched in 2009, aimed at developing a food sovereignty policy for Canada (Kneen 2011).[4] The PFPP organized consultations across the country to engage consumers and urban food systems activists in developing food sovereignty language to redefine food and agricultural policies for Canada. While some Indigenous peoples actively participated in the PFPP, several

---

[1]The NFU also includes non-farmer (Associate) members, comprising about 8 percent of the membership in 2012. Overall, the rural landscape in Canada is populated by numerous agricultural commodity organizations that function primarily to improve the marketing and increase sales of a specific commodity for an integrated national and international market. Examples of such organizations are the Canadian Cattlemen's Association, Western Canadian Barley Association and the Canadian Canola Growers Association; (See Canadian Agricultural Human Resource Council, n.d.)

[2]*Malbouffe*, literally meaning 'bad food', is usually translated as junk food. It is a concept used by the Confédération Paysanne in France in its struggle against industrial agriculture. Shortly after the Union Paysanne was formed they invited José Bové, then spokesperson for the Confédération Paysanne, to Québec to exchange ideas about organizing strategies.

[3]The non-farmer members of the Union Paysanne have their own space along with an administrative council and full voting privileges at the Annual Congress.

[4]While Food Secure Canada was instrumental in supporting the People's Food Policy Project, these operated as distinct entities.

indigenous organizations sought to deepen their own indigenous food sovereignty frameworks. Some of these indigenous frameworks are highly critical of a version of food sovereignty they view as agriculture- and state-centric. Indigenous food sovereignty activists stress the importance of decolonization, self-determination and the inclusion of fishing, hunting and gathering as key elements of a food sovereignty approach to sustainable food systems in Canada, and highlight the complexity of issues of sovereignty, authority, individual and collective rights, equity, culture and (re)distribution of land and other resources (e.g. Morrison 2006, 2011).

This contribution explores the various meanings of food sovereignty developed by distinct actors in Canada to better understand existing challenges, tensions, convergences and divergences in developing a national movement for food sovereignty. We begin with some theoretical reflections on food sovereignty that have informed our analysis of food sovereignty movements in Canada. We then focus on how food sovereignty is manifested in Canada by exploring how three distinct sectors of society – farmers, foodies and Indigenous peoples – use food sovereignty discourse.[5] We then critically assess how the 'unity in diversity' principle of food sovereignty functions in the Canadian context, paying particular attention to the policy implications of debates about the meaning of food sovereignty.

Food sovereignty: some theoretical considerations

The framework for food sovereignty is evolving continually, but at its core is a set of goals comprised of strengthening community, livelihoods and social and environmental sustainability in the production, consumption and distribution of nutritious and culturally appropriate food. The pursuit of these goals is informed by a range of strategies: respect for place and diversity, acceptance of difference, understanding the role of nature in production, human agency, equitable distribution of resources, dismantling asymmetrical power relations and building participatory democratic institutions.

To better understand what food sovereignty is – its potential, challenges and limitations as a framework for food system change – we need to look carefully at the social actors involved. As the social movement literature confirms, concepts that have transformatory potential do not appear in a vacuum as disembodied intellectual exercises. Food sovereignty, as La Vía Campesina initially conceptualized it, is an idea deeply grounded in the lives of peasants, Indigenous peoples and farmers in the Global North and South. It has since been collaboratively reworked with city-based groups for relevance to urban contexts.

Food sovereignty emerged in the debates held within La Vía Campesina as communities in the Global South and the Global North engaged in a collective struggle to define alternatives to the globalization of a neoliberal, highly capitalized, corporate-led model of agricultural development (Desmarais 2007). La Vía Campesina first articulated the basic principles entailed in food sovereignty at its Second International Conference held in Tlaxcala, Mexico (La Vía Campesina 1996a) and then introduced it in the international arena at the civil society conference held in conjunction with the World Food Summit in 1996 (La Vía Campesina 1996b).[6] The only Canadian social actor involved

---

[5]In the Canadian context, 'First Nations' refers to aboriginal peoples who are recognized by the constitution. First Nations are distinct from the Inuit and the Métis; while First Nations is a contested term, many Indigenous peoples refer to their communities as First Nations. In this contribution we use First Nations and Indigenous peoples interchangeably.

[6]Among some peasant organizations, there had been some references to earlier articulations of food sovereignty by ASOCODE in Central America (Edelman 1999), and also in Mexico. Further

in defining food sovereignty in this early stage was the NFU, one of the founding members of La Vía Campesina.

As this collection of the *Journal of Peasant Studies* confirms, there is a growing litera-ture that seeks to explore some of the theoretical dimensions and political implications of food sovereignty.[7] Windfuhr and Jonsén (2005) initially highlighted the significant ways in which food sovereignty differs from the right to food and food security while also providing an early analysis of the potential and constraints of a food sovereignty policy approach. Others have demonstrated how food sovereignty is much more encompassing than food security and the right to food because it places questions of what food is produced, where, how, by whom, and at what scale at the centre of public debate, and also raises similar questions about food consumption and distribution (Desmarais 2007, McMichael 2009, Patel 2009, Wittman *et al.* 2010).[8] Claeys (2012) sheds light on how the food sover-eignty movement's claims to new rights reflect an alternative conception of rights that is more collective and decentralized, with implementation depending not just on states, but also on communities, peoples and international bodies. Empirically, Isakson's (2009) study in Guatemala and Rosset *et al.*'s (2011) work on agriculture in Cuba provide key insights concerning the multiple social and environmental benefits of, and the links between, agroecological practices, biodiversity conservation and food sovereignty. These works highlight the role of peasant movements in shifting agricultural development to focus on small-scale production for local markets in efforts to sustain viable livelihoods and rural communities. Other research highlights specific elements of food sovereignty such as agrarian reform (Borras and Franco 2010), rural movements' struggles (Borras *et al.* 2008), international human rights campaigns (Edelman and James 2011), and food security and food justice (Alkon and Mares 2012).

Food sovereignty proponents seek fundamental social change, a transformation of society as a whole that can be achieved through the vehicle of food and agriculture. To better under-stand food sovereignty as an organizing frame for transformative social change, it is useful to conceptualize it as a process involving persistent, diverse and interconnected struggles. Ramon Vera (2010), a long-time agrarian activist in Mexico, puts it like this:

> Clearly there is evidence of food sovereignty in the struggles of many around the world. You will not encounter it only in one place and be able to point to concrete examples. . . . Instead, it is a continual struggle. In a place as devastated as Mexico, it is a struggle that you lose and you win every day, little by little. Food sovereignty means working on the health of something that has been deeply devastated and is in need of great repair. . . . Food sovereignty is about the struggles for autonomy, for territorial control, to build strong people's assemblies, to recuperate *lo comunitario*; it means building movements to care for the forests, water, recuperate the soil, preservation of ancestral seeds, stopping the entrance of GMOs [genetically modified organ-isms]. These are everyday and permanent struggles.

How are we to understand this diversity of food sovereignty struggles? What Vera is stres-sing here is the need to pay attention to the multiplicity of sites and the multifaceted nature of

---

consolidation of the meaning of food sovereignty emerged as a result of debates within La Vía Cam-pesina. For discussions of the origins of food sovereignty within La Vía Campesina see Desmarais (2007) and Wittman *et al.* (2010).

[7]Due to space limitations we mention only several key contributions. For a recent and more complete review see Wittman (2011).

[8]For a discussion of the conceptual limitations of food security, see Fairbairn (2010) who situates the neoliberal foundations of household food security in the corporate food regime.

resistance to dispossession and inequality. Clearly, food sovereignty in Saskatchewan, Canada, will look different than in Indonesia or Peru. A range of factors, including history, social relations (class, race, gender, age), ecology, politics and culture, shapes the particular nature of each food sovereignty struggle in any given place. Importantly, however, we also need to understand how these various struggles are connected and how they shape one another.

An analysis of food sovereignty also takes into account the different stages of struggle. On the one hand, in many places, communities might not be using the language of food sovereignty but in fact are engaged in initiatives that fit within a food sovereignty framework. When peasant communities in Mexico are fighting to keep Canadian mining companies from accessing land because mining will affect the quality and access to the land and water available for producing food, are they not involved in a food sovereignty struggle? On the other hand, many Vía Campesina organizations have been engaged in food sovereignty work for decades. Most were fighting to have a greater say in decision-making about food and agriculture, for the creation of more just policies to ensure the well-being of rural communities, control of markets and agrarian reform.

La Vía Campesina's notion of food sovereignty emerged in the international public space that peasants, Indigenous peoples and farmers created and consolidated as a transnational community of resistance. That process of imagination, contestation and negotiation involved a deep understanding of a global food system that was creating a crisis of global proportions. There was also a deep understanding that problems arising from this system simultaneously involved both *local* and *national* struggles of dispossession and destruction of livelihoods (e.g Bush 2010). The production, distribution and consumption of food all take place in specific locales. Food sovereignty is very much situated; it occurs in particular places and how it is expressed is determined largely by local dynamics, but also in response to changing global dynamics.

This understanding of food sovereignty recognizes what Doreen Massey (1991) has called 'a global sense of place' or what Simon Springer (2011, 525) calls the 'relational geographies of resistance' which recognize that the global and local are rarely separable. La Vía Campesina's role in internationalizing place-based movements (Desmarais 2007), while at the same time giving global scope to communities' diverse visions, hopes and struggles for food sovereignty, is a concrete example of local struggles being transformed through engagement with actors and contexts outside their immediate sphere of influence. Thus, the transformative potential of movements for food sovereignty lie in their broad vision for social change, a collective vision that is shaped by understanding the particularity, diversity and connectedness of food sovereignty struggles.

This means that food sovereignty will be addressed differently in places like Canada, where farm operators in 2011 constituted less than 1 percent of the population, production is intensely commercial, and has been organized around international as well as local and national markets since the colonial period.[9] Yet, in Canada, many of the issues that prompted the emergence of a food sovereignty alternative are deeply felt: collapsing rural communities as a result of the ongoing farm income crisis leading to rural exodus, an aging farming population and a decline in public services; farmers' loss of power in the marketplace and in policy development, accompanied by the corporatization of agriculture, and growing concerns from both consumers and producers about human and animal health and welfare, and the environmental, social and economic sustainability of industrial

---

[9]Farm owners/operators plus paid farmworkers comprised less than 2 percent of Canada's total population in 2011.

agriculture. These are precisely the issues that have broadened the reach of the food sovereignty discourse to other actors in Canada – consumers, urban food organizations and Indigenous peoples (Wittman et al. 2011).

Farmers – cultivating an idea

Agriculture in Canada is regionally specific. Large farms in the prairie provinces produce the bulk of the country's grains, oilseeds and beef, while smaller farms in British Columbia, Québec and Ontario grow commodities such as dairy, vegetables and fruit, and the coastal provinces provide fish and fish products. As a whole the agriculture and agri-food sector is 'modern, highly complex, integrated, [and] internationally competitive' (AAFC 2013). Canada exports approximately 45 percent of its domestic food and agricultural production (AAFC 2010, quoted in Qualman 2011). As is the case with other industrialized countries, Canadian agricultural policy development over the past three decades reverted from a state-assistance perspective adopted during the Second World War back to a 'market-liberal paradigm' (Skogstad 2008). The roots of this transition can be traced to the 1969 Report of the Federal Task Force on Agriculture which advised that it was 'desirable to end farming by the individual farmer and shift to capitalist farming . . . In sketching out this kind of model for agriculture circa 1990, we are of course rejecting the "Public utility" or socialized concept of agriculture' (quoted in Warnock 1971, 9). Subsequent policies have emphasized the building of a 'more market-oriented agri-food industry'. Farmers are prompted to be more 'self-reliant' and 'market responsive' (Agriculture Canada 1989, 30–37), all the while producing more, especially for export markets increasingly controlled by vertically and horizontally integrated transnational agri-business corporations.

The landscape of rural Canada is also ideologically diverse. While some farmer organizations embrace neoliberal ideals of free trade and privatization, others approach food and agriculture from a social and economic justice perspective. The NFU emerged in 1969 as an amalgamation of the provincial farmers' unions of Alberta, Saskatchewan, British Columbia, Ontario and maritime farmers who had not yet formed a union. It has a long history of struggles to support the continuation of alternatives to neoliberal globalization, such as orderly marketing boards (i.e. single-desk selling/collective marketing though the Canadian Wheat Board) and supply management systems.[10] One of the NFU's main goals is to 'work together to achieve agricultural policies which will ensure dignity and security of income for farm families while enhancing the land for future generations' (National Farmers Union, n.d.). To this end, the organization 'strives for a system of food production, processing, and distribution that is, in all stages, economically viable, socially just, and ecologically sound. The current system does not meet these criteria and, thus, is not sustainable' (NFU, 'Policy on Sustainable Agriculture' n.d. quoted in Beingessner 2013).

Many market-oriented, commodity-based groups reject the NFU's critiques of neoliberal policies that aim to dismantle orderly marketing and supply management while further consolidating the privatization, industrialization and corporatization of the food system. For

---

[10]Supply management is a legislated marketing tool designed to stabilize supply and prices for producers and consumers. In Canada, supply management is used to control the production of dairy, eggs and poultry by allocating a quota. Unlike the other unregulated commodities, farmers in this system are able to recover costs of production because prices are set by a government agency (i.e. the Dairy Commission) that uses a cost-of-production analysis reflecting real on-farm costs. Single desk selling refers to the system whereby the Canadian Wheat Board had a legal monopoly on the sale of wheat and barley from the western provinces in Canada.

instance, the Western Canadian Wheat Growers' Association (WCWGA) – whose membership has 'a strong business focus' and 'believe open and competitive markets, innovation and investment are key to creating a stronger and more prosperous agricultural sector' (WCWGA n.d.) – mounted a multi-year vocal campaign aimed at eliminating the monopoly of the Canadian Wheat Board (CWB), a farmer-controlled, state-sponsored collective marketing agency that sells on behalf of farmers all of the wheat and barley grown on the prairie provinces for export and domestic human consumption. Rejecting single-desk selling and arguing instead for 'freedom to market' and dual marketing, the campaign against the CWB escalated throughout the 1990s and 2000s. This included direct actions such as illegally trucking grain across the Canadian border into the United States of America.[11] Meanwhile, the NFU saw farmer-controlled, collective marketing – elements central to the effective functioning of the CWB – as expressions of food sovereignty. In efforts to maintain and strengthen the CWB, the NFU worked with allies, including the Canadian Federation of Agriculture, to demonstrate how dual marketing would lead to the demise of the CWB and demand that farmers be allowed to vote on whether or not the monopoly of the CWB should be maintained. The NFU also spearheaded the formation of the Friends of the Canadian Wheat Board, a coalition of farm organizations and individuals, including non-farmers, that has legally challenged the Government of Canada (FCWB n.d).

In essence, the fight to keep the CWB can be considered a long-standing food sovereignty struggle in Canada, but it gets more complicated when moving beyond the Canadian border. It was initially waged by the NFU's predecessors, the provincial prairie farmers' unions, that fought for a stronger farmers' voice and collective marketing against the increasing market power of private corporations involved in the export-based grain trade in Western Canada (Magnan 2011, 118). As Magnan explains, the more recent conflicts over the CWB 'intersect with food sovereignty by pitting collective marketing against neoliberal ideals of market efficiency, free enterprise and free trade' (2011, 116) while seeking to strengthen farmers' 'market power and democratic control over farmers' own marketing arm' (2011, 129).[12] It is not clear, however, how the presence of the CWB in the

---

[11]Resistance to the CWB began much earlier, from several fronts. The Palliser Wheat Growers Association, formed in 1970 and predecessor to the WCWGA, sought the outright abolishment of the CWB (Magnan 2011, 116). Magnan (2011) suggests that the WCWGA together with the provincial government of Alberta and conservative federal governments attacked the CWB's single-desk selling monopoly primarily because they saw it as an 'illegitimate infringement on the right of farmers to market their grain independently', and argued for dual marketing within the CWB. That is, marketing through the CWB should be voluntary to enable farmers to exercise the right to choose how they want their grain marketed, either through the CWB or through private companies. Foreign interests such as commodity groups and transnational grain companies have also tried to end the CWB's single-desk selling power and they have enlisted government support to do so. The government of the United States of America has pursued numerous (14 to date) legal trade challenges – all have been unsuccessful (Magnan 2011, 117).

[12]This farmer market power and democratic decision is now on hold. The NFU reports: 'In 2011 the federal government passed a law, Bill C-18, to dismantle the 75-year-old Canadian Wheat Board . . . . The law was passed in defiance of a Federal Court ruling that deemed the introduction of the bill to be contrary to the rule of law, because the binding farmer vote on proposed changes to the single desk was not held as required under the Canadian Wheat Board Act in force at the time. The federal government began implementing Bill C-18 regardless of the court ruling, yet it is also appealing the ruling. Farmers have launched a class action lawsuit to overturn Bill C-18 (see www.cwbclassaction.ca). Their claim includes charges under Canada's Charter of Rights and Freedoms, including breach of the Right to Freedom of Association and of the Right to Freedom of Expression' (NFU 2012b).

international markets affects food sovereignty struggles elsewhere. While there is recognition that the purpose of the CWB is to protect the interests of Canadian farmers, some NFU members acknowledge that greater understanding of the consequences of the CWB's marketing practices for farmers elsewhere is needed. One member of the NFU suggested,

> some of the things that we are fighting for don't fall into food sovereignty. The CWB had a huge campaign about white flour and noodles in foreign markets (rice growing areas). This is in direct opposition of what we are fighting for. (NFU workshop 2011)

Ideological divergences are also at the heart of the struggle to maintain supply management in the production of dairy, eggs and poultry, a system under increasing threat at the World Trade Organization (WTO) deliberations and at even greater risk in the current Canada-European Comprehensive Trade and Economic Agreement (CETA) and Trans-Pacific Partnership trade negotiations. The NFU and the Union Paysanne support supply management as an effective mechanism to implement food sovereignty, and are calling to expand this system to other commodities. However, both organizations recognize deep flaws in how supply management is practiced in Canada. The overcapitalization of quota has led to a significant increase in the size of existing dairy and poultry farms while the high cost of the quota effectively blocks the entry of new farmers into the supply-managed sector. Rather than abandoning the idea of supply management, the NFU argues that the whole system needs to be overhauled to remain true to its original purpose:

> Under no circumstances should quotas be marketable or negotiable between producers. All production quotas should revert to the market agency for reallocation when no longer required by a producer. Priorities should be given to small and new producers, provided the new producers do not fall into the agribusiness category. . . . . Quotas now held by agribusiness and other commercial corporate entities should be frozen (NFU 2011).

In Québec, the Union Paysanne (n.d.) has a similar position, stressing the importance of a system that supports small-scale production.[13] The organization was a vocal and visible actor in the struggle over intensive livestock operations in Québec that helped lead to a moratorium on large hog operations by the Government of Québec. The Union Paysanne was formed in May 2001 as an alternative to the mainstream and dominant Union de Producteurs Agricoles du Québec (UPA), an organization that also uses the language of food sovereignty but calls for supply management to be maintained largely as is. The UPA claims that it is 'actually the single mouthpiece, the official voice that speaks on behalf of all Québec farmers' (UPA, n.d). This claim was facilitated by a provincial law introduced in 1972 that formally recognized the UPA as the province's only legitimate farm organization. While the UPA also defends collective marketing and supply management, it is an organization that 'has a history of supporting industrial agriculture' (Kneen 2011, 89) and represents the interests of a number of large producer cooperatives, although it also has members who are small- and medium-scale farmers.

---

[13]Special thanks to Stephanie Wang for reviewing carefully our discussion of farm politics in Québec and the Union Paysanne's work.

In many ways, the Union Paysanne ideologically represents everything that the UPA is not.[14] Both use the language of food sovereignty, albeit with very different meanings. The Union Paysanne's demands for a peoples' food sovereignty that emphasizes social and environmental sustainability including, most notably, producers' control over the factors of production, appear to be drowned out by the more prominent voices for a state-led food sovereignty as expressed by Québec's large *Coalition Souveraineté Alimentaire*, a group that pulls together 86 organizations including members of the UPA. In May 2013 the Parti Québecois, referencing La Vía Campesina, officially launched a food sovereignty policy as a framework for all future decision-making on agriculture and food in Québec (MAPAQ 2013). The impetus for this policy is twofold. The Parti Québecois is undoubtedly using the idea of state-led food sovereignty to oppose federal government attempts to push through CETA, which threatens the supply-managed industry in Québec. Secondly, the language of food sovereignty resonates in the historical and contemporary context of a strong political movement in Québec, *le mouvement souverainiste*, led by the Parti Québecois, for national sovereignty for the province of Québec.

The Union Paysanne's vision, like that of La Vía Campesina, sees the state as having a critical role in building food sovereignty. But for the Union Paysanne, food sovereignty is a bottom-up, rather than top-down, process in which communities define what kind of food systems are wanted, to which the state would respond accordingly. Consequently, while the organization sees some positive aspects to Québec's food sovereignty policy – it supports the aim, among other things, to have 50 percent of the food consumed in the province be sourced within the province – the Union Paysanne is voicing strong opposition to the latest government policy. The Union Paysanne argues that the Government of Québec is misappropriating and instrumentalizing food sovereignty language to introduce a policy that reinforces aspects of large-scale industrial agricultural production and processing, rather than one that would help transform the food system in Québec (Union Paysanne 2013). For the Union Paysanne, introducing a policy geared to have more food produced for local consumption also necessarily entails democratizing the food system so that citizens are involved in deciding what food is produced, where and how it is grown and who grows it. Second, it claims that taking steps towards food sovereignty would entail implementing the more substantial recommendations that emerged from the two-year consultative process (2006–2008) that yielded the Pronovost Report.[15] Among the report's 50 recommendations are dismantling the UPA's monopoly on farmer representation, changing the collective marketing mechanisms to allow for on-farm sales, restructuring the Farm Income Stabilization Insurance Program that currently favours large-scale production,

---

[14]These ideological divergences exhibited at the local and national levels are also manifested at the international level, mainly through La Vía Campesina and the International Federation of Agricultural Producers (IFAP) which had diametrically opposing positions and strategies on key agricultural issues (Desmarais 2007, Borras 2010). The Union Paysanne formally joined La Vía Campesina in 2004 and the UPA, through its membership to the Canadian Federation of Agriculture, had been a member of the IFAP for many years. IFAP was formally dissolved in November 2010 (ILO 2012).

[15]In 2006, the Government of Québec constituted the *Commission sur l'Avenir de l'Agriculture et de l'Agroalimentaire Québecois* (The Commission on the Future of Agriculture and Agri-food of Québec) to examine current challenges and existing public policies and make recommendations for improvements within the agriculture and agrifood sector. The Commission, headed by Jean Pronovost, engaged in extensive consultations holding public sessions (in 15 regions and 27 municipalities) that included 770 presentations by different stakeholders. The 2008 report (Agriculture and agrifood: securing and building the future) is most often referred to as the Pronovost Report. (See Commission sur L'Avenir de l'Agriculture et de l'Agroalimentaire Québecois 2008)

replacing it with a mechanism that is universal but also places a cap on the amount allocated, and compensating those using environmentally sound practices. The Union Paysanne claims that the new food sovereignty policy is in fact 'greenwashing' and it is demanding that the Government of Québec retract 'food sovereignty' and, instead, call it a policy of food self-sufficiency (Radio-Canada 2013).

Although divergences exist in demands among farmer organizations in Canada, these organizations have occasionally joined together in resistance movements focused on particular issues. In doing so they have made important links with urban-based civil society, non-profit, charitable and consumer-based organizations to wage campaigns around cross-cutting issues of agriculture, health and environmental protection. One example is the successful farmer-led struggle against genetically modified (GM) wheat that involved the participation of environmental groups (including Greenpeace Canada and the Sierra Club of Canada), the National Health Coalition, the Council of Canadians and the NFU along with some mainstream farm organizations like the Agricultural Producers Association of Saskatchewan and the Keystone Agricultural Producers (Eaton 2013, 100–101, Peekhaus 2013).[16] A prior example is the broad grassroots movement that engaged in a decade-long struggle between 1987 and 1998 to successfully block the registration of recombinant bovine somatotropin (rBST), or rBGH, in Canada (Sharratt 2001). In this case the NFU initially worked at consolidating joint positions among different farm organizations and then subsequently garnered the support of the Council of Canadians, a 35,000-strong citizens' organization that had formed primarily to expand the notion and practice of democracy and resist the Canadian government's embrace of free trade and privatization. Eventually, resistance grew to include consumer groups, food policy councils and community-based organizations. As Sharratt's study of the decade-long struggle explained,

> The diversity of the opposition was its greatest strength; farmers spoke out against animal ill-health and threats to the dairy industry, consumers demanded safe milk, and government scientists exposed industry pressure and inadequate science. Each voice in opposition was a strong and legitimate voice for a constituency of people who were actively opposed to rBGH. . . . With a truly grassroots and national movement against rBGH, Monsanto was unable to target individuals or groups to discredit. Canadians organized to defeat rBGH without a national organization concerned with food issues or a visible consumer's movement. The scrutiny of rBGH by both MPs and Senators restored hope in Canada that the mechanisms of the parliamentary system can function for the public interest. (Sharratt 2001, 394–5)

Foodies: bringing farmers and eaters to a shared table

Historically, governments have used a cheap food policy to enable low industrial wages. In the current environment, however, much of the low-priced food in Canada is imported and discipline in wages is accomplished through the possibility of exporting jobs. At the same time that Canadians spend on average just over 10 percent of their income on food, food insecurity is growing. Between 2007 and 2011, the percentage of Canadians accessing food banks increased from 7.7 to 8.2 percent of the population; in 2011 over 900,000 Canadians accessed the Food Bank each month (UNHRC 2012). Recognizing the need to

---

[16]The anti-GM wheat struggle occurred some years after GM canola had been accepted and spread quickly and widely across the Canadian rural landscape. The Action Group on Erosion, Technology and Concentration (ETC Group), formerly known as the Rural Advancement Foundation International, has played a key role in the Canadian resistance to biotechnology (and nanotechnology) in agriculture and food (Peekhaus 2013).

politicize problems of both production and consumption within a common food policy framework, in 2004 a national food movement began to emerge as food activists, farmers, members of community-based organizations, Indigenous peoples, nutritionists and researchers from across the country defined a three-pronged organizational strategy aimed at zero hunger, building a sustainable food system and ensuring healthy and safe food (Kneen 2011).

Formally constituted in 2006, Food Secure Canada/*Réseau pour une alimentation durable*[17] initially voiced its concerns mainly through a food security lens. A more recent shift to using the language of food sovereignty is due to three main developments. First, the NFU, as a founding member of Food Secure Canada, was increasingly using the language of food sovereignty. Simultaneously, Indigenous peoples within the movement brought to the table discussions of indigenous food sovereignty, forming an Indigenous Circle within Food Secure Canada. Second, several members of Food Secure Canada participated in the Nyéléni Forum on Food Sovereignty and returned to Canada convinced that the language and conceptual framework of food sovereignty captured more effectively the kind of food systems they were striving to build. Third, that conviction led to the development of the PFPP, which was geared to collectively define a national food sovereignty policy for Canada. The PFPP organized various consultation spaces including 350 kitchen table meetings involving approximately 3500 people across the country, submission of individual and group policy position papers, conference calls and three conferences.[18] This two-year participatory process (2009–2011) led to the publication of a consultative document entitled 'Resetting the table: a people's food policy for Canada' (PFFP 2011). This is described by Food Secure Canada as a 'living' document that is expected to evolve and change as new issues arise and/or new approaches are agreed upon.

At the same time that national-level civil-society mobilization around the framework of food sovereignty was occurring through the work of Food Secure Canada, a food sovereignty discourse was increasingly taking root in local and regional non-profit, charitable and consumer-based organizations like the Young Agrarians, Slow Food convivia, faith-based groups including Unitarian Service Committee (USC) of Canada and the United Church of Canada (United Church of Canada 2013), as well as urban food distribution networks like FoodShare Toronto (Johnston and Baker 2005) and The Stop Food Distribution Centre.[19] These groups take on the framework of food sovereignty primarily from the perspective of food consumers with an active desire to connect to local and regional food production systems. For example, the NFU Youth Coalition was instrumental in instigating the formation of the Young Agrarians network in British Columbia. This community-building project initiates farm tours, potlucks and land-linking events, as well as online resources such as a farmer resource map and blog to 'engage young farmers, would-be farmers and the public in the reshaping of our food system'.[20]

The consumer-citizens (also known as locavores or foodies) who populate many of Canada's urban alternative food networks are often initially concerned with issues of

---

[17]Until September 2013, the French name of the organization was *Sécurité Alimentaire*.
[18]A similar consultative and participatory cross-sectoral process, called the People's Food Commission, had been organized by civil society organizations in the late 1970s in Canada (People's Food Commission 1980).
[19]See http://www.foodshare.net and http://www.thestop.org/. For analysis of various food initiatives in Ontario see Friedmann (2007 and 2011).
[20]youngagrarians.org/about.

taste, health and the local environment that affect their daily lives and those of their immediate communities (Johnston 2008, Johnston and Baumann 2010).[21] In response, these networks tend to advocate the construction of very local (e.g. 100-mile diet) food systems that are intended to make fresher and nutritious food more available while celebrating local and regional cultures (e.g. Gibb and Wittman 2013). This ethic is expressed in the explosion of citizen-driven municipal food policy councils across Canada that have been instrumental in increasing the scale and scope of farmers' markets, community gardens, farm-to-school lunch programs and the diversification of municipal landscaping to include edible plants (McRae and Donahue 2013). But unlike the work of organizations like the NFU, the Union Paysanne and Food Secure Canada, which advocate changes in provincial and international policy around agri-food systems, as well as local initiatives, the policy demands among most local food networks in Canada are relatively understated, despite using language echoing food sovereignty concerns in local organizing, events and websites. The consumer-oriented focus on the principles of individual ethical consumption may sideline a focus on 'structural causes and collective solutions required to fix the industrial food system', leading urban foodies to be perhaps less likely to advocate for specific policies and programs like supply management that would lead to broader food system change at the national and international levels (Johnston and Baumann 2010, 129). This local food movement narrative tends to celebrate local food, rather than criticizing food injustice. In the words of one member of a Canadian local food non-profit:

> We are for, rather than against. For example, we are for local and sustainable, supports for farmers to access land, freely traded and shared seeds rather than against GE [genetic engineering]... Food banks tend not to use 'food sovereignty'; they use 'food security'. But to take one step further is take it to a power place, and not many food banks do that. Little grassroots organizations do, of course, and societies that aren't charities. Non-profit societies have a lot more freedom. (Interview 4/23/2013)

Highly visible 'foodie' organizations focus their efforts on voluntarily constructing localized food systems from the bottom up – building farmers' markets, guerilla gardening, local food potlucks, community gardens. Nevertheless, the things foodies care about ('geographic specificity, "simplicity", personal connection, history and tradition, and ethnic connection' (Johnston and Baumann 2010, 73)), along with environmental and health issues, are congruent with the food sovereignty framework. In this sense, the scaling up of food sovereignty discourse and activity by consumers and urban-based food justice organizations like Food Secure Canada has given a new focus and constituency to the movement beyond the traditional food-producing members of La Vía Campesina. As Cathleen Kneen, the co-founder of Food Secure Canada, argues, the

> [People's Food Policy Project] builds on the local organizing that is already going on in the multiplicity of food self-reliance projects in both rural and urban areas, and its method is to overcome the 'individual' by starting with the personal ... They can then begin to think in terms of policies that will actually support food sovereignty. (2010, 234)

---

[21]The term 'foodie' is politically contested, perceived by some as a symbol of elitism and exclusion divorced from the issues of social justice, and by others as simply a term that describes an 'eater' who is engaged with learning about food and the food system (cf. Johnston and Baumann 2010). We use it here in the latter sense.

First Nations – decolonizing food sovereignty in Canada?

Several organizations in Canada, including the British Columbia Food Systems Network (BCFSN) Working Group on Indigenous Food Sovereignty and the Food Secure Canada Indigenous Circle, are approaching the framework of food sovereignty from yet another direction. Indigenous communities in Canada have had a long and critical engagement with the concept of sovereignty, questioning to what extent this (Western) concept reflects indigenous self-determination and the relationship between autonomy and respectful inter-dependency between communities (c.f. Alfred 1999). Rather than building a new 'loca-lized' (and agriculture-centric) food system as an alternative to the global, industrial system – the language of many of the civil society food networks referenced above – Indi-genous communities seek to honor, value and protect traditional food practices and net-works in the face of ongoing pressures of colonization. These values and practices are evident, for example, in traditional indigenous food trading networks that extend far beyond the '100 mile-diet' and that were key nodes of exchange of knowledge as well as food (Turner and Loewen 1998).

Indigenous peoples in Canada also face a significantly different set of challenges related to food sovereignty compared to most Canadian farmers or members of urban and local food advocacy groups. These include disproportionate experiences of ill-health compared with the rest of the population, with shorter life expectancies a result of unequal access to health, education and other public services, higher poverty rates, and diet-related issues (Adelson 2005, Estey *et al.* 2007). Food insecurity rates for Indigenous peoples living off reserve are 33 percent – three times higher than the national average – and in some Indigenous communities, particularly in Canada's north, levels of food insecurity reach 75 percent (Reading and Wien 2009, Thompson *et al.* 2011, Fieldhouse and Thomp-son 2012).

Colonization and unresolved treaty processes have resulted in the loss of widespread access to traditional territories and relationships supporting the hunting, gathering, fishing, cultivation and trading of traditional indigenous foods (Turner and Loewen 1998, Turner and Turner 2008, Morrison 2011). The disruption of traditional indigenous food trading and knowledge networks have resulted in high food prices in remote commu-nities, a decline in the use of traditional foods by young people, in particular, and escalating transport costs (Thompson *et al.* 2011). Even so, 40–50 percent of indigenous communities in British Columbia, for example, still obtain some food locally through harvesting, hunting, fishing and gathering (FNHC 2009). In these communities, over 200 different types of traditional foods are regularly harvested (Chan *et al.* 2011), and contemporary food sharing and trading relationships exist among and between distinct First Nations (Turner and Loewen 1998, Morrison 2011).

Community consultations with Indigenous peoples have documented the continued importance of traditional foods and foodways to indigenous health and cultural well-being in both rural/remote and urban areas and have drawn attention to problems of lack of access to these (Morrison 2006, Mundel and Chapman 2010, Elliott *et al.* 2012). These consultations have resulted in the self-definition of a concept of indigenous food sovereignty, a framework that explicitly recognizes the social, cultural and economic relationships that underlie inter-community food sharing and trading as a mechanism for indigenous health and well-being. In the words of Dawn Morrison, the coordinator of the British Columbia Working Group on Indigenous Food Sovereignty,

> Indigenous food sovereignty describes, rather than defines, the present day strategies that enable and support the ability of Indigenous communities to sustain traditional hunting,

fishing, gathering, farming and distribution practices, the way we have done for thousands of years prior to contact with the first European settlers ... We have rejected a formal universal definition of sovereignty in favour of one that respects the sovereign rights and power of each distinct nation to identify the characteristics of our cultures and what it means to be Indigenous. (Morrison 2011, 97–8)

The Indigenous Circle within Food Secure Canada brought these discussions to the PFPP, resulting in the addition of a seventh pillar, beyond the six pillars of food sovereignty developed at Nyéléni. The project's Indigenous Circle emphasized that 'Food sovereignty understands food as sacred, part of the web of relationships with the natural world that define culture and community' (People's Food Policy Project 2011). Kneen says this seventh pillar is 'foundational' because

If food is sacred, it cannot be treated as a mere commodity, manipulated into junk foods or taken from people's mouths to feed animals or vehicles. If the ways in which we get food are similarly sacred, Mother Earth cannot be enslaved and forced to produce what we want, when and where we want it, through our technological tools. And of course, if food is sacred, the role of those who provide food is respected and supported. (Kneen 2011, 92)

To translate the elements of indigenous food sovereignty into a policy framework, Morrison (2011) summarizes four main principles that Elders, traditional harvesters and community members have identified within the BCFSN to guide work on Indigenous food sovereignty. In addition to the idea that *Food is sacred*, these discussions have emphasized the importance of *Participation* at individual, family, community, and regional levels. *Self-determination* refers to the 'freedom and ability to respond to our own needs for healthy, culturally-adapted indigenous foods. It represents the freedom and ability to make decisions over the amount and quality of food we hunt, fish, gather, grow and eat' (Morrison 2011, 100). Finally, *Legislation and policy reform* attempts to 'reconcile Indigenous food and cultural values with colonial laws, policies and mainstream economic activities' (101). This principle has resulted in significant mobilization around policy reform in forestry, fisheries and health programming.

In several important recent court cases, indigenous communities have been successful in re-establishing a framework for self-determined access to traditional fishing and hunting grounds. The Nuu chah nulth Fisheries case (finalized in 2009 after a decade in court) challenged federal Department of Fisheries and Oceans restrictions on indigenous commercial fisheries, affirming 'the nation's right to implement fishing and harvesting strategies according to its own unique cultural, economic and ecological considerations' (Dolha 2009, Morrison 2011, 108). More recently, indigenous food sovereignty proponents have joined with local food networks and environmental organizations to protest the effects of open-pen farmed Atlantic salmon on the British Columbia coast. Over 90 percent controlled by three Norwegian companies, farmed salmon has been BC's largest agricultural export since 2005, but a number of studies now provide evidence that fish farming in BC contributes to the erosion of wild salmon runs throughout the province, primarily via the infestations of sea lice, which are transferred to out-migrating wild juvenile salmon (Krkosek *et al.* 2006, Frazer 2009).

In the fall of 2012, the passage of a federal omnibus bill made sweeping changes to a range of legislative policies, including the Fisheries Act and the Indian Act. Bill C-45 reduced protections for millions of waterways and made it easier to force indigenous communities to surrender reserve land to extractive industries, catalyzing the Idle No More indigenous sovereignty movement.[22] Through numerous demonstrations across Canada during the winter of late 2012 and early 2013, Idle No More brought to public attention a range of policy initiatives that threaten treaty rights and indigenous sovereignty. Arguing that 'we are in a critical time where lives, lands, waters and Creation are at-risk and they must be protected' (Idle No More and Defenders of the Land 2013), members of the movement sought alliances with non-indigenous allies and environmental groups around the common themes of indigenous sovereignty and environmental protection. The NFU (2013), Food Secure Canada and the Union Paysanne each expressed solidarity, as exemplified by a Food Secure Canada resolution:

> We stand with Idle No More and call upon the Government of Canada to remedy its historical and current policies of colonization, assimilation and destruction, and work with each Nation to define and engage in an appropriate relationship based on respect and responsibility and full recognition of the right to self-determination. Healing and rebuilding contemporary relationships between Indigenous peoples and the Canadian government and honouring original nation-to-nation agreements are crucial steps towards achieving food sovereignty and food security for all. (Food Secure Canada 2013)

Reshaping the political

A universal conceptualization of food sovereignty is challenged by the diversity of communities using the language of food sovereignty in Canada. Distinct national, provincial, regional and cultural concerns in terms of community identity and subjectivity, and relationships to political and institutional authority, mean food sovereignty doesn't map tidily onto a national, or even provincial, scale. This poses significant challenges to working together to build food sovereignty in Canada. However, the expanding discourse around food sovereignty in Canada has resulted in a reshaping of the political spaces in which decisions and values shift concerning issues related to how and what food is produced, accessed and consumed. For the NFU, this means continuing its engagement with national politics around international trade agreements like CETA and TPP (Trans-Pacific Partnership). It also includes ongoing work at the provincial and municipal levels while reaching out to new constituencies, like small-scale fruit and vegetable producers in BC and Ontario, and urban consumers who self-identify as members of local food movements. Finally, for indigenous communities engaged in their own struggles to reclaim traditional territories and rights related to self-determination around their food systems, the use of food sovereignty discourse requires detaching the word 'sovereignty' from its historical and legal meanings and reconstructing elements of popular control, autonomy and interdependence (Alfred 1999, 59).

Do current mobilizations for Food Sovereignty in Canada exhibit a 'unity in diversity' to share an organizing frame for transformative food system change? There are contradictory positions: for example, the UPA, the Coalition Souveraineté Alimentaire and the Union Paysanne do not agree on the definition and purpose of food sovereignty. On the other hand, members of Food Secure Canada – which include more than 50 provincial and 12 national organizations and a growing number of individual members – have consolidated a set of

---

[22]The Idle No More movement 'revolves around Indigenous Ways of Knowing rooted in Indigenous Sovereignty to protect water, air, land and all creation for future generations'. The movement seeks the 'revitalization of Indigenous peoples through Awareness and Empowerment' (Idle no more 2013). See http://idlenomore.ca for more information.

policy demands framed as food sovereignty. These demands encompass the work of regional organizations for localized food economies, but are clearly situated within the national and global food system. Emphasizing that 'the core of food sovereignty is reclaiming public decision-making power in the food system' (PFPP 2011, 9), the policy demands resulting from the PFPP include:

- Ensuring that food is eaten as close as possible to where it is produced (domestic/regional purchasing policies for institutions and large food retailers, community-supported agriculture, farmers markets).
- Supporting food providers in a widespread shift to ecological production in both urban and rural settings (organic agriculture, community-managed fisheries, indigenous food systems, etc.), including policies for the entry of new farmers into agriculture.
- Enacting a strong federal poverty elimination and prevention program, with measurable targets and timelines, to ensure Canadians can better afford healthy food.
- Creating a nationally funded Children and Food strategy (including school meal programs, school gardens, and food literacy programs) to ensure that all children at all times have access to the food required for healthy lives.
- Ensuring that the public, especially the most marginalized, are actively involved in decisions that affect the food system. (PFPP 2011, 2)

The current negotiating text of CETA indicates that 'local governments will no longer be legally able to give preference to local or Canadian suppliers', a key demand of locavore and municipal food policy councils (Shrybman 2010). The NFU, for example, has articulated a position on CETA, but urban proponents of municipal and school food programs do not often articulate clear demands around international trade policy as a threat to food sovereignty. Similarly, vibrant movements and campaigns for an expansion of urban agriculture are occupying unused urban lots and advocating for changes to municipal bylaws to allow the sale of produce from backyard gardens. But to date, these groups demonstrate little visible engagement or connection with the Farmland Defense League and other movements seeking to protect access to farmland threatened by urban sprawl, or with indigenous groups advocating for hunting and fishing reserves, or with environmental and indigenous groups to protect salmon fisheries from habitat degradation resulting from mining and resource extraction. Unlike the farmer, indigenous and food-insecure populations also involved with Food Secure Canada, some urban consumer constituency groups operate from a position of relative privilege, and are less present in political advocacy work at the national and international scale (the work of the Toronto Food Policy Council on national food policy and social justice issues is an important exception). Municipal food policy councils are also limited in the scale/scope of their policy arena, rarely getting into issues of labour or international trade (Toronto Public Heath 2010, City of Vancouver 2013, Mansfield and Mendes 2013, McRae and Donahue 2013).

Even so, food sovereignty discourse is in Canada is changing, no longer concerned primarily with production and marketing concerns like supply management, orderly marketing and international trade policy. It is making inroads in civil society-based and urban food networks like Food Secure Canada who support farmer- and indigenous-led struggles over the shape and direction of food sovereignty, but who also lead initiatives around socially-just food consumption that bridges the conceptual gap between food producers and marginalized/food-insecure populations. One example is Edmonton's Good Food Box Programme

(GFB), originally designed in 2009 as a non-profit social enterprise to expand access to locally produced food to urban residents, to provide 'fair market value to producers ... to be accessible to all and to create jobs for low-income residents' (Connelly *et al.* 2011, 314). Capitalizing on the growing urban demand for local food, the GFB has expanded its offerings to include prepared and specialized foods oriented towards 'niche foodie and middle class-markets' to achieve a critical mass to support additional investment in local food infrastructure (315). In this example, food system transformation happened at a local scale through the political education of an urban consumer population. This consumer base then began to engage with the broader food system, by participating in local food policy councils, locavore and Slow Food events and healthy eating initiatives.

In addition to embracing Resetting the Table as a people's national food policy for Canada, Food Secure Canada – in cooperation with indigenous organizations, the NFU (2012) and other groups – facilitated broad consultations with the United Nations (UN) Special Rapporteur during his Right to Food country fact-finding mission to Canada in 2012, the first such mission in an Organisation for Economic Co-operation and Development (OECD) country. These organizations saw the mission to Canada as a unique opportunity to give visibility to the human rights concerns of the industrial food system and inadequate social policies in Canada, particularly around food insecurity and indigenous access to traditional food provisioning systems. The response from Canada's federal Conservative majority party was altogether different. Some high-level federal Conservative government officials refused to meet with the Special Rapporteur, while others criticized him for being 'ill-informed, patronizing' (Whittington 2012). Other officials dismissed the visit to Canada for investigating questions related to the human right to food as inappropriate.

What is most evident in examining the demands of a wide range of actors using food sovereignty language in Canada is their shared goal to reclaim a public voice in shaping the food system. There is a growing convergence around a discourse and practice of social justice, ethical foods and cultural diversity – all key elements of the People's Food Policy Framework. There are also examples of alliances based on food sovereignty concerns between diverse groups self-identifying as farmers, foodies and First Nations, which offer prospects for future solidarity-building. How that power is claimed is diverse, and occurs at different locations and scales, through: demands to address the structural causes of unjust and environmentally damaging agri-food and trade policies at local, provincial, national and international policy levels; the ability to make more sustainable choices as individual consumers within both local and globalized food systems, and struggles for decolonization and self-determination by Indigenous peoples. There are also, however, strong divergences in the meaning and goals of food sovereignty as was clearly the case in the province of Québec, and differences between agriculture-centric vs. indigenous food sovereignty perspectives. As the locus of food sovereignty activism shifts from (rural) issues of production and traditional foodways to (urban) issues of consumption, it is still unclear if and how this will affect struggles over access to and control over productive resources. It is also still unclear whether these distinct manifestations of food sovereignty in Canada – each in their own way and to different degrees working towards the transformation of existing structures of food production and food access – will make inroads into a broader food system transformation. Thus, if food sovereignty is about fundamental transformation of existing structures, ways of thinking and being, then this implies a constant process of struggle that is at its initial stages in Canada.

References

Adelson, N. 2005. The embodiment of inequity: health disparities in Aboriginal Canada. *Canadian Journal of Public Health*, March/April 2005. S45–S61.

Agriculture and Agri-food Canada (AAFC). 2013. *An overview of the Canadian agriculture and agri-food system*. Ottawa: AAFC. Available from: http://www4.agr.gc.ca/AAFC-AAC/display-afficher.do?id=1331319696826

Agriculture Canada. 1989. *Growing together: a vision for Canada's agri-food industry*. Ottawa: Government of Canada.

Alfred, T. 1999. *Peace, power, righteousness: an indigenous manifesto*. Don Mills, Ontario: Oxford University Press.

Alkon, A.H., and Mares, T.M. 2012. Food sovereignty in US food movements: radical visions and neoliberal constraints. *Agriculture and Human Values*, 29(3), 347–359.

Beingessner, N. 2013. Alternative Land Tenure: A Path Towards Food Sovereignty in Saskatchewan? Unpublished Masters Thesis, Department of Justice Studies, University of Regina. Saskatchewan.

Borras, S. 2010. The politics of transnational agrarian movements. *Development and Change*, 41(5), 771–803.

Borras, S. and J. Franco. 2010. Food sovereignty and redistributive land policies. In: H. Wittman *et al.*, eds. *Food sovereignty: reconnecting food, nature and community*. Halifax: Fernwood Publishing, pp. 106–119.

Borras, S., M. Edelman and C. Kay. 2008. *Transnational agrarian movements: confronting globalization*. Southern Gate, Chichester: Wiley-Blackwell.

Bush, R. 2010. Food riots: poverty, power and protest. *Journal of Agrarian Change*, 10(1), 119–129.

Canadian Agricultural Human Resource Council. n.d. Directory of Canadian Agricultural Associations. Available at http://www.agriguide.ca/home

Chan, L., O. Receveur, D. Sharp, H. Schwartz, A. Ing and C. Tikhonov. 2011. *First Nations food, nutrition and environment study (FNFNES): results from British Columbia (2008/2009)*. Vancouver: University of Northern British Columbia, pp. 1–216.

City of Vancouver. 2013. *What feeds us: Vancouver food strategy*. Vancouver, BC: City of Vancouver, pp. 1–150.

Claeys, P. 2012. The creation of new rights by the food sovereignty movement: the challenge of institutionalizing subversion. *Sociology*, 46(5), 844–860.

Commission sur l'Avenir de l'Agriculture et de l'Agroalimentaire Québecois. 2008. Agriculture and agrifood: Securing and building the future. Department of Agriculture, Government of Québec. Available from: http://www.caaaq.gouv.qc.ca/userfiles/File/Dossiers%2012%20fevrier/Rapport%20CAAAQ%20anglais.pdf

Connelly, S., S. Markey and M. Roseland. 2011. Bridging sustainability and the social economy: achieving community transformation through local food initiatives. *Critical Social Policy*, 31 (2), 308–324.

Desmarais, A.A. 2007. *La Vía Campesina: globalization and the power of peasants*. Halifax and London: Fernwood Publishing and Pluto Press.

Dolha, L. 2009. 'Nuu-Chah-Nulth Celebrate Landmark Fisheries Decision'. *First Nations Drum* 19, 11 (November). Available from: http://www.firstnationsdrum.com/2009/11/nuu-chah-nulth-celebrate-landmark-fisheries-decision/ [Accessed 10 January 2014].

Eaton, E. 2013. *Growing resistance: Canadian farmers and the politics of genetically modified wheat*. Winnipeg: University of Manitoba Press.

Edelman, Marc. 1999. *Peasants against globalization. Rural social movements in Costa Rica*. Stanford, California: Stanford University Press.

Edelman, M. and C. James. 2011. Peasants' rights and the UN system: quixotic struggle? Or emancipatory idea whose time has come? *Journal of Peasant Studies*, 38(1), 81–108.

Elliott, B., D. Jayatilaka, C. Brown, L. Varley and K.K. Corbett. 2012. 'We are not being heard': aboriginal perspectives on traditional foods access and food security. *Journal of Environmental and Public Health*, 2012(6), 1–9.

Estey, E.A., A.M. Kmetic, and J. Reading. 2007. Innovative approaches in public health research: applying life course epidemiology to aboriginal health research. *Canadian Journal of Public Health*, 98, 444–446.

Fairbairn, M. 2010. Framing resistance: International food regimes and the roots of food sovereignty. In: H. Wittman, A.A. Desmarais and N. Wiebe, eds. *Food sovereignty: Reconnecting food, nature and community.* Halifax: Fernwood Publishing. pp. 15–32.

FCWB. (Friends of the Canadian Wheat Board). N.d. Available from: http://friendsofcwb.ca/ [Accessed 24 May 2013].

Food Secure Canada. 2013. Food Secure Canada Stands in Solidarity with Idle No More. Press release, January 10, Toronto: Food Secure Canada.

Fieldhouse, P. and S. Thompson. 2012. Tackling food security issues in indigenous communities in Canada: the Manitoba experience. *Nutrition & Dietetics,* 69(3), 217–221.

First Nations Health Council (FNHC). 2009. *BC First Nation Community Nutrition Needs and Assets Survey.* West Vancouver, BC: First Nations Health Council.

Frazer, L.N. 2009. Sea-cage aquaculture, sea lice, and declines of wild fish. *Conservation Biology,* 23, 599–607.

Friedmann, H. 2007. Scaling up: bringing public institutions and food service corporations into the project for a local, sustainable food system in Ontario. *Agriculture and Human Values,* 24(3), 389–398.

Friedmann, H. 2011. Food sovereignty in the Golden Horseshoe region of Ontario. In: H. Wittman, A. A. Desmarais and N. Wiebe, eds. *Food sovereignty in Canada: creating just and sustainable food systems.* Halifax: Fernwood Publishing, pp. 169–189.

Gibb, N., and Wittman, H. 2013. Parallel alternatives: Chinese-Canadian farmers and the Metro Vancouver local food movement. *Local Environment,* 18(1), 1–19.

Idle No More. 2013. 'Idle No More World Day of Action – January 28,' Press release issued January 10.

Idle No More, and Defenders of the Land. 2013. From solidarity spring to sovereignty summer: An international callout to all indigenous peoples, supporters, allies of Idle No More and Defenders of the Land, Available from: http://idlenomore.ca/articles/latest-news/global-news/item/225-sovereignty-summer. [Accessed 27 May].

ILO. 2012. Governing Body, 315th Session, June 15, Geneva. GB.315/INS/INF/1 Available from: www.ilo.org/wcmsp5/groups/public/—ed.../wcms_183413.pdf [Accessed 15 June 2013].

Isakson, S. R. 2009. No hay ganancia en la milpa: the agrarian question, food sovereignty, and the on-farm conservation of agrobiodiversity in the Guatemalan highlands. *Journal of Peasant Studies,* 36(4), 725–759.

Johnston, J. 2008. The citizen-consumer hybrid: ideological tensions and the case of Whole Foods Market. *Theory and Society,* 37(3), 229–270.

Johnston, J. and L. Baker. 2005. Eating outside the box: foodshare's good food box and the challenge of scale. *Agriculture and Human Values,* 22(3), 313–325.

Johnston, J. and S. Baumann. 2010. *Foodies: democracy and distinction in the gourmet foodscape.* New York: Routledge.

Kneen, C. 2010. Mobilisation and convergence in a wealthy northern country. *Journal of Peasant Studies,* 37(1), 229–235.

Kneen, C. 2011. Food Secure Canada: where agriculture, environment, health, food and justice inter-sect. In: H. Wittman, A.A. Desmarais and N. Wiebe, eds. *Food sovereignty in Canada: Creating just and sustainable food systems.* Halifax: Fernwood Publishing, pp. 80–96.

Krkosek, M., Lewis, M. A., Morton, A., Frazer, L. N., & Volpe, J. P. (2006). Epizootics of wild fish induced by farm fish. *Proceedings of the National Academy of Sciences,* 103(42), 15506–15510.

La Vía Campesina. 1996a. Proceedings of the II international conference of the Vía Campesina. Brussles: NCOS Publications.

La Vía Campesina. 1996b. The right to produce and access to land. Position of the Vía Campesina on food sovereignty presented at the World Food Summit, November 13-17, Rome.

Magnan, A. 2011. The limits of farmer-control: food sovereignty and conflicts over the Canadian Wheat Board. In: H. Wittman, A.A. Desmarais and N. Wiebe, eds. *Food sovereignty in Canada: Creating just and sustainable food systems.* Halifax: Fernwood Publishing, pp. 114–133.

Mansfield, B. and W. Mendes. 2013. Municipal food strategies and integrated approaches to urban agriculture: exploring three cases from the global North. *International Planning Studies,* 18(1), 37–60.

MAPAQ. (Ministère d'Agriculture, Pêcheries *et al*imentation de Québec). 2013. 'Politique de souveraineté alimentaire.' Ministere d'Agriculture, Pecheries *et al*imentation du Québec,

Available from: http://www.mapaq.gouv.qc.ca/fr/ministere/politiquesouverainetealimentaire/ Pages/Politiquedesouverainetealimentaire.aspx [Accessed 26 May 2013].

Massey, Doreen. 1991. A Global Sense of Place. *Marxism Today*, June 1991. Available from: http:// www.amielandmelburn.org.uk/collections/mt/index_frame.htm

McMichael, P. 2009. Food sovereignty, social reproduction and the agrarian question. In: A.H. Akram-lodhi and C. Kay, eds. *Peasants and globalization: political economy, rural transformation and the agrarian question*. London: Routledge, pp. 288–312.

McRae, R. and K. Donahue. 2013. *Municipal food policy entrepreneurs: a preliminary analysis of how Canadian cities and regional districts are involved in food system change* (pp. 1–36). Toronto: Toronto Food Policy Council; Vancouver Food Policy Council; CAPI-ICPA.

Morrison, D. 2006. *First Annual Interior of BC Indigenous Food Sovereignty Conference Report*. B. C. Food Systems Network.

Morrison, D. 2011. Indigenous food sovereignty – A model for social learning. In: H. Wittman, A.A. Desmarais and N. Wiebe, eds. *Food sovereignty in Canada: creating just and sustainable food systems*. Halifax: Fernwood Publishing, pp. 97–113.

Mundel, E. and G.E. Chapman. 2010. A decolonizing approach to health promotion in Canada: the case of the Urban aboriginal community kitchen garden project. *Health Promotion International*, 25(2), 166–173.

NFU (National Farmers Union). 2011. NFU Policy Book, NFU National Office, Saskatoon, SK. Canada.

NFU (National Farmers Union). 2012. 'Farmers, the Food Chain and Agriculture Policies in Canada in Relation to the Right to Food,' Submission to the Special Rapporteur On The Right To Food, Mr. Olivier De Schutter, Mission to Canada, May 10, Winnipeg, Manitoba.

NFU. 2013. NFU in solidarity with Idle No More. Press release, January 15, Saskatoon, SK. Available from: http://www.nfu.ca/story/national-farmers-union-solidarity-idle-no-more [Accessed 28 May 2013].

NFU (National Farmers Union). n.d. National Farmers Union Policy on Sustainable Agriculture. Available from http://www.nfu.ca/policy/national-farmers-union-policy-sustainable-agriculture. [Accessed 12 May 2013].

NFU (National Farmers Union). n.d. 'National Farmers Union Canada – Home.' National Farmers Union. Available from: www.nfu.ca. [Accessed 12 May 2013].

Patel, Raj. 2009. What does food sovereignty look like? *Journal of Peasant Studies*, 36(3), 663–673.

Peekhaus, Wilhelm. 2013. *Resistance is fertile: Canadian struggles on the BioCommons*. Vancouver: University of British Columbia Press.

People's Food Commission. 1980. *The land of milk and money: the national report of the People's Food Commission*. Toronto: Between the Lines.

PPFP People's Food Policy Project. 2011. Resetting the table: a people's food policy for Canada. Available at www.peoplesfoodpolicy.ca. [Accessed on May 13, 2013].

Qualman, Darrin. 2011. Advancing agriculture by destroying farms? The state of agriculture in Canada. In: H. Wittman, A.A. Desmarais and N. Wiebe, eds. *Food sovereignty in Canada: creating just and sustainable food systems*. Halifax: Fernwood Publishing, pp. 20–42.

Radio-Canada. 2013. En quête d'une politique de souveraineté alimentaire. May 16, Available from: http://www.radio-canada.ca/nouvelles/Politique/2013/05/15/007-quebec-en-quete-politique-souverainete-alimentaire.shtml. [Accessed 26 May 2013].

Reading, C.L. and F. Wien. 2009. *Health Inequalities and Social Determinants of Aboriginal Peoples' Health*. Prince George, BC: National Collaborating Centre for Aboriginal Health.

Rosset, P., B. Machin Sosa, A.M. Roque Jaime, and D.R. Avila Lozano. 2011. The Campesino-to-Campesino agroecology movement of ANAP in Cuba: social process methodology in the construction of sustainable peasant agriculture and food sovereignty. *Journal of Peasant Studies*, 38(1), 161–191.

Sharratt, L. 2001. No to bovine growth hormone: a story of resistance from Canada. In: B. Tokar, ed. *Redesigning life? The worldwide challenge to genetic engineering*. London: Zed Books, pp. 385–396.

Shaw, K. 2008. *Indigeneity and Political Theory: sovereignty and the limits of the political*. New York: Routledge.

Shrybman, S. 2010. Municipal procurement implications of the proposed Comprehenive Econoimc and Trade Agreement (CETA) between Canada and the European Union. Legal Opinion prepared for the Centre for Civic Governance at Columbia Institute. www.civicgovernance.ca

Skogstad, Grace. 2008. *Internationalization and Canadian agriculture: policy and governing paradigms*. Toronto: University of Toronto Press.

Springer, Simon. 2011. Public space as emancipation: meditations on anarchism, radical democracy, neoliberalism and violence. *Antipode: A Radical Journal of Geography*, 43(2), 525–562.

Thompson, S., A. Gulrukh, M. Ballard, B. Beardy, D. Islam, V. Lozeznik and K. Wong. 2011. Is community economic development putting healthy food on the table? Food sovereignty in northern Manitoba's aboriginal communities. *Journal of Aboriginal Economic Development*, 7(2), 14–39.

Toronto Public Health. 2010. *Cultivating food connections: toward a healthy and sustainable food system for Toronto)*. Toronto: City of Toronto, pp. 1–42.

Turner, N.J. and D.C. Loewen. 1998. The original 'free trade': exchange of botanical products and associated plant knowledge in Northwestern North America. *Anthropologica*, 40(1), 49–70.

Turner, N.J. and K.L. Turner. 2008. Where our women used to get the food: cumulative effects and loss of ethnobotanical knowledge and practice; case study from coastal British Columbia. *Botany*, 86(2), 103–115.

United Church of Canada. 2013. Toward food sovereignty for all. Available from: http://www.united-church.ca/files/general-council/gce/2013/gce_1305_food.pdf [Accessed 8 January 2014].

Union Paysanne. N.d. Available from: http://www.unionpaysanne.com/images/stories/Doc/fiches/gestion_de_l_offre.pdf [Accessed 25 May 2013].

Union Paysanne. 2013. 'L'Union paysanne boycottera la rencontre du ministre Gendron,' Press release, March 21, Saint-Hyacinthe, Québec. Available from: http://www.unionpaysanne.com/communiques/661-lunion-paysanne-boycottera-la-rencontre-du-ministre-gendron. [Accessed 23 May 2013].

United Nations Human Rights Council. 2012. *Report of the Special Rapporteur on the right to Food, Olivier de Schutter: Mission to Canada* (No. A/HRC/22/50/Add.1) Geneva: United Nations General Assembly.

Vera, Ramon. 2010. Interview conducted by Annette Desmarais, February 22, 2011, Mexico City.

Warnock, John. 1971. The farm crisis. In: L. LaPierre, J. McLeod, C. Taylor and W. Young, eds. *Essays on the left*. Toronto: McClelland and Stewart Ltd.

WCWGA (Western Canadian Wheat Growers Association. N.d. http://www.wheatgrowers.ca/. [Accessed May 21, 2013].

Whittington, L. 2012. UN food envoy blasts inequality, poverty in Canada | Toronto Star. The Star. May 16. Available from: http://www.thestar.com/news/canada/2012/05/16/un_food_envoy_blasts_inequality_poverty_in_canada.html [Accessed 1 June 2013].

Windfuhr, M. and J. Jonsén. 2005. *Food sovereignty: towards democracy in localized food systems*. Rugby, Warwickshire: ITDG Publishing.

Wittman, H. 2011. Food sovereignty: a new rights framework for food and nature? *Environment and Society: Advances in Research*, 2(1), 87–105.

Wittman, H., A.A. Desmarais and N. Wiebe. 2011. *Food sovereignty in Canada: building just and sustainable food systems*. Halifax: Fernwood Publishing.

Wittman, H., A.A. Desmarais and N. Wiebe. 2010. *Food sovereignty: reconnecting food, nature and community*. Halifax and Oakland: Fernwood Publishing and Food First Books.

Annette Aurélie Desmarais is Canada Research Chair in Human Rights, Social Justice and Food Sovereignty at the University of Manitoba. She is the author of *La Vía Campesina: globalization and the power of peasants* (Fernwood Publishing and Pluto Press, 2007) which has been published in various languages. Annette is also co-editor of *Food sovereignty: reconnecting food, nature, and community*, and *Food sovereignty in Canada: creating just and sustainable food systems*.

Hannah Wittman is an Associate Professor at the Faculty of Land and Food Systems and Institute for Resources, Environment and Sustainability at the University of British Columbia. She conducts collaborative research on food sovereignty, local food systems and agrarian citizenship in Brazil and Canada and is co-editor of *Environment and citizenship in Latin America: natures, subjects, and struggles, Food sovereignty: reconnecting food, nature, and community* and *Food sovereignty in Canada*.

The 'state' of food sovereignty in Latin America: political projects and alternative pathways in Venezuela, Ecuador and Bolivia

Ben McKay, Ryan Nehring and Marygold Walsh-Dilley

The concept of food sovereignty has been enshrined in the constitutions of a number of countries around the world without any clear consensus around what state-sponsored 'food sovereignty' might entail. At the forefront of this movement are the countries of the so-called 'pink tide' of Latin America – chiefly Venezuela, Ecuador and Bolivia. This paper examines how state commitments to food sovereignty have been put into practice in these three countries, asking if and how efforts by the state contribute to significant transformation or if they simply serve the political purposes of elites. Understanding the state as a complex arena of class struggle, we suggest that state efforts around food sovereignty open up new political spaces in an ongoing struggle around control over food systems at different scales. Embedded in food sovereignty is a contradictory notion of sovereignty, requiring simultaneously a strong developmentalist state and the redistribution of power to facilitate direct control over food systems in ways that may threaten the state. State-society relations, particularly across scales, are therefore a central problematic of food sovereignty projects.

Introduction

While its origins can be traced back to the early 1980s (Edelman 2014), the concept of food sovereignty most commonly deployed by social movements today emerged in a 1996 declaration presented by La Via Campesina at the World Food Summit of the Food and Agriculture Organization (FAO) in Rome. In this document, food sovereignty is defined as 'the right of each *nation* to maintain and develop its own capacity to produce its basic foods, respecting cultural and productive diversity' (Via Campesina 1996, emphasis added). This notion echoes earlier conceptions of food sovereignty used in Mexico to imply 'national control over diverse aspects of the food chain, thus reducing dependency on foreign capital and imports of basic foods, inputs, and technologies' (Heath 1985, 115, quoted in Edelman 2014, 6). In good part, Via Campesina's 1996 declaration was motivated by the failure of the World Trade Organization's 1995 Agreement on Agriculture (AoA) to adequately address the issue of agricultural subsidies in the United States and Europe, and in

---

An early version of this paper was presented at the Yale Conference on Food Sovereignty, and benefited from the comments received there. The authors would also like to acknowledge the editors of this special collection, chiefly Saturnino M. Borras Jr., and three anonymous reviewers as well as Sara Keene and Stalin Herrera, who provided helpful comments and constructive criticism. Authors are listed in alphabetical order.

particular the flooding of developing country markets with heavily subsidized agricultural goods. Rather than solve the subsidy issue, the AoA had the effect of institutionalizing the disparity between the two agricultural powerhouses (the United States and the European Union) and the rest of the world (Bello 2005, 38). This agreement marked a turning point in the assault on small-scale agriculture, particularly in the developing world, and Via Campesina's declaration was issued in response to this failure.

Just five years later, in a 2001 Declaration on Food Sovereignty, Via Campesina redefined the concept as

> the right of *peoples* to define their own agriculture and food policies, to protect and regulate domestic agricultural production and trade in order to achieve sustainable development objectives, to determine the extent to which they want to be self-reliant, and to restrict the dumping of products in their markets. (Via Campesina 2001, emphasis added)

A similar definition is found in the 2007 International Forum on Food Sovereignty, which defines food sovereignty as 'the right of peoples to healthy and culturally appropriate food produced through ecologically sound and sustainable methods, and their right to define their own food and agriculture systems' (Nyéléni 2007). These definitions emphasize direct, even 'local', control over food production and consumption. Here, food sovereignty is understood as a set of commitments leading to a food system that (1) provides sufficient, healthy, nutritious and culturally- and locally-appropriate food for all; (2) values and supports food providers, with a particular focus on small-scale family farmers, peasants etc.; (3) localizes the food system; (4) localizes control over and access to land resources; (5) values and contributes to local knowledge and skills; and (6) works with nature, with a focus on agroecological production (Nyéléni 2007).

This subtle change in the scale and location of sovereignty – from the national to the local and from the accrual of sovereignty in the hands of the nation-state to those of 'peoples' – marks an important definitional shift in mobilizing food sovereignty as a tool for political change. At the same time, food sovereignty has been taken up at the national level by a number of countries, which have written the concept into their constitutions as a guaranteed right. In Latin America, the constitutional inclusion of food sovereignty emerged in the context of a political shift to the left – the so-called 'pink tide' – that has united social movements protesting against the neoliberal reforms of the 1990s with progressive governments that are more responsive to public demands. That is, food sovereignty is being brought into the state precisely as many Latin American states become more explicitly linked to civil society groups and movements.

These overlapping shifts, both definitional and constitutional, raise important questions and tensions, not least about the role of the state in generating and supporting food sovereignty within its national borders. In what ways does food sovereignty as a concept and a practice call upon and mobilize – or reject – the state? And how do state-level interventions in the name of food sovereignty intersect with and/or contradict the goals of social movement proponents and the 'local peoples' that food sovereignty is ultimately intended to serve? These questions become particularly important in a context of 'distinct national, provincial, regional and cultural concerns in terms of community identity and subjectivity, and relationships to political and institutional authority', meaning that 'food sovereignty doesn't map tidily onto a national, or even provincial, scale' (Desmarais and Wittman 2014, 16). At the same time, however, visions of food sovereignty outlined in the Nyéléni Declaration and elsewhere require institutional, infrastructural and legal support and protections, which will rely at least to some degree on state involvement.

In this paper, we interrogate the 'state' of food sovereignty through a comparative analysis of the three countries in Latin America where food sovereignty has been enshrined as a constitutionally guaranteed right: Venezuela, Ecuador and Bolivia. We rely principally on secondary sources, archival documents such as newspapers and legal documents, and, to a smaller degree, on the experiences of the authors living, working and conducting qualitative fieldwork in each of the three countries. We outline the political processes through which constitutional, legal and policy measures were adopted, how food sovereignty was conceived in this process and to what degree food sovereignty objectives were achieved. We focus on state-society interactions, and ask how efforts by the state contribute to transformative aspirations or if they simply serve the political purposes of elites. The case studies presented here are necessarily (for space and comparative considerations) drawn in broad strokes, but nonetheless we find such a comparison helpful for addressing this question of how the state fits into food sovereignty aspirations.

Food sovereignty cannot be conceived of as a finite outcome; it is a political space and terrain of struggle around control over food systems. As such, state efforts around food sovereignty open up new political spaces in this ongoing contest. To unpack the transformative potential of such state-led food sovereignty efforts, we draw from Edelman's (2014) work that asks 'who is the sovereign in food sovereignty', and add as well a question about against whom or what this sovereignty is exercised. We suggest that state engagement in food sovereignty projects – and how well they are able to achieve their own stated goals or contribute to transformative reform – depends in large part on how the state interprets these questions.

Struggles around *food* sovereignty are struggles over *sovereignty* (i.e. self-determination, see Clark 2013; Mesner 2013) at different scales. Sovereignty in this context simultaneously accrues to both state and communities (broadly defined). Clearly, food sovereignty at the regional or community level depends in large part on the sovereignty of the state. But the accrual of sovereignty at sub-national scales does not necessarily complement state sovereignty, and may be seen as a threat to it. Embedded in food sovereignty, then, is a contradictory notion of sovereignty – a contradiction that has the potential to create significant tensions as states pursue national food sovereignty frameworks and policies. State-society relations, particularly across scales, are therefore a central problematic of food sovereignty projects.

The state cannot 'stand alone' on food sovereignty, but neither can 'local' communities, groups or people. If food sovereignty is to be about the ability of 'local' peoples to have a say in defining, managing and controlling their own food and agricultural systems, then state efforts to support food sovereignty must involve some degree of structural reform to distribute power in ways that facilitate such local autonomy. State efforts around food sovereignty thus depend on the nature of state-society interaction and the ability of reformists to engage in symbiotic, mutually empowering relationships (see Fox 1993; Borras 2007). But this shifting distribution of power is necessarily shot through with conflicts and tensions, as actors across the state-society terrain interpret food sovereignty goals differently and place them against other priorities.

In Venezuela, the inclusion of food sovereignty in the national constitution has been accompanied by significant structural changes in governance systems, most notably with the decentralization of governance into community hands. This process has allowed greater local control over food and other systems, ultimately contributing to the sovereignty of *local* communities vis-à-vis the Venezuelan national state as well as foreign capital or political interests. In Bolivia, food sovereignty has been taken up by the state as part of a de-colonial project in ways that assert Bolivian state control over food systems vis-à-vis foreign governments and international institutions. While a central element in this process is the rhetorical elevation of indigenous models of community, thus far there has been relatively little devolution of this control to the regional or community level. Indeed, the state in Bolivia is critiqued for failing to bring structural changes to the extractivist and disequalizing models that have guided rural development in the country thus far, relying instead on consolidating power and state-led redistribution of mineral wealth to historically excluded populations. Finally, in Ecuador, food sovereignty has been mobilized neither as part of a radical shift in governance that gives local spaces more power, nor as part of a sovereignty project vis-à-vis foreign powers, but rather as a state consolidation project to simplify, and ultimately adjudicate between, different visions of food sovereignty.

These cases demonstrate how the food sovereignty concept is used by state actors in particular ways to support their own strategies and goals. Not all of these strategies have the same potential for transformative change of the sort promoted by the rural and peasant movements that make up La Via Campesina. Indeed, the political project of the Bolivian state and the simplification strategies of the Correa administration in Ecuador have arguably done little to support such goals. Food sovereignty in these contexts has been used to galvanize consent and popular support, with state actors co-opting or consolidating food sovereignty as their own in ways that result in state-society power dynamics that significantly favour the former. In this context, food sovereignty becomes little more than a legitimating discourse (Kerssen 2013) and/or, as in Ecuador, is simplified and standardized (see Scott 1998) in ways that transform food sovereignty into 'one-size-fits-all', manageable projects.

Among the cases examined here – the three countries that have a constitutional guarantee of food sovereignty for their citizens – only in Venezuela are these nominal rights accompanied by partial structural changes that contribute to empowering people at the local level to have greater control over their own food production and consumption. This has been achieved through a radical re-envisioning of the locus of governance, creating and supporting community-level structures that put political power in the hands of the people in a new way.[1] This strategy is transforming relations around access to resources and decision-making control in favour of participatory institutions in communities, resulting in a symbiotic relationship between state and society that contributes to institutional reform and empowers local producers and consumers (see Fox 1993, 2005 for general background discussion).

The 'state' of food sovereignty

Food sovereignty is, unlike other popular concepts aimed at enabling stable access to food, 'essentially a political concept' (Windfuhr and Jonsén 2005, 15), and the state is necessarily part of the food sovereignty process. Nonetheless, Bernstein (2014) calls the relationship between state and society 'the elephant in the room of the programmatic aspirations of Food Sovereignty' (24). There is no consensus about what effective state action would look like or what policies effectively support food sovereignty – though this question has certainly generated debate (Rosset 2003; Rosset 2008; McMichael 2008; Patel 2009; Martinez-Torres and Rosset 2010). But as Schiavoni (2014a, 2) reminds us, 'the state has often been a *facilitator* of many of the very policies and structures that the food

---

[1]This, however, is not a point of consensus among observers and researchers. See Kappeler (2013) for a very different take and argument on the Venezuelan case.

sovereignty movement seeks to dismantle, from land grabs to free trade agreements', complicating the question of what role the state might take in support of food sovereignty goals. Supportive state policies might include: protection against dumping, trade and speculation in agriculture; supply management; floor prices; marketing boards; agrarian reform; farmer-owned food inventories; hoarding controls; a moratorium on agrofuels; a shift to agroecology; and state-directed food provisioning (Rosset 2008; McMichael 2014). The food sovereignty goals of localizing and domesticating trade and maintaining limited farm sizes will similarly require strong regulatory controls (Edelman 2014, 17). While such policies might facilitate spaces for building food sovereignty, they require a radical political transformation (Holt Giménez and Shattuck 2011) that is much easier said than done. Further, there is the distinct potential that such 'food sovereignty' policies actually strengthen the state vis-à-vis food sovereignty advocates or local communities (Edelman 2014).

This raises a central tension regarding the possibilities for state action in supporting food sovereignty: food sovereignty requires a simultaneous 'developmentalist' state and a redistribution of power to facilitate direct control over food systems in ways that may threaten the state. If food sovereignty necessarily involves the 'right to self-determination, for communities to redefine for themselves the substance of the food relations appropriate to their geographies' (Patel and McMichael 2004, 249), how might food sovereignty be defined, led, controlled, or implemented by the state? Indeed, this implies what Patel and McMichael (2004, 249) call a 'contradictory understanding of rights' with the state as guarantor but not author of food sovereignty rights.

The concept of food sovereignty entails a reformulation of the formal, Westphalian vision of the sovereignty of nation-states (McMichael 2009), while at the same time calling upon it. Indeed, it seems to rely upon 'multiple sovereignties' (McMichael 2009), which may in turn be harmonious or competing. How can you have a powerful notion of food sovereignty at the level of the nation state, particularly in the context of plurinationality like in Bolivia and Ecuador, when different groups (peoples, nations or communities) have divergent ideas about what food sovereignty means and looks like in practice? Food sovereignty involves, as McMichael writes in this collection (2014; see also McMichael 2012), a form of strategic essentialism that calls upon the idea of sovereignty to claim juridical ground in the short run, but, in forcing a rethinking of the locus of sovereignty, it also has the potential to reformulate the meaning of sovereignty itself in the long run. The actual forms and visions for food sovereignty are quite diverse and its meaning has an elasticity as it is taken up by groups (including states) beyond its roots in the countryside (McMichael 2014, see also Hospes 2014; Edelman 2014). These visions of what food sovereignty looks like are sometimes corresponding or approximate enough to be brought together, but are just as likely (as the Ecuador case discussed below demonstrates) to be too dissimilar. This multiplicity of forms indicates that a one-size-fits-all pathway to food sovereignty is impossible. Indeed, framing food sovereignty as an objective and achievable outcome unproductively reifies what is essentially a terrain of contestation, a political space and project – complicating our questions as to the role of the state in building and supporting food sovereignty.

The state is understood here an arena of complex, strategic relations between political and social spheres (Gramsci 1971; Poulantzas 1978; Jessop 2007). That is, we do not conceive of the state as a monolithic entity, but rather a contested system of social relations. The possibility of reform is influenced by the degree of autonomy and capacity of pro-reform state and societal actors and the nature of their interaction (see Fox 1993). That is, reformers must be both free to form and pursue goals independently (autonomously) as well as able to get people 'to do what they want them to' (Migdal 188, xi). Distinguishing between these two dimensions of power is important because they are both necessary in order for reforms to be implemented. For example, state or societal actors may have the autonomy to pursue a food sovereignty agenda, but lack the capacity to implement such reforms, or vice-versa. In both instances, it is unlikely that a pro-poor reform will be carried out (Borras 2007, 70). However, these two relational dimensions of power – autonomy and capacity – are not pre-determined or unchanging; they are shaped and reshaped by actors in both the state and society. Strategic interaction between pro-reform state and societal actors can mutually reinforce reform agendas and alter degrees of autonomy and capacity.

Nominal rights to food sovereignty potentially open up spaces for the pursuit of a trans-formative agenda, but are not sufficient. A transformative agenda requires both the rights and the pro-empowerment institutional reforms that make these rights meaningful. Fox notes (2005, 7) that

> Institutions may nominally recognize rights that actors, because of imbalances in power relations, are not able to exercise in practice. Conversely, actors may be empowered in the sense of having the experience and capacity to exercise rights, while lacking institutionally recognized opportunities to do so.

Our task is to examine the ways in which state frameworks for food sovereignty in Vene-zuela, Ecuador and Bolivia are accompanied by institutional reforms which empower non-state actors to define the substance of their food-related institutions and capacities. Under-standing that there are variations within pro-reform (interested in structural change in support of food sovereignty goals) and anti-reform (attempting to block such changes) groups within both state and society, the challenge is to create environments in which pro-reformists within the state and society can enact mutually reinforcing agendas (Fox 1993; Borras 2007). However, this is no easy task, as it requires a continuity of perceived shared interests from reformists both 'above' and 'below' (see Fox 2005). Indeed, this must be an ongoing project, as 'anti-reform forces attempt to block the reform process through their own state-society alliances' (Borras 2007, 279). The alignment of reformist goals and strategies across levels benefits from the inclusion of intended beneficiaries in the design, implementation and resource allocation for reform agendas (Fox and Gershman 2000; Fox 2005). Hence the importance of state-society interaction around food sovereignty or other empowerment reforms.

Food sovereignty in Latin America: three cases

The election of leftist leaders in Latin America signified a new regional shift in anti-US imperialism and the reintroduction of the state into development planning and policy. Notably, the election of Hugo Chavez in 1998 defied the Monroe doctrine and historical precedent of maintaining US interests within Latin American capitals. After the turn of the last decade, the elections of Rafael Correa in Ecuador, Evo Morales in Bolivia, Daniel Ortega in Nicaragua, Fernando Lugo in Paraguay and Luis Inácio 'Lula' da Silva in Brazil (among others) represented a significant defiant bloc united around a reinvigorated civil society and anti-imperialist discourse (Cockcroft 2006). At the same time, increased transnational ties between rural social movements helped bring agrarian concerns to the national and international political stage (Borras et al. 2008).

In Venezuela (1999), Ecuador (2008) and Bolivia (2009), new constitutions were adopted as part of this turn to the left, and a 'new Andean Constitutionalism' emerged (Schilling-Vacaflor 2011). While these governments nationalized key industries, strengthening their control of the economy, they also increased social spending, created legislation aimed to increase participation and representation, and adopted measures to increase the fulfillment of human rights – including the right to food sovereignty. There is still doubt as to whether these measures signify an alternative to free market principles or a 'bending and moulding' of existing political and economic structures that is more 'pro-regulation' than 'anti-capitalist' (Arditi 2008; Panizza 2005). In the following section, we critically review each country's insertion of food sovereignty into its consti-tution and their subsequent policies and programmes. We examine the tensions around the various forms of sovereignty, paying particular attention to how state-society inter-actions have developed around state-level food sovereignty efforts. Since the pursuit of food sovereignty ultimately requires changing the relations of access to and control over food and agricultural systems (from decision-making to productive resources), it is impera-tive that food sovereignty strategies are approached in a relational way – changing 'social relations of production and reproduction, of property and power' (Bernstein et al. 1992, 24).

Venezuela

Background

After a failed coup attempt in 1992, Lieutenant Colonel Hugo Chavez continued a move-ment 'from below' against years of social and economic exploitation by elite classes, before spending two years in prison. Declining socio-economic conditions amongst the middle and lower classes created a conducive environment for a dramatic transformative change. From 1979 to 1999, real per capita income declined by 27 percent – the worst in the region – while poverty increased from 17 percent in 1980 to 65 percent in 1996 (Wilpert 2007, 13). In 1998, Chavez was elected as President with 56 percent of the vote, marking the start of a political, social and economic transformation. Approving a new Constitution in 1999, President Hugo Chavez consolidated state power, while simultaneously opening up spaces to facilitate decentralized participatory democratic processes at the local level through social 'Misiones' and Communal Councils. While these reforms are intended to be redistributive and empower the marginalized, the highly contentious and conflicting 'dual power' that persists within and between state and societal forces has produced uneven, inconsistent and contested outcomes (Enriquez 2013, also see Kappeler 2013). This dual power is characterized by the co-existence of class powers which frequently exert conflicting influences over the state apparatus, presenting both opportunities and bar-riers to food sovereignty and other reformist agendas. When reformists within the state engage with like-minded societal actors in a mutually reinforcing way, pro-poor reformist agendas like food sovereignty can be realized (see Schiavoni 2014b).

Although Venezuela's Organic Law of Agro-food Security and Sovereignty was only approved in 2008, elements of food sovereignty were enshrined in its 1999 Constitution, specifically in Articles 305, 306 and 307. The 1999 Constitution was written by a consti-tutional assembly comprising 24 members elected nationally, three indigenous representa-tives and 104 elected representatives from their respective states (Wilpert 2003). 'Chavistas' represented 95% of the total representatives, and within six months the new constitution was subjected to a national vote where 71.8 percent approved, with an abstention rate of 55.6 percent (Wilpert 2003). Venezuela's 2008 Law, however, is a com-prehensive 143-page document covering many key principles inherent in a food sover-eignty concept (Gaceta Oficial 2008). Instead of outlining a few specific programmes, Venezuela has a variety of complementary initiatives that seek to build a pathway towards food sovereignty. Despite being a major net importer of food based on a history of urban-biased industrialization policies and an extremely high rate of urbanization, Venezuela has demonstrated significant structural reforms that distribute power in ways that support self-determination of food systems.

One element of Venezuela's food sovereignty strategy has been its state-led redistributive agrarian reform programme (see McKay 2011; Enríquez 2013 for the details of this programme). This programme encompasses a multitude of complementary programmes and policies for credit (FONDAS,[2] INDER,[3] BAV[4]), technical assistance (INTI,[5] CIARA,[6] FONDAS, *Misión Ché Guevara*, Cuban-Venezuela Agreement for agro-technical expertise), agroecology (INIA,[7] INSAI,[8] Cuba-Venezuela Agreement), infrastructure development (INDER), marketing (CVAL,[9] MERCAL[10]), and even a government agency established to defend the rights of agrarian reform beneficiaries for legal disputes free of charge (Enríquez 2013). This programme is oriented towards improving access to land, food and markets.

Access to land. In 2001, *Misión Zamora* was established under the Land Law with the following key objectives: set limits on the size of landholdings; tax unused property as an incentive to spur agricultural growth; redistribute state-owned land to peasant families and cooperatives; and lastly, as of 2005, to expropriate/recover fallow/illegally-held land from the private sector for the purpose of redistribution (Delong 2005). While in 2001 land subject to expropriation was defined as 'only high-quality idle agricultural land of over 100 hectares or lower quality idle agricultural land of over 5000 hectares (*latifundia*)' (Wilpert 2007, 111), as of 2010, *latifundia* is defined as being 'a piece of land that is larger than the average in its region or is not producing at 80 percent of its productive capacity' (Suggett 2010). This agrarian reform programme is designed to dismantle the *latifundia* and reinvigorate the countryside with more equitable resource distribution. From 2001 to 2010, over 5.5 million hectares of arable land has been 'recovered', benefitting over 1 million people (Wilpert 2011; Enríquez 2013, 622). While this radical reform programme has not gone uncontested by capitalist elites within and outside the state, the most recent modification integrates rural workers into implementing the reform themselves by giving ownership to those working (renting) land and thus incorporating a 'land to the tiller' element in the Land Law (Enríquez 2013, 631). This modification cedes a certain degree of responsibility and political power to rural workers to hold state and societal actors accountable to reformist measures, therefore interacting with efforts by pro-reform state actors in a mutually reinforcing way (see Fox 1993).

Access to food and markets. Under the Ministry of Food, *Misión Mercal* was established as a state-run food company, initially to combat the food shortages that plagued the country during the corporate lock-out in December 2002. *Misión Mercal* is a chain of

---

[2]Development Fund for Socialist Agriculture.
[3]Rural Development Institute.
[4]Agricultural Bank of Venezuela.
[5]National Land Institute.
[6]Foundation for Training and Innovation for Rural Development.
[7]National Institute of Agricultural Research.
[8]National Institute of Integral Agricultural Health.
[9]Venezuelan Food Corporation.
[10]Mercados de Alimentos.

government-subsidized grocery stores that sell food at prices 'roughly 39 percent below traditional supermarkets' (Isaacs et al. 2009). The Mercals, along with PDVAL,[11] are distribution links of the state-run intermediary chain which provide low-income Venezuelans with food staples at affordable rates. Large storage spaces, distribution centres and transportation networks have also been set up to combat food speculation, hoarding and sabotage (Isaacs et al. 2009). In 2010, there were 16,600 Mercals nationwide, employing roughly 85,000 workers (Smith 2010). In addition to Mercals, the Mission has set up 6075 *Casas de Alimentación*, or food banks, which provide free meals to roughly 900,000 people in need (Schiavoni and Camacaro 2009). Mercals account for roughly 20–30 percent of total food sales in Venezuela, with roughly two-thirds of the population visiting the stores regularly (Government of Canada 2011).

Despite these notable successes, including being recognized by the FAO as one of the 16 countries to reach the 1996 World Food Summit's goal of halving the total number of their undernourished, processes of agrarian transformation in Venezuela are not without problems (FAO 2013). Kappeler, for example, highlights the struggles in incentivizing urbanites to move to the countryside and notes the many failures when urbanites with 'little practical experience in the field of agriculture' resettled to work on rural cooperatives (2013, 6). Kappeler also points to the contradictory processes that exist with Venezuela's agro-industrial state enterprises and the food sovereignty agenda. Despite replacing the *latifundia* in many parts of the country, Kappeler argues that these state enterprises have 'not reduced divisions of labor in the agriculture sector (as many supporters of food sovereignty suggest is required), but replaced one set of tensions with another' (2013, 12). While one could argue that eliminating private capital's control over a country's food and agricultural systems could be a first step towards a food sovereignty process, Kappeler rightly points out the unevenness and inconsistencies related to Venezuela's current food sovereignty agenda.

While these efforts towards improving access to land, food and markets are often held up as the principal state mechanisms supporting food sovereignty in Venezuela (e.g. Kappeler 2013), we suggest that a third arena, the Communal Councils, provides the most significant space for empowerment and social transformation around food systems (see also Marcano 2009; Schiavoni 2014b). Indeed, it is in the Communal Councils that we can see the most significant structural reforms, as well as the creation of spaces for sovereignty at smaller scales.

Sovereignty of whom relative to what?

One central element of Venezuela's food sovereignty strategy is its Communal Councils, which are designed to foster a high degree of empowerment, participatory spaces and decentralized decision-making. Communal Councils began forming in 2005 and were officially recognized in 2006 with the Law of Communal Councils, which was reformed in 2009. Communal Councils are locally run organizations which enable people to exercise community governance and directly manage their own self-defined development needs over a self-defined geographic space.[12] The latest government figures indicate that there are 41,783 Communal Councils registered to date, each of which consists of between 150 and 400 families in urban areas, a minimum of 20 families in rural areas and at least 10 families in indigenous

---

[11]Productora y Distribuidora Venezolana de Alimentos.
[12]Communal Councils are not defined geographically by municipal boundaries.

zones (MPComunas 2014). Through a participatory decision-making process, all members of a community over the age of 15 can participate in the citizens' assembly, which is the council's principal decision-making body. Development plans and specific projects are put forward and voted on by the citizens' assembly who also elect representatives for two-year periods to work in a variety of committees which focus on issues such as health, education, natural resource management, finance, social control and monitoring, among others. Once approved by the assembly, financing from the government and state-funded foundations is transferred to the council's finance commission, bypassing any regional, provincial or municipal organs. Further, these councils are now combining in their respective geographic areas to create 'Socialist Communes'. As of the time of writing, 612 communes have been officially registered, which collectively integrate their local Communal Council initiatives to cover larger social and geographic scales over longer periods of time (MPComunas 2014). These systems of self-management are intended to empower the formerly excluded classes in political processes, enhancing local social capital and 'the capacity of the poor to network and organize collectively' (Petras and Veltmeyer 2006, 84).

According to Venezuelan school teacher and community organizer Jesus Rojas – who is also a member of the planning committee for his Communal Council in Rio Tocuyo, Lara, Venezuela – the 'formation of Communal Councils and Socialist Communes are constantly growing and are playing the most important role in local community empowerment and the revolutionary process' (interview, 10 August 2013). As a member of the planning committee, Rojas explained how the 14 Communal Councils in his region have officially registered as a Socialist Commune and are in the process of implementing larger-scale projects including expanding and improving infrastructure, electricity, water access and sewage systems, but also providing agricultural inputs and technical assistance for farmers, and expanding '*los centros acopios*' (collection centres) where farmers can sell their crops and receive a better price than the market alternative. This is one part of the state-owned Venezuelan Agricultural Corporation's initiative that procures crops from farmers and distributes them to several socialist food markets. Farmers are therefore more able to control their own production needs and directly take charge of their own situation in terms of inputs, production and access to markets. For small farmers, one of the most important components of this process is that 'they are free from the exploitative private intermediaries who used to reap all the profits and take advantage of both producers and consumer' (interview, Jesus Rojas, 10 August 2013).

While Communal Councils and Communes are dependent on financial resources from the state, they represent a new organ and space which work in parallel with traditional municipal and state-level government structures. This type of arrangement exemplifies the multiple dimensions of sovereignty across scales and the dynamic state-society relationship which uses 'state power at one level to sustain activities at another plane' (Iles and Montenegro 2013, 9). Communal Councils and their extended networks of Socialist Communes are therefore characteristic of a polycentric system wherein constituting elements act independently yet are capable of ordering relationships to each other (Ostrom 1972). As long as the state continues to guarantee the rights and autonomy of the Communal Councils and Socialist Communes to define, manage and control their own local and regional development needs, this kind of polycentric system may be a model for 'building new institutional conduits' for food sovereignty (Iles and Montenegro 2013, 9).

At the same time, decision-making within Communal Councils can be tense and contested, and struggles over diverging interests mean that councils are also an arena of debate and contestation. Forms of class struggle therefore play out during Communal Council and Socialist Commune assemblies as societal actors with diverse interests negotiate the community's development needs in a participatory way. While we cannot assume that food sovereignty is being advanced in all of the Communal Councils, this type of participatory democratic decision-making and degree of local sovereignty over development processes by the community promote the types of political spaces that food sovereignty movements seek to engender.

Lessons from Venezuela

The process of transformation in Venezuela is certainly not without its flaws as deeply entrenched class conflicts continue and a 'dual power' endures (Enriquez 2013). However, the continued expansion of Communal Councils, Socialist Communes and redistributive agrarian reform programme is shifting power and autonomy to organized communities and creating dynamic spaces for new forms of state-society collaboration. An important aspect of this process is that it is not just based on investment injection or socio-economic protection. Public spaces for political participation are being created through Communal Councils, which allow newly empowered pro-reformists within society to engage and make demands to the state. Further, the agrarian reform programme, though uneven and inconsistent in certain places, is reshaping rural power relations through direct resource-based transfers of wealth. These pro-poor initiatives are leading to empowering environments which enable people to not only fulfil their rights, but push for further reforms. The combination of reforms which have facilitated spaces of interaction between pro-reform state and societal actors and zero-sum resource-based transfers of wealth have led to forms of empowerment and, despite tensions and inconsistencies, are creating conditions for a transition to food sovereignty.[13]

Ecuador

Background

The election of Rafael Correa in 2006 was built on his campaign of a Citizen's Revolution (*Revolución Cuidania*) that promised, among other things, a redrafting of the constitution in order to redefine national development objectives and citizenship rights. His populist rise followed decades of rural neglect and limited political participation of peasant and indigenous peoples. Following widespread privatization and economic liberalization in the mid-1990s, rural organizations launched massive protests that put them, and their demands, on the national political agenda. In his first year in office, Correa promised a constituent assembly to incorporate citizen participation in rewriting the constitution which was widely supported through a public referendum. The referendum was also a democratic means to elect the constituent assembly itself, of which 80 out of 130 members were from Correa's party (*Movimiento Alianza Pais*) (Conaghan 2008). As the constitution was rewritten through this assembly, one of the strongest demands from social movements and civil society was for the constitutional right to food sovereignty and agrarian reform (Fernández and Puente 2012).

The new constitution was ratified and signed into law on 28 September 2008. In it, food sovereignty and agrarian reform are principally addressed in Chapter IV, which defines food sovereignty as 'a strategic objective and an obligation of the *state* that persons, communities, peoples and nations achieve self-sufficiency with respect to healthy and culturally appropriate food on a permanent basis' (Asamblea Nacional 2008, emphasis added). The 14

---

[13]These new spaces developed during the Chávez era. How and the extent to which they continue to evolve in the post-Chávez period remains an open-ended question as a shift in the 'dual power' of the state and extreme class conflict in society could roll back these important spaces.

'responsibilities of the state' include the adoption of fiscal policies to prevent reliance on food imports; redistributive policies that permit peasants access to land, water and other productive resources; development of scientific research and technological innovation to guarantee food sovereignty; and the development and regulation of biotechnology, among others (see Asemblea Nacional 2008, 138–9).

The explicit responsibilities of the state listed in the constitution are articulated into policy initiatives through the National Plan of Good Living (*Plan Nacional de Buen Vivir*) (SEN-PLADES 2009) and the Food Sovereignty Law (LORSA). This national development plan establishes a more definitive 'call to action' by proposing a framework that outlines the government's objectives for ensuring all citizens a right to good living and their constitutional promises. The term Good Living (*Buen Vivir/Sumak Kawsay*) is intended to reflect an indigenous worldview of how to organize society around the community, environment and living within socially determined needs (see Gudynas 2011; Flor 2013). What is particularly interesting about the inclusion of the concept of Good Living in the constitution is that it has enabled a shared political discourse of resource nationalization to integrate the interests of indigenous social movements, peasant organizations and the Ecuadorian state. One of the ways this has been translated in state policies is through the LORSA, which intends to bridge the interests of civil society with the state in the implementation of the constitutional mandate for food sovereignty and Good Living development objectives.

Land redistribution. Issues of land use and distribution are central to the way the new constitution addresses food sovereignty. Immediately following the discussion of food sovereignty, the constitution states that 'the state will determine the use and access to land that should fulfill a social and environmental function' (Article 282, 138). However, despite the imperative for land redistribution in the new constitution and the continued calls for peasant-led agrarian reform, little progress on policies and programmes that significantly influence the distribution of land has been made (Giunta 2013).

The primary mechanism oriented towards land distribution is the National Land Fund, which is intended to 'regulate the equitable access of land for peasants' (Article 282, 138). However, while the newly drafted constitution identifies the state as the principal arbiter of the distribution of land, it does little to elaborate how agrarian reform can and should take place. In other words, there is no mention of what actors should be involved and what lands are to be (re)distributed. The same article also prohibits the existence of *latifundia* and the hoarding or privatization of water and its sources, but does not elaborate on how lands would be expropriated (Giunta 2013).

The country's post-2008 agrarian reform (Land Plan – *Plan Tierras*) was designed by the Ministry of Agriculture, Livestock, Aquaculture and Fisheries (MAGAP) with several ambitious and misleading promises on expropriating *lantifundia* and redistributing land (both state-owned and expropriations). Publically, MAGAP has said it plans to transfer 2.5 million hectares to landless peasants through offering state land and expropriating private and unused land. However, estimates of land in the hands of the state vary, both by top government officials, and data in the Land Plan itself, from 69,000 hectares to 200,000 hectares (Peralta 2011, 44). Around 1 million hectares were supposed to be purchased through the Land Fund; however, these promises have not been fulfilled (the Land Plan ended in 2013). The latest budget evaluation in 2010 showed that only USD 4 million went to land redistribution despite an original proposition of USD 10 million (Herrera et al. 2010). The plan also calls for a budget of USD 38 million over four years to carry out the reform. As of March 2013, out of the over 2 million hectares promised to peasants, the state has only distributed 25,000 hectares (MAGAP 2013).

Despite the lack of comprehensive agrarian reform, the government has implemented what it calls an 'Agrarian Revolution' that utilizes a territorial strategy of increasing federal resources for agrarian schools and incentivizing farmer organization. A number of programs and policies complement this strategy by seeking to expand market access by farmers and their organizations through expanded social spending. However, even these programs have been subject to scrutiny as federal funding levels have been grossly unequal between different regions. While overall spending in agriculture has almost doubled under Correa, his home province of Manabí received 71 percent of all agricultural funds from 2005 to 2009 (Herrera et al. 2010).

Historically, MAGAP has been a political arm of Ecuador's *latifundia*, and large private interests continue to have a strong influence. These anti-reform actors have constrained the potential for any structural change through agrarian reform efforts despite public commitments of the president and his political allies. Indeed, MAGAP's failure regarding agrarian reform comes after decades of unfulfilled promises to peasant and indigenous agriculturalists (Yashar 2005). Thus, even though agrarian reform and food sovereignty is presented as a goal of the state, there is little to show that MAGAP will substantially change in order to put these goals into practice (Clark 2013). Even the most recently appointed minister of MAGAP said, in May of 2011, that 'peasants should have no illusions regarding the management [of MAGAP] and that a center-right institution is aiming to increase the productivity and competitiveness of Ecuadorian agriculture in the global market' (Rosero et al. 2011). Overall, the Ecuadorian constitution fell short of translating the discursive power of food sovereignty as an ongoing and contested political arena into substantive political and economic change through agrarian reform.

Sovereignty of whom relative to what?

One of the key tensions with regards to food sovereignty in national politics in Ecuador is that there are many civil society actors in Ecuador demanding food sovereignty and agrarian reform. These groups have divergent conceptions of sovereignty and appropriate land use, and vary in their approach to negotiate with state bureaucrats and bureaucracies (Yashar 2005, 72, 138–40). Indigenous groups have played an important role in particular, having gained significant political strength and contributed to Correa's electoral success (Becker 2011a, 2011b). Some of the most prominent organizations that have contributed to communicating demands to the constituent assembly have been: CONAIE,[14] FENOCIN,[15] FEINE,[16] CONFEUNASSC-CNC[17] and Ecuarunari.[18] These movements presented their long list of demands to the assembly, which included explicit objectives

---

[14]National Indigenous Confederation of Ecuador (*Confederación Nacional de Indígenas del Ecuador – CONAIE*) is a confederation that includes some of the organizations also involved in the constituent assembly (i.e. Ecuanari).
[15]National Federation of Indigenous and Afro-descendant Peasants of Ecuador (*Federación Nacional de Organizaciones Campesinas, Indígenas e Negras del Ecuador*).
[16]Ecuadorian Federation of Indigenous Evangelicals (*Federación Nacional de Indígenas Evangelicas*).
[17]National Affiliated Confederation of Peasant Social Security – National Peasant Coordination (Confederación Nacional de Afiliados al Seguro Social Campesino – Coordinadora Nacional Campesina).
[18]National Confederation of the Quichua Community (*Confederación de los Pueblos de Nacionalidad de Kichua del Ecuador*).

for food sovereignty (see CONAIE 2007 and FENOCIN, n.d.),[19] and called on the state to play a central role by nationalizing natural resources, supporting small-scale agriculture through policy initiatives, and redistributing land. The organization of the constituent assembly was divided into several groups with specific tasks to coordinate and integrate the various demands of civil society into the constitution. The sixth assembly took up food sovereignty and agrarian issues and was specifically tasked with listening to indigenous and peasant organizations. This assembly was where issues of sovereignty – both in terms of food sovereignty and the sovereignty of indigenous nations – were raised and contested. The various organizations included in this assembly used different strategies for including their members and representing their voices to the assembly. For example, while CONAIE sought to unify more generally around broad 'themes' of food sovereignty and insisted on weekly discussions with the assembly, FENOCIN was fixed on land reform and made demands in a more unidirectional manner (Rosero et al. 2011). Beyond these divergent strategies, the organizations also had different understandings of what 'nation' meant and how and to what degree 'sovereignty' was based on collective nation building independent of the state (in the context of plurinationality). These organizations differed racially, geographically, demographically, economically and culturally, but were ultimately required to negotiate and agree upon a coherent national conception of food sovereignty.

From November 2007 until January 2008, the sixth assembly established a 'citizens' forum' throughout numerous towns and cities across Ecuador that resulted in around 250 proposals for food sovereignty and other agrarian issues. Two prominent academics from Correa's party analysed the proposals and drafted a synthesized report that was presented to the assembly (Rosero 2008). After this report passed with a majority vote in the assembly, a meeting was held with leaders of peasant organizations and social movements to validate the results. During this meeting, there were significant disagreements over the understandings of what food sovereignty meant for each organization – what was described as 'putting personal interests [of the organizations] over that of the collective good of the Ecuadorian people' (Andrango 2008 cited in Rosero et al. 2011). When the organizations finally arrived at an agreement (what is called the 'Consensus of Quito'), many concessions had been made in order to approve a final plan for the assembly. Conceptually, they all agreed that food sovereignty and its policies were the right of communities but should be executed through state policies. Agrarian reform, and the expropriation of 'unproductive or unused lands', was demanded but met with resistance within the assembly, which informed civil society leaders that such a reform would be dealt with through legal measures and carried out by MAGAP (Herrera et al. 2010; Rosero et al. 2011). Thus, while the Constituent Assembly opened up a novel space of democratic engagement around food sovereignty, the execution of the resulting vision was left in the hands of the same old structures and bureaucracy. As described above, the execution of the food sovereignty vision from the constitution was ultimately unsuccessful. The necessity to produce a single government document in a short amount of time was undoubtedly a problematic task for civil society. As a result of these conditions and concessions, a strong alliance did not form between these organizations and the pro-reform members of the constituent assembly.

---

[19]CONAIE's proposal can be read here: http://www.iee.org.ec/publicaciones/INDIGENA/ConaieAsamblea.pdf;
    FENOCIN'S proposal can be read here: http://www.fenocin.org/.

Lessons from Ecuador

While the constituent assembly opened the opportunity for both state and societal actors to participate in the rethinking of national development priorities, the structural transformations of society and the economy as envisioned in the constitution have yet to be realized. Many indigenous organizations and peasant movements have since withdrawn support from the Correa government, with CONAIE's president even calling his administration 'capitalist and neoliberal', as early as 2009 (El Universal 2009). While the constitution should be celebrated as a significant victory for citizens' rights to food sovereignty, the guarantor of those rights will need to revisit longstanding demands for structural change to fulfil its constitutional duties.

Rather than facilitating spaces for communities to construct and define their own food systems, constitutional food sovereignty in Ecuador relies almost exclusively on the state as sovereign rather than any kind of mutually empowering state-society synergy. In other words, '[t]he shift in state-society relations in Ecuador has largely strengthened the power of the state vis-à-vis civil society' (Clark 2013, 26). Though the food sovereignty concept provided a means through which social movements and peasant organizations could make demands for reform, state-level food sovereignty efforts failed to change existing relations of production and power (see Giunta 2013). In this context, food sovereignty was viewed as potential mechanism of agrarian reform, rather than as an end in itself. A critical obstacle was that redistributive agrarian reform did not materialize, in large part due to political contestations within the state apparatus (i.e. MAGAP). Nevertheless, the process of rewriting the constitution did open up what Deborah Yashar (2005, 29) calls 'political associational space', or the ability for organizations to dialogue and 'engage in sustained legal organizing'. Yet this political moment failed to produce a coherent and compelling enough vision to ensure the restructuring of political and economic resources in the country. The historical and ongoing constraints of government bureaucracies erected insurmountable structural barriers that prevented the radical redistribution of power and material resources. That is, in this case the state had the autonomy to establish constitutional goals around food sovereignty that were quite radical, but pro-reform state and societal actors lacked the capacity, or strong 'social networks', to take advantage of the political opportunity and transform these goals into the kind of change that significantly alter food systems in ways that support food sovereignty (see Yashar 2005, 79).

Bolivia

Background

Bolivia's military dictatorships in the 1970s and early 1980s, followed by the onset of neoliberal policies through the structural adjustment programme's 'New Economic Policy' (NEP) in 1985, dismantled public services and exposed vulnerable rural livelihoods to foreign competition and capital accumulation. This was compounded by what Kohl and Farthing call a 'perfect economic storm' consisting of:

> the inability of two successive governments to generate jobs and significant economic growth; an aggressive coca eradication programme that destroyed the regional economy of Cochabamba; the collapse of the Argentine economy, eliminating Bolivia's largest labour market and, as important, terminating workers' remittances; and the decline in government revenue occasioned by privatization of the state oil company. (Kohl and Farthing 2006, 149)

The privatization of the state-owned water company SEMAPA *(Servicio Municipal de Agua Potable y Alcantarillado)* and the resulting 'Cochabamba Water War' (Olivera and Lewis 2004), combined with massive protests by Bolivia's largest union of peasants, CSUTCB[20] and a general strike called by Bolivia's Worker's Confederation (COB), reflected the general discontent among the Bolivian middle and lower classes. This led to a tumultuous three years of clashes between protesters and the state, including violent military repressions of protests and the death of over 60 protesters, and ultimately, the overthrow of two Bolivian presidents. The 2005 election saw the clear victory of Evo Morales, leader of the coca growers' union and a central figure in negotiating the transition of power from former President Gonzalo Sanchez de Lozada and his Vice-President turned President Carlos Mesa. This launched a new era in Bolivian politics, led by Morales' party, the Movement Towards Socialism (MAS), which was closely linked to the emergent indigenous, anti-colonial and populist social movements that had come together in opposition to the neo-liberal reforms of the 1990s and beyond. This broad coalition of peasant, worker and indigenous organizations came to form the *Pacto de Unidad* (Unity Pact) which was essential in Morales' rise to power and became integrated, to varying degrees, within the new regime.

One of Morales' first priorities was to initiate a process through which a new constitution would be written. This followed up on the demands for a constituent assembly made by increasingly visible indigenous and peasant organizations beginning in the early 2000s, which sought to ensure the protection of indigenous territory in light of the new recognition of Bolivia as a multicultural and pluri-ethnic state (Assies 2006). A Constituent Assembly was convened in 2006, but the struggles of this assembly to write a constitution that captured the goals of its highly varied members – 255 elected constituents – reflect the deep divisions within the country and the difficulties of shifting towards inclusive and participatory democracy. When the constitution was written and finally approved in 2009, it included food sovereignty as a central element of several sections. It first refers to food sovereignty in the context of international relations and treaties, suggesting that they must function to meet the interests and sovereignty – including food sovereignty – of the people. Article 255 (Constitución Política del Estado Plurinacional de Bolivia, 2009) stipulates:

> negotiation, signing, and ratification of international treaties shall be governed by the principles of ... food security and food sovereignty for all; prohibiting the import, production and marketing of GMOs [genetically modified organisms] and toxic elements that can harm human health and the environment.

Further, the chapter on 'Sustainable Integrated Rural Development' emphasizes food sovereignty as integral to rural development, laying out the objective to 'ensure food security and sovereignty, prioritizing domestic production and consumption ... and establishing mechanisms to protect Bolivian agriculture' (Constitución Política del Estado Plurinacional de Bolivia, 2009, art. 405, 406).

The constitutional presence of food sovereignty follows up on the inclusion of the concept in the other important policy documents of Morales' administration. For instance, in the first National Development Plan elaborated under Morales in 2006, food sovereignty

---

[20]Confederación Sindical Única de Trabajadores Campesinas de Bolivia, or the Confederated Union of Rural Workers of Bolivia.

was laid out as a key element of a new vision of development. In 2008, this was elaborated into the Rural Development and Food Sovereignty and Security policy (PSSA), which was to be implemented through four main programs: (1) SEMBRAR,[21] which promotes private-public partnerships and is largely dependent on overseas development assistance for short-term investment projects designed to increase food production (MDRyT 2010, 63, Liendo 2011); (2) CRIAR,[22] which finances community-led initiatives to support small-scale agriculture (MDRyT 2010); (3) EMPODERAR,[23] which funds agro-entrepreneurial development projects (Liendo 2011, MDRyT 2010); and (4) Promotion of Agroecological Production (*Fomento a la Produccion Ecologica/Organica*), which supports agroecological producers with production and marketing {MDRyT 2010, 66). These programs relied upon external financing and did not significantly restructure agriculture or governance, nor did they transform relations of production. Thus, the programs had limited impact on food sovereignty goals.

A more direct potential pathway to supporting food sovereignty was Bolivia's 'Agrarian Revolution' under the 2006 *Ley de Reconduccion* no. 3545 (Extension Law), which redefines natural resources as state property, and puts more emphasis on state control and oversight over land consolidation and labour relations (Valdivia 2010, 74). The programme is characterized by four main policy aims: (1) distribution of state-owned land and redistribution by expropriation of land not serving a 'socio-economic function' (FES) to indigenous peoples and peasant communities; (2) mechanization of agriculture; (3) subsidized credits for small-scale producers; and (4) markets for the products of peasant origin (Urioste 2010). By 2010, the agrarian reform appeared to be relatively successful; more than 31 million hectares were titled and over 100,000 of these titles were distributed to 174,249 beneficiaries (INRA 2010; Redo et al. 2011). However, in the Department of Santa Cruz, where over two thirds of total cultivated land is located including 98 percent of large-scale soy plantations, a mere 12 percent of the territory has been regularized (Redo et al. 2011, 234). In addition, 91 percent of titled land has 'been endowed by the state and are composed entirely of forest reserves' (Redo et al. 2011, 237). Thus, while the Agrarian Revolution was intended to challenge the prevailing unequal agrarian structure, it has failed to do so, while also contributing to widespread deforestation as new frontiers expand into Bolivia's rich biodiverse areas of Amazonian, Andean and Chaco forests (Hecht 2005, 377).

This inability to dismantle unequal agrarian structures is related to a historical consolidation of elite power, particularly in the eastern lowlands region referred to as the '*Media Luna*' for its shape that looks like a half moon. Bolivia's eastern lowlands of Santa Cruz have been dominated by a capitalist class of agro-elites since the agrarian reform of 1953. This reform, devised by the US-designed Bohan Plan's 'march to the east', distributed large-scale landholdings between 500 and 50,000 hectares to well-connected capitalist elites (Valdivia 2010, 69). This was followed by fraudulent land and resource concentration by the dictatorships from 1971 to 1982 (Webber 2008; Urioste 2010), and the subsequent neoliberal-era reforms prior to the election of Evo Morales in 2006 (Kay and Urioste 2007). A high degree of territorial dominance and structural inequality in the lowlands has therefore been rooted in historical processes and institutionalized socially through decades of political and economic influences.

---

[21]Meaning 'to plant' or 'to sow'.
[22]Creación de Iniciativas Alimentarias Rurales.
[23]Emprendimientos Organizados para el Desarrollo Rural Autogestionario.

Though the historical class inequalities undoubtedly have created barriers for pro-reform social forces, the current 'Agrarian Revolution' has also failed to dismantle such structures. The land ceiling of 5000 ha, for example, is essentially rendered obsolete by Article 315 (II) which states that if a corporation has several 'owners' or 'partners' each can have up to a maximum of 5000 hectares, making land-size limits virtually non-existent. Furthermore, the land ceiling only applies to land acquired after 2009, adding to its ineffectiveness (Article 399). The 'Agrarian Revolution' also encourages and provides credit for farmers to mechanize their production methods, failing to foresee the increased dependence on petroleum-based inputs and debt creation this would entail for the majority of family farmers who control under 0.7 ha of land each[24] (Urioste 2010, 9; INE 2011; World Bank 2007). These shortcomings in transforming the unequal land-based social structure impede a pathway towards food sovereignty. This is compounded by the fact that the externally funded project-based PSSA programmes are established through temporary capital injection for relatively short-term project goals.

Sovereignty of whom relative to what?

The Morales administration has mobilized food sovereignty as an element in a broader project of decolonization. In the newly rewritten constitution and recent framework laws, they draw upon indigenous and social movement ontologies – like *Sumaq Kawsay*[25] and food sovereignty – that contest Northern visions of development (Gudynas 2011). The uses of these concepts are both strategic and essentializing, but are an attempt to build an anti-colonial foundation while also seeking to address poverty, particularly in the rural sector, within that global structural environment. However, the Morales administration has been heavily critiqued for failing to follow through on its radical positions and promises, suggesting that this move is simply symbolic, at best, or a strategy to shore up supporters and expand power, at worst. For instance, Bolivian sociologist and social critic Silvia Rivera Cusicanqui argues that Morales' claims of indigeneity and his calls for decolonization are purely rhetorical, and that the work of his administration has done little to disrupt the 'hegemonic models that places [Bolivia] as the back yard of the large transnational companies' (quoted in Erbol 2014).

Morales has used the threat of the conservative lowland politics as a way to keep social movements in line and remove their ability to exert pressure over the direction his administration takes – ultimately silencing the social movement threat while at the same time keeping up the appearance of widespread social movement support and involvement (Silva 2014). Despite this, however, social movement groups in Bolivia are increasingly stepping away from Morales and vocalizing a critique that his administration is failing to put into policy and practice any real structural change that reflects the indigenous ontologies Morales purports to support. For instance, these groups heavily criticize the continued resource extraction model of development (Weinberg 2010a, 2010b; Fabricant 2013), which Morales relies upon to generate the funds to support the expansion of social protections for the poor and rural sector (Postero 2010). This emerging schism was visible at the 2011 World People's Conference on the Rights of Mother Earth, hosted by Morales in Cochabamba, Bolivia, which

---

[24]Authors' calculation based on data from INE (2011) and World Bank (2007, 19) [(2,861,330 ha total arable land × 14%)/(660,000 total farm units × 87% smallholders) = 0.698 ha per unit].
[25]Closely related to the Good Living concept deployed in Ecuador, discussed above.

brought together government representatives and delegates from social movements around the world. A discussion on resource extraction within the Morales administration was pushed out of the official conference (see Albro 2013), with the official organizers of the conference seeking to silence these critiques of the Morales government.

Overall, as Morales' decolonization project unfolds, there is the explicit focus on building Bolivian sovereignty vis-à-vis international institutions and powers, particularly the United States. But there is also the threat to national sovereignty from the elites in the eastern lowlands. In this context, the state policies are guided by defending sovereignty at the national level such that a significant redistribution of power has not emerged. At the same time, while there is the appearance of productive state-society relations – particularly with social movements – in fact these relations have led to a high degree of co-optation by the state, resulting in a loss of autonomy amongst social movements and thus a lack of empowerment.

Lessons from Bolivia

While in the constitution and elsewhere, such as the National Development Plans, the Law of Mother Earth and the Integral Development for Living Well, food sovereignty has been enshrined as a right of Bolivian peoples, the actual policies put into effect erode the possibilities to enact food sovereignty goals in practice. For example, in a follow-up to the Law of Mother Earth, Law 337 seeks to reduce deforestation and improve agricultural productivity in the Amazon region of the country. But this law was supported by the large agribusiness lobby as it actually has the effect of encouraging agribusiness expansion in the region because it creates the expectations of future pardon for illegal deforestation and sets very low fines for such transgressions (Mongabay 2013). Despite a general commitment to food sovereignty, there has been an inability to enact meaningful structural changes that might contribute to the achievement of food sovereignty on the ground.

Thus, in Bolivia, these commitments to support food sovereignty have largely failed to create spaces for participatory democratic decision-making and control over resources, or to give local peoples the opportunity to carry out a food sovereignty strategy as defined by them. Nonetheless, Morales has worked to throw off the mantle of control by global elites, consolidating state power over national resources and pushing back against control by external state and international institutions. However, the high degree of control over land and resources by agro-industrial elites in the 'Media Luna' has constrained the capacity of the state to put forth and carry out food sovereignty reforms. While the Morales administration is much more sympathetic than previous governments in Bolivia to the concerns, needs and ideas of rural and indigenous peoples and popular classes, the challenge of creating a space for alternative notions of development and exercising sovereignty in the face of global and national elites has constrained the state's capacity towards structural change. Furthermore, many of the key social movements have lost a certain degree of autonomy through their alliance and direct affiliation with the MAS. While recent developments have led to divisions within the *Pacto de Unidad*, perhaps the most important organization for food sovereignty, the CSUTCB, has maintained a strong alliance with the MAS and has arguably lost much of its autonomy to push the state for more reforms.

State pathways towards food sovereignty

The rights to food sovereignty as expressed by La Via Campesina and federal governments in Venezuela, Bolivia and Ecuador appear relatively similar in description. However, the alignment of state and social forces and the character of state power (state autonomy and capacity) differ within each case, leading to different outcomes. In this paper, we argue that despite similar state-level rhetorical and constitutional uses of food sovereignty in these three countries, the concept has been carried out according to particular goals, strategies and processes with very different results.

The case studies examined here demonstrate that legal and constitutional frameworks alone fail to create conditions for food sovereignty. Laws and rights alone do not lead to social justice, which depends as well on a way to put these nominal protections into practice. As Patel (2009, 669) argues, 'it is insufficient to consider only the structures that might guarantee the rights that constitute food sovereignty – it is also vital to consider the substantive policies, process, and politics that go to make up food sovereignty'. This is particularly true in relation to rural spaces and poor or marginalized peoples. These legal frames and protections are interpreted and implemented in a matter that reflects the prevailing social relations of power in the countryside and nation more broadly. Laws and policies are, as Borras and Franco (2010, 9; see also Franco 2008) point out,

> not self-interpreting and not self-implementing. It is during the interaction between various, often conflicting, actors within the state and in society that land policies are actually interpreted, activated and implemented (or not) in a variety of ways from one place to another over time.

This is why it is helpful to think of food sovereignty efforts in terms of autonomy and capacity, to examine how the ability to undertake meaningful reforms is promoted or constrained along these two dimensions of power.

If state food sovereignty efforts are going to truly promote peoples' 'right to self-determination ... to redefine for themselves the substance of the food relations appropriate to their geographies' (Patel and McMichael 2004, 249; see above), they must put into place radically new policies, processes and politics that facilitate these goals. This will necessarily entail rethinking the contemporary structures through which governance around food and agricultural systems takes place. Thus, food sovereignty is a space of political and social struggle to radically restructure relations of resource access and control. Creating such space depends upon a political restructuring that allows for the democratic conversation about food policy, rather than being the force that brings about such changes (Patel 2009, 679). Bolivian and Ecuadorian attempts to implement food sovereignty projects, such as Bolivia's public-private partnerships for food production strategies (SEMBRAR) and their emphasis on agricultural modernization and mechanization, or Ecuador's reliance on expanded agricultural credit as a central element of their agrarian reform, are more aptly described as temporary residual solutions than a significant restructuring of social relations. Indeed, while such initiatives may help to resolve immediate needs and bring greater public and political attention to the rural sector, they fail to directly contribute to the creation of participatory democratic decision-making or lead to the transfers of wealth and power that are much more likely to generate the restructuring of social relations necessary for food sovereignty. These efforts to create favourable market conditions, technological transfers and the injection of short-term investment represent residual approaches that repackage market-oriented strategies of food security as food sovereignty rather than facilitate structural change (see Bernstein et al. 1992). Without any transformative processes being pursued, food sovereignty as a discourse has been used to galvanize support across agrarian and indigenous populations. Food sovereignty strategies have therefore been 'simplified' as temporary projects and capital injections, which ultimately fail to address the structural inequalities that govern capitalist food systems. While this may contribute to state sovereignty relative to both internal and external forces, it does not contribute to sovereignty at the community or local level.

Among the three cases examined here, the attempts by the Venezuelan state have come the closest to facilitating a structural shift that promotes local control over food and food systems. Venezuela's Communal Councils have been instrumental in empowering previously excluded local people through participatory democratic processes. Combined with a redistributive state-led agrarian reform programme that is working to dismantle an unequal agrarian structure, Venezuela is undergoing a process of structural transformation and creating spaces for people to define, determine, manage and implement their food and agricultural systems in a decentralized, participatory way. In other words, the state is establishing conditions with the onus on the people to define and create food sovereignty. Pro-reformist state actors are attempting to restructure the social relations of production through land-based transfers of power as well as political transfers of power through Communal Councils and Socialist Communes. Though these processes are not without tensions and are unravelling unevenly across geographic space and between government initiatives (see Kappeler 2013), they are facilitating local empowerment through participation and are conducive to establishing mutually reinforcing symbiotic state-society relations that can reshape existing power structures. Approaching problems of food systems and unequal agrarian structures in such a relational way has contributed to the ability of Venezuela to instigate the transformative change required do develop a viable pathway toward food sovereignty.

Contemporary corporate assault on land resources and labour in the context of multiple crises (food, climate, fuel, finance) and the related global land rush provide evidence that the state has an important role to play regarding access to and control over land and its productive resources (Borras et al. 2012; Wolford et al. 2013). While state action can promote, prevent, reverse and/or divert pro-poor reforms, societal actors can influence and shape such actions (see Barraclough 1999). Thus, where opportunities exist for the initiation of, or engagement in, spaces of participatory involvement, it is important that politically mobilized and organized societal actors engage in such processes and, where possible, interact with pro-reform state actors. Food sovereignty entails, thus, a dynamic state-society interaction – indeed, an interplay of sovereignty at different scales.

Conclusion

In this paper, we examine the state-level actions in three Latin American countries that have instituted a constitutional right to food sovereignty. We acknowledge that the state is a necessary component of food sovereignty efforts, since it is only through state-level action that structural transformations necessary for food sovereignty can be pursued. But the state cannot stand alone on food sovereignty. After all, food sovereignty as a contested terrain entails multiple sovereignties – at the local/community level and the state level. Thus, the continuous symbiotic interaction between empowered pro-reform state and societal actors is a necessary prerequisite for food sovereignty.

Even with a shared leftist orientation and commitment in the three countries examined here, food sovereignty efforts took place within particular contexts, goals and strategies. In Bolivia, the concept of food sovereignty was integrated into a decolonizing project vis-à-vis the United States aimed at building up the sovereignty of the nation-state. But this sovereignty project ultimately did not involve a devolution of power internally, and, indeed,

Bolivia's food and agricultural policy has relied on and reproduced existing inequalities. In Ecuador, state-level attempts to be inclusive ended up placing state institutions in a position to adjudicate between differing visions of food sovereignty, ultimately reducing or 'simplifying' food sovereignty into pro-poor 'residual' projects rather than a broader transformative pathway with comprehensive agrarian reform. Additionally, political tensions within government institutions failed to effectively translate and carry out the redistributive demands of civil society. In Venezuela, however, pro-reform state actors are pursuing a strategy oriented at dismantling existing unequal agrarian structures and transforming relations of access and control, while simultaneously opening up space for participatory democratic decision-making at the local level. We suggest this presents the most promising trajectory for transformative change around food sovereignty. While such a structural transformation of society and the economy does not necessarily ensure that food sovereignty be realized (indeed, sovereignty is an ongoing political project), these changes 'sow the seeds' for *peoples* to cultivate food sovereignty in ways that enable communities to 'have the democratic conversation about food policy in the first place' (Patel 2009, 670).

References

Albro, R. 2013. 'Living Well' at home and abroad: indigenous politics, climate change, and the limits of governance in Bolivia. Paper presented at the Annual Meeting of the Latin American Studies Association, Washington DC. May 31.

Andrango, L. 2008. Carta de invitación a la reunión del 29 de mayo, Ciudad Alfaro, 26 de mayo.

Arditi, B. 2008. Arguments about the left turn in Latin America: a post-liberal politics? *Latin American Research Review* 43, no. 3: 59–81.

Asamblea Nacional. 2008. *La Consitución del Ecuador.* Quito, Ecuador, Asamblea Nacional. http://www.asambleanacional.gov.ec/documentos/Constitucion-2008.pdf (accessed January 14, 2014).

Assies, W. 2006. Land tenure legislation in a pluri-cultural and multi-ethnic society: the case of Bolivia. *The Journal of Peasant Studies* 33, no. 4: 569–611.

Barraclough, S. 1999. The role of the state and other actors in land reform. Discussion Paper, No. 101. London: URISD.

Becker, M. 2011a. Correa, indigenous movements, and the writing of a new constitution in Ecuador. *Latin American Perspectives* 38, no. 1: 47–62.

Becker, M. 2011b. *Pachakutik: Indigenous movements and electoral politics in Ecuador.* New York: Rowman and Littlefield.

Bello, W.F. 2005. *Dilemmas of domination: The unmaking of the American empire.* New York: Metropolitan Books.

Bernstein, H. 2014. Food sovereignty via the 'peasant way': a sceptical view. *The Journal of Peasant Studies.*

Bernstein, H., B. Crow and H. Johnson, eds. 1992. *Rural livelihoods: Crises and responses.* Oxford: Oxford University Press in association with The Open University.

Borras, S.M. 2007. *Pro-poor land reform: a critique.* Ottawa: University of Ottawa Press.

Borras, S.M. Jr., C. Kay, S. Gómez, and J. Wilkinson. 2012. Land grabbing and global capitalist accumulation key features in Latin America. *Canadian Journal of Development Studies/Revue Canadienne D'études du Développement* 33, no. 4: 402–416.

Borras, S.M. and J.C. Franco. 2010. Contemporary discourses and contestations around pro-poor land policies and land governance. *Journal of Agrarian Change* 10, no. 1: 1–32.

Borras, S. Jr., M. Edelman, and C. Kay. 2008. Transnational agrarian movements confronting globalization. *Journal of Agrarian Change* 8, nos. 2–3: 169–204.

Clark, P. 2013. Food Sovereignty, Post-Neoliberalism, campesino organizations and the state in Ecuador. Paper presented at *Food Sovereignty: A Critical Dialogue,* International Conference, Yale University. http://www.yale.edu/agrarianstudies/foodsovereignty/pprs/34_Clark_2013.pdf (accessed February 14, 2014).

Constitución Política del Estado Plurinacional de Bolivia. 2009. http://www.presidencia.gob.bo/documentos/publicaciones/constitucion.pdf (accessed August 16, 2013).

Cockcroft, J.D. 2006. Imperalism, state and social Movements in Latin America. *Critical Sociology* 32, no. 1: 67–81

Conaghan, C.M. 2008. Ecuador: Correa's plebiscitary presidency. *Journal of Democracy* 19, no. 2: 46–60.

CONAIE. 2007. Propuesta de la CONAIE frente a la Asamblea Constituyente. Quito: Confederación de las Nacionalidades y Pueblos Indigenas del Ecuador.

Delong, S. 2005. Venezuela's agrarian land reform: More like Lincoln than Lenin. *Venezuela Analysis*. http://venezuelanalysis.com/analysis/963 (accessed January 18, 2014).

Desmarais, A. and H. Wittman. 2014. Farmers, foodies & First Nations: getting to food sovereignty in Canada. *The Journal of Peasant Studies* 41, no. 6. DOI:10.1080/03066150.2013.876623.

Edelman, M. 2014. Food sovereignty: forgotten genealogies and future regulatory challenges. *The Journal of Peasant Studies* 41, no. 6. DOI:10.1080/03066150.2013.876998.

El Universal. 2009. Conaie acusa el gobierno de Correa de 'capitalista y neoliberal. *El Universal*, 11 Sept.

Enríquez, L. 2013. The paradoxes of Latin America's 'pink tide': Venezuela and the project of agrarian reform. *The Journal of Peasant Studies* 40, no. 4: 611–38.

Erbol. 2014. 'No hay ningún gobierno indígena en América Latina'. http://www.erbol.com.bo/noticia/politica/04012014/no_hay_ningun_gobierno_indigena_en_america_latina (accessed February 14, 2014).

Fabricant, Nicole. 2013. Good Living for Whom? Paper presented at the Latin American Studies Association Annual Meetings, Washington, DC. May 31.

FENOCIN, n.d. website of Confederación Nacional de Organizaciones Campesinas, Indigenas y Negras. www.fenocin.org.

Fernández, B.S. and F. Puente. 2012. Configuración y demandas de los movimientos sociales hacia la Asamblea Constituyente en Bolivia y Ecuador. *Revista de Ciencas Sociales* 44: 49–65.

Food and Agriculture Organization (FAO). 2013. Reconocimiento de la FAO a Venezuela. Santiago de Chile: Oficina Regional de la FAO para América Latina y el Caribe. http://www.rlc.fao.org/es/paises/venezuela/noticias/reconocimiento-de-la-fao-a-venezuela/ (accessed February 3, 2014).

Flor, F.H. 2013. Tierra: Soberanía Alimentaria y Buen Vivir of *Tierra urgente, ed.* F. Hidalgo and M. Laforge., Quito: SIPAE: 145–158.

Fox, J. 1993. *The politics of food in Mexico: State power and social mobilization.* Ithaca: Cornell University Press.

Fox, J. 2005. *Empowerment and institutional change: Mapping 'virtuous circles' of state-society interaction. Volume 2 of Serie Análisis del Desarrollo.* Mexico: Universidad Iberoamericana, Instituto de Investigaciones sobre Desarrollo Sustentable y Equidad Social.

Fox, J. and J. Gershman. 2000. The World Bank and social capital: Lessons from ten rural development projects in the Philippines and Mexico. *Policy Sciences* 33, nos. 3–4: 399–419.

Franco, J.C. 2008. Peripheral justice? Rethinking justice sector reform in the Philippines. *World Development* 36, no. 10: 1858–73.

Gaceta Oficial. 2008. *Ley Organica de Seguridad y Soberania Agroalimentaria.* No. 5,891. 31 July, 2008. http://www.pgrfa.org/gpa/ven/ley_soberania.pdf (accessed August 16, 2013).

Giunta, Isabella. 2013. Food sovereignty in Ecuador: The gap between the constitutionalization of the principles and their materialization in the official agri-food strategies. Paper presented at *Food Sovereignty: A Critical Dialogue*, International Conference, Yale University. http://www.yale.edu/agrarianstudies/foodsovereignty/pprs/50_Giunta_2013.pdf (accessed February 21, 2014).

Government of Canada. 2011. *Agri-Food past, present & future report: Venezuela.* Agriculture and Agri-Food Canada. http://www.ats.agr.gc.ca/lat/4215-eng.htm (accessed August 8, 2013).

Gramsci, A. 1971. *Selections from the prison notebooks of Antonio Gramsci.* Edited and Translated by Quintin Hoare and Geoffrey Nowell Smith. London: Lawrence and Wishart.

Gudynas, E. 2011. Buen vivir: Today's concept. *Development* 54, no. 4: 441–447.

Heath, J.R. 1985. El Programa Nacional de Alimentación y la crisis de alimentos. *Revista Mexicana de Sociología* 47, no. 3: 115–135.

Hecht, S. 2005. Soybeans, development and conservation on the Amazon Frontier. *Development and Change* 36, no. 2: 375–404.

Herrera, S., D. Carrín, J. Flores, M.L. Larrera, and J. Rodríguez. 2010. *Análisis de la Inversión y la Política Pública para Agricultura en Ecuador.* Quito: Oxfam International – Instituto de Estudios Ecuatorianos.

Holt Giménez, E. and A. Shattuck. 2011. Food crises, food regimes and food movements: rumblings of reform or tides of transformation? *The Journal of Peasant Studies* 38, no. 1: 109–144.

Hospes, O. 2014. Food sovereignty the debate, the deadlock, and a suggested detour. *Journal of Agriculture and Human Values* 31, no. 1: 119–130.

Iles, A. and M. Montenegro. 2013. 'Building relational food sovereignty across scales: An example from the Peruvian Andes'. Paper presented at *Food Sovereignty: A Critical Dialogue*, International Conference, Yale University. http://www.yale.edu/agrarianstudies/foodsoverei gnty/pprs/67_Iles_Montenegro_2013.pdf (accessed February 4, 2014).

Instituto Nacional de Estadistica (INE). 2011. *Informacion Estadistica*. http://www.ine.gob.bo (accessed August 16, 2013).

Instituto Nacional de Reforma Agraria (INRA). 2010. *La tierra vuelve a manos indígenas y campesinas*. La Paz: INRA.

Isaacs, A., B. Weiner, G. Bell, C. Frantz, and K. Bowen. 2009. 'The food sovereignty movement in Venezuela, part 1' *Venezuelan Analysis*. http://venezuelanalysis.com/analysis/4952 (accessed September 20, 2013).

Jessop, B. 2007. *State power*. Cambridge: Polity Press.

Kappeler, A. 2013. Perils of peasant populism: why redistributive land reform and 'food fovereignty' can't feed Venezuela. Paper present at *Food Sovereignty: A Critical Dialogue*, International Conference, Yale University. http://www.yale.edu/agrarianstudies/foodsovereignty/pprs/65_Kappeler_2013.pdf (accessed February 4, 2014).

Kay, C. and M. Urioste. 2007. Bolivia's unfinished agrarian reform: Rural poverty and development policies. *In*: A.H. Akram-Lodhi, S.M. Borras and C. Kay, eds. *Land, poverty and livelihoods in the era of globalization: Perspectives from developing and transition countries*. London and New York: Routledge, pp .41–79.

Kerssen, T. 2013. Food sovereignty and the quinoa boom in Bolivia. Paper present at *Food Sovereignty: A Critical Dialogue*, International Conference, Yale University. http://www.yale.edu/agrarianstudies/foodsovereignty/pprs/79_Kerssen_2013b.pdf (accessed February 4, 2014). (Cited with permission from author).

Kohl, B.H. and L.C. Farthing. 2006. *Impasse in Bolivia: Neoliberal hegemony and popular resistance*. London: Zed Books.

Liendo, R. 2011. *Politicas publicas de desarollo rural y reguridad alimentaria 2006–2011. Tierra, territorio y seguridad alimentaria en Bolivia*. La Paz, Bolivia: Fundacion Tierra.

Marcano, L.C. 2009. From the neo-liberal barrio to the socialist commune. *Human Geography: A New Radical Journal* 2, no. 3: 75–88.

Martinez-Torres, M.E., and P.M. Rosset. 2010. La Via Campesina: The birth and evolution of a transnational social movement. *The Journal of Peasant Studie* 37, no. 1: 149–75.

MAGAP. 2013. Plan Tierras. http://servicios.agricultura.gob.ec/mag01/magapaldia/2013/Pdf,%20banner,%20eventos/PLAN%20TIERRAS%20REPORT..pdf (accessed March 10, 2014).

McKay, B. 2011. Assessing the impacts of Venezuela's state-led agrarian reform programme on rural livelihoods. M.A. Thesis, Halifax: Saint Mary's University (Canada).

McMichael, P. 2008. Peasants make their own history, but not just as they please … *Journal of Agrarian Change* 8, no. 2: 205–28.

McMichael, P. 2009. Global citizenship and multiple sovereignties: reconstituting modernity. *In*: *Hegemonic Transitions, the State and Crisis in Neoliberal Capitalism*, ed. Y. Atasoy, 23–42. New York: Routledge.

McMichael, P. 2012. Food regime crisis and revaluing the agrarian question. *Research in Rural Sociology and Development* 18: 99–122.

McMichael, P. 2014. Historicizing food sovereignty. *The Journal of Peasant Studies* 41, no. 6. DOI:10.1080/03066150.2013.876999.

Mesner, M. 2013. The territory of self-determination: social reproduction, agroecology, and the role of the state. In *Globalization and food sovereignty: Global and local change in the new politics of food*, ed. M.J Massicotte, Peter Andrée, Jeffrey Ayres, and Michael Bosnia. Toronto: University of Toronto Press, pp. 53–83.

Ministerio del Poder Popular para las Comunas y los Movimientos Sociales (MPComunas). 2014. *Consulta Pública*. Gobierno Bolivariano de Venezuela. http://consulta.mpcomunas.gob.ve/ (accessed April 5, 2014).

Ministerio de Desarrollo Rural y Tierras (MDRyT). 2010. *Revolución rural y agraria, Plan del sector desarrollo agropecuario*. La Paz: MDRyT.

Mongabay. 2013. 'Bolivia takes step to boost agriculture and curb surging deforestation'. Mongabay. com. January 28. http://news.mongabay.com/2013/0128-bolivia-land-use-law.html (accessed February 14, 2014).

Nyéléni Forum. 2007. Nyéléni 2007: Forum for Food Sovereignty. http://www.nyeleni.org/spip.php?article290 (accessed August 18, 2013).

Olivera, O., and T. Lewis. 2004. *Cochabamba! water war in Bolivia.* Cambridge: South End Press.

Ostrom, V. 1972. Polycentricity. Paper presented at the 1972 Annual Meeting of the American Political Science Association, Washington Hilton Hotel, Washington, D.C., September 5–9.

Panizza, F. 2005. Unarmed utopia revisited: the resurgence of left-of-centre politics in Latin America. *Political Studies* 53: 716–734.

Patel, R. 2009. Food sovereignty. *The Journal of Peasant Studies* 36, no. 3: 663–706.

Patel, R. and P. McMichael. 2004. Third Worldism and the lineages of global facism: the regrouping of the global South in the neoliberal era. *Third World Quarterly* 25, no. 1: 231–54.

Peralta, P.O. 2011. La redistribución agrarian en la Revolución Ciudadania of *Tierra urgente,* ed. F. Hidalgo and M. Laforge. Quito: La Isla.

Petras, J. and H. Veltmeyer. 2006. Social movements and the state: Political power dynamics in Latin America. *Critical Sociology* 32, no. 1: 83–104.

Poulantzas, N. 1978. *State, power, socialism.* London: NLB.

Postero, N. 2010. The Struggle to Create a Radical Democracy in Bolivia. *Latin American Research Review* 45S: 59–78.

Redo, D., A.C. Millington, and D. Hindery. 2011. Deforestation dynamics and policy changes in Bolivia's post-neoliberal era. *Land Use Policy* 28: 227–241.

Rosero, F. 2008. La asamblea nacional constituyente: tensiones entre la utopia deseada y el cambio posible, Paris: Instituto de Investigación y debate sobre la gobernanza. http://www.institut-gouvernance.org/es/analyse/fiche-analyse-448.html (accessed March 15, 2014).

Rosero, G.F., C.Y. Yonfá, and R.F. Villaroel. 2011. *Soberanía alimentaria, modelos de desarrollo y tierras en Ecuador.* Quito: CAFOLIS.

Rosset, P.M. 2008. Food Sovereignty and the contemporary food crisis. *Development* 51, no. 4: 460–463.

Rosset, P.M. 2003. Food sovereignty: global rallying cry or farmer movements. *Food First Backgrounder* 9, no. 4: 1–4.

Schiavoni, C. 2014a. Competing sovereignties in the political construction of food sovereignty. Paper present at *Food Sovereignty: A Critical Dialogue*, International Conference, International Institute of Social Studies, http://www.iss.nl/fileadmin/ASSETS/iss/Research_and_projects/Research_networks/ICAS/90_Schiavoni.pdf (accessed February 2, 2014).

Schiavoni, C. 2014b. Competing sovereignties, contested processes: the politics of food sovereignty construction. Working Paper 583. The Hague: International Institute of Social Studies.

Schiavoni, C. and W. Camacaro. 2009. The Venezuelan effort to build a new food and agriculture system. *Monthly Review* 61, no. 3: 129–141.

Schilling-Vacaflor, A. 2011. Bolivia's new constitution: towards participatory democracy and political pluralism? *European review of Latin American and Caribbean studies* 90: 3–22.

Scott, J. 1998. *Seeing like a state: How certain schemes to improve the human condition have failed.* New Haven: Yale University Press.

SENPLADES. 2009. *Plan Nacional para el Buen Vivir.* Quito: SENPLADES.

Silva, E. 2014. Social movements, policy, and conflict in post-neoliberal Latin America: Bolivia in the time of Evo Morales. *Research in Political Sociology* 21: 51–76.

Smith, G. 2010. A Food Fight for Hugo Chavez. *Bloomberg Businessweek.* http://www.businessweek.com/magazine/content/10_12/b4171046603604.htm (accessed June 8, 2011).

Suggett, J. 2010. Venezuelan Land Law reform promises 'Land for those who work on it'. *Venezuelan Analysis.* http://venezuelanalysis.com/news/5432. (accessed August 10, 2013).

Urioste, M. 2010. *Land governance in Bolivia.* La Paz: Fundacion TIERRA.

Valdivia, G. 2010. Agrarian capitalism and struggles over hegemony in the Bolivian lowlands. *Latin American Perspectives* 37: 67–87.

Vía Campesina. 1996. *La Vía Campesina: Proceedings from the II International Conference of the Vía Campesina,* Tlaxcala, Mexico, April 18–21, 1996. Brussels: NCOS Publications.

Via Campesina. 2001. *Our world is not for sale: Priority to peoples' Food Sovereignty, WTO out of Food and Agriculture.* http://www.voiceoftheturtle.org/library/2001–11–1%20Peoples%20foodsovereignty-en.htm (accessed July 10, 2013).

Webber, J. 2008. Rebellion to reform in Bolivia (Part I): domestic class structures, Latin American trends, and capitalist imperialism. *Historical Materialism* 16, no. 2: 23–58.

Weinberg, B. 2010a. Bolivia's New Water Wars: Climate Change and Indigenous Struggle. *NACLA Report on the Americas* 43, no. 5: 19–24.

Weinberg, B. 2010b. Beyond exctractivism: an interview with Rafael Quispe. *NACLA Report on the Americas* 43, no. 5: 21.

Wilpert, G. 2003. Venezuela's new constitution. *Venezuela Analysis*. http://venezuelanalysis.com/analysis/70 (accessed February 2, 2014).

Wilpert, G. 2007. *Changing Venezuela by taking power: The history and policies of the Chavez government*. London: Verso.

Wilpert, G. 2011. An Assessment of Venezuela's Bolivarian revolution at twelve years. *Venezuelan Analysis*. :http://venezuelanalysis.com/analysis/5971 (accessed August 10, 2013).

Windfuhr, M. and J. Jonsén. 2005. *Food Sovereignty: Towards democracy in localised food systems*. Rugby: ITDG Publishing.

Wolford, W., S.M. Borras Jr., R. Hall, I. Scoones, and B. White. 2013. Governing global land deals: the role of the state in the rush for land. *Development and Change* 44, no. 2: 189–210.

World Bank. 2007. *Bolivia - land for agricultural development project*. Washington, DC: The World Bank. http://documents.worldbank.org/curated/en/2007/09/8476438/bolivia-land-agricultural-development-project (accessed January 10, 2014).

Yashar, D. 2005. *Contesting citizenship in Latin America: The rise of indigenous movements and the postliberal challenge*. Cambridge: Cambridge University Press.

Ben McKay is a PhD candidate at the International Institute of Social Studies (ISS) in The Hague, and is part of the research programme Political Economy of Resources, Environment and Populations Studies. He is currently researching agrarian transformation in Bolivia in the context of the 'soy complex' and the rise of BRICS (Brazil, Russia, India, China, South Africa) countries.

Ryan Nehring is a PhD student at Cornell University in the Department of Development Sociology. His research interests include the political economy of rural development in Latin America and, more recently, the emergence of Brazilian South-South Cooperation in African agriculture.

Marygold Walsh-Dilley is a postdoctoral associate in the Department of Development Sociology at Cornell University. Her research interests include agriculture and rural development, social-ecological change and globalization, and food and land politics, with a particular focus on agrarian change among indigenous communities in Andean Bolivia.

Food sovereignty in Ecuador: peasant struggles and the challenge of institutionalization

Isabella Giunta

The Ecuadorian Constitution (2008) declared food sovereignty a strategic goal and a government obligation, embracing many of the proposals put forth since the late 1990s by Ecuadorian federations linked to Vía Campesina. The issue of food sovereignty has expanded from the inner circles of peasant organizations to the wider context of the whole Ecuadorian society. The paper provides an overview of this process, describing the collective actions that made it possible. Moreover, it attempts to explain the reasons why the 'Agrarian Revolution' is currently evaluated as weak, and the motivations for a gap between constitutional mandates and the ongoing official policies.

Introduction

The Ecuadorian Constitution (2008) declared food sovereignty as a strategic goal and a government obligation, institutionalizing – although partially – the proposal put forward by the international peasant movement Vía Campesina in 1996. The aim of this paper[1] is to critically reflect on the impact of collective actions (especially those promoted by organizations linked to this movement) carried out to institutionalize the principles of food sovereignty in Ecuador, including an analysis of the gap that exists between the formal and the material constitution of the official strategies.[2]

The first part of this paper outlines the situation before the Constituent Assembly (mandated with drafting a new constitution) met. It shows how the inclusion of food sovereignty principles in the new constitution occurred not just as a result of an advantageous political conjuncture but derived as well from struggles against neoliberal reforms and from alternative practices carried out by social movements over the last few decades.[3] In this framework, the paper outlines the role played by the Ecuadorian federations (affiliated with

The author is grateful for the helpful comments given by the anonymous reviewers at the *JPS*. Moreover, she is thankful to the leaders of the Ecuadorian organizations linked to Vía Campesina for their cooperation, and to Annamaria Vitale for supervising ongoing research and for all her suggestions.

[1]The paper is based on preliminary results of field research conducted between 2012 and 2013.
[2]In this paper *formal constitution* refers to the written norm, while *material constitution* to the concrete conditions determined by relations of power.
[3]A focus centred only on the event (Constituent Assembly) would reduce the analysis to the collective action at that circumscribed time and to the ability of institutions to embrace the movement's agenda, omitting the role played by social actors in creating the conditions necessary for the implementation of the constituent process.

Vía Campesina) which, by the late 1990s, had placed food sovereignty as a priority of their specific and common political agendas, through platforms such as Mesa Agraria.

The paper then provides a brief account of how these federations participated actively in the Constituent Assembly process. The new Constitution established radical changes in the agri-food sector and embraced, within the rights of *buen vivir*, many of the proposals claimed by the federations and organizations linked to Vía Campesina. Thus, during and after the Constituent Assembly stage, the issue of food sovereignty expanded from the inner circles of certain peasant organizations to the wider context of the whole Ecuadorian society, achieving centrality in the political arena.

In addition to a review of the constitutionalization process, the paper explores the reasons why, five years later, the process of redesigning public institutions and agri-food policies does not appear consistent with the constitutional mandates. The so-called 'Agrarian Revolution' is considered a weak process, not only by social organizations but also by the governmental sector, although it is a component of the so-called Citizens' Revolution promoted by the 'progressive' government of Rafael Correa. The discussion of fundamental issues (especially access to land, water, productive models, use of genetically modified organisms [GMOs] and agrofuels), which began during the Constituent Assembly period, had become even more heated during the approval of the Organic Law of the Food Sovereignty Regime (2009). A reduction in the capacity for mobilization of peasant organizations and the more general shift of power relations in favour of agro-industry, which controls the national food chains, have contributed to postpone the regulation of more sensitive topics. Meanwhile, some official initiatives have been launched, but they do not appear to be fully inscribed within a transition in the food regime.

In this framework, the paper argues that there is a gap between the success of social movements in winning certain innovative normative frameworks and rights (*buen vivir* and, within its rights, the food sovereignty) and the limitations on their institutionalization, formalization and implementation as they bump up against the power structure that marks the agri-food system. This led to some continuity in the neoliberal policies. Indeed, the still-competing currents, in both society and the state, make difficult a transition in the agri-food policies, generating a de facto combination of food sovereignty and agricultural modernization approaches (or, in other terms, between *buen vivir* and developmentalist paradigms) and a tension between revolution (a transition in the food regime) and reform (policies focused on peasants and inspired by food sovereignty principles). Finally, as occurred in other Latin-American countries (e.g. Bolivia, Venezuela or Brazil) a debate arose on the role of social movements in the ongoing change processes, as well as on how their relationship with the state should be moulded.

However, despite the contradictions pointed out, the Ecuadorian institutionalization of food sovereignty – as embedded within a broader transformative vision, grounded in *buen vivir* – brings significant elements to the global debate on food sovereignty paradigm and the efforts to make it more inclusive, overcoming a more 'productionist' approach.

A mosaic of anti-neoliberal struggles

Agriculture is quite relevant in the Ecuadorian economy: including livestock, it represents 8.2 percent of the real gross domestic product (GDP),[4] and employs about 30 percent of the

---

[4]In 2010, with an average of 9 percent for the period 2000–2010.

workforce, a percentage that increases significantly (69.2 percent) if we consider the rural population.

These data, however, fail to recognize the real importance of agriculture. First of all, the distortion caused by the importance of petroleum in the economy should be taken into consideration: agriculture represented 13.2 percent in 2010 and an average of 15.46 percent for the period 2000–2010 of 'non-oil GDP' (Carrión and Herrera 2012).

An analysis conducted exclusively using GDP does not take into account other crucial dimensions, such as production for self-consumption and transactions not carried out within conventional markets (that is, transactions that are not invoiced, and non-monetary exchanges). This becomes more relevant in countries such as Ecuador, where the production earmarked for self-consumption is considerable and the informal economy employs 47.2 percent of the urban Economically Active Population (INEC 2013). Similarly, the official statistics underestimate the capacity of agriculture to generate employment, since they do not consider domestic work, indirect employment and employment in agriculture as secondary activities (Carrión and Herrera 2012).

On the other hand, the data related to GDP are often translated as evidence of a trend towards low productivity and of the impelling need to modernize Ecuadorian agriculture, especially the peasant sector. García Pascual (2006) notes that in the last few decades, the gap between Ecuador and other countries grew in terms of productivity levels (e.g. for cereals/USA). The same author observes that the global Ecuadorian production increase (27 percent between 1990 and 2004) was only half due to the improvement in productivity, the rest being attributable to the expansion of cultivated area. Using these arguments, García Pascual critically analyzes the effectiveness of the modernization policies already implemented in Ecuador. Indeed, from an agro-ecological point of view, the low productivity trends are linked mainly to the lack of investments in research, infrastructure and technical assistance in agriculture as well as to the predominance of production models which do not facilitate the regeneration of soil fertility, are not adapted to local ecosystems and result in more vulnerability to recurrent adverse climatic events (Altieri 2009; Martínez-Alier 2011; Carrión and Herrera 2012; ECLAC et al. 2012).[5]

National appraisals report that the value of food exports significantly exceeds that of imports. Carrión and Herrera (2012) state that there is a high degree of self-sufficiency to cover internal food demand (e.g. in strategic products such as vegetables, milk or rice), even if there is a deficiency of certain products, which represents an alarming trend that in the future, if it continues, could seriously affect national food security. The latter phenomenon is related mostly to the agri-food policies that have been implemented. Indeed, in promoting agro-industrial production and exportation, these policies have neglected part of the production allocated to domestic consumption (especially those traditionally managed by peasants), with effects on food security and on the production and reproduction conditions for small producers, who have been increasingly excluded from access to fertile land, infrastructures and public support (Guerrero and Ospina 2003; Chiriboga 2004; Kay 2004; García Pascual 2006; Martínez Valle 2008). In particular, this trend refers to products such as wheat (94 percent), barley (62 percent), oats (86 percent), lentils (73 percent) and apples (66 percent) (Carrión and Herrera 2012). The case of wheat is emblematic since its deficit has risen despite the increase in demand, as

---

[5]In this framework, it is key to add that peasants compete in unequal conditions with agro-industry (e.g. in terms of access to land, mechanization, services or infrastructures).

a result of policies that have favoured imports (from the USA) instead of support for peasant producers and national production (Peltre-Wurtz 1989).

The Green Revolution and structural adjustment plans promoted by the World Bank and the International Monetary Fund in the 1980s favoured monoculture (at the expense of food security and agrobiodiversity in this mega-diverse country) and the economic groups dedicated to the export of exotic products (especially shrimp, bananas, flowers and cocoa). Government support for peasants whose work aimed at production for the domestic market decreased drastically, as did the prices of their products, while input costs increased. The Agrarian Reform process stopped, and was replaced by land privatization strategies; meanwhile, peasants were being excluded from the modernization of the rural sector, based on capital-intensive technologies, and thus also from market competition. In this way, neoliberalism has led to important changes in land tenure as well as in rural labour and livelihoods (Larrea et al. 1996; Kay 2004; Martínez Valle 2004).

Nowadays, there is strong inequality in the distribution of wealth and in the access to productive factors. In rural areas, poverty hovers around 49.1 percent, while extreme poverty is 23.3 percent (BCE 2012). As regards the access to land, 64.4 percent of the smaller productive units (less than 5 hectares) only cover 6.3 percent of the agricultural surface, while the biggest properties (more than 200 hectares), which represent 0.1 percent of the total, control 29 percent of the overall surface (Carrión and Herrera 2012; Eclac et al. 2012).

However, the imposition of neoliberal policies, aimed at an indiscriminate opening of the economy to the logics and capitals of international markets, faced many obstacles, in particular the effects related to the decline in the prices of raw material and the debt crisis (Acosta 2006), as well as the conflict with Peru (1981, 1995) and the recurrence of disasters.[6]

In addition, the expansion of the 'petroleum frontier' produced huge social and environmental impacts, particularly in Amazonia. The forced displacement of indigenous peoples, as well as deforestation, oil contamination and spills, the indiscriminate spread of agro-industrial monoculture and biodiversity erosion are among those phenomena which are often referred to as the 'environmental disaster' of eastern Ecuador. Unfortunately, deforestation and the loss of biodiversity has become a widespread phenomenon across the country; the destruction of mangroves in the Pacific coast, for the production of shrimp for export, is only one example.

In reaction to these transformations imposed by neoliberalism, several social conflicts have taken place since the early 1990s. Other factors which contributed to exacerbating social tensions as well as fostering general distrust in the political system were the vicious cycle of debt and the drastic reduction of welfare spending,[7] the renewed concentration of wealth, pervasive tax evasion, the progressive collapse of the domestic banking system, the violation of democratic institutions, and their inefficiency and widespread (public and private) corruption (Acosta 2006).

Furthermore, by the late 1980s, a new phenomenon significantly altered the political panorama: indigenous people emerged as political actors reacting vigorously to the subordination imposed on them for centuries. Thus, ethnic demands gained a pivotal role along

---

[6]*El Niño* (1982–1983, 1997–1998), an earthquake (1987) and volcanic eruptions (1999).

[7]Between 1971 and 1981, foreign debt increased by 22 times. The payment of debt services increased progressively from 18 percent in 1980 to more than 50 percent of the national budget in 2000; meanwhile, social spending fell from 50 percent to 15 percent (Acosta 2006).

with classist demands (peasants); the main claims were: access to land, legalization and protection of ancestral territories (starting with the Amazonian), bilingual education and the plurinationality of the state as a strategy against domination, violence and invisibility (Dávalos 2005). In addition, there was a consistent rejection of the violent transformations caused by neoliberal policies (Guerrero and Ospina 2003). The Confederación de Nacionalidades Indígenas del Ecuador (CONAIE) undoubtedly led the innovative movement, even if other organizations, such as Federación Nacional de Organizaciones Campesinas e Indígenas (FENOC-I) and Federación Ecuatoriana de Indígenas (FEI), participated in it.

The indigenous movement became the emblem of the reaction to the economic crisis and to the structural adjustment package. The claim to the right to diversity and the criticism of the dominant models of democracy and development, which were ethnocentric and exclusionary, played a crucial role in the symbolic opposition against the neoliberal *pensée unique* (Larrea et al. 1996; Dávalos 2005; Zamosc 2009). Thus, the indigenous movement broke onto the national scene, catalyzing social protests and aggregating multiple social actors: organizations of peasants and Afro-Ecuadorians, women and human rights associations and public trade unions, as well as environmental and ecological activists.

Protests started in the 1990s with the occupation of *Iglesia de Santo Domingo* in Quito (May 1990) followed by the first *levantamiento* led by CONAIE (June 1990) with thousands of indigenous peasants, mostly from the highlands, who occupied roads and institutions. In 1992, a march on the capital demanded the protection of indigenous territories in Amazonia. In addition, numerous actions were organized within the *Campaña Continental 500 Años de Resistencia Indígena, Negra y Popular* (1992), which criticized the commemoration of Spanish colonization, denouncing its impacts and announcing the counter-offensive of indigenous and Afro-descendants. In 1994, a *levantamiento* opposed the *Ley de Desarrollo Agrario* and its privatization of land. This general strike organized by the Coordinadora Agraria Nacional (integrated by CONAIE, FENOC-I, the Federación Nacional de Trabajadores Agroindustriales, Campesinos e Indígenas Libres del Ecuador [FENACLE] and FEI), paralyzed the country for 10 days, forcing the government to modify the law (Larrea et al. 1996). Thanks to broad alliances in 1995, social movements achieved victory in the referendum against the privatization of Social Security that had just preceded the constitution of the *Pachakutik-Nuevo País* (1996).[8] In 1997, social movements were actively involved in the fall of President Bucaram, as well as in the 1998 Constituent Assembly process, without, however, being able to set an anti-neoliberal agenda (Ramírez Gallegos 2010).[9]

At the end of the 1990s, environmental campaigns grew around the defence of tropical forests and mangroves. Within this framework, Acción Ecológica launched the concept of 'ecological debt' to the world, in order to make the 'North' face its responsibilities for the global environmental degradation towards the 'Third World' and to assert the illegitimacy of the country's foreign debt (Paredis et al. 2007).

Nevertheless, between 1992 and 1996, the main neoliberal adjustments were put in place, such as: privatization, macroeconomic measures related to currency exchange and

---

[8]This movement entered the political-electoral arena, marking the transition from an agenda based essentially on indigenous issues to a 'national project' to gather the demands of all the *excluded* in the country and to promote new radical forms of democracy and state (Larrea Maldonado 2004).
[9]While some important social rights (e.g. women, lesbian, gay, bisexual, and transgender) and collective rights of indigenous people were recognized.

interest rates, trade liberalization, financial deregulation and the dismantling of the state as the leading figure in development (Acosta 2006; Falconí and Muñoz 2012). The economic crisis continued to worsen until the end of the 1990s, when the country suffered a recession and accelerated impoverishment, never before experienced.[10] Emigration increased, with a diaspora in the USA, Spain and, to a lesser extent, Italy. A 'bank holiday' (March 1999) led to the freezing of all deposits, inducing a massive rescue operation with public funds. In January 2000, Jamil Mahuad announced dollarization, sacrificing national monetary sovereignty (Acosta 2006).

Against this recession and the measures taken by the government, new protests took place: a March 1999 strike against rising fuel prices and the freezing of bank deposits precipitated a new uprising in July 1999. Indigenous people and peasants, along with transport workers, occupied Quito; for a week, they picketed the parliament and the government palace, forcing the members to dialogue, which was interrupted in September due to the -escalation of the crisis. On 21 January 2000, 10 days after the dollarization decree, mobilizations exploded and a triumvirate, integrated by the CONAIE president (A. Vargas) and the Army Colonel Gutiérrez, took over power (for few hours), forcing Mahuad to abandon the presidency. Vice-president Noboa, appointed as successor, ratified the dollarization, but in January 2001 faced a massive new *levantamiento* against the new economic measures (increasing prices for transport, fuel and gas for domestic use). Several local governments adhered to it, but its peculiarity was the unity of the so-called 'rural front', due to the joint convocation of CONAIE, Confederación Nacional de Organizaciones Campesinas, Indígenas y Negras (FENOCIN), Confederación Nacional del Seguro Social Campesino- Coordinadora Nacional Campesina (CONFEUNASSC-CNC) and Consejo de Pueblos y Organizaciones Indígenas Evangélicos del Ecuador (FEINE). Connections and supplies to Quito were paralyzed for two weeks, and seven protesters were killed (Guerrero and Ospina 2003).

Electoral competitions as well as the direct participation of some organizations (including CONAIE) in the government of Lucio Gutiérrez (2003–2005), rifts within CONAIE and Pachakutik, and the process of 'normalization' directed towards indigenous and peasant organizations via projects financed by international funds (such as PRODEPINE), are among the factors that contributed to the weakening of social mobilizations in the first decade of the twenty-first century.[11]

With the exception of the mostly urban mobilization of *forajidos* (2005) which led to the ousting of president Gutiérrez (Ospina 2009; Ramírez Gallegos 2010), after 2001, the bigger protests were animated by indigenous, peasant and environmental organizations. Focused against the regional Free Trade Area of the Americas (especially in 2002) and then the bilateral Free Trade Agreement (2004–2006) with the USA, the mobilizations denounced the impacts (on peasants and biodiversity as well as in the increasing of privatizations) of signing these free-trade agreements.

So, after more than a decade of deep and recurrent economic, political and social crisis, the innovative proposal led by Rafael Correa (the so-called Citizens' Revolution) received wide consensus. Correa first achieved electoral victory in 2006, embracing some of the main demands of social movements, but without establishing broad and stable alliances

---

[10]GDP fell 31 percent between 1998 and 2000; in 1999, devaluation reached 216 percent and inflation 52 percent. In 2000, the incidence of poverty doubled compared to 1995 (reaching 71 percent) as did extreme poverty (35 percent) (Acosta 2006).
[11]Ospina (2009) presents a literature overview of these factors, suggesting the addition of the inability to manage the differences inside the indigenous movement, which prevented it from acquiring the political strength necessary to promote more structural changes in Ecuador.

with them. Among other things, there was the request to start the Constituent Assembly process to radically transform the institutions and the social pact.

Practices and actions aimed at promoting the principles of food sovereignty

The innovation in conceiving of a radical social, economic and productive transformation (Carrión and Herrera 2012) that took place in Ecuador during the writing of a new Constitution (2008) was largely based on resistance processes that social movements had carried out in the country since the 1990s. In opposition to neoliberal policies, they fought for the defence of diversity (with proposals such as plurinationality and interculturality), territories and natural heritage (with innovative paradigms such as *buen vivir* and food sovereignty or claiming ecological debt) as well as to re-found the models of democracy, state rule and economy on the basis of equity and social justice.

As for the food issue, the goal of the constitutionalization of food sovereignty principles does not appear exclusively ascribable to President Correa's embrace of the movement's agenda or, more generally, to a momentarily favourable political climate as favourable as transient.[12] It can also be explained by retracing previous resistance processes that promoted this innovative paradigm through struggles and piloted alternative practices implemented in the territories. In this context, it seems reasonable to point to the leading role that four federations have played since the late 1990s when they introduced food sovereignty in their political agenda as an explicit priority. These are FENOCIN, the Coorporación (ex Coordinadora) Nacional Campesina-Eloy Alfaro (CNC-EA), the Confederación Nacional del Seguro Social Campesino (CONFEUNASSC) and FENACLE.

FENOCIN, despite the crises faced since its establishment (1968), has played a considerable organizational and political role, becoming, cyclically, one of the main representatives of the national agrarian issue. Over the years, it has changed its acronym, from the initial FENOC, which referred to its peasant composition, to FENOC-I in 1988, marking the transition to the inclusion of ethnic claims (under the banner of interculturalism) along with classist ones, to the current name FENOCIN, adopted in 1997 to highlight Afro-Ecuadorian people's participation. The latter shift represents a significant break with the subalternity of blacks, historically relegated to the lowest level of the racialized and hierarchical structure of Ecuadorian social classification, which considered them subordinates to indigenous people (Walsh 2009). FENOCIN succeeded in uniting within its organization different social classes and groups, in giving explicit visibility to and politicizing the rich cultural and social diversity of the country, and in building a stable and enduring alliance between the indigenous-peasant people of the highlands, *montubios* (coastal peasants), Afro-descendents and, to a lesser extent, settlers and indigenous people of Amazonia. This is, probably, a unique case in the country as well as on the continent.

The CNC-EA started in 1992 and brings together indigenous and peasant organizations, associations of producers and communitarian irrigation groups on the coast and in the highlands. Founded at the same time, CONFEUNASSC mainly unites members of *Seguro*

---

[12]Ramírez Gallegos (2010) refers to an 'arena for change' that has been favoured by a 'mega bloc' in the Constituent Assembly, a big and heterogeneous coalition. Moreover, Rafael Correa, as part of this coalition, was interested in pursuing an anti-neoliberal discourse as well as an opposition to the traditional party system.This favourable political conjuncture has permitted a significant dialogue and cooperation between social organizations and the democratic representative institutions. However, several contrasts have appeared within this 'mega bloc', especially on development model and environmental issues, plurinationality of the state and sexual and reproductive rights.

Social Campesino. Both federations were part of CONFEUNASCC-CNC (a rupture occurred in the mid-2000s),[13] which played a crucial role in the struggles against the privatization of social security in 1995 and in general for the expansion and improvement of its coverage for peasants. CONFEUNASSC-CNC actively promoted the indigenous-peasant alliance within the movement of the 1990s, with social mobilization as well as through the experience of Pachakutik, which they helped to establish, together with the CONAIE and the Coordinadora de Movimientos Sociales. Both CNC-EA and CONFEU-NASSC were engaged in a political agenda that combined the classist peasant claims (access to land and productive factors as well as to a fair market) with a larger framework concerning rural development, conducting battles to claim social security (in particular CONFEUNASSC) and access to better education and health in the countryside (especially the CNC-EA).

Finally, FENACLE, established in 1969, represents a peculiar aspect of Ecuadorian rurality: it participated in the struggles for land in the 1970s, then focused more on the organization of landless rural workers and, to a lesser extent, peasants (about 20 percent). Its members are from the areas of short-cycle monoculture (maize and rice) and plantations (bananas and sugar cane) on the coast and, to a lesser extent, in the highlands (floriculture). Its main struggles are for the rights of rural workers, although claims for land and support for peasants are included in its agenda.

These four federations belong to the international peasant movement Vía Campesina,[14] whose food sovereignty proposal has become the federations' organizing principle for reshaping the national agrarian issue. They are also related to a continental network called Coordinadora Latinoamericana de las Organizaciones del Campo (CLOC), which first appeared between 1989 and 1992 within the *Campaña Continental 500 Años de Resistencia Indígena, Negra y Popular*, and then officially formed in 1994 (CLOC n.d.). CLOC has a dual role: that of regrouping rural organizations in the Americas (but not those of the USA and Canada), and of serving as a further contact point for dialogue and participation of these same organizations within Vía Campesina.

FENOCIN is a direct participant in the creation of these spaces of continental and international organization. FENOCIN, still denominated FENOC-I at the time, was one of the signatories both of the Mons Declaration in 1993, linked to the official establishment of Vía Campesina, and that of Lima, which in 1994 made the founding of CLOC public. FENOC-I was also one of the supporters of the Tlaxcala Declaration of 1996, with which Vía Campesina, at the conclusion of its second international conference, officially launched, on a global scale, the proposal of food sovereignty as antagonist to the dominant view of food security (Vía Campesina 1996).

These four Ecuadorian federations, in the last 15 years, beyond campaigns and mobilizations, have developed practices to disseminate and concretize the principles of food sovereignty, combining the recovery and revaluation of peasant farming practices with ecological innovations, through the so-called *knowledge dialogue* (*diálogo de saberes*). In this way, they have contributed to disseminating initiatives such as agro-ecological farming, diversified farming systems, organic agriculture, intercropping and agroforestry systems in the country. Local organizations affiliated with the national federations – such as Unión de Organizaciones Campesinas e Indígenas de Cotacachi – UNORCAC and Unión de Organizaciones Campesinas de Quevedo – UOCQ (FENOCIN) or Unión Provincial de

---

[13]After the break-up, the CNC called itself CNC-Eloy Alfaro.
[14]Since 2010, also FEI.

Organizaciones Campesinas de Manabí-UPOCAM (CNC-EA) among others – promoted: the recovery of agrobiodiversity (by seed banks and in-situ), the combination of crops with farm animal production, reforestation, soil covering and fertility recovering, as well as the substitution and reduction of agrochemicals. The common objectives of these initiatives were the reduction of external input dependence, the improvement of peasant autonomy, the promotion of solidarity and social cooperation, and environmental sustainability. To complement the above, projects for the transformation, distribution and commercialization of peasant products were implemented. Moreover, training was promoted in the three regions (The Coast, the Andean highlands and Amazonia) on diverse issues, from agro-ecological production (e.g. the program *campesino-a-campesino* adopted by FENOCIN) to formal rural education (e.g. *Unidad Educativa Popular Particular a Distancia 'Nuestra Tierra'* of CNC-EA) to political leadership (*Escuelas de Liderazgo* promoted by CONFEUNASSC, CNC-EA, FENACLE and FENOCIN), all aimed at improving the know-how and the abilities of the peasants to influence local and national policies. Planned in contradiction to the current neoliberal agri-food policies, all these enterprises were mostly self-managed and promoted by local organizations and federations, with the support of local and international non-governmental organizations (NGOs) rather than public funds.

These processes are part of a broader phenomenon experienced by Ecuador during the 1990s: a gradual spread of networks for social innovation inspired towards sustainable agriculture as well as solidarity economy. Several initiatives appeared aimed at promoting the processing and commercialization of peasant products, by means of food fairs, peasant markets and shops, in an attempt to revitalize local food systems, overcoming market intermediaries through the direct relation between producers with consumers. In more recent years, urban-marginal consumer groups appeared, organizing themselves for food purchasing and distribution, through the so-called *canastas comunitarias*. In rare cases, these groups were able to establish mechanisms of direct supply units from local peasants.

The federations linked to Vía Campesina have also concentrated efforts to organize themselves in order to boost their claims, and to influence institutions related to the agrarian issue, as illustrated in the following section.

The dynamics of resistance and creation, briefly described above, as well as the effort placed on regrouping in joint platforms, is necessary background needed to explain the ability to be proactive and the advocacy that federations involved in the fight for food sovereignty exercised in Ecuador during the Constituent Assembly of 2007/2008. However, it is interesting to note that this happened despite the fact that individual federations have undergone recurrent crises, making their collective actions, as well as their networking, discontinuous.[15]

Mesa Agraria: in search of 'unity in diversity' for a joint agrarian agenda

Beginning in the late 1990s, in Ecuador, the Mesa Agraria evolved into a national space which brought together peasant, indigenous and rural worker federations as well as their local member organizations. Initially, the participants were FENOCIN, CONFEUNASSC-CNC and ECUARUNARI.[16] The latter, however, quit the Mesa in 2003; meanwhile, in

---

[15]This discontinuity of both networking and collective action, which increased after the Constituent Assembly phase, probably contributes to the future weakness in terms of implementation of food sovereignty principles, as we summarize in the last section of this paper.

[16]Affiliated to CONAIE, Ecuarunari is not a member of Vía Campesina (unlike the other federations).

2005, FENACLE joined and in 2007 CONFEUNASSC substantially reduced its participation.

Mesa Agraria is defined as a 'consensus-building space' by the same promoting entities, to emphasize their non-fusion and to maintain the freedom of action of each federation – individually or within additional networks – with regards to the issues identified as shared.[17] Indeed, the aim of Mesa Agraria was to reach, in a participative way, a common understanding of the agrarian question, as a preliminary step to establishing a joint political agenda as well as a consequent repertoire of unified actions.

Mesa Agraria, before its dissolution in 2009, was marked by a continuous succession of intense coordination periods and 'freezing' stages, mostly dictated by 'external' political circumstances that affected organizations and distanced them.[18]

However, during its existence, this network was able to combine different dimensions and create a dialogue. First was a territorial dimension, as it set up a cooperative and bidirectional flow between national leaderships and local militants aimed at processing and validating proposals and actions. In this way, it collected the contributions of national federations as well as grassroots organizations affiliated with them in different areas (several hundred decentralized entities). This allowed, among other things, a dialogue between different territories in the nation's three regions, whose geographies are characterized by a rich social and cultural diversity. Secondly, different 'identitarian' constructions were combined, due to the significant differences between the federations in terms of self-representation, representativeness, geographic coverage and affinity to political parties.[19]

Moreover, the Mesa Agraria had to build the internal agreements needed to forge its collective action. This was enacted in two principal dimensions according to the circumstances, similar to Vía Campesina (Borras 2004), protests or dialogues and participation with institutions in order to influence their policies.

Nevertheless, these federations, over several years, have been able to dialogue and regroup around a shared innovative Agrarian Agenda through a permanent process of negotiation and construction of *unity in diversity*, also characteristic of Vía Campesina (Borras 2008; Desmarais 2008, 2009; McMichael 2008). This process, which is not trouble-free, leads to common goals and discursive practices that politicize and integrate different perspectives on the agrarian issue and, overall, reflect the socio-cultural and ecological diversity of the country.

In the early 1990s, FENOC-I and FENACLE, along with CONAIE and FEI, created a similar network for political deliberation and joint action, the Coordinadora Agraria Nacional (Coordinadora Agraria Nacional 1993; Muñoz 2010). However, with Mesa Agraria, a decade later, the perspective changed: the struggle was no longer meant to include peasants in the dominant agrarian model – chasing 'modernization and development of indigenous

---

[17]During Mesa Agraria's existence, the federations also collaborated with other networks engaged in similar issues (e.g. Foro de Recursos Hídricos, Colectivo Agrario [from 2007] or roundtables promoted by NGOs [such as Centro Andino para la Formación de Líderes Sociales (CAFOLIS)]).

[18]After the constituent assembly phase, Mesa Agraria was engaged in the debate on the law called Ley Organica de Soberania Alimentaria (LORSA), as well as the initial debate on water and land laws. After 2009, the meetings became less frequent, until the coordinating group completely dissolved, without any official statement. Federations then joined renewed areas of coordination, some founded spontaneously and others were promoted by the government, including the Red Agraria.

[19]FENOCIN is historically related to the Socialist Party, while the CONFEUNASSC and CNC were founders of the Pachakutik-Nuevo País, which they later quit. Since 2006, they have all maintained relations, even if in different manners and unstably, with the current governing party, Alianza País.

and peasant economies' (Coordinadora Agraria Nacional 1994) – but rather aspired to a transition towards food sovereignty as an alternative to neo-liberal policies.

Since 2000, the federations intensified their meetings and some NGOs started to technically and financially support this newborn coordination and to participate in the internal debate; at any rate, representation as well as deliberation, according to the approved rules of operation, remained an exclusive prerogative of the participating rural federations.[20]

Given the impact of free trade in terms of deepening the economic and productive marginalization in the national peasant sector, the anti-free trade opposition was a priority that involved the Mesa Agraria between 2001 and 2006. During that five-year period, the whole country was impacted by social mobilization in opposition to US economic integration policies, initially by the regional FTAA and then its bilateral version, between the USA and Ecuador, the FTA. The Mesa Agraria endorsed demands expressed at continental and regional levels,[21] promoted training and awareness campaigns among its member organizations and organized media campaigns, demonstrations and symbolic occupations of public entities. Its mobilizations stood alongside numerous others promoted by several Ecuadorian social actors, including CONAIE and a network called Ecuador Decide.

In addition to the struggle against FTAA, in 2002 the Mesa Agraria started an internal process of analysis and debate that led to the elaboration of an *Agenda Agraria de las Organizaciones del Campo del Ecuador* (first version dated 2003, then revised in 2006). The document is based on the food sovereignty paradigm and demands measures for an agrifood transition, as well as the relative and indispensable access to productive factors. Planning was followed (between 2003 and 2006) by a decentralized campaign within the local member organizations, specifically targeted at their communitarian leaderships, for the diffusion of the agenda and the improvement of their political action skills.

In 2003 the *Agenda Agraria* was recognized as a reference point in the elaboration of the *Minga para el agro* plan launched by the Ecuadorian government under the leadership of the indigenous leader Luis Macas, Minister of Agriculture from January to August 2003, during the presidency of Lucio Gutiérrez. At this stage, a round-table discussion was established between social actors and the Ministry, with the aim of discussing the texts of the General Law on Seed and the Law on Nutritional and Food Security. The first bulwark of agro-industry interests was then withdrawn due to pressure from indigenous, peasant and environmental organizations (including the Mesa Agraria) aimed at defending farmers' rights to seeds and avoiding GMO introduction. The second was approved in April 2006 with a text that inaugurated the use of the term 'food sovereignty' in Ecuadorian legislation.

In August 2003, the alliance between Sociedad Patriótica, Lucio Gutiérrez's party and Pachakutik (which both CONAIE and CONFEUNASCC-CNC joined) collapsed; from that moment until 2006, Mesa Agraria recoiled from dialogue spaces with the government and

---

[20]Over the years, the Mesa Agraria received the support of various Ecuadorian NGOs, such as Acción Ecológica, Fundación de Campesinos María Luisa Gómez de la Torre (FMLGT), Heifer Ecuador, Terranueva and international organizations such as Centro Regionale d'Intervento per la Cooperazione (CRIC), Terra Nuova, Intermón Oxfam or Solidaridad Suecia-América Latina (SAL). Terranueva was designated to take on the 'technical-operational secretariat' but operating on the basis of the political mandate of the federations. It would be interesting to analyze this kind of alliance with NGOs, especially compared to what it has implied in terms of expanding the capacity for the federations' action and, also, with respect to their autonomy.

[21]In meetings against the Área de Libre Comercio de las Américas (ALCA) such as the 'Encuentro Hemisférico de lucha contra el ALCA' (La Habana, November 2001), the Andean meeting 'El ALCA y sus impactos económicos y ecológicos' (Quito, March 2001), the Third Congress of CLOC (México, August 2001) and even the World Social Forum in Porto Alegre (Brazil, February 2002).

decided to focus its action on mobilization against the FTA, internal training and dissemi-nation of the *Agenda Agraria* at national and local levels.

Before the presidential election of 2006, Mesa Agraria drew up a proposal and invited the candidates to dialogue: it is in this context that, in September of the same year, the pre-sidents of the federations signed an agreement with Rafael Correa. He committed – in case of election – to promoting an 'Agrarian Revolution' that would democratize access to land, prevent water privatization, and in general foster access to strategic resources for the 'reac-tivation' of the peasant sector. In early 2007, after Correa became president, Mesa Agraria participated in the promotion of a Constituent Assembly, which was also a central request from other Ecuadorian social actors (e.g. CONAIE).

The constituent action of peasants

Mesa Agraria supported the campaign for the Constituent Assembly with human and finan-cial resources (on 15 April 2007, more than 81 percent of voters voted 'yes' in the referen-dum). This commitment was renewed in the campaign for candidates (September 2007), when two of its leaders were elected: Pedro De La Cruz (president of FENOCIN) and Guil-lermo Touma (president of FENACLE).

The federations then concentrated their efforts on signing agreements with various members of the Constituent Assembly in order to engage them in the promotion of food sovereignty. In the meantime, a participatory and deliberative debate – using regional and national forums – started among federations and their local organizations, aimed at developing a consensual proposal for the new Constitution. Rather than being a text outlin-ing the constitutional articles in detail, it referred to 'key ideas, the meanings, the spirit that we believe should animate the new Magna Carta, in particular referring to those aspects related to food sovereignty and security, territorial development with equity and workers' rights' (Mesa Agraria 2007, 4).[22] In a nutshell, it refers to five guidelines: a guar-antee of food sovereignty, a promotion of an agrarian revolution, a model of sustainable and equitable territorial development, a guarantee of workers' rights, in general and specifically of agricultural employees, and, finally, the necessity of re-establishing a sovereign and intercultural state. As explained in the same text, at the basis of the proposal is the 'unob-jectionable need to abandon neoliberalism' (Mesa Agraria 2007, 6), to move towards a different economic and social model,

> to change social, economic and productive relationships in the countryside making it more equitable, just and sustainable. To contrast productively, culturally, ideologically and by prac-tices, with the agro-industrial model of corporations and the national rural elites. (Mesa Agraria 2007, 21)

In the coastal town of Montecristi, from 30 November 2007, the Constituent Assembly commenced operating and continued until September of the following year. From that moment, the members of Mesa Agraria increased their actions, both individually and in coordination, aimed at disseminating, on a social level, the proposals through public events, media campaigns and lobbying efforts targeted at the Assembly as well as to other social actors and public opinion. A team of leaders focused on a direct and permanent dialogue with the Constituent Assembly Workgroups, while forums, food and seed festivals

---

[22]Translated by the author.

and other events were organized around the headquarters of the Assembly and during the Assembly sessions.

Among the main events, beyond various parades organized in Quito and Montecristi, was the *Feria por la Soberanía Alimentaria* (7 May 2008). A hundred producers connected to Mesa Agraria invaded the Constituent Assembly's headquarters to exhibit their seeds and products and to distribute leaflets. The climax of the day was when they offered lunch based on produce from the extremely varied food culture existing in the country. Members of the Constituent Assembly, their consultants and media reporters (more than 500 people) flocked in massive form to partake, thus commemorating the day as a crucial moment for the positioning of food sovereignty proposals.

In any case, Mesa Agraria was not the only space engaged in the promotion of the constitutionalization of food sovereignty; there were also other actors with whom the federations often discussed and collaborated. Among them were Acción Ecológica, Red Guardianes de las Semillas and Coordinadora Ecuatoriana de Agroecología. In collaboration with them, in March 2008, la Mesa Agraria organized a forum (with more than 100 delegates) to negotiate a common declaration on food sovereignty and seed defence, which was later jointly presented to the Constituent Assembly and spread widely by the media and publications.

During the Constituent Assembly process, the participation of the organizations linked to Mesa Agraria, coming from different parts of the country, was enthusiastic. There was eagerness to show the wealth of the culinary and agro-biodiversity heritage of the territories that they had helped preserve. It suggested the peasants' willingness to prove that they were key productive and political subjects able to rethink a different society.

Food sovereignty, *buen vivir* and rights of Nature: challenges of constitutionalization

At the end of the process, the balance was positive: the new Constitution includes the proposals regarding food sovereignty in a consistent way. It responds undoubtedly to an 'external' favourable political trend, but at the same time it is evidence of the ability for argumentation, communication and advocacy that peasant organizations exercised within Ecuadorian society, giving new focus and content to the agrarian question while redrafting the social contract. Since that moment, food sovereignty has expanded from the inner circles of organizations to the wider context of the whole Ecuadorian society.

In this way, it is not just a demand of social movement organizations, but a national issue that gains centrality in the political debate.

Food sovereignty was institutionalized by the new Constitution of Ecuador as part of the rights to *buen vivir* (or *sumak kawsay*); which is a concept borrowed from the Andean cosmovision, but redefined and politicized particularly by the indigenous movement, together with other social movements and critical intellectuals. The introduction of this concept represents an epistemic shift, which is able to cross the borders of Ecuador to broaden, in an innovative way, the global debate on 'development' and the capitalist mode of production.

Buen vivir is a plural and pluridimensional concept under construction (Quijano 2010; Gudynas 2011; Gudynas and Acosta 2011), based on principles such as reciprocity, solidarity and relationality (Walsh 2009; Villalba 2013) and understood not as an 'alternative development', but rather as a regime 'alternative to development' (Villalba 2013). Able to decolonize the conceptualization of history, it proposes a multi-dimensional perspective that breaks with the linear and univocal understanding imposed by the Western modernity paradigm. Far from an individualistic approach, the subject of *buen vivir* is communitarian, and constructed ontologically upon a harmonic relationship among humans and between them and the ecosystems in which they live.

This leads to pluralism and interculturalism, as ways of rethinking social relations and the state (Walsh 2009; Fatheuer 2011).

Moreover, it is important to stress that the adoption of *buen vivir* implies overcoming the logic of endless accumulation and growth as well as the extraction-oriented development paradigm. It is an innovative ontological understanding of the relationship between human and extra-human nature that recognizes their mutual penetration and suggests an overcoming of the metabolic rift that is part of capitalism. According to this perspective, Nature becomes a subject of rights, and is conceived not as an external factor of production to subjugate and exploit, but as an 'intrinsic' patrimony to respect and reproduce (Dávalos 2008). Thus, the constitutionalization of *buen vivir* entails the obsolescence of the logic of 'accumulation by dispossession' (Harvey 2003) and the commodification of nature (and with it of agriculture and food), encouraging Ecuador to overcome its historical dependence on the exploitation of natural resources. In this challenge, the debate on whether or not to extract oil found in Yasuní National Park is emblematic (Fatheuer 2011).

The economy, as conceptualized in the new constitutional text, recognizes humans as subjects and gravitates toward a dynamic and balanced relationship between society, state and market, in harmony with Nature. In this way, the market is not considered to be the exclusive social regulator, while the state is conceived as a guarantor of the right to *buen vivir* of the population and the rights of Nature (Gobierno del Ecuador 2008).

Within this innovative model of conceiving the world and social reproduction, food sovereignty becomes the framework used to change the agri-food model, placing the agrarian issue out of the hegemonic discourse of modernization and productivity.

However, a question remains: to what extent has the concept of food sovereignty been included in the Constitution respecting all its original implications in terms of rethinking the agrarian issue (McMichael 2006, 2008; Desmarais 2009; Patel 2009)? In particular, this question focuses on two main elements inherent in the proposal of food sovereignty and its epistemic fracture:

(1) the recognition of food as a right that cannot be mediated (or organized) by the market, but must reside within the free discretion of the 'people, nations and states' (Declaration of Nyeleni 2007);

(2) the affirmation of the rights of people and countries not only to food but also to the production of appropriate food, claiming, thus, the essential re-appropriation, to the hands of those who produce, of production factors such as land, water and seeds.

In opposition to the policies historically implemented in Ecuador, which aimed at the production of exotic commodities (fruit, flowers, shrimp, etc.) for foreign markets, the new Constitution establishes radical changes in the agri-food sector.

Article 13 of the Preamble affirms the rights of individuals and communities to the secure and permanent access to appropriate food, preferably locally produced, according to different identities and cultures. This article ends by assigning the role of food sovereignty promoter to the state (Gobierno del Ecuador 2008). This first statement, however, does not develop a full definition of what food sovereignty means (Giunta and Vitale 2013). Parts of the elements that characterize and establish the dichotomy of food sovereignty versus food security (Cavazzani 2008) were included in the body of the constitutional text, especially in reference to 'by whom' and 'how' to produce food, through a chapter specifically dedicated to food sovereignty. Article 281 establishes food sovereignty as a 'strategic goal and governmental obligation to ensure that persons, communities, peoples and nationalities reach self-sufficiency of healthy and culturally appropriate food, on a permanent basis' (Gobierno del Ecuador 2008, 281).[23]

Also detailed are the desirable measures as well as the responsibilities of the state. According to the claims of peasant organizations, it promotes:

(1) short food chains and a greater national self-sufficiency;
(2) the agro-ecological conversion and free use of seeds;
(3) Ecuador as a country free of GMO seeds (raw material or finished products not included);
(4) support to peasants aimed at the access to land, water and credit;
(5) prohibition of latifundium and a social and ecological function for land use;
(6) prohibition of monopolistic and speculative practices around food;
(7) primacy of production for food sovereignty rather than for agro-fuels;
(8) fair economy and direct relationship between producers and consumers.

The inclusion of these regulations certainly means a radical rethinking of the agri-food system. However, the Constitution includes points of 'no determination'. A significant example is given by its demand for the redistribution of land or water without solving how to promote fair access to these productive factors. Perhaps by market rules? Or by an agrarian reform which proceeds to expropriate lands? This is a fundamental matter in the food sovereignty proposal of Vía Campesina and is the key to changing the strong inequalities that cross rural Ecuadorian areas.

In addition, a leading role is assigned to the state as a guarantor of food sovereignty. At first glance, this undoubtedly appears to be a significant achievement for organizations and social movements who fought for the state to take on these responsibilities.

In fact, the concept of food sovereignty promoted by Vía Campesina implies 'the necessity of governments and states to protect and stimulate family, peasant and cooperative farming with adequate agricultural pricing policies, technical assistance and market guarantees' (Vía Campesina 2009, 59).

In this way, it claims a central role for the state, although global governance has undermined sovereignty and reduced (but not reset) the centrality of the states. Vía Campesina explains this position, which could be considered a return to nationalism, referring to the 'national purpose' of the state and therefore the responsibility of parties and governments in the 'administration of the so-called "common good"' (Vía Campesina 2009, 95), pointing out that:

the true solution to the problems within agriculture will not always be resolved by governments and political forces. This statement does not mean that our social movement must construct its own model, parallel to the one of the state, or must construct basic participating alternatives, not related to the political institutionalism or to the market. We must stress that these policies must reach the agricultural sector and rural areas without inequality nor exclusion. (Vía Campesina 2009, 96)

This position implies the affirmation of two issues as a priority: (1) sovereignty of the state over national policies and (2) centrality of the role of the state in the transition of the development model. However, at the same time, it is accompanied by a persistent claim by Vía

---

[23]Translated by the author.

Campesina of a (3) leading role in decision-making and over the control of resources held by communities, peoples and nations.

The first two principles are widely found within the Ecuadorian Constitution. As regards the first, the constitutional text claims a 'plural notion of sovereignty', considering it as popular, national and referring to food, energy and international relations (Acosta and Martínez 2010; SENPLADES 2013a). As for the second principle, the entire Constitution is founded on state centrality, including the sections dedicated to food sovereignty.

In reference to the third aspect, people and communities hold the right to access to food. However, it is not explicit whether they hold the right to decide, on a permanent and systematic basis, on their agri-food systems and policies, a right that is a fundamental part of food sovereignty as conceptualized by Vía Campesina.

The Constitution generally provides the guarantee of 'participation of persons, communities, peoples and nationalities' (Gobierno del Ecuador 2008, Art. 85), through a permanent construction of the so-called *poder ciudadano* (citizen power) (Art. 95). Here, participation is clearly understood as a right of all citizens to be actively engaged in all matters of public interest through mechanisms of 'representative, direct and communitarian democracy'. The effectiveness of the instruments provided for this participation remains an open question but, in any case, the constitutional text introduces the paradigm of food sovereignty without explicitly identifying the community as essential subjects of the hoped-for transition, and as politically recognized and visible actors along with the state. This leads to the question of whether the state is able to implement a transition to a food sovereignty regime on its own – without social mobilization and participation – overturning power relations and acquiring, in the meantime, the technical skills needed to transform the agri-food system.

Clearly, open issues are not fortuities, but marked by conflicting interests that clashed during the Constituent Assembly. In fact, the constitutional text must be read as the result of tension and negotiations between pro-change sectors and groups concentrated on the defence of their privileges (Acosta and Martínez 2011), which even occurred within the governing party, Alianza País (Muñoz 2010; Ramírez Gallegos 2010). In this way, during the Constituent Assembly the power relations, as they were, allowed the constitutionalization of a significant part of the pro-food sovereignty proposals, but not to the extent that they led to success for the more controversial issues, such as a total regulation of the agrarian reform and GMOs. Due to this impasse, the choice was to postpone the resolution on the points of disagreement to the consequent legislative regulation (Rosero Garcés et al. 2011), as promoted by executive and Constituent Assembly forces.

The enabling legislation: avoiding the nodal points of conflict

At the beginning of 2009, the LORSA (Organic Law of the Food Sovereignty Regime) was approved by National Assembly, then modified by a partial presidential veto and entered in force in May 2009.[24]

Local members of Vía Campesina continued their influencing action, but in a more dispersed manner and showed a decreased deliberative and proactive ability; on the other hand, reactionary sectors – opposed to a food sovereignty regime – strived to reduce the constitutional mandate, taking advantage of a political situation which was more favourable to them, due to contradictory positions within the same government, as well as a relative

---

[24]The LORSA, as modified by the presidential partial veto, entered into force without a previous review, within the 30 days established, by the National Assembly (Rosero Garcés et al. 2011).

repositioning of the opposition forces. The result of the process, in itself very short, is the entry in force of a 'law of mediation' that put aside most of the sensitive, even if key, issues, despite the fact that it was a framework legislation aimed at establishing the mechanisms by which the state must undertake the obligations and objectives provided in the constitutional text (Muñoz 2010).

Access to land, understood as one of the main demands of peasant organizations, was ratified in Article 6 on the basis of its social and environmental function and through the inclusion of measures in favour of small producers, including the ones specifically related to women producers and breadwinners (Gobierno del Ecuador 2009). However, the Law does not outline the guidelines and modalities to implement it, or the resources needed to create the National Land Fund. Even the fundamental right to water is ratified, but its regulation was postponed to the corresponding law, which is one of the legislative projects that have generated greater social conflict during the transition period after the Constituent Assembly (Ramírez Gallegos et al. 2013). The free use, interchange and conservation of seeds are once again recognized as a responsibility of the state and society; here LORSA added, however, the specification of 'native' which would exclude locally improved foreign varieties (such as rice). Explicitly mentioned is the conversion to agro-ecological systems and diversification as well as that priority should be given to small and medium productions for public agri-food purchases.

However, by the partial presidential veto of the Law, some critical points were introduced, in reference to: (1) inserting greater flexibility for the production of agro-fuels, that must be avoided 'as much as possible'; (2) granting a time-span of one year for illegal owners to regularize their shrimp production (about 44,642 hectares of mangroves); (3) foreseeing subsidies for big producers in case of market distortions; (4) deleting the specification of destroying the GMO seeds (if entered as raw materials) and, to put it more generally, as disabling their reproductive capacity, without specifying how (Rosero Garcés et al. 2011).

The Conferencia Nacional de Soberanía Alimentaria (COPISA) was founded with members appointed through a competition based on merits and not endowed with a completely autonomous status (as initially proposed by organizations); indeed the COPISA was then ascribed to the Ministry of Agriculture. The task assigned to this entity was to coordinate a participatory debate for the design of subordinate laws (use and access to land, seeds, agricultural development, agro-industry and agricultural employment, animal and plant health, public access to credit, insurance and subsidies).

As in the Constituent Assembly phase, the debate on the points of greatest conflict was postponed to the approbation of the laws subordinated to LORSA.[26]

Several drafts of the bill were presented; some were promoted by COPISA or supported by it. One instance is the proposal of Land and Territories Law presented by Red Agraria (integrated by CNC-EA, FENOCIN, FENACLE and FEI with other organizations) through a citizen initiative of gathering petition signatures. Implemented between October 2011 and March 2012, it reached a wide social consensus with over 40,000 endorsements when 25,000 would have been sufficient for the legislative qualification. The text – discussed in several workshops by organizations and communities of the three regions – handled the most critical issue of land redistribution, advancing concrete proposals.

---

[26]They are: land, water, productive model, use of GMOs and agro-fuels.

In fact, this bill set the maximum extension for private property,[27] anything beyond would be turned into agro-productive enterprises (with 40 percent of the stocks sold to the workers involved), or the surplus would have to be sold, otherwise it would be expropriated. It is one of the most debated topics, due to its relevance in defining which properties should be considered as latifundium, and therefore illegal according to Article 282 of the Constitution. This bill also promoted the redistribution of state lands, to be assigned exclusively to associative property (by at least five people) and free of charge, or, at the most, after paying a symbolic price. In addition, it proposed the establishment of a Ministry for Food Sovereignty as a necessary institution to implement the agrarian reform process and, in general, to safeguard the hoped-for transition in the agri-food system.

In total, at least six bills were drawn up (Rosero Garcés et al. 2011), including one by the Chamber of Agriculture that was presented to the National Assembly in March 2012 by a member of the ruling party (who quit a few months later). This text quoted some of the constitutional watchwords, referring to the concept of food sovereignty and the need to regulate latifundism, but was careful to set limits for private property. It proposed to qualify the latifundium only on the basis of its non-productivity or in presence of unused public infrastructure for irrigation. Finally, it provided the transaction on the market as a unique mechanism for land redistribution.

However, the more sensitive subordinate laws were still not approved, probably due to the lack of agreements among (and within) the legislative groups and between them and the executive groups. Land tenure (regulation of latifundium and mechanisms for access to land) and agricultural model (specifically GMOs and agrofuels) appear to be as the most controversial issues, as parts of the more general dichotomy between continuity of the neoliberal approach and transition towards agro-ecological and food sovereignty models. This is a contention experienced also by the same government and ruling party, which is integrated by conservative as well as more pro-change trends.[28]

Another factor causing delay was probably that in 2009–2013, the governmental block did not reach an absolute majority in National Assembly, having to find a way to gain support for each law approved (Ramírez Gallegos et al. 2013).

In this context, sensitive issues that would leave social movements or, in contrast, powerful economic groups unsatisfied, were intentionally avoided during the campaign for the presidential election (February 2013).

In the light of the legislative majority won by re-elected president Rafael Correa, an acceleration was predictable for the new period of government (2013–2017), as well as a complicated resolution of the differences on central issues experienced within the same government and ruling party, which we have outlined above. Due to the complexity as well as the dynamism of the political arena, predictions are not easy; however, in the next sections, we present some reflections that could contribute to consideration of the different options.

---

[27]Coast and Amazonia: 500 hectares, highlands: 200. Moreover, it distinguishes between properties exceeding those limits as either productive or unproductive, each receiving different treatment (processing, sale or expropriation).
[28]The composition of Alianza País is heterogeneous: it has been promoted by leaders of traditional leftist parties, leftist intellectuals, ecologists, social and women activists as well as people without political trajectory but aligned to Correa or coming from catholic and center-right sectors. This diversity, held together and governed by Correa, has generated tensions, during and after the Constituent Assembly (see e.g. Ramírez Gallegos 2010; Ramírez Gallegos et al. 2013).

Will the 'Agrarian Revolution' start?

Since the beginning, an 'Agrarian Revolution' has been considered as a strategic component of the Citizens' Revolution promoted by the government of Rafael Correa. However, five years after the approval of the Constitution, the balance of this 'Agrarian Revolution', in terms of implementation of public policies and strategies, is frequently critically evaluated, even by the same government sector.[29]

The official plans, including the Plan of *buen vivir* (the National Development Plan) for the period 2013–2017, continue to claim food sovereignty as part of a radical change of the productive matrix. However, the current situation is quite different.

In recent years the agribusiness has been strengthened and exports have increased, due to higher global food prices, but also thanks to a clear continuity in the agri-food policies.

Meanwhile, an aid policy, based on packages tailored to traditional monoculture and targeted at small producers, continue to retain sizeable public support.

As for the innovative level, 'Schools of the Agrarian Revolution' (aimed at improving food sovereignty and productivity by the promotion of dialogue between local and scientific knowledge) have been implemented, as well as projects designed to facilitate access to credit and land. Yet these might seem to be encouraging a status of peasant dependence, since they are not clearly associated with processes of agro-ecological conversion. The land program (*Plan Tierras*) addresses, in an innovative way, the issue of land tenure, promoting acquisition by associative models rather than by individuals.

Despite this innovation, mechanisms of the commodification of land and financialization of the rural areas are reproduced by plans which lead the peasants into debt (with the Banco Nacional de Fomento) in order to purchase land on the market.

Moreover, this could generate significant increases of the land price on the market.

This seems to be in contradiction with the proposal of food sovereignty as interpreted by Vía Campesina, which affirms the necessity of 'altering power relations in society in favour of peasants and the coalitions which support them and which have nothing to do with the private patrimonial transactions financed by the state', a position that involves a severe critique of the strategy of agrarian reform promoted by the World Bank and is based 'on the liberalization of agricultural markets' (Vía Campesina 2009, 131).

Moreover, some initiatives, called 'rural inclusive businesses', have been promoted with the aim of connecting producers with agro-industry and the big distribution chains, but they do not automatically imply a conversion to the model of production or the traditional accumulation regime.

As for his commitment, President Correa has repeatedly emphasized the need to modernize the Ecuadorian rural sector to increase productivity, including the use of GMOs, and has announced the necessary constitutional reforms to allow it.

In the meantime, social organizations (including those linked to Vía Campesina that animated Mesa Agraria and then Red Agraria) have suffered reshaping of their organizational ability and political action. This is probably due to the inherent cycles of latency and visibility of the collective action and to the necessity to redefine objectives and strategies in a context that has changed radically in a few years. The current leadership is no longer a classic government of the neoliberal era, therefore organizations cannot act as they usually do: they have to reinvent their strategies and political agendas. Autonomous action is complex, especially for those organizations that support Correa's government

---

[29]In this regard, Rafael Correa has declared, on several occasions, that the launching of drastic transformations in rural development is the biggest debt that the government owes to Ecuadorians.

and that are in a precarious balance in the attempt to publicly report the inertia in official agri-food policies without being in opposition to the government – a government that is engaged in the promotion of significant transformations in the country, especially regarding the improvement of social policies, the redistribution of wealth, the defence of the state and its role as regulator. For these reasons, it continues to enjoy high levels of support from the population and from the organizations linked to Vía Campesina.

In this regard, a trend to governmental centralism could reduce the space for dialogue, while at the same time promoting a direct relationship between the state and single producers by means of official programs. In this way, organizations experiment with a reduction of their intermediary role and their abilities to influence the decision-making process. This trend informs, in general, the modalities of relationship between the state and the social actors in a government that, even if 'progressive', is far from building itself as a 'government of social movements'. Indeed, as we have noticed, organized social actors and individuals seem to play an ambiguous role in the institutionalization of food sovereignty principles. This vagueness – in the phase following the Constituent Assembly – leads to the marginalization of those who were the main actors of this innovative constitutionalization.[30] Meanwhile, international cooperation has reduced its financial support, further weakening the possibility of 'autonomous' action, at least from the state, of these social actors.

In the early phase (2009–2012) following the Constituent Assembly there were some mobilizations (conflicting and pro-active), such as the protests for water and against mining or, as stressed above, the peasant proposal of the Land Law. However, peasant organizations and federations that have promoted the institutionalization of food sovereignty face difficulties in gaining visibility on the political scene and in the media.

They must cope with the risk of being used by several actors: on the one hand, the government itself, which might be interested in treating them as 'pacified' allies and, on the other hand, the opposition, particularly by those interested in generating a perception of widespread antagonism towards the government (such as the private media, angered by regulatory policies on information conducted by Correa). The result is that little attention is obtained in the political scene, as occurred in March 2012, on the occasion of the official presentation of the Land Bill, when public attention was fragmented mostly between the *Marcha por la vida* protest (promoted by CONAIE and the left opposition) and the counter-march supported by the government. On that occasion, the third possibility sponsored by Red Agraria – aimed at making its voice heard by demanding radical changes in the agri-food system by means of dialogue rather than protest – attracted modest attention, if not outright rejection, from those groups in conflict.

In this context, it seems that power relations are not settling favourably for pro-food sovereignty organizations. If this is true, the space of negotiation – for enabling legislation and policies – will probably turn from the fight for an overall transition in the agri-food system to more moderate challenges.[31] These could be some elements of a food sovereignty agenda that allow greater access to productive resources and to the food chains, by focused policies for peasants.

---

[30]Which are, as argued in the first part of this paper, FENOCIN, CNC-EA, CONFEUNASSC and FENACLE, among others.

[31]In this sense, the latest demand of peasant organizations for the establishment of a Ministry of Food Sovereignty, rather than persisting with a transformation of the Ministry of Agriculture, could be an indicator.

Conclusions

Currently, in Ecuador, food sovereignty is part of the national political debate and a contentious issue for the whole society, not only for peasant organizations.

However, the redesign of public institutions and agri-food policies does not appear consistent with the mandates positioned in the Constituent Assembly phase. This is conceivable in light of the slow pace in materializing those challenges (by enabling legislation and official policies) and the persistence of the logic of rural industrialization and modernization within certain strategic components of the government. All this is accompanied by a reduced centrality of social actors that originally sponsored the proposal for food sovereignty.

Nevertheless, food sovereignty remains a collective goal, constitutionalized and therefore legitimate, towards which Ecuadorian society should head. This embodies not only a victory for the Ecuadorian and international movements that have made it their battleground, but also a crucial step that marks the relations of power in the agri-food sector.

A 'return of the state' in rural development, after the drastic reduction due to adjustment, is certain, including radical improvements in welfare.[32] Moreover, it is necessary to recognize that the Constitution represents a roadmap. Meanwhile, the transition is complex, considering the structural inequality inside the country and its dependent integration in the global dimension. However, the inconsistency between the challenges constitutionalized or included in government plans (such as the National Development Plan), and the slowdown in the adoption of legislations and policies clearly influenced by them, must also be understood as the result of contradiction between divergent interests and concrete power relations in the Ecuadorian agri-food sector. The resistance to food transition is animated, clearly, by powerful groups dedicated to agro-industry and agro-export, which historically grew at the expense of the mass of peasants, indigenous and rural workers. The effects are differences on crucial issues within the same governmental block, between the more conservative elements and those committed to the need for radical changes.

In Ecuador, there is an ongoing conflict related to the control of resources which results in the struggle between two ideas of social production: '*buen vivir*', as an alternative to development, versus a reinvention of 'developmentism', where market maintains primacy and the transformation process is based on an intensive exploitation of nature and modernization.

The result of this clash is yet not clear, just as whether or not the second model (developmentism) is transitionally necessary to reach the first one (*buen vivir*), as even the most optimists would argue. In this sense, it is interesting to critically reflect on this clash and recognize the role of social movements in the promotion and materialization of new models, as well as in their ability to gain a concrete engagement of the government in order to change power relations. It would imply a rethinking of the role of the state and

---

[32]Welfare spending quadrupled between 2006 and 2012; the promotion of gratuity improved significantly the access to education and health while poverty (income based) decreased by 10 percent. The regained centrality of the state in the planning and implementing of development strategies led the launching of significant plans to improve mobility and transport infrastructures as well as the quality of human settlements (e.g. housing, water, sanitation) and the increase of cash transfer programs (see e.g. SENPLADES 2013b). All these measures were focused on more vulnerable populations, including those in the rural areas.

materializing more participative forms of governance for the transition, that clearly include all social actors.

The food sovereignty proposal offers the possibility of reestablishing the relationship between humans and nature, as well as between cities and the countryside. In this regard, Ecuador, with the institutionalization of the paradigms of *buen vivir* and food sovereignty, has redefined the route, opting for a break that must radically transform the overall productive matrix.

References

Acosta, A. 2006. *Breve historia económica del Ecuador*. 3rd ed. Quito: CEN.

Acosta, A., and E. Martínez, eds. 2010. *Soberanías*. Quito: Abya-Yala.

Acosta, A., and E. Martínez, eds. 2011. *Economía social y solidaria. El trabajo antes que el capital. José Luis Coraggio*. Quito: Abya-Yala.

Altieri, M.A. 2009. Agroecology, small farms, and food sovereignty. *Monthly Review* 61, no. 3: 102–11.

BCE (Banco Central del Ecuador). 2012. Reporte de pobreza, desigualdad y mercado laboral. BCE. http://www.bce.fin.ec/documentos/Estadisticas/SectorReal/Previsiones/IndCoyuntura/Empleo/PobrezaDic2012.pdf (accessed August 12, 2013).

Borras, S.M. Jr. 2004. La Vía Campesina: An evolving transnational social movement. *Transnational Institute (TNI) Briefing Paper*, November 2004. Amsterdam: Transnational Institute (TNI).

Borras, S.M. Jr. 2008. La Vía Campesina and its Global Campaign for Agrarian Reform. *Journal of Agrarian Change* 8, no. 2–3: 258–89.

Carrión, D., and S. Herrera. 2012. *Ecuador rural del siglo XXI. Soberanía alimentaria, inversión pública y política agraria*. Quito: IEE.

Cavazzani, A. 2008. Tra sicurezza e sovranità alimentare. *Sociologia Urbana e Rurale* 30, no. 87: 43–7.

Chiriboga, M. 2004. Mercados, mercadeo y economías campesinas. *Ecuador Debate* 61: 217–34.

CLOC (Coordinadora Latinoamericana de Organizaciones del Campo). n.d. Quienes somos? http://www.cloc-viacampesina.net/es/quienes-somos (accessed August 2013).

Coordinadora Agraria Nacional. 1993. Manifiesto de la Coordinadora Agraria Nacional. http://abyayala.nativeweb.org/ecuador/agrarian/agrar1.html (accessed August 2013).

Coordinadora Agraria Nacional. 1994. *Proyecto de Ley Agraria Integral*. Quito: CONAIE, FEPP.

Dávalos, P. 2005. Movimiento indígena ecuatoriano: construcción política y epistémica. In *Cultura, política y sociedad. Perspectivas latinoamericanas*, ed. D. Mato, pp. 337–57. Buenos Aires: CLACSO.

Dávalos, P. 2008. *Reflexiones sobre el sumak kawsay (el buen vivir) y las teorías del desarrollo*. Quito: ALAI. http://alainet.org/active/25617&lang=es (accessed May 8, 2013).

Desmarais, A.A. 2008. The power of peasants: Reflections on the meanings of La Vía Campesina. *Journal of Rural Studies* 24, no. 2: 138–49.

Desmarais, A.A. 2009. *La Vía Campesina. La globalizzazione e il potere dei contadini*. Milano: Jaca Book.

ECLAC, FAO, and IICA. 2012. *The Outlook for Agriculture and Rural Development in the Americas: A Perspective on Latin America and the Caribbean. 2013*. Santiago, Chile: FAO.

Falconí, F., and P. Muñoz. 2012. Ecuador: de la receta del 'Consenso de Washington' al Posneoliberalismo. In *Rafael Correa, balance de la Revolución Ciudadana*, ed. S. Mantilla and S. Mejía, pp. 75–96. Quito: Editorial Planeta.

Fatheuer, T. 2011. Buen Vivir. A brief introduction to Latin America's new concepts for the good life and the rights of nature. *Publication Series on Ecology* Vol. 17. Berlin: Heinrich Böll Foundation.

García Pascual, F. 2006. El sector agrario del Ecuador. Incertidumbres (riesgos) ante la globalización. *Íconos* 10, no. 24: 71–88.

Giunta, I., and A. Vitale. 2013. Politiche e pratiche di sovranità alimentare. *Agriregionieuropa* 9, no. 33: 81–3.

Gobierno del Ecuador. 2008. *Constitución de la República del Ecuador*. Quito: Asamblea Nacional Constituyente.

Gobierno del Ecuador. 2009. *Ley orgánica del Régimen de la Soberanía Alimentaria.* Quito: Asamblea Nacional.

Gudynas, E. 2011. Desarrollo, derechos de la naturaleza y Buen Vivir despúes de Montecristi. In *Debates sobre cooperación y modelos de desarrollo. Perspectivas desde la sociedad civil en el Ecuador,* ed. G. Weber, pp. 83–102. Quito: CIUDAD.

Gudynas, E., and A. Acosta. 2011. La renovación de la crítica al desarrollo y el buen vivir como alternativa. *Utopía y Praxis Latinoamericana* 16, no. 53: 71–83.

Guerrero, C.F., and P.P. Ospina. 2003. *El poder de la comunidad. Ajuste estructural y movimiento indígena en los Andes ecuatorianos.* Buenos Aires: CLACSO.

Harvey, D. 2003. *The New Imperialism.* Oxford: Oxford University Press.

INEC. 2013. *Evolución de los Indicadores Laborales Septiembre-2013.* Quito: INEC. http://www.inec. gob.ec/estadisticas/?option=com_content&view=article&id=92&Itemid=57 (accessed October 31, 2013).

Kay, C. 2004. Rural livelihoods and peasant futures. In *Latin America Transformed: Globalization and Modernity.* 2nd ed., eds. R.N. Gwynne and C. Kay, pp. 232–50. London: Arnold.

Larrea, F., A. Andrango, and J.P. Muñoz. 1996. Rupturas y consensos: la lucha del movimiento indígena en el Ecuador en el marco del proceso de modernización agraria. *Cuadernos Agrarios* 50, no. 11–12: 255–62.

Larrea Maldonado, A.M. 2004. El movimiento indígena ecuatoriano: participación y resistencia. *OSAL* 5, no. 13: 67–76.

Martínez-Alier, J. 2011. The EROI of agriculture and its use by the Via Campesina. *Journal of Peasant Studies* 38, no. 1: 145–60.

Martínez Valle, L. 2004. Trabajo flexible en la nuevas zonas bananeras de Ecuador. In *Effectos sociales de la globalización. Petróleo, banano y flores en Ecuador,* ed. T. Korovkin, pp. 129–55. Quito: Cedime, Abya-Yala.

Martínez Valle, L. 2008. Respuestas endógenas de los campesinos frente al ajuste estructural. Ecuador desde la perspectiva andina comparativa. In *Desarrollo rural y neoliberalismo,* ed. L.L. North and J.D. Cameron, pp. 105–27. Quito: CEN- UASB.

McMichael, P. 2006. Reframing development: Global peasant movements and the new agrarian question. *Canadian Journal of Development Studies* 27, no. 4: 471–83.

McMichael, P. 2008. Peasants make their own history, but not just as they please . . . *Journal of Agrarian Change* 8, no. 2-3: 205–28.

Mesa Agraria. 2007. *Soberanía Alimentaria: propuestas a la Asamblea Nacional Constituyente.* Quito: Ecuador.

Muñoz, J.P. 2010. Constituyente, gobierno de transición y soberanía alimentaria en Ecuador. In *Cambio de rumbo en las políticas agrarias latinoamericanas? Estado, movimientos sociales campesinos y soberanía alimentaria,* eds. J. Gascón and X. Montagut, pp. 151–68. Barcelona: Icaria Editorial.

Ospina, P. 2009. 'Nos vino un huracán politico': la crisis de la CONAIE. In *Los Andes en movimiento. Identidad y poder en el nuevo paisaje político,* eds. P. Ospina et al., pp. 123–46. Quito: UASB-UB-CEN.

Paredis, E., G. Goeminne, and W. Vanhove. 2007. *The Concept of Ecological Debt: Its Meaning and Applicability in International Policy.* Ghent: Academia Press.

Patel, R. 2009. What does Food Sovereignty look like?. *Journal of Peasant Studies* 36, no. 3: 663–706.

Peltre-Wurtz, J. 1989. El pan que comemos es estadounidense. In *Flujos geográficos en el Ecuador. Intercambios de bienes, personas e información,* eds. J.V. León et al., pp. 7–16. Quito: Corporación Editora Naciónal.

Quijano, A. 2010. 'Bien Vivir' para REDISTRIBUIR el poder. Los pueblos indígenas y su propuesta alternativa en tiempos de dominación global. In OXFAM, *Informe 2009–2010 Oxfam. Pobreza, desigualdad y desarrollo en el Perú.* Lima: OXFAM, pp. 112–121.

Ramírez Gallegos, F. 2010. Fragmentación, reflujo y desconcierto. Movimientos sociales y cambio político en el Ecuador (2000–2010). *OSAL* 11, no. 28: 17–47.

Ramírez Gallegos, F., M. Le Quang, and C. Bastidas Redín. 2013. *Investigaciones Legislativas-Coaliciones parlamentarias y conflictividad social en el Ecuador 2009–2011.* Quito: ANE-AG.

Rosero Garcés, F., Y. Carbonell Yonfá, and F. Regalado Villaroel. 2011. *Soberanía alimentaria, modelos de desarrollo y tierras en Ecuador.* Quito: CAFOLIS.

SENPLADES. 2013a. *Plan Nacional de Desarrollo / Plan Nacional para el Buen Vivir 2013–2017*. Quito: SENPLADES.

SENPLADES. 2013b. *6 años Revolución Ciudadana*. Quito: SENPLADES.

Vía Campesina. 1996. II International Conference of the Vía Campesina Tlaxcala, Mexico, April 18–21. http://viacampesina.org/en/index.php/our-conferences-mainmenu-28/2-tlaxcala-1996-mainmenu-48/425-ii-international-conference-of-the-via-campesina-tlaxcala-mexico-april-18-2 (accessed August 2013).

Vía Campesina. 2009. *La Vía Campesina Policy Documents- 5th Conference Mozambique, October, 2008*, Jakarta: Indonesia.

Villalba, U. 2013. Buen Vivir vs development: A paradigm shift in the Andes? *Third World Quarterly* 34, no. 8: 1427–42.

Walsh, C. 2009. *Interculturalidad, estado, sociedad. Luchas (de) coloniales de nuestra época*. Quito: UASB-Abya Yala.

Zamosc, L. 2009. Ciudadanía indígena y cohesión social en América Latina. In *Los Andes en movimiento. Identidad y poder en el nuevo paisaje político*, eds. P. Ospina et al., pp. 13–39. Quito: UASB-UB-CEN.

Isabella Giunta is a PhD candidate, Doctoral School in Knowledge and Innovation for Development, A. Gunder Frank, Department of Political and Social Sciences, University of Calabria (Italy). A graduate in Social Anthropology, Ms. Giunta lived for more than 10 years in Ecuador working on cooperation and research projects, conducted mainly with indigenous and peasant organizations. She is currently carrying out comparative research between Ecuador and Italy on the collective actions of organizations linked to Vía Campesina.

Re-purposing the master's tools: the open source seed initiative and the struggle for seed sovereignty

Jack Kloppenburg

'Food sovereignty' must necessarily encompass 'seed sovereignty'. Corporate appropriation of plant genetic resources, development of transgenic crops and the global imposition of intellectual property rights are now widely recognized as serious constraints on the free exchange of seeds and the development of new cultivars by farmers, public breeders and small seed companies. In response, an Open Source Seed Initiative (OSSI) has been launched in the United States to apply legal mechanisms drawn from the open source software movement to plant breeding. An open source license is a tool constituted by the provisions of contract law. It is a tool of the master inasmuch as the structure of the legal system has been designed to facilitate the activities of the dominant stakeholders in the overarching social formation. This paper assesses the problematics of re-purposing such a tool by examining the issues that have been raised in OSSI's efforts to develop its licenses and to transmit its sense of their potential to prospective allies. Through an examination of the expressed positions of La Vía Campesina and Navdanya on the nature of 'seed sovereignty', the compatibilities and disjunctures of OSSI's stance with those of potential allies in the food sovereignty movement are assessed.

Introduction

For the master's tools will never dismantle the master's house. They may allow us to temporarily beat him at his own game, but they will never enable us to bring about genuine change.

–Audre Lorde (1984)

Open source is a development methodology. Free software is a social movement.

–Richard Stallman (2013)

Given the position of the seed as part of the irreducible core of agricultural production, it is difficult to imagine any form of 'food sovereignty' that does not include a necessary and concomitant dimension of what might be called 'seed sovereignty'. The erosion of farmer sovereignty over seed – via corporate appropriation of plant genetic resources, growing monopoly power in the seed industry, the development of transgenic crops and the global imposition of intellectual property rights – has become a pivotal issue for farmers the world over. Whatever their many differences, primary agricultural producers of *all* types and in (almost) *all* places find themselves confronting Monsanto (and/or its corporate analogs) in similar fashion, with similar implications for their access to and use of seed. The seed and its attendant political ecology are now a potential vector for development of the sort of shared consciousness envisioned by Marx (1998, 45) and wel-comed by La Vía Campesina (LVC) leaders as 'a common base … for globalising the struggle' (Nicholson in Wittman 2009, 678) against the corporate food regime.

Nor are farmers the only ones subject to the conscientizing influence of the way capital has assumed sovereignty over the seed. Plant breeders in public institutions now find them-selves in a position very similar to that of farmers. Increasingly, their access to genetic material, and even breeding methods, are constrained by the proliferation of intellectual property rights which are concentrated disproportionately among a narrow set of large and powerful firms. The debilitating effect of such limitations on these breeders' 'freedom to operate' is accompanied by declining funding and by institutional pressures to shape their research in ways that complement – rather than compete with or provide alternatives to – the objectives and interests of the 'Gene Giants'. For at least some public breeders, the mismatch between their normative commitment to public service and the demands for accommodation with industry is a motivation to seek another path.

A material expression of this tendency can be seen in the creation in the United States of the Open Source Seed Initiative (OSSI), of which I am a founding member. Organized by a working group of public plant breeders, private breeders, non-governmental organ-izations (NGOs) and sustainable food system advocates, OSSI intends to encourage and reward the sharing rather than the restriction of germplasm, to revitalize public plant breeding and to integrate the skills and capacities of farmer breeders with those of plant scientists. A key tool for achieving these goals is development of 'open source' licenses that preserve the right to use material for breeding and the right of farmers to save and replant seed. Modeled on the legal arrangements successfully deployed by the free and open source software movement, OSSI hopes that its licenses might under-gird the creation of a 'protected commons' populated by farmers and plant breeders whose materials would be freely available and widely exchanged but would be protected from appropriation by those who would monopolize them. Although constituted as a North American initiative in the first instance, it is OSSI's ambition to catalyze the estab-lishment of allied initiatives among indigenous peoples, in the Global South and in Europe.

That sounds nice in theory (Kloppenburg 2010). The actual process of implementation has been rather more complicated than we of OSSI had hoped. And here the quotation from poet Audre Lorde is germane. An open source license is a tool constituted by the provisions of contract law, backed by the authority of the state. As Lorde warns, it is a tool of the master inasmuch as the structure and provisions of the legal system have for the most part been designed to facilitate the activities of the dominant stakeholders in the overarching social formation. That does not mean that space for progressive and liberatory action is absent, for taking Lorde at face value is to subscribe to a species of determinism. But we at OSSI should surely take her caution seriously. Re-purposing contract law is not simple, and it is prudent to assess the degree to which it implicates us in relationships we might prefer to avoid as well as the degree to which it might produce the genuine change that we desire.

This paper represents an initiation of that assessment through engagement with some of the key issues that have been raised in our efforts to develop OSSI licenses and to transmit our sense of possibility to potential allies and cooperators. At a practical level, we have encountered a variety of technical, legal obstacles to drafting workable licenses that are making us rethink our relative emphasis on the normative goal of reintroducing an ethos of sharing for germplasm exchange versus the pragmatic goal of creating a legally enforce-able mandate for sharing. Quite apart from these practical considerations, the open source route to recovery of seed sovereignty looks different, and is differentially appealing, depending upon location in the geo-social landscape. Especially in the Global South, among food sovereignty advocates with whom OSSI would like to make common cause, there is distrust of an initiative whose dependence on a formal license appears as one more application of the legal tools of the master which have already been so destructive of farmer sovereignty over seeds.

Further, the genesis of OSSI in a North American political economic context lends the project a distinctive structural orientation. The public breeders, farmer breeders and private breeders who constitute OSSI's core membership are committed to the twin principles of farmers' right to save and replant seed and to open access to material for breeding purposes. But they also believe that breeders of new, commercially available plant varieties should be rewarded for their contributions. Therefore, OSSI is developing a royalty-bearing 'open source' license. This is unacceptable to some in the Global South (and North), but others welcome a proactive approach that could provide opportunities for the development of small-scale and cooperative seed businesses. Additionally, while OSSI members are oriented to the organic sector and to participatory breeding, they do not share the uncompromisingly rejectionist stance toward genetic engineering that is common to many advocacy organizations in the North and South.

So, while the OSSI initiative might hope to be useful beyond its North American integument, there are fault lines that need to be recognized and addressed as it looks further afield for allies. Here again, the experience of the free and open source software movement is relevant. Whatever the potentialities of a tool, the scope of its effects depends mostly on how it is used and by whom. Richard Stallman – a principal progenitor and major figure of the free software movement – decries the loss of a normative emphasis on 'freedom' associated with the emergent prominence of an 'open source' tendency which he suggests is framed narrowly as a 'development methodology' designed to 'appeal to business executives by highlighting the software's practical benefits, while not raising issues of right and wrong' (Stallman 2013). Whether OSSI supports a mere 'development methodology' or contributes to Lorde's 'genuine change' will depend on how it negotiates these tensions.

The master's toolbox

If we are to assess the ways in which some of the master's tools – licensing and contract law – might be used in ways that the master didn't necessarily intend, we need to examine the character and operation of those instruments. For capital, the challenge has been to find ways to separate farmers from the autonomous reproduction of planting material and to bring them into the market for seed every growing season. There are two routes to this objective, one technical and one social. The technical path involves the plant breeding method of hybridization which renders the resulting crop economically (though not biologically) sterile. The development of hybridization has been extensively discussed (Kloppenburg 1988) and need not be rehearsed here except for the observation that the profits produced by hybrids financed the growth of a robust private seed industry that then had both the resources and motivation to continue the commodification of the seed. Because many important crops cannot be easily hybridized (e.g. soybeans, wheat), a second path to corporate seed sovereignty was pursued: control via legislative fiat.

And for capital the law has been a consistent and powerful mechanism for commodification of the seed in the United States, in Europe and globally. As early as the 1890s, seed companies in the US had begun agitating for application of intellectual property rights to new crop varieties. In 1930, they settled for a Plant Patent Act covering some asexually reproducing species. European seed companies, no less interested in the commodification of germplasm than their American counterparts, introduced patent-like 'plant breeders' rights' (PBR) through the creation of the Union for the Protection of New Varieties of Plants (UPOV) in 1961. UPOV became both the model and justification for passage of the similar US Plant Variety Protection Act (PVPA) in 1970. A major difference between US and European approaches to restricting farmers' access to germplasm has been the use in the European Union (EU) of a 'Common Catalogue' which has prohibited the exchange or sale of any but the officially approved and listed cultivars (Bocci 2009). In the US, the seed industry vigorously opposed application of varietal quality standards or limitations on its marketing strategies.

Though revisions have further circumscribed their original rights under UPOV and PVPA, farmers can still save and replant seed of protected varieties for their own use, and breeders can employ those materials for the production of new cultivars. However, neither a 'farmer's exemption' nor a 'research exemption' is available for material protected under US utility patent law. And with the 1980 *Diamond v. Chakrabarty* decision of the US Supreme Court, plants became patentable subject matter. A series of legal challenges over the past 15 years (i.e. *Asgrow Seed Co. Winterboer*, 1995; *J.E.M. Ag Supply, Inc. v. Pioneer Hi-Bred*, 2001; *Bowman v. Monsanto Co.*, 2013) have served only to confirm and reinforce the status of new crop varieties – and genes, and gene sequences, and tissue, and plants and seeds – as intellectual property. Although the European Patent Office has held that patents on plant varieties *per se* should not be issued, genes and gene sequences are patentable and their insertion in plant varieties redounds to a *de facto* patenting of the variety (Louwaars *et al.* 2009). With a few exceptions (Australia, Japan, Korea), patenting plants and/or plant genes is not countenanced outside North America and the EU. However, the 'trade-related aspects of intellectual property rights' (TRIPS) provisions of the World Trade Organization (WTO) require that member nations institute some form of intellectual property rights (IPR) for plants. Many countries simply accede to UPOV (Blakeney 2012), while others are coming under direct bilateral pressure from the US and EU nations to institute 'TRIPS-plus' arrangements that go beyond UPOV to more closely approximate patent regimes (Vivas-Egui and Oliva 2010).

The availability of utility patent protection for plants and plant improvement processes and technologies has been aggressively embraced by both public and private interests. Even as applications for PBR have risen constantly since 1980, they have now been overtaken by an enormous pulse of utility patent applications which began in 1990 (Graf *et al.* 2003, Pardey *et al.* 2013). Although the number of patents applied for annually is increasing in both the US and Europe, the number of applicants is decreasing. In the period 2004–2008 the five so-called 'Gene Giants' (Monsanto, DuPont, Syngenta, Bayer, Dow) accounted for 83.4 percent of patent applications in the US (Pardey *et al.* 2013, 28) and 35 percent of applications in the EU in the years 2003–2007 (Louwaars *et al.* 2009, 36). These patterns reflect a continuation of the historical increase in the level of concentration in the seed industry. Consolidation by dominant firms has been extended domestically and internationally, with a new emphasis on acquiring vegetable seed companies (see especially Howard 2009). The leading six companies now enjoy an estimated 66 percent market share of global commercial seed sales which are valued now in excess of $US35 billion (ETC Group 2013, 3). This market power is both enabled and enhanced by the ownership of key patents on enabling technologies used in the production of cultivars containing genetically modified (GM) traits which are themselves patented. The need to license these traits ties remaining local and regional seed companies to the Gene Giants and also acts as a barrier to entry for potential new firms.

The mutually reinforcing effects of concentration and patenting have had significant effects on farmers, perhaps most clearly in the US. The rapid adoption of genetically modified organism (GMO) varieties of maize and soy is well established. Less well recognized is that this widespread acceptance of transgenics by producers has less to do with increased yield than with a desire on the part of hard-pressed farmers to simplify their managerial options (Zilberman *et al.* 2013). As 'treadmill' theory explains, farmers have faced difficulty retaining the economic gains from adoption of the new varieties in the face of prices for corn and soy seed that more than doubled between 2001 and 2010 (Fuglie *et al.* 2012). The practice of 'stacking' multiple GM traits in one variety raises prices further and ensures that features that might be going off-patent are connected to one for which a patent is still in effect. Though a growing number of farmers would like to return to less complex or even non-GM varieties, concentration in the industry now means that there are few alternative sources of seed. Moreover, most of the surviving independent seed companies have little capacity for research and have few alternative varieties to offer. The possibility of saving seed for plant-back in the next growing season is limited by utility patent law under which there is no farmer exemption. The aggressive character of Monsanto's systematic campaign against such use is surely designed as an object lesson for all producers (Center for Food Safety 2004). The recent unanimous decision of the US Supreme Court in *Bowman v. Monsanto Co.* clearly establishes the position of the juridical superstructure in support of the principle that saving and growing seed from a patented plant is indeed a prohibited making.

Concentration in the seed industry has now proceeded so far – at least in the United States – that intellectual property arrangements need no longer even be the chief means for disciplining the farmer. Indeed, when competing companies and varieties are effectively absent, the dominant oligopolists are in a position to dictate to farmers the very conditions of access to seed. The mechanism for this is what legal scholars call 'private ordering' which relies not on patent law but on contract law. The concrete form this takes is the 'bag tag' or, formally, the 'Technology/Stewardship Agreement' as Monsanto terms it. The 'bag tag' is a 'shrink-wrap' license accompanying a bag of seed. Opening the bag constitutes agreement to the terms of the license which include, at length and explicitly, not to save or replant seed or to hold Monsanto accountable for any form of liability. Note that the farmer does not buy or own the seed, the farmer *licenses* its *use* (Winston 2008). Such licenses are now in common use for grain crops in the US by Monsanto, DuPont, Syngenta and Dow, and surely others. Seminis, a vegetable seed company owned by Monsanto, has developed and deployed a streamlined version of its license suitable for printing on a consumer-sized seed packet. It is not clear how extensively this form of licensing is used in Europe, though the European Seed Association's *IP Enforcement Tool-kit* does include instructions on the use of language for contractual sales terms to disallow 'further production and/or reproduction' (European Seed Association 2011, 3).

Although a great deal of attention has been focused on Monsanto for its dogged pursuit of farmers allegedly violating contracts or infringing its patents, many more companies are actually deeply but less visibly involved in global enforcement of the privileges to which IPR and contract law entitle them. The February 2013 issue of the trade journal *Seed World* carries full-page advertisements from each of two companies – Agro Protection USA Inc., and Seed Technology Education Program – which offer their services for ensuring grower 'compliance' with IPR requirements. Rather than outsource such enquiries, some companies have banded together to encourage farmers to inform on one another.

The Farmers Yield Initiative (FYI) is a coalition of 37 private and public partners which 'has the collective goal of advancing wheat research, education, seed certification, and the enforcement of intellectual property rights under the Plant Variety Protection Act (PVP) and patent laws' (Farmers Yield Initiative 2013). The FYI website provides a link to 'Submit a Tip' via snail-mail, email or a 'toll free number' which (at least when I called it) connects to a private law office in Arkansas. Although FYI may appear to be an example of typically American excess, the Anti-Infringement Bureau for Intellectual Property Rights on Plant Material (AIB) – a group of 14 European and Japanese seed companies, plus Monsanto – prominently places a large, red 'Report Piracy Now!' button on *all* of its web pages (Anti-Infringement Bureau 2013). Similar enforcement activities have emerged in Colombia and Brazil.

What does give the American FYI project an especially Orwellian flavor is the participation of 14 public agencies: eight land grant universities, three state crop improvement associations, a university research foundation, a state seed department and the United States Department of Agriculture's Plant Variety Protection Office. The active involvement of these institutions in so ethically problematic an initiative is an indication of how powerful the chronic debilitating pressures on public plant breeding have been. Foremost among these has been a long-term decline in federal and state funding for public agricultural science generally and for classical plant breeding in particular. Public institutions have been powerfully attracted to contractual relationships with industry in order to replace diminishing resources, and public plant breeders have often found it necessary to depend on royalty-bearing germplasm releases to maintain their programs. Closer financial and intellectual ties to a concentrated commercial seed sector compound historic pressures for public researchers to move away from the production of finished cultivars in favor of basic research and germplasm enhancement that complements rather than competes with private work (Coffman *et al.* 2007).

Public breeders who persist in a commitment to serve more diverse clients or broader objectives in their work are constrained – no less than farmers – by the tools of the master. Widespread patenting of germplasm, research technologies and breeding methods has resulted in a 'patent thicket' whose effects have been characterized as a 'tragedy of the anti-commons' (Heller and Heisenberg 1998). Negotiating the dense accumulation of intellectual property rights that potentially surrounds the material and methods of their work in order to assess and to obtain 'freedom to operate' is now a substantial transaction cost for breeders. Since such costs are independent of size of enterprise, their discouraging effect is greatest on public researchers, small seed companies and farmer breeders (Graf *et al.* 2004). In any case, access to patent-protected genetic or technical resources is not assured. Unlike PBR and PVPA, under utility patent law there is no research exemption and any use of patented material – even of seed for a simple variety trial – cannot be undertaken without the permission of the patent owner, and this is not uncommonly refused (Pollack 2009).

Universities have taken to mimicking private practice, and any exchange of materials, even between public scientists, is now accompanied by another expression of contract law, the Material Transfer Agreement (MTA). An MTA sets out provisions of permitted use and specifies ownership of the research results flowing from use of the material. Uncertainty as to what is patented or what is even patentable creates yet another level of constraint. Breeders who are part of OSSI cite multiple instances of traits that they are familiar with and currently using, but which have now been patented by the Gene Giants. The OSSI breeders would like to continue to use or release lines incorporating those traits, but they are refraining from doing so because of potential patent infringement issues. The intellectual property offices of the public institutions which employ these breeders agree that the patent claims made by the companies are likely not defensible in court. But the breeders are nonetheless advised not to proceed with their work, because the cost of even a successful lawsuit involving a deep-pocket transnational would be prohibitive. Monopoly power is being used to obstruct research and impede innovation, a clear inversion of the intent of patent legislation.

The reduction of capacity and reorientation of effort by public research has proceeded in Europe and the Global South as well as in the US, though in somewhat different form. In the United Kingdom, public breeding has been almost non-existent since the privatization of the Cambridge Plant Breeding Institute in the late 1980s (Murphy 2007, see especially Chapter 9). Other European countries retain a significant public plant breeding presence, especially in the area of participatory plant breeding, which is almost entirely absent in the US and which presents a very fertile platform for farmers and scientists to mobilize to work for new modes of plant improvement (Almekinders and Hardon 2006). The Gene Giants are, of course, influential in Europe. But the power of Monsanto *et al.* is to a significant degree diluted by a robust mid-scale contingent of mostly vegetable seed companies that are the backbone of the European Seed Association. These companies share with the Gene Giants a taste for PBR and a distaste for farmer plant-back, but are considerably less enthusiastic about patents because of the way they have seen patents used in the US to accelerate concentration and enhance the market power of a few firms.

Although there is growing momentum toward the US model of patenting (Louwaars *et al.* 2009), the principal thrust of European intellectual property rights in plant breeding has historically been centered on PBR as codified by UPOV, but in a distinctive and critical synergy with the Common Catalogue. Like PVPA, the provisions of UPOV have been tightened to prevent farmers from saving quantities of seed larger than what would service their own land. But the Common Catalogue requirements prohibit event the exchange, much less the sale, of seed of varieties not approved and listed in the Catalogue. Listing entails a variety of administrative obligations and requires that a variety be distinct, uniform and stable (DUS). The DUS criteria effectively disqualify many cultivars bred by farmers and/or those bred for alternative cropping systems such as organics. For a European farm population far more accustomed to seed sharing and on-farm selection than its American counterparts, this restriction is a major concern over and above the continuing efforts of the seed industry to force them to respect PBR. Ironically, in the US, there are no (very few) farmer breeders but, if there were, they could sell what they bred; in Europe there are many farmer breeders but they cannot sell what they breed.

For seed sovereignty advocates in the Global South, the threat to farmers and breeders of the US patent model is well recognized, and only a few nations now countenance that practice. Nevertheless, the pressures to accept utility patenting, often justified as a means of accessing proprietary material and methods, will continue. An example of the sort of stealth decisions that may gradually erode resistance is the recent change in 'Management of Intellectual Assets' by the CGIAR (Consultative Group on International Agricultural Research) system. The CGIAR centers may now establish – or even allow third parties to establish – intellectual property rights over their assets when such action is 'necessary for the further improvement of such Intellectual Assets or to enhance the scale or scope of impact on target beneficiaries' (CGIAR 2013). The implications of adherence to the UPOV convention are actually the more immediate issue. Already many Latin American nations have joined UPOV, and a strict interpretation of its language would prohibit saving seed or a protected variety for any purpose but use on the farmers' own holding. Actually, the European experience with the Common Catalogue may contain the most important lesson for maintenance of free exchange and continued development of farmer varieties in the Global South. The introduction of seed quality and phytosanitary laws not directly tied to intellectual property rights are now ubiquitous and relatively uncontested worldwide. While they are commonly justified by the alleged need to maintain seed purity and ensure varietal quality, their requirements for registration and certification determine what is legally marketable and too often have the effect – as with the Common Catalogue – of disadvantaging or excluding farmers and small seed producers (GRAIN 2005, Santilli 2012).

Over the course of nearly a century, legal arrangements have been used very effectively as a tool to achieve and maintain a quite considerable degree of corporate sovereignty over the seed. The tools of intellectual property law, contract law and regulation have been deployed to separate farmers from the autonomous reproduction of seed and to emasculate public sector breeders who could – and should – be providing alternatives to corporate cultivars. The loss of seed sovereignty to the Gene Giants is by no means complete. But it would be an error – and a serious misreading of historical momentum – to imagine that an increasingly narrow set of masters will not continue to wield the legal tools available to them in the service of achieving total sovereignty over the seed.

No to the tools of the master, yes to seed sovereignty

These contours of the commodification of the seed detailed above have been widely recognized and extensively analyzed for more than 20 years (see, e.g., Mooney 1979, Kloppenburg 1988, Shiva 1997, Mgbeoji 2006, Mushita and Thompson 2007, Aoki 2009). Nor are these issues new to the peasants, farmers and indigenous peoples who have for decades directly experienced the effects of the privatization of plant genetic resources. The challenge now is not so much to understand what is happening – that's been pretty clear for a long time – but to determine what is to be done about it. And deciding what *is* to be done can usefully be informed by recalling what *has* been done.

Pat Roy Mooney's 1979 book, *Seeds of the Earth: a private or public resource?*, framed the central issues clearly, brought international attention to the political economy of plant genetic resources and catalyzed a movement that sought redress for asymmetric patterns of North/South seed flow in the Food and Agriculture Organization (FAO) of the United Nations. In 1983, FAO members voted to establish an International Undertaking on Plant Genetic Resources that declared commercial cultivars and breeding lines as no less the 'common heritage of mankind' than the landraces and farmer varieties that have been so abundantly collected for so long under that rubric by the companies and research agencies of the Global North. This initiative set off a long and complex series of geopolitical negotiations intended to create an equitable multilateral framework for managing 'facilitated access' under an acceptable form of 'benefit sharing'. These talks finally produced the International Treaty on Plant Genetic Resources for Food and Agriculture (ITPGRFA) in 2002, an agreement that to date has still not been ratified by the US.

As protracted negotiations ensued in the FAO, other modalities for providing a reciprocal flow of benefits to providers of useful plant genetic material were explored. A surge of activity in 'bioprospecting' during the 1990s generated many proposals for bilateral agreements through which indigenous and farm communities might be compensated for their willingness to supply genetic resources. Deployed in a number of instances, these arrangements not only failed to deliver any significant benefits but frequently caused considerable social disruption and were actively damaging to the contracting communities (Nigh 2002, Hayden 2003, Greene 2004). The TRIPS requirement for *sui generis* provision of some form of intellectual property protection for plants appears to offer a means for incorporating some recognition of community or traditional resource rights in national laws. Such efforts – in places as diverse as India (Shiva *et al.* 2013) and Italy (Bertacchini 2009) – have so far resulted in rhetorical affirmations of farmers' rights or represent quite modest gains which are diluted by and/or subordinated to conventional property law. The foremost example of this latter process is surely the final version of the ITPGRFA itself which makes Farmers' Rights subject to national legislation, permits patenting of lines derived from material in the multilateral system and fails to provide a workable and legally defensible framework for benefit sharing. US Secretary of State John Kerry can now advise the US Senate that it ought to ratify the Treaty since, he argues, it effectively changes nothing and full participation will put his State Department negotiators 'in the best position to protect the interests of US farmers, researchers and industry' (US Senate 2010).

A wide variety of academic and policy analysts have been grappling with what to do about the asymmetric and unjust character of plant germplasm use and exchange. Some are so overwhelmed by practical complexities and moral ambiguities that they fail to provide any effective guidance at all (Gepts 2004, Eyzaguirre and Dennis 2007). Some agree that *something* needs to be done about the injustices, but that the realities of corporate power and a hegemonic capitalism require a situational pragmatism that involves cutting the best deal you can. Dusting off an old seed industry apologia, Brush (2007, 11) concludes that existing mechanisms of development assistance and technology transfer represent sufficient means of ensuring 'reciprocity' and 'benefit sharing'. Cary Fowler, of the Global Crop Diversity Trust, flatly declares that 'for better or worse, the debate concerning whether the international community will sanction the existence and use of IPRs in relation to germplasm … is over' and that 'Anyone who is not happy will remain unhappy' (Fowler 2003, 3, 11).

Fowler's conclusion is not very satisfactory for most farmers and peasants. Nor is it satisfactory for a significant number of citizens worldwide who may have never put a seed in the ground but who do eat and who are part of the quite robust movement opposed to 'biotechnology' in particular and corporate globalization more generally. The seed has become a key nexus in awareness of and opposition to the neoliberal project of restructuring the social and natural worlds around the narrow logic of the market (Kloppenburg 2004, Schurman and Kelso 2003). Nevertheless direct agricultural producers do have a focused interest in seed that has led them to organize – and to be organized – in distinctive fashion.

There are many organizations around the world working on seed matters, but two of the most prominent are La Vía Campesina (LVC; http://viacampesina.org/en/) and Navdanya (http://www.navdanya.org/). Both initiatives were begun about the same time: Navdanya in 1987, and La Vía Campesina in 1992. Navdanya is dedicated explicitly to achieving 'seed freedom' and its activities are geared principally to programs in India. However, through the charismatic personality, prolific writing and international connections of its founder, Vandana Shiva, it has global discursive influence. LVC, by contrast, is an organization of organizations, a network of peasant/farmer and indigenous groups which is broadly committed to a bundle of structural objectives summarized under the term 'food sovereignty' (Desmarais 2007). Between them, Navdanya and LVC express understandings of the nature and dimensions of 'seed sovereignty' that are widely held among producers and advocacy groups in the Global North and, especially, the Global South. If OSSI has ambitions to contribute to a social movement rather than supporting a mere development methodology, it needs to understand how its approach is compatible with or diverges from the positions and perspectives of its projected movement allies.

Although this paper foregrounds the phrase 'seed sovereignty', it is important to note that neither Navdanya nor LVC commonly use that formulation to refer to their approach to seed issues. The term has recently begun to appear in Navdanya's materials as another way of expressing their more ubiquitously deployed concept of 'seed freedom'. It is almost entirely absent in LVC's discourse, perhaps because even though seed is a central concern, LVC's conception of what constitutes food sovereignty also embraces land tenure, gender, water rights, demilitarization and migration. This lacuna in usage gives me an opportunity to use 'seed sovereignty' as a heuristic domain into which I will place features that seem to me common to the perspectives of both Navdanya and LVC.

Of course, LVC has always recognized control over genetic resources as a key component of its struggle, and early on identified 'seeds as the fourth resource ... after land, water and air' (LVC 2013a). The core elements of LVC's stance on biodiversity and genetic resources were laid down in a position paper written in October 2000 (LVC 2001), and have not changed materially. In the last two years, seed issues have come to the fore for LVC as a meeting of the governing body of the ITPGRFA galvanized publication of the 'Bali Seed Declaration' (LVC 2011), *Our seeds, our future* (LVC 2013a) and the 'Jakarta Call' (LVC 2013c) for food sovereignty. Navdanya has always been about seeds, first and foremost ('navdanya' means nine seeds). Although 'Seed Freedom' has long been its organizing metaphor, 'seed sovereignty' (along with 'food sovereignty', water sovereignty and 'land sovereignty') has now made its way onto Navdanya's web home page as one of the core elements of its overarching goal of 'Earth Democracy'. In 2013, Navdanya published *The law of the seed* (Shiva *et al.* 2013), an updating of the 2006 *Manifesto on the future of seeds*. Both publications reflect the ideas of a set of the international advocacy associates of Vandana Shiva. More recently, Shiva issued a statement on 'The seed emergency: the threat to food and democracy' (Shiva 2012a) and invited supporters to sign on to a 'Declaration on seed freedom' (Shiva 2012b). In what follows, I draw upon these documents to draw the outlines of what I will call 'seed sovereignty'.

From a review of Navdanya and LVC materials, I distill four principal and constitutive dimensions of seed sovereignty:

- *The right to save and replant seed*. The irreducible monad of what LVC (2011) describes as 'a war for control over seeds' is the right to save and replant seed. It is precisely this circuit that capital seeks to sunder using both technical and legal tools. The ur-principle of seed sovereignty is that farmers 'must be autonomous in terms of seed' (LVC 2013b). From this core commitment flow a number of linked propositions.
- *The right to share seed*. Following closely on the right to save and replant one's own seeds is the right to share those seeds with others and to receive seeds from others. It is on this foundation of open, reciprocal exchange that crop genetic diversity has, for millennia, been maintained and increased. While it is fundamental that farmer-to-farmer exchange should be unimpeded, there is also a clear sense that plant genetic resources are a 'treasure that we farmers generously place at the service of humanity' at large (LVC 2011). Preserving the shared access of the global community to these materials requires the 'safeguarding of commons against privatization' (LVC 2013c), or their treatment as a 'public good' (Shiva 2012a, 2012b). But the various and contested meanings of 'commons' and 'public good' are never engaged and a framework for sharing beyond the farm is not explored.
- *The right to use seed to breed new varieties*. The right to save, replant and share seed is linked to the capacity of farmers to generate new cultivars adapted to their own production system. To the extent that farmer breeders respond – as they must – to the

pest, disease and agronomic challenges posed by a rapidly changing ecosphere, they will be developing genetic material of significant utility for a necessary shift to a more resilient, sustainable agriculture. 'We will continue to share seeds knowing that our knowledge, our science, our practice as guardians of seed diversity are crucial to adapting to climate change' (LVC 2013c).

• *The right to participate in shaping policies for seed.* The foregoing rights to save, replant, share and breed are precisely the activities that UPOV, PVPA, 'bag tag' licenses and utility patents are intended to abridge. As manifestations of a legal super-structure, reform or repeal of such arrangements must be undertaken in the political realm. Accordingly, Shiva and her colleagues propose a 'Law of the seed' (Shiva *et al.* 2013), though less as a serious attempt to formulate a concrete regulation than as a discursive device to focus attention on policy options. In its 'Bali seed declaration,' LVC demands the 'enshrining in the laws of each country and at the global level the recognition of the inalienable rights of peasant and family farmers to conserve, use, exchange, sell and protect their seeds' (LVC 2013a). No less than 'food sovereignty', 'seed sovereignty' is to be achieved through democratic par-ticipation and legislative action.

As organizations directly engaged in struggle, both LVC and Navdanya understand that change is achieved not given. Further, effort must be twofold; that is, the aggressions of the neoliberal project must be opposed, and alternatives must be established, even if only pro-visionally. Two key platforms for opposition are apparent:

• *Opposition to intellectual property rights.* The leading and most efficacious modality for corporate appropriation of the seed is the imposition of IPR. The effects of IPR mechanisms have been so severe that there is no tolerance for them in any configur-ation: 'industrial property over seeds, including patents and plant variety certificates are but different forms of theft … All forms of patents; plant variety protection and its royalties on farm-produced seeds; as well as other forms of industrial property must be banned' (LVC 2011). This uncompromising attitude toward IPRs often given an epistemological justification that carries ethical weight: 'We oppose intellectual prop-erty over any form of life. We want to elevate to a universal principle the fact that genes, as the essence of life, cannot be owned' (LVC 2001, 49); and 'patents on seeds are ethically wrong because seeds are life forms' (Shiva *et al.* 2013, 5).

• *Opposition to genetically modified organisms.* Opposition to IPRs is linked to and almost completely coterminous with opposition to GMOs: 'GMOs and patents con-taminate our fields and then prohibit us from using our own seeds' (LVC 2013a). GMOs are understood as the vector through which both the technical and the social imperatives of the Gene Giants are simultaneously introduced. And just as with IPRs, an epistemological stance adds ethical weight to more material concerns: 'Life forms, plants and seeds are all evolving, self-organized, sovereign beings' (Shiva *et al.* 2013, 5). GMOs are opposed not simply because they have problematic or undesirable environmental or social effects, but because genetic engineering vio-lates the integrity of a sovereign entity.

A firm rejectionist stance in relation to IPRs and GMOs is complemented by an affir-mative orientation to several core initiatives:

- *Community seed saving and exchange.* LVC categorically scorns the ITPGRFA framework for the multilateral collection, conservation and exchange of plant genetic resources as 'a contradictory and ambiguous treaty, which in the final analysis comes down on the side of theft' (LVC 2011). Instead, LVC is committed to strengthening channels for 'exchanging know-how from farmer to farmer, and organizing collectively to produce and conserve locally our own seeds intended for small-scale farming and organic farming' (LVC 2013a, 3). Similarly, the central axis of Navdanya's on-the-ground programs has long been oriented to community-based, *in situ*, dynamic maintenance of farmer cultivars (Shiva *et al.* 2013).
- *Agroecology and participatory breeding.* While farmers' seeds and knowledge ought to be the foundation for seed sovereignty, there is a clear willingness to develop these resources through a complementary relationship with formal science, scientists and scientific institutions. A distinctive feature of both LVC and Navdanya is their quite recent adoption in discourse of the now mainstreamed term 'agroecology' as a referent of the sort of just and sustainable socio-technical forms of production they are working toward. 'Participatory plant breeding' (PPB) appears as a fertile vehicle for establishing mutually respectful, power-balanced and synergistic relationships between farmers and plant scientists. LVC's 'Bali seed declaration' (LVC formulation) calls specifically for an 'agroecology' involving 'participative research in farmers' fields and under the control of farmers' organizations'. Shiva *et al.* devote three full Articles in their 'Law of the seed' to the melding of indigenous and scientific knowledge and practice (Shiva *et al.* 2013, 32–4).
- *Legal sovereignty over seed.* The most powerful expression of 'seed sovereignty' would, of course, be some actual and concrete juridical mandate. Both LVC and Navdanya have long demanded recognition of 'farmers' rights', and this is what the 'farmers' rights' clauses of the ITPGRFA were supposed to have affirmed. But, as LVC well understands, 20 years of struggle over the form of the treaty produced little more than an affirmation of the primacy of intellectual property rights. LVC now appears to be placing its energies into the development of an international convention on peasants' rights broadly conceived (LVC 2011). Shiva *et al.* (2013, 35), in their 'Law of the seed' – which is really a discursive intervention rather than a serious juridical proposal – do little more than call for 'collective ownership of local varieties'. And though LVC also asserted farmer 'ownership' in its early formulations (LVC 2001, 49), it is not at all clear what that term means, or how it would be operationalized, or reconciled with objectionable forms of ownership or with the principle of sharing or with the concept of the commons/public good.
- *Openness to allies.* Neither Navdanya nor LVC anticipate realizing their goals without the active participation and material assistance of allied organizations and interests. Navdanya has long worked with a wide range of advocacy and activist groups and most of its outreach is intended to engage and mobilize citizens' and advocacy groups. LVC is not an organization, but a 'movement of organizations' (Nicholson 2012, 2). Although LVC limits its membership to small farmer/peasant organizations, it welcomes 'strategic alliances' (LVC 2013c). According to LVC leader Paul Nicholson (2012, 4), 'We need NGOS, but our alliances must be based on strategic agreements and political objectives in order to accomplish a priority task'. LVC can be thought of as autonomous, but not autochthonous.

From this heuristic exercise, 'seed sovereignty' emerges as a coherent set of linked features. What is perhaps most apparent is a robust rejection of the technical (GMOs) and legal

(IPRs) tools of the master. This oppositional stance is balanced by a clear set of affirmative tendencies that are informed by a core set of foundational principles. Plant genetic resources are understood as a broadly social product, a collective heritage of farming communities that should be freely exchanged and disseminated for the benefit of all. Seed sovereignty would ideally be manifest in a legally defined space in which sharing is unimpeded by IPRs. This space is further envisioned as a space in which farmers can continue to apply their local knowledge and ingenuity in the service of an agriculture that sustains not only their communities but the environment. In this, farmers are not expected to work alone, but could look to formal scientific institutions to cooperate in the enterprise of plant breeding and improvement, albeit in a more equitable manner that embraces participatory engagement with farmers themselves and is directed to the production of diverse range of socially and environmentally appropriate plant varieties. It sounds nice. Could OSSI be a part of moving that vision forward?

OSSI: seeds should be free as in speech, not as in beer

My own enthusiasm for OSSI is rooted in the same frustrations that so thoroughly inform LVC's spurning of the 'benefit sharing' provisions of the ITPGRFA as being 'offered the proceeds from the theft of our seeds' (LVC 2011). The legitimacy of plant genetic resources as the 'common heritage of mankind' was called into question at the FAO during the 1980s because, as it expanded globally, the seed industry had begun using IPRs to exclude others from access to their varieties for multiplication and breeding purposes. The problem was not that seed companies were obtaining and using crop genetic resources, or even that they were selling seed, but that they were restricting access to and preventing the use of materials that, as a matter of reciprocity, ought to have been shared. It is this failure of reciprocity – and, with patenting, the elimination of the right to replant and to use for further breeding, the loss of the *derivative right to use* – that is regarded as asymmetrical and therefore unjust. The inequitable nature of this practice has been compounded as corporations have used IPRs over genetic materials not just to accrue monopoly rents, but to actively undermine the independence of farmers and the integrity and capacity of public plant science. Significantly, the initial strategic response at the FAO in 1983 was not to make companies pay for genetic resources but to declare that what they claimed as proprietary lines were in fact part of common heritage. This position was deemed impractical by many and the debate was soon transformed from how to enlarge the commons to how make industry pay for its raw materials.

I was one of those who in the 1980s argued for what I now regard as a marketized and therefore misconceived and inadequate response (Kloppenburg and Kleinman 1987, Kloppenburg 1988). The logical outcomes of that strategy are the flawed, compensationist approaches to 'access and benefit sharing' that have neither protected farmers and indigenous peoples from biopiracy nor brought them any benefit, but have functioned mostly to legitimate and institutionalize their continued expropriation. The really radical route to reestablishing symmetry in flows of crop germplasm was not to arrange payment for access to genetic resources in addition to IPR lines, but to work for reconstitution of the commons for both types of germplasm. But I *was* correct, back in 1988, in my judgment that pulling the companies' breeding lines into the status of common heritage was not a workable approach, and that continuing to maintaining peasant landraces as a freely accessed mine for genetic resources was unjust. Is there a way out of this conundrum? Perhaps what is required is a mechanism for germplasm exchange that allows sharing among those who will reciprocally share, but excludes those who will not. What is needed is not recreation of the inadequate *open-access commons*, but creation of a *'protected commons'*.

A 'protected commons', as Richard Jefferson (2006, 23) has so aptly phrased it, is precisely what an open source approach is designed to create. Frustrated by expanding constraints on their ability to add to, modify and share as freely as seemed personally and socially desirable, individual software developers have sought ways to create space in which they could develop content and code that could be liberally exchanged and built upon by others, but not appropriated and privatized by corporations. As Richard Stallman so memorably explains, '"free software" is a matter of liberty, not price. To understand the concept, you should think of "free" as in "free speech", not as in "free beer"' (Stallman 2002, 43). The right to derivative use is the core of free and open source software (but note that Stallman refuses to accept 'open source' as an adequate descriptor since it does not explicitly reference 'freedom').

The tool for achieving this freedom of derivative use is a license, a form of contract. Open source software is copyrighted and then made available under a license that permits further modification and distribution as long as the modified software is distributed under the same license. This arrangement produces a 'viral' effect that, critically, enforces continued sharing as the program and any derivatives and modifications are disseminated. Also critically, the virality of the license also prevents appropriation by companies that would make modifications for proprietary purposes since any software building on the licensed code is required by the license to be openly accessible. This feature – called 'copyleft' – is what distinguishes 'open source' from mere 'open innovation'. Thus, software developed under an open source license is released not into an open innovation/open access commons, but into a 'protected commons' populated by those who agree to share but effectively inaccessible to those who will not. In this way 'copyright or patent rights are exercised to share and socialize intellectual property – counter to the very meaning of the exclusivity that characterizes it' (Dusollier 2007, 1394). That is, the tools of the master are re-purposed in a way that the master did not intend and which actively subverts the master's hegemony.

Such re-purposing of the legal tools of the master has been proven very fruitful in the software sector (Weber 2004). Thousands of open source programs are now available, among them the email program Thunderbird, the web browser Firefox, and the operating system known as Linux. The success of these open source software initiatives has inspired a variety of analysts to propose application of open source principles and practices to plant breeding and the seed sector. These ideas emerged more or less independently from a variety of disciplines – plant breeding itself (Michaels 1999), molecular biology (Jefferson 2006), sociology (Kloppenburg 2010), law (Aoki 2009, Hope 2008) – and from diverse geopolitical positions – North America (Michaels 1999), Europe (Hughes and Deibel 2006/7) and the Global South (Douthwaite 2002, Srinivas 2002). Elsewhere, I too have suggested that development and deployment of a copyleft, open source license for germplasm appears to offer a 'fecund modality for impeding further dispossession and for the pursuit of concrete initiatives for the actual repossession' of seed sovereignty (Kloppenburg 2010, 385–6). But, how might such a project actually be undertaken?

In April 2010, a small meeting was held in Madison, Wisconsin, USA, to explore the prospects for implementing some sort of open source initiative for seeds. Attending were six North American public plant breeders, one North American farmer breeder, one North American social scientist and three representatives of a Global South advocacy NGO with deep experience with participatory breeding (a fourth Global South participant representing a prominent indigenous NGO was invited but unable to attend). Enthusiasm for the idea led to targeted recruitment for attendance at a second meeting held in May 2011 in Minneapolis, Maryland, USA. Participation was expanded to include additional public breeders, farmers, indigenous groups from North and South, a small seed company and several non-profit advocacy organizations. Those attending the Minneapolis meeting constituted themselves as the Open Source Seed Initiative (OSSI), discussed principles and objectives and outlined a course of action. The priority task was determined to be creation of OSSI open source licenses, including one that is royalty bearing. Over the past year, OSSI has refined its constitutive principles, retained *pro bono* legal representation and drafted licenses, and has plans to release material under those licenses.

The objectives that OSSI intends to achieve are specified as follows in the latest draft of 'OSSI basic principles' (OSSI 2013):

(1) A germplasm licensing framework with no breeding restrictions on the germplasm released through its auspices other than that derivatives must also be released with the same license.
(2) A robust, vibrant and well-supported public and community plant breeding sector producing germplasm and cultivars that can be equitably grown, sold, changed and distributed.
(3) A plurality of sources from which farmers, gardeners and breeders can obtain seed.
(4) Integration of the skills and capacities of farmers with those of plant scientists for enhancing and enlarging participatory plant breeding.
(5) Respect for the rights and sovereignty of indigenous communities over their seeds and genetic resources.

On the whole, OSSI's objectives have considerable goodness of fit with the visions of 'seed sovereignty' distilled from the positions of LVC and Navdanya. Although it would be pleased if its project would find traction in other parts of the world and looks forward to supporting sister initiatives elsewhere, OSSI also understands that perspectives shift depending upon geo-social positioning. Indeed, from the first discussions in Madison in 2011, we have been aware of a number of fault lines that potentially restrict the OSSI project – at least as it is presently constituted – to a specifically North American context. Preliminary conversations with representatives of Global South organizations that have long been involved in genetic resource issues – including LVC and some of its key NGO allies – have illuminated those fault lines and have precipitated this consideration of how well the tools of the master can really be used effectively against their creators.

The objections we've heard from our potential allies turn not on OSSI's overall objectives, but specifically on OSSI's proposals for the use of a license as its performative vehicle. OSSI has been warned that the practical requirements for operation of a license are not workable, that as a restrictive covenant a license is *prima facie* a form of ownership, that no form of ownership should be used or applied to living beings and that a royalty-bearing license is simply another form of PBR.

OSSI's approach is shaped in significant ways by its genesis in a North American context. Notably, it has emerged from the milieu of institutionalized plant breeding rather than as a project of primary producers. Further, the membership is dominated by plant breeders employed by public, 'land grant' universities although it also includes a few breeders from small seed companies and a non-profit organization. The foundational interest in the right of 'derivative use' is therefore oriented principally to the use of material for purposes of breeding rather than for planting. In North America, there is virtually no farmer breeding. With declining levels of state support, public breeders now often rely on royalty revenue for maintenance of their programs. The decay of institutional mechanisms for release of public cultivars and concentration in the seed industry can mean that if public breeders do not provide what companies want, their materials will never be used. OSSI's public breeders are involved in organic and participatory breeding (see Murphy *et al.* 2004), but these projects are difficult to sustain under current funding priorities. OSSI's private breeders are seed vendors whose survival depends on sales. Both public and private breeders are offended and frustrated by concentration, constraints on access to breeding material and the appropriation of their lines by competitors. While they are normatively disposed to a maximally unencumbered flow of plant genetic resources, they are now embedded in a robust market system in which they feel they have no option but to participate; hence their interest in a royalty-bearing license.

As a result, there is in OSSI a significant tension between two tendencies: one for completely unencumbered, 'free' seed, and one for seed carrying some obligation for reward to the breeder. This tension is manifest not only between breeders, but also within each breeder depending on the type of material in question (populations and breeding lines versus finished, commercially valuable cultivars). OSSI therefore decided to develop model licenses for both alternatives with the intent to allow breeders to choose the option that best fits their situation. Believing that only a truly functional license would recruit support and stimulate use, OSSI instructed its legal team to draft licenses that were both 'copyleft' and maximally defensible in court.

Drafts of a 'free seed' and a 'royalty-bearing' license have been completed. What makes both licenses 'open source,' according to OSSI's thinking, is the 'copyleft' requirement in both licenses that all derivative lines and combinations of the licensed material also be free for breeding. Briefly,

- The 'free' license provides the widest degree of freedom of use. As with 'free software', the only restriction is that licensees may not restrict the freedom of others to use the seed in whatever way they wish. Originators of genetic material transferred under this license may not collect royalties and may not restrict usage in any way. Recipients of genetic material transferred under this license may grow the seed, may reproduce the seed, may share the seed, may sell the seed, may conduct research with the seed and may breed new varieties with the seed, and farmers may save and replant the seed.
- The 'royalty-bearing' license allows collection of royalties on the seed, but may not restrict usage in any other way. Recipients of genetic material transferred from the originator under this license may be required to pay royalties on commercial sale of the seed, but may grow the seed, may reproduce the seed, may share the seed, may sell the seed, may conduct research with the seed and may breed new varieties with the seed, and farmers may save and replant the seed.

OSSI has indeed found that the tools of the master are technically very cumbersome, at least for OSSI's purposes. A license is a private contract which, by law, prospective licensees must have an opportunity to read in its entirety. That means that the complete language of the license would have to appear on every package or container of seed sold or exchanged. Moreover, if licensed material is received or acquired without knowledge of the license, the license cannot be enforced in relation to that recipient. Further, in order to achieve robust defensibility, the licenses run seven pages in language that none but an attorney can understand. The probability that such a license will be transmitted for more than a few iterations is very low. This failure to virally propagate would negate the key and most powerful feature of the open source license approach. Compounding these technical obstacles was a sense among OSSI members that implementing a mandatory, legally binding, lengthy, confusing, unwieldy, restrictive license would bring us perilously close in style and substance to the practices characteristic of the Gene Giants.

These deficiencies were felt to be most debilitating in regard to the 'free seed' license which OSSI had hoped would be used liberally among breeders, farmers and gardeners. OSSI is now exploring how the license might be shortened sufficiently to fit on a conventional seed packet *and* retain its legal enforceability. A second – though less appealing prospect – would be to shift to a 'free seed pledge' (the actual choice of an appropriate term – pledge, commitment, declaration – is not yet clear). The pledge would consist of a simple, very short, affirmatively phrased statement expressing a commitment to allowing unrestricted use of the seed and its derivative progeny lines. Notably, the 'pledge' is not a 'license' and would not be legally binding. OSSI is also continuing to develop a royalty-bearing license, which, it is anticipated, could be used for breeding material containing high-value traits or for finished cultivars. Seed companies and institutional breeders are already familiar with complex legal documents (e.g. licenses, MTAs) and it is those actors, rather than farmers and gardeners, who would be the principal targets of a legally enforceable mandate to keep materials freely available.

The objection to a license as a form of intellectual property is a complex issue. For free and open source software, the license is the necessary and indispensable instrument that ensures that anyone who redistributes free software *must* pass along the freedom to use it in any way *except* that the distribution terms cannot be altered. This single restriction on freedom to use (that is, you can only distribute under the original license) is balanced by the preservation of a much larger range of freedoms. The Free Software Foundation addresses this contradiction directly: 'Proprietary software developers use copyright to take away users' freedom; we use copyright to guarantee their freedom' (Free Software Foundation 2012). OSSI's proposed licenses are based on this same principle. There is surely good reason to be skeptical of an initiative that employs a form of ownership to challenge exclusion and propagate an ideology of sharing. Still, the narrative of the seed as a 'commons' (LVC 2013c) or 'public good' (Shiva 2012a) is not without its own parallel contradictions. Open access (which is open source without copyleft provisions) neither assures equal access nor prevents appropriation and privatization. Further, 'property' is properly understood not as some undifferentiated form of commoditized 'ownership' but as a complicated 'bundle of rights' to possess and use an object or resource. 'Farmers' rights' are a form of property, as are 'traditional resource rights' or 'community rights'. One of the affirmative features of seed sovereignty is the objective, clearly expressed by both LVC and Navdanya, of establishing some form of legal sovereignty over seed.

It is clear, however, that OSSI's proposed royalty-bearing license is very close indeed to the forms of IPR that have proven so problematic. Indeed, it might be regarded as 'PVPA-plus' inasmuch as its provisions are almost isomorphic with that federal law. The key – and critical – difference is that OSSI's license contains a copyleft clause that renders any derivative line freely available for breeding and so effectively impedes patenting or locking up of its genetics. A license containing a royalty-bearing option is seen by some OSSI members as a necessary complement to the free seed license. Were public breeders adequately funded, they would not need or desire a royalty flow. But public breeders are not now adequately funded and their extant channels for germplasm release almost always are linked to seed companies. Farmer breeders, small private seed companies, and non-profit institutions involved in cultivar development also see a necessity to have their work rewarded. Their goals are an adequate and legitimate return to their labor, not monopoly profit. Still, within OSSI itself there is continuing debate over the desirability of pursuing an arrangement that so closely mimics the tools of the master.

In principle, OSSI envisions its royalty-bearing license being applied to agreements with firms reproducing seed for commercial sale, and farmers will be free to save and replant for their own purposes. Royalties are often regarded by Global South movement groups as synonymous with IPRs and as a form of theft (LVC 2011, 3). They surely can be. But OSSI members are also aware of individuals, groups and communities in Latin America and Southeast Asia that are interested in underwriting their activities through development of a market for their seeds (SEARICE 2009). If OSSI can craft a reward system that is fair and preserves access to material for breeding and on-farm use, it may be useful for communities and cooperatives outside North America.

A final cautionary note is that while some may find OSSI licenses too restrictive, others may find them too *free*. Although OSSI's royalty-bearing license violates the Free Software Foundation (FSF)'s definition of adequate 'freedom', we follow FSF's model in placing no other restrictions on derivative uses. This means that once situated in the 'protected commons' by an open source license, materials might be used for purposes unpalatable to the donor. Prominent among these purposes would be genetic engineering, for which many agricultural and sustainablility advocacy organizations – and specifically LVC and Navdanya – profess an uncompromising and enduring antipathy. The almost complete identification of the tool (GMOs) with the tool user (the Gene Giants) is understandable, but misconstrued. There is no question that the tool of transgenics has been wielded very effectively by the corporations to advance their particular interests. But their ability to use the tool is a function of their power rather than an endogenous characteristic of the technology itself. Though concerned with how genetic engineering is being deployed, and especially the degree to which it has displaced classical breeding, most OSSI members do not oppose use of transgenics *per se*. Moreover, farmers in India and Vietnam have themselves appropriated the tools of the master and introgressed GM traits into their own cultivars (Stone 2007). The focus of attention on opposition to transgenics has diverted attention from the development of novel genetic technologies for plant breeding which do not involve inter-specific transfers. These techniques, already being touted and justified as non-transgenic, are being aggressively patented according to a familiar pattern (Lusser *et al.* 2012).

Conclusion: the primacy of process

So where does this leave us? I began this paper by asking if the tool of an open source license, birthed within a particular social formation and therefore bearing the marks of that social formation, could nevertheless be re-purposed to liberatory or at least progressive ends. It's not like this question hasn't been asked time and again over the years, as a matter of both strategy and tactics. I've always liked Erik Olin Wright's framing: 'What is needed is what used to be called "nonreformist reforms", social changes that are feasible in the world as it is (thus they are reforms), but which prefigure in important ways more emancipatory possibilities' (Wright in Kirby 2001, 21). An open source license for germplasm appears to be feasible, especially given the example of software. Emancipatory? Well, I've argued that, in a kind of institutional Aikido, an open source license for germplasm could use the structure and the momentum of the legal system itself to move that system in directions its corporate architects didn't intend and which undermine their hegemony (Kloppenburg 2010).

But will it really do that? How does one recognize an 'emancipatory' change? Esping-Andersen *et al.* (1976) suggest that a key feature is a 'noncommodified' stance that places struggle in a political rather than a market setting. Their admonition works for a 'free seed' license which possesses a truly transmogrifying potential. But the 'feasibility' of that license is in question. Additionally, some members of OSSI feel that, in the world as it is, we need a royalty-bearing license, at least in North America. And so, *pace* Esping-Anderson *et al.* (1976), we find ourselves with a commodified component to our struggle. And, despite quite broad congruence between the overall objectives of OSSI and advocates of 'seed sovereignty', there are nevertheless some serious fault lines that may preclude the emergence and advance of common global initiatives.

The attraction of an open source initiative for me has much to do with the frustration of watching 20 years of non-commodified political struggle for farmers' rights produce the impotent, and perhaps actively meretricious, ITPGRFA which, after an additional 10 years, the United States still has not condescended to sign. Meanwhile, a concentrating capital has extended its reach into the genescape despite a few symbolically important but functionally largely meaningless rollbacks of the most egregious examples of raw bio-piracy (e.g. the Enola bean, Basmati rice). Open source offers at least the prospect of a shift from continuous defensive actions to the creation of a positive, relatively autonomous space in which capital might be effectively prohibited – by its own rules – from trespassing.

But, as I've outlined in this paper, achieving that sort of emancipatory outcome will not be easy. Nevertheless, there is growing international interest in 'open source' in its many manifestations. I have just learned of a parallel initiative to OSSI's that has been organized in Germany (see Kotschi and Kaiser 2012). The concept now has sufficient traction among some plant breeders, seed companies and advocacy groups in the United States to have permitted the founding and elaboration of OSSI. OSSI's expansive visioning of a legally binding free seed license has been adapted to the realities of 'the world as it is'. OSSI's royalty-bearing license conforms even further to 'the world as it is'. However, I am not ready to assign OSSI to Richard Stallman's category of 'development methodology' rather than 'social movement'. Really, it is very difficult to anticipate what the future holds for innovative initiatives. The point, it seems to me, is to generate options to be tried.

I think that Paul Nicholson's insistence that 'food sovereignty' need not be definitively rendered '*because FS is dynamic, it's a process*' (Nicholson 2012, 7) is useful here. Else-where, Nicholson observes that for LVC there are 'spaces of reflection and debate, and spaces of organic articulation of these strategies' (Nicholson in Wittman 2009, 680). What OSSI is or is not will become clear as it articulates, that is, as it acts. And this process is entirely consistent with what plant breeders do. Plant breeders refer to the 'G × E' (gene × environment) interaction which generates the diversity to which they apply the creative power of selection (see especially Tracy 2003). They put the seed into the ground and see what kinds of plants emerge from the chancy interaction of genes and environment. The members of OSSI representing the Global South gave us similar advice: implement OSSI in the US and let's see what happens. That's a plan – well, that's a process.

References

Almekinders, C. and J. Hardon, eds. 2006. *Bringing farmers back into breeding.* Wageningen: Agromisa Foundation.

Anti-Infringement Bureau for Intellectual Property Rights on Plant Material. 2013. Home. http://www.aib-seeds.com/en/home/31.aib [Accessed on 21 August 2013].

Aoki, K. 2009. 'Free seeds not free beer': Participatory plant breeding, open source seeds, and acknowledging user innovation in agriculture. *Fordham Law Review*, 77(5), 2275–2310.

Bertacchini, E. 2009. Regional legislation in Italy for the protection of local varieties. *Journal of Agriculture for International Development*, 103(1/2), 51–63.

Blakeney, M. 2012. Patenting of plant varieties and plant breeding methods. *Journal of Experimental Botany*, 63(3), 1069–1074.

Bocci, R. 2009. Seed legislation and agrobiodiversity: Conservation varieties. *Journal of Agriculture and Environment for International Development*, 103(1–2), 31–49.

Brush, S.B. 2007. Farmers' rights and protection of traditional agricultural knowledge. *World Development*, 35(9), 1499–1514.

Center for Food Safety. 2004. *Monsanto vs. US farmers*. Washington, DC: Center for Food Safety.

CGIAR (Consultative Group on International Agricultural Research). 2013. Managing CGIAR intellectual assets for the benefit of smallholder farmers. Available at http://www.cgiar.org/consortium-news/managing-cgiar-intellectual-assets-for-the-benefit-of-smallholder-farmers/ [Accessed 22 August 2013].

Coffman, W.R., W.H. Lesser, and S.R. McCouch. 2007. Commercialization and the scientific research process: The example of plant breeding. *In*: P.E. Stephan and R.G. Ehrenburg, eds. *Science and the university*. Madison, WI: University of Wisconsin Press.

Desmarais, A. 2007. *La Vía Campesina: Globalization and the power of peasants*. Halifax: Fernwood Press.

Douthwaite, B. 2002. *Enabling innovation: A practical guide to understanding and fostering technical change*. Boston, MA: Zed Books.

Dusollier, S. 2007. Sharing access to intellectual property through private ordering. *Chicago-Kent Law Review*, 82(3), 1391–1435.

Esping-Andersen, G., R. Friedland, and E.O. Wright. 1976. Modes of class struggle and the capitalist state. *Kapitalistate*, 4–5, 186–220.

ETC Group. 2013. Gene giants seek 'philanthrogopoly'. *ETC Group Communiqué* Issue #10.

European Seed Association. 2011. *IP enforcement tool-kit for vegetable seed companies*. European Seed Association. Available at http://www.euroseeds.org/publications/position-papers/intellectual-property/esa_11.0068.7 [Accessed 15 August 2013].

Eyzaguirre, P.B. and E. Dennis. 2007. The impacts of collective action and property rights on plant genetic resources'. *World Development*, 35(9), 1489–1498.

Farmers Yield Initiative. 2013. Farmers yield initiative. Available from http://www.farmers yieldinitiative.com/ [Accessed on 21 August 2013].

Fowler, C. 2003. The status of public and proprietary germplasm and information: An aassessment of recent developments at FAO. IP Strategy Today No. 7-2003. Ithaca, NY: *bio*Developments-International Institute, Inc.

Free Software Foundation. 2012. What is copyleft? Available at http://www.gnu.org/copyleft/ [Accessed on 22 July 2012].

Fuglie, K., P. Heisey, J. King, and D. Schimmelpfennig. 2012. Rising concentration in agricultural input industries influences new farm technologies. Available from http://www.ers.usda.gov/amber-waves/2012-december/rising-concentration-in-agricultural-input-industries-influences-new-technologies.aspx#.UiU5UD_pySo [Accessed on 2 July 2013].

Gepts, P. 2004. Who owns biodiversity, and how should the owners be compensated? *Plant Physiology*, 134(April), 1295–1307.

Graf, G., S. Cullen, K. Bradford, D. Zilberman, and A.B. Bennet. 2003. The public-private structure of intellectual property ownership in agricultural biotechnology. *Nature Biotechnology*, 21, 989–995.

Graf, G.D., B.D. Wright, A.B. Bennet, and D. Zilberman. 2004. Access to intellectual property is a major obstacle to developing transgenic horticultural crops. *California Agriculture*, 58(2), 120–126.

GRAIN (Genetic Resources Action International). 2005. Latin America: The mantra of privatisation. *Seedling*, July, 36–40.

Greene, S. 2004. Indigenous people incorporated? Culture as politics, culture as property in biopharmaceutical bioprospecting. *Current Anthropology*, 45(2 April), 211–237.

Hayden, C. 2003. *When nature goes public: The making and unmaking of bioprospecting in Mexico*. Princeton, NJ: Princeton University Press.

Heller, M. and R. Heisenberg. 1998. Can patents deter innovation? The anticommons in biomedical research. *Science*, 280, 698–701.

Hope, J. 2008. *Biobazaar: The open source revolution and biotechnology*. Cambridge, MA: Harvard University Press.

Howard, P. 2009. Visualizing consolidation in the global seed industry: 1996–2008. *Sustainability*, 1, 1266–1287.

Hughes, S. and E. Deibel. 2006/7. Opinion piece: Plant breeder's rights, room for maneuver? *Tailoring Biotechnologies*, 2(3 Winter), 77–86.

Jefferson, R. 2006. Science as a social enterprise: The CAMBIA BiOS initiative. *Innovations*, Fall, 11–42.

Kirby, M. 2001. 'An interview with Erik Olin Wright.' Available from http://www.ssc.wisc.edu/~wright/kirby_wright.pdf [Accessed on 2 September 2013].

Kloppenburg, J. 1988. *First the seed: The political economy of plant biotechnology, 1492–2000*. New York, NY: Cambridge University Press.

Kloppenburg, J. 2004. *First the seed: The political economy of plant biotechnology, 1492–2000*. Madison, WI: University of Wisconsin Press.

Kloppenburg, J. 2010. Impeding dispossession, enabling repossession: Biological open source and the recovery of seed sovereignty. *Journal of Agrarian Change*, 10(3 July), 367–388.

Kloppenburg, Jr. and D. Kleinman. 1987. Seed wars: Common heritage, private property, and political strategy'. *Socialist Review*, 95(September-October), 7–41.

Kotschi, J. and G. Kaiser. 2012. *Open-source für saatgut: Diskussionspapier*. Göttingen: AGRECOL.

Lorde, A. 1984. *Sister outsider*. Berkeley, CA: Crossing Press.

Louwaars, N., H. Dons, G. Van Overwalle, H. Raven, A. Arundel, D. Eaton, and A. Nelis. 2009. *Breeding business: The future of plant breeding in the light of developments in patent rights and plant breeder's rights*. CGN Report 2009–14, Wageningen: Centre for Genetic Resources.

Lusser, M., C. Parisi, D. Plan, and E. Rodriguez-Cerezo. 2012. Deployment of new technologies in plant Breeding. *Nature Biotechnology*, 30(3 March), 231–239.

LVC (La Vía Campesina). 2001. The position of Vía Campesina on biodiversity, biosafety and genetic resources. *Development*, 44(4), 47–51.

LVC (La Vía Campesina). 2011. La Vía Campesina Bali Seed Dclaration. Available at http://climateandcapitalism.com/2011/03/20/la-via-campesina-the-bali-seed-declaration/ [Accessed 18 March 2011].

LVC (La Vía Campesina). 2013a. La Vía Campesina: Our seeds, our future. Available at http://viacampesina.org/downloads/pdf/en/EN-notebook6.pdf [Accessed 15 August 2013].

LVC (La Vía Campesina). 2013b. Tunis 2013: If we rely on corporate seed, we lose food sovereignty. Available at http://viacampesina.org/en/index.php/actions-and-events-mainmenu-26/world-social-forum-mainmenu-34/1394-tunis-2013-if-we-rely-on-corporate-seed-we-lose-food-sovereignty [Accessed 25 August 2013].

LVC (La Vía Campesina). 2013c. The Jakarta call. Available at http://viacampesina.org/en/index.php/our-conferences-mainmenu-28/6-jakarta-2013/resolutions-and-declarations/1428-the-jakarta-call [Accessed 14 June 2013].

Marx, K. 1998. *The communist manifesto*. New York, NY: Verso.

Mgbeoji, I. 2006. *Global biopiracy: Patents, plants, and indigenous knowledge*. Ithaca, NY: Cornell University Press.

Michaels, T. 1999. General Public License for Plant Germplasm: A proposal by Tom Michaels. Paper presented at the 1999 Bean Improvement Cooperative Conference, Calgary, Alberta.

Mooney, P.R. 1979. *Seeds of the earth: A private or a public resource*. Ottawa: Inter Pares.

Murphy, D. 2007. *Plant breeding and biotechnology: Societal context and the future of agriculture*. Cambridge, UK: Cambridge University Press.

Murphy, K., D. Lammer, S. Lyon, B. Carter, and S. Jones. 2004. Breeding for organic and low-input farming systems: An evolutionary-participatory breeding method for inbred cereal grains. *Renewable Agriculture and Food Systems*, 20(1), 48–55.

Mushita, A. and C.B. Thompson. 2007. *Biopiracy of biodiversity: Global exchange as enclosure*. Trenton, NJ: Africa World Press.

Nicholson, P. 2012. Food sovereignty, a basis for transforming the dominant economic and social model: An interview of Paul Nicholson, La Vía Campesina. Geneva: CETIM.

Nigh, R. 2002. Maya medicine in the biological gaze: Bioprospecting research as herbal fetishism. *Current Anthropology*, 43(3), 451–477.

OSSI (Open Source Seed Initiative). 2013. OSSI basic principles.

Pardey, P., B. Koo, J. Drew, J. Horwich, and C. Nottenburg. 2013. The evolving landscape of plant varietal rights in the United States, 1930–2008. *Nature Biotechnology*, 31(1 January), 25–29.

Pollack, S. 2009. Crop scientists say biotechnology seed companies are thwarting research. *The New York Times*, (February 20), B3.

Santilli, J. 2012. *Agrobiodiversity and the law*. New York: Earthscan.

Schurman, R. and D. Kelso. 2003. *Engineering trouble: Biotechnology and its discontents*. Berkeley, CA: University of California Press.

SEARICE (Southeast Asia Regional Initiatives for Community Empowerment). 2009. *Revisiting the streams of participatory plant breeding*. Quezon City, Philippines: SEARICE.

Shiva, V. 1997. *Biopiracy: The plunder of nature and knowledge*. Boston, MA: South End Press.

Shiva, V. 2012a. The seed emergency: The threat to food and democracy. Available at http://www.aljazeera.com/indepth/opinion/2012/02/201224152439941847.html [Accessed 20 August 2013].

Shiva, V. 2012b. Defending seed freedom. Available at http://seedfreedom.in/declaration/ [Accessed 25 August 2013].

Shiva, V., C. Lockhart, and R. Schroff (eds.) 2013. *The law of the seed*. New Delhi, India: Navdanya International.

Srinivas, K. 2002. The case for BioLinuxes: And other pro-commons innovations. In *Sarai reader 2002: The cities of everyday life*. New Delhi: Center for the Study of Developing Societies, 321–328.

Stallman, R. 2002. *Free software definition. In free software, free society: Selected essays of Richard M. Stallman*. Boston, MA: GNU Press.

Stallman, R. 2013. Why open source misses the point of free software. Available from http://www.gnu.org/philospohy/open-soruce-misses-the-point.html [Accessed on 19 December 2012].

Stone, G. 2007. The birth and death of traditional knowledge: Paradoxical effects of biotechnology in India. *In*: C. McManis, ed. *Biodiversity and the law: Intellectual property, biotechnology and traditional knowledge*. Earthscan.

Tracy, W.F. 2003. What is plant breeding? *In*: M. Sligh and L. Lauffer, eds. *Summit proceedings: Summit on seeds and breeds for 21st century agriculture*. Pittsboro, NC: Rural Advancement Foundation International.

U.S. Senate. 2010. *International treaty on plant genetic resources for agriculture, report to accompany treaty doc. 110–19*. Committee on Foreign Relations, U.S. Senate, Washington, DC: USGPO.

Vivas-Egui, D. and M.J. Oliva. 2010. *Biodiversity related intellectual property provisions in free trade agreements*. Issue Paper No. 4, Geneva: International Centre for Trade and Sustainable Development.

Weber, S. 2004. *The success of open source*. Cambridge, MA: Harvard University Press.

Winston, E. 2008. What if seeds were not patentable? *Michigan State Las Review*, 2008, 321–344.

Wittman, H. 2009. Interview: Paul Nicholson, La Vía Campesina. *The Journal of Peasant Studies*, 36 (3 July), 676–682.

Zilberman, D., S.E. Sexton, M. Marra, and J. Fernandez-Conejo. 2013. The economic impact of genetically engineered crops. *Choices*. Available from http://ecnr.berkeley.edu/vfs/PPs/Sexton-Ste/web/choices.pdf [Accessed on 2 July 2013].

Jack Kloppenburg works in the Department of Community and Environmental Sociology at the University of Wisconsin-Madison. He has studied the social impacts of biotechnology, the controversy over control of genetic resources and the prospects for framing 'foodsheds' as an analytical basis for developing sustainable food systems. He is currently jazzed by the potential of 'food sovereignty' and by the possible application of 'open source' principles to plant breeding. He is a founder of the Open Source Seed Initiative.

Food sovereignty, food security and democratic choice: critical contradictions, difficult conciliations

Bina Agarwal

In recent years, the concept of 'food sovereignty' has gained increasing ground among grassroots groups, taking the form of a global movement. But there is no uniform conceptualization of what food sovereignty constitutes. Indeed, the definition has been expanding over time. It has moved from its initial focus on national self-sufficiency in food production ('the right of nations') to local self-sufficiency ('the rights of peoples'). There is also a growing emphasis on the rights of women and other disadvantaged groups, and on consensus building and democratic choice. This paper provides a critique of some of the major tenets of the food sovereignty movement. It recognizes that many developing countries may wish to pursue the goal of self-sufficiency in the context of the global food crises, and that it is important to promote social equality and democratic choice. Taken together, however, there can be serious contradictions between the key features of the food sovereignty vision, such as between the goals of national and local food self-sufficiency; between promoting food crops and a farmer's freedom to choose to what extent to farm, which crops to grow, and how to grow them; between strengthening family farming and achieving gender equality; and between collective and individual rights, especially over land ownership. The paper also reflects on the ways in which some of the food sovereignty goals could be better achieved through innovative institutional change, without sacrificing an individual's freedom to choose.

1. Food sovereignty: shifting definitions

In 1996, when it mooted the concept of food sovereignty, La Via Campesina focused on national self-sufficiency and diversity in food systems: 'Food sovereignty is the right of each nation to maintain and develop its own capacity to produce its basic foods, respecting cultural and productive diversity.' But as the idea of food sovereignty spread globally, embraced by a variety of groups, the definition broadened. In 2002, food sovereignty was envisioned as follows:

> The rights of peoples to define their own food and agriculture; to protect and regulate domestic agricultural production and trade in order to achieve sustainable development objectives; to determine the extent to which they want to be self-reliant .... (Cited in Patel 2009)

This article was originally published online with an error. This version has been corrected. Please see corrigendum: (http://dx.doi.org/10.1080/03066150.2014.961269)

This is a revised version of a paper presented at the International Conference on 'Food Sovereignty: A Critical Dialogue', sponsored by the *Journal of Peasant Studies* and the Program on Agrarian Studies at Yale University, New Haven, September 14–15, 2013. I am grateful to Jun Borras for inviting me to give a keynote address at this interesting conference, and to the two anonymous referees of JPS for their helpful comments.

In February 2007, the definition became all encompassing, as elaborated in the Nyéléni declaration of the forum for food sovereignty, held by La Via Campesina in Nyéléni, Mali:

> Food sovereignty is the right of peoples to healthy and culturally appropriate food produced through ecologically sound and sustainable methods, and their right to define their own food and agriculture systems. It puts the aspirations and needs of those who produce, distribute and consume food at the heart of food systems and policies, rather than the demands of markets and corporations. It offers a strategy to resist and dismantle the current corporate and food regime ... It defends the interests and inclusion of the next generation ... Food sovereignty prioritises local and national economies and markets, and empowers peasant and family farmer-driven agriculture. ... It ensures ... the rights to use and manage lands ... [It] implies new social relations free of oppression and inequality between men and women, peoples, racial groups, social and economic classes and generations. (For the full text, see Patel 2009, 673–4)

This expanding definition first moves from the right of self-reliance of *nations* (1996), to the rights of people to define domestic production and trade, as well as determine the extent to which they *want to be self-reliant* (2002). It then embraces everyone who is involved in the food chain – from producers to distributors to consumers (2007). This last definition also includes a range of other rights, such as the right to manage land, and emphasizes peasant empowerment, family farming, and freedom from gender-related and other inequalities.

There are many contradictory strains in this last definition, some of which have been discussed by Patel (2009), such as the inclusion of the rights of *all* producers and distributors without distinction between large and small, or between farm owners and landless farm workers. For the purpose of my discussion, however, there are other issues (which Patel does not touch upon) that can prove especially problematic, if all that is promised here is sought to be operationalized. First, there is the shift from an emphasis on national self-sufficiency (as a cry against global hegemony and dependency in access to food) in the 1996 definition, to arguing for local self-sufficiency in the 2002 definition, although it is not clear how small 'local' may be – it could even be read as meaning household self-sufficiency. The 2002 definition may also be seen as directed at state policies within countries and against multinational corporations controlling the food chains, but the necessity and even feasibility of local self-sufficiency is debatable. Second, although in both 2002 and 2007 there is an emphasis on democratic decision-making, the thrust is not the same. The 2002 definition allows people to be self-sufficient to the extent they want to be, giving primacy to individual choice, but in 2007 it is group decisions that matter. Paul Nicholson's elaboration of La Via Campesina's vision in his interview with Hannah Wittman (2009, 682), highlights this:

> We have to move forward, making sure that our decisions and declarations are made well. This requires long debates and reflection because decisions have to be made deliberately. Consensus is fundamental ... We have a long-term vision and this means that our declarations and principles require lots of discussion. For this reason, the internal process within La Via Campesina is very important. It has to be based on debate. ...

But we may ask: how representative are those who have framed this vision? Can consensus really be reached or would we merely get majoritarianism? What space would dissenting voices have? How would perspectives stemming from gender, caste, ethnicity, and so on be incorporated, if they diverge from one another or from the majority? Although these are general questions of presence and representation that can apply to many contexts, they are particularly complex when applied to issues of livelihood and survival under substantial inequality and diversity between peoples and nations.

Third, the 2007 declaration forefronts *family* farming, even while emphasizing gender equality. But how will unequal gender relations embedded within families be tackled? Indeed an emphasis on family farming, which often depends on women's unpaid labour, could go in the opposite direction, unless intra-household inequalities are addressed. In addition, how does family farming gel with the idea of collective ownership of land?

These shifting/broadening definitions reflect what Patel succinctly calls 'definition by committee', a definition into which a diversity of people can read themselves. This may help in mobilizing people around a campaign, but is it workable on the ground?

This paper argues that La Via Campesina's 1997 definition of food sovereignty, namely the efforts by nation states to attain self-reliance, has some relevance in the wake of the 2007–2008 world food crises and the overdependence of many (especially southern) countries on others (especially northern countries) for their food security; although the balance of imports and home production would need to be worked out. There is also much merit in La Via Campesina's emphasis on environmentally sustainable agriculture. But it would be difficult to operationalize the 2007 definition in so far as farm households, based on their specific constraints and priorities, may choose options that are contrary to the vision, whereas limiting their choice would go contrary to the democratic principles of the right to choose that the declaration forefronts. In fact, in particular contexts, restrictions on choice could – paradoxically – be detrimental in economic terms precisely for the small farmers whose interests the declaration seeks to represent, but who were not all party to its framing. The issue of gender inequality is especially complex and may be difficult to address by prioritizing individual family farming. Alternative institutional arrangements based on proactive farmer cooperation in production, especially cooperation among women farmers, may be more conducive to gender equality, but that could go contrary to individual family farming.

Section 2 of the contribution spells out the nature of global interdependency in food production and distribution, thus examining the issues embedded in the 1996 definition – 'the right of nations'. The subsequent two sections then critically examine some key aspects of the 2007 vision of food sovereignty, namely the potential for achieving self-sufficiency given serious supply constraints faced by small farmers; the question of women farmers and gender equality; and the issue of democratic choice. Section 3 focuses on changing agrarian structures and the growing feminization of agriculture across the world's regions. It also outlines the constraints that small farmers and especially women face, in making a subsistence living or taking advantage of new opportunities, thus underlining the challenges of increasing production and achieving gender equality. Section 4 points to the difficulties of reconciling democratic choice and the promotion of a particular kind of agriculture. Evidence from India illustrates that the choices farmers want to make, given the constraints they face, can diverge substantially from La Via Campesina's vision of food sovereignty. It also highlights the contradictions between the democratic freedoms of individuals and the programmes identified on their behalf by global movements. Section 5 then presents a way by which small farmers could overcome their resource constraints, such as through local cooperation and resource sharing which would prove both economically and socially empowering. The issue of democratic choice nevertheless remains unresolved – will the cooperating farmers choose a path that is in line with the food sovereignty vision or will they follow other paths to fulfil their livelihood needs? The concluding Section 6 pulls together the various threads of the argument while raising further questions.

2. The right of nations: self-sufficiency?

A dramatic rise in food prices in 2007–2008 shook the world out of its complacency. There was nearly a 40 percent increase in the food price index relative to 9 percent in 2006 (von Braun 2008). Wheat prices almost quadrupled and maize prices almost tripled between 2000 and 2008. The adverse effects of this price rise fell on foodgrain importing countries and on net buyers of foodgrains within countries (Quisumbing et al. 2008, von Braun 2008–09). The poor, and especially women and children in poor households, were the most adversely affected. The price rise, by some estimates, added 105 million to the poor, mostly in South Asia and sub-Saharan Africa (Ivanic and Martin 2008). Although the price spike in 2007–2008 was especially sharp, the overall upward trend in food prices is expected to continue. This, along with the prospect of price volatility, remains a major global concern.

An important factor underlying the price rise is the regional concentration of foodgrain production and exports. In 2008, Asian farmers produced 90 percent of the world's rice and around 40 percent of its wheat and total cereals. But most Asian countries consume what they produce – the exports come from only a few. For instance, although over 80 percent of rice exports came from Asia in 2008, the exporters were primarily Thailand, Vietnam, India and Pakistan and, beyond Asia, the USA. Similarly, 85 percent of wheat exports came from only four regions – North America, Russia, Europe and Australia; and 81 percent of maize exports came from North America and Latin America (especially Argentina and Brazil). Taking all cereal exports together, 65 percent came from North America and Europe (Figure 1).

This regional concentration not only makes food-deficit countries over-dependent on a few countries for fulfilling their needs, it also leaves them vulnerable to the vagaries of policy shifts in the exporting countries. This can influence global availability and prices

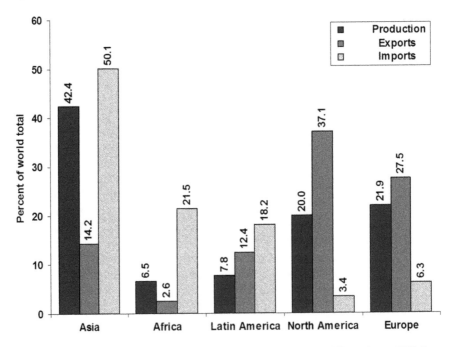

Figure 1. Production, exports and imports of total cereals by the world's regions, 2008 (percentages).

Source: Based on FAO Statistics (http: /faostat.fao.org). Also reproduced in Agarwal (2013).

of foodgrains. Foodgrain supplies will fall and prices rise, for example, if the exporting countries shift large areas earlier devoted to foodgrains to biofuels, or reduce exports to cater to the needs of their own populations, or manage their agriculture inefficiently, or fail to control speculative hoarding. Adverse weather conditions can add to these negative effects. Such factors were important in the 2007–2008 price rise.

In that year, almost 100 million tonnes, or 4.8 percent of all cereals produced, went into ethanol production. Thirty-three percent of the corn production in the United States in 2008–2009 was similarly used.[1] Facilitated especially by government subsidies for growing energy crops, American farmers shifted large areas from soybean and wheat to maize for biofuel. Moreover, several countries in Asia (e.g. China and India) and Latin America restricted their exports as a short-term response, further reducing foodgrain supply for importing countries.

In the long-term, we must also factor in climate change (CC) as a substantial threat to global food security. Although estimates of the extent of CC impact vary, they are consistent in their predictions that South Asia and sub-Saharan Africa will be the worst affected (Table 1; see also Wheeler and von Braun 2013). And these are also the regions where most of the world's poor live.[2]

Moreover, a rise in crop prices will not work as an incentive for higher production unless small farmers (typically cultivating under 2 hectares), who constitute the vast majority of farmers in developing countries, can overcome their supply constraints. In addition, if output lags behind population increase, the per capita calories available in 2050 will be lower than in 2000 throughout the developing world (IFPRI 2009). The poor will again face the brunt of this gap. Food security for the estimated 9 billion people by 2050 will need an extraordinary effort, even without climate change. With climate change, even with the best efforts at mitigation, poor farmers and especially women and children are likely to be affected adversely (IFPRI 2009, Wheeler and von Braun 2013).

In this scenario, La Via Campesina's argument for food sovereignty in terms of 'the right of each nation' (and of deficit nations in particular) to seek self-sufficiency, resonates. But how will food deficit regions, especially those most vulnerable to adverse climate change – namely South Asia and sub-Saharan Africa – move towards sufficiency?

It is important to recognize at the onset that not every nation can be self-reliant in food, given obvious restrictions imposed by limited arable land, irrigation water and other essential resources, especially in geographically small countries. Hence trade cannot be eliminated,[3] nor would it be desirable to do so, given the ecological, climatic and other location specificities that make some crop division of global production beneficial. But let us consider a more limited goal, namely of countries seeking to raise food production to their best capacity. For increasing production, two contrasting models are being mooted globally with divergent visions of agrarian transitions. One vision privileges large corporate farms feeding a growing number of city dwellers. The other envisions the vast body of small and marginal farmers enhancing their productivity and making a smooth transition from agriculture to non-agriculture, or choosing to stay in agriculture as an attractive livelihood option. La Via Campesina roots for the latter. But there can be many difficulties in realizing this idea.

---

[1]The figures for all cereals were obtained directly from Ramesh Chand, Director, National Centre for Agricultural Economics and Policy (Delhi), and those relating to maize from Chand (2009).
[2]For an elaboration of these arguments, see Agarwal (2011).
[3]See also, Burnett and Murphy (2013).

Table 1. Estimated climate change effect on 2050 crop production relative to no climate change effect (percentage difference).

Region	Rice	Wheat	Maize
South Asia	−14.5	−48.8	−8.9
East Asia and Pacific	−11.3	1.8	8.9
Sub-Saharan Africa	−15.2	−35.8	−7.1
Latin America	−19.2	17.4	−4.0
World	−13.5	−27.4	−0.4

Source: IFPRI (2009).

To begin with, as elaborated in the next section, there are supply side constraints in the ability of small farmers to raise production. The issue of gender is linked with these constraints given the growing feminization of agriculture and the specific problems that women farmers face. Moreover, nations seeking self-sufficiency have to cater to the needs of all their citizens, including those who are working in the non-farm sector (rural or urban) or as landless agricultural labourers. This means that food producers need to go beyond self-sufficiency to producing a surplus. As elaborated in Section 4, however, those who are currently in farming, if given a choice, may choose not to grow food crops at all. But consider first the constraints to increasing production and the interconnected issue of gender.

3. The small farmer and her constraints

The majority of farmers in developing countries are small, often marginal, and increasingly women. And most are trapped in low productivity cycles. This is especially so in Asia and Africa where almost 60 percent of the workforce remains in agriculture, although agriculture's contribution to GDP is under 10 percent in Asia and under 20 percent in Africa. This divergence between agriculture's GDP contribution and the population it supports means that many remain dependent on low yield, subsistence farming.

And this trap is gendered, given women's disproportionate dependence on agriculture for their livelihood. In Asia, for example, in 2008, 57 percent of female workers relative to 48 percent of male workers depended on agriculture-related livelihoods. In Africa, these percentages were 63 and 48 respectively. Women also constitute a substantial proportion of the *total* agricultural workforce. In Asia, 43 percent of all farm workers in 2008 were female, with percentages close to 50 in many countries (Table 2). In the world's major rice producing and exporting countries, therefore, almost half the agricultural workforce is female. In Africa, again, almost 50 percent of agricultural workers are women. Further, aggregating the time spent on producing, processing and preparing food, women are estimated to contribute 60–70 percent of the total labour needed to bring food to the table in large parts of sub-Saharan Africa, India and China (Doss 2010, 9).

Moreover, over the past 40 years, across the world (with the exception of Europe) women workers have been rising as a proportion of the total agricultural workforce, since more men than women have moved to non-farm jobs (Figure 2). In effect, we are seeing a feminization of agriculture (namely, a rise in the proportion of women in the total agricultural workforce, even if the absolute proportion remains half or below).

Small farmers and especially women farmers thus have a central role to play in reviving agriculture and increasing its capacity to withstand the onslaughts of climate change. But they also face substantial constraints – insecure rights in the land they cultivate; lack of an assured

Table 2.   Percentage of females in the total agricultural labour force: Asian countries.

Region/Country	1971	1981	1991	2001	2005	2008
South-East Asia						
Cambodia	52.7	57.7	55.5	54.0	52.3	51.6
Indonesia	30.0	33.9	38.9	38.9	39.2	39.2
Lao People's Democratic Republic	48.1	51.4	51.3	52.1	52.6	52.5
Malaysia	38.6	41.1	31.3	25.6	23.3	21.9
Philippines	23.0	27.5	24.2	24.9	24.3	24.0
Thailand	49.9	49.2	47.3	46.1	46.0	45.3
Viet Nam	47.4	50.7	51.1	50.3	49.8	49.4
South Asia						
Bangladesh	42.9	42.8	45.7	46.2	48.3	50.0
Bhutan	39.7	25.9	22.6	24.4	30.0	34.2
India	39.3	32.3	32.5	32.3	39.7[a]	39.7[a]
Nepal	41.5	35.4	39.9	44.3	46.6	47.6
Pakistan	29.9	17.0	19.4	22.6	26.1	28.3
Sri Lanka	20.2	34.6	36.4	34.6	36.1	37.2
East Asia						
China	44.3	45.8	47.3	47.9	48.0	48.0
Asia	41.9	40.9	42.3	42.4	42.6	42.6

[a]Figures for India for these two years have been calculated from the 2004–2005 National Sample Survey data (NSSO 2005a) and population projections given in GoI (2006).

Sources: Calculations based on FAO Statistics (http://faostat.fao.org), except for 2005 and 2008 for India.

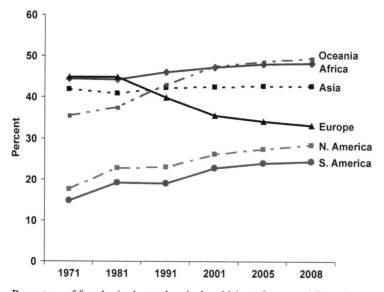

Figure 2.   Percentage of females in the total agricultural labour force: world's regions.

Source: Based on FAO Statistics (http: /faostat.fao.org). Also reproduced in Agarwal (2013).

water supply; little access to formal credit; and limited access to inputs such as fertilizers, or to technology, information on new agricultural practices and marketing infrastructure.[4]

---

[4]See World Bank (2007) for a global picture, and GoI (2011), for India.

These constraints affect small farmers of both genders. But women face additional difficulties. The vast proportion of them own little or no land themselves in developing countries.[5] Most of them therefore work as unpaid labour on family farms owned by male relatives, or as labourers on the fields of others, or under insecure tenure arrangements on land obtained through male family members or markets (World Bank 2007, 80). In Nepal, in 2001, women owned land in only 14 percent of landowning rural households (Allendorf 2007). In India, in 2010–2011 women held 12.8 percent of all operational (that is, cultivated) land holdings, which constituted only 10.4 percent of the cultivated area (GoI 2010–11). In rural China, in the early 2000s, women constituted an estimated 70 percent of the effectively landless, since they usually failed to receive allotments of community land under the household responsibility system, when they relocated upon marriage or divorce (Li 2003, 4). Recent legal changes have further reduced the chances of such allotments. Within Asia as a whole, the gender gap in access to land is much greater in South Asia than in Southeast Asia; and within South Asia it is greater in the northern belt (e.g. northwest India, Bangladesh and Pakistan), than in the southern (e.g. south India and Sri Lanka). Laws, culture, religion, ecology, and cropping patterns all contribute to this geographic variation (Agarwal 1994). For instance, women are found to be much more visibly involved in rice and millet cultivation than in wheat.

Similarly, Africa reveals substantial gender gaps in access to land. In Kenya, women constitute 5 percent of registered landholders. In Ghana, women hold land in 10 percent of the households and men in 16–23 percent (Deere and Doss 2006). Latin America does relatively better, but is still far from gender equal in land ownership (Deere and de Leon 2001, Lastarria-Cornhiel and Manji 2010). Moreover, even when women have access to land, their control over it in terms of rights to lease, mortgage, or sell it, or use it as collateral tends to be more restricted than men's (Agarwal 1994, Saito et al. 1994). Household surveys, compiled by the FAO (2011, 23) for 20 countries, also show that male-headed households (MHHs) operate much larger farms on average than female-headed households (FHHs).

In addition, women farmers face well-documented gender inequalities and male bias in accessing the range of essential inputs and services mentioned earlier.[6] Members of rural cooperatives providing inputs are predominantly men in most countries (see Saito et al. 1994, among others). Women farmers are also less likely to own agricultural tools than male farmers (Saito et al. 1994, 23, Peterman et al. 2009, 28). In addition, their public participation and mobility is socially restricted in many countries. This limits their ability to procure inputs or labour, or sell their produce profitably (Agarwal 1994, World Bank 2009, FAO 2011).

Constraints in access to land, inputs and technical support systems can significantly affect the productivity of all small and marginal farmers, but especially of women farmers given the gendered constraints. For instance, in sub-Saharan Africa where men and women often cultivate both separate and joint plots, the majority of the 22 studies that I examined, which measured productivity differences between male and female farmers, found lower yields on women's plots/farms (see Agarwal 2013 for details),

---

[5]Although few countries collect country-level gender-disaggregated data on land or asset ownership, information gleaned from those that do, and from small-scale studies in others, shows a substantial gender inequality.
[6]See World Bank (2009), FAO (2011), and Peterman et al. (2009) for global information; and Doss (2001) for Africa.

while a few found no statistically significant difference in yields or overall output.[7] The studies showing lower yields for women attribute this variously to women's insecure land rights or their lower access to inputs (especially fertilizers), male labour, oxen or extension services. A few studies also show that women would have higher outputs than male farmers, if they had access to the same inputs and extension services as men.[8] Based on a wide review of evidence for Kenya, Quisumbing (1996) concluded that women's crop yields could have been raised by up to 23 percent if their access to production inputs and experience had been the same as men's. In Burkina Faso, Udry et al. (1995) estimated that output could be increased by 10–15 percent if inputs such as manure and fertilizers were reallocated from men's plots to women's plots in the same household.

Beyond individual countries, FAO's 2011 *State of Food and Agriculture Report* has assessed that reducing the constraints faced by women farmers could raise yields on their farms by 20–30 percent and raise total agricultural output in developing countries by 2.5–4 percent, thus making a significant impact on national food availability (FAO 2011).[9] A failure to bridge the gender gaps in access to inputs and services, however, would not only confine a large proportion of farmers to low productivity agriculture, it would also impact adversely on national efforts to attain food security.

What does this imply for the food sovereignty discussion? First, in order to increase national food output based on small-holder agriculture, most developing countries will require serious efforts to enable small farmers (and especially the rising proportion of women farmers) to overcome their production constraints. The food sovereignty movement thus needs to focus much more than it appears to have done on how these constraints – which often vary by country and context – can be overcome. Second, the Nyéléni declaration argues for gender equality and a recognition of women's roles and rights in food production, as well as women's representation in decision-making. At the same time, it gives centre stage to the 'family farm'. This emphasis is problematic on several counts. To begin with, given that male members have shifted disproportionately either to cities or to non-farm jobs within rural areas, many family farms are effectively managed by women, but most (as noted) have no direct rights over the land or other assets. More particularly, family farms do not provide autonomy to women workers or the means to realize their potential as farmers. Hence a nod toward gender equality is not enough. The problems women face as farmers are structural and deep-rooted, and would need to be addressed specifically. This would include redistributing productive assets such as land and inputs *within* peasant households in gender-equal ways, and directing state services to cater better to the needs of women farmers, such as services relating to credit, extension, training, information on new technology, field trials, input supply, storage and marketing. Institutional innovations involving only women rather than entire families, as discussed in Section 5 of this paper, could also hold potential gains, both in terms of productivity and equity. But to achieve this would require a much more complex approach to production, gender and the state than is to be found so far in La Via Campesina's elaborations.

---

[7]These were studies by Adesina and Djato (1997), Adeleke et al. (2008), Kumase et al. (2008), Moock (1976), Bindlish, Evenson and Gbetibouo (1993), Quisumbing et al. (2001) and Hill and Vigneri (2009).
[8]See Kumase et al. (2008), Moock (1976), Dey (1992) and Udry et al. (1995).
[9]I have focused on crops, but the argument that improving women's resource access can increase output could also be extended to other types of food, such as fish.

Moreover, achieving national self-reliance in food availability depends not only on overcoming small farmer production constraints. It also depends on what the farmers choose to do.

4. The right of democratic choice

The food sovereignty vision gives considerable weight to democratic choice and debate. Of course all choices can be structurally constrained by the economic, political and social limitations within which they are exercised. Nevertheless, the 2002 definition (as noted above) at least allows scope for individual choice, recognizing that people can be self-sufficient *to the extent they wish to be*. The 2007 definition, however, focuses more on collective processes of democratic deliberation and consensus building. Both issues – consensus building and individual choice – are little addressed in practice.

None would deny the merit of democratic deliberation. But this would require more than information, persuasion and argument. A key question is: how would inequalities based on gender, ethnicity and class be addressed? La Via Campesina is constituted of an estimated 148 member organizations across 69 countries (Martinez-Torres and Rosset 2010, 165). Its members are heterogeneous on all the mentioned counts, as well as ideologically (Borras 2008). In particular, the landless and near-landless are not well represented even in Brazil, where the movement is strong. In India, the Karnataka State Farmers Association – the most visible face of La Via Campesina in South Asia – is constituted of well-off farmers who have resisted redistributive land reform and other measures that could benefit the landless and near-landless. The latter therefore do not see the organization as representing their interests (Borras 2008). There is also rather little integration between La Via Campesina and the many other global movements that address the interests of particular constituents of the rural working classes.[10] Hence, notwithstanding the commonality across difference which clearly exists and keeps the movement alive, it is valid to ask: is it possible to build consensus among such disparate constituents?

Moreover, what if a significant proportion of farmers make choices (admittedly within the constraints they face) that diverge notably from those desired by the food sovereignty movement for a presumed common good? There are farmers who may be disillusioned with farming itself, or be compelled for reasons of economic viability to eschew food production for self-sufficiency. Do they have a democratic right to choose what they have reason to value?[11]

By way of illustration, consider some examples from India. In 2003, a nationwide survey carried out by the Government of India (NSSO 2005b) of 51,770 farm households (0.286 million persons) living in 6638 villages found that some 40 percent of them did not like farming, and given a choice, would prefer another source of livelihood.[12] The question

---

[10]La Via Campesina is only one (albeit one of the best known today) of many transnational agrarian movements that have emerged in recent decades, representing a diverse constituency of peasants, small farmers, consumers and producers, concerned variously with food politics, land and related issues (for a useful overview of such movements, see especially Borras et al. 2008).

[11]For an elaboration on human capability, defined in terms of the freedom to choose what a person has reason to value, see Sen (1999).

[12]The total sample is slightly smaller when we exclude missing information, and also apply the definition of 'farmer' strictly to exclude those who are not cultivating any land even if they own some, or are landless and not leasing in land in the year of the survey. This corrected sample has been used for Tables 3, 4 and 5.

Table 3. Attitudes towards farming by farm size.

Farm size (operated area)	Like farming	Don't like farming	All farmers
(hectares)	(*N*=30,294)	(*N*=21,075)	(*N*= 51,369)
>0.0 – ≤ 1.0	60.5	76.1	66.9
>1.0 – ≤ 2.0	19.0	13.8	16.9
>2.0	20.5	10.1	16.2
Total	100.0	100.0	100.0

Source: B. Agarwal and A. Agrawal, 'Choosing' not to farm?, ongoing analysis.

they were asked was: 'Do you like farming as a profession?' The survey defined a farmer as someone who not only operated some land but was engaged in agricultural activities during the 365 days preceding the day of the survey. Landless agricultural labourers who were not leasing in land and those owning but not cultivating land were excluded. A farm household was defined as one where at least one of its members was cultivating. Agricultural activities included crop cultivation, animal husbandry, poultry, fishing and sericulture.

Who were the farmers who did not like farming?[13] Some 76 percent of them operated one hectare (ha) or less. Their average operated area was 0.9 ha and average owned area was 0.8 ha, compared with 1.4 ha and 1. 3 ha respectively of those who said they liked farming (Table 3). Those disliking farming were also less likely to be aware of government measures such as minimum support prices; have crop insurance; be members in a farmers' organization or a self-help group (SHG); know about bio-fertilizers; or come from a household where at least one household member was a graduate or had had formal training in agriculture (Table 4). This suggests that the most vulnerable and resource poor are the most likely to want to leave agriculture.

The survey also asked those who said they did not like farming to select from four possible reasons for their view – low profitability, riskiness, low social status and 'other'. The respondents opted mainly for low profitability (two-thirds mentioned this) and the risk involved in the occupation (one-fifth said this) – profitability being more of an issue for the farmers cultivating 1 ha or less than with those cultivating over 2 ha (Table 5). Farmers in a higher farm size group (>2 ha) were somewhat more likely to mention risk and less likely to mention profitability, compared with the lowest farm size category of 1 ha or less, but the differences across land size groups were not dramatic. It is likely that the farmers would have given different responses if farming were more profitable and less risk-prone, or if they were less resource constrained.

Beyond the survey, there is also considerable evidence that farmers when faced with difficult economic choices do not want to undertake food production. In my ongoing research on women's group farming in Andhra Pradesh (discussed in more detail in the next section), for instance, I found that a number of women's group farms had stopped cultivating collectively. An important reason was the mandate by the local quasi-NGO, which had catalysed group formation, that the women should grow food crops in order to enhance household food security (not dissimilar to the food sovereignty approach). But food crops often failed due to lack of irrigation under drought conditions. The women's groups wanted to cultivate non-food crops, especially cotton, and many among them who were also doing

---

[13]The results presented here are part of an ongoing analysis by the author and a colleague, Ankush Agrawal.

Table 4. Characteristics of farm households liking/not liking farming.

Characteristics of farm households	Like farming	Don't like farming	All farmers
Average area operated (ha)	1.41	0.89	1.20
Average area owned (ha)	1.27	0.79	1.08
Percentages			
Aware of minimum support price	32.0	24.9	29.1
Have crop insurance	4.5	2.7	3.8
Are members of a farmers' organization	2.7	1.9	2.4
Are members of a Self Help Group	6.4	4.1	5.4
Are aware of bio-fertilizers	22.9	17.4	20.7
At least one household member is a graduate	36.2	31.7	34.4
At least one household member has formal training in agriculture	3.4	2.1	2.9

Source: B. Agarwal and A. Agrawal, 'Choosing' not to farm?, ongoing analysis.

Table 5. Reasons for not liking farming by farm size.

	Reasons for not liking farming (%)				
Farm size (operated area: ha)	Not profitable	Risky	Social status	Other	All
>0.0 − ≤ 1.0	67.2	17.8	5.2	9.8	100.0
>1.0 − ≤ 2.0	65.5	22.1	6.0	6.4	100.0
>2.0	60.3	26.8	5.0	7.9	100.0
Total	66.2	19.3	5.3	9.1	100.0

Source: B. Agarwal and A. Agrawal, 'Choosing' not to farm?, ongoing analysis.

family farming alongside were growing cotton on their family plots. Restricted to food crops under group cultivation, some had stopped group activity altogether when the crop failed.[14] The potential profit from farming was also a consideration. The groups needed cash to pay for the high cash rents on the land they leased in. Some illustrative voices from Karimnagar district (Andhra Pradesh) are given below, based on interviews conducted in 2013 with groups that had not undertaken collective farming for the last two years:

> We want more profits from agriculture. The MS (NGO) staff restricted us to food crops. Because there were no rains for a third year running we only cultivated pulses in 2 acres, but got no yield. Then we decided to do individual farming with cotton which allows us to get a profit even when rains are scarce. All of us have taken land on lease and are cultivating cotton now. (Women's group farm, village 1)

> We did want to continue with group farming, but we have to pay a high lease rate for the land. The land owners are demanding Rs. 15,000 per acre without irrigation facilities. For maize cultivation we need water. We lost the maize crop entirely due to the drought. Cotton would have given us some profit even under drought conditions, but MS [the NGO] insisted we cultivate only food crops. If they permit us to cultivate cotton we could still do group farming, since we can then recover the cost of investment and the lease paid. (Women's group farm, village 2)

---

[14]Although this was not the only reason for the groups becoming inactive – sometimes intra-group conflicts also led to a breakup – but the lack of freedom to grow non-food crops was identified as the main reason in this region.

Investment in agriculture has increased but profits from food crops are low. MS will not let us cultivate cotton which is viable on this land, so we are no longer interested in continuing with group farming. (Women's group farm, village 3)

We are interested in group farming but we are not interested in growing food crops. If MS allowed us, we would like to cultivate flowers as a group, as there is much demand for flowers in the market. (Women's group farm, village 4)

There is also a popular assumption that women prefer to cultivate food crops. Examples such as those above, as well as those from other regions such as parts of sub-Saharan Africa where women are successfully cultivating commercial crops like cocoa, indicate that this is a misplaced assumption.[15] Food security does not necessarily need food self-sufficiency at the local or household level. Landless rural dwellers and most urban dwellers buy food and have no means to grow their own. For them, a living wage is what matters for food security. Moreover, *nutritional* health depends not only on the quantity of foodgrains consumed and their diversity, but also on other nutritious food items, which cannot all be grown for self-consumption, as well as access to adequate and clean cooking fuel, clean water, sanitation, etc.

The issue of non-chemical farming (undoubtedly desirable both environmentally and for consumer health) is again complex and not everyone's choice. In India, for instance, according to the 2013 statistics from the *World of Organic Agriculture*, only 0.6 percent of agricultural land is under certified organic production, despite policies in many states to promote low chemical farming.[16] Of course these figures are likely to be a gross underestimate of organic farming per se, in that the vast proportion of Indian farmers are organic *by default* rather than by choice, since they cannot afford to buy chemical inputs. Comparable figures on agricultural land under certified organic production are 0.36 percent in China, 0.27 percent in Brazil and 19.6 percent in Austria (which is the highest percentage in Europe).

Choosing not to farm for self-sufficiency, choosing not to grow food crops, choosing not to grow organically – these are all democratic choices, subject to the constraints that farmers face. There can thus be a serious conflict between the aims of the food sovereignty movement and what many farmers may choose to do.

5. Cooperation and collectivities

Consider now the issue of collective versus individual rights. In his elaboration on the Nyéléni declaration, Paul Nicholson notes (Wittman 2009, 679): ' … we hold collective rights above an individual ownership model of land.' It is not clear, however, what this would mean in practice. The tension between individual and collective rights could potentially be serious. How would individual ownership be converted into collective rights? The process of socialist collectivization has been widely eschewed for its high human and production costs. The food sovereignty movement, however, provides no clear pathways or alternatives.

Alternatives do exist, however. As will be discussed below, voluntary cooperation to constitute collectivities could be one way forward for smallholders to overcome their supply constraints. The institutional forms I discuss here are a far cry from the idea of

---

[15]Also see Whitehead (2005) on the complex crop division of labour by gender in sub-Saharan Africa.
[16]See FIBL & IFOAM (2013), and Bhattacharyya and Chakroborty (2005, 116). For additional discussion, see also Willer and Yussefi (2007).

Table 6.   Levels and nature of cooperation: a typology.

Level of cooperation	Nature of cooperation	Illustrative examples[a]
Single purpose minimal cooperation	Membership in cooperatives or producer companies for marketing or input purchase, but individual cultivation	Many countries globally, including both developing and developed economies
Single purpose medium cooperation	Joint investment in private irrigation or large machinery, but individual cultivation	India (in many states) France and Canada: CUMA (cooperatives for the use of agricultural equipment) Cuba
Multipurpose limited cooperation	Collective crop planning, purchase of inputs and sale of outputs, but individual cultivation	India, Cuba[b]
Multipurpose comprehensive cooperation	Group farming: pooling privately owned or leased in land along with labour and capital, for joint cultivation, marketing, and profit sharing.	*Current*: India, France, Japan. *Late 1990s, early 2000s*: the transition economies of Romania, Kyrgyzstan, East Germany, and Nicaragua

[a]These examples are only illustrative. There could also be cases in other countries.
[b]These are outside the context of collectives and are constituted of peasant families who own their farms, cultivate separately, but cooperate in sharing farm machinery, obtaining credit and marketing their crops.
Source: Bina Agarwal, ongoing research.

collective *ownership* of a major resource such as land. In fact, individual rights can live comfortably with collective approaches through a voluntary pooling of private resources for production, without forfeiting ownership. But this would involve moving beyond the model of individual family farming which the food sovereignty movement has been emphasizing.

Potentially, a group approach to agricultural production can take many forms, involving varying degrees of cooperation and benefits (see typology in Table 6). Single purpose cooperation at the end of the production process, such as for marketing, is common and can be found in many regions and countries through various types of collective arrangements. But marketing cooperatives with individual production involve little everyday cooperation. A somewhat higher level of cooperation is involved in jointly investing in movable machinery such as tractors and combine harvesters, or immovables such as irrigation wells. In fact, joint investment in irrigation wells by small farmers goes back historically a century or more in South Asia (see, for example, Darling 1947, Goyal 1966), and has taken new forms in recent decades. For instance, in the late 1980s, during my fieldwork in a village in India's Alwar district, Rajasthan, I found many farmers who despite owning small and scattered plots had been able to irrigate them fully, by investing in tubewells in groups of eight where their plots were located. As one such farmer who owned 75 cents of land in three fragments located in different parts of the village told me – I now own three-eighths of a tubewell! Investing in a tubewell would not have been affordable or efficient for such farmers on an individual basis. Another variation on this is machine cooperatives, which invest in large machines that can be hired by farmers – examples can be found in countries as diverse as Canada, France, Cuba and India. Joint crop planning and pooling finances to buy inputs, machinery and crop insurance (what I term multipurpose limited cooperation in Table 6) is also beginning to emerge through the support of NGOs or quasi-NGOs in parts of India. Such collective planning can also take account of local ecology in deciding on cropping patterns. More generally, operating in groups can improve small farmers' bargaining power with government agencies and so increase their access to formal credit, inputs and information (Braverman et al. 1991).

However, the most integrated form of cooperation, with the potential for most benefit in terms of productivity and social empowerment, involves the pooling of land (owned or leased in), labour and capital. Potentially, this can bring economies of scale; spread the risks of farming among a larger number; facilitate crop experimentation and diversification; add to the pool of knowledge and managerial skills; and help individual families overcome peak labour shortages by increasing labour supply. Land consolidation alone can lead to substantial labour saving through a better division of tasks.[17] We would also expect groups to be better cushioned for short-term shocks such as rising input prices, and to adapt more effectively to climate change since conserving soils, water and forests usually requires collective effort.

For women farmers, these economic advantages could prove particularly substantial since these women face the most constraints. Also, as a group it would be easier for them to overcome the social restrictions on public interaction and mobility that they face in many cultures. A critical mass of 25–30 percent women, for instance, is found to empower rural women in South Asia to participate more effectively in mixed gender groups, such as those managing local forests (Agarwal 2010a, 2010b).

Overall, therefore, as a group, we would expect small and marginal farmers to be better protected as producers. A range of examples of small farmer cooperation indicate that this could work in practice, at least in particular contexts, if not everywhere. We find both old and current examples of group farming with land pooling especially in Asia and Europe. France, for instance, has had a long tradition of farmers pooling their land and other resources to constitute group farms called GAECs (Groupements d'Exploitation en Commune). This was catalysed by a law passed by the State in 1962.[18] Even today many thousand GAECs sustain and are attracting a new generation of farmers. There is also evidence of farmers coming together in small groups for cooperative farming after de-collectivization in East Germany (Mathijs and Swinnen 2001). In particular, my current research in South Asia and explorations in the transition economies of central Asia and Europe reveal a range of illustrative cases. In the latter regions the groups are constituted of families and in South Asia only of women (see Agarwal 2010c for details).

In several parts of Central Asia and Eastern Europe where the large collective farms of the 1950s–1970s were de-collectivized in the 1980s and 1990s, farmers could revert to individual family farming if they wished to. But not all chose to. Many farming families in Kyrgyzstan, Romania and East Germany, for instance, voluntarily formed new group enterprises (with friends, relatives or neighbours), by pooling their land, capital and labour to farm collectively in small groups on the restituted land, or in downsized former collectives. They did this to overcome scarcity of machinery and labour, or inadequate experience or skills in individual farm management. In the early 2000s, these group enterprises were found to be significantly more productive than individual family farms.[19] Since then the scene has been changing. For instance, my recent field visit in Kyrgyzstan (in July 2013) with Malcolm Childress (who was involved in the earlier study on that country) to a few

---

[17]Land consolidation alone can lead to substantial labour saving (Foster and Rosenzweig 2010)

[18]I am currently researching this.

[19]See, for example, Sabates-Wheeler (2002); Sabates-Wheeler and Childress (2004), and Mathijs and Swinnen (2001). See also Agarwal (2010c) for a detailed discussion.

of the same enterprises as studied earlier, revealed shifts away from group to more indivi-dualized family farms. They mentioned difficulties faced in drought years, high taxes and fees imposed by the government on collectives, or internal conflicts. At the same time, the fact that the groups served an important transitional function and survived for several years is, in itself, of no small importance. And my planned follow-up research on the earlier groups could provide further insights on those that have sustained.

In South Asia we find a very different model. Here there are women-only groups cat-alysed by NGOs or local governments. In India, some initiatives date to the 1980s. In Andhra Pradesh (south India), for example, with support from the Deccan Development Society (DDS, an NGO), poor, low-caste women in drought-prone Medak district began to lease in or purchase land in groups of 5–15, through various government schemes that provided subsidized credit and/or grants for this purpose (Agarwal 2003, 2010c). They cul-tivated the land collectively, aiming to achieve food security in an environmentally friendly way, through organic farming and crop diversification. In fact DDS's Director, P.V. Satheesh, is a strong advocate of food sovereignty in India,[20] and has been at the forefront of a 'grow millet' campaign.[21]

In 2008, DDS's group leasing programme covered around 85 hectares in 26 villages. In addition, women's groups were cultivating about 225 ha of land that they had purchased in 21 villages using the government's land-cum-grant scheme. They could not have bought the land through their individual resources. The groups are formed voluntarily. Decision-making is democratic. All the women know each other and share field tasks and produce equitably. They plant multiple crops and crop varieties (using seeds they preserve). This reduces their risk of total crop failure and provides a balanced diet. The group members I interviewed in the late 1990s said that by working together they could overcome their pro-duction constraints, access government officials and enjoy flexibility in the use of their time. They also said they ate better, although whether they are fully self-sufficient needs to be assessed.

A second example from India is again drawn from Andhra Pradesh. This was one of three states where group farming was catalysed in 2000 by the United Nations Development Programme and the Government of India (Burra, 2004). In Andhra, the programme was implemented locally with the help of the Andhra Pradesh Mahila Samatha Society (which runs the Education for Empowerment of Women programme of the government of India). In this five year project, start-up capital funds, implements and technical support were provided to the groups during the project period (one group was formed per project village). After project support ended in 2005, the groups continued to function in many villages under the umbrella of the Mahila Samatha Society. Today, about 250 of the original 500 groups are still active. Here, about 7500 women farmers from scheduled caste communities are farming in groups of around 15–20 women each.[22] In my ongoing research here I found that the land is typically taken on lease from one or more of the group members and somewhat more rarely from non-members. The groups were directed to cultivate only or mainly food crops to enhance family food security. As noted, some groups ceased to work together but many have sustained for some 13 years, although not all have farmed continuously every year. They have faced difficulties in

---

[20]See, for example, Mazhar et al. (2007).
[21]See, for example, http://www.thehindu.com/news/national/andhra-pradesh/from-pastapur-to-senegal-widening-the-network-of-millets/article5396601.ece
[22]Figures provided in 2011 by the head of the Andhra Pradesh Mahila Samatha programme.

procuring land to lease as well as in obtaining inputs, but most of the groups report reaping some form of social and economic benefit.

Another notable example from India is the Kudumbashree programme, launched by the Government of Kerala to support landless and land-poor women lease land and undertake group farming. Since 2010, the Joint Liability Group (JLG) scheme of the National Bank for Agriculture and Rural Development (NABARD) has helped link the groups with sub-sidized credit and various economic incentives. An estimated 34,000 groups are leasing in land for group farming in all districts of the state. Here there are no external restrictions on which crops women can grow. Women choose crops based on ecology, profitability, con-sumption needs, and production incentives. In some parts of the state, they grow crops for both self-consumption and sale, but elsewhere they grow a range of crops (including veg-etables and bananas) mainly for the market, choosing their markets (local or distant) based on transaction costs and prices.[23] Interestingly, unlike in Andhra Pradesh, there are fewer differences here in the crops grown by group farms and family farms. To the extent that the groups tend to grow mainly paddy while individual farmers more often grow veg-etables, the women's choice is based primarily on the type of land they have and the avail-ability of irrigation, as well as the economic incentives extended to them by the Kudumbashree Mission, rather than by mandate.[24]

These varied examples demonstrate the potential of small farmers (women and men) cooperating for overcoming their resource constraints. In the former socialist regimes, the cooperation is between farming families that receive little direct external support from the State. In South Asia the cooperation is between women from farming families, with support from the local government or NGOs. The gender implications of these efforts can be mixed. In inter-family cooperation there is no clear mechanism for tackling intra-family inequalities. In the women-only group farms there is a basis for women's empowerment outside the family structure, but women's claims on family land and labour for their collective efforts remain weak. Nevertheless, it is interesting that many groups (especially in Kerala) do receive support from the husbands of some of the women involved in finding land to lease, or in terms of technical advice and help in market-ing their crops. In other words, women's group farming ventures are typically seen by spouses as bringing additional income or food in kind, rather than as conflicting with family farm production. In Kerala, the Kudumbashree programme has also brought many women into active work participation outside the home who were earlier involved mainly in domestic chores.

Of course group farming is not being suggested as a panacea, nor as the only possible alternative. But it is a model whose potential has received rather little attention as an alterna-tive to the dominant model of individual family farms – an alternative that could help small farmers who are severely resource-constrained to find decent work and livelihoods in situ-ations of economic and climate uncertainty. Certainly it is an alternative about which we hear little in the food sovereignty debates. This form of collective action (which I call 'coop-erative collective action') is also more difficult to sustain, and is different from what I term 'agitational collective action' that is common to social movements (See also Agarwal,

---

[23]See also Vorley et al. (2012) who uses examples from several countries to emphasize the need to recognize and enhance small farmers' agency, and understand how they negotiate a mix in global, national and local markets.

[24]In Bangladesh too, we can find examples of women's groups leasing in land for joint cultivation (see IFAD 2009).

2000). Agitations are typically sporadic and situation-specific, such as for calling upon the State to implement redistributive land reform. In contrast, multipurpose cooperation in farming requires regular interaction, decision-making and monitoring. In a sense this is an institutional innovation that is needed in the *post*-agitation phase of a movement for, say, land rights.

In addition, there are at least three points of note in the ground examples of group farming cited above. First, the land (where individually owned) is not forfeited when the group is formed, in contrast to the collectives envisioned by La Via Campesina (as articulated by Paul Nicholson). Rather, farmers keep their individual rights but farm collectively. The land they farm can come from within the group or from outside it. Sometimes members keep part of their land for self-cultivation and pool a part.

Second, as outlined in Section 4, many of the women's groups (active and inactive) that I have been researching in Andhra Pradesh feel they would have been more productive (or less at risk) if they could have grown non-food crops such as cotton. For them, food security does not necessarily arise from growing their own food, but from having economic access to food, including through purchase. They give weight to higher incomes, rather than food self-sufficiency through production alone. This is also reflected in their growing cotton on many of their family farms. In other words, given a choice (within their resource constraints) they would have gone for commercial crops rather than subsistence food crops.

Moreover, very few of the 710 groups and individual farmers (including male farmers) interviewed in my survey in Andhra Pradesh and the approximately 250 interviewed in Kerala wanted their children to take up farming. Consistently, they preferred their children to be educated and take up other jobs. The idea of education for more lucrative farming found no place in their aspirations for the next generation.

Third, these initiatives did not arise from a global vision of what peasant economies should do or be. They arose out of local visions and institutional support systems. Groups that are free to choose what they grow and how, based on economic returns or any other objective they value, appear more likely to survive as a collectivity than those who have a particular vision of self-sufficiency imposed from above. The food sovereignty approach emphasizes horizontal rather than hierarchical interactions but, paradoxically, farmers with equal say may go their own way.

6. Concluding comments

The La Via Campesina vision of food sovereignty, with its emphasis on food self-sufficiency, diversity, agroecology, community, democracy and equality is undeniably attractive and important, but some elements can also be in serious conflict with others in practice.

The goal of food self-sufficiency at the national level, for instance, has resonance as a means of reducing vulnerabilities arising from the over-dependency of food importing countries on food exporting ones. Much of the developing world depends on food imports from the developed world and a few developing countries for fulfilling its food needs. Given the uncertainties arising from such dependence, rising and volatile food prices, and the effects of climate change, national efforts to achieve some degree of food sufficiency and move towards low chemical, environmentally sustainable agriculture – both important cornerstones of the food sovereignty argument – clearly appear desirable, although not all countries can or may want to aim at full sufficiency.

But national self-sufficiency goals cannot translate simply into local or household self-sufficiency goals. Nations have to provide for all citizens, many of whom are in non-farm or urban jobs, and farmers may not make choices that move a country towards food self-sufficiency. It is of course legitimate to argue that the choices farmers make are subject to the constraints they face and the alternatives before them. It is therefore important to identify those constraints – economic, institutional, technical, informational and political – and to reflect on alternatives, in particular on little discussed alternatives based on small farmer cooperation. But it is equally important to recognize that the valuable rights of voice and choice, exercised by the disadvantaged in local contexts, cannot always fall in line with preconceived trajectories defined by global movements on behalf of the disadvantaged. Therein lies the paradox.

In the agrarian transitions we are currently witnessing, an increasing proportion of small farmers (men more than women) are leaving agriculture; many others (of both genders) would like to do so; and most hope their children will find a future in another occupation. Among those who choose to stay, many would like to opt for commercially viable crops rather than subsistence crops; to use some chemicals rather than none; and to connect with a range of marketing outlets depending on the crops grown, the prices offered and the transaction costs incurred, rather than depend solely on local markets. Also, increasingly as countries urbanize, food security for millions will depend on their ability to buy food, rather than producing it themselves.

All this raises critical questions about the realistic nature of the food sovereignty vision. Undeniably, the vision is an important reminder of the environmental and other risks following the excesses of green revolution technology, and the need to build diversity, ecology and community, but the framework for this is far from clear. Group approaches based on voluntary cooperation and democratic principles, such as those discussed in this paper, could be a way forward. But these approaches are markedly different from former socialist collectives and are not built on Paul Nicolson/La Via Campesina's idea of collective land ownership. And they necessitate a shift away from the individual family farming model emphasized in the food sovereignty vision. Group approaches also require adaptation to context and support from governments and civil society.

The importance of contextual adaptation of any global vision raises issues of individual choice and democratic freedoms, which cannot simply be set aside. Here, significant challenges arise from questions such as: who represents the many? By what processes are decisions taken? And can institutions that promote voice and choice lead to a convergence of individual and collective priorities, or promote individual freedoms while defining collective responsibilities?

References

Adeleke, O.A., O.I. Adesiyan, O.A. Olaniyi, K.O. Adelalu, and H.M. Matanmi. 2008. Gender differentials in the productivity of cereal crop farmers: a case study of maize farmers in Oluyole Local Government Area of Oyo State. *Agricultural Journal*, 3(3), 193–198.

Adesina, A.A. and K.K. Djato. 1997. Relative efficiency of women as farm managers: Profit function analysis in Côte d'Ivoire. *Agricultural Economics*, 16(1), 47–53.

Agarwal, B. 1994. *A field of one's own: Gender and land rights in South Asia*. Cambridge: Cambridge University Press.

Agarwal, B. 2000. Conceptualising environmental collective action: Why gender matters. *Cambridge Journal of Economics*, 24, 283–310.

Agarwal, B. 2003. Gender and Land rights revisited: Exploring new prospects via the state, family and market. *Journal of Agrarian Change*, 3(1–2), 184–224.

Agarwal, B. 2010a. *Gender and green governance: The political economy of women's presence within and beyond community forestry*. Oxford: Oxford University Press.

Agarwal, B. 2010b. Does women's proportional strength affect their participation? Governing local forests in South Asia. *World Development*, 38(1), 98–112.

Agarwal, B. 2010c. Rethinking agricultural production collectivities. *Economic and Political Weekly*, 27 February, 55(9), 64–78.

Agarwal, B. 2011. Food crises and gender inequality, Working Paper No 107, United Nations Department of Economic and Social Affairs, New York.

Agarwal, B. 2013. Food security, productivity and gender inequality. In: R. Herring, ed. *Handbook of Food Politics and Society*. Accessible online. New York: Oxford University Press.

Allendorf, K. 2007. Do women's land rights promote empowerment and child health in Nepal? *World Development*, 35(11), 1975–1988.

Bhattacharyya, P. and G. Chakraborty. 2005. Current status of organic farming in India and other countries'. *Indian Journal of Fertilisers*, 1(9), 111–123.

Bindlish, V., R. Evenson, and M. Gbetibouo. 1993. Evaluation of T and V-based extension in Burkina Faso, World Bank Technical Paper No. 226, Africa Technical Department Series, World Bank, Washington, DC.

Borras, Jr., S.M. 2008. La Via Campesina and its global campaign for agrarian reform. *Journal of Agrarian Change*, 8(2 & 3), 258–289.

Borras, Jr., S.M., M. Edelman, and C. Kay. 2008. Transnational agrarian movements: Origins and politics, campaigns and impact. *Journal of Agrarian Change*, 8(2&3), 169–204.

Braverman, A., J.L. Guasch, M. Huppi, and L. Pohlmeier. 1991. Promoting rural cooperatives in developing countries, discussion Paper No. 121, World Bank, Washington DC.

von Braun, J. 2008. Rising food prices: What should be done? *Eurochoices*, 7(2), 30–35.

von Braun, J. 2008–09. Food-security risks must be comprehensively addressed, Annual Report Essay 2008–09, IFPRI, Washington, DC.

Burnett, Kim and Sophia Murphy. 2013. What place for international trade in food sovereignty? Paper presented at the International conference on 'Food sovereignty: A critical dialogue' September 14–15, 2013, Yale University, New Haven, CT.

Burra, N. 2004. Empowering women for household food security: UNDP's Experience, United Nations Development Programme, Delhi.

Chand, R. 2009. Challenges to ensuring food security through wheat. CAB Reviews: Perspectives in Agriculture, *Veterinary Science, Nutrition and Natural Resources*, 4 (65): 1–13. See http://www.cabi.org/cabreviews.

Darling, M.L. 1947. *The Punjab peasant in prosperity and debt*. Lahore: Vanguard Books.

Deere, C.D. and Magdalena de Leon. 2001. *Empowering women: Land and property rights in Latin America*. Pittsburgh: University of Pittsburgh Press.

Deere, C.D. and C.R. Doss. 2006. The gender asset gap: What do we know and why does it matter? *Feminist Economics*, 12(1–2), 1–50.

Dey, J. 1992. Gender asymmetries in intra-household resource allocation in sub-Saharan Africa: Some policy implications for land and labour productivity', paper presented at an IFPRI workshop on Intra-household resource allocation.

Doss, C.R. 2001. Designing agricultural technology for African women farmers: Lessons from 25 years of experience. *World Development*, 29(12), 2075–2092.

Doss, C.R. 2010. If women hold up half the sky, how much of the world's food do they produce? Background paper, 2011 *State of Food and Agriculture Report (SOFA Report)*, FAO, Rome.

FAO. 2011. *The State of Food and Agriculture* (SOFA Report). Rome: FAO.

FIBL & IFOAM. 2013. *The World of Organic Agriculture*. Available from: http://www.organic-world.net/fileadmin/documents/yearbook/2013/web-fibl-ifoam-2013–318-321.pdf

Foster, A.D. and M.R. Rosenzweig. 2010. Is there surplus labour in rural India, Discussion Paper No. 991, Economic Growth Centre, Yale University, New Haven.

GoI. 2006. *Census of India 2001: Population projections for India and States 2001–2026*, Report of the technical group on population projections, National Commission on Population, GoI, Delhi.

GoI (Government of India). 2010–11. *Agricultural Census 2010–11* All India Report on Number and Area of Operational Holdings, Agriculture Census Division, Department of Agriculture and Co- Operation, Ministry of Agriculture, New Delhi.

Goyal, S.K. 1966. *Cooperative farming in India*. Bombay: Asia Publishing House.

Hill, R.V. and M. Vigneri. 2009. Mainstreaming gender sensitivity in cash crop market supply chains, Background paper, 2011 *SOFA Report*. FAO, Rome.

IFAD (International Fund for Agricultural Development). 2009. *Evaluation: Bangladesh*. Available from: www.ifad.org/evaluation/public_html/eksyst/doc/country/pi/bangladesh/cesba94e_3.htm. [Accessed 14 September 2009].

IFPRI (International Food Policy Research Institute). 2009. *Climate change: Impact on agriculture and costs of adaptation*. Washington, DC: IFPRI.

Ivanic, M. and W. Martin. 2008. Implications of higher global food prices for poverty in low-income countries, Policy Research Working Paper Series 4594, World Bank, Washington DC.

Kumase, W.N., H. Bisseleua and S. Klasen. 2008. Opportunities and Constraints in Agriculture: A Gendered Analysis of Cocoa Production in Southern Cameroon, Discussion Paper No. 27. Courant Research Centre, University of Göttingen.

Lastarria-Cornhiel, S. and A. Manji. 2010. Land Tenure, Land Policy, and Gender in Rural Areas, background paper, 2011 *SOFA Report*, FAO, Rome.

Li, Z. 2003. *Women's land tenure rights in rural China: A synthesis*. Beijing: Mimeo, Ford Foundation.

Martinez-Torres, M.E. and P.M. Rosset. 2010. La Via Campesina: The birth and evolution of á transnational social movement. *The Journal of Peasant Studies*, 37(1), 149–175.

Mathijs, E. and J.F.M. Swinnen. 2001. Production organization and efficiency during transition: An empirical analysis of East German agriculture. *Review of Economics and Statistics*, 83(1), 100–107.

Mazhar, F., D. Buckles, P.V. Satheesh, and F. Akhter. 2007. *Food sovereignty and uncultivated biodiversity in South Asia*. Ottawa: IDRC.

Moock, P.R. 1976. The efficiency of women farm managers Kenya. *American Journal of Agricultural Economics*, 58(5), 831–835.

NSSO (National Sample Survey Organisation). 2005a. *Employment and unemployment situation in India* (July 2004 - June 2005), NSS 61th Round, NSSO, New Delhi: Government of India (GoI).

NSSO. 2005b. *Some aspects of farming: Situation assessment survey of farmers*. New Delhi: Department of Statistics, Government of India.

Patel, R. 2009. Grassroots voices: What does food sovereignty look like? *Journal of Peasant Studies*, 36(3), 663–706.

Peterman, A., J. Behrman, and A.R. Quisumbing. 2009. A review of empirical evidence on gender differences in non-land agricultural inputs, technology and services in developing countries, background paper, 2011 *SOFA Report*, FAO, Rome.

Quisumbing, A.R. 1996. Male-female differences in agricultural productivity: Methodological issues and empirical evidence. *World Development*, 24(10), 1579–1595.

Quisumbing, A.R., Ellen Payongayong, J.B. Aidoo, and Keijiro Otsuka. 2001. Women's land rights in the transition to individualized ownership: Implications for the management of tree resources in Western Ghana. *Economic Development and CulturalChange*, 50(1), 157–182.

Quisumbing, A.R., R.S. Meinzen-Dick, L. Bassett, M. Usnick, L. Pandolfelli, C. Morden, and H. Alderman. 2008. Helping women respond to the global food price crises, Policy Brief 7, IFPRI, Washington DC.

Sabates-Wheeler, R. 2002. Farm strategy, self-selection and productivity: Can small farming groups offer production benefits to farmers in post-socialist Romania. *World Development*, 30(10), 1737–1753.

Sabates-Wheeler, R. and M.D. Childress. 2004. Asset-pooling in uncertain times: Implications of small-group farming for agricultural restructuring in the Kyrgyz Republic, Working Paper 239, Institute of Development Studies, Sussex.

Saito, K.A., H. Mekonnen, and D. Spurling. 1994. Raising the productivity of women farmers in sub-Saharan Africa, World Bank Discussion Papers, Africa Technical Department Series No. 230, World Bank, Washington DC.

Sen, A.K. 1999. *Development as freedom*. New York: Knopf.

Udry, C., J. Hoddinott, H. Alderman, and L. Haddad. 1995. Differentials in farm productivity: Implications for household efficiency and agricultural policy. *Food Policy*, 20(5), 407–423.

Vorley, B., E. del Pozo-Vergnes, and A. Barnett. 2012. Small producer agency in the globalised market: making choices in a changing world, IIED/HIVOS. Downloaded from http://pubs.iied.org/16521IIED.html

Wheeler, T. and J. von Braun. 2013. Climate change impacts on global food security. *Science*, 341, 508–513.

Whitehead, A. 2005. The gendered impacts of liberalisation policies on African agricultural econom-
ies and rural livelihoods, background paper for UNRISD Report on gender equality: Striving for
justice in an unequal world (Geneva: UNRISD).
Willer, H. and M. Yussefi, eds. 2007. *The world of organic agriculture statistics and emerging trends.*
Available from: http://www.orgprints.org/10506
Wittman, H. 2009. Interview: Paul Nicholson, La Via Campesina. *The Journal of Peasant Studies*, 36
(3), 676–682.
World Bank. 2007. *World development report 2008: agriculture for development.* Washington, DC:
World Bank.
World Bank. 2009. *Gender in agriculture sourcebook.* Vols 1 and 2. Washington, DC: World Bank.

Bina Agarwal is Professor of Development Economics and Environment at the School of Environment, Education and Development, University of Manchester. She was earlier Director of the Institute
of Economic Growth, Delhi. She is also President of the International Society for Ecological Economics and an award-winning author. Among her publications are several books, including *A Field
of One's Own: Gender and Land Rights in South Asia* (1994) and *Gender and Green Governance*
(2010).

Index

For Product Safety Concerns and Information please contact our EU
representative GPSR@taylorandfrancis.com
Taylor & Francis Verlag GmbH, Kaufingerstraße 24, 80331 München, Germany

www.ingramcontent.com/pod-product-compliance
Ingram Content Group UK Ltd.
Pitfield, Milton Keynes, MK11 3LW, UK
UKHW051830180425
457613UK00022B/1175